NB 6188060 4

D1638158

A LITERARY HISTORY OF ENGLAND

A LITERARY HISTORY OF ENGLAND

—VOLUME I—

The Middle Ages (to 1500)

KEMP MALONE

Johns Hopkins University

ALBERT C. BAUGH

University of Pennsylvania

—VOLUME II—

The Renaissance (1500–1660)

TUCKER BROOKE

MATTHIAS A. SHAABER

University of Pennsylvania

—VOLUME III—

The Restoration and Eighteenth Century (1660–1789)

GEORGE SHERBURN

DONALD F. BOND

The University of Chicago

—VOLUME IV—

The Nineteenth Century and After (1789–1939)

SAMUEL C. CHEW

RICHARD D. ALTICK

The Ohio State University

A LITERARY HISTORY OF ENGLAND

Second Edition

Edited by Albert C. Baugh

VOLUME III

THE RESTORATION

and

EIGHTEENTH CENTURY

(1660-1789)

by

GEORGE SHERBURN

&

DONALD F. BOND

NORTH EASTERN LIBRARY SERVICE
AREA LIBRARY, DEMESNE AVENUE
BALLYMENA, Co. ANTRIM BT43 7BG
NUMBER 6188060
CLASS 820.9004

London

First published in Great Britain in 1948 by
Routledge & Kegan Paul Ltd
Second edition 1967
First published in paperback 1972
Reprinted three times

Reprinted 1993 by
Routledge
11 New Fetter Lane, London EC4P 4EE

© *1948 by Appleton-Century-Crofts, Inc.*
© *1967 by Meredith Publishing Company*

Printed and bound in Great Britain by
Hartnolls Ltd, Bodmin, Cornwall

All rights reserved. No part of this book may be
reprinted or reproduced or utilized in any form or
by any electronic, mechanical, or other means, now
known or hereafter invented, including
photocopying and recording, or in any information
storage or retrieval system, without permission in
writing from the publishers.

ISBN 0-415-10454-8

Preface to the First Edition

The purpose of the work of which the present volume forms a part is to provide a comprehensive history of the literature of England, an account that is at once scholarly and readable, capable of meeting the needs of mature students and of appealing to cultivated readers generally. The extent of English literature is so great that no one can hope to read more than a fraction of it, and the accumulated scholarship—biographical, critical, and historical—by which writers and their works, and the forms and movements and periods of English literature have been interpreted, is so vast that no single scholar can control it. A literary history by one author, a history that is comprehensive and authoritative over the whole field, is next to impossible. Hence, the plan of the present work. A general harmony of treatment among the five contributors, rather than rigid uniformity of method, has seemed desirable, and there is quite properly some difference of emphasis in different sections. It is hoped that the approach to the different periods will seem to be that best suited to the literature concerned. The original plan brought the history to an end with the year 1939 (the outbreak of the Second World War); but delay in publication caused by the war has permitted reference to a few events of a date subsequent to 1939.

Since it is expected that those who read this history or consult it will wish for further acquaintance with the writings and authors discussed, it has been a part of the plan to draw attention, by the generous use of footnotes, to standard editions, to significant biographical and critical works, and to the most important books and articles in which the reader may pursue further the matters that interest him. A few references to very recent publications have been added in proof in an effort to record the present state of scholarly and critical opinion.

As for the present volume, all that is necessary here is to record again the author's indebtedness to Professors Rodney M. Baine and Walter J. Bate, who made corrections in the manuscript, and to Professors Donald F. Bond and Arthur Friedman, who helped with the proof as well as the copy.

G. S.

NOTE TO SECOND EDITION

The reception of the *Literary History of England* has been so gratifying as to call for a number of successive printings, and these have permitted minor corrections to be made. The present edition has a further aim—to bring the book in line with the most recent scholarship. Small changes have been made in the plates wherever possible, but most of the additions, factual and bibliographical, are recorded in a Supplement. The text, Supplement, and Index are correlated by means of several typographical devices. Explanations of these devices appear on each part-title page as well as at the beginning of the Supplement and the Index.

The editor regrets that the authors of Books II, III, and IV did not live to carry out the revisions of those books, but their places have been ably taken by the scholars whose names appear with theirs in the list of collaborators. It has been the desire of the editor, as well as of those who have joined him, that each of these books should remain essentially as the original author wrote it, and we believe that other scholars would concur. Any new points of view, it is hoped, are adequately represented in the Supplement.

A. C. B.

Contents

List of Abbreviations

AJP	American Journal of Philology
Archiv	Archiv für das Studium der neueren Sprachen und Literaturen
ARS	Augustan Reprint Society
CBEL	Cambridge Bibliography of English Literature (4v, Cambridge, 1941)
CFMA	Les Classiques français du moyen âge
CHEL	Cambridge History of English Literature (14v, 1907–17)
CL	Comparative Literature
E&S	Essays and Studies by Members of the English Association
EETS	Early English Text Society, Original Series
EETSES	Early English Text Society, Extra Series
EHR	English Historical Review
EIC	Essays in Criticism
ELH	*ELH*, A Journal of English Literary History
ELN	English Language Notes
EML Series	English Men of Letters Series
ES	English Studies
ESt	Englische Studien
GR	Germanic Review
HLQ	Huntington Library Quarterly
Hist. Litt.	Histoire littéraire de la France (38v, 1733–1941, in progress)
JAAC	Journal of Aesthetics and Art Criticism
JEGP	Journal of English and Germanic Philology
JHI	Journal of the History of Ideas
KSJ	Keats-Shelley Journal
LTLS	(London) Times Literary Supplement
MA	Medium Ævum
MLN	Modern Language Notes
MLQ	Modern Language Quarterly
MLR	Modern Language Review
MP	Modern Philology
N&Q	Notes and Queries
NCF	Nineteenth-Century Fiction
PMLA	Publications of the Modern Language Association of America
PQ	Philological Quarterly

REL	Review of English Literature
RES	Review of English Studies
RLC	Revue de littérature comparée
RR	Romanic Review
SAB	Shakespeare Association Bulletin
SATF	Societé des anciens textes français
SEL	Studies in English Literature, 1500–1900 (Rice Univ.)
SF&R	Scholars' Facsimiles and Reprints
ShS	Shakespeare Survey
SP	Studies in Philology
SQ	Shakespeare Quarterly
SRen	Studies in the Renaissance
STS	Scottish Text Society
UTQ	University of Toronto Quarterly
VP	Victorian Poetry
VS	Victorian Studies

BOOK III

The Restoration and Eighteenth Century (1660-1789)

~⁌~

PART I

The Rise of Classicism

Guide to reference marks

Throughout the text of this book, a point • set beside a page number indicates that references to new critical material will be found under an identical paragraph/page number (set in **boldface**) in the BIBLIOGRAPHICAL SUPPLEMENT.

In the Index, a number preceded by an **S** indicates a paragraph/page number in the BIBLIOGRAPHICAL SUPPLEMENT.

I

The Spirit of the Restoration

In May, 1660, invited by Parliament, King Charles II returned from exile, and the Restoration of monarchy in England became a fact.[1] Amidst the spontaneous outbursts of joy, poets and others were not slow in asserting a parallel between this Restoration and the imperial establishment, after civil wars, of Octavius Augustus Caesar in Rome (31 B.C.). This attitude of mind is implicit in the title of Dryden's poem, *Astræa Redux,* composed for the occasion, and explicit in the concluding lines of the effort:

Neo-Augustanism

> Oh Happy Age! Oh times like those alone,
> By Fate reserv'd for great *Augustus'* Throne!
> When the joint growth of Arms and Arts forshew
> The World a Monarch, and that Monarch *You.*

The author (Francis Atterbury?) of the preface to *The Second Part of Mr. Waller's Poems* (1690) more magisterially says, "I question whether in *Charles* the Second's Reign, *English* did not come to its full perfection; and whether it has not had its *Augustan Age,* as well as the *Latin.*" This neo-Augustanism, so promptly recognized and acclaimed, we call neo-classicism. It implies a veneration for the Roman classics, thought, and way of life. It values highly a noble Roman tone. The stately enthusiasm of the time Dryden caught in retrospect as he penned his *Threnodia Augustalis* (1685):

> Men met each other with erected look,
> The steps were higher that they took;
> Friends to congratulate their friends made haste,
> And long-inveterate foes saluted as they pass'd.

The dignity and stateliness outlived the enthusiasm. The new Augustus, Charles II, proved to be both lazy and lecherous, and in spite of his undoubted wit and intelligence (seldom has an English monarch been personally friendly to so many distinguished intellectuals!) disillusionment soon attended his reign. In 1667 Samuel Pepys summed up this attitude:

[1] For general aids on the history of the literature of this period consult A. Beljame, *Le Public et les hommes de lettres en Angleterre, 1660-1744* (Paris, 1881); Richard Garnett, *The Age of Dryden* (1903); Sir Herbert Grierson, *Cross Currents in English Literature of the XVIIth Century* (1929); Sherard Vines, *The Course of English Classicism* (1930); Louis Cazamian, "Modern Times 1660-1932," in *A History of English Literature* (translated from the French [Paris, 1924] in 1927, rev. ed., 1935). — For general bibliographies see Robert Watt, *Bibliotheca Britannica; or, a General Index to British and Foreign Literature* (4v, Edinburgh, 1824); *Annual Bibliography of English Language and Literature,* edited for the MHRA (Cambridge, 1921-   ); Ronald S. Crane, Louis I. Bredvold, Richmond P. Bond, Allen T. Hazen, Arthur Friedman, and Louis A. Landa (successively), "English Literature of the Restoration and Eighteenth Century: A Current Bibliography," annually since 1926 in *PQ*

It is strange how ... every body do now-a-days reflect upon Oliver, and commend him, what brave things he did, and made all the neighbour princes fear him; while here a prince, come in with all the love and prayers and good liking of his people, who have given greater signs of loyalty and willingness to serve him with their estates than ever was done by any people, hath lost all so soon, that it is a miracle what way a man could devise to lose so much in so little time.

The Court and French Influence

Charles and his court had brought back from their Continental exile a love of French wit, gallantry, elegance, and artistic deftness. Doubtless Virgil, Horace, Cicero, Ovid, and Juvenal meant more to the literate English gentleman of the period than did his French contemporaries, Descartes, Molière, Corneille, and Boileau—though it would be wrong to underestimate the French influence.[2] But the necessary social, economic, and religious readjustments crowded in upon the minds of men: their realistic, common-sense, and at times even cynical evaluation of life was at wide variance from Roman stateliness and French refinement. The spirit of the age was far from unified; and in reaction against its complexity Restoration intellectuals thirsted for a rational simplification of their existence. To understand their divergent efforts to reduce confusion to a lucid simplicity it is necessary to have some awareness of their thinking in the fields of science, religion, and politics, as well as their tendencies in the arts.[3]

The Influence of Science

In science the most important work was done by men connected with the Royal Society of London.[4] This organization emerged in 1660, or shortly thereafter, from groups meeting earlier in London at Gresham College or in Oxford at Wadham. Its technical achievements lie chiefly, but by no means exclusively, in the field of mathematics as applied to the motion of the heavenly bodies. For our purposes it cannot too constantly be remembered that the leading fellows of the Society were devoutly religious men: the work of Robert Boyle (1627-91) in chemistry, of John Ray (1627-1705) in other natural sciences, of Sir Isaac Newton [5] (1642-1727) in mathe-

for April; *CBEL*, esp. Vol. II. — For detailed political histories of the Restoration period see Lord Macaulay's *History of England from the Accession of James II* (5v, 1849-61; ed. Sir Charles H. Firth, 6v, 1913-15); George M. Trevelyan, *England under the Stuarts* (1904 ff.); David Ogg, *England in the Reign of Charles II* (2v, Oxford, 1934); and George N. Clark, *The Later Stuarts, 1660-1714* (1934). Among the shorter, one-volume histories of England may be recommended those by Arthur L. Cross (1914) and by George M. Trevelyan (1926). For bibliography see Godfrey Davies (ed.), *Bibliography of British History: Stuart Period, 1603-1714* (Oxford, 1928).

[2] L. Charlanne, *L'Influence française en Angleterre au XVIIᵉ siècle* (Paris, 1906).

[3] For general treatments of this field see Basil Willey, *The Seventeenth Century Background* (1934) and Preserved Smith, *A History of Modern Culture*, Vol. II, "The Enlightenment" (1934). On the more specialized theme of the thirst for simplification see Richard F. Jones, "The Moral Sense of Simplicity," *Studies in Honor of Frederick W. Shipley* (St. Louis, 1942), pp. 265-287.

[4] Important early accounts of the Royal Society are found in Thomas Sprat, *A History of the Royal Society* (1667) and in Joseph Glanvill, *Plus Ultra* (1668). More recently we have Henry B. Wheatley, *The Early History of the Royal Society* (1905) and Sir W. Huggins, *The Royal Society* (1906). Richard F. Jones in his *Ancients and Moderns* (St. Louis, 1936) analyzes the intellectual background of science. Very illuminating also are Edwin A. Burtt's *Metaphysical Foundations of Modern Physical Science* (1925) and Sir Henry Lyons's *The Royal Society, 1660-1940* (Cambridge, 1944).

[5] Sir Isaac was a fellow of the Royal Society after 1671 and President from 1703 until his death in 1727. His *Principia* appeared in 1687.

matics and astronomy—all was designed to support religious orthodoxy, and had no subversive or eccentric ends in view. Great as were their known scientific achievements, for us their significance lies rather in their ability to popularize certain methods of thinking and writing. The motto of the Society, *nullius in verba*—"on the word of no one"—is a direct challenge to historians who, however wrongly, regard English neo-classicism as an appeal to the ancients as authorities. The Royal Society was experimental and empirical in method; assent to a proposition had to be suspended until the evidence was examined. They shunned purely a priori reasoning, and preached the necessity of having a hesitant or "open" mind. Frequently this attitude approached skepticism as method if not as ultimate end. The indirect influence of the Society through the Boyle lectures, founded in 1692 by Robert Boyle's will, "to prove the truth of the Christian Religion," was great in furthering the "physico-theology" that was the answering challenge of the orthodox to certain types of deists. In general, the Society purposed to substitute experiment for disputation as a road to truth. Eventually their method would transfer attention from the pursuit of humane learning to the study of things, but at the start that was far from the intention of scientists, who at times disparaged Aristotle as a student of nature, but were seldom hostile to his efforts as a moralist or a literary critic. They tended to believe in the progress of man through the illumination of the new science; and this idea of progress was gradually to preoccupy later generations.[6]

Science and English Prose

It has been regarded as significant of the practical and perhaps even materialistic bent of the English mind that while seventeenth-century France created in its celebrated Académie Française (1635) a literary foundation, England organized a society for scientific research. The Royal Society, however, concerned itself with more than scientific experimentation. The inclusiveness of its conception of science perhaps forestalled efforts to establish an academy. It had as fellows many literary men who had slight interest in science, and it actively promoted the study and reform of English prose style, and like the French Academy was eager to improve and fix standards in language. Late in 1664 it appointed, "for improving the English language," a committee that included, among others, Dryden, Evelyn, Waller, and Sprat. Meetings of this committee were held with such other literati present as Cowley, Villiers, Duke of Buckingham, and "Matt" Clifford. Because of the death of Cowley and the interruption caused by the plague of 1665, the committee, so Evelyn wrote in 1689, "crumbled away and came to nothing." The statement is not perfectly accurate; for though the committee seems never to have reported formally to the Society, its ideals of style became of very great importance.[7] In a well-known passage in his *History of the Royal Society* (1667) Bishop Sprat has summarized these ideals:

[6] The origin and history of *The Idea of Progress* can be found treated in the book of that title by an ardent believer in the idea, John B. Bury (1920; 1932).

[7] Richard F. Jones, "Science and English Prose Style in the Third Quarter of the Seventeenth Century," *PMLA*, xlv (1930). 977-1009; significantly reviewed in *PQ*, x (1931). 184-186.

They [the Society] have therefore been most rigorous in putting in execution the only Remedy that can be found for this *extravagance,* and that has been a constant Resolution to reject all amplifications, digressions, and swellings of style; to return back to the primitive purity and shortness, when men deliver'd so many *things* almost in an equal number of *words.* They have exacted from all their members a close, naked, natural way of speaking, positive expressions, clear senses, a native easiness, bringing all things as near the Mathematical plainness as they can, and preferring the language of Artizans, Countrymen, and Merchants, before that of Wits or Scholars.

These ideals, obviously essential to scientific exposition, were reinforced by the conversational tradition of elegant French prose, and became outside scientific circles a part of the reaction from baroque magnificence to neo-Palladian simplicity. Hobbes, who interestingly enough was not approved by the Royal Society, worked "non ut floride sed ut Latine posset scribere"; and Glanvill, who was converted to the stylistic ideals of the Society, urged upon parsons the quality of *plainness* as opposed "First, to *hard words;* Secondly, to *deep* and *mysterious notions;* Thirdly, to *affected Rhetorications;* and Fourthly, to *Phantastical Phrases."*

Genteel Tolerance

Under the influence of the new science, then, the useful and the plain were replacing the ornate, the rich, the complex. At first sight it may seem strange that a similar tendency to simplification can be traced in the religious thinking of the time. Certainly religious controversy—"polemical divinity" it was called—was a chief product of the fecund printing press; but gentlemen were becoming bored by such zeal. The religion of all true gentlemen was ideally something that no true gentleman ever argued about: argument might be left to the parsons! As ambassador to Holland Sir William Temple admired the effects of toleration in that country, and in his *Observations upon the United Provinces* (1673) he remarks concerning Dutch composure in religious controversy:

They argue without interest or anger; They differ without enmity or scorn, And They agree without confederacy. Men live together like Citizens of the World, associated by the common ties of Humanity.... The Power of Religion among them, where it is, lies in every Man's heart. . . .

In England this beatific condition seemed more than a channel-crossing distant; but remotely the ideal was perceived and valued as the coil of varied controversy incessantly renewed itself at home. Weary of disputation and eager for a simplified, reasonable creed Dryden could write:

> Faith is not built on disquisitions vain;
> The things we *must* believe are *few* and *plain.*

But no great number of Englishmen followed Dryden's search for "unsuspected ancients" to serve as authoritative sanctions in faith. The age was prejudiced against any *ipse dixit* authority.

There were complicated positions taken.[8] The Catholics, disliked largely

[8] Louis I. Bredvold in his *Intellectual Milieu of John Dryden* (Ann Arbor, 1934) gives an admirable picture of this confusion.

for political rather than doctrinal reasons, were at times willing even to *Religious*
undermine the authority of Scripture, since by so doing they undermined *Animosities*
the chief orthodox basis for Protestant faith. The Puritans were still assailing
Anglicans on questions of church government; but many dissenters and
Anglicans, both largely Calvinists, would unite against the rising tide of
Arminianism. In the forefront of its 1629 Protestation the House of Commons had asserted: "Whosoever shall bring in innovation of religion, or
by favour or countenance seek to extend or introduce popery or Arminianism, or other opinion disagreeing from the true and orthodox Church,
shall be reputed a capital enemy to this kingdom and commonwealth." [9]
At the end of the century a kindlier attitude towards practical moral sanctions as opposed to the Calvinist covenant of grace would have made such
a protest impossible.[10] The blood and tears of war, controversy, and political
intrigue had led gradually to a practical, if not always a reasoned, spirit
of toleration.

To civic life the great contribution of "the people called Quakers" was
doubtless their insistent belief in religious toleration.[11] Their contribution
to religious life was their mystical emphasis on experience—on the life of
God in the soul of man. To them religion ideally was a pleasant psychological *The*
state rather than a terror-stricken argument. An astonishing number of *Quakers*
journals, autobiographies, and histories, some of them by hardly literate *and Reason*
authors, testify to the zeal of the Friends in promoting religious experience.
Most notable among these would be the *Journal* (1694) of the first great
Quaker, George Fox (1624-1691), for which William Penn (1644-1718)
wrote an important introduction. Penn was no skilful writer, but his *No
Cross No Crown* (1669) and especially his *Some Fruits of Solitude* (1693)
are effectively simple and fervent. The theologian of the Society of
Friends was Robert Barclay (1648-1690), whose *Apology for the True
Christian Divinity* (1678) represents Quaker logic at its best. The mystical
sense of divine immanence, however, was more valued by Friends than was
reasoned theology. In this matter their position was sharply at variance from
that of seventeenth-century Protestants and Catholics, who could agree in
basing faith on reason. Strong in their concept of "the light of reason,"
which the orthodox insisted was uniform and universal, both Protestants
and Catholics were bitterly scornful of the "inner" or private light so valued
by the Quakers and by some other sects—and called by their enemies "enthusiasm." Subjectivity was antithetical to the ideal of constant and universal
reason.

The most effective voice raised in favor of the sanction of common ex- *Locke and*
perience as opposed to the vagaries of "enthusiasm" was that of John Locke *Empiricism*
(1632-1704). His most important work—perhaps the most important in

[9] Godfrey Davies, "Arminian vs. Puritan," *Huntington Library Bull.,* v (1934). 157-179.
Here p. 172 is quoted.
[10] Harry G. Plum, *Restoration Puritanism: A Study in the Growth of English Liberty* (Chapel
Hill, 1943).
[11] Luella M. Wright, *The Literary Life of the Early Friends, 1650-1725* (1932).

English philosophy—was his *Essay concerning Human Understanding* (1690). In the first three books of this work Locke strove to demolish the theory of innate ideas, to define the true nature of ideas, and to explain the relation of language to thought. Finally, in the last and most important book, he developed his theory of knowledge—as coming only from sense experience and from reflection upon that experience. His ability to write with clarity and order as well as his use of the methods of the New Science in philosophical thinking made him the great empirical rationalist of modern philosophy and (unintentionally) the father of much skeptical thinking in the century to follow. He demonstrated the need of an historical revelation of religion; but his psychological approach to the relation of reason to faith (Book IV, chapter XVIII) ultimately weakened reason and strangled faith. His method in the *Essay* and in *The Reasonableness of Christianity* (1695) was seized upon by the deist John Toland, whose *Christianity Not Mysterious* (1696) showed, according to its title-page, "that there is nothing in the Gospel contrary to reason, nor above it, and that no Christian doctrine can be properly called a mystery." Thus while aimed against the subjective enthusiasts, Locke's rationalism unintentionally played into the hands of the great enemy on the other flank, the deists. Locke's influence on deistic thinking, on psychology, and on the new field to be called epistemology, was to be enormous throughout the eighteenth century.[12]

The Deists   Apart from the Quakers, the deists were perhaps the chief religious novelty in the period, and all the professed Christian sects disparaged the deist position. The divergences between the "natural religion" of the deists and the "revealed religion" of their opponents are not always easy to establish. The orthodox Christians asserted that the deists denied the historical revelation made through Jesus Christ and recorded in the Holy Scriptures, and believed only in a revelation seen by human reason in God's created universe. In general the deists certainly stressed their belief in the Creation, the "Book of Nature," as evidently God's handiwork and thus a revelation of Himself. They said little about the Scriptures. John Toland and some others, to be sure, openly attacked the integrity of the Bible. Privately, many deists regarded the historical aspects of the biblical revelation with suspicion; overtly, they annoyed orthodox scientists by stealing and perhaps misapplying some of their thunder. John Ray's book, *The Wisdom of God Manifested in the Works of the Creation* (1691) had a title that might please some deists as much as it clearly did the orthodox "physico-theologians" of the Royal Society. The deists glorified reason, but frequently identified it with common sense or the almost intuitional "light of reason." They could find attributes of deity manifested in the works of the Creation or revealed axiomatically in the minds of all men. They questioned the worth of a local revelation, long past, and stressed the universal

---

[12] S. G. Hefelbower gives a useful, if simplified, account in his *Relation of John Locke to Deism* (Chicago, 1918). On the less tangible matter of Locke and literature see Kenneth Mac-Lean's *John Locke and English Literature of the Eighteenth Century* (New Haven, 1936).

religious perceptions or intuitions of men. As Professor Lovejoy states the deist's position:

Precisely this was the ostensible procedure of Herbert of Cherbury. *Summa veritatis norma est consensus universalis;* true religion consists solely of *notitiae communes,* things that everybody knows; and to judge how far a "particular faith" coincides with this norm you must ask, among other things, whether any of its articles "be not controverted among foreign nations, among whom other faiths are received." Thus alone is to be determined the doctrine of the *Ecclesia vere catholica sive universalis,* the only church *quae errare non potest,* because it alone utters the judgment of all mankind with respect to those truths of which they have self-evident knowledge by the light of nature. As Voltaire said, "Sans doute [Dieu] a parlé; mais c'est à l'Univers."

The spectrum of religious opinion would thus range from this belief in a universal, uniform perception of truth through the light of reason to a belief in private revelations of an inner light, which was purely individual; it would range from the argumentative theologians, such as the Cambridge Platonists, to the quietism of the Quaker or the intellectual libertinism of the fine gentleman, such as Sir William Temple. The Anglicans, torn by divergences among themselves, had to oppose Catholics, deists, and dissenters of many different stripes. The perplexed mind sought various ways out of this confusion, ways including rational simplifications, pure fideism, and, at the other extreme, many types of skepticism. Such escapes frequently tended to undermine the prestige of "polemical divines" and of rational theology itself, and thus aided anti-rational tendencies destined remotely to eventuate in sentimentalism or evangelicalism.

In the field of politics there was similar confusion. A strong and perhaps even pharisaical satisfaction was felt that the English, unlike their neighbors, the French, were not "born to serve" an absolute monarch like Louis XIV. *Political* Yet absolutism and divine right were strongly defended in the *Patriarcha* *Contro-* (1680) and other popular writings of Sir Robert Filmer, who died in 1653. *versies* Divinely constituted authority was Filmer's refuge from the confusion of conflicting parties, and of parliaments divided against themselves. Thomas Hobbes's *Leviathan* (1651) substituted for the divine sanction of sovereignty a materialistic absolutism based on an original compact that irrevocably delegated to one person power over the governed. Far from granting any religious or ecclesiastical sanction for sovereignty Hobbes made the Church entirely the creature of the monarch. His absolutism, his materialism, and his anti-clericalism—which seemed to go to the length of atheism—as well as his irritatingly systematic thinking, made Hobbes's doctrines the object of loud and continual anathemas throughout the period, and yet the fundamental purpose of his work was, again, the gratification of a love (quite a selfish love in Hobbes's psychology) for a settled peace.

In a period when Parliament was establishing its control over the throne by inviting Charles II to return and William and Mary to displace James II, absolutism might too readily be thought a dead issue. It was, however, the

Locke's Treatises

accession of James II, coupled with Continental set-backs to liberty [13] that stimulated John Locke to publish his great works, some of which were of supreme political importance. His views had long been formed, but, appearing at the troubled moment of the Revolution of 1688, they were its cogent defense. A protégé of the great Earl of Shaftesbury, Locke was an intellectual Whig. He had long been for toleration in religion; and his *Two Treatises of Government* (1690) was the best answer to the absolutism of Filmer and Hobbes. Locke's influence on constitutional theories both in England and America was destined to be enormous. He emphatically gave the legislative branch of government supreme power. The authority of the governor, he said, derived solely from the consent of the governed, and the bound of his power was the welfare of those governed by him. *Salus populi suprema lex*. Government thus became in some sense a matter of expediency, and expediency might determine policy—as it did in Locke's denial of toleration to Catholics while extending it to dissenters.

Political Parties

Any political expediency in Locke was only a faint effect of what went on in the actual politics of his day. The laziness of Charles II had allowed the rise of government by cabinet ministers to become remarkable, and in the heat of the sensational Popish Plot (1678) there had emerged the troublesome and irrational party labels, *Whig* and *Tory*. The Whigs claimed to protect the liberties of the subject, and they certainly attempted to help the dissenters; the Tories, likely to be ardent Churchmen, professed a devotion to royal prerogative and to the legitimate line of succession to the throne. The Tories, with some injustice, accused the Whigs of being republicans, disciples of Oliver, the late Protector; the Whigs retaliated more unjustly after 1688 by calling the Tories Jacobites, that is, supporters of the deposed James II. The necessity of a Protestant succession had provoked endless controversy, even reviving notions of divine right which had to be abandoned upon the accession of William and Mary as joint rulers. The principle of allegiance and the meaning of oaths of allegiance were topics of bitter dispute when, led by Sancroft, Archbishop of Canterbury, many clerics refused to violate their allegiance already sworn to James II by taking the required oaths of allegiance to the new rulers. Such Jacobites were called non-jurors; and they included eminent literary scholars like George Hickes (1642-1715) and Thomas Hearne (1678-1735), and the essayist and critic Jeremy Collier (1650-1726). Hickes and Collier in turn succeeded Sancroft as head of the Jacobite episcopacy: Collier at times signed himself as "Primus Anglo-Britanniae Episcopus."

All this troubled activity of political, religious, and scientific unrest was,

[13] "Europe in 1685 was passing through a political and religious crisis such as she had not passed through since 1588. In February of that year James II had declared himself a Catholic. In June, on the death of its Elector, the Palatinate passed into the hands of the Catholic family of Neubourg. In October Louis XIV revoked the Edict of Nantes; and in December the Duke of Savoy withdrew his grant of toleration to the Vaudois. On every side the Reformation and liberty seemed threatened as never before." — C. H. Driver, "John Locke," in *The Social and Political Ideas of Some English Thinkers of the Augustan Age*, ed. F. J. C. Hearnshaw (1928), p. 85.

of course, primarily the concern of the upper classes, especially of university men. Normally, after a period of varying length spent at either university, the young gentleman traveled on the Continent, and then returned to an active life in London or to a retired life in the country. The citizen and the country squire are outstanding types of the period, frequently burlesqued in comedy or in fiction. Men like John Evelyn and Sir William Temple loved the country and viewed eventual retirement there as a desired goal. Men like Samuel Pepys loved London and the amusements it and its environs afforded. As a whole, England must have presented an almost entirely rural aspect. London, to be sure, was the completely dominant metropolis, and contained somewhat less than two-thirds of a million inhabitants—which would be about one-tenth of the whole country's population. Norwich and Bristol had each perhaps 30,000 inhabitants, and York and Exeter had hardly more than 10,000. The great Midland manufacturing towns, already growing, would not be large for more than a century.[14] For the rest the country was sprinkled with small towns, villages, and country seats of gentlemen or noblemen. If we believe Macaulay (and it is not necessary to give him complete credence), the country squire of this period was practically illiterate. In the Restoration comedies, on the other hand, a valet may be presented as about the most intelligent person in the play. Such pictures are not to be trusted. The classes at times were curiously scrambled. One recalls Pepys's sister Pall, who became briefly a member of his household, "not as a sister but as a servant" who did not sit at table with the family. Pall grew proud and idle, however, and had to be sent back to the country. Unprivileged countryfolk frequently looked on London as a heavenly city; and it is certain that if the population of the island was rural, the arts were very largely urban. In the literature of the period class demarcations were especially strong. Restoration comedy was for courtiers and (perhaps) for rising citizens of London; Bunyan, on the other hand, was for the semi-literate dissenter, and he made his way very slowly towards a just recognition outside of his own class. He was, however, evidently read by other classes, as were the chapbooks of the period, which correspond roughly to the pulp fiction of the present day, to which in many respects they are greatly superior. Naturally, different classes—whether the class distinction is based on social position, on religious bias, or on a town or country background—had different tastes. It is, however, probably wrong to assume rigid demarcations in taste: the population was shifting from class to class, as the career of Pepys amply shows. Prudent Quakers and able dissenters were acquiring fortunes in trade, and were forming a new aristocracy, for which the Civil Wars and other causes had made room. New monarchs had new favorites to reward, and thus the nobility itself was being reconstituted towards the end of the century. In the first edition of Arthur

Social Conditions

---

[14] J. N. L. Baker, "England in the Seventeenth Century," in *An Historical Geography of England before 1800*, ed. Henry C. Darby (Cambridge, 1936), pp. 435-443 on "The Population of England."

Collins's *Peerage* (1709) twenty-one dukes are listed as living: of these only four represented ducal creations antedating 1660.

New dignities, whether of title or of wealth, encouraged new ways of life and renewed respect for Augustan decorum and for the arts of conspicuous consumption. Like the newly created duke, the wealthy citizen or the country squire developed an interest in the beauty of his house—his physical refuge from the turmoil of the day.[15] Of the care bestowed upon country seats Defoe in his *Compleat English Gentleman* (written *c.* 1730) remarks, "Nothing is forgotten to improve the estate, nothing entirely neglected but the heir." Macaulay, who like Defoe had a prejudice against country squires as Tories, in chapter III of his *History* has given a not too kind account of these squires and their homes; but in spite of such opinion and in spite of more real jocose remarks in Restoration comedies slurring country life, the weight of evidence indicates that the gentry and nobility of the time were proud of their country seats and spent large sums on remodeling old Gothic mansions into classical houses. Magnificent palaces such as Longleat and Chatsworth were being built, and the French-Italian axial garden was already becoming a frequent pattern in landscaping before the end of the century. Restoration houses and gardens were pictured in large numbers in extensive works such as James Beeverell's *Délices de la Grand' Bretagne et de l'Irlande* (1707) and Johannes Kip's *Britannia Illustrata* (1707-8). These elaborate productions were the result of pride as well as a cause of increasing pride in domestic architecture and landscaping in the eighteenth century. In the seventeenth century the best English architectural tradition was the Palladian style used by Inigo Jones (d. 1652). The greatest Restoration architect was Sir Christopher Wren (1632-1723), who in a more ornate style labored chiefly on public buildings; and these, from the Sheldonian Theatre in Oxford to the City churches and St. Paul's Cathedral in London, show Italian classicism at its English best.[16] Such of these edifices as now remain after troubled years constitute the best English monuments of architectural Augustanism. The most exquisite details in many Wren interiors are secured by the unbelievably delicate and elaborate wood-carving that is a feature of this late baroque period. The carvings of Grinling Gibbons (1648-1720) are the supreme achievement in this art. Painting in the Restoration period was inferior: Van Dyck, the most distinguished Continental painter working in England during the early century, was dead; and the visiting successors were Sir Peter Lely (1618-1680) and Sir Godfrey Kneller (1646-1723).

Marginal note: Stately Homes Are Built

> Lely on animated canvas stole
> The sleepy eye, that spoke the melting soul—

[15] The authoritative work on this problem is that of Beverley Sprague Allen, *Tides in English Taste (1619-1800): A Background for the Study of Literature* (2v, Cambridge, Mass., 1937).
[16] Sir Reginald Blomfield, *A History of Renaissance Architecture in England, 1500-1800* (2v, 1897), J. A. Gotch, *The English Home from Charles I to George IV* (1918), and Henry A. Tipping, *English Homes, Period IV (1649-1714)* (2v, 1920-28).

such was Pope's verdict on an art that he understood and practised. In childhood Pope inherited from his aunt the painting implements of her husband, Samuel Cooper (1609-72), perhaps the most notable of the skilful miniaturists of the time.

Of the fine arts music was practised with the most distinction. The keen *Music* eye of Samuel Pepys, watching at the waterside as citizens removed their goods by boat during the great London fire, on September 2, 1666, "observed that hardly one lighter or boat in three...but there was a pair of Virginalls [a sort of spinet] in it." Pepys himself, with his collection of viols, his harpsichord, and his flageolet, was passionately fond of music, and was not merely a performer but also a pleasing composer of songs. To contradict facile assertions of emotional deficiencies and artificialities of the period it may be well to quote Pepys's account of some incidental music for Massinger's *Virgin Martyr,* which he heard on February 27, 1667-8:

> That which did please me beyond any thing in the whole world was the wind-musique when the angel comes down, which is so sweet that it ravished me, and indeed, in a word, did wrap up my soul so that it made me really sick, just as I have formerly been when in love with my wife; that neither then, nor all the evening going home, and at home, I was able to think of anything, but remained all night transported, so as I could not believe that ever any musick hath that real command over the soul of a man as this did upon me: and makes me resolve to practice wind-musick, and to make my wife do the like.

Music was the Londoner's diversion at home as well as his delight in the theatre. Pepys was a friend of the composers Matthew Locke (1630?-1677) and Henry Purcell (1658?-1695), the last named one of the greatest England has yet produced. His opera *Dido and Aeneas* (*c.* 1690), with Dido's poignant final air, "When I am laid in earth," reinforces the impression made by Pepys's reaction to music—that Restoration lovers of music were far from emotionally callous. Others of the Purcell family were musicians of note; but the introduction of Italian opera rapidly undermined the English musical tradition, and early in the eighteenth century and thereafter London was largely an El Dorado for the best Continental artists, most of whom could be heard there.

These, then, are the principal intellectual and artistic interests of Restoration England. Of the literary achievements the ensuing chapters will attempt to tell the story.

II

Literary Criticism of the Restoration

In the mid-seventeenth century English literary criticism was formulating neo-classical dogma out of ideas long current in Italy and France, and familiar earlier in English academic circles and in such groups as those presided over by Ben Jonson and by "Sidney's sister, Pembroke's mother."

Tradition-alism and Rationalism

The doctrines were marked primarily by traditionalism and secondarily by a common-sense rationalism.[1] Naturally, in view of the great influence of Aristotle, Horace, Cicero, and Quintilian, as well as of Castelvetro, Scaliger, and, later, Boileau, the doctrines have been regarded as not native to English thinking. Although many of the dogmas imported from the Continent were never completely accepted in England, the common-sense aspect of neo-classicism easily domesticated itself. To follow the distinguished methods of the best ancients, that is, to follow "the rules" deduced by common sense from ancient procedure, seemed obviously practical. It was the function of critics to establish these laws for authors and to administer them with equity as judges. But the ancients when fantastic or parochial in habit might properly be disregarded, and no really eminent English critic ever wholeheartedly accepted all the French rules, the "foreign laws" (as Pope called them), laid down for the art of poetry. On the other hand, few were the critics of the period 1650-1750 who did not pay excessive attention to these rules.

Analysis and Rhetoric

The methods of these traditionalist critics were in general analytical or rhetorical. Aristotle, as interpreted by Renaissance commentators, gave doctrines for analytical critics, while Horace, Cicero, and Quintilian (and their disciples) largely originated the rhetorical tradition, which regarded poetry

[1] Perhaps the best single source of information about Restoration criticism is Joel E. Spingarn's *Critical Essays of the Seventeenth Century* (3v, Oxford, 1908-9) with its excellent introduction, texts, and notes. — For general discussions: F. E. Schelling, "Ben Jonson and the Classical School," *PMLA*, XIII (1898). 221-249; reprinted in *Shakespeare and Demi-Science* (Philadelphia, 1927); George Saintsbury, *A History of Criticism* (3v, Edinburgh, 1900-4); W. G. Howard, "Ut Pictura Poesis," *PMLA*, XXIV (1909). 40-123; James E. Routh, *The Rise of Classical English Criticism to the Death of Dryden* (New Orleans, 1915); Donald L. Clark, *Rhetoric and Poetry in the Renaissance* (1922); P. S. Wood, "Native Elements in English Neo-Classicism," *MP*, XXIV (1926). 201-208; René Bray, *La Formation de la doctrine classique en France* (Paris, 1927); P. S. Wood, "The Opposition to Neo-Classicism in England, 1660-1700," *PMLA*, XLIII (1928). 182-197; Marvin T. Herrick, *The Poetics of Aristotle in England* (New Haven, 1930); Arthur O. Lovejoy, "The Parallel of Deism and Classicism," *MP*, XXIX (1932). 281-299; Louis I. Bredvold, "The Tendency towards Platonism in Neo-Classical Esthetics," *ELH*, I (1934). 91-119; Ronald S. Crane, "Neo-Classical Criticism," in *Dictionary of World Literature*, ed. Joseph T. Shipley (1943), pp. 193-203. — For bibliographical aids see *CBEL*, II. 3-31 and John W. Draper, *Eighteenth Century English Aesthetics: A Bibliography* (Heidelberg, 1931).

as a superior refinement on the persuasive arts of oratory. The analytical and rhetorical methods were mutually helpful, and in some ways mutually destructive. Aristotle focused attention on the nature of poetry as existent in certain forms, notably epic and tragedy. He gave a method for analyzing poems of these types. He did not stress either the genetics or the effectiveness of poetry, but concentrated on its component parts and its structural principles. The rhetorical tradition, deriving strength from the fact that in the schools poetry was taught as a sub-topic under rhetoric, stressed creative processes and methods of affecting the mind of a reader. Neoclassical poetry was essentially rhetorical in that it spoke to an audience and attempted to move or to modify the mental state of its audience. Normally it did not, like later, romantic poetry, tend to be soliloquy. The composition of an oration from Greek times had been viewed under three aspects: *invention,* or the finding of material; *disposition,* or the arrangement of material; and *eloquence,* or the embodying of matter in fit style. As applied to the composition of poetry the first of these three aspects of creation was not necessarily cold-blooded. The prologue of the most epical of Shakespeare's plays, *Henry V,* begins,

> O for a Muse of fire, that would ascend
> The brightest heaven of invention;

and usually—but not always—in neo-classical criticism invention is not mere ingenuity but is associated with fire and elevation. It is a favorite word with Dryden; and for most English critics before 1750 it carried a meaning at times approaching that of the term so popular and so undefined in romantic criticism, "creative imagination." From rhetorical theory also, as well as from Bacon, Hobbes, and other psychological writers, the poet learned that to affect his readers he must through his own imaginative deftness appeal to "the passions" (as emotions were termed) of his reader. The principles of criticism changed less in the seventeenth century than the abilities of poets, but in the case of both critics and poets what change there was tended towards admiration of simplicity, sound sense, and propriety, and away from fantasy or anything like imaginative eccentricity. The poet was to sing in perfect full tone; he was not to try for "original" or individual tonal effects.

Before proceeding to discuss the major critics of the period it may be well to mention certain recurring topics sometimes regarded as subjects of universal agreement. While it is true that the belief, current at that time, *The Pur-* in the uniformity of human reason led critics to announce principles as if *pose of* axiomatically self-evident, hardly more unanimity was evident in this period *Poets* than in most ages. There was widespread agreement in the Horatian dogma that poets wished to profit or to please.

> Aut prodesse volunt aut delectare poetae,

Horace had written, and the moderns approved the dictum. Most, to be sure, assumed (as did Horace himself) that the best poetry afforded *both* delight and moral instruction, delight being the immediate and instruction the ultimate end. In 1668 Dryden evoked dissent from Shadwell by saying that "delight is the chief, if not the only, end of poesy: instruction can be admitted but in the second place, for poesy only instructs as it delights." Rymer believed in pleasure alone as object, but he stressed moral instruction as inherent in the higher sorts of poetry. Most critics seem to have regarded instruction as the ultimate end of the art, and poetry in practice frequently became a sort of wisdom-writing. Ten-syllable aphorisms, or even *pensées* in the general fashion of Pascal's, were features in the writing of most authors from Dryden to Blake.

Theories of Imitation   Imitation was the accepted method of poetry, but there was no uniformly accepted meaning attached to the term itself. To Aristotle poetic *mimesis,* badly translated into Latin as *imitatio,* had meant the representation of the actions of men. To Renaissance critics it had meant at times the imitation of one's predecessors, especially ancient classical authors. Its materials were the actions or manners of men, and the process of representation involved two things: depiction of an action and of an implicit principle of action. Critics of the epic, such as René Le Bossu,[2] thought a poet first selected a principle of action or a passion (disunity due to the wrath of Achilles, for example), and then wove a fable to illustrate it. The criteria of imitation were verisimilitude and decorum, and both might refer either to the action itself or to the principle of the action. Other criteria, much appealed to, were Truth, Reason, and Nature—terms used practically as synonyms representing a not too well-defined ultimate of excellence. Poetic mimesis might be idealistic and portray men not as they are but rather as they ought to be. There was no idea that the poet should attempt photographic realism. "Holding the mirror up to nature" might perfectly apply to the art of the actor, but it was less apt with reference to the more intellectual and ideal art of the poet. The meaning of human action as portrayed rather than the appearance of it was what appealed to poets with an abstractionist and moral bias. A further concept, expressed in the phrase *la belle nature,* involved a nature purged of its worthless or trivial dross and in a sense pre-fabricated and tested by the experience of (usually) the ancients. It was in this sense, according to Pope, that the young Virgil found Nature and Homer "the same." [3] Homer was in fact preferable to nature because he had supposedly sloughed off the crudeness of all but *la belle nature.*

The Rules   The criterion of art later most deplored by romantic critics was the rules. Admiration of one's predecessors made one a traditionalist, and critics attempted to judge the intelligence and tact of a poet's imitation by deducing general rules or "methodizing" the tradition followed. One might, at one's peril, depart from the rules; but if the departure did not surprise, delight,

---

[2] René Le Bossu's *Treatise of the Epick Poem* appeared in French in 1675, and was englished by "W. J." in 1695. It became the standard work on the epic, and in 1719 was reprinted. For a recent and thorough treatment of these matters see Hugh T. Swedenberg, Jr., *The Theory of the Epic in England, 1650-1800* (Berkeley, 1944).

[3] *Essay on Criticism,* line 135.

and enrich the tradition, it was likely to be bitterly condemned. The rules varied greatly in nature, but they prescribed, sometimes minutely, the procedure proper for each of the poetic genres. The fundamental trouble with "rules critics," apart from their less accountable absurdities, was summarized later by Dr. Johnson: they judged by principles and not by perceptions. They did not ask what was in a poem, but told what had to be in such a poem if it fulfilled traditional prerequisites. Such critics were early the objects of ridicule. Professor Spingarn found a French critic, the Chevalier de Méré, remarking: "I have noticed that those who lay the most stress on rules have little taste; and yet it is good taste which alone can create good rules." [4] Perception was bound to have its innings, and taste was to become by the turn of the century a word of power. It could modify the rules or defy analysis by insisting on the indefinable grace, the *je ne sais quoi*, as an eminent French critic, the Père Bouhours, called it in a famous essay.[5]

Traditionalist criticism worked through the various genres that French critics had deduced from the classics. Aristotle had hardly treated, in his fragmentary *Poetics*, more than the epic and tragedy; but by the middle of *The Genres* the seventeenth century the accepted genres had been both defined and evaluated. In 1704 John Dennis stated the net results with commendable bluntness:

1. The greater Poetry is an Art by which a Poet justly and reasonably excites great Passion, that he may please and instruct; and comprehends Epick, Tragick, and the greater Lyrick Poetry [i.e., the Pindaric ode].
2. The less Poetry is an Art by which a Poet excites less Passion for the foremention'd Ends; and includes in it Comedy and Satire, and the little Ode, and Elegiack and Pastoral Poems.[6]

The types Dennis lists, it should be noted, are arranged in order of descending importance. In the dedication of his *Aeneis* Dryden had remarked, "A Heroic Poem, truly such, is undoubtedly the greatest work which the soul of man is capable to perform." In the words "truly such" Dryden nods amicably to the traditionalism of his day, to the rules of the epic. But such a nod is not mere pedantry. On Dryden's opinion, his editor, W. P. Ker, comments:

The 'Heroic Poem' is not commonly mentioned in histories of Europe as a matter of serious interest: yet from the days of Petrarch and Boccaccio to those of

---

[4] Spingarn, *op. cit.*, I, p. xcv.

[5] In *Spectator* No. 62 Addison characterized Dominique Bouhours (d. 1702) as "the most penetrating of all the French critics." In his beautifully written *Entretiens d'Ariste et d'Eugène* (1671), ed. René Radouant (Paris, 1920), occur two essays at least, "Le Bel esprit," and "Le Je ne sais quoi," which are often echoed by English authors. In "Le Bel esprit" Bouhours describes wit as *un corps solide qui brille,* and this concept of wit is much quoted. In 1688 Dryden translated Bouhours' *Life of St. Francis Xavier*, and his *Manière de bien penser dans les ouvrages d'esprit* (1687) was translated into English in 1705 and 1728. On the history of this doctrine see Samuel H. Monk, "A Grace beyond the Reach of Art," *JHI*, v (1944). 131-150.

[6] "The Grounds of Criticism in Poetry," in *The Critical Works of John Dennis*, ed. Edward N. Hooker (2v, Baltimore, 1939-43), I. 338. With Dennis's ranking of the genres other critics would tend to agree. Possibly they would not make the excitement of passion the sole criterion for this ranking.

Dr. Johnson, and more especially from the sixteenth century onward, it was a subject that engaged some of the strongest intellects in the world (among them, Hobbes, Gibbon, and Hume); it was studied and discussed as fully and with as much thought as any of the problems by which the face of the world was changed in those centuries. There might be difference of opinion about the essence of the Heroic Poem or the Tragedy, but there was no doubt about their value. Truth about them was ascertainable, and truth about them was necessary to the intellect of man, for they were the noblest things belonging to him.[7]

It was in this lofty Augustan mood that critics at their best accepted the doctrines of neo-classical traditionalism. At their best they never in theory seriously disparaged the imaginative and emotional aspects of literary art; but they did subject these mercurial factors to the rigorous control of judgment. No critic is constantly at his best, and Restoration critics at times *Imagination* made the subjection of imagination to judgment excessive,[8] and at times *and Judg-* were too moralistic or too much devoted to a prosaic common-sense attitude *ment* towards life. With the rules that concerned unity in structure and plainness in poetic style they struggled not very effectually. Unity is a late and perhaps a rare aesthetic quality, and the problem of appropriate decoration in style is as thorny as that of morals in art. We shall get further light on some of these problems if we examine individually some of Dryden's contemporaries —as well as Dryden himself, who has been called "the first great modern critic."

Davenant   An early outburst of neo-classical pronouncement occurred in the prose *as Critic* discourses that preceded (1650) Davenant's *Gondibert* on its first appearance. Davenant[9] wrote a long prefatory epistle to his friend Thomas Hobbes,[10] which is in a sense a "defense of poetry" as well as of his own dull epic; and Hobbes contributed a friendly "Answer" to this prefatory epistle. It is significant that the focus of attention here, as in Cowley's critical writing,

[7] *Essays of John Dryden* (2v, Oxford, 1900), I, p. xvi.

[8] On control of the imagination by judgment see George Williamson, "The Restoration Revolt against Enthusiasm," *SP*, xxx (1933). 571-603, and two articles by Donald F. Bond: " 'Distrust' of the Imagination in English Neo-classicism," *PQ*, xiv (1935). 54-69, and "The Neo-classical Psychology of the Imagination," *ELH*, iv (1937). 245-264.

[9] For Davenant's career and works, see below, ch. v, n. 5. The present account of the critical writing of Davenant and Hobbes may be thought to undervalue their work. For other accounts see Spingarn, *op. cit.*, and Cornell M. Dowlin, *Sir William Davenant's Gondibert, its Preface and Hobbes's Answer* (Philadelphia, 1934), and Clarence D. Thorpe, *The Aesthetic Theory of Thomas Hobbes* (Ann Arbor, 1940).

[10] Thomas Hobbes (1588-1679) was born at Malmesbury, the son of a clergyman. After attending local schools from the age of four and learning Latin and Greek at six, he in 1603 entered Magdalen Hall, Oxford, and was graduated in 1608. For most of the rest of his life he was practically a member of the Cavendish family, since he served as tutor and companion to both the second and the third Earls. On his Continental travels Hobbes made many friends— among them, Gassendi and Galileo. Among his English friends were Bacon, Harvey, Selden, Cowley, Waller, Davenant, and Ben Jonson. His enemies were equally numerous: he was among the first to flee to Paris after the Long Parliament met in 1640; and after the publication of *Leviathan* (1651), fearful of French charges of atheism, he returned to England. Here too he underwent this accusation, and his replies as well as his mathematical controversies with Seth Ward, John Wallis, and Robert Boyle, extended over decades. From Clarendon and the church party he was protected by Charles II, who in Paris had been his pupil in mathematics, and who granted him a pension of £100. After a long and disputatious career Hobbes in 1675 retired to the Cavendish country estates at Chatsworth and Hardwick. He died at the age of ninety-one. — *Opera philosophica quae Latine scripsit* (Amsterdam, 1668); ed. Sir William Molesworth (5v, 1839-45); *The English Works*, ed. Sir William Molesworth (11v, 1839-45).

was the epic. In Davenant's opinion "Heroick Poesie...yeelds not to any other humane work"; and the philosophical Hobbes, agreeing, undermined his integrity as critic by such enthusiastic praise of *Gondibert* as "I never yet saw Poem that had so much shape of Art, health of Morality, and vigour and beauty of Expression as this of yours." These were doubtless the qualities that Hobbes and his age felt should exist in great poetry. Davenant found the function of "heroic" poets comparable to that of divines, generals, statesmen, and lawgivers as an aid to "government"; that is, to the control of manners and morals. "And as Poesy is the best Expositor of Nature, Nature being misterious to such as use not to consider, so Nature is the best Interpreter of God, and more cannot be said of Religion."

The apparent nobility of these ideas can be overvalued. Hobbes's "Answer" asserts a high intellectual concept of poetry when he says "That which giveth a Poem the true and natural Colour consisteth in two things, which are, *To know well,* that is, to have images of nature in the memory distinct and clear, and *To know much." To know well* is the basis of decorum; *The to know much* is the source of delightful variety resulting from the well- *"Answer"* stored mind. But this high level is not maintained: an unimaginative, *of Hobbes* matter-of-fact disapproval of scenes that take us into fantastic localities, "even into Heaven and Hell...where Nature never comes," shows the really pedestrian concepts involved. The criterion of "truth" is invoked, and Davenant prefers truth of passion (fiction?) to truth of fact: the poet is not bound as is the historian, but he must remain within the limits of the probable. Hobbes dissents "from those that think the Beauty of a Poem consisteth in the exorbitancy of the fiction. For as truth is the bound of Historical, so the Resemblance of truth is the utmost limit of Poeticall Liberty." Thus in critical theory romantic "exorbitancy" was making its exit. A little more than a century later Richard Hurd at the end of his *Letters on Chivalry and Romance* (1762) summed up the results and indicated a counter-change in remarking: "What we have gotten by this revolution, you will say, is a great deal of good sense. What we have lost, is a world of fine fabling."

Few writers have acquired so much reputation in the field of criticism *Hobbes a* on so little bulk of critical writing as has Thomas Hobbes. His philosophical *Rhetorical* thinking was doubtless of great negative influence in the period: it spurred *Critic* all the other major thinkers of England to antagonism. In criticism his influence is less clear. His "Answer" to Davenant's preface, his own preface to his translation of the *Odyssey* (1675), and a few pages in his philosophical writings have caused him to be regarded as the father of neo-classical rationalistic aesthetics, and more recently as a forerunner of modern psychological theory concerning poetic creation. A true rhetorician, Hobbes regarded poetry as a means of modifying the minds of others: he studied the task as a psychological problem. "Invention" is an imaginative process; "disposition" is stressed as judgment, and "eloquence" is associated with certain ornamental functions of "fancy." His terminology is shifting, but his description of the creative process is not with all his meanings essentially novel. "Wit"—a valued faculty—consists of *"Celerity of Imagining,* (that is, swift succession of one thought to another;) and *steddy direction* to some approved end." "A good wit" is called "a good fancy." "But," he says, "without Steddiness, and Direction to some End, a great Fancy is one kind of Madnesse." Wit associates and combines; judgment discerns and differentiates. It is Hobbes's insistence on control in art, on judgment as a check to exorbitancy of fancy, that is his chief contribution to the aesthetics of his day.

Dryden's Critical Merit

The most valuable criticism of the period was that written by John Dryden.[11] The high excellence of his critical writing derives, first, from a mental incisiveness that led him at times with inspired directness to the heart of a problem and, secondly, from an unusually catholic sensitiveness to the merits of several divergent literary traditions. Amongst these traditions his mind has seemed to some merely blown about by various winds of doctrine inconsistently. The truth is that he is almost phenomenally able to see merits in all literary camps.

His Development

There is also the problem of development; for Dryden was writing criticism (chiefly in prefaces, there being at the time no other well established vehicles of criticism, except perhaps pamphlets) at frequent intervals throughout a career of almost forty years, and one might expect changes in his position. The temptation is to exaggerate a progressive detachment from Elizabethan "romanticism" in favor of neo-classical "orthodoxy." It is doubtful if any orthodox and tangible neo-classical *credo* was ever widely held; certainly Dryden is no consistent adherent to any such formulated doctrine. His prefaces are, at first sight, preoccupied with transitory, even topical, matters, and this fact makes it difficult to trace development surely, and makes it wise to focus on the aesthetic values basic in his thinking.

Of Dramatic Poesy

His fundamental skeptical independence in dogmatizing is perhaps best seen in his masterpiece in critical writing, the early *Essay of Dramatic Poesy,* written in 1665 and published in 1668, as a part of his argument with his brother-in-law, Sir Robert Howard, over the advisability of writing plays in rime. In form it is a Ciceronian dialogue; the four speakers present diverse points of view, for most of which Dryden felt both sympathy and reservation. The first speaker, Crites, defends the ancients (for whom Dryden has great

---

11 For Dryden's career see below, ch. III, esp. n. 2. The best of his critical writings are all in *Essays of John Dryden,* ed. W. P. Ker (2v, Oxford, 1900), and Professor Ker's introduction is still the best brief commentary. Other commentaries include: P. H. Frye, "Dryden and the Critical Canons of the Eighteenth Century," *Nebraska Univ. Stud.,* VII (1907). 1-39; John H. Smith, "Dryden's Critical Temper," *Washington Univ. Stud., Humanistic Series,* XII (1925). 201-220; O. F. Emerson, "John Dryden and a British Academy," *Proceedings of the British Academy,* X (1921). 45-58; F. G. Walcott, "John Dryden's Answer to Thomas Rymer's *The Tragedies of the Last Age,*" *PQ,* XV (1936). 194-214; J. O. Eidson, "Dryden's Criticism of Shakespeare," *SP,* XXXIII (1936). 273-280; Pierre Legouis, "Corneille and Dryden as Dramatic Critics," in *Seventeenth Century Studies Presented to Sir Herbert Grierson* (Oxford, 1938), pp. 269-291; Guy Montgomery, "Dryden and the Battle of the Books," *Essays and Studies by Members of the English Department, University of California, Univ. of Calif. Pub. in English,* XIV (1943). 57-72; Hoyt Trowbridge, "Dryden's *Essay on the Dramatic Poetry of the Last Age,*" *PQ,* XXII (1943). 240-250.

admiration); Eugenius, who like Dryden believes in progress in the arts, defends the superiority of contemporary English drama; Lisideius prefers French drama to English and prefers Elizabethan drama to that of the early Restoration period; and Neander, who most nearly is Dryden himself among the speakers, finally defends the English as opposed to the French, gives a glowing account of Jonson, Beaumont and Fletcher, and Shakespeare, but defends the recent use of rime in plays.

Here, and usually, Dryden believes in progress and modernity. He objects to the triteness of Roman comic plots, their faulty moral instruction, their weak wit, and their lack of warmth in love scenes; he praises their excellent contrivance of situation, their structural regularity—which the French imitate but which, he thinks, may easily lead to thinness of action. Irregularity in structure may contribute invaluable variety, but the paths of irregularity are difficult. One of Dryden's triumphant sentences is: "Now what, I beseech you, is more easy than to write a regular French play, or more difficult than write an irregular English one, like those of Fletcher, or of Shakespeare?" He can respect and even overvalue French rules, but he feels that the French are "too strictly tied up" with these formalistic matters; so he loyally asserts that "in most of the irregular plays of Shakespeare or Fletcher ... there is a more masculine fancy and greater spirit in the writing, than there is in any of the French." Dryden is relatively consistent, if somewhat prejudiced, in his evaluation of French drama; his notion of progress led him at times to overvalue his own age as compared with Elizabethan drama, notably in his Epilogue to the Second Part of *The Conquest of Granada* and in the prose "Defence" of the Epilogue (1672), where he asserts that the Elizabethans— often actually "low"—failed to produce polite or courtly dialogue because they were not, like the Restoration comic writers, frequenters of the best school of manners, the court! Normally he recognizes the merits as well as the defects of the Elizabethans. He sums up in his preface to the *Examen Poeticum* (1693), where he exclaims: "Peace be to the venerable shades of Shakespeare and Ben Johnson! none of the living will presume to have any competition with them; as they were our predecessors, so they were our masters."

Dryden swerved from minor positions, such as the use of rime in plays or rant in his heroic dramas; but he is reputably constant in his catholic appreciation of naturalness, "refined" wit, structural neatness (and such rules as conduce to it) as well as of variety (disparaging such rules as constrict genius), of "bold strokes," and of "masculine fancy." These last two values he admires in the Elizabethans, though at times excessively aware of the incorrectness found with them. "Shakespeare," he says, "who many times has written better than any poet, in any language ... is the very Janus of poets; he wears almost everywhere two faces; and you have scarce begun to admire the one, ere you despise the other." Similarly Dryden finds many faults among ancient writers, but yet holds them to be the best teachers for moderns. He believes in a spirited and emulous imitation of Nature as shown

Dryden's Consistency

by the ancients, but abhors a constricted imitation—"all that is dull, insipid, languishing, and without sinews." He ranges himself among the Aristotelians in his "Grounds of Criticism in Tragedy" (1679), and urges classical restraint in diction in his dedication to *The Spanish Friar* (1681). Both these works are influenced by Thomas Rymer's *Tragedies of the Last Age Consider'd* (1678)—a work to which Dryden planned a reply,[12] and by which he was considerably influenced. In the last decade of his career such prefaces as those to his translations of Juvenal (1693) and Virgil (1697) naturally stress classical topics; but even in the first extreme phase of Rymer's influence— seen in the dedication to *The Spanish Friar*—we find Dryden declaring firmly for tragicomedy as opposed to pure genres, and in one of his last dedications (to his *Aeneis,* 1697) he exclaims, "Let the French and Italians value themselves on their regularity; strength and elevation are our standard." Throughout his career he is likely to be boldly independent.

On such topics as the heroic poem or wit or such a neo-classical ultimate as "Nature," Dryden's thought is always vital and incisive; but a great deal of his impressiveness derives from his directness and pungency of expression.

His Prose Style He seasons his assertions with apt and illuminating metaphor or with a summarizing aphorism. Of tragicomedy he concludes: "the feast is too dull and solemn without the fiddles," and his glowing remarks about Shakespeare ("he needed not the spectacles of books to read Nature") and Chaucer ("here is God's plenty") are known examples. Of Ben Jonson's indebtedness to the ancients he says, "You track him everywhere in their snow"; of Jonson's borrowings: "He invades authors like a monarch; and what would be theft in other poets, is only victory in him." A final apt metaphor in the preface to his *Evening's Love* (1671) expresses neatly the neo-classical concept of emulous imitation:

But in general, the employment of a poet is like that of a curious gunsmith, or watchmaker: the iron or silver is not his own; but they are the least part of that which gives the value: the price lies wholly in the workmanship. And he who works dully on a story, without moving laughter in a comedy, or raising concernment in a serious play, is no more to be accounted a good poet, than a gunsmith of the Minories is to be compared with the best workman of the town.

Obviously Dryden understands not merely poetic expression but also what he himself calls "the other harmony of prose." The frequency with which his phrases turn up in later authors indicates a considerable and appropriate amount of influence.

Apart from Dryden the most notable critic of the Restoration period was probably Thomas Rymer [13] (1641-1713), who, trained for the bar and per-

12 See Hugh Macdonald, *John Dryden, a Bibliography* (Oxford, 1939), p. 179, and James M. Osborn, *John Dryden* (1940), pp. 267-269 ("Dryden's 'Heads of an Answer to Rymer' ").

13 Thomas Rymer (1641-1713), son of a prominent Roundhead who in 1664 was executed after a Presbyterian uprising, was himself a consistent royalist. He attended loyal schools, including Sidney-Sussex College, Cambridge, where, however, he took no degree. A member of Gray's Inn, he was called to the bar in 1673; but thereafter for a time devoted himself to literature rather than to law. He acquired a great and deserved reputation for learning, and in 1692 was appointed historiographer royal, in 1693 editor of diplomatic documents and treaties.

suaded that of all the "Noble Exercises of Humane Understanding. ...   *Thomas*
Experimental Philosophy is the most noble, beneficial, and satisfactory,"   *Rymer*
became in criticism the standard-bearer of unimaginative neo-classical rationalism. Rymer had a deservedly great reputation as a historical antiquarian; his *Foedera* (1704-35 in 20 volumes), an enormous collection of
English state papers from the Middle Ages down to 1654, is still a major
landmark in the development of English historical studies. His achievement
as a critic has been from the start debatable. His translation (1674) of René
Rapin's *Reflections on Aristotle's Treatise of Poesie* indicates his regard both
for Aristotle and for French criticism. In his preface to this work he exhibits
his predilection for "exquisite sense" rather than "variety of matter," for neat,
unified plotting rather than for Elizabethan richness or humanity, and for
judgment rather than fancy. In his *Tragedies of the Last Age Consider'd*
he tersely announces, "Common sense suffices," and while this principle is
unimaginatively prominent, an austere sense of decorum is rather what
causes him in this work to castigate three plays of Beaumont and Fletcher.
In 1692 he published *A Short View of Tragedy* (dated 1693), one section of
which contains his notorious attack on *Othello*. His opinions of Shakespeare
seem generally, and justly, to have been regarded by his contemporaries as
extremely severe; [14] his obviously great learning was, however, widely
respected. He had an unusual knowledge of Greek tragedy, and the *Short
View* shows an astonishing diversity of reading. In his *Essay concerning
Critical and Curious Learning* (1698) he involved himself in the controversy
between Sir William Temple and the wits of Christ Church, Oxford, over
ancient and modern learning. Here he neatly states the nature of his adherence to Aristotle, of whom he was perhaps the most bigoted follower in his
day:

Using as model his friend Leibniz's *Codex Juris Gentium Diplomaticus* (1693), he labored for
the rest of his life, often at his own expense, on the arduous undertaking that is his real
monument, his *Foedera*. — *Reflections on Aristotle's Treatise of Poesie by R. Rapin* (translated
by Rymer, 1674); *Edgar, an Heroick Tragedy* (1678); *The Tragedies of the Last Age Consider'd
and Examin'd by the Practice of the Ancients and by the Common Sense of All Ages, in a
Letter to Fleetwood Shepheard, Esq.* (1678); *A Short View of Tragedy: It's Original, Excellency,
and Corruption, with Some Reflections on Shakespear, and Other Practitioners for the Stage*
(1693); *An Essay concerning Critical and Curious Learning: In which are Contained Some
Short Reflections on the Controversie betwixt Sir William Temple and Mr. Wotton; and that
betwixt Dr. Bentley and Mr. Boyl. By T. R.* (1698) [ascribed to Rymer]; *A Vindication of
an Essay concerning Critical and Curious Learning ... by the Author of the Essay* (1698);
Foedera (15v, 1704-13; Vols. XVI-XX [in part by Robert Sanderson], 1715-35). — Sir T. Duffus
Hardy, "Memoir," in Vol. I of his Syllabus of the *Foedera* (1869); A. Hofherr, *Thomas Rymers
Dramatische Kritik* (Heidelberg, 1908); G. B. Dutton, "The French Aristotelian Formalists and
Thomas Rymer," *PMLA*, XXIX (1914). 152-188.

14 The work attracted great attention. It is reviewed in P. Motteux's *Gentleman's Journal* for
December, 1692 (p. 15), and in Richard Wolley's *Compleat Library* for the same month (pp.
58-66) the work gets a long summary—which omits the whole section on *Othello*. John Dennis's
Impartial Critick (1693) is a spirited reply. Samuel Butler's lines "Upon Critics who Judge of
Modern Plays Precisely by the Rules of the Antients" (Spingarn, *Critical Essays*, II. 278-281) is
a reply to *The Tragedies of the Last Age Consider'd*, and a reply to the *Short View* is addressed
to Dryden, presumably by Charles Gildon, under the title of "Some Reflections on Mr. Rymer's
Short View," in *Miscellaneous Letters* (1694), pp. 64-118. Concerning Dryden's reaction to this
earlier work see Fred G. Walcott in *PQ*, XV (1936). 194-214. Shakespeare was not without
friends!

Critical Learning, in the Modern Acception, is commonly taken for a thorough Understanding of Classick Authors, and an Exact Knowledge of those Rules, by which Men judge and determine nicely of all the finer Parts and Branches of Humane Literature. *Aristotle* was the first that drew these Rules up into Compass, and made Criticism an Art; and the Philosopher took such Care to form his Precepts upon the Practice of the best Writers, and to reduce them withal to the severest Test of Nature and Reason; that he scarcely left any thing for succeeding Ages to do. . . . But in short, he is esteemed a good Critick, who can distinguish the Beauties and Excellencies of an Author; and discover likewise his Failures and Imperfections. When he makes his Judgment of a Book; he takes it in pieces, and considers the whole Structure and Oeconomy of it.

Rymer was analytical: he took tragedies to "pieces"; he is also especially to be noted as a "verbal critic," meticulous and unimaginative in reducing poetic language to "common sense." His devotion to the rules plus an exaggerated evaluation of probability and decorum and an insensitiveness to the richness of human nature in the Elizabethan drama subverted his great learning and his keen sense of the importance of design or plotting in both epic and tragedy. He resented the tendency to regard the "monstrous irregularities" of Shakespeare as "shining beauties." "Good Conduct in War," he pontificates, "is no hindrance to the boldest Undertakings. . . . And a due observation of critical rules, that is, a strict attendance to the rules of nature and reason, can never impede or clog an author's fancy." Here Rymer differs from Dryden and other critics of the time; but it is observable that even for him reason and nature were higher than Aristotle.

Rymer was consistently of the party of the ancients, and thus naturally an ally of Sir William Temple in the campaign against modern writers that arose from Sir William's championing of antiquity in his *Essay upon the Ancient and Modern Learning* (1690). Sir William was a widely but superficially read statesman and man of the world, whose essay, if it had not annoyed certain scholars (William Wotton and Richard Bentley) by its faulty dating of Aesop's *Fables* and the *Epistles* of Phalaris, might have been praised and neglected for its suave and cadenced periods. After Temple's secretary, a young man named Jonathan Swift, reduced the controversy to acrid laughter in his *Battle of the Books* (1704), this essay was less regarded than another, *Of Poetry,* published in the same volume with it. Here Temple is the elegant amateur rather than the pedantic Aristotelian, but he is on the whole very much of his own day. Poetry has something in it "too libertine to be confined to so many rules" as the modern French critics invent; Sir William will content himself with the easier prescriptions of Aristotle and Horace, neglecting their commentators. Yet he agrees that to "the heat of invention and liveliness of wit" poetry must add "the coldness of good sense and soundness of judgment." In three other respects he is significant: (1) The earliest poets were thought to be the best; nature decays; and civilization knows cyclic change, but not progress. Dryden and many contemporaries did not agree here, and Temple's denial of the idea of progress did not deter

Temple and the Ancients

others from espousing it. (2) On the basis of the old psychology that regarded heat as precondition for imagination and cold as fostering judgment Temple popularized the idea that genius depended in part on climate. This became a favorite eighteenth-century idea, and encouraged a tendency to think in relative rather than absolute terms. (3) Temple's polished amateurism promoted an aristocratic pose on the part of poets. This was perhaps inherent in the central concept of Augustanism, but it developed the belief that poetry was the most elegant of leisurely and genteel employments: its function was to amuse. So naturally Temple concluded his essay *Of Poetry* with the famous sentence that so well illustrates his pleasingly rhythmical style:

When all is done, Human Life is, at the greatest and the best, but like a froward Child, that must be Play'd with and Humor'd a little to keep it quiet till it falls asleep, and then the Care is over.

In the last two decades of the seventeenth century, verse was increasingly *Criticism* used as a vehicle for criticism in the Horatian tradition. The Earl of Ros- *in Verse* common published a metrical translation of Horace's *Art of Poetry* (1680), and a year later John Oldham also printed a modernized adaptation of the poem. In 1682 John Sheffield (later Duke of Buckinghamshire) published a metrical *Essay upon Poetry,* and in 1683 Sir William Soames and Dryden helped popularize Boileau's recent *Art Poétique* (1674) by an English translation. In 1684 Roscommon brought out his *Essay on Translated Verse,* and other poets followed with various satirical or didactic poems concerned with criticism. In 1700 Sir Richard Blackmore published his *Satyr against Wit,* and his admirer Samuel Wesley (1662-1735), the father of the founder of Methodism, brought out *An Epistle to a Friend concerning Poetry.* Somewhat more interesting was the *Essay upon Unnatural Flights in Poetry,* which, with elaborate prose annotations, "Granville the polite" (Lord Lansdowne) published in 1701. The path was open and well trodden that was to lead to Pope's *Essay on Criticism.* The critic was tied down to decorum, to the natural, to pedestrian common sense. The fantastic was "out"!

III

The Poetry of Dryden

The General Nature of Dryden's Poetry

Taste in poetry has changed so extremely in the last century and a half that for many persons John Dryden and his school are practically unreadable. For the intelligent student of poetry this is not true. Dryden is one of the most significant figures in the history of English verse; for he perhaps more than any other single person formulated a method for poetry that has appealed to disciples (some of them, to be sure, only metrical imitators) as different as Pope, Gray, Churchill, Byron, Keats, and T. S. Eliot; a method that for two generations after his death dominated English verse. Dryden's way was not that of the sensuous romantic, "tremblingly alive all o'er," unlocking his heart of hearts for the public to see; it is rather an impersonal, almost editorial, criticism of life. Much of the time it hardly seems to be "the language of the emotions," and seldom is it merely that of the senses. It is a method that conceives of poetry as intellectual utterance emotionally or imaginatively suffused so as to persuade a public "audience." It is, in short, the poetry of eloquence, which, in spite of John Stuart Mill and his followers, is not merely a reputable but an essential method for poets living as Dryden did in times of public emergency. His poetry is "occasional"; and the occasions which it celebrates are public and important—or were in his day. As time passes, however, the importance of occasions fades; the obvious journalistic character of such poetry requires annotation, and annotation is insufferable tedium to later casual readers of verse.

The Element of Control

Basically, the school of Dryden is devoted to a belief in *control* as essential to art, to a disbelief in "unpremeditated art." One's imagination was controlled by the procedure of the ancients and by thinking in terms of genres. Accidentally, the school is devoted to translation and to satire; but Dryden—and Pope as well—realized that satire and didactic verse were "low" genres; and each aspired to produce an epic—to Dryden's mind "undoubtedly the greatest work which the soul of man is capable to perform." But the need to gratify patrons, to defend "sacred truth," and to make a living, compelled both Dryden and Pope to inhabit, in Swift's phrase, "the lowlands of Parnassus." Both poets made excellent translations of the greatest epics; but their own epics were never written.

The love of control operated also in the field of metrics, and the closed heroic couplet became the favored metre for Dryden and his followers. One must remember, however, that Dryden excelled all other English poets in the Cowleyan Pindaric, and that the stanza forms used for songs in his plays are both neat and varied. But the bulk of his work was in the couplet, which, though he did not invent, he did in a sense perfect. His chief predecessors in the evolution of the closed couplet as the container for Augustan wit were Ben Jonson, Waller, Denham, and Sandys.[1] Early prosodists to theorize the form were the author of *The Arte of English Poesie* (1589), usually ascribed to George Puttenham, and the author of an essay signed "J. D." in Joshua Poole's *English Parnassus* (1657). Such influences in addition to closing the couplet tended to make verse accent coincide with that of speech, to regulate the placing of the caesura, and to further the frequent use of rhetorical devices of various sorts. Dominated by an ideal of correctness, these tendencies resulted in verse notable for deft artifice and for mechanical perfection. Variety in metrical effect was a quality that Dryden achieved by a frequent use of triplets and of Alexandrines to break the monotony. Along with these metrical mannerisms came attendant rhetorical habits, such as parallelism, balance, antithesis, repetition, and other similar patterns. Aphoristic lines were much favored, especially such as involved epigrammatic surprise. From the early century's love of conceits Dryden derived a habit of illustrative and at times decorative tropes that are a feature of his method. The poetic vocabulary was rigidly restricted by excluding neologisms, archaisms, "low" words, or technical words. To the modern reader the use of Latinate words or idioms and the constant repetition of a few much used epithets—*sad, murmuring, alternate, trembling,* etc.—as well as the love of adjectives ending in -y (*wavy, paly,* for example) seem unfortunate mannerisms. They occur more commonly in the second-flight poets of the period than in Dryden.

A curious combination of frequently prosaic matter and a vigorous and lofty manner—of journalistic material in Augustan form—marks much of Dryden's work.[2] At times these two elements are beautifully fused, but in

---

[1] See George Williamson, "The Rhetorical Pattern of Neo-classical Wit," *MP,* xxxiii (1935). 55-81; and Ruth Wallerstein, "The Development of the Rhetoric and Metre of the Heroic Couplet, especially in 1625-1645," *PMLA,* l (1935). 166-209.

[2] John Dryden (1631-1700) was born in Northamptonshire and was reared there in a Puritan family environment. He was sent (*c.* 1644) to Westminster School, which, under the celebrated headmaster, Dr. Busby, gave the best secondary education and the fiercest floggings that England then afforded its young aristocrats. From Trinity College, Cambridge, he was graduated B.A. in 1654, and before 1660 he was settled in London. After other employment he turned to writing, lodged with his publisher, was elected to the Royal Society (1662), married above his station, and turned playwright to make money. From 1663 to 1678 he averaged something like a play a year, pausing hardly at all when in 1671 powerful wits burlesqued him in *The Rehearsal.* He achieved great fame and won official recognitions, some of them lucrative. Theatrical and political animosities caused him (as well as the rest of the nation) no end of trouble, and in December 1679 he was set upon and beaten for a satire written by another. Attacks on him grew more numerous when, soon after the accession of the Catholic James II in 1685, he became a Catholic. The sincerity of his conversion has been questioned, but without sure reason. After the Revolution of 1688 he lost, as a Catholic, the laureateship and all his other places, and was forced in old age to turn again to his pen for a livelihood. — *Works,* ed. Sir Walter Scott and George Saintsbury (18v, Edinburgh, 1882-92); *Essays,* ed. W. P. Ker (2v, Oxford, 1900; 1926); *Poetical Works,* ed. George R. Noyes (Boston, 1908); *Poems,* ed. John Sargeaunt (1910, 1935); *Poetry and Prose,* ed. David Nichol Smith (1925); *Dramatic Works,* ed. Montague Summers (6v, 1931-32); *The Best of Dryden,* ed. Louis I. Bredvold (1933); *The Letters of John Dryden, with Letters Addressed to Him,* ed. Charles E. Ward (Durham, N. C., 1942). — Hugh Macdonald, *John Dryden: a Bibliography* (Oxford, 1939); reviewed by James M. Osborn, *MP,* xxxix (1941-2). 69-98, 197-212, 313-319. — Samuel Johnson, *Lives of the Poets,*

Dryden's
Early
Poems

his early poems their incongruity shrieks at one. While still a schoolboy at Westminster, for example, he contributed lines *Upon the Death of Lord Hastings* (a fellow student), remarkable for their grotesquely ingenious conceits about smallpox; and possibly at Cambridge he composed (but did not print) harmlessly flirtatious verses to Honor Dryden, his cousin. In 1659 with Waller and Sprat he published *Three Poems* upon the death of Cromwell. Dryden's effort was entitled *Heroique Stanzas Consecrated to the Glorious Memory of his most Serene and Renowned Highnesse Oliver Late Lord Protector* ... and years later these were more than once reprinted by Dryden's enemies to discredit him politically. A cousin of Dryden's had been among the judges who tried King Charles I, and one line (48) of Dryden's heroics was perversely supposed to imply approval of the regicide. When the sky changed a year and a half later, Dryden, like many another, was eager to celebrate the restoration of the monarchy. This he did finely in his poem *Astræa Redux* (1660), a poem which later led enemies to remind him of his celerity in tergiversation. In an epistle of the same date *To Sir Robert Howard* (whose sister in 1663 became Dryden's wife) is a couplet that sums up, doubtless, the attitude of both Dryden and the nation:

> All will at length in this opinion rest:
> "A sober prince's government is best."

The success of *Astræa Redux* as a poem on a "heroic" public occasion was followed by a panegyric on the coronation of Charles II entitled *To his Sacred Majesty,* and presently Dryden, after his speedy success as a playwright was assured, became a hopeful courtier, graciously regarded by royalty itself. This panegyric is ingenious wit-writing, with half-fused conceits and encrustations of imagery: it was good business but not very good poetry. His epistle addressed *To Dr. Charleton* (1663) about Stonehenge is of more interest since it shows Dryden's attitude towards the new science as opposed to ancient science, and because it was not merely another poem addressed to a great personage in the hope of possible rewards in patronage.

In the last poem of this early group, *Annus Mirabilis* (the wonders of the year 1666) Dryden is also glowingly eulogistic of the Royal Society, in which he obviously had some faith and interest even if he never paid his dues. The poem, descriptive of the naval war against the Dutch and also of the great

Annus
Mirabilis

fire of London (2-6 September 1666), again makes use of the heroic quatrain, which in his preface Dryden judges to be "more noble, and of greater dignity, both for the sound and number, than any other verse in use amongst us"— and which he does not use again! He regards his matter as historical rather than epic, but insists on the lofty heroic quality of the events, and he makes

ed. G. B. Hill (1905); George Saintsbury, *Dryden* (1881); A. W. Verrall, *Lectures on Dryden* (Cambridge, 1914); Mark VanDoren, *The Poetry of John Dryden* (1920; rev. 1945); Allardyce Nicoll, *Dryden and his Poetry* (1923); T. S. Eliot, *Homage to John Dryden* (1924); T. S. Eliot, *John Dryden: the Poet, the Dramatist, the Critic* (1932); Louis I. Bredvold, *The Intellectual Milieu of John Dryden* (Ann Arbor, 1934); James M. Osborn, *John Dryden: Some Biographical Facts and Problems* (1940). On Dryden's principal plays see Part I, ch. v; on his chief prefatory essays see above, ch. II.

them majestic both by the sound of the verse and by the use of grandiose imagery:

> Then, we upon our globe's last verge shall go,
> And view the ocean leaning on the sky:
> From thence our rolling neighbors we shall know,
> And on the lunar world securely pry.

The poem as a whole is less interesting than its preface, which illuminates Dryden's notion of poetic imagination:

The composition of all poems is, or ought to be, of wit; and wit in the poet . . . is no other than the faculty of imagination in the writer, which, like a nimble spaniel, beats over and ranges thro' the field of memory, till it springs the quarry it hunted after. . . . But to proceed . . . to the proper wit of an heroic or historical poem, I judge it chiefly to consist in the delightful imaging of persons, actions, passions, or things.

The spaniel is active and self-consciously industrious, but if Dr. Johnson justly condemned those who "lay on the watch for novelty," Dryden's nimble faculty seems to deserve a similar censure. Conscious effort is perhaps overvalued here. For one of his school Dryden is in this poem at times daringly descriptive; but generally in description he lacks vivid, specific detail, and so misses delight.

With *Annus Mirabilis* Dryden's first poetical period terminates. He had already gone over to the definitely lucrative career of popular dramatist. Between 1663 and 1681 he produced nearly a score of plays, which aided both his fortune and his reputation. In 1668 he was made poet laureate and in 1670 historiographer royal. A second poetic period, far more distinguished for its non-dramatic poems, falls in the years 1681-87. These years, lurid with political and religious controversy (especially with regard to the succession *Satire* to the throne of England) and ending in the expulsion of the Catholic King James II in 1688, saw Dryden turning brilliantly to political satire and religious argument in verse as well as to translation and to lyric poetry.

The great political satires include *Absalom and Achitophel, The Medal,* *Absalom* and *Mac Flecknoe,* a literary satire born of politics. Somewhat lacking in *and* structure and overweighted with prolonged "scolding," these pieces are all *Achitophel* magnificent in their vigorous dignity, their boisterous vituperation, and their incisive satirical portraiture. After the excitement of the Popish Plot (1678) there had been repeated attempts to force a bill through Parliament excluding Catholics (and thus the legitimate heir, the Duke of York) from the throne of England. The villain in these attempts was the Whig leader, the Earl of Shaftesbury, who in the summer of 1681 was under arrest charged with high treason.[3] At the suggestion of the King, *Absalom and Achitophel* was written and its publication timed to fall just a week before Shaftesbury's fruitless arraignment. The poem makes use of biblical story to suggest how Achitophel (Shaftesbury) is tempting to rebellion Absalom (the Duke of Monmouth,

---

[3] Ruth Wallerstein, "To Madness Near Allied: Shaftesbury and His Place in the Design and Thought of *Absalom and Achitophel,*" *Huntington Library Quar.,* VI (1943). 445-471.

illegitimate son of Charles II and the Whig candidate to succeed his father). Since Monmouth had not yet rebelled, the poem lacks action, but not tenseness. It consists largely of satirical portraits and of eloquent argumentative speeches in Dryden's epical style. Satirical portraits, or characters, were a favorite device of the day, but no one has ever surpassed Dryden's work in this art. Most of the portraits are enlivened merely by political animus; the famous character of Zimri, however, is further spiced by personal pique, for Villiers, Duke of Buckingham, who is Zimri, had satirized Dryden as "Bayes" in the dramatic burlesque *The Rehearsal* (1671). The lines on Zimri—

> A man so various, that he seem'd to be
> Not one, but all mankind's epitome—

are certainly among the most telling ever written in the vein of personal satire.

The Medal and Mac Flecknoe

Four months after this successful party piece Dryden published *The Medal* (March, 1682), another satire on Shaftesbury, whose followers upon his release from the charge of treason had cast a commemorative medal in honor of his triumph. The poem, less brilliant than its predecessor, gains force from being centered on a single person, but it lacks the edge of the earlier poem. It was answered, but not in kind, two months after its appearance by a scurrilous and gossipy retort, *The Medal of John Bayes,* probably from the pen of Thomas Shadwell. This dramatist, formerly a close friend, was now among the most venomous of Dryden's many personal and political enemies. In turn, a few months later, Dryden's opinions concerning Shadwell were published twice; first in *Mac Flecknoe,* apparently written in 1678, and secondly in passages inserted by Dryden in Nahum Tate's *Second Part of Absalom and Achitophel.* In his treatment of Shadwell Dryden drops at times his heroics and becomes roundly but still incisively abusive. His picture of Og (Shadwell) in Tate's poem begins:

> Now stop your noses, readers, all and some,
> For here's a tun of midnight work to come,
> Og, from a treason-tavern rolling home.
> Round as a globe, and liquor'd ev'ry chink,
> Goodly and great he sails behind his link.
> With all this bulk there's nothing lost in Og,
> For ev'ry inch that is not fool is rogue:
> A monstrous mass of foul corrupted matter,
> As all the devils had spew'd to make the batter. . . .
> The midwife laid her hand on his thick skull,
> With this prophetic blessing: *Be thou dull!*

The last three words here quoted echo the theme of the earlier *Mac Flecknoe,* certainly one of Dryden's most effective and most influential poems. *Mac Flecknoe* appeared anonymously, but was acknowledged by Dryden in 1693. About 1678, upon the decease of a secular priest, Richard Flecknoe, known as a bad versifier, it had occurred to Dryden to nominate Shadwell successor to the throne of Nonsense. Flecknoe, who

> In prose and verse, was own'd, without dispute,
> Thro' all the realms of *Nonsense,* absolute —

chooses Shadwell to succeed him as the perfect nadir of genius:

> The rest to some faint meaning make pretense,
> But Sh—— never deviates into sense.
> Some beams of wit on other souls may fall,
> Strike thro', and make a lucid interval;
> But Sh——'s genuine night admits no ray,
> His rising fogs prevail upon the day.

Satire on dullness of authors here reaches that high plateau of caustic and relentless phrasing, the other boundary of which might be Pope's *Dunciad*— a poem clearly much indebted to *Mac Flecknoe,* as were the works of other poets and even dramatists, Henry Fielding among them. The *genus irritabile vatum* were embattled over matters of their art with an ardor that hardly can be seen in any other period. For Dryden these excursions into political and personal satire brought a swift and abundant harvest of scurrilous abuse— and doubtless a considerable respect from intelligent and from Tory readers.

The Roman gravity and intellectual quality of Dryden's art, evident in these keen satires, are even more evident in the two great poems that concern his religion. The first of these, *Religio Laici,* published late in 1682, was occasioned by a translation from the French of Father Simon's *Critical History of the Old Testament* earlier in the year. The *Critical History* was ***Religious*** a sensational and learned attack on the textual integrity of the Bible, the "one ***Poems:*** sacred book" of Protestants, and an assertion of ecclesiastical authority or Religio infallibility as the only sure guide to faith. The book would have come to Laici Dryden's attention partly because translated by a young friend, Henry Dickinson, and partly because of Dryden's skeptical interest in theological arguments on faith. In his political poems Dryden had, like a good Tory, tied up with a strong principle of authority in government. Certainly in 1682 he was no Catholic apologist, but he is obviously respectful of authority in religion—which in spite of Father Simon he still places in the Scriptures. He rejects the reason and the universality claimed by the deists; he rejects the Catholic claim of infallibility as preferable to textually faulty Scriptures, and he shrewdly argues that infallibility, if operative, ought to emend and explicate such texts easily—though "no council dare pretend to do" such a thing! While longing for an "omniscient church" and asserting that

> In doubtful questions 'tis the safest way
> To learn what unsuspected ancients say,

he professes himself a good Anglican and a believer perhaps in the light of reason but not in the rationalizing divines, a believer whose compromise is built on the typical principle: "common quiet is mankind's concern." The poem is earnest and smooth in tone. It has less of wit and less of encrusted imagery than almost any other poem of equal length that Dryden wrote. His conclusion is, therefore, very significant:

> And this unpolish'd, rugged verse, I chose;
> As fittest for discourse, and nearest prose.

Nowadays probably any aesthetician would think this poem, as executed, essentially unpoetical. To Dryden evidently there was no impassable gulf between eloquent prose and poetry. In stating "sacred truth" he was writing *discourse,* and yet the use of metre and a grave dignity of more than prosaic utterance he deemed appropriate. To realize this is essential in understanding both Dryden and the neo-classical tradition. But the adagio movement of the opening lines of the poem is grand poetry, according to any tradition.

The Hind and the Panther

In the months following the accession of the Catholic King James II (1685), Dryden like many others became a Roman Catholic. This act has been regarded as gross time-serving, and it has been defended as a natural development of Dryden's earlier quest for "unsuspected ancients" and an "omniscient" or infallible church. It is undisputed that he remained from 1686 to his death a devout Catholic and that as such in 1688 he lost all of his "places" given by Charles II or James II. In 1687 he argued his change of faith in *The Hind and the Panther.* This curious blend of animal fable and religious controversy illustrates Dryden's aesthetic courage rather than his tact. The Milk-white Hind is the Roman Church; the Panther is the Anglican Church, and the various dissenting sects are symbolized also in animal shapes. The First Part characterizes all these allegorical persons with discursive reflections on the problems each presents. At the end of the section the Lion (the King) commands the fiercer beasts to allow the timid Hind to approach the watering place—an allegory of the recent Declaration of Indulgence (April, 1687); and it is this act that thereafter lessens the Hind's timidity. The Second Part is a controversial dialogue between the Hind and the Panther as they stroll together towards the Hind's "lonely cell," a dialogue which covers somewhat the same intellectual issues as *Religio Laici.* In Part Three the argument lasts most of the night, and centers now on more pragmatic English points of controversy. Here the Panther relates the story of the Swallows who were destroyed because they followed the ill counsels of the Martins (the extremists in the Roman clergy, whose influence on James II Dryden perhaps feared), and the Hind retorts with the fable of the Buzzard (Bishop Burnet), which shows the savageness of the extreme Anglican party.

This poem might have been as quaintly amusing as such a medieval *débat* as *The Owl and the Nightingale,* but Dryden was somewhat too earnest in his polemics for that. Arguments between allegorical animals have been frequent in literature, and the absurdity of Dryden's fundamental fable has been too easily ridiculed ever since the early spoofing indulged in by those two young wits, Charles Montagu, Earl of Halifax (1661-1715) and Matthew Prior, in *The Hind and the Panther Transvers'd to the Story of the Country-*

Mouse and the City-Mouse (1687). Doubtless there are at times absurdities; but these are so extremely superficial (or possibly so extremely fundamental) that they do not matter much. The poem has a rich diversity, a complex variety beyond Dryden's imaginative habit. Pope was right, also, in thinking the poem showed at its best the poet's marvelous command of the couplet. The quiet but mannered ease of the opening lines is perfectly melodic:

> A milk-white Hind, immortal and unchang'd,
> Fed on the lawns,[4] and in the forest rang'd;
> Without unspotted, innocent within,
> She fear'd no danger, for she knew no sin.

Shortly, a plain passage on "private reason" is followed by a piece of autobiography unusual in itself and in its devout and passionate appeal:

> Thy throne is darkness in th' abyss of light,
> A blaze of glory that forbids the sight.
> O teach me to believe thee thus conceal'd,
> And search no farther than thyself reveal'd;
> But her alone for my director take,
> Whom thou hast promis'd never to forsake!
> My thoughtless youth was wing'd with vain desires,
> My manhood, long misled by wand'ring fires,
> Follow'd false lights; and, when their glimpse was gone,
> My pride struck out new sparkles of her own.
> Such was I, such by nature still I am;
> Be thine the glory, and be mine the shame.
> Good life be now my task: my doubts are done.

In general in the poem the metrical effects subconsciously are fitted to the mood; the "panic fright" of the huddled sparrows, for example, produces a twittering hesitancy of caesuras and verbal re-echoings that overflow from the couplet to a triplet:

> Night came, but unattended with repose;
> Alone she came, no sleep their eyes to close:
> Alone, and black she came; no friendly stars arose.

The poem is nowadays for poets rather than for theological polemics; it is one of Dryden's most impressive attempts at fusing disparate elements. Here he worked (like his misguided Martin)

> Till grosser atoms, tumbling in the stream
> Of fancy, madly met, and clubb'd into a dream.

Possibly *clubb'd* is a more exact metaphor than *fused;* but even if a conglomerate, the work certainly elevates the author far above the status of a mere "inaugurator of an age of prose and reason."

Dryden was also a lyric poet of considerable ability. His comedies and

---

[4] A *lawn* in Dryden's day was a grassy open space between woods.

Dryden's Songs and Odes

Miscellanies are sprinkled with deftly turned witty songs in the Cavalier tradition. Love is the favored theme, and Restoration love is likely to be stereotyped in cynical, physical, or artificially coquettish detail. When Dryden recounts the amorous play of "Fair Iris and her Swain" he elegantly leers both at the lovers and at his readers. The metres are very apt and nimble, Dryden being curiously expert in triple rhythms. His "Sea Fight" in *Amboyna* approaches roughly the rhythms of free verse. In Dryden's day, however, a song was less valued as poetry than was "the greater lyric," by which term was meant the Cowleyan Pindaric, a rimed poem of irregular verses arranged in strophes of no fixed structure. In this form the cult of irregularity, sublimity, and enthusiasm was to express itself for many a year. Against the irregularity protest was to rise, notably in Congreve's *Ode on the Victorious Progress of Her Majesty's Arms* (1706), the prefatory "Discourse" of which condemned Cowley's simplification of the true Pindaric. Yet the Cowleyan form was long popular, and Dryden contributed much to its vogue by his poems of the type.

The Great Odes

Two of these, the *Threnodia Augustalis* (1685), in memory of Charles II, and the ode *To the Pious Memory of Mrs. Anne Killigrew* (1686) are dignified and restrained threnodies. In the latter poem Dryden expresses loud repentance for his part in augmenting the "fat pollutions" of the stage. Three other odes were libretti set to music. That *On the Death of Mr. Henry Purcell* is perhaps adequate for the commemoration of the loss of England's greatest composer. The two written for the Musical Society's celebrations of St. Cecilia's day are among Dryden's noblest efforts. The first strophe of the *Song for St. Cecilia's Day,* set by Draghi in 1687, begins and ends with full rich-toned majesty:

> From harmony, from heav'nly harmony
> This universal frame began:
> From harmony to harmony
> Thro' all the compass of the notes it ran,
> The diapason closing full in Man.

There is nothing superior to this in the more famous ode, *Alexander's Feast* (1697), which after two less distinguished musical settings gained added glory when Handel in 1736 composed for it a magnificent score. The effectiveness of the poem, however, is not dependent on musical setting. It has a neatly handled story; it has spirit; and its movement is direct, varied, and speedy as in much of Dryden's best work. It partakes perhaps of the theatrical and the obviously ingenious; it furthermore lacks the gravity of Dryden's best work; but its effectiveness is indubitable, and it remains not Dryden's best but certainly his most popular poem. There is something to be said for a poetic art and a manner of life that enable a poet to produce his most vigorous and attractive lyric at the age of sixty-six.

With the accession of William and Mary, naturally, Dryden lost his pension and the laureateship. The latter went to the "true blue" poet Tom Shadwell! Now, as he was entering old age, Dryden again had to write for a living.

He got a half dozen dramatic pieces staged, but he had lost touch with *Transla-*
audiences and had a personal "loathing" for such employment. His main *tions*
resource became translation both in verse and prose. In 1684 he had begun
editing for Jacob Tonson a series of volumes of miscellanies "by the Most
Eminent Hands." In these he collected his original poems and published
many translations. As early as 1680 he had made notable contributions to a
translation of *Ovid's Epistles* done "by Several Hands"; in the second
miscellany, *Sylvae* (1685), he attempted Lucretius with distinction and also
Theocritus and some small pieces of Horace; but his major classical translations were those of Juvenal and Persius (1693) and the tremendous task of
doing Virgil into English (1697). The *Æneid* was for Dryden a most lucrative and a most distinguished venture in translation.[5] In prose meanwhile he
did various translations from the French and from the classics did at least
prefatory sections for versions of Plutarch's *Lives* (1683), Polybius (1693),
Tacitus (1698), and Lucian (1711). He was in all this drudgery industrious,
conscientious, and, thanks to long practice, usually apt, elegant, vigorous, and
spirited in his renditions.

Along with these noble pot-boiling efforts Dryden found time to make
modern English versions of a variety of poetic narratives, which shortly
before his death in 1700 he published as *Fables Ancient and Modern*.[6] These *Dryden's*
include the First Book of the *Iliad,* eight tales from Ovid, three from *Fables*
Chaucer, and three from Boccaccio, as well as other non-narrative poems.
Throughout the eighteenth century the *Fables* were apparently the most
popular of Dryden's poems. Doubtless there was more about Chaucer than
metre that Dryden did not comprehend as he should: simplicity, lightness are
traits in which Dryden was comparatively deficient; but it is clear that he
had a warm and keen appreciation of Chaucer's humanity. With Ovid he is
excellent, and Boccaccio suits his genius well. It is a pity that Dryden did so
little narrative verse; for his speed and his dramatic gift shown here are most
suitable for such work. For a poet of almost seventy years the vitality is
astonishing.

All this must have made a very busy old age, and yet the work seems not
to have kept Dryden from his normal coffee-house pleasures. The tradition is
that he wrote mornings, dined at home, and spent the afternoon and early *Dryden's*
evening at Will's Coffee-house, where he had his "winter seat" near the fire *Last Years*
and his "summer seat" in the balcony. In 1682 Shadwell had given an ill-
natured picture of this life in *The Medal of John Bayes:*

You who would know him better, go to the Coffee-house (where he may be said
almost to inhabit) and you shall find him holding forth to half a score young
fellows, (who clap him on the back, spit in his mouth, and loo him on upon the
Whiggs, as they call 'em) puft up, and swelling with their praise: and the great
Subject of his Discourse shall be of himself, and his *Poetry;* What Diet he uses
for *Epick* what for *Comick;* what course he is in for *Libel,* and what for *Tragedy.*

[5] See J. McG. Bottkol, "Dryden's Latin Scholarship," *MP,* XL (1943). 241-254.
[6] Herbert G. Wright, "Some Sidelights on the Reputation and Influence of Dryden's Fables,"
RES, XXI (1945). 23-37.

Thus in the company of such friends as Wycherley, Dennis, Southerne, Garth, Walsh, Lockier, Granville, Congreve, and others, Dryden passed the evening of his days. Diet apart, the talk might well have been the best since the days of Ben Jonson at the Mermaid. Enemies Dryden had, but when the virulent Whig, Bishop Burnet (the Buzzard in *The Hind and the Panther*), called Dryden in print "a monster of immodesty and impurity of all sorts," Dryden's remaining friends almost to a man went on record as giving the lie direct to the Bishop. To them Dryden was modesty and kindness itself. There is even an (improbable) anecdote to the effect that on one occasion he gave a very small lad named Alexander Pope a shilling for a boyish effort in translation. *Virgilium tantum vidi* was Pope's later reverent comment concerning the poet who was of all others Pope's master as well as the master of the Restoration period.

IV

Minor Poets of the Restoration

The greater poets of the Restoration period clearly were John Milton and John Dryden. These men represent two developments at the end of the Renaissance. Milton preserved the elevation and glowing richness of the humanist intellect, while Dryden developed in the realistic, critical, and skeptical tradition initiated in part by Montaigne. Milton in his post-restoration poems thought and worked in terms of the higher genres, epic and tragedy, and he thus achieved the acme of English neo-classical distinction.[1] Dryden worked in inferior genres, and the lesser poets in general followed Dryden in this respect. At the end of the century, to be sure, Sir Richard Blackmore (*c.* 1655-1729) was pouring forth interminable epic strains; but these were not highly regarded. The most acclaimed poems, apart from Milton's, were in general satirical or didactic. There was, of course, much writing and singing of popular political songs and ballads as well as songs of love and drinking; but these were regarded much of the time as non-literary. Normally poems in these lower genres were written in a familiar, facetious, and at times even a vulgar or actually indecent tone: the dignity of Augustanism tended to be slighted, but it was still valued for nobler efforts.

Higher and Lower Genres

The most eminent of these lesser poets—for very different reasons—were Samuel Butler and John Wilmot, Earl of Rochester. These men were poets of distinction and permanent interest. We may well discuss Butler [2] first

[1] For the influence of Milton in the period see Raymond D. Havens, *The Influence of Milton on English Poetry* (Cambridge, Mass., 1922).

[2] Samuel Butler (1612/13-1680) was born the son of a well-to-do Worcestershire yeoman, who valued books and learning. The son was educated at King's School, Worcester, and possibly later became a member of Gray's Inn. He was in 1661 steward of Ludlow Castle for the Earl of Carbery, Lord President of Wales. Except for the first two parts of *Hudibras* most of his writing was done after 1667. His "characters," published in 1759, were composed between 1667 and 1669. He was secretary to George Villiers, Duke of Buckingham, for all or part of the time when his grace was Chancellor of the University of Cambridge (1671-4). Anthony Wood asserts that Butler helped write *The Rehearsal*. The popularity of Part III of *Hudibras* (1678) caused the King to give Butler £100 and to order an annual pension of that sum paid to him. Among the poet's friends were Thomas Hobbes, John Cleveland the poet, Samuel Cooper the miniaturist, and Sir William Davenant; surviving him were such other friends as John Aubrey, Tom Shadwell, and Dr. Charles Davenant the economist. Butler's traditional poverty has probably been exaggerated. Many of the above details are taken from the careful article by E. S. de Beer, "The Later Life of Samuel Butler," *RES*, IV (1928). 159-166. Another good source for Butler's family and early life is René Lamar, "Du Nouveau sur l'auteur d'*Hudibras*," *Revue Anglo-Américaine*, I (1924). 213-227. — *Poetical Works*, ed. Reginald B. Johnson (2v, 1893); *Collected Works* (3v [I and II, ed. A. R. Waller; III, ed. René Lamar], 1905, 1908, 1928). — *Lord Roos His Answer to the Marquess of Dorchester's Letter* (1660; see *LTLS*, March 21, 1936, p. 244); *Hudibras*, Part I (1663); *Hudibras*, Part II (1664); *To the Memory of ... DuVall* (1671); *Two Letters* (1672); "Heroical Epistle of Hudibras to Sidrophel," in *Hudibras*, Parts I and II (1674); *Hudibras*, Part III (1678). — Samuel Johnson, *Lives of the Poets* (1779), ed. George Birkbeck Hill (1905); Hardin Craig, "*Hudibras, Part I*, and the Politics of 1647,"

and the practical and journalistic poetry of the day, and later turn to Rochester and the court poets.

Butler's
Hudibras

Butler's contemporary reputation was almost exclusively based on *Hudibras*,[3] since most of his other works were first published in 1759 long after his death, and *Hudibras* is still his major work. A friend and contemporary in 1663 called Part I of the poem "the most admired piece of drollery that ever came forth," and this was a common verdict. A drollery was an attack— or a miscellany largely filled with attacks—on Puritans. The completed poem consists of three parts each containing three cantos, with *An Heroical Epistle of Hudibras to Sidrophel* appended to Part II and two epistles added at the very end of the poem. Ostensibly *Hudibras* is a mock-heroic, and as antiheroes Butler presented a Presbyterian colonel and knight, named Hudibras, and Ralpho, an Independent in religion, who is the knight's squire. The two remotely resemble Don Quixote and Sancho Panza, but their arguments over theology and church government are more vituperative than the chivalry of Cervantes' hero would have allowed. The action is less amusing now in its loose episodic flow than it was in its own day. Part I, starting slowly, tells how Hudibras and Ralpho tried to stop a bear-baiting in a "western" town. They win the first battle, but in a later encounter Hudibras and Ralpho lose and are imprisoned in place of their foes. Meanwhile, Hudibras has fallen in love with a widow's jointure-land, and so also with the widow. In Parts II and III we have his fruitless adventures in trying to win the widow. In one striking episode he visits a Rosicrucian prognosticator, Sidrophel—a visit that ends in a battle disastrous to second-sight.

The purpose of the whole is obviously satirical, and the action simply a loose thread upon which arguments, reflections, and caustic portraits are strung. Recently there has come to light an important account of the poem in a letter written by Butler in 1663, to accompany a copy of *Hudibras,* Part I, that he was sending to a friend in India. Of his poem he says:

It was written not long before the time when I had first the honor to be acquainted with you, and Hudibras, whose name it bears, was a West Country knight, then a Colonel in the Parliament army, and a committee man, with whom I became acquainted lodging in the same house with him in Holborn. I found his humor so pleasant that, I know not how, I fell into the way of scribbling, which I was never guilty of before nor since. I did my endeavor to render his character as like as I could, which all that know him say is so right that they found him out by it at the first view. For his esquire Ralpho, he was his clerk and an Independent, between whom and the knight there fell out such perpetual disputes about religion as you will find up and down in the book for as near as I could set down their very words. As for the story, I had it from the

---

Manly Anniversary Studies (Chicago, 1923), pp. 145-155; Jan Veldkamp, *Samuel Butler* (Hilversum, 1923); Beverley Chew, "Some Notes on the Three Parts of Hudibras" [bibliographical], *Essays & Verses about Books* (1926), pp. 65-97; J. T. Curtiss, "Butler's Sidrophel," *PMLA*, XLIV (1929). 1066-1078; Dan Gibson, "Samuel Butler," *Seventeenth Century Studies by Members of the Graduate School, University of Cincinnati,* ed. Robert Shafer (Princeton, 1933), pp. 279-335; Ricardo Quintana, "The Butler-Oxenden Correspondence," *MLN,* XLVIII (1933). 1-11.
[3] Only the ignorant fail to pronounce the final *s* in the name of this very English hero!

knight's own mouth, and is so far from being feigned that it is upon record; for there was a suit of law upon it between the knight and the fiddler, in which the knight was overthrown to his great shame and discontent, for which he left the country and came up to settle at London. The other persons, as Orsin a bearward, Talgot a Butcher, Magnano a Tinker, Cerdon a Cobbler, Colon a Clown etc., are such as commonly make up bear-baitings, though some curious wits pretend to discover certain persons of quality with whom they say those characters agree; but since I do not know who they are, I cannot tell you till I see their commentaries, but am content (since I cannot help it) that everyman should make what applications he pleases of it, either to himself or others. But I assure you my chief design was only to give the world a just account of the ridiculous folly and knavery of the Presbyterian and Independent factions then in power and whether I have performed it well or no I cannot tell, only I have had the good fortune to have it generally esteemed so, especially by the King and the best of his subjects. It had the ill fortune to be printed when I was absent from this town, whereby many mistakes were committed, but I have corrected this book which you will receive myself, with which, Sir, I send you the best wishes and real affections of / Your humble and faithful / Servant Sam: Butler.[4]

From the letter we infer that from the start readers made personal applications of the characters and probably allegorical interpretations of the action. Of this last matter Butler says nothing; of his persons, Hudibras and Ralpho are thus from life, and they come to London from the "West Country" after discomfiture probably resembling that recounted in Part 1 of *Hudibras*. Butler somewhat coyly deprecates identification of minor persons of the story with actual people. Sir Samuel Luke, commonly regarded as the prototype of Hudibras, was from Bedfordshire and not from a western county. Neither the story nor the depiction of actual persons, however, was Butler's "chief design." That was to expose "the ridiculous folly and knavery" of Puritans.

His usual methods are burlesque, through distortion, and travesty, through *Butler's* vulgarization. There are long grotesque "characters" of all the persons *Methods* involved; there is author's comment by way of analysis or history; and there are interminable violent disputes between Hudibras and Ralpho, Hudibras and Sidrophel—or any other opponent who offers. The knight was, we are told,

> in Logic a great critic,
> Profoundly skill'd in Analytic;
> He could distinguish, and divide
> A hair 'twixt south and south-west side;
> On either which he would dispute,
> Confute, change hands, and still confute;
> He'd undertake to prove by force
> Of argument a man's no horse;
> He'd prove a buzzard is no fowl,
> And that a Lord may be an owl; . . .
> All this by syllogism, true
> In mood and figure, he would do.

[4] Modernized from Quintana's text, *MLN*, XLVIII (1933). 4.

He was also skilled in the pedantries (not the practical aspects) of rhetoric, mathematics, philosophy, and "school-divinity." The famous lines on his religion show the vigor of Butler's animus:

> For his Religion it was fit
> To match his learning and his wit:
> 'Twas Presbyterian true blue,
> For he was of that stubborn crew
> Of errant saints, whom all men grant
> To be the true Church *Militant:*
> Such as do build their faith upon
> The holy text of pike and gun;
> Decide all controversies by
> Infallible artillery;
> And prove their doctrine orthodox
> By apostolic blows and knocks;
> Call fire and sword and desolation,
> A godly-thorough-Reformation,
> Which always must be carry'd on,
> And still be doing, never done:
> As if Religion were intended
> For nothing else but to be mended.

The burlesque also has objects other than Puritanism. Chivalry, as in *Don Quixote,* and heroism, as in Scarron, are disparaged. The fighting always is far from decorous, and intellectual combat is similarly made cheap. Butler abhors logic-chopping, and is so skeptical by nature that he can doubt the sincerity of conviction through argument. In one passage he asks,

> *What makes all doctrines plain and clear?*
> About two hundred pounds a year.
> *And that which was prov'd true before,*
> *Prove false again?* — Two hundred more.

One of his more significant poems, it may be noted, is an unfinished *Satire in Two Parts upon the Imperfections and Abuse of Human Learning.*

Defects of Hudibras

The defects of *Hudibras* are obvious. It lacks structure, and is only a series of desultory, drifting—and brilliant—passages. In these passages, furthermore, Butler is too leisurely: he spins a dozen couplets where a better artist would have made one do. Forty lines devoted to describing Hudibras's beard have been rightly thought excessive, and there are many such dilated descriptions. The truth was that in the period 1663-78 almost anything was good for a laugh against Puritans, and Butler had no need to restrain himself. Again, Butler is often guilty of bad taste. Admittedly, he has the art of making bad taste amusing, but he goes too far—for example, in the "nasty pickle" that makes Hudibras and Ralpho offensive in the end of II, ii, where he is enforcing the obvious moral:

> That man is sure to lose,
> That fouls his hands with dirty foes.

His taste for unsavory realism persists when he turns to burlesquing the arts of poetry, meretricious or otherwise. Here he maintains a vulgar, anti-heroic, anti-poetic attitude towards his material. He loves to cheapen poetic "imagery":

> The sun had long since, in the lap
> Of Thetis, taken out his nap,
> And like a lobster boil'd, the morn
> From black to red began to turn.

Since Chaucer's day at least this sort of thing has been good fun, though the lobster is doubtless a bold stroke. So likewise Butler burlesques the So-have-I-seen tropes so popular at the time, and he ends passages with aphoristic bits of wisdom much as playwrights punctuated passages with a couplet. His fights mix the grotesque with the mock-heroic. Obviously vulgar brawls, they are called combats or conquests and treated in lofty terms. Most obviously he burlesques poetic arts in his rhythms and double rimes. The jolting effects of his octosyllabic couplets underline the awkwardness of the actions—whether physical or intellectual. Sober folk, like Joseph Addison,[5] would prefer neater rhythms and less screaming rimes; but Addison confesses that "the generality of his [Butler's] readers are so wonderfully pleased with the double rhymes" that they will not approve Mr. Spectator's opinion.

The power of the burlesque lies precisely in these externals, just as the subtlety of it lies in the allusiveness of the text. Clearly the cheap format of the early editions of *Hudibras* Part i indicates that it pleased not only Charles II and the court but "the generality of readers" also. It had a proletarian action; but it had also an appeal to bookish men. It glances at chapbook *The Appeal* stories and at Homer and Virgil as well. It mocks the pedantries of the *of* Hudibras schools, the absurdity of astrology and the new science, and the irrationality of synods and of the "inward light." Butler was a very learned man, and the whole scope of his reading is drawn upon for themes, famous passages, or methods of thinking and writing that might aid his burlesque. He has a remarkable gift for portraiture. The schools of Dutch realism and French travesty meet in his work, which anticipates and rivals the graphic art of his later illustrator, William Hogarth. His favorite classical satirist was Juvenal; but he owed fully as much in theme and method to such moderns as Rabelais, Cervantes, and Scarron. Among English poets he is less a buffoon than he is a jester such as Shakespeare might have created in his later plays.

Butler's intellectual quality, if not his full genius, is seen also in his other works which largely lack the grotesqueness of *Hudibras*. *The Elephant in the Moon,* a facetious satire on Sir Paul Neale, and the *Satire on the Royal* *Butler's Society* both show his unsympathetic attitude towards the new learning. *Intellectual* Butler is that contradiction, the complete skeptic combined with the com- *Quality* plete conservative. He hated silly new mechanical ways of doing things. Hudibras,

[5] *Spectator*, No. 249.

> by geometric scale,
> Could take the size of pots of ale;
> Resolve by sines and tangents straight,
> If bread or butter wanted weight;
> And wisely tell what hour o' th' day
> The clock does strike, by algebra.

One suspects that Gulliver's Laputan tailor had had hints of his trade from Hudibras. Butler and his knight lived in days obsessed with the need of progress—

> No sow-gelder did blow his horn
> To geld a cat, but cry'd Reform.

Self-consciously pious folk nasally intoned new doctrines—

> As if Religion were intended
> For nothing else but to be mended.

Butler was loudly contemptuous of all new doctrine; he even contemned human reason itself because of all these unstable aberrations. At a high point in the satire on Hudibras's mind we are told

> He understood b' implicit faith,
> Whatever Skeptic could inquire for;
> For every *why* he had a *wherefore.*

For such intellectual self-sufficiency Butler's contempt was unbounded. He was on the losing side: the idea of progress through science and a complete trust in human powers was to triumph: his lot was to go down fighting scurrilously. He stimulated many to imitate the surfaces of his work; the cast of his mind was less frequently copied. As a whole he is a unique figure, an intellectual in the burlesque tradition. John Dennis in writing an epitaph for Butler summed it up well:

> He was a whole species of poets in one:
> Admirable in a manner
> In which no one else has been tolerable. . . .

Butler, it is true, had no worthy, avowed disciple. Tom D'Urfey, Ned Ward, Tom Brown, and nameless writers in miscellanies emulated his less desirable traits, but lacking the intellectual quality of his substance, merely vulgarized his manner. Charles Cotton's *Scarronides: or, Virgile Travestie* (1664) perhaps owed some of its great popularity to the vogue of *Hudibras,* but *Scarronides* owed none of its nature to Butler. In formal satire as distinguished from travesty or burlesque the more reputable tradition—formal, Augustan, or neo-classical—swept over and past Samuel Butler.[6]

In this formal tradition appears the work of John Oldham,[7] who followed

---

[6] Butler and Oldham (and later satirists) are well placed in their satirical tradition by C. W. Previté-Orton in his *Political Satire in English Poetry* (Cambridge, 1910).

[7] John Oldham (1653-1683), son of a Gloucestershire nonconformist clergyman, was educated at home, at Tetbury Grammar School, and (1670-74) at St. Edmund Hall, Oxford. Upon graduation he returned to Gloucestershire, probably to teach, and in 1676 became usher at Croydon School, the headmaster of which was a relative of Oldham's college friend, Charles

Andrew Marvell (better known for his non-satirical work) and perhaps *Formal*
slightly anticipated Dryden's satires—though of course Dryden's reputation *Satire:*
as poet was quite established before Oldham began to publish in 1677. A *John*
half-dozen years make up the period in which Oldham was publishing; and *Oldham*
since these years were those of the excitement over the Popish Plot, Oldham
was naturally led into political satire. He was the foremost and most furious
of those who fought on the side of Titus Oates and the Whigs. His *Satyrs
upon the Jesuits* (1681), avoiding mock-heroic narrative, made use of a
dramatic monologue that gives high heroic eloquence but unfortunately lacks
variety and change of pace in its vituperation. With these satires he printed
a Pindaric "Ode," already published under the lurid title *A Satyr against
Vertue* (1679). Here we meet that dangerous quality irony, which while
pretending to glorify vice actually scourges rakes who glory in their vicious-
ness. Oldham's purpose seems not to have been understood by all, and indeed when he ironically curses virtuous fools,

> Who think to fetter free-born souls,
> And tie 'em to dull morality, and rules —

he is expressing a love of freedom which elsewhere in his work is not ironical.
He abhorred the servitude of teaching school, and declined the too menial
office of chaplain to the Earl of Kingston; he was too proud to dedicate
poems fulsomely for a price, as his friend Dryden practically did. In the satire
*Addressed to a Friend that is about to Leave the University and Come
Abroad in the World,* Oldham affirms this love of freedom eloquently in
the inserted fable of the wolf that wanted food but would not endure the
indignity of collar and chain put upon the civilized and well-fed Towzer.
It is the furious sweep of Oldham's satiric rage that is most impressive, but
this fable, and other passages that might seem autobiographical, have a charm
that is more amiable. Although his Pindaric odes have more fervor and
imagination than the average of his day, and although in *The Careless Good
Fellow* he shows ability to turn out a jolly, fiery drinking song, his true
medium is the closed heroic couplet, which he uses with an abruptness and
ruggedness of rhythm that are individual and sincere but not always pleasantly smooth. Dryden's touching lines *To the Memory of Mr. Oldham* are

Morwent, upon whose death Oldham had composed an early ode. Because of poems circulated
in manuscript the Earl of Rochester is said to have visited Oldham at Croydon, and here also
was written the ode *Upon the Marriage of the Prince of Orange with the Lady Mary* (1677),
which won no recognition. In the years 1679-81 he was tutor to a young gentleman, and in
1681, "set up for a wit" in London. His *Satyrs upon the Jesuits* (1681) was a great success;
but presently Oldham had again to become a tutor. At the end of his life he enjoyed the
patronage of the young Earl of Kingston; he died of smallpox at Kingston's seat, Holme
Pierrepont in Nottingham. — Oldham's *Works* were first collected in 1684, and were reprinted
several times down to 1722. His *Compositions in Prose and Verse* were edited by E. Thompson
(1770) and his *Poetical Works* by R. Bell (1854, 1871); *Some New Pieces* by him appeared in
1681; *Poems and Translations* in 1683, and *Remains . . . in Verse and Prose* in 1684. — See
H. F. Brooks, "A Bibliography of John Oldham," *Oxford Bibliographical Soc. Proc.,* v (1936).
1-38 (with a biographical and critical introduction); Weldon M. Williams, "The Genesis of
John Oldham's *Satyrs upon the Jesuits*," *PMLA,* LVIII (1943). 958-970; W. M. Williams, "The
Influence of Ben Jonson's *Catiline* upon John Oldham's *Satyrs upon the Jesuits*," *ELH,* XI
(1944). 38-62.

Oldham's most enduring monument: they show how the finished, mellow artist in couplet-making viewed an able apprentice:

> Farewell, too little and too lately known,
> Whom I began to think and call my own:
> For sure our souls were near allied, and thine
> Cast in the same poetic mold with mine. . . .
> O early ripe! to thy abundant store
> What could advancing age have added more?
> It might (what nature never gives the young)
> Have taught the numbers of thy native tongue.
> But satire needs not those, and wit will shine
> Thro' the harsh cadence of a rugged line.

Court Poets   Butler and Oldham were almost "professional" poets whom the court condescended to patronize. The chief court poets, the last of the cavalier breed, were Rochester, Sedley, Dorset, and, apart from this group of rakes, Charles Cotton. In this group (but not as lyrists) would come also John Sheffield, Earl of Mulgrave (and later Duke of Buckinghamshire) and Wentworth Dillon, Earl of Roscommon. The most notable and the most notorious of all these was the young Earl of Rochester.[8] If one could blot out his mad debaucheries and the corollary obscene poems, Rochester's more reputable verse would give him a very high place in English poetry. On paper his personality seems brilliant but unlovely. He was a patron of at least a half-dozen poets, on most of whom he turned maliciously after some friendly gestures. He was thought to have embraced the dangerous doctrines of Hobbes; and indeed he was a skeptic, a materialist, a selfish pleasure-loving sensationalist, who doubtless aped the self-love of which Hobbes was regarded as the apostle. He was a young nobleman of sensual appetites so strong that his health was early ruined, and upon his death, aged thirty-three, he became not only the symbol of the grossest debaucheries the time could devise but also a black warning to youthful lords, through the pamphlet

---

[8] John Wilmot, second Earl of Rochester (1647-1680), was born at Ditchley, Oxfordshire, and at the age of eleven he succeeded his father to the earldom. At Wadham College (1660-61) he began writing verse. He traveled in France and Italy, returned to England in 1664, and fought in the war against the Dutch in 1665. Back in London he became intimate with Sedley, Dorset, and Villiers, Duke of Buckingham; and, despite his youth, he speedily became somehow the most notorious of this group of rakes. He rapidly became famous also as a wit and satirist, and he was briefly a fickle patron to several poets, including Dryden. — *Poems on Several Occasions, by the Rt. Hon. the E. of R.* (Antwerpen [i.e., London], 1680); *Poems . . . with Valentinian* (ed. by Rochester's friends; the preface is by Rymer, 1691); *Miscellaneous Works*, with Memoirs by Mons. St. Évremond (1707, etc., esp. 1731, 1939); *Collected Works*, ed. John Hayward (1926); *Poetical Works*, ed. Quilter Johns (1933). — *A Satyr against Mankind* (1675); *The Enjoyment* (1679); *A Letter to Dr. Burnet* (1680); *Upon Nothing* (1711); *Valentinian* (1685); *Familiar Letters* (2v, 1697); *The Rochester-Savile Letters*, ed. John H. Wilson (Columbus, Ohio, 1941). — T. Longueville, *Rochester and other Literary Rakes* (1902); J. Prinz, *John Wilmot, Earl of Rochester* (Leipzig, 1927); V. de Sola Pinto, *Rochester* (1935); Charles Williams, *Rochester* (1935); S. F. Crocker, "Rochester's *Satire against Mankind*: a Study of Certain Aspects of the Background," *West Virginia Univ. Stud., Philological Papers*, II (1937). 57-73; Kenneth B. Murdock, " 'A Very Profane Wit,' " in *The Sun at Noon* (1939), pp. 269-306; 317-318. An excellent text in which to read the worth-while poems by Rochester is the attractive volume called *A Satire against Mankind & Other Poems by John Wilmot Earl of Rochester*, edited by Harry Levin with an introductory essay (Norfolk, Conn., 1942).

on his death-bed repentance by Bishop Burnet, who had saved his soul but perhaps darkened his reputation.

As poet Rochester was primarily a vigorous and mordant satirist in the fields of philosophy, literature, manners, and politics. In the first of these fields fall two of his best works, the *Satyr against Mankind* (1675) and the lines *Upon Nothing. A Satyr against Mankind* attacks both man and man's reasoning powers. It begins impetuously:

The Earl of Rochester

> Were I, who to my cost already am
> One of those strange, prodigious Creatures *Man,*
> A Spirit free, to choose for my own share
> What sort of Flesh and Blood I pleased to wear,
> I'd be a Dog, a Monkey or a Bear,
> Or any thing, but that vain Animal,
> Who is so proud of being rational.

If this seems extreme or childish misanthropy, one must recall the fact that complacent praise of the nobility and even the divinity of Reason had been common in the earlier Renaissance; and one may also perceive, as Rochester did, that human reason had hardly kept England from shipwreck during much of the thirty years of Rochester's life. Such anti-rationalist utterance was common in the critical revulsion of the later Renaissance. Rochester had found a general suggestion for the form of his poem in Boileau's eighth satire; but the skepticism of all reason (Boileau satirizes the *abuses* of reason) comes from Montaigne and others [9] rather than from Boileau. The attitude is common in English before 1675, but it was nowhere (before Swift's time) stated with such burning energy as here. *Upon Nothing,* which Dr. Johnson thought his lordship's "strongest effort," excels in its ingenious and brilliant playfulness and cynicism. The Stoics held that all creation was derived from an original universal Something. Rochester ironically asserts the precedence of Nothing:

> Ere Time and Place were, Time and Place were not,
> When primitive Nothing Something straight begot,
> Then all proceeded from the great united — What.

The poem is an exceedingly clever witticism at the expense of metaphysics, or at least of Stoic metaphysics. The implications are skeptical to a degree that Dr. Johnson perhaps did not perceive. Rochester is no great thinker, but he is an intellectual. If in these two poems he aims paradox and witticism against sober philosophy and reason, he does it with an intense impulsion that suggests an intellect capable of changing its direction radically and turning towards faith.

Rochester's most important piece of literary satire is his *Allusion to Horace's 10th Satyr of the First Book.* This hasty and unpolished piece is personal satire rather than literary criticism. It is simply an episode in the running battle his lordship was carrying on with many poets, from Dryden

Literary Quarrels

[9] See S. F. Crocker, *op. cit.*

to the negligible Sir Carr Scrope (1649-80). The rugged opening lines and other passages indicate his recurring and not very valid attitude towards Dryden, who seems to glance back at Rochester in his preface to *All for Love* (1678). Sir Carr Scrope and Otway, among others, replied to Rochester's *Allusion,* and Rochester retorted most abusively on Sir Carr in *An Answer to the Defence of Satyr.* In these poetic essays in literary criticism there was little intellectual or critical merit. Shortly thereafter Roscommon in 1680 translated Horace's *Art of Poetry,* and in 1684 he published his *Essay on Translated Verse;* Mulgrave (John Sheffield) in 1682 brought out his *Essay upon Poetry:* these poems show something as to the climate of literary opinion in its cooler moments. Rochester's *Allusion* and *Tryal of the Poets,* and Mulgrave's *Essay upon Satyr* (not to mention Scrope's *Defence of Satyr*) may make spicier reading, but their chief importance is to indicate the extreme irascibility of the *genus irritabile vatum* whose flowery ease on occasion became vitriolic.

Rochester as the scourge of manners is hardly wiser than Rochester the critic of poets; but he is here more equable and perceptive. In *A Letter from Artemisa in the Town to Cloe in the Country* he has more smooth elegance of finish than in other satires and a more dramatic power of depicting society. *Tunbridge Wells* also has remarkable realism; but these

Social and Political Satire

two pieces and most of his social satires tend to deal with the love-life of Restoration "quality," and they are consequently crude in matter and usually hasty and unpolished in manner. The political satires, closely related to the social, are remarkable for their blunt and obscene attacks on the King (Charles II) and his mistresses and advisers. The Marquis of Halifax (Savile) has left us an unflattering account of the monarch's love of filthy wit in conversation, and Rochester evidently was a master here. For the gross indecorums of these satires Rochester was more than once banished from the court, but was speedily pardoned. One must assume that the Merry Monarch, like King Lear, affected the wit of a "bitter fool," who was a pestilent gall, outstanding for his daring and insight. How else shall we explain his tolerance of Rochester's epigrammatic epitaph?

> Here lies a Great and Mighty King
> Whose Promise none relies on,
> Who never said a Foolish Thing
> Nor ever did a Wise One.

At times, as in *The Commons Petition to King Charles II,* Rochester's wit must have been of welcome service; and in such poems as *The History of Insipids (The Restoration)* his personal attacks on royal advisers were perhaps ostensibly disinterested.

In most of these satires Rochester uses the heroic couplet with so natural a rough vigor and resonance that he takes his place high among the users of this metre, the tune of which a century after his death every warbler was to have learned by heart and to have made tediously commonplace. For

Rochester the couplet is a flexible and exciting vehicle. He must also be set down as a notable writer of songs in an age when, as Mulgrave thought,

> Without his Song no Fop is to be found.

He might well have included Rochester (said by some to be the prototype *Rochester's* of his friend Etherege's Dorimant) and all the flowery courtiers with the *Songs* fops. No one can read Rochester's satires without a sense of his gifts of phrasing, and these served him well also in his songs. But in the satires phrasing is heightened by fiery, spontaneous scorn; and in Rochester's songs, which are chiefly amorous, there is no parallel poetic or sexual fury behind the phrases. He gives us graceful and effective approximations of passion, and shows that he is a wit who cleverly counterfeits. In his very pretty *Strephon and Daphne* he gives his frank philosophy of love:

> Love, like other little Boys,
> Cries for Hearts, as they for Toys:
> Which, when gain'd, in Childish Play,
> Wantonly are thrown away.

At times he seems less like the hard Dorimant. In briefer songs such as *My dear Mistress has a Heart* and in *Love and Life* he shows at least a beautifully firm finish that few lyrists of his day could equal. *Love and Life*, like many cavalier songs, begins with a perfect stanza:

> All my past Life is mine no more,
>   The flying Hours are gone:
> Like Transitory Dreams giv'n o'er,
> Whose Images are kept in store
>   By Memory alone.

One must confess, however, that the poet seems as much like his metrically boisterous self in such a satirical song as that beginning

> Room, room, for a Blade of the Town
>   That takes Delight in Roaring,
> Who all Day long rambles up and down,
>   And at Night in the Street lies Snoaring.

It was insight, impulsive vigor, and an appearance of blunt, unflattering honesty that gave this rake of a lord the charms he must have had to counteract his selfishness or his utter lack of idealistic illusion, and make him an admired type of his time as well as a dominant storm-center in his bleak, brief day.

Sir Charles Sedley [10] (1639?-1701) was admired by Rochester as a fellow *Sir Charles* rake and poet, perhaps chiefly because of his indecorous pranks—notorious *Sedley* before Rochester dawned upon the Town. Sedley was the author of three plays and some satirical poems, but what Rochester and posterity have

---

[10] V. de Sola Pinto has ably edited *The Poetical and Dramatic Works of Sir Charles Sedley* (2v, 1928), including "A Bibliography of Works by or Ascribed to Sir Charles Sedley" (II. 235-261); and has written an excellent life called *Sir Charles Sedley* (1927).

agreed in praising is his songs. These are love poems of at least two types. The first is pleading, ingratiating, and yet witty, solicitation, seen charmingly in the song beginning

> Not, Celia, that I juster am,
>   Or better than the rest,
> For I would change each hour like them,
>   Were not my heart at rest —

and seen at its best in the rich, almost Elizabethan, melody and fancy of

> Love still has something of the sea,
>   From whence his mother rose;
> No time his slaves from doubt can free
>   Nor give their thoughts repose!

His second type of love lyric is the playful, almost satiric, song, such as that *To a Devout Young Gentlewoman,* who is overacting her piety and is told,

> 'Tis early to begin to fear
>   The devil at fifteen.

Another poem, addressed, let us hope, to an older Phillis, opens with the gay protestation—

> Phillis is my only joy,
>   Faithless as the winds or seas.

The Earl of Dorset (1638-1706) Such pieces establish Sedley as one of the best gay lyric poets in his century. Charles Sackville,[11] Lord Buckhurst—after 1677 Earl of Dorset—tends to be caustic rather than playful in his songs. His friend Rochester described him as a pointed satirist, "the best Good Man with the worst-natur'd Muse." He wrote relatively few satirical poems but several are tinged with satire. His lines on *The British Princes* of Edward Howard were profusely abusive and his stanzas *On the Countess of Dorchester* ("Dorinda") are strong but unpleasant in their epigrammatic sting. His one famous song is that which is wrongly captioned "Written at Sea, in the first Dutch War, 1665, the night before an Engagement." The rollicking stanzas of this poem are all that remain of Dorset's once very great reputation:

> To all you ladies now at land
>   We men at sea indite;
> But first wou'd have you understand
>   How hard it is to write;
> The Muses now, and Neptune too,
> We must implore to write to you,
>   With a fa, la, la, la, la.

[11] Dorset's poems will be found in the collections of English poets made by Samuel Johnson (Vol. xi, 1779), Robert Anderson (Vol. vi, 1795), and Alexander Chalmers (Vol. viii, 1810). They were first collected in *The Works of Rochester, Roscommon, Dorset,* etc. (2v, 1714). For comments on the canon of his works see *MLN,* xlvii (1932). 454-461 (by H. A. Bagley) and l (1935). 457-459 (by R. G. Howarth); Brice Harris, *Charles Sackville Sixth Earl of Dorset* (Urbana, 1940; *Univ. of Illinois Studies in Lang. and Lit..* xxvi).

The last of these cavalier lyrists to achieve a reputation as such was Charles Cotton [12] (1630-1687). In his own lifetime his moderate fame was based on his burlesques, especially *Scarronides,* on his translations, the most notable of which was his excellent version of Montaigne's *Essays,* and on his treatise on fly-fishing, thought worthy in 1676 to be added to his friend Izaak Walton's *Compleat Angler* as Part II. But since the praise of Words- worth, Coleridge, and Lamb made famous the nature lyrics of Cotton, pub- lished first in 1689 as *Poems on Several Occasions,* his delicately simple artistry in lyric poetry has been much admired. He was no court poet, but was in some sense a disciple of Herrick and Carew. His Staffordshire estates were encumbered with debts, but he loved the country and frequented London probably as a publishing center. Instead of cultivating rakish aristo- crats, he made friends of more modest geniuses in verse, but chiefly Izaak Walton (1593-1683), whom he called "my most worthy father and friend." Wordsworth and his group admired the simplicity and profusion of *The Retirement* and *The Ode to Winter.* In the former poem Cotton has escaped from the Town and relaxes in his native environment—particularly praising his river, the silver Dove. He is surprisingly fond of describing storms, espe- cially at sea, perhaps as a result of his voyage to Ireland as a captain in the army (1670?), on which occasion he barely escaped shipwreck. His four sets of quatrains for Morning, Noon, Evening, and Night are at once exquisite in their natural reality and in their fancy. Watching the sheep coming to fold at sunset he describes the shadows:

Charles Cotton

> A very little, little flock
> Shades thrice the ground that it would stock;
> Whilst the small stripling foilowing them,
> Appears a mighty Polypheme.

His love poems, natural and genuine, and his other verses are influenced frequently by French lyrists of the century, and while he produces charming effects in these imitations and translations, the country details of his de- scriptive poems are what one values most.

It remains to add something concerning a device used in the publication of short poems, a device not invented in the Restoration period but one greatly popularized then. This was the method of combining a few poems by each of several authors to make a single volume, called a "miscellany." [13] It was more frequently a publisher's device than it was an author's trick,

Miscellanies and Song Books

[12] Cotton's *Genuine Works* (1715); *Poems,* ed. J. Beresford (1923); *Poems* [selected] (illus- trated by Lovat Fraser, 1925). — *The Compleat Gamester* (1674); *The Morall Philosophy of the Stoicks* (transl. from Guillaume Du Vair, 1664); *Scarronides* (2v, 1664-5); *Horace* (transl. from Corneille, 1671); *Burlesque upon Burlesque* (1675); *Essays of Montaigne* (transl. 3v, 1685). — Charles J. Sembower, *The Life and Poetry of Charles Cotton* (1911); J. Beresford, "The Poetry of Charles Cotton," *London Mercury,* v (1921). 57-69; Gerald G. P. Heywood, *Charles Cotton and his River* (Manchester, 1928).
[13] Bibliographies of miscellanies exist as follows: Arthur E. Case, *A Bibliography of English Poetical Miscellanies, 1521-1750* (Bibliographical Soc., Oxford, 1935), and Norman Ault, for the years 1660-1800, in *CBEL,* II. 173-256.

though it enabled satirists and modest poets to appear anonymously and thus to escape a certain amount of personal censure. The most reputable series of miscellany volumes were those published in 1684 and thereafter by the bookseller Jacob Tonson with the advice and aid of John Dryden.[14] These were advertised at times as "published by Mr. Dryden," and they were popularly referred to (even the additions published after the poet's death) as "Dryden's Miscellanies." The series ran to Volume VI (1709), and had no consistent uniformity of title-page. In contrast to these, the least dignified of the miscellanies was a type called *drollery*,[15] which may be said to exist from the time (1655) when "H. H." published the *Musarum Deliciae* of Sir John Mennes and Dr. James Smith to the *Merry Drollery Compleat* (1691). A drollery might contain first-rate poetry, but normally it specialized in printing fugitive manuscript pieces or reprinting broadsides and ballads that attacked the Puritans scoffingly and indecently. Of somewhat more dignity is a series of miscellanies called *Poems on Affairs of State*, which are dominantly but not exclusively political.[16] Begun in 1689, these by 1707 had increased to four volumes with the contents varying somewhat in successive editions. The announced purpose of these volumes was "to remove those pernicious Principles which lead us directly to Slavery." Here James II and the Catholic party replace the Puritans as undesirables. Still another development of this general sort was the songbook.[17] Such very numerous collections, frequently with tunes included, were enormously popular. They unfortunately tended to separate lyrics, the words of songs, from other types of poetry, and then to subordinate lyrics to music. The most notable publishers of popular songs in the period were John Playford and his son Henry. By all odds the most prolific and successful song writer was Tom D'Urfey (1653-1723), author of loyalist satires, of many plays, and of some very bad Pindaric odes, but chiefly a song writer.[18] D'Urfey summed up his own vogue in his stammering remark (recorded or invented by Tom Brown): "The Town may da-da-damn me for a Poet, but they si-si-sing my Songs for all that."

All these types of miscellanies are storehouses for preserving fugitive pieces, and because of the danger in avowing authorship of any spicy political writing the ascriptions of authorship given in these volumes should command very skeptical respect. The publication of poems in miscellany volumes (frequently mixed with short prose pieces) continued to be popular through-

---

[14] See Hugh Macdonald, *John Dryden, a Bibliography* (Oxford, 1939), pp. 67-83. Also R. D. Havens, "Changing Taste in the Eighteenth Century: A Study of Dryden's and Dodsley's Miscellanies," *PMLA*, XLIV (1929). 501-536.

[15] Harvard University has an unpublished dissertation by Courtney D. C. Smith on *The Seventeenth-century Drolleries* (1943).

[16] Macdonald, *John Dryden, a Bibliography*, pp. 316-322.

[17] Cyrus L. Day and Eleanore B. Murrie, "English Song-Books, 1651-1702, and their Publishers," *Library*, XVI (1936). 355-401.

[18] Cyrus L. Day, *The Songs of Thomas D'Urfey* (Cambridge, Mass., 1933); Willard Thorp, *Songs from the Restoration Theater* (Princeton, 1934). For an excellent bibliography see Cyrus L. Day and Eleanore B. Murrie, *English Song-Books, 1651-1702: A Bibliography with a First-Line Index of Songs* (1940).

out the eighteenth century, and it has been used to the present day. It is, however, especially notable as a popular Augustan device, which in ultimate effect complicates the establishment of the canon of an author's work, and makes difficult the study of the history of short poems. The popularity of a poem or type of poem cannot be inferred from its appearance in a single miscellany; but if reprinted in several its popularity must be assumed.

V

Restoration Drama: I. Heroic Plays and Tragedies

Restoration drama [1] has been regarded as both the glory and the shame of the period. The comedies handle wit, satire, and neat situation in a manner hardly surpassed elsewhere in English drama; but they are notoriously deficient in moral decency, though very sensitive to a superficial norm in manners. In the more serious plays produced shortly after the Restoration there is an artificial declamatory elevation which, joined with bustling action and elaborate spectacle, for some years dazzled audiences. Later this "heroic" type of play yielded to dramas of pathos and domestic sentimentality. The conditions of the theatre that fostered these serious plays and the nature of the plays themselves will be the subject of the present chapter.[2] The comedies will be reserved for the next chapter, although it must be noted that few dramatists specialized either in comedy or tragedy. They thought, however, in terms of genres, and we may well follow their example.

The Inter-regnum Officially the theatres of London had been closed from the autumn of 1642 until after the Restoration of Charles II. Actually, there were, in Cromwell's time, dramatic performances in the houses of noblemen and even privately among cultivated Puritans. The lower classes, too, still delighted in "mummings," rope-dances, acrobatic acts, and drolls—which last were farcical fragments of plays.[3] At least one of the more proletarian Elizabethan playhouses, the Red Bull, was not dismantled by the Puritans, and was

---

[1] In the chapters on the drama that cover dramatic history from 1660 to 1789 the dates of plays given in the footnotes are supposed always to be dates of publication. In the text of these chapters the dates of first performances, when known, are given.

[2] General materials on the drama of this period may be found in Allardyce Nicoll, *A History of Restoration Drama, 1660-1700* (Cambridge, 1923; 2d ed., 1928). This is the standard history. Other histories are D. E. Baker, Isaac Reed, and Stephen Jones, *Biographia Dramatica; or, a Companion to the Playhouse* (3v, 1812; a dictionary of [*a*] playwrights and [*b*] plays); J. Genest, *Some Account of the English Stage* (10v, Bath, 1832; still exceedingly useful for details about minor plays or about actors and acting); Sir Adolphus W. Ward, *A History of English Dramatic Literature to the Death of Queen Anne* (3v, 1899); Ashley H. Thorndike, *Tragedy* (Boston, 1908); George H. Nettleton, *English Drama of the Restoration and Eighteenth Century* (1914; a readable and reliable brief survey); Bonamy Dobrée, *Restoration Tragedy* (Oxford, 1929; useful for history and criticism). For the influences of the drama of the earlier seventeenth century on Restoration playwrights see Alfred Harbage, *Cavalier Drama* (Philadelphia, 1936). On the theatres of the time see the authoritative studies of Eleanore Boswell, *The Restoration Court Stage* (Cambridge, Mass., 1932) and Leslie Hotson, *The Commonwealth and Restoration Stage* (Cambridge, Mass., 1928). Three books by Montague Summers are useful, if used with caution: *A Bibliography of the Restoration Drama* (1935), *The Restoration Theatre* (1934), *The Playhouse of Pepys* (1935). Very useful is Alfred Harbage's *Annals of the English Drama, 975-1700: An Analytical Record of All Plays, Extant and Lost, Chronologically Arranged* (Philadelphia, 1940).

[3] Hyder E. Rollins, "A Contribution to the History of English Commonwealth Drama," *SP*, XVIII (1921). 267-333.

used briefly after the Restoration, and frequently during the interregnum. In 1673 Francis Kirkman recorded his memories of plebeian performances there in the forbidden period: "I have seen the Red Bull Play-House, which was a large one, so full, that as many went back for want of room as had entered; and as meanly as you may now think of these Drols, they were then Acted by the best Comedians then and now in being." [4] Although the tradition of legitimate drama was mangled rather than killed, evidently the proletarian taste for farce and bustle endured along with a taste for poetic drama.

But Puritanism had worked so well—aided doubtless by the repellent neurotic sensationalism of Jacobean drama—that after the Restoration the theatre was not the popular institution it had been in 1600. At the beginning of the century London could support a half-dozen playhouses; after 1660, if we shut our eyes to two or three years of free-for-all competition in producing plays, only two theatres maintained a struggling existence, and for the period 1682-95 only one continued regular seasons. Such conditions prevailed in spite of a considerable royal patronage. In the summer of 1660 the King issued "patents" to his friends Sir William Davenant [5] and Thomas Killigrew, which gave them a virtual monopoly in organizing companies of actors and producing plays. Killigrew's company became known as the King's players, and after 1674 they were housed in the Theatre Royal in Drury Lane. Of Davenant's company the King's brother, the Duke of York (later James II), was patron, and it acted after 1671 in a new theatre in Dorset Garden. The very predominance of court influence and courtier management tended perhaps to diminish the appeal of the theatre to the merchant classes. The wealthy citizen of London and his wife were in fact frequently objects of mirth in the comedies of the time; yet it is not altogether clear that the ridicule was offensive to this ambitious and rising social class.

But the citizens were morally respectable—or tended to be; and the theatre

Puritan and Court Influences

---

[4] *The Wits*, ed. John J. Elson (Ithaca, N. Y., 1932), p. 268; see also Charles R. Baskervill, *The Elizabethan Jig* (Chicago, 1929), p. 122.

[5] Sir William Davenant (1606-1668), the son of a tavern-keeper, was born at Oxford, and about 1620-21 he was a member of Lincoln College, Oxford. He was for a few years in the service of the Duchess of Richmond and later of Fulke Greville, Lord Brooke. At court he became acquainted with Endymion Porter, Henry Jermyn, and others of influence, and rapidly gained favor as poet and dramatist until in 1638 he succeeded Ben Jonson as poet laureate. An active royalist during the Civil War, he was knighted at the siege of Gloucester (1643). With the court he withdrew to France after the defeat of the royal army, and it was there that he began *Gondibert* and first published the *Discourse on Gondibert* with Hobbes's *Answer* (1650). Sailing for America on a royal mission (1650), he was captured and imprisoned in the Tower. Freed in 1654, Davenant devoted himself to tactful dramatic productions and, after 1660, to the management of his ("the Duke's") company of comedians. As a writer for the stage his real achievement was operatic—in his *Siege of Rhodes* (acted first in 1656) and in his operatic adaptations of Shakespeare's *Tempest* and *Macbeth*. — *Works* (1673); *Dramatic Works*, ed. J. Maidment and W. H. Logan (5v, Edinburgh, 1872-4); *Love and Honour and The Siege of Rhodes*, ed. James W. Tupper (Boston, 1909). — Hazelton Spencer, *Shakespeare Improved* (Cambridge, Mass., 1927); Leslie Hotson, *The Commonwealth and Restoration Stage* (Cambridge, Mass., 1928); Alfred Harbage, *Thomas Killigrew* (Philadelphia, 1930); Friederich Laig, *Englische und Französische Elemente in Sir William Davenants Dramatischer Kunst* (Emsdetten, 1934); Alfred Harbage, *Sir William Davenant* (Philadelphia, 1935); Arthur H. Nethercot, *Sir William D'Avenant* (Chicago, 1938).

The Players

tended in the other direction! It was a shock, for example, when after 1660, in imitation of the French theatre, women, and not boys, played female rôles on the English stage. The actresses were often the avowed mistresses of noblemen or even of royalty itself. It is perhaps natural that, if we except Thomas Betterton (1635?-1710), the period produced no great histrionic geniuses. Preëminent among his fellow actors Betterton created most of the "heavy" heroic rôles of the period and acted comedy parts as well. He was a most important link in a Shakespearean acting tradition in so far as any such tradition survived the interregnum. Michael Mohun in Killigrew's company was the corresponding tragedian: he had acted before 1642. Later Mrs. Barry and Mrs. Bracegirdle were important actresses. Edward Kynaston had a long and significant career that began by his playing female parts: "the loveliest lady that ever I saw in my life," was the verdict of that connoisseur in ladies, Samuel Pepys. Kynaston's later career was devoted to dignified paternal rôles. Among the popular performers were several excellent low comedians: John Lacy, Cave Underhill, James Nokes, Thomas Doggett, and Joe Haynes—the last famous as a practical jester and clown, especially in "stunt" prologues and epilogues. It is this last type of actor that chiefly shows that sophisticated courtiers were not the only audience towards whom appeal was directed.

The Theatres

The theatres themselves are a development from the private theatres of the Elizabethan age—a rectangular roofed-in hall with a proscenium arch framing the back stage but not framing the wide apron that still projected well into the pit. Davenant featured elaborate scenery, back drops with side flats that slid in grooves, thus opening or closing to change scenes on occasion. Machines, enabling Jupiter to descend in a cloud or aiding spirits, sylphs, or fairies to float through the air, were most elaborate, and "made" many a very popular play or opera. Because of these complicated machines it became increasingly desirable to exclude spectators from the stage. The audience, frequently inattentive and noisy, was not seldom even turbulent. On benches in the pit sat the aristocratic sparks and "ladies of the town." Pinchwife in *The Country Wife* (Act II, Scene 1) made his Margery sit in a box, though she, to his horror, liked the gaily dressed pit. "We sat amongst ugly people," she says. "He would not let me come near the gentry, who sat under us, so that I could not see 'em. He told me, none but naughty women sat there, whom they toused and moused. But I would have ventured, for all that." Pepys, who was almost as jealous as Pinchwife, preferred for many reasons to go to the theatre without his Elizabeth, yet he normally took her to the pit. On October 19, 1667, they went to the première of Lord Orrery's *Black Prince*—

where, though we came by two o'clock, yet there was no room in the pit, but we were forced to go into one of the upper boxes, at 4s. a piece, which is the first time I ever sat in a box in my life. And in the same box came, by and by, behind me, my Lord Barkeley and his lady, but I did not turn my face to them to be known, so that I was excused from giving them my seat; and this pleasure

I had, that from this place the scenes do appear very fine indeed, and much better than in the pit.

The scenes, the music, the "naughty women" in the audience were features as well as the plays themselves. On the stage the chief early developments were operas and heroic plays. Early operas were promoted and at times written by Sir William Davenant, the patentee. Sir William had written masques and romantic plays for fifteen years before the theatres were closed, and had been made governor of the Cockpit company of actors in 1639. During the interregnum he had evaded restrictions by producing operas and entertainments—not technically plays.[6] The most significant of these was *The Siege of Rhodes,* which was performed in various states and finally, in two parts, in 1661. This opera ("the story sung in Recitative Musick") derives dramatically from romances such as Beaumont and Fletcher had popularized.[7] A literary origin is seen in its relation to the heroic poem: it strives for epic elevation. It anticipates neo-classical conventions in its use of balancing characters and situations. Solyman the Magnificent, a sultan, contrasts with Alphonso, a Christian hero, and there is similar balance between the sultaness and Alphonso's wife. There are long moments of self-communings and arguments over "costly scruples" and typical psychological perplexities, such as the difficulty of reconciling love and honor [8]—all of which were soon to be stereotyped in the so-called "heroic play."

The Begin-nings of Opera

Under Davenant's influence developed both the heroic play and the English opera.[9] Foreign opera was perhaps first heard in England during this period. Perrin's *Ariadne* was heard in French at the Theatre Royal in 1674, and Italian singers performed at court. English opera usually eschewed the new recitative style and interspersed spoken lines with song. Although the appeal of opera derived from the music and spectacular mechanical effects, it is notable that some of the most popular English operas were adapted from Shakespeare: *Macbeth* by Davenant in 1673; *The Tempest* by Davenant and Dryden in 1667, and, more successfully, by Shadwell in 1674; and *The Fairy Queen,* adapted by Settle from *Midsummer Night's Dream* in 1692, with music by Henry Purcell. In general the operas lack literary importance: Nahum Tate's libretto for Purcell's beautifully set *Dido and Aeneas* (1689), for example, has no value apart from what the composer gave it in his rare music.

Davenant's other foster child, the heroic play,[10] is also in some sense a cultural phenomenon rather than a literary achievement, even though Dryden himself enjoyed writing such plays. Dryden, in fact, is not only the chief playwright in this type but also the principal contemporary com-

The Heroic Play

---

[6] See Alfred Harbage, *Sir William Davenant* (Philadelphia, 1935).

[7] A complete survey of such influence on the Restoration drama is given by Arthur C. Sprague in his *Beaumont and Fletcher on the Restoration Stage* (Cambridge, Mass., 1926).

[8] *Love and Honour* was the title of an early play by Davenant, acted in 1634 and published in 1649; ed. J. W. Tupper, as noted above.

[9] Edward J. Dent, *Foundations of English Opera* (Cambridge, 1928).

[10] For discussions of the heroic play see the books and articles listed in *CBEL,* II. 396, and Alfred Harbage, *Cavalier Drama* (Philadelphia, 1936), pp. 48-71.

mentator on it. In his essay *Of Heroic Plays,* prefixed to *The Conquest of Granada* (1672), he analyzes and defends the type; in the prefaces to *All for Love* (1678) and *The Spanish Friar* (1681) he recants. Davenant he regarded as the father of the type, though he recognized it as a development both of the Elizabethan tradition and of the tradition "of Corneille and some French poets." He also recognized the influence of Ariosto and the heroic poem, observing that "an heroic play ought to be an imitation, in little, of an heroic poem; and, consequently, that Love and Valour ought to be the subject of it." This observation in part accounts for the more than Augustan elevation that makes much of the dialogue in these plays frankly ridiculous. Dryden thought Davenant's plays lacked this elevation as well as the fullness of plot and variety of characters desirable.

The Earl of Orrery

In a period of somewhat more than a decade (1664-77 are Professor Nicoll's dates) these qualities were achieved by a group of authors, many of whom elected to write their heroic tragedies in rime. This habit, reintroduced from France and favored by Charles II, was taken up by Roger Boyle, Earl of Orrery (1621-1679), who among the first writers of heroic tragedy exercised considerable influence.[11] He used English materials in two historical plays, *Henry V* (1664) and *The Black Prince* (1667), but cast them in the form of French tragedy and used the popular device of antithetical emotions to tear the souls of his persons between the conflicting duties due to a mistress and to a friend or between love and filial piety. In *The General* (1664) the hero is torn between love and honor, and the emotional conflicts in *Mustapha* (1665), perhaps his most typical play, are exceedingly complex. The political and domestic intrigues of an Oriental royal family seen in swiftly shifting situation and heard in lofty, declamatory rhetoric characterize the work. Orrery uses a strong but artificial style. The love of antithetical wit causes one character, wishing to convey the idea that the sultaness will be merciful, to say:

> Madam, she will not now by one mean act,
> A future stain on her past fame contact.

The play contains much luridly Machiavellian action, much heroic artifice, and some heroic pathos in the death of Mustapha.

The Indian Queen

But some months before Orrery's first play was acted in London,[12] Dryden, collaborating with his saturnine brother-in-law, Sir Robert Howard, had in January, 1664, produced *The Indian Queen,* and for more than a decade thereafter Dryden was the master-author of heroic plays.[13] In *The Indian*

11 *The Dramatic Works of Roger Boyle, Earl of Orrery,* ed. William S. Clark (2v, Cambridge, Mass., 1937), contains texts, a bibliography, and a long historical preface.

12 It had been acted in Dublin at least as early as 1662.

13 *Works,* ed. Sir Walter Scott and George Saintsbury (18v, 1882-92); *Dramatic Works,* ed. Montague Summers (6v, 1931-2); *Selected Dramas,* ed. George R. Noyes (Chicago, 1910). There is no really satisfactory edition of all Dryden's plays. — G. R. Noyes, introduction to *Selected Dramas;* M. Sherwood, *Dryden's Dramatic Theory and Practice* (Boston, 1898); Allardyce Nicoll, *Dryden as an Adapter of Shakespeare* (Shakespeare Association, 1922); B. J. Pendlebury, *Dryden's Heroic Plays* (1923); Cecil V. Deane, *Dramatic Theory and the Rhymed Heroic Play* (1931); H. Granville-Barker, "Wycherley and Dryden," in *On Dramatic Method*

Queen love and valor, the prescribed motives,[14] are the conflicting forces. Montezuma, the general of the Inca's forces, defeats the Mexicans, and wishes the hand· of the Inca's daughter, Orazia, as his reward. Not being of royal blood he is deemed ineligible; but at the end of the play it turns out that he is the son of the true (exiled) Queen of Mexico; and hence these two lovers, who throughout the play have both been persecuted by unwanted proffers of affection, noble or lustful, are finally made happy. Evil characters obligingly commit suicide. It is notable that Montezuma, stung when the Inca refuses to give him Orazia, changes sides, and fights for the Mexicans: such a change of allegiance, used more than once in Dryden's later plays, is here fairly plausible. The characters are familiar types: Acacis, the young Mexican idealist, noble, though a prisoner of war ("Virtue is calm in him but rough in me," says Montezuma); Traxalla, the villain-general, whose fame is shaded by Montezuma's and whose love is lust; Zempoalla and Amexia, rival and contrasting queens of Mexico—all these types were soon to be familiar in later heroic plays: the emperor of a remote land, the ever-victorious hero, with a "swelled mind," the rival villain, the dazzlingly virtuous heroine, and the pseudo-royal villainess are all here. A conjuring scene, aerial spirits, and other masque-like, romantic elements, aid the spectacle, which, for the rest, consists of minds audibly and rhetorically torn by emotion or by "cruel circumstance." It was natural that the great success of this play, Howard's third and Dryden's second, should encourage Dryden to bring on a sequel, *The Indian Emperor,* a year later. This very popular play added no technical developments to the type; it used advantageously the richly exotic scenery painted for *The Indian Queen.*

During the next four years Dryden produced three comedies, but in 1669 he returned to the heroic play in producing *Tyrannick Love, or, The Royal Martyr,* with significant modifications of the type. The plot introduces us to the tyrant Maximin as protagonist and ranter. There is no villainess; and St. Catharine of Alexandria (as "captive queen") introduces an element of Christian apologetics, later more significant in Dryden's nondramatic poetry. St. Catharine gives certain scenes a more intellectual quality than is found in other heroic plays, and her threatened tortures add a new gruesomeness. Porphyrius, the worthy general, who is the only possible hero in the play, hardly rants at all. Maximin's rages are at times super-imperial; he dies contemning the gods—

Tyrannick Love

> And after thee I go
> Revenging still, and following ev'n to the other world my blow;
> And shoving back this earth on which I sit,
> I'll mount, and scatter all the Gods I hit.

(1931); Ned B. Allen, *The Sources of Dryden's Comedies* (Ann Arbor, 1935); Mildred E. Hartsock, "Dryden's Plays: A Study in Ideas," *Seventeenth Century Studies, Second Series, by Members of the Graduate School, Univ. of Cincinnati,* ed. Robert Shafer (Princeton, 1937), pp. 71-176; D. W. Jefferson, "The Significance of Dryden's Heroic Plays," *Proceedings of the Leeds Phil. and Lit. Soc.,* v (1940). 125-139.

[14] Prescribed, that is, in Dryden's later essay "Of Heroic Plays," *Essays of Dryden,* ed. W. P. Ker (1900), I. 148-159.

The play is an amazing fusion of complicated rant, love, rationalistic argu-
fying, with, finally, an amusing epilogue spoken by no less a personage than
the King's "Protestant whore," Mrs. Nell Gwyn, who played the emperor's
daughter, Valeria. She ends with the lines:

> As for my epitaph when I am gone,
> I'll trust no poet, but will write my own: —
> Here Nelly lies, who, though she lived a slattern,
> Yet died a princess, acting in S. Catharine.

The Con-
quest of
Granada
    Thrilling as the final rants of Maximin were (the play ran for fourteen
days), they were less varied and effective than the poetical rhetoric of Dryden's most elaborate heroic play, *The Conquest of Granada,* a play in two
parts (1670, 1671) filling ten highly complicated acts. The moral instruction
seems to be that a nation divided against itself, as were the Moors in Granada,
is easy prey for armies led by a supernaturally effective general such as
Almanzor, who is Dryden's loudest realization of a full-blown hero. The
characters and their complications in love are for the most part familiar.
Boabdelin, the weak ruler of Granada, is betrothed to the lovely Almahide
(Nell Gwyn again), but obviously her ultimate destiny is the arms of
Almanzor. Contrasting with Almahide is the beauteous serpent Lyndaraxa,
of whom one of her male victims, the king's brother, remarks:

> Her tears, her smiles, her very look's a net.
> Her voice is like a Siren's of the land;
> And bloody hearts lie panting in her hand.

This fair creature and her plotting brother are responsible for most of the
villainy in the play. A contrasting and sweetly different couple are Ozmyn
and Benzayda, who illustrate the sentimental appeal of innocent, simple,
idyllic love and the painful contest between love and filial duty.

The Char-
acter of
Almanzor
    The character of Almanzor and the poetry in which it is expressed are
most remarkable. It is true that Almanzor is frequently absurd: he changes
sides in the wars until he makes one dizzy, and his titanic rants are grotesque.
But, curiously enough, they have a basis in reason and are at the same time
thoroughly romantic. The king's brother sketches the character briefly:

> Vast is his courage, boundless is his mind,
> Rough as a storm, and humorous as wind:
> Honor's the only idol of his eyes;
> The charms of beauty like a pest he flies;
> And, rais'd by valor from a birth unknown,
> Acknowledges no pow'r above his own.

When condemned to death by the king he remarks:

> No man has more contempt than I of breath,
> But whence hast thou the right to give me death?
> Obey'd as sovereign by thy subjects be,
> But know that I alone am king of me.

I am as free as nature first made man,
Ere the base laws of servitude began,
When wild in woods the noble savage ran. . . .
If thou pretend'st to be a prince like me,
Blame not an act which should thy pattern be.
I saw th' oppress'd, and thought it did belong
To a king's office to redress the wrong:
I brought that succor which thou ought'st to bring,
And so, in nature, am thy subjects' king.

When the king, unmoved by this reasoning, orders the guards to execute Almanzor "instantly," the hero replies—

Stand off; I have not leisure yet to die.

Clearly, such a man has something!

The audience's delight in this play was probably not diminished by the burlesque *Rehearsal* [15] (1671), which, composed much earlier to ridicule Sir Robert Howard and Davenant, was now remade as an attack on Dryden (Bayes, in the play) and heroic plays. The ingenious and biting satire, based on a common-sense reaction to the excesses of Almanzor and his sort, seems not immediately to have affected Dryden's reputation or the popularity of the plays satirized. At any rate in 1675 Dryden produced another (his last) rimed heroic play, *Aureng-Zebe,* which followed closely the pattern of the earlier plays in its stock characters, its multiplication of love-complications, with villainy defeated and the two reputable lovers left to live while carnage and madness remove most of the other principals. Indamora, the captive queen of this play, is pursued by three unwanted lovers in addition to the hero: in no other play has Dryden more ingeniously tortured his love affairs. There is here less of rant; the poetry is frequently reflective in substance and more sinuous in its rhythms. Aureng-Zebe's meditations at times are quiet even to melancholy:

Aureng-Zebe and Dramatic Adaptations

When I consider life, 'tis all a cheat;
Yet, fooled with hope, men favor the deceit,
Trust on, and think to-morrow will repay.
To-morrow's falser than the former day —
Lies worse, and, while it says we shall be blest
With some new joys, cuts off what we possessed.
Strange cozenage!

Such a passage indicates the mastery Dryden has achieved in adapting the rimed couplet to dramatic verse; yet this was his last play in rime to be

[15] *The Rehearsal,* written by George Villiers, Duke of Buckingham, with the aid of Thomas Sprat, Martin Clifford, Samuel Butler, and perhaps others, invents the device, used later delightfully by Fielding and Sheridan, of having friends of the playwright (Bayes) attend the rehearsal of his play: the rehearsal goes badly; the play itself is absurd, as are the author's explications of it, and the comments of the "friends" add savor in caustic wit. — See the ed. of Montague Summers (Stratford-on-Avon, 1914). Dane F. Smith in his *Plays about the Theatre in England* (1936) comments on the play. According to Emmett L. Avery, "The Stage Popularity of *The Rehearsal,* 1671-1777," *Research Studies of the State College of Washington,* VII (1939). 201-204, there were 291 performances of the play in the period studied. The most popular eighteenth-century portrayers of Bayes were Estcourt, the two Cibbers, and David Garrick.

acted. He did, to be sure, with Milton's permission, base a rimed opera, *The State of Innocence* (1677), on *Paradise Lost;* but this was not performed. Others continued to use the couplet, and it is conceivable that Dryden abandoned rime and ranting heroism together when he found that inferiors (notably Settle) could prove rivals in such a field.[16] Even in his later tragedies, however, Dryden could not escape the epic-heroic elevation that dominated much of his nondramatic work. His tragedies suffer from the fact that they remind us of better things. His adaptations of Shakespeare, *All for Love* (1677) from *Antony and Cleopatra,* and his *Troilus and Cressida* (1679), unlike Tate's popular reworking of *King Lear,* do remain tragedies; but their humanity is artificialized in heroic terms—Troilus and Antony are cousins or brothers of Almanzor and Aureng-Zebe, and Cleopatra much resembles a captive queen in her worries. Yet *All for Love* remains the best of the plays that pour Elizabethan material into neo-classic French molds. Its blank verse is noble, its unity effective; if Shakespeare had never written, it would seem one of the most impressive monuments in English drama. It remains, in fact, from a literary point of view, the most dignified English tragedy in the tradition of the three unities. Dryden's last plays— *Cleomenes* (1692) and *Love Triumphant* (1694)—had little success.

An unfortunate episode in Dryden's career as heroic playwright was the animosity resulting from the great success of *The Empress of Morocco* (1673), the second play of young Elkanah Settle.[17] This was twice success- fully acted at court, and was then presented publicly in London. Its success was engineered (at least aided) by noblemen who had been Dryden's patrons, and the success seemed a deliberate challenge to Dryden's fame. The play is hardly more absurd than some of Dryden's, but its plotting, which concerns the successful intrigues of a wicked empress and her lover against her son, is less well knit than Dryden's work, and its poetry is obviously inferior. Its theatrical merit lay in its highly spectacular scenic effects. Dryden and his friends of the moment, Crowne and Shadwell, at- tacked the absurdities of the play; Settle retorted in kind on *The Conquest of Granada,* and much controversy resulted. Between 1671 and 1718 Settle was to produce almost a score of plays; but from this career of almost unequaled length, he emerges with the reputation of having been scorned by both Dryden and Pope—as well as by lesser authors.

All for Love

Elkanah Settle

16 Professor Nicoll (*Restoration Drama,* p. 90) tells us that from 1660-70 there were 18 new plays in the couplet; from 1670-80, 24; in the next decade he found only one; in the last decade of the century, only 4; and in the early eighteenth century, 6.

17 Elkanah Settle (1648-1724), born at Dunstable, entered Trinity College, Oxford in 1666, but soon left without a degree, and proceeded to London. His first tragedy, *Cambyses* (1671), met with considerable success and for some years his plays were popular. An artificially created rivalry with Dryden led to scurrilous attacks and replies. In 1691 Settle was appointed City Poet, and as such produced the annual pageants for the Lord Mayor's Day. In a long and poverty-stricken old age he did hack work of various sorts. He even wrote drolls for Barthol- omew Fair and, according to legend, acted in them. About 1718 he secured admission to the Charterhouse, and he died there in 1724. — His plays are listed in Nicoll's *Restoration Drama.* A biography has been written by Frank C. Brown, *Elkanah Settle* (Chicago, 1910), and Ros- well G. Ham has treated the quarrel with Dryden in "Dryden vs. Settle," *MP,* xxv (1928). 409-416.

The chief tragic writers of the period were Lee, Otway, and Southerne. John Banks, with seven or eight tragedies, and Crowne, with eleven, are definitely inferior to these three.[18] All these men are influenced by the *Tragedy* heroic play, by Elizabethan tragedy (especially by the "tragedy of blood"), and by the French tradition formulated from Aristotle and Seneca in the early part of the seventeenth century. Corneille, whose plays date 1629-74, was negligent of the rules, and Racine, whose plays date 1664-91, triumphed by means of the rules: both these great tragic poets exercised much influence in England. Their tradition, allowing nothing to be accidental, neglected external action in favor of portraying the passions or states of mind of heroic personages. This necessitated the use of narrative relations for events off-stage, and extreme focus of action on a final fateful day. All tragedies of this sort might begin on the note sounded early in Lee's *Rival Queens,* "The morning rises black"; and so many did begin in this fashion that the device was easily burlesqued. The persons devote much time to rhetorical displays of feeling and are likely to get casuistically involved in stating moderately simple reactions.

Nathaniel Lee [19] was one of the few specialized dramatists of the period. *Nat Lee* Between 1674 and 1684 he produced eleven tragedies and no comedies. In two additional tragedies, *Oedipus* (1678) and *The Duke of Guise* (1682), he collaborated with Dryden. Nine of these plays were based on stories about Greeks or Romans, some of them found, however, in the French romances of Lee's day. Since Lee mentions Shakespeare, Fletcher, and Jonson in his prefaces, one must conclude that he was consciously attentive to diverse traditions. Like Dryden, his friend, he tried to fuse the Elizabethan idiom with that of French tragedy and French heroic romance. Love was his theme, and in Langbaine's opinion, "His Muse indeed seem'd destin'd for the Diversion of the Fair Sex; so soft and passionately moving are his scenes of Love written." [20] Three of his plays were dedicated to royal mistresses, and *Mithridates* he himself calls a lady's play. It was one of his best. In the crucial years after 1678 he naturally wavered into political innuendo, and one of his very best plays, *Lucius Junius Brutus* (1680), was banned after three performances. Over others he had trouble with the censor.

---

18 For John Crowne (1640?-1712?) see Arthur F. White, *John Crowne* (Cleveland, 1922), and for John Banks (*c.* 1652-1706) our best account is the Introduction to Thomas M. H. Blair's edition of Banks's *Unhappy Favourite* (1939).

19 Nathaniel Lee (*c.* 1649-1692), the son of a clergyman, was educated at Westminster School and at Trinity College, Cambridge (1665-68). Leaving Cambridge, Lee went to London, and in spite of poverty speedily moved in fashionable society. He tried acting, but after a few months abandoned it for the writing of tragedies, at which he was highly successful. His intemperate habits became extreme, and in 1684 his mind failed completely. He was confined in Bedlam for five years (1684-89) and died in 1692. — *Works* (1694; 2v, 1713; 3v, 1734); *Nero* (1675); *Sophonisba* (1675); *Gloriana* (1676); *The Rival Queens, or the Death of Alexander the Great* (1677); *Mithridates* (1678); *Oedipus* (with Dryden, 1679); *Caesar Borgia* (1680); *Theodosius* (1680); *Lucius Junius Brutus* (1681); *The Duke of Guise* (1683); *Constantine the Great* (1684); *The Princess of Cleve* (1689); *The Massacre of Paris* (1689). — Bonamy Dobrée, *Restoration Tragedy* (Oxford, 1929); R. G. Ham, *Otway and Lee* (New Haven, 1931); W. B. VanLennep, "Nathaniel Lee," *Harvard Summaries of Theses* (Cambridge, Mass., 1935), pp. 337-341.

20 Gerard Langbaine, *An Account of the English Dramatick Poets* (Oxford, 1691), p. 321.

In the essential nature of his tragedies Lee seems an apt illustration of his friend's dictum, "Great wits are sure to madness near allied"; for in his work tragic rant and imagery seem tainted with wildness and confusion. His first tragedy, *Nero,* dealt with the gruesome crimes of that emperor's day; almost his last was based on Mme de Lafayette's *Princesse de Clèves;* and Lee turns her picture of the French court into something almost as distasteful as *Nero.* In Lee the heroic recovered a sort of Jacobean decadence. Certainly he lacked control in his flights. In his dedication to *Theodosius* he says: "It has been often observed against me, That I abound in ungovern'd Fancy; but, I hope, the World will pardon the Sallies of Youth: Age, Despondence, and Dulness come too fast of themselves." And in the dedication to *Lucius Junius Brutus* he thinks a critic of such a story must be a Longinus "or nothing." Sublime flights were his objective; "furious fustian and turgid rants" were his achievement, so Cibber thought; and Cibber gave the added ungenerous opinion that only the dignity of Betterton's utterance as Alexander in *The Rival Queens* could have kept the play on the stage for so many succeeding years. It is easier to make a long list of Lee's faults than to perceive his merits steadily. His characters do rage rather than speak; situations change with absurd rapidity; at times motivation of important deeds is sadly deficient; and there is an almost unvarying high emotional tension. His Alexander, so Crowne thought, was "continually on the fret"; and the observation applies to many of his leading persons. But on the stage the plays had great effect. The fluency and speed of action, the torrent of violent imagery, the introduction of gruesome tableaux, and the fact that the stories of his plays have a strong, crude fascination account for much. His poetic gift, above all, might often make a minor Elizabethan envy him. There is also, along with the impetuosity of it all, a quiet sentimentality, an exaggerated stress on more or less innocent tears and pathos that was in effect somewhat akin to the lachrymose comedies soon to be in vogue.

Thomas Otway

Otway [21] in his brief career (1675-1683) strengthens the tendency remarked in Lee to develop away from heroics towards sentimental pathos. His first play, the typically heroic *Alcibiades* done in rime, apparently had no great success; but his second, *Don Carlos,* was a great hit, and remained one of his most popular works. Though written in rime and in the fast staling heroic conventions—such as making a tyrant father and his son rivals in

21 Thomas Otway (1652-1685), born in Sussex, was educated at Winchester (1665-68) and Christ Church, Oxford (1669-71). In 1671 he left for London, where he first attempted acting (with little success) and soon devoted himself to writing plays under the not very rewarding patronage of the Earl of Rochester. In 1678 he was in Flanders as an army officer; but he returned to London the following year with pockets still empty. The remaining five years of his career as distinguished writer were spent in dissipation and extreme destitution. — *Works* (1692; 2v, 1712); *Complete Works,* ed. Montague Summers (3v, 1926); *Works,* ed. J. C. Ghosh [the best edition] (2v, Oxford, 1932). *Alcibiades* (1675); *Don Carlos* (1676); *Titus and Berenice* (1677); *Friendship in Fashion* (1678); *The History and Fall of Caius Marius* (1680); *The Orphan* (1680); *The Poet's Complaint of his Muse* (1680); *The Souldier's Fortune* (1681); *Venice Preserv'd* (1682); *The Atheist* (1684); *Windsor Castle* (1685). — *Otway's Orphan and Venice Preserv'd,* ed. Charles F. McClumpha (Boston, 1908), an edition with critical and historical comment; Roswell G. Ham, *Otway and Lee* (New Haven, 1931).

love and using a scorned lady (the Duchess of Eboli) as a plotting villainess
—the play excelled because Otway treated his exalted personages as if they
were human. In his dialogue they spoke the natural language of the heart
more nearly than their type predecessors, and with a literary flavoring
borrowed, as in the case of Lee, from Shakespeare. Like others of his day
Otway could also adapt from the French, and in 1676 he brought out two
short pieces, *Titus and Berenice,* based on Racine's *Bérénice* (1670), and a
long-popular farce afterpiece, *The Cheats of Scapin,* from Molière. In 1679
he tried to blend two traditions by fusing the story of *Romeo and Juliet*
with episodes from Roman history in his *Caius Marius,* a tragedy that had
much popularity. He kept his Sulpitius (Mercutio) alive to the end, and
expanded and diluted his pathos by having Lavinia (Juliet) revive in the
tomb before Young Marius (Romeo) died. Naturally the play is far from
being true Shakespeare; but in its day it had popularity.

The Orphan and *Venice Preserv'd,* however, both had and deserved a far **The**
greater esteem than these earlier plays. As a domestic tragedy *The Orphan* **Orphan**
admirably suited Otway's gifts for pervasive pathos. Twin brothers, Castalio
and Polydore, "both of nature mild and full of sweetness," are rivals for
the love of Monimia. Castalio, somewhat too considerate of his brother's
probable pain in losing Monimia, is married to her secretly; but the lustful
Polydore, unaware of the marriage, overhears the nocturnal plans of the
newly wedded couple, and, thinking what he hears is merely an agreement
for an illicit assignation, contrives in the darkness to substitute himself
for his brother in the marriage bed. The last two acts are a protracted expiation of this crime through successive suicides. The rôle of Monimia was
written for Mrs. Barry, with whom Otway had fallen hopelessly in love;
she was another's; but the pathos of Otway's heart was transferred to
Monimia's lips and made the rôle infallible for any audience's tears for
many decades.

Venice Preserv'd, or a Plot Discover'd is similarly focused on pathos. It **Venice**
has two added sources of interest: certain indecent comic scenes and a **Preserv'd**
topical political aspect. The corruptness of the Venetian senate, symbolized
in the animalism of Antonio—thought comic in 1681 as a satire on the Earl
of Shaftesbury—stimulates patriots to a rebellious plot. Jaffeir, the harmless
tragic hero, has (like Othello) by marriage robbed another senator, Priuli,
of his daughter Belvidera, and is scorned by her father. Hence he falls into
the conspiracy, which ultimately costs him his friendship with Pierre and
his own and his wife's honor—and of course their lives. Torn by divergent
loyalties (that sworn to his bosom companion, Pierre, and that pledged to
his wife Belvidera) Jaffeir finds himself in one tense dramatic situation
after another until on the scaffold itself he first, in order to save his friend
from the tortures, stabs Pierre and then himself. Belvidera goes mad—

> Say not a word of this to my old father,
> Murmuring streams, soft shades, and springing flowers,
> Lutes, Laurells, Seas of Milk, and ships of Amber.

With these words, often quoted in the century to follow, her reason leaves her, and soon she dies, haunted in her last moments by the ghosts of Jaffeir and Pierre. The contemporary popularity of this tragedy was in part due to the atmosphere of plotting and counter-plotting that enveloped the last years of Charles II. Otway's attitude expresses a serious condemnation of cabals and plots in a tone that gave the play dignity. But the fact that it has been revived oftener than any English non-Shakespearean tragedy is due, not to political purpose but to its powerful emotional appeal. The play was, in the admirable remark of Dr. Johnson, the work "of one who conceived forcibly and drew originally by consulting nature in his own breast." It may be recalled that in 1756 Joseph Warton in "grading" the English poets placed Otway among the best "sublime and pathetic poets," and ranked him with Lee, behind only Spenser, Shakespeare, and Milton. If six years later, in reprinting the dedication of his *Essay on the Writings and Genius of Pope,* Warton omitted all mention of Otway and Lee in his rankings, the omission is probably due to the disagreement of friendly critics as to the proper placing of these writers rather than to any sudden decline of esteem.

Thomas Southerne

The charming actress Mrs. Barry, who inspired and created the distressed innocence of Monimia and Belvidera, found a third rôle of great popular appeal in the Isabella of Thomas Southerne's *Fatal Marriage* (1694).[22] Here Southerne avoided the political objectives that limited the popularity of his first serious play, *The Loyal Brother* (1682), and made a notable addition to the tradition of bourgeois tragedy. Although his gifts for comedy more than equaled those for tragedy, he is perhaps best known by *The Fatal Marriage* and by *Oroonoko* (1695). Both these plays are tragicomedies in the sense that a serious story of tragic ending is sandwiched in (and not too smoothly) with an independent comic plot. The serious plots came from short stories by Mrs. Aphra Behn,[23] as Southerne himself tells us; and they emphasize the progress of the last decade of the century through pathos towards sentimentalism. The "passionate distress" of Isabella— innocently wedded to two husbands, one of whom returns after seven years of supposed death—and the more philosophical, as well as more brutal, woes of "the royal slave", Oroonoko, are still moving. There is nothing bourgeois about Oroonoko and his spotless Imoinda—except their appeal! Evidently before 1700 the enslaved "noble savage" or noble exotic greatly attracted English lovers of liberty. Southerne's tragic idiom is most uneven; at times

---

22 Thomas Southerne (1660-1746) was born in Dublin, the son of a prosperous brewer. After attending Trinity College, Dublin, he went to London and entered the Middle Temple, which seems to have been a cradle for dramatists. He left the Temple, probably about 1682, and, except for a brief career as an army officer (1685-88), devoted himself to dramatic writing. After 1700 he wrote little, but lived quietly in London for the most part. — *Works* (2v, 1713); *Plays* (3v, 1774); *The Loyal Brother* (1682); *The Disappointment* (1684); *Sir Anthony Love* (1691); *The Wives Excuse* (1692); *The Maid's Last Prayer* (1693); *The Fatal Marriage* (1694); *Oroonoko* (1696); *The Fate of Capua* (1700); *The Spartan Dame* (with John Stafford, 1719); *Money the Mistress* (1726). — John W. Dodds, *Thomas Southerne, Dramatist* (New Haven, 1933).
23 On Mrs. Behn's novels see below, Part I, ch. VIII, n. 20.

high and dignified passion is coupled with awkward pedestrian phrasing. His sense of structure is a violent return to early Elizabethan love of variety: the French unities have slight influence here.

Southerne, therefore, is a sort of milestone by which to measure development in tragedy. His deficient sense of structure is exceptional; and the shifting taste of the time is signalized in the fact that Congreve's *Mourning Bride,* one of the most popular of neo-classical "unified" tragedies, was staged in 1697 about a year after *Oroonoko.* But clearly in Otway, Lee, and Southerne the English tradition preserved itself and moved away from the heroics encouraged by French romances and by Dryden's successes, towards a love of strained and intense pathos, based upon private, family emotions akin to those most played upon by sentimentalists. Southerne as well as Lee and Otway made use of ancient classical stories; all of them were influenced by French drama, and all were more concerned with situations that depicted and appealed to the passions than they were with nice motivation of character or with neat construction of unified plots. The popularity of tragic actresses and the increasing number of ladies in the audience encouraged the use of sentimental distress as the vital force in their plays. Other circumstances will further motivate a somewhat similar development in comedy.

VI

Restoration Drama: II. Comedy

Blending
Traditions

Diverse elements went to the making of Restoration comedy.[1] When the theatres were reopened in 1660, Davenant's company revived plays of Beaumont and Fletcher, Shakespeare, and less famous Elizabethans, but no Ben Jonson. Killigrew controlled Jonson, of whose plays he used seven. The critics praised chiefly Jonson,[2] Beaumont and Fletcher,[3] and Shakespeare—the last of whom had much influence on tragedy but less on comedy. Jonson contributed a popular type of low comedy, and his method of characterization by means of humors was common throughout the whole century. Idealistic romanticism was "out" in comedy; in its place appeared a somewhat skeptical attitude towards life, derived perhaps from the romances of Beaumont and Fletcher and from such realistic intrigues as those in Fletcher's *Wild-Goose Chase* and *The Chances*—which last the Duke of Buckingham, in February, 1667, made into a very typical Restoration comedy. Writers like Middleton and Shirley showed the way to knotted intrigues and to local color within the environs of London. For plot materials and for a sense of the comedy inherent in social aberration Molière was enormously influential on all the English comic writers of the period.[4] Spanish comedy, too, encouraged bustling plots, and the Spanish *novelas* furnished tricks of intrigue for many plays. Plautus and Terence had long since been absorbed into both the English and the French comic traditions; but in their own right the Romans still had direct influence.

All these elements unite; but something is added to give the true Restora-

---

[1] General references to books and articles on Restoration drama will be found above, ch. v, n. 2. To these may be added the following that deal more specifically with comedy: Charles Lamb, "On the Artificial Comedy of the Last Century" (1822; in "Elia," *Works,* ed. Thomas Hutchinson, Oxford, 1908, I. 648-656); Thomas Babington (Lord) Macaulay, "The Dramatic Works of Wycherley, Congreve, Vanbrugh, and Farquhar," *Edinburgh Review,* LXXII (1841). 490-528; reprinted among his "Critical Essays," see *Complete Writings* (Boston, 1900), xv. 47-100; John Palmer, *The Comedy of Manners* (1913); Bonamy Dobrée, *Restoration Comedy* (Oxford, 1924); Henry T. E. Perry, *The Comic Spirit in Restoration Drama* (1925); Kathleen M. Lynch, *The Social Mode of Restoration Comedy* (1926); Gellert S. Alleman, *Matrimonial Law and the Materials of Restoration Comedy* (Wallingford, Penn., 1942); Clarence S. Paine, *The Comedy of Manners (1660-1700): A Reference Guide to the Comedy of the Restoration* (Boston, 1941); and Elizabeth L. Mignon, *Crabbed Age and Youth: The Old Men and Women in the Restoration Comedy of Manners* (Durham, N. C., 1947).

[2] Gerald E. Bentley, *Shakespeare and Jonson: Their Reputations in the Seventeenth Century Compared* (2v, Chicago, 1945).

[3] Arthur C. Sprague, *Beaumont and Fletcher on the Restoration Stage* (Cambridge, Mass., 1926).

[4] J. E. Gillet, *Molière en Angleterre, 1660-70* (Bruxelles and Paris, 1913), and Dudley H. Miles, *The Influence of Molière on Restoration Comedy* (1910); and John Wilcox, *The Relation of Molière to Restoration Comedy* (1938).

tion flavor. Although dramatists and critics alike agreed that moral in- *Court* struction, through social criticism, was the aim of literature, and that comedy *Influence* was a corrective of vices and follies, undoubtedly laughter or entertainment, and not moral improvement, was the true objective of Restoration comedy. The manners of the court were highly corrupt, and the comedy that the court patronized was unblushing, hard, cynical, and immoral. Among the notable playwrights Dryden, Sedley, Etherege, Wycherley, Congreve, and Vanbrugh were men of fashion or courtiers; and the less aristocratic writers, such as Otway and Mrs. Behn, were as crudely indecent as the courtiers. No French play was adapted into English in this period without a notable increment of grossness. The element of idealism was replaced by a cynical and frequently explicit denial or at least a disregard of healthy values.

Perhaps because of the corruptness of court circles, perhaps because of a *The Social* more general extreme revulsion against all Puritanism, it was good business *Mode of* to present on the stage shamelessly emancipated people. But the real source *Comedy* of comic effect concerns manners rather than morals. It was thought generally that there was or should be an explicit pattern of conduct or decorum for every station in life: for the monarch and for the beggar, for the gentleman and for his valet, for the fine lady and for the bawd. If like Congreve's Witwoud (*The Way of the World*) one pretended to a pattern for which one was unqualified (in this case the dullard pretending to wit), one was comic; if like many boorish country squires one pretended to be a gentleman, one's manner of pretending might be comic. Sir Fopling Flutter, like all the fops that he begot in later plays, was not a gentleman, but a gentleman *manqué*. He was as sure of his exquisite quality as is the drunkard of his dignity of bearing; but at every point he missed the true pattern, with complete unawareness of the fact. As for the ladies—all at heart engrossed in a man-hunt but always industrous to conceal the fact—their hypocritical coyness as well as their not infrequent sudden blunt remarks about sexual appetites seemed comical. Whatever is shocking is a deviation from pattern: some shocks are painful; some that are painful to us were comical to the Restoration. Nowadays it is wise to regret the grossness of situation and of repartee in these comedies and to try to recapture the fine sense of social protocol that made any unconscious singing off key—violating the pattern —amusing.

Elizabethan comedy had been an imaginative representation of men liv- *Portrayal* ing; Restoration comedy is rather an anatomy of life, not more a repre- *by* sentation than a commentary on life and on various social schematisms. *Analysis* The persons frequently are not so much men as specialized humors in Jonson's fashion. They are specialized in type or function: the inelegant country squire, the rake as hero, the male bawd (Otway's Sir Jolly Jumble and Vanbrugh's Old Coupler), the furious rejected mistress—there is no end to the obvious "type" characters habitually used. The dramatists also are conscious of class patterns. Etherege's *Comical Revenge* has four plots: a noble plot (presented in rime) concerning the loves of Lord Bevill's daughters; a genteel plot that presents Sir Frederick's wooing of his widow; a low comedy plot in the gulling of the Cromwellian knight, Sir Nicholas Culley; and lastly a servant plot involving the discomfiture of the valet, Dufoy. Comic implications arising from patterns of social class are common. There are schematic motivations of intrigue: the younger brother or spend-thrift heir must trick a frugal father out of necessary funds; the neglected wife must reclaim her husband's attentions by making him jealous (jealousy is, as Mrs. Loveit in *The Man of Mode* remarks, "the strongest Cordial we can give to dying Love"); most common of all intrigues are the varying devices for disentangling oneself from a love affair or for indemnifying oneself against the boredom of matrimony. The married state is loudly and commonly made a subject for uncomplimentary laughter. Thus one concludes that Restoration comedy is rather less a representation of life than it is a commentary upon manners.

Comic Techniques Used   The techniques involved have in part been hinted. Plots are double or triple; seldom is there perfect unity of action. The unities of time and place are vaguely observed and always strongly influential. Romantic plots may be in rime; most of the comedies are in prose, and are realistic rather than romantic or idealistic. Repartee is much valued, and frequently plot is neg-lected for discussion of proper conditions for marital happiness, of cuckoldry, and, very commonly, of the nature of wit. In such "conversations" Congreve is the supreme artist. Pepys found no wit in Etherege's first play, and Pope thought Farquhar's dialogue pert and low; yet to an unpractised reader Etherege and Farquhar may now pass as artists in dialogue; to a more experienced reader the superiority of Congreve in finished, formal precision and in brilliant marksmanship will be apparent. There was no steady development towards this perfection of witty comedy: Congreve was a supreme moment in a period remarkable for its gift at repartee. The two outstanding "moments" in Restoration comedy, so far as chronology goes, are found in the years 1668-76 and 1693-1707.

It is natural that the years 1660-1667 should be marked by the revival of old plays and experimentation in the new plays. Of these early efforts Sir

The Early Comedies of Manners   Robert Howard's political comedy *The Committee* (1662) had decided topical appeal, and Sir Samuel Tuke's adaptation from the Spanish of *The Adventures of Five Hours* (1663) was a contrasting type of happily ending drama of romantic intrigue. Dryden, not too highly endowed for comedy, began his dramatic career with his *Wild Gallant* (1663), a play of Jonsonian humors and confused intrigue, in which Isabelle's campaign for a husband is the lively driving force. In *Sir Martin Mar-all* (1667) he borrows his material from Molière without borrowing much sparkle of wit. These plays were prophetic of Dryden's tendency to concentrate in comedies on plot-intrigue rather than on "manners." Etherege's first play shows little more tendency towards the typical comedy of manners. His *Comical Revenge* (1664) has a lightness of touch that is promising, but in plot and character-ization Etherege will soon do better. The Duke of Buckingham's reshaping of Fletcher's *Chances* (1667) gave indication of the callous morality, the astonishing gift of manipulating situation swiftly, and the keen, shameless facetiousness of dialogue that was to characterize the true Restoration comedy, and yet this play is fully as Jacobean as it is Restoration in method.

The year 1668 saw several new comedies of some distinction, and the eight years following include the best early achievements in genuine Restora- *New* tion comedy. The period saw Dryden's reputation increased by heroic plays *Achieve-* rather than by comedies, though *Marriage à la Mode* (1671) is one of his *ments* best. *The Assignation* (1672) is negligible. *Marriage à la Mode* deals with typical material, but in an independent fashion. The intrigue is romantic rather than cynical in tone: Dryden has a sympathetic interest in his flirtatious couples and lacks the aloofness of Etherege and Congreve. Melantha's passion for French words is most innocently amusing, and the casual comments on the wit of polite conversation are admirably comic.

But these eight years saw more significant developments in the work of Etherege, Wycherley, and Shadwell. Of this trio Etherege and Wycherley were courtiers and wrote respectively only three and four plays. Shadwell in a long career produced eighteen. The work of these three is significantly different.

Etherege's *Comical Revenge* (1664) coming at a period when new come- *She Wou'd* dies were rare, had perhaps undeserved success.[5] *She Wou'd if She Cou'd* *if She* (1668) came in a season that offered competition, and being badly acted *Cou'd* at first was ill received. Later the play achieved popularity. Shadwell in the preface to his third play, *The Humorists* (1670), called *She Wou'd* "the best comedy that has been written since the Restoration of the Stage," —an interesting opinion from one who in his Preface to *The Sullen Lovers* (1668) had abused the witty, impudent lechery of current plays that lacked humorous Jonsonian characters. In Lady Cockwood, however, Etherege had come as near to a humorous personage as he ever did, and possibly she appealed to Shadwell. Etherege's characters here are rationally defined rather than imaginatively created: of two country knights Sir Oliver Cockwood has a hypocritical wife who seeks adventure, and Sir Joslin Jolley has two young kinswomen—Ariana, sly and pretty, and Gatty, wild and witty —who are pursued by "two honest gentlemen of the town," and are finally wedded to them. The plotting is not too deft, but the light conversation is charming. Contemporary versifiers who said Etherege had "writ two

---

[5] Sir George Etherege (*c.* 1635-1691) came of a genteel family of Berkshire. His father died in France (1649), and the son was reared by his grandfather. As a young man he traveled abroad, and for a time studied law. After 1664 he was a man about town who occasionally wrote a witty comedy; after 1668 he had an intermittent career as diplomat. He was secretary to the Ambassador in Constantinople (1668-71), and returned to marry a fortune and to be knighted. He was James II's envoy to the Diet of Ratisbon (1685-89), from which place he wrote the letters preserved in his *Letterbook* (ed. Sybil Rosenfeld, Oxford, 1928). As a Jacobite he lived in France and died in Paris. — *Works,* ed. A. W. Verity (1888); ed. H. F. B. Brett-Smith (2v, Oxford, 1927). For biographical materials see Sybil Rosenfeld, "Sir George Etherege in Ratisbon," *RES,* x (1934). 177-189; and especially Dorothy Foster, "Sir George Etherege," *LTLS,* May 31, 1928, p. 412, and *RES,* VIII (1932). 458-459, where several other contributions by Miss Foster are referred to. Critical and historical comment is found in the introduction to Mr. Brett-Smith's excellent edition.

Talking Plays without one Plot," were perhaps wrong: there were numerous episodic intrigues, though these, particularly in his first play, were not too well fused. "A single intrigue in love," he causes a gentleman to say in *She Wou'd*, "is as dull as a single plot in a play." In this second play all the persons are "dancers on the ropes," a fall from which would mean an awkward betrayal of intrigue. They make use of a dialogue that is easy, airy, and witty, and its cool finish together with the relaxed, objective attitude of the author towards his material—a cavalier detachment from emotion—gave the true Etherege savor, characteristic of the best in the period.

The Man
of Mode

Of Etherege's three comedies the third, *The Man of Mode, or Sir Fopling Flutter* (1676), has caused most comment, and is doubtless the best. The plot is basically unified, being the rake Dorimant's progress in his amours. It is, in fact, summarized by his remark (1. i. 200): "Next to the coming to a good understanding with a new Mistress, I love a quarrel with an old one." Modern readers find Dorimant cruel to Mrs. Loveit and Bellinda, but the scenes involving these ladies doubtless were comic to a generation that had no sympathy for ladies who took their light loves seriously. The scene that shows us Dorimant in his dressing gown and Bellinda just ready to leave after their first assignation is in implication most gross; but in its action—with the valet "tying up linen"—doubtless provoked laughter. The better parts of the play are really a succession of episodic scenes that are delightfully comic and most skilfully written. Loveit's rages, Old Bellair's fumbling advances to Emilia, the dissembling love scene of Young Bellair and Harriet, the first appearance of the overdressed Sir Fopling—tactfully referred to in Act III—Lady Woodvill's first meeting with Dorimant in the Mall, Sir Fopling's adventures there with Loveit: all these are handled with a keen sense of the comic. The trick of using a not too important plot to support a succession of such scenes was to teach Congreve much. Dorimant apparently became in theatrical circles the accepted type of fine gentleman of the Restoration, and one of the central objectives of Richard Steele's *Conscious Lovers* (1723) was the desire to correct that acceptance. Dorimant was certainly far from the sentimental ideal, and Etherege himself evidently had qualms about his hero; for he left him on probation with Harriet as the play ended.

William Wycherley [6] probably learned little from Etherege's cynical avoid-

---

[6] William Wycherley (1641-1716) was born at Clive near Shrewsbury. At about the age of fifteen he was sent to France, where he frequented refined circles and where he became a Catholic. In 1660 he was briefly at Oxford; presently he was in London in the Inner Temple. His first play, acted in 1671, gained him the intimacy of a royal mistress, the Duchess of Cleveland, through whose interest he secured a commission in a foot regiment (1672). His marriage with the Countess of Drogheda (1679 or 1680) displeased Charles II, who had just offered him the tutorship of his son, the Duke of Richmond. Because of debts Wycherley was for some time in Fleet Prison; but he was released by the proceeds of a benefit performance at Whitehall (December 14, 1685) of his *Plain Dealer*. After 1704 he formed a friendship with young Alexander Pope, who, somewhat too zealously, revised many of Wycherley's later verses. On his deathbed Wycherley married again, ostensibly in order to prevent his property from passing to his nephew. — *Miscellany Poems* (1704); *Posthumous Works* (Vol. 1, ed. Theobald, 1728; Vol. 11, ed. Pope, 1729); *Plays*, ed. William C. Ward (1888); *Complete Works*, ed. Montague

ance of genuine emotion or from his use of successive light satirical vignettes *Wycherley's*
of polite society—which would impede more engrossing plots—or from his *Independ-*
flexible empty dialogue. After his first play, Etherege's art in the transcrip- *ence*
tion of life as he actually saw it about him was probably characteristic of
the moment rather than a clear case of pioneering: he transcribed life, but
he lacked philosophy. To him life was a frivolous game, and to become
emotionally engrossed therein was perhaps slightly vulgar. Between *She
Wou'd if She Cou'd* and *The Man of Mode* Wycherley produced three of
his four plays, and these took a graver view of life, and offered more in
the way of commentary on life.

His first play, *Love in a Wood* (1671) was like *The Comical Revenge* Love in
in that it presented a series of love intrigues as seen in different classes of a Wood
society; but Wycherley focused more on citizens and less on the life of
fashion. Alderman Gripe, a hypocritical Puritan, ultimately marries a
wench; he is a perfectly Jonsonian comic figure. Lady Flippant, his sister,
is the amorous widow whose eager quest for a husband was to be reproduced in many later spinsters. Dapperwit, a fop of wit, as the later Sir
Fopling Flutter was to be the fop of mode or dress, gets Gripe's daughter
for his wife, but, being a fool, justly misses getting her fortune. Ranger,
a moderately uninteresting man about town, temporarily forsakes his mistress Lydia in order, apparently, to complicate the course of true love for
the romantic (almost sentimental) couple, Valentine and Christina, who
hardly come from the same realistic world as do the other persons. The
sardonic philosophy of the play seems to be that in the scale of being every
one is someone else's cully or dupe. "Every wit has his cully, as every squire
his led captain"; but "the best wits of the town are but cullies themselves
. . . to sempstresses and bawds." Among set conversations in the play that
between Lydia and Dapperwit concerning wit is very striking, and this
foppish poet is throughout the play a rich study in "false wit"—anticipating
Congreve's more casually conceived Witwoud.

The Gentleman Dancing-Master (1672) is the simplest and least sardonic The
of Wycherley's plays. It concentrates on a single intrigue, that of Hippolita, Gentleman
who, to avoid marriage with a frenchified fop, finds herself a true gentleman Dancing-
who poses as her dancing-master and finally becomes her husband. Subordi- Master
nate intrigues are almost completely lacking. The comedy arises from the
fact that the fop, though English, burlesques French manners, by being more
French than the French, while Hippolita's father (an English merchant)
is more Spanish than a grandee. Mrs. Caution, as the suspicious aunt and
critical sister, is an admirably comic person. The scenes in which Mr.
Gerrard, who "can't dance a step" or play the violin, is compelled to show

Summers (4v, 1924); *Epistles to the King and Duke* (1683); *On his Grace the Duke of Marlborough* (1707). — Charles Perromat, *William Wycherley, sa vie—son œuvre* (Paris, 1921);
George B. Churchill, "The Originality of Wycherley," *Schelling Anniversary Papers* (1923),
pp. 65-85; Willard Connely, *Brawny Wycherley* (1930); H. P. Vincent, "The Date of Wycherley's Birth," *LTLS*, March 3, 1932, p. 155, and "The Death of William Wycherley," *Harvard
Studies & Notes in Phil. & Lit.*, xv (1933). 219-242 (a new explanation of the deathbed
marriage).

Hippolita the steps of the coranto in the presence of suspicious relatives must have been uproarious farce. Though Wycherley's gayest and slightest piece, its lack of satiric direction and of multiplicity of intrigue caused it to be perhaps undervalued.

The Country Wife

His third play, *The Country Wife* (1675), has recently been thought his best. It involves two intrigues. The first is that by which Horner, recently returned from France in a condition deceitfully described as "bad as an eunuch," practises promiscuous cuckolding and, chiefly, wins the favor of the Country Wife (Margery) whom the superannuated sensualist, Pinchwife, has married. Pinchwife, by temperament and experience made suspicious and jealous, has had to come to London to marry his sister Alithea to the fop Sparkish. The more polite but less distinguished intrigue of the play concerns her ultimate gulling of Sparkish and marrying with Harcourt. The broad indecency of the leading farcical situation—the alleged impotence of Horner—dominates the play, which is a whimsical gulling of cuckolds, and especially of the distasteful Pinchwife. Margery's country frankness continually punctures the polite duplicity of London social pretense, most notably at the end when she insists on Horner's physical integrity until she finds she can't be rid of her "musty husband," and so will—"since you'll have me tell more lies"—acquiesce in politeness. The central device of the play is doubtless highly indecent: Wycherley's manipulation of it is brilliant. It is notable also that here, as in *Love in a Wood,* he makes his spectators partisans in condemning selfish, pretentious, or hypocritical persons (Pinchwife, Sparkish) and enjoying their discomfiture.

The Plain Dealer

This trick becomes central in his last play, *The Plain Dealer* (1676), which in his own day was thought his finest achievement. Manly, the Plain Dealer, has been robbed and wronged by his mistress Olivia and his closest friend, Vernish. He is aided throughout his misfortunes by the virtuous and lovely Fidelia, who has long followed him disguised as a man. From Racine's *Les Plaideurs* (1668) Wycherley has derived the fantastic litigious Widow Blackacre, who is gulled by Freeman. The play is most sardonic. Manly, derived in part from Molière's *Misanthrope* (1666), rivals the railing malcontents of Elizabethan drama in bleak bitterness. But, on the other hand, Manly anticipates some of the traits of the eighteenth-century good man or benevolist: he is easily gulled and is honest in the extreme, but his tone is misanthropic rather than benevolent. In all his plays, except the second, Wycherley exposes the absurdities of mere pretenders to wit and lashes the hypocrisies of mankind: he paints a dark picture of the men and women of his age. Lacking the aloofness and unconcern of Etherege and Congreve, he is vehement in scorning the backbiting of Dapperwit, the hypocrisy of Alderman Gripe, and the falseness of Olivia. On the other side, in Christina, Hippolita, and Fidelia, he presents more virtuous charm than one can find in the other leading comedies of the time. His scenes are laid in general in the homes of citizens or in the lodgings of impecunious young gentlemen, or in eating houses or other places of recreation. For a man educated in

France he surprisingly lacks aristocratic tone and a regard for modishness. Evidently he did not respect the class in which he moved; probably he did not even respect certain aspects of his own character, and so was not unwilling to expose blackly those who might seem to themselves and to others better than himself. In any case he never wrote without both imaginative and intellectual conviction. If he could have been as refined and easy as he was penetrating and amusing, he might well have been the foremost among English comic writers. One can disregard the prejudice and squeamishness of Macaulay and other Victorians towards Wycherley as a moralist, and yet his pictures of "real life" are, as such, most repugnant.

After 1677 Etherege and Wycherley wrote no more for the stage, and *Shadwell* Dryden produced little comedy of importance except his *Spanish Friar* (1680). In the years 1677-92, furthermore, hardly a single new comic playwright of distinction appeared: these years were a plateau of mediocrity, except perhaps for the work of Thomas Shadwell.[7] During the years of Etherege and Wycherley, Shadwell had produced nine plays and by 1692 his total was eighteen. In the preface to his first play, *The Sullen Lovers* (1668), he had announced his program: he was against the frivolities of wit or repartee, against the love-and-honor clichés, and against the use of either romantic or modishly disreputable lovers; he adhered to the school of Ben Jonson, the comedy of humors. Yet he admired Etherege and at times almost equaled Wycherley in brutality or vulgarity. In his prefaces, prologues, and epilogues he frequently wrote of dramatic art, and was more explicitly concerned with obeying the rules than were the witty comic writers of the time. He pictures the bourgeoisie vividly and amusingly, and more than other dramatists preceding Farquhar lays his scenes in the country, though what he shows us there (as in *Epsom Wells*) are Londoners on a holiday. He was a professional dramatist rather than a gentleman who wrote a few plays. The frankly coarse and low material typical of Jonsonian comedy was less acceptable by 1680 than it had been in 1608, and although Shadwell succeeded with audiences, he did not win too much critical esteem. This failure has been blamed on Dryden's animosity, perhaps too exclusively.

Among his early works *The Sullen Lovers,* a satire on the Howard family of wits, was very successful, as was the more vulgar *Epsom Wells* (1672). In *The Virtuoso* (1676) he had fun with the supposed absurdities of the new science with its strange experiments and its love of theory—as seen in Sir Nicholas Gimcrack's devotion to "the speculative part of swimming" and

---

[7] Thomas Shadwell (*c.* 1642-1692) was born at Santon Hall, Norfolk, and educated in Bury St. Edmunds, Caius College, Cambridge (1656-58), and the Middle Temple. After some travel abroad he devoted himself to literature, and after 1668 for fifteen years produced a new play almost every year. In 1682 began his feud with Dryden, whom at the Revolution of 1688 he had the pleasure to succeed as poet laureate and historiographer royal. — *Dramatick Works* (4v, 1720); *Complete Works,* ed. Montague Summers (5v, 1927). In addition to the plays mentioned here in the text Shadwell wrote *The Royal Shepherdess* (1669); *The Humorists* (1671); *The Miser* (1672); *Psyche* (1675); *The Libertine* (1676); *The History of Timon of Athens* (1678); *A True Widow* (1679); *The Woman-Captain* (1680); *The Medal of John Bayes* (1682); *A Lenten Prologue* (1683); *The Scowrers* (1691); *The Volunteers* (1693). See Albert S. Borgman, *Thomas Shadwell* (1928).

other such picturesque vagaries. The preface to this play condemned false uses of humor in a way that touched more than one contemporary. Naturally in the years after the Popish Plot, Shadwell as a "true blue" Whig won partisan popularity with two political comedies, *The Lancashire Witches* (1681) and *The Amorous Bigotte* (1690). Of his later plays *The Squire of Alsatia* (1688) and *Bury Fair* (1689) are the best. Alsatia was a low section of London, and in its environment Shadwell developed a discussion as to the best way of rearing a son. The contrasting pairs of fathers and sons were as old as the *Adelphi* of Terence; but they came to new life, commonly sentimentalized, in later generations. *The Squire of Alsatia* was enormously popular in its first run, having, one suspects, in parts the appeal of a gangster play of our days.

Aphra Behn   Apart from the work of Shadwell these middle years (1677-92) saw the continuation of the work of other professional playwrights. Mrs. Aphra Behn's productive career began in 1670 (before Wycherley's), and her last play (1696) was her nineteenth.[8] Only one of these nineteen (*Abdelazer,* 1676) was a tragedy. Much under the influence of Spanish novels, she wrote stories herself and comedies of adventurous intrigue derived from Spanish *novelas*. Typical would be *The Dutch Lover* (1673) and *The Rover,* a play in two parts (1677, 1681). Disguisings, farce elements, and even characters from the *commedia dell' arte* (Harlequin and Scaramouch in *The Rover,* Part II) are used in her plays. Naturally she also included political hits, as, for example, in *The City Heiress* (1682). In character Mrs. Behn was definitely emancipated; and her compliance with the taste of the time, together with the prime fact that her plays came from a woman's pen, gave her a reputation for shocking indecencies as a dramatist. She simply tried to write like the men, whom she in no way surpassed.

Ravenscroft   Edward Ravenscroft (*c.* 1650-1697) between 1672 and the end of the century produced a dozen plays, about half of them in this middle period. For invention, which he lacked, he substituted adaptation, especially from the French, or even plagiarism. His first plays, *The Citizen Turn'd Gentleman* (1672) and *The Careless Lovers* (1673), were synthesized from Molière in a fashion such as to stress the bustle of situation and even farce and to minimize characterization or wit. He borrowed from the Spanish also, and in *Scaramouch a Philosopher* (1677) he made for the Drury Lane Company an adaptation from Molière's *Scapin* six months after Otway had brought out his very popular *Cheats of Scapin* at the other house. In general Ravenscroft was more competent in farce than in anything subtle enough to be called comedy.

From this middle period of mediocrity (1677-92) we pass to the final brilliant outburst of comedies composed in the Restoration spirit by Congreve, Vanbrugh, and Farquhar, and staged in the years 1693-1707. Chronologically these men—who were small boys when the last plays of Etherege

---

[8] For the life of Aphra Behn (1640-1689) see Part I, ch. VIII. n. 20. A list of her plays will be found in Allardyce Nicoll's *History of Restoration Drama*, pp. 352-353, and in *CBEL*, II. 417-418.

and Wycherley were first produced—hardly belong to the Restoration; but that they are in the spirit of the Restoration can be seen by examining their plays and observing the steadiness with which they persevered in that spirit in spite of a notably rising tide of moral criticism. The focal work in this attack on the theatre was that of the non-juror, Jeremy Collier, who in 1698 published *A Short View of the Immorality and Profaneness of the English Stage*.[9] Collier's chief victims were Dryden, Wycherley, Congreve, Vanbrugh, D'Urfey, and Otway (*The Orphan*). What he most objected to was the use of profanity in stage dialogue and the unfavorable portrayals of clergymen; but he also held (chapter IV) that the popular plays of the time encouraged immorality. He urged, in orthodox neo-classical fashion, that comedy should correct vice and not promote it. His work attracted more attention than any other single book or pamphlet; but it is notable that Shadwell in the preface of his first play (1668) had criticized the morals of comedy, and Dryden in his *Ode to Mrs. Anne Killigrew* (1686) had admitted gross faults. Both these dramatists, however, were obvious offenders. The newly founded Society for the Reformation of Manners had denounced the theatre before Collier's book appeared, and its members very likely were behind the practical attempts at censorship made through presentments to the Grand Jury or through the arrests of actors or through orders from the long-suffering Lord Chamberlain. The controversy lasted long, and Collier's reforms were still agitated by his friend and fellow non-juror Richard Russell in *The Grub-street Journal* (1730-37). Independent playwrights continued to produce "unreformed" plays, but certain professional playwrights, Colley Cibber, for example, had begun to produce dramas ostensibly less offensive. Cibber was a shrewd producer rather than a sincere moralist, as we shall see later—at least no one in his own day took his moralizing seriously.

William Congreve [10] was definitely among the unregenerate. Doubtless he

[9] The standard work on the Collier controversy is that by Joseph W. Krutch, *Comedy and Conscience after the Restoration* (1924). See also Sister Rose Anthony's *The Jeremy Collier Stage Controversy* (Milwaukee, 1937). A brief list of documents in the controversy is found in the *CBEL*, II. 400-402.

[10] William Congreve (1670-1729) was born at Bardsey, Yorkshire; but his childhood was spent in Ireland, where his father's military service took the family. He studied at Kilkenny School (with Jonathan Swift), and attended Trinity College, Dublin. In London he was admitted to the Middle Temple in 1691, but he had little interest in the law, and began a gentlemanly career as author. He produced four comedies and one tragedy, the first two for Drury Lane and the last three for Betterton's company in the new theatre in Lincoln's Inn Fields. He replied to Jeremy Collier's attack on his plays, but after the cool reception of *The Way of the World* (1700) he wrote virtually nothing for the theatre. He held various government sinecures, and lived politely with many friends and practically no enemies. Much time during his later years he spent with Henrietta, Duchess of Marlborough, to whom he bequeathed the bulk of his estate, apparently with a private understanding that the Duchess was in turn to bequeath it, as she did, to her (and possibly Congreve's) daughter, Lady Mary Godolphin. — *Works* (3v, 1710); *Complete Works,* ed. Montague Summers (4v, 1923); *Comedies,* ed. Bonamy Dobrée (Oxford, 1925); *The Mourning Bride* (and other works), ed. Bonamy Dobrée (Oxford, 1928); *Works,* ed. F. W. Bateson (1930); *Incognita* (1692; ed. H. F. B. Brett-Smith, 1922); *The Mourning Muse of Alexis* (1695); *A Pindarique Ode to the King* (1695); *Letters upon Several Occasions* [some by Congreve], ed. John Dennis (1696); *The Birth of the Muse* (1698); *Amendments of Mr. Collier's False and Imperfect Citations* (1698); *The Judgement of Paris* (1701); *A Hymn to Harmony* (1703); *The Tears of Amaryllis* (1703); *A Pindarique Ode on the Victorious Progress of Her Majesties Arms* [with a prefatory "Discourse of the Pindarique Ode"] (1706); *An Impossible Thing* (1720); *A Letter . . . to the Viscount Cobham*

Congreve's Merits was shocked and annoyed to find his work rather ineptly attacked by Collier. Congreve regarded himself as a reformer of the stage; and that he was so regarded by others is evident from the fact that he (with Vanbrugh, another sinner) was chosen to direct the new theatre in the Haymarket, which was opened in 1705 and was supposedly devoted to theatrical uplift. Early in his career Congreve had been praised by Dryden and Southerne, who helped get his first play produced, and by Addison, Swift, and doubtless many others. But his reform was concerned with the technique of drama—its wit, its structure, its dialogue. Perhaps because he became aware that his sort of reform did not catch on, perhaps because he did not care to compete with less genteel, less acute playwrights, he ceased from writing for the stage at the age of thirty. His prefaces, as well as Swift's rimed epistle to him, indicate that Congreve felt superior to his audiences. Far be it from him to cut blocks with a razor! So he became an elegant minor poet, a gouty man about town, and the gallant of a wealthy duchess. If there was something of the snob in Congreve, he was still an amiable snob, one of the best liked of literary men during a period of nearly forty years (1692-1729), in which very few wits were generally beloved.

Clearly Congreve was a formalist, a technician, a man of artistic rather than moral conscience. He learned much from such predecessors as Etherege, Wycherley, Shadwell, and Molière. That his characters were subtler than Etherege's can be seen by comparing his gentlemen, Vainlove and Mirabell, with the celebrated Dorimant. Congreve's heroes do not love a quarrel with a cast mistress, do not condescend to berate their servants, and are not vain of their inconstancy in love—though they are inconstant. He has, again, none of Wycherley's vehemence, and yet the actions of his plays, especially of the *Double Dealer,* are far from being inherently comic. " 'Tis but the way of the world" might have been said of any of his sophisticated characters in any of his plays, and the way of the world evidently is not a pretty way. With the superficialities of the world, however, the comic writer may safely and amusingly play. "There are," he recognizes, like a true neo-classicist, "Crimes too daring and too horrid for Comedy. But the Vices most frequent, and which are the common Practice of the looser sort of Livers, are the subject Matter of Comedy." So among the affectations and follies of men Congreve works, leaving more serious matters to be corrected by the courts ecclesiastical or civil. "Unmasking," wrote his friend Swift, almost at the same moment when Congreve was defending his plays against Collier, "I think, has never been allowed fair usage, either in the world or the playhouse." But the unmasking of follies is Congreve's forte.

His Plots Congreve's highest excellences are not seen in his plots, although he pays more attention to the three unities than his contemporaries did. In the important unity of action this statement is perhaps contradicted by his first play,

---

(1729). — George Meredith, *An Essay on Comedy* (1877; 1897); Edmund Gosse, *A Life of William Congreve* (1888; rev. 1924); D. C. Taylor, *William Congreve* (Oxford, 1931); John C. Hodges, *William Congreve the Man* (1941).

The Old Bachelor (1693), which like Etherege's *Comical Revenge* involves
a series of intrigues on different social levels. Neatly blended with the one
that gives the play its name is the gulling of Sir Joseph Wittol (a fool who
has offended Vainlove) by marrying him to a common woman after Heart-
well, the old bachelor and misogynist, has hardly been saved from her
charms. Meanwhile Bellmour, in love with Bellinda, takes time off to disguise
himself as the fanatic preacher Tribulation Spintext and thus to cuckold
the Puritan banker Fondlewife. Vainlove has a relatively easy time in winning the one honorable woman in the cast, Araminta. The play was an
enormous success, and the reputation of the young playwright seemed
assured. Later in the same year, however, his second play, *The Double Dealer*
(1693), failed. This failure is hardly accountable. The plot is far more unified, being merely the struggle of Mellefont against the jealous Lady Touch-
wood and the Iago-like Maskwell to win his charming Cynthia. There are
thrilling episodes, but no divergent intrigues as in the first play. The darkness of the villainy makes the play hardly more than tragicomic, and possibly
this fact explains its cool reception. *Love for Love* (April, 1695) was long the
most popular of Congreve's plays. The plot here tells how Valentine, at odds
with a critical father, is likely to lose his estate to a sea-going younger brother
and thus miss getting his beloved heiress, Angelica. The intrigue is deftly
suspensive, turning largely on the ultimate triumph of the intelligent younger
couple over a star-crazed uncle and an unnatural father, with, in the last
act, a masked marriage that tricks the fop Tattle into wedding the blemished
Mrs. Frail instead of the expected Angelica. This plot is, in comic effect,
Congreve's best. In *The Way of the World* (1700), his best comedy, he
had an excellent plot but treated it negligently: he had too much love of
topical conversation to waste time in telling the story of how Mirabell evades
the malicious plotting of Lady Wishfort, Mrs. Marwood, and her lover
Fainall, and persuades the aloof but charming Millamant to marry him.
Obviously all these plots are conventional: we have a comedy, not of love, but
of the love-chase. Financial reverses, irate fathers, jealous cast mistresses
(particularly coquettish aunts of the pursued lady), are the chief obstacles to
success, and legal documents, signed or unsigned, disguisings, and masked
marriages that involve mistaken identities, are frequent episodes. It is the
same old deck of cards, but Congreve does clever tricks with them.

His characters likewise tend to be conventional. Frequently he gives us *His*
relatively flat, two-dimensional persons; but at other times his imagination *Characters*
works more vividly than we realize. In Act II of *The Way of the World*
Mirabell, talking to Mrs. Fainall about her husband, remarks, "When you
are weary of him you know your remedy." The significance of the remark is
apparent only at the final discovery in Act v that before marrying Fainall
the lady had with remarkable prescience deeded her whole estate in trust to
Mirabell. She would never have done that to Dorimant: the Congreve gentleman can be trusted. His top ladies—the virtuous heroine of each play—are
not finely imagined. Millamant alone has color and charm, and Millamant

above the other three heroines is the clear victim of affectation: the thought of a husband is too, too tedious! In her case it is perhaps Congreve's wit rather than her charm that is truly vivid. Her entry (Act II) in full sail with "a shoal of fools for tenders" is unsurpassable, as is her capitulation to Mirabell at the end. Early in the play Mirabell and Fainall talk of her, and when Fainall opines that she has wit, Mirabell replies: "She has beauty enough to make any man think so, and complaisance enough not to contradict him who shall tell her so." Yet he goes on to say that even her affectations make her more agreeable. The passage is in Congreve's finest vein.

In general, however, it is the incidental or inferior persons that Congreve best delineates. His second gentlemen are negligible plot-ridden sketches; his villains and scorned ladies (except perhaps Lady Wishfort) are melodramatic creatures who belong in heroic plays; but his valets, his gulls, and his fops—who are literary and not, like Sir Fopling Flutter, addicted to overdressing merely—are likely to be superbly conceived. His one worthy country squire, Sir Wilfull Witwoud, is much underrated as a character. Sir Wilfull's eagerness to get his boots off in the drawing-room or to get at his sack, and his lack of eagerness to get at his wooing are all broadly yet finely turned. When critics talk of Congreve's artifice and elegance, they should recall this roistering drunken squire, who nevertheless so pleases Congreve that he is made before the end of the play a friend and ally to Millamant—far more acceptable than his affected, foppish brother. The dramatist's portraits of the gentleman's gentleman are original and unexpected. The admirable Waitwell can disguise himself as Sir Rowland and come a-wooing Lady Wishfort most genteelly. Of his lawfully wedded wife—another of Mirabell's thoughtful precautions to protect Lady Wishfort—Waitwell can say with Jeeves-like dignity: "With submission, we have indeed been solacing in lawful delights; but still with an eye to business, sir. I have instructed her as well as I could." But if Waitwell is prophetic of the Victorian butler, Jeremy of *Love for Love* surpasses prophecy. Watch him in Act V as he underlines the contrast between himself and his "betters":

Jeremy. Sir, I have the seeds of rhetoric and oratory in my head; I have been at Cambridge.
Tattle. Ay! 'tis well enough for a servant to be bred at a university: but the education is a little too pedantic for a gentleman. I hope you are secret in your nature, private, close, ha?
Jer. O sir, for that, sir, 'tis my chief talent: I'm as secret as the head of Nilus.
Tat. Ay! who is he, though? a privy counsellor?
Jer. [Aside] O ignorance! — [Aloud.] A cunning Egyptian, sir, that with his arms would overrun the country: yet nobody could ever find out his headquarters.
Tat. Close dog! a good whoremaster, I warrant him. . . .

His Wit   Such a passage illuminates Congreve's unrealistic but amusing characterizations, also his gifts in wit, and above all his eagerness to take time out, even in a final act, for superfluous verbal by-play. It is from these incidental passages, which overlay his plots always, that Congreve's rather sorry and not very comic stories gain life and sparkle. These superadded social vignettes are the quintessence of Congreve's genius. He dabbles incessantly in witticism, sometimes antithetical in structure, sometimes pungent in repartee, usually deftly humorous in its implications. If in the scale of being there had to be a maidservant called Mincing, she would inevitably announce dinner as Congreve makes her: "Mem, I am come to acquaint your la'ship that dinner is impatient." And her la'ship, who has "a mortal terror at the apprehension of offending against decorums," bravely trusts that "Sir Rowland" will not think her "prone to any iteration of nuptials." Verbal wit was perhaps Congreve's highest value, and apparently it was that of all his gentleman fools (not of his servants), who aspire to wit but for whom it is, as Swift said, "the lost language." For Congreve words danced with stately precision or with gay levity; no English dramatic writer has surpassed him in cool intellectual mastery of diction. He was perhaps too subtle for his own good.

For comedy, as we shall see in the work of Vanbrugh and Farquhar, was tending in another direction, somewhat cheaper, which stressed story element and social "problems" that became a serious interest rather than a cause for brilliant witticism.

Vanbrugh [11] was concerned in somewhat less than a dozen plays, practically all of which were translated or adapted from contemporary French comedies. His career was that of a man who had the interests of good theatre at heart but who lacked either inventiveness or leisure—and it was certainly the latter of these—for the composition of original dramas. *The Pilgrim* (1700) was a reworking of Fletcher; *Aesop* (1696-7) was adapted from Boursault; *The False Friend* (1702) came from Le Sage, who had it from the Spanish; *The Country House* (1703) and *The Confederacy* (1705) were racy translations from Dancourt; while *Squire Trelooby* (1704, in collaboration with Congreve and Walsh), *The Mistake* (1705), and *The Cuckold in Conceit* (1707) were from Molière. Of these the earlier ones had in general the greatest popularity. Of his two original plays both he and the public justly thought more highly of *The Relapse* (1696) than of *The Provok'd Wife* (1697). After Vanbrugh's death Colley Cibber in 1728 completed the fragmentary *Journey to London*, which as *The Provok'd Husband* was acted with great success in spite of the fact that Cibber's verbal ineptitudes both in his preface and in the dialogue caused considerable mirth among critics.

Vanbrugh's first play, *The Relapse*, also had an accidental connection with

Sir John Vanbrugh

[11] Sir John Vanbrugh (1664-1726) was born in London, the grandson of a Flemish merchant, a refugee from the persecutions of the Duke of Alva. Little is known of his early life except that he was for two years in France (1683-85), where he became interested in architecture. He was for some years in the army, and divided his later career between writing and architecture. He was made Comptroller of the Royal Works in 1702, and thereafter he built Castle Howard for the Earl of Carlisle and Blenheim Palace for the Duke of Marlborough. He also designed the Haymarket Theatre, of which he was manager for two years. He was knighted in 1714. — *Plays* (2v, 1719); *Complete Works*, ed. Bonamy Dobrée and Geoffrey Webb (4v, 1927-28). — G. H. Lovegrove, *The Life, Work, and Influence of Sir John Vanbrugh* (1902); John C. Hodges, "The Authorship of *Squire Trelooby*," *RES*, IV (1928). 404-413; Paul Mueschke and Jeannette Fleisher, "A Re-Evaluation of Vanbrugh," *PMLA*, XLIX (1934). 848-889; Laurence Whistler, *Sir John Vanbrugh* (1938).

The
Relapse

Cibber, whose first play, *Love's Last Shift,* had been very successful at the beginning of 1696. *The Relapse* was a somewhat cynical sequel to Cibber's comedy. Cibber had shown a debauched and faithless husband, Loveless, reclaimed by the beauty of virtue as seen in Amanda, his wife, whom he failed to recognize after eight years of separation, but whose faithfulness in love most improbably restored him to constancy. This sentimental device of reforming dissolute characters with sudden facility in the last act was popular: it gave the lie to those who thought the stage negligent of morality. But it did not convince Vanbrugh, who taking much the same cast, constructed his *Relapse* to show Loveless's later instability after reform, and to subject the virtuous Amanda to extreme temptation by Worthy. Amanda's virtue survives the test in a crucial scene designed to excite the inflammable spectators by its nearness to a rape and to content the sentimental by the triumph of virtue. In replying to Collier, Vanbrugh alleged speciously that the play was a dramatic discussion of the text "Lead us not into temptation." The subplot shows Young Fashion tricking his elder brother (Sir Novelty, now Lord Foppington) out of his bride, Miss Hoyden, by the aid of Coupler, with whom Young Fashion has made a bargain unmentionable, and unmentioned by Collier and later critics. A chaplain named Bull gave just offense to respecters of the priesthood. Both *The Relapse* and *The Provok'd Wife* are specious and cynical. Marriage, to be sure, is not so much the dull clog as it is a mordant problem. Loveless and Sir John Brute are completely culpable and disgusting as husbands.

Vanbrugh's
Social
Problems

Vanbrugh has a concern with social problems, which he poses only to jeer at them. He does show the tendency of the day to depend on story rather than on witty dialogue, and his characters, while never completely realized, have more human interest than do the persons of the greater plays that preceded his. In dialogue he lacked the chiseled precision and acuteness of Congreve. There was not, as Cibber remarked, "the least Smell of the Lamp in it"; and Cibber adds the opinion of "all the Actors of [his] Time, that the Style of no Author whatsoever gave their Memory less trouble than that of Sir John Vanbrugh." One suspects that whereas the actors had to memorize Congreve's lines exactly, a slip in a speech from Sir John's pen mattered less. As the architect, part-owner, and briefly as manager of the new theatre in the Haymarket, he represented still the aristocratic tradition in the drama, and quite apart from his plays was an influential figure in theatrical affairs.

Farquhar,[12] the last notable figure in the Restoration tradition, really

[12] George Farquhar (1677?-1707) was born in north Ireland, the son of a clergyman, and completed his education with a year at Trinity College, Dublin (1694-5). After working for a short time as a corrector for the press of a bookseller, he became an actor, but upon his arrival in London (c. 1697) he devoted himself to writing comedies. In 1703 he married a young lady who had given herself out to be a fortune but who was not. Farquhar, in spite of the trick and of his own penniless state, harbored no resentment. He died in poverty just after the success of his last play. — *Comedies* (1710); *Works* (2v, 1711); *Dramatic Works,* ed. A. C. Ewald (2v, 1892); *Complete Works,* ed. C. A. Stonehill (2v, 1930). *The Adventures of Covent Garden* (1699); *Sir Harry Wildair* (1701); *Familiar and Courtly Letters* (2v, 1700-1); *The Inconstant* (1702); *Love and Business in a Collection of Occasional Verse and Epistolary Prose. A Discourse likewise upon Comedy* (1702); *The Stage-Coach* (1704); *Barcellona: a Poem* (1710). — William Archer, *George Farquhar,* ed. for the Mermaid Series with an ex-

belongs to the eighteenth century. In the years 1698-1707 he produced seven *George*
comedies and a farce afterpiece; and this brief career of a highly gifted young *Farquhar*
dramatist (he died aged 29) indicates definitely a transitional trend. Farquhar
observes in the preface to his least popular play, *The Twin Rivals,* that "A
play without a beau, cully, cuckold, or coquette, is as poor an entertainment to
some palates, as their Sunday's dinner would be without beef and pudding."
Normally, though somewhat influenced by Collier's protest, he tried to give
his audience its favored fare, but with a difference. He does not picture his
drawing-room characters merely as such; his gentlemen are more human,
have more red corpuscles, and are less mere illustrations of the manners of
the day than were the gentlefolk of his wittier predecessors. The fact that
many of his characters are less modish than those of his predecessors is perhaps referable to the example of Shadwell: certainly the bawds, midwives,
constables, citizens, and soldiers that made brief appearances in other plays
are here given considerable scenes and organic rôles. The element of story
is stressed; only in *The Recruiting Officer* do we get scenes that approach
the satirical episodes or conversations so common in Wycherley and Congreve; and in Farquhar's hands such scenes either verge on farce or aid the
plot. Like Shadwell he occasionally leaves the City, and gives us a breath of
country air—that of Shrewsbury in *The Recruiting Officer* and Lichfield in
The Beaux' Stratagem.

Even in his short career something of development in skill appears. His
first play, *Love and a Bottle* (1698), and his fifth, *The Twin Rivals* (1702),
were from the start regarded as inferior, very likely because of their lack of *New*
modish elegance. In *The Twin Rivals,* where a younger, deformed brother *Norms of*
intrigues to steal his virtuous (elder) twin's title and estate, we see senti- *Conduct*
mental elements elbowing and joining hands with the cynically comic tradition. For elegance Farquhar substitutes naturalness as the desideratum in
manners. One of his ladies, Aurelia, here says, "I take good manners to be
nothing but a natural desire to be easy and agreeable to whatever conversation we fall into"; and this principle she thinks as fitting for a porter as for
a duke. Her friend Constance, similarly, believing her lover dead, remarks,
"I have no rule nor method for my grief.... I am content with the slight
·mourning of a broken heart." Even more clearly sentimental is the surprising dénouement of the second plot of the play. Richmore, a wealthy fine
gentleman, is in the nick of time (Farquhar uses the situation more than
once) prevented from raping Aurelia by the intervention of Trueman, who
proceeds to reproach Richmore with the wrongs done to another lady, Clelia.
A quarter of an hour after his failure with Aurelia, much impressed by Trueman's eloquence, Richmore suddenly announces, "Your youthful virtue
warms my breast, and melts it into tenderness"—and forthwith agrees to
marry the wronged Clelia! This reform through melting tenderness might
be pure Cibber!

cellent introduction (1906); J. R. Sutherland, "New Light on George Farquhar," *LTLS,*
March 6, 1937, p. 171.

But while sentimental tendencies in comedy led Farquhar to an increased and sincere sympathy with his characters as well as to increased insistence on the story element as compared with social satire, his true and skilful gifts for comedy and his lack of any excessive love for moral instruction kept him most of the time within the Restoration tradition. This allegiance can be seen in his three most popular comedies. His second play, *The Constant Couple* (1699), was very successful, probably because of its varied and bustling action rather than because the dubious virtue of the long-separated couple is ultimately rewarded. Gentlemen in Farquhar's plays fall to fisticuffs much more readily than in Etherege or Congreve; Sir Harry Wildair, perhaps Farquhar's most attractive gentleman, and Colonel Standard both have occasion in this play to beat scorned lovers, and such physical activities are common in Farquhar's plays. Lady Lurewell undergoes a reform towards the end, which, however, is well motivated. The success of the rôle of Sir Harry led to a sequel called *Sir Harry Wildair* (1701), which at the time was successful but is clearly inferior to *The Recruiting Officer* (1706) and *The Beaux' Stratagem* (1707).

The Army Appears

In *The Recruiting Officer* Farquhar is on sure ground. The disbanded officer (Colonel Standard) had been a familiar figure since Otway's days, and now in Serjeant Kite, recruiting at Shrewsbury, masquerading à la Rochester as a fortune-teller, and serving as pimp for his master Captain Plume, Farquhar gave the stage its most richly comic soldier. A comparison of the rôle of Sylvia with that of Wycherley's Fidelia (both following their lovers disguised as men) will indicate how little there is to choose morally between the two writers. This play hardly classes as high comedy, but in richness of effect and diversity of action, all well fused, it is certainly superior to anything by Shadwell, of whom it remotely reminds one.

His Last Success

The Beaux' Stratagem, which with *The Constant Couple* and *The Recruiting Officer* kept the English stage as well as almost any English comedies have done, tells its story with ease and high spirits. The fortune-hunters, Archer and Aimwell, win our sympathies and keep them; their success, though somewhat accidental, is most pleasing. Lady Bountiful with relatively few lines lives perfectly as a type, and so do other minor persons. The drunken Squire Sullen is shown with brutal vividness, essential, perhaps, to justify the concluding divorce. This formal separation might not have been necessary in Etherege's circle. Times have changed, however, and even in Farquhar's plays one sees a substitution of human interest and somewhat vulgar "character" for the witty, depraved aristocrats of the earlier Restoration. Pope's often quoted line, "What pert, low dialogue has Farquhar writ," contains an element of truth if we remember that he spoke as the close friend of Wycherley and Congreve. Farquhar's scenes are socially (not morally) lower than those of his predecessors—Shadwell excepted; and the lack of attention to rigid social decorum might seem in 1737 to make for something like pertness. But, even if partly just, Pope's line neglects the vivid liveliness, the eager, easy flow of situation, and the true *vis comica* that sets Farquhar apart from and above his actual contemporaries, Cibber and Steele. If there had been more Farquhars or if this one had lived to write more plays, the acceleration towards decline in English comedy might have been arrested. A great decline in comic wit had already taken place when the audiences failed to appreciate *The Way of the World*.

VII
Patterns in Historical Writing

Not all the comedy of the Restoration was played on the stage. Life itself was dazzling and theatrical; it might be a merry farce, but it inclined to a serious realization that destiny—whether honor, love, fortune, Heaven, or Hell—depended on manipulation of the present moment. This preoccupation with immediacy results in the common use of Restoration daily life as material for literature and in frequent attempts to elevate this daily life to an ancient Augustan level or at least to draw moral education from it. History, as Bacon and most analysts of the seventeenth century agreed, included three patterns: chronicles, lives, and narrations. The century was so much in love with diary-writing that Bacon might almost have added it as a pattern: doubtless it is included under lives. Diarists of necessity deal with contemporary material; but at this time biographers and even narrative historians in general limit themselves to the familiar matter of their own day. They are obsessed by the present moment either as a delight or as a warning—sometimes as both.

Preoccupation with the Present Moment

The instinct to live for the moment lyrically and at the same time prudently is seen nowhere better than in the *Diary* of Samuel Pepys [1] (1633-1703). Since the *Diary* is written in Thomas Shelton's system of shorthand, what we have is a transcript improved by successive editors. We are at least one remove from Pepys himself, but the *Diary* is so intimate that we feel closer to Pepys than we do to almost any man who has ever written. The *Diary* covers the years 1660-69, and gives a beautifully detailed account of stirring public events—the return of King Charles, his coronation, the plague of 1665, the London fire of 1666, and the Dutch wars. For its period it pictures also, and most vividly, private life in London and in an average well-to-do house-

Pepys's Diary

---

[1] Pepys's *Diary* has been edited as *Memoirs of Samuel Pepys*, ed. Lord Braybrooke (2v, 1825; 5v, 1828; 5v, 1848-9); as *Diary and Correspondence*, ed. Lord Braybrooke and Mynors Bright (6v, 1875-9); as *Diary*, ed. Henry B. Wheatley (10v, 1893-9). His other published writings include *Memoires Relating to the State of the Royal Navy* (1690), ed. J. R. Tanner (1906); *Private Correspondence and Miscellaneous Papers*, ed. Joseph R. Tanner (2v, 1926); *Further Correspondence*, ed. Joseph R. Tanner (1929); *Letters and Second Diary*, ed. R. G. Howarth (1932); *Shorthand Letters*, ed. Edwin Chappell (Cambridge, 1933); *The Tangier Papers of Samuel Pepys*, ed. Edwin Chappell (1935). A new and unabridged transcript of the *Diary*, to be edited by William Matthews and Robert Latham is eagerly awaited.—Among biographical aids the following are the best: Henry B. Wheatley, *Samuel Pepys and the World He Lived In* (2d ed., 1880); *Occasional Papers Read by Members at Meetings of the Samuel Pepys Club* (2v, 1917-25); Joseph R. Tanner, *Samuel Pepys and the Royal Navy* (Cambridge, 1920); Joseph R. Tanner, *Mr. Pepys: An Introduction to the Diary* (1925); Arthur, Lord Ponsonby, *Samuel Pepys* (1928); John Drinkwater, *Pepys: His Life and Character* (1930); Clara Marburg, *Mr. Pepys and Mr. Evelyn* (Philadelphia, 1935); Arthur Bryant, *Samuel Pepys* (3v, Cambridge, 1933-38).

hold. In richness and humaneness of detail it is hardly rivaled elsewhere in literature.

Pepys was born and passed most of his life in London. His father was a *His* tailor, and the family was sound but modest stock from Huntingdonshire. *Career* Samuel was educated at St. Paul's School, and at Trinity Hall and Magdalene College, Cambridge. At the age of twenty-two he had made a mad love-match with a penniless French beauty, Elizabeth St. Michel; hence he needed, as he got, considerable help from his fortunate cousin, Edward Montagu, who had been a trusted servant of Cromwell in the Admiralty, and who now as Admiral, with cousin Pepys in attendance, brought King Charles over from Holland in May, 1660. Montagu was shortly thereafter created Earl of Sandwich, and he was long to remain Pepys's "Lord" and patron. He got Pepys made Clerk of the Acts in the Navy Office and got him other places as well. Pepys throughout his active life was practically always in the service of the navy, although his career was interrupted dangerously during the uproar over the Popish Plot, when his life was in jeopardy, and he was briefly in 1679 imprisoned in the Tower. In 1683 he accompanied Lord Dartmouth to Tangier, aided in its demolition, and wrote a valuable and interesting journal of the voyage. In 1684 he was President of the Royal Society, and from 1684 to 1689 he was again Secretary of the Admiralty. After the Revolution of 1688 he lived in retirement in "paradisial Clapham," as Evelyn called it. If his devotion to James II now kept him from public employment, his active civic interest still showed itself with regard to Christ's Hospital[2] and possibly other institutions.

The first entry in his *Diary* was dated January 1, 1660—when Pepys was twenty-seven years old. He wrote, one may guess, purely for the pleasure of rehearsing briefly and secretly the joys of the day: there is no evidence that he later reread what he had written or that he ever revised it. Certainly, at the time of writing, the idea of publication would have horrified him. When he died, he left his papers, his books, and his extensive collections of prints, ballads, and broadsides, to go to his college, Magdalene, Cambridge; and there his six volumes of shorthand remained substantially unregarded until John Evelyn's *Diary*, published in 1818, called attention to Evelyn's friend, Pepys. Presently an undergraduate named John Smith was employed to decipher Pepys's shorthand, and in 1825 a much abbreviated edition of the *Diary* was first published.[3]

A year after he began his *Diary* Pepys could set down in his annual sum- *Pepys's Joy* mary of the state of his affairs: "Myself in constant good health, and in a *in His* most handsome and thriving condition. Blessed be Almighty God for it." *Possessions* His cousin had placed him well. The house provided for the Clerk of the Acts was already his pride and joy: life seemed aglow with dignity, prosperity, and delight. He came to feel an exquisite pleasure in his possessions—his

[2] Rudolph Kirk, *Mr. Pepys upon the State of Christ-Hospital* (Philadelphia, 1935).
[3] For a history of the text see Arthur Bryant's *Samuel Pepys, the Man in the Making*, pp. 392-393. This book is the first volume of what is by all odds the most readable and detailed account of Pepys.

books, his bookcases, the hangings in his best room, the dinners he gave, with "all things mighty noble; and to my great content." He loved his beautiful wife passionately, and after her death he had her bust placed in St. Olave's Church, where it was in full view from Pepys's pew. Meanwhile he was madly jealous of Pembleton, her dancing-master, and was at the same sad moment frankly conscious of his own failings in his amours with numerous other ladies.

His Slavery to the Senses
Another man in another age might have made a grimy record out of this diary. Pepys was eager for financial gain, and if his pleasure in his increase of goods had not been so naïve and unalloyed, it might have seemed tedious or even grasping. Then too, he was eager to gratify promiscuously his love of fondling pretty women ("God forgive me," he writes, "I had a mind to something more."); and his frank revelations of these flirtations or infidelities, which might have been repellent, are uniformly amusing and at times even comic. Witness, for example, his attempts in St. Dunstan's Church, August 18, 1667:

turned into St. Dunstan's Church, where I heard an able sermon of the minister of the place; and stood by a pretty, modest maid, whom I did labour to take by the hand and the body; but she would not, but got further and further from me; and, at last, I could perceive her to take pins out of her pocket to prick me if I should touch her again — which seeing I did forbear, and was glad I did spy her design. And then I fell to gaze upon another pretty maid in a pew close to me, and she on me; and I did go about to take her by the hand, which she suffered a little and then withdrew. So the sermon ended, and the church broke up, and my amours ended also. . . .

"A strange slavery that I stand in to beauty," he had earlier confessed, "that I value nothing near it." Even in his grosser moments there is a shamefastness or even delicacy that marks him as a connoisseur in sensation, one almost unaware of the tawdry side of experience. Another man, for example, after riding all day in the mud would have been annoyed at night to have his sleep broken; but Pepys in full sense of comfort was pleased to be made conscious of that comfort. He records:

I never did pass a night with more epicurism of sleep; there being now and then a noise of people stirring that waked me, and then it was a very rainy night, and then I was a little weary, that what between waking and then sleeping again, one after another, I never had so much content in all my life. . . .

He savored the bouquet of all experience, from sleep to the ecstasy that he felt for the woodwind music in Massinger's *Virgin Martyr*. Among the arts music was his favorite,[4] and in his household a servant with musical gifts was at once a companion and a pupil. Pepys himself composed at least four songs, and he performed on the viols, the flageolet, and the harpsichord at least. At home music was a frequent pleasure. In the Christmas season (January 3, 1666) he records:

¹ See Sir J. F. Bridge, *Samuel Pepys, Lover of Musique* (1903).

So home, and find all my good company I had bespoke. . . . and good musique we had, and, among other things, Mrs. Coleman sang my words I set of "Beauty retire," and I think it is a good song, and they praise it mightily. Then to dancing and supper, and mighty merry till Mr. Rolt come in, whose pain of the tooth-ake made him no company, and spoilt ours; so he away, and then my wife's teeth fell of akeing, and she to bed. So forced to break up all with a good song, and so to bed.

Abroad he frequented James Harrington's Rota Club or intellectual society wherever found. The theatre he enjoyed and disparaged by turns; occasionally he swore to stay away entirely, but in a few weeks or months there he would be again.

Pepys's "epicurism" in all the life of sensation easily blinds a reader of the *Diary* to the fact that he was a hard-working Clerk and an able servant to the Royal Navy—one of the very ablest in its history. He put in long hours in the office, scrutinized expenditures watchfully, studied the history of the navy, meddled in rope making and in naval architecture, and became truly an expert administrator. When thirty-two he was made Treasurer of Tangier, a crown possession in the affairs of which he was to have for years an important part. In the same year he was elected to the Royal Society. During the plague of 1665 Pepys remained at his post trying to keep the fleet supplied and active against the Dutch. The King himself, after the terror was over, thanked Pepys: "I do give you thanks for your good service all this year, and I assure you I am very sensible of it." For long years Pepys was to render better and better service. He was to be twice Secretary of the Admiralty Commission, was to be historian of its activities for the decade 1679-88 in his *Memoires Relating to the State of the Royal Navy* (1690), and according to his recent brilliant biographer, Bryant, he was largely responsible for England's naval tradition in modern times. *His Public Service*

The appeal of his *Diary*, then, lies not in the fact that Pepys had a petty, gossip-loving mind: he was not that kind of man. It lies in the fact that Pepys, Puritan bred though he was, coupled with a tremendous business efficiency a ready capacity for delight in all aspects of life—feminine beauty, food, music, architecture, the playhouse, and a cultivated home life. Along with stirring pictures of public events he gives a vivid self-betrayal of his own weakness and strength; above all he shows as no one else ever has shown in complete detail how everyday life may be lived both prudently and glowingly. *The Nature of the Diary*

The publication of Pepys's *Diary*, it has been noted, was due to the earlier publication (1818) of the parallel work of John Evelyn, who had mentioned Pepys many times.[5] Evelyn has none of the tantalizing charm of Pepys, but

---

[5] John Evelyn (1620-1706) was born at Wotton (Sussex); he studied (1637-40) both at Oxford and in the Middle Temple. During the troubled forties he spent much time on the Continent, but in 1647 he returned to England, and in 1652 took up residence at Sayes Court, Deptford. He laid plans with Robert Boyle for founding the Royal Society, and in 1659, less successfully, planned with Col. Herbert Morley for the Restoration of the monarchy. In 1653 he had begun to lay out his famous garden at Sayes Court—later ruined by his tenant, Peter

John Evelyn on a more sober level he shared many of Pepys's interests. Pepys was a servant of the court; Evelyn—a product of the squirearchy that Macaulay so abused—was rather a member of the court, one with a zeal for improving and beautifying the life of his day. A sane and reputable virtuoso and projector, he was diversely engrossed in gardening, in city-planning (for London after the fire), in numismatics, in forestry, and in experimental science.

His
Writings:
Their Public
Service

His works, in general, are directed to specific practical purposes. Among them *Fumifugium* (1661) was directed against the smoke nuisance of London (in 1661!), *Sculptura* (1662) described the new method of mezzotint engraving, soon to be perfected and known as "the English method," and *Sylva* (1664) urged the necessity of reforestation in England, and was his most regarded work in his day. He wrote a few poems, translated the First Book of Lucretius (1656), and entered the field of social morals in *Liberty and Servitude* (1649); in *A Character of England* (1659), which attempted to engraft French politeness on the less refined English stock; and in *Publick Employment and an Active Life preferred to Solitude* (1667), where he broaches again the subject treated by Cowley, Sir George Mackenzie, and many others. His most praised work in recent times is *The Life of Mrs. Godolphin*,[6] a private memorial (first published in 1847) of a saintly Maid of Honor, Margaret Blagge, who married Sidney Godolphin and died in 1678 at the age of twenty-five. She was the Pamela of her age and was renowned as such. When Crowne's *Calisto, or the Chaste Nimph* was to be presented at court in 1674, Mrs. Blagge (as she was called even after her marriage) was commanded both by the King and by the Duke of York to return to court and appear as the chaste heroine—which she did "to admiration ... covered with jewels." The Platonic passion felt by Evelyn and this young woman for each other is a phenomenon reverentially recorded by her biographer.

Apart from writing, Evelyn had a dignified and active interest in the repair or improvement of practically everything from Old St. Paul's[7] to the English garden and even to the English language. He was a charter member of the Royal Society and continued as a devoted fellow and councilor throughout his career. On two occasions the presidency of the Society might have

---

the Great of Russia. In 1694 Evelyn removed to the family seat at Wotton, and he died there in 1706. — *Miscellaneous Works*, ed. William Upcott (1825). Evelyn's *Diary* has been printed from the transcript of William Bray by editors who have selected different passages to publish. A complete edition by E. S. de Beer is in prospect. The four differing texts available are (*a*) ed. William Bray (2v, 1818); (*b*) 2v, 1819, and in the Chandos Classics [1879?]; (*c*) 5v, 1827; ed. Henry B. Wheatley (4v, 1879, 1906); (*d*) ed. John Forster (4v, 1850-52); ed. Austin Dobson (3v, 1906; Globe ed., 1908; Everyman's Library, 2v, n. d.). See *CBEL*, II. 830. — E. Gordon Craig, "John Evelyn and the Theatre," in *Books and Theatres* (1925), pp. 1-68; Arthur, Lord Ponsonby, *John Evelyn* (1933); Clara Marburg, *Mr. Pepys and Mr. Evelyn* (Philadelphia, 1935); Geoffrey Keynes, *John Evelyn: A Study in Bibliophily and a Bibliography of his Writings* (Cambridge, 1937).

6 Ed. Samuel Wilberforce (1847); ed. Harriet Sampson (Oxford, 1939).

7 See Evelyn's "Londinium Redivivum, or London Restored," in *Jour. Royal Inst. Brit. Architects*, XXVII (1919-20). 467-470; ed. E. S. de Beer as *London Revived. Considerations for its Rebuilding in 1666* (Oxford, 1938).

been his if he had wished.[8] His distinction was not that of a public official, although he was a member of various commissions. During the Dutch wars he impoverished himself as a member of the Commission for the Sick and Wounded. The highest civic office that he achieved was to be briefly one of three commissioners to execute the office of Privy Seal. His true rôle was that of a model country gentleman actuated by the widest and most intelligent "public spirit."

His *Diary* covers more time, but is less revealing, than that of Pepys. It *Evelyn's* lacks the "confessions" aspect of Pepys's work. If Evelyn was guilty of *Diary* indiscretion (and one may doubt it), he was not so indiscreet as to record the fact. His *Diary* tends to become a history of his own times, and as such is invaluable because of its balance and sobriety. Much of the first third of it deals with his travels or residence on the Continent during the Commonwealth, at which time he was acquainted with Waller, Hobbes, Denham, Hyde (later Earl of Clarendon), and other royalists.[9] Here also in 1647 he found an estimable if very youthful bride. The richest section of the *Diary* is that dealing with his life at Sayes Court and in London between the years 1652 and 1694. At this last date he retired to his birthplace Wotton, where the remainder of his life was passed. The latest entries in the *Diary* are for January, 1706, a month before Evelyn's death. It was the quiet harmony of this rural existence that he really loved. In a letter to another fellow of the Royal Society, John Beale (July 11, 1679), Evelyn had lamented that for ten years he had been in "perpetual motion, and hardly two months in a year at my own habitation." From Wotton at the age of seventy-seven he wrote to another friend concerning life there:

We have here a very convenient apartment of five rooms together, besides a pretty closet, which we have furnished with the spoils of Sayes Court, and is the raree-show of the whole neighborhood, and in truth we live easy as to all domestic cares. Wednesday and Saturday nights we call Lecture Nights, when my Wife and myself take our turns to read the packets of all the news sent constantly from London, which serves us for discourse till fresh news comes; and so you have the history of an old man and his no young companion, whose society I have enjoyed more to my satisfaction these three years here, than in almost fifty before, but am now every day trussing up to be gone, I hope to a better place.[10]

Preoccupation with London newspapers—appearing with new liberty since 1695—with his comfortable household, and with the Heavenly City—for his

---

[8] Margaret Denny, "The Early Program of the Royal Society and John Evelyn," *MLQ*, I (1940). 481-497. On Evelyn's connection with the project of an Academy in England see J. E. Spingarn, *Critical Essays of the Seventeenth Century* (1908), II. 337-338; B. S. Monroe, "An English Academy," *MP*, VIII (1910). 107-122; and Edmund Freeman, "A Proposal for an English Academy in 1660," *MLR*, XIX (1924). 291-300.

[9] Evelyn was ambitious to seem to be *the* man to bring about the Restoration and was later envious of General Monck. See E. S. de Beer, "Evelyn and Colonel Herbert Morley in 1659 and 1660," *Sussex Archaeological Collections*, LXXVIII (1937). 177-183, and Arthur H. Nethercot in *HLQ*, I (1938). 439-446.

[10] Letter to Dr. Bohun, January 18, 1697, in the *Diary* (ed. Austin Dobson, 1906), I, pp. lxi-lxii.

journey to which he was "every day trussing up"—these three interests form a trinity quite typical of the better aspects of the Restoration.

Minor Diaries

There were many other diaries kept in this general period,[11] but either they are of little vividness or importance, or else they are specialized in their interest and lack literary quality. For Parliamentary history *The Journal of Sir Simonds D'Ewes,* which "from the beginning of the Long Parliament to the opening of the Trial of the Earl of Strafford" was published in 1933,[12] has great importance—as has also *The Diary of Thomas Burton* (1828) covering the doings of Parliament from 1656-59. Narcissus Luttrell's *Brief Historical Relation of State Affairs* (1678-1714), published in 1857, is compiled frequently from newsletters such as Evelyn and his wife read at Wotton. Luttrell was not always an eye-witness, but his work has some historical value as coming from a notable scholar and collector of pamphlets, ballads, and broadsides. With him we pass to the field of *materiel*—to the work of men who felt it a duty to assemble and preserve data from which history could be written. Such men were numerous. Sir William Dugdale (1605-86) wrote an autobiography as well as important historical works. His son-in-law, Elias Ashmole (1617-92), founder of the Ashmolean Museum, kept a diary, published as his *Memoirs* (1717), and produced an antiquarian history, *The Institution of...the Order of the Garter* (1672). Sir Roger Manley (1626?-1688) produced various works of contemporary history, and Sir Paul Rycaut (1628-1700) capitalized on his knowledge of the recent history of the eastern Mediterranean countries. The ecclesiastical historian, John Strype (1643-1737), was also a great collector of facts; but he, like most of these persons here enumerated, lacked literary and philosophical quality. One aimed, it seems, to collect data that might make history full and accurate or might at least enable one to support a controversial position in historical writing.

There were, however, two men in this period who achieved some quality of distinction other than the merely factual in their historical writing—the first Earl of Clarendon and Gilbert Burnet, Bishop of Salisbury.

The Earl of Clarendon

Edward Hyde (1609-1674), created first Earl of Clarendon in 1661, was one of the most distinguished statesmen of the mid-seventeenth century. He derived his education from Oxford, from the Middle Temple, and from companionship with such scholars and literati as Ben Jonson, John Selden, John Hales, Edmund Waller, and Lord Falkland. He was early engaged in politics, and the keynote to his whole career was respect for constitutional monarchy and for the Church, positions which led to a firm adherence to the royalist cause. He was Chancellor of the Exchequer in 1643, and in 1645 became one of the guardians of the Prince of Wales (Charles II). While hiding with the Prince in the Scilly Islands in 1646, he first conceived the idea of his *History.* At the Restoration his influence as Lord Chancellor was enormous; but he had many enemies in Parliament and at court (where,

---

[11] Arthur, Lord Ponsonby in his *English Diaries* (1923) lists and reviews some thirty diaries of the seventeenth century. His *More English Diaries* (1927) adds a half-dozen others. His lists are not complete.
[12] Ed. Wallace Notestein (New Haven, 1933).

Evelyn records, he was "an eye-sore" to the mistresses and revelers), and in 1667 he was dismissed from office and exiled to France. In France he finished his *History,* did some other writing, and there he died in 1674.[13]

Clarendon's *History of the Rebellion* is certainly the noblest example of formal historical writing in the period. Covering the years of strife between Charles I and the Parliament and ending with the Restoration—years during which Clarendon as a royal councilor played a most important part, the sixteen books of the *History* deal with highly controversial matter. Originally it was conceived as a defense of the constitutional royalists who advised Charles I and as a source of counsel for royal action. It was not designed for contemporary publication. Additional material for it, as the project grew, was drawn from the *Life* of himself that Clarendon composed (1668-70) during his exile. The last books of the *History* also were written in France in 1671-2.[14] In reliability the work varies greatly according as the original sources were or were not at hand. The materials from the *Life* are least trustworthy, and Book ix is the most respected section of the work. The object—self-defense, defense of constitutional monarchy, of the crown, and of royal advisers—did not always make for unbiased presentation; and the facts that composition was spread over a period of about thirty years and that Clarendon was constantly distracted from this task by his public employments make the distinguished result somewhat surprising. *Clarendon's History*

The distinction of the *History* depends largely on its neo-classical ideals. It is a formal, elaborate piece of architecture. It led one, so Evelyn wrote to Pepys, "by the courts, avenues, and porches into the fabric." In spite of its imperfections it was and is a noble structure. Much solid merit resides in its expert insight into constitutional problems; much in its clear, forward-moving narrative strength; but its chief delight is its many "characters." [15] To recreate "the eminency and virtue" of leading personages (and such men rather than political issues Clarendon chose to regard as the cause of the Civil Wars) was as much "the true end of history" as the recording of counsels and actions. The author's evident moderation in these characters is perhaps due to his tolerance of human nature in general. In his essay *Of Human Nature* (1668) he concluded that "nature is as much the creation of

[13] From 1660-67 Clarendon served ably as Chancellor of Oxford University, and worthy memorials of him still remain, notably the distinguished Clarendon Press. Through the marriage (1660) of his daughter Anne to the Duke of York (later James II), he became the grandfather of Queen Mary II and Queen Anne. He bequeathed his manuscripts to the University, which in 1702-4 published *The History of the Rebellion and Civil Wars in England* in three volumes. The best modern edition is that of W. D. Macray (6v, Oxford, 1888). *The Life of Edward, Earl of Clarendon* appeared in 1759, and was reprinted from the MS in 1857 (2v). See also Thomas H. Lister, *Life and Administration of Edward, First Earl of Clarendon* (3v, 1837-38); *Calendar of the Clarendon State Papers Preserved in the Bodleian Library,* ed. O. Ogle, W. H. Bliss, W. D. Macray, and F. J. Routledge (1872-1932); Sir Charles H. Firth, "Clarendon's *History of the Rebellion,*" *EHR,* xix (1904). 26-54, 246-262, 464-483; Sir Henry Craik, *Life of Edward, Earl of Clarendon* (2v, 1911).

[14] On the composition of the *History* see Sir Charles H. Firth's articles in *EHR,* as cited above.

[15] Many of the best of these are reprinted, with admirable comment, in D. Nichol Smith's *Characters from the Histories and Memoirs of the Seventeenth Century, with an Essay on the Character* (Oxford, 1918).

God as grace is; and it is his bounty that he created nature in that integrity, and hath since restored it to that innocence, or annexed that innocence to it, if it be not maliciously ravished, or let loose, from it." And so his lordship could reprehend Pym's "power of doing shrewd turns" in masterly under-statement, and could similarly regret "some unpopular natural infirmities" on the part of Archbishop Laud.[16] In commendation Clarendon was no less even-tempered. His portraiture of his intimate friend, Lord Falkland,[17] is his most glowing work; but he treats the merits of an opponent, John Hamp-den for instance, with dignity and high respect. His contemporaries are conceived as successors and fellows of the great heroes portrayed by Sallust, Tacitus, or Plutarch. The style lacks the crispness and brevity of the "new prose" of his day, but it is stately, easy, and flowing. Although the sentences are neither so varied, so settled, nor so finely chiseled as those of Gibbon were to be a century later, their effect is true Roman.

Gilbert Burnet

Definitely less of this nobility is seen slightly later in the historical work of Gilbert Burnet,[18] who also writes of his own times and of his own cause—the cause being in his case Protestantism as embodied in latitudinarian Anglicanism. Burnet, a downright, hard-headed Scot, stood in the relation of guide and counselor to William and Mary, as Clarendon had done to Charles II. To the merry monarch himself, however, on January 29, 1680, Burnet had addressed an astonishing letter—which King Charles burned and forgave—urging upon the King the necessity of a change of heart and of manners: "And now, Sir," he remarks, ". . . suffer me . . . to tell you that all the distrust your people have of you, all the necessities you are now in, all the indignation of Heaven that is on you, and appears in the defeating of all your counsels, flow from this, that you have not feared nor served God, but have given yourself up to so many sinful pleasures." There was nothing delicate or fine about Burnet; but his assurance, obnoxious as it was to many, was courageous and at times tolerant. He was a power in battles for the material well-being of the Church during the reigns of William and Mary and of Queen Anne; but he was cordially detested by all High Church Tories. Gross materialism is a charge that these antagonists often brought against him. If he congratulated the anti-Romanist Whig clergy on being "a wall for their church and country," the Tories would sneer, as Jonathan

---

[16] As antithetical to the point of view of eighteenth-century sentimentalism it is notable that a chief "infirmity" was that Laud "believed innocence of heart, and integrity of manners, was a guard strong enough to secure any man in his voyage through this world."

[17] On Viscount Falkland see Kenneth B. Murdock, *The Sun at Noon* (1939), pp. 1-38.

[18] Gilbert Burnet (1643-1715) was born in Edinburgh. A precocious student, he entered Marischall College at the age of ten, and was graduated M.A. in 1657. After the Restoration he mediated between the Crown and the Presbyterians, and in 1673 he became a royal chaplain. His strictures on court life and royal morals made him at times unpopular in court circles, and at the accession of James II he retired to the Continent, where he soon became a close and influential adviser to William of Orange. In 1689 he became Bishop of Salisbury and leader of the Whiggish latitudinarians in the Church. One of the more learned men of his day, he was very active in political and religious writing, strongly anti-Catholic in bias and opportunist in method. — The best *Life* of Burnet is that by T. E. S. Clarke and H. C. Foxcroft (Cambridge, 1907).

Swift did, "A south wall, I suppose, for all the best fruit of the church and country to be nailed on."

From his great mass of miscellaneous writing, chiefly controversial and religious but in part scientific, a few historical works demand attention here, not for their complete trustworthiness but because of an advance at times in method. In 1677 after some years of delay he published his *Memoirs of the* *His* *Lives and Actions of James and William, Dukes of Hamilton.* This work, *Histories* really a continuation [19] of John Spottiswoode's *History of the Church of Scotland* (1655), was based on documents, many of which were printed in the text or at the end of the volume—a procedure not usual at the time in such works but necessary in the case of controversial history. In 1679 appeared Part 1 of Burnet's *History of the Reformation of the Church in England,*[20] designed both as honest history and as a blast against the papist writers, who were just then agog over a recent French translation of Nicholas Sanders's (d. 1581) *English Schism.* Although an atmosphere of Popish Plots hardly made for unbiased production of such a work, Burnet had done much research on the subject, even advertising in modern fashion in the *London Gazette* (January 1, 1680) for documentary aids, and he was doubtless unaware of any blameworthy prejudice. By the Whig faction and by Low Churchmen the work was highly approved. It marked in some ways a change in the methods of historical writing. Burnet was aware that modern history could not be written in the manner of the ancients with one's eye chiefly on personal and moral lessons of heroic behavior. For him history lost its large or educational function and adopted a precise and limited controversial objective. Evidence both as to conduct and as to analysis of issues became thus indispensable, and factual research was imperative. Here Burnet shows awareness of the antiquarian tendencies arising in the scholarship of his day.

Just as in his *Reformation* Burnet patterned after Paolo Sarpi and Sleidan rather than after the ancients, so in his most important work, the *History of His Own Time* (begun in 1683),[21] his master was the great Frenchman Thuanus (De Thou). Though the work is self-effacing, it partakes at times of the quality of a diary or a collection of *ana* or of anecdotes. As a high-class gossip, Burnet recorded the sources of his tales frequently, and wrote more commonly with credibility than one might at first expect. His memory was prodigious. He was rash and crude in style and method, and here, as in his "characters," he fell far short of Clarendon. His greatest value arises where Clarendon ceased, and for the last quarter of the century he gave an invaluable, if prejudiced, record. The epilogue to the *History* and his *Some Passages of the Life and Death of the . . . Earl of Rochester* (whose notable deathbed repentance Burnet witnessed and here in 1680 recorded) have been praised as well written. In general his style, rapid, easy, and careless, is undistin-

---

[19] So printed in the fourth ed. of Spotiswood (1677) and similarly reprinted, Oxford, 1852.
[20] Part II appeared in 1681; Part III in 1714. Ed. N. Pocock (7v. Oxford, 1865).
[21] *Bishop Burnet's History of His Own Time* (2v, 1724-34; 4v, 1753); ed. M. J. Routh (7v, Oxford, 1823); ed. O. Airy (Vols. I and II only, Oxford, 1897-1900).

guished. One need not go so far as his inveterate enemy, Jonathan Swift, who was constantly jibing at "that peculiar manner of expressing himself, which the poverty of our language compels me to call [his] style." Swift's best quip was his note on Burnet's remark that *Paradise Lost* "was esteemed the beautifullest and perfectest poem that ever was writ, at least in *our* language." In the margin Swift here wrote: "A mistake, for it is in *English.*" Rapier work, elegance, or polish was not Burnet's forte.

Biography and Auto-biography

In the Restoration period history as a type of writing was obviously close to biography and autobiography. Clarendon's *Life* was in part merged with his *History.* Distinguished personages as varied in character and interest as Margaret Cavendish, Duchess of Newcastle, Sir Simonds D'Ewes, and Richard Baxter, wrote autobiographies, and in general this method of self-record is either designed to adumbrate history or, as in the case of Baxter and many other Puritans, to reveal the dangers and triumphs of the spiritual life. Its techniques are variable and unsettled.[22] The word *biography* was new in English at this time, and its intention varies from the private document meant for no circulation, at least outside the family itself, to the public biographical eulogy of a funeral sermon, or to formal biography as generally practised. The best examples are those that blend public with private history, and this can be tactfully done by an intelligent but adoring wife. Margaret Cavendish, Duchess of Newcastle, wrote her own life and that of her husband the Duke.[23] His Grace's life was published in folio in 1667 while he was still alive, and the autobiography of the Duchess herself had appeared much earlier. Such publication, like much else about this learned and literary lady, was unusual. Lady Fanshawe[24] was more in accord with tradition; for in portraying the unblemished worth of her Sir Richard, who in public life met poverty with distinction and the vicissitudes of travel with high courage, she wrote only for the private instruction of her son. Similarly Mrs. Lucy Hutchinson in her clean-cut *Memoirs of Colonel Hutchinson*[25] was erecting a private family memorial to her "murdered" husband, but with a consciousness that some day the defense of a regicide would not be scorned. She writes his *Memoirs* in the third person, and with an objectivity more apparent than real. She stresses the public career of her husband and hence seems to write history; but she writes with a tactfully managed personal interest in what she does. She has an admirable reserved sense of appropriate detail, and is vivid without being trivial or intimate. The argument over what gave significance to small details was already under way.

22 Ch. IV of Waldo H. Dunn's *English Biography* (1916) deals with the period 1500-1700. A fuller treatment is found in Donald A. Stauffer's *English Biography before 1700* (Cambridge, Mass., 1930).

23 The Duchess of Newcastle's sketch of her own life appeared first in Book XI of her *Nature's Pictures Drawn by Fancie's Pencil to the Life* (1655). Her life of her husband was entitled (in part) *The Life of the Thrice Noble, High and Puissant Prince William Cavendishe, Duke, Marquess, and Earl of Newcastle* ... (1667); ed. Sir Charles H. Firth (1886); in Everyman's Library (1915).

24 Anne, Lady Fanshawe's *Memoirs* (written in 1676) were first printed in 1829; they were reëdited from the MS in 1907.

25 First printed in 1806; well edited by Sir Charles H. Firth (1906). Mrs. Hutchinson's fragment of autobiography is printed with the *Memoirs.*

Burnet condemned trivialities; Dryden in his *Life of Plutarch* was keen for them. Richard Baxter in the beautiful *Breviate of the Life of Margaret Baxter* (1681) [26] memorializes his wife's passion for spirituality, suppresses practically all details of her virtuous "creature" love for himself, and yet contrives to create an atmosphere of passionate intimacy. Effects and techniques must vary when the life deals with public affairs or when it is concerned with spiritual experience. Except as a stimulus to spirituality it would have been indecorous to publish a life of Margaret Baxter only twenty years after her death. The Puritan fervor of the *Breviate* parallels interestingly the *Life,* hardly more worldly than the *Breviate,* in which the Maid of Honor Margaret Blagge (Mrs. Godolphin) was beatified by Evelyn.

However varied the techniques of biography may be, the purposes sought *Short Lives* are usually obvious. It may have historical, spiritual, or ethical interest, or it may, as in the case of "rogue" biographies, be largely mere entertainment. A significant and rather novel development in the period is the prefatory biography that introduces the reader to an author's work and that tends to get collected into something that by the end of the century takes on the likeness of a specialized biographical dictionary. The best of these brief independent or prefatory lives are doubtless those of Richard Hooker (1665) and of George Herbert (1670), both written by Izaak Walton. On a more mundane level Bishop Thomas Sprat's *Life* of Abraham Cowley (prefixed to Cowley's *Works* in 1668) represents an obvious confusion of biography with literary criticism, but is one of the best of the prefatory lives of the time.

Collections of lives perhaps are the distinctive development in biography *Collections* during this half century. Most such collections have a less natural and more *of Biogra-* specialized field than Thomas Fuller's *History of the Worthies of England* *phies* (1662), which in wit and incisiveness equals anything that was soon to follow. At the opposite extreme is Thomas Pope Blount's imitation of Continental "polyhistors" in his *Censura Celebriorum Authorum* (1690) in which he compiles biographical data for the history of scholarship throughout Europe. He writes in Latin for a European audience, but the interest is thinly antiquarian. Chiefly in all these collections it is the clergy, especially the nonconformist saints, who are treated. Samuel Clarke (1599-1683) had issued in 1650 his *Marrow of Ecclesiastical History,* a farrago of lives of Puritan clergymen, Christian rulers, and "Christians of Inferiour Rank"; he followed this with *A General Martyrologie* (1651). *A Loyall Martyrology* (1662) was produced by William Winstanley (1628?-1698), who in 1687 brought out a thin and not very valuable volume of *Lives of the Most Famous English Poets.* Other collections of literary biographies were *Theatrum Poetarum* (1675) by Milton's nephew, Edward Phillips,

---

[26] Reprinted in 1826 (as *Memoirs...*) and in 1928 by John T. Wilkinson, *Richard Baxter and Margaret Charlton, a Puritan Love Story. The Reliquiae Baxterianae: or, Mr. Richard Baxter's Narrative of the Most Memorable Passages of his Life and Times* was first published in 1696. A useful abridgment under the title *The Autobiography of Richard Baxter* (ed. J. M. Lloyd Thomas) appeared in 1925 (and in Everyman's Library [1931]).

and Gerard Langbaine's *Account of the English Dramatick Poets* (1691), revised in 1699 by Gildon as *Lives and Characters of the English Dramatick Poets*. All of these were very humble but not quite despicable beginnings in the field of literature. Here the outstanding achievement was that of Anthony Wood (1632-1695) in his two volumes of *Athenae Oxonienses: An Exact History of all the Writers and Bishops who have had their Education in ... Oxford from 1500, to the End of the Year 1690*. These volumes (1691-2) were the results of much antiquarian research, in which Wood was indefatigable.[27] Ill-natured and ill-considered statements made his work obnoxious to Oxford, and certain pages accusing the late Chancellor Clarendon of selling offices caused a lawsuit. When Wood was found guilty, his expulsion from the University resulted. The "evidence" against Clarendon came really from notes supplied by an assistant antiquary, John Aubrey (1626-1697), who was as relaxed and amiable as Wood was intense and quarrelsome. Both men had been inspired to antiquarianism by Dugdale's *Warwickshire* (1656). Wood's early ambition was to do a similar history for Oxfordshire, and Aubrey worked to the same end for Wiltshire. But Aubrey's lack of method kept him from achievement of his goal. His collections made over a period of twenty-five years largely for Wood's *Athenae* were edited as *Brief Lives* in 1898. They display the collecting of anecdotes at its best. The trivial details are delightful gossip and yet apparently maintain a high degree of truthfulness. Here as in Pepys and in other witty writers of the period we have the amused observer of life setting down details that delight both the antiquarian and the gossip. The taste of the age, as of all ages, was described by Dryden in remarks concerning intimate biography in his *Life of Plutarch* (1683):

You may behold a *Scipio* and a *Lelius* gathering Cockle-shells on the shore, *Augustus* playing at bounding stones with *Boyes;* and *Agesilaus* riding on a Hobby-horse among his Children. The Pageantry of Life is taken away; you see the poor reasonable Animal, as naked as ever nature made him; are made acquainted with his passions and his follies, and find the *Demy-God* a *Man*.

Aubrey is highly successful in this unbuttoned style, just as Clarendon and others had charmed by a reverse process, in which the men of their day became if not demigods at least heroes of Augustan stature.

[27] Extensive and fascinating autobiographical materials were edited by the Rev. Andrew Clark for the Oxford Historical Society from Wood's papers under the title *The Life and Times of Anthony Wood ... described by Himself, Collected from his Diaries and Other Papers* (5v, 1891-1900).

VIII
Types of Prose Fiction

It is notable that in a period when aristocratic playwrights excelled, writers *Fiction for* of fictitious narrative at the same social level were practically non-existent *Various* or lacking in merit. The only English writer of prose fiction to achieve *Classes* permanent distinction as such in this period was the "mechanick" preacher John Bunyan; and for his work the court circles, so influential in the drama, had naturally no regard. Courtly fiction of the moment was imported, and came largely from France, the home of the elegant refinement that was then so highly regarded. One must not assume that fiction was rigidly specialized for class consumption; but clearly there were types of fiction devised for aristocratic, for pious, or for popular lower-class readers. But an aristocrat might be pious, and probably all classes, and not merely the less learned, read chapbooks on occasion. There is a specialization; but it cannot be rigidly asserted.[1]

The lofty French romances by D'Urfé, Gomberville, Mlle de Scudéry, *French* and La Calprenède had undoubtedly a considerable polite vogue. Enormously *Romances* long (eight or ten volumes is a fair average), tediously complicated, and loosely organized, one of these romances was a fiction library in itself. The stories were an escape from the vulgarities of a court where the King fondled his mistresses in public, and where one of them (Castlemaine), doubtless *toute ereintée*, drove in Hyde Park and "lay impudently upon her back in her coach asleep, with her mouth open." [2] The escape, however, was to a world of aristocratic artificiality, a world where the protocol of elegant love or of heroism totally replaced average human behavior. Because of escapism or some other appeal most of the more popular French romances found English translators and readers. La Calprenède's *Cassandra* was englished in part in 1652 and completely translated by Sir Charles Cotterell in 1667, and abridged by other hands in 1703. His *Cleopatra* was gracefully translated by R. Loveday and others (1652-59), and versions of *Pharamond*

---

[1] For bibliographies of Restoration fiction see *CBEL*, II. 488-495, 529-535, and Arundell Esdaile, *A List of English Tales and Prose Romances Printed before 1740* (The Bibliographical Society, 1912). For the French fiction of the time see Ralph C. Williams, *A Bibliography of the Seventeenth-Century Novel in France* (1931). The largest history is Ernest A. Baker's *History of the English Novel*, Vol. III (1929). John C. Dunlop's *History of Prose Fiction* (3v, Edinburgh, 1814; 2v, 1906) summarizes several seventeenth-century romances. Frank W. Chandler's *Literature of Roguery* (2v, 1907) is excellent in its field, as is Charlotte E. Morgan's *Rise of the Novel of Manners* (1911). On French influence in fiction Thomas P. Haviland's *"Roman de Longue Haleine" on English Soil* (Philadelphia, 1931) is useful. For shorter general histories of the English novel, which naturally devote little space to this period, see below, Part II, ch. x, n. 1.

[2] *The Diary of Samuel Pepys* for March 19, 1665.

were made by John Davies (1662) and by John Phillips (1677). Mlle de Scudéry's *Ibrahim* appeared in English (by Henry Cogan) in 1652 and in 1674; and of others from her pen there appeared *Artamenes, or the Grand Cyrus* (translated by "F. G.", 1653-55 in five folio volumes), *Clelia* (translated by John Davies and George Havers, 1655-61, in five volumes), and *Almahide* ("done into English by J. Phillips, Gent." in 1677). There were other similar but less gigantic French works that had a vogue in England —notably the semi-historical stories of Mme de Lafayette.

That the vogue of these romances was immediate, widespread, and enduring cannot be doubted. The heroic plays of the time frequently made use of materials from these epics in prose. Gallant letter writers bandied about the names of the heroes and heroines familiarly. Dorothy Osborne, later wife of Sir William Temple, in her *Letters* was continually discussing the characters of these romances, and poor Mrs. Pepys by ineptly retelling tedious episodes from *The Grand Cyrus* brought wrath to her husband and then tears to herself. Horace Walpole, born in 1717, as a child lived with these romances, and the same was evidently true of the American-born Charlotte Lennox, author of *The Female Quixote* (1752). The nature of the influence of these stories on eighteenth-century fiction is fairly obvious: they encouraged an artificial idealism in decorum, emotional scenes ornamented with *beaux sentiments,* and perhaps the concept of prose fiction as related to the heroic poem, as the "epic in prose." It is also true that some of the eighteenth-century *romans à clef* (or "scandal chronicles") owe their romantic veneer to this tradition.

English Romances   English romance diverges somewhat from the French pattern. John Reynolds's *Flower of Fidelitie* (1650) and John Crowne's *Pandion and Amphigenia* (1665) are greatly, if ineptly, indebted to Sidney's *Arcadia;* and the anonymous *Eromena* (1683) draws its substance from William Chamberlayne's *Pharonnida* (1659): Roger Boyle's *Parthenissa* (1654-69; 1676) is the most pretentious and tedious example of the French pattern. An earlier independent and intellectual tradition is seen following somewhat after Bacon's *New Atlantis* and John Barclay's *Argenis.* Such works furthered philosophical or educational romance. *Aretina* (Edinburgh, 1660), by Sir George Mackenzie, later known as the "bloody advocate" of covenanting persecution, rejoices in the sub-title of "the serious romance," and shows that its author was rather essayist than story-teller. In 1666 Margaret Cavendish, the learned Duchess of Newcastle, published her imitation of Lucian, *The Blazing World,* as an appendage to her *Observations upon Experimental Philosophy.* The story seems an appalling confusion of episode with no clear philosophy emerging.[3] This love for serious romancing is seen also in the religious effort of the Rev. Nathaniel Ingelo (1621?-1683), *Bentivolio and Urania* (1660-64), which went through four editions by 1682, possibly aided by the fact that the title-page advertises that "all the Obscure Words

---

[3] See Henry Ten Eyck Perry, *The First Duchess of Newcastle and Her Husband* (Boston, 1918), pp. 252-258, for a summary of the story.

throughout the Book are interpreted in the Margin." Evidently the religious counsels so lavishly inserted are directed towards the less literate of the sexes!

Even in heavily didactic romances English authors were inferior at the *Philo-* time to those on the Continent. As the secularization of thought increased, *sophical* there was great interest in how far human reason aided only by "the light *Romances* of nature" could go. Speculatists in these fields found comfort in the accounts of self-taught philosophers such as the medieval Arabic *Hai Ebn Yokdan* by Abi Jaafar Ebn Tophail and its Spanish imitation, Gracian's *Critick*. The Arabic work, translated into Latin by the Rev. Edward Pococke in 1671, was made English in 1674, again in 1686, and again in 1708. Yokdan, exposed new born in a desert island, grows up in solitude, and through contemplation and observation alone arrives at a sophisticated grasp of divine essence and other similar metaphysical concepts. Gracian's romance was made English by Sir Paul Rycaut (1681). His autodidact, Andrenio, is brought up by animals in an underground den: when adult he is suddenly projected by an earthquake to the surface of his desert island (St. Helena), where he meets "the experienced naufrage" Critilo. Their travels and comments on society seen in the light of nature make up the volume. A less exotic educational romance that had later influence was the Abbé Fénelon's *Adventures of Telemachus,* first translated in 1699-1700 and reprinted thereafter many times. A perfect specimen of neo-classicism, written in the tradition of Xenophon's *Cyropaedia* for the edification of the French dauphin, this work stimulated simplified benevolist thinking, and, with its obvious Homeric echoes, increased an awareness that epics might be written in prose. But neither this nor any of the works just mentioned has much relation to skilful narrative art.

Another aspect of polite fiction that has French affiliations is the use of private letters for story-telling.[4] Letters in the tradition of Pliny the Younger relate to the essay rather than to narrative fiction—such letters, for example, as the curious *CCXI Sociable Letters* (1664) by the Duchess of Newcastle. *Epistolary* These, however, as well as the translation of the witty epistles of Balzac *Narratives* and Voiture, indicate that the English were learning from abroad in part that the personal letter might possibly be an elegant literary composition. Three types which thus early began to influence fiction were the news letter, the travel letter, and the love letter. In such miscellanies as Charles Gildon's *Post Boy Rob'd of his Mail* (1692-93) letters that tell gossiping episodes are found, and in Tom Brown's popular *Adventures of Lindamira* (1702) this use of letters is full fledged.[5] The travel letter, popularized by the Italian G. P. Marana, whose *Letters Writ by a Turkish Spy* were made English in 1687,[6] may be at times narratives and at times essays in social criticism. A very popular translation of travel letters was Mme d'Aulnoy's

---

[4] See Helen Sard Hughes, "English Epistolary Fiction before *Pamela*," *Manly Anniversary Studies* (Chicago, 1923), pp. 156-169, and also Godfrey F. Singer, *The Epistolary Novel* (Philadelphia, 1933).

[5] Benjamin Boyce, *Tom Brown of Facetious Memory* (Cambridge, Mass., 1939), pp. 103-108.

[6] 7v, 1687; Vol. VIII, 1694. A discussion of the authorship that is illuminating is found in *DNB* under Robert Midgley (1655?-1723).

Ingenious and Diverting Letters of the Lady ——*'s Travels into Spain*
(1691-92), of which a reprint in 1708 called itself the "eighth edition." More
romantic, normally, were the love letters. The vogue of these for narrative
—known in France for a century—became notable in England after Sir
Roger L'Estrange translated *Five Love-Letters from a Nun to a Cavalier*
and *Seven Portuguese Letters* (1678-81). In this vein English genius can
show Mrs. Aphra Behn's *Love Letters between a Nobleman and his Sister*
(1684), which went through many editions, and Mrs. Mary Manley's *Letters*
(1696), which like others in this kind tend to make love lurid rather than
tender.[7] Here we find at times a sentimental tone and at times the cynical
mood of Restoration gentlefolk.

Crime and   Less depraved but equally bleak is the rogue literature of the time. This
Adventure appealed to readers who had no great concern with elegance or decorum
as they read. A most popular series of crime stories by a merchant named
John Reynolds, first published in 1621 as *The Triumphs of God's Revenge
against the Crying and Execrable Sin of Murther in Thirty Severall Tragicall
Histories,* went through several editions, and was augmented for Restoration
readers by ten histories showing "God's Revenge against the Abominable
Sin of Adultery" (1679). The popularity of this pious work lasted into the
nineteenth century. Lives of rogues from Elizabethan times down had been
written with the pretense of warning one against roguery, with the object
of exposing the tricks of rogues, or with the actual object of thrilling readers
by the sensationalism of crime. Crimes so notorious as to need no embroidering easily expanded from the pamphlet or chapbook state into something
approaching fiction. The career, for example, of Mary Moders or Carleton,
"the German Princess" from Canterbury, became the subject of many
narratives both before and after she was hanged in 1673.[8] The best of these,
by Francis Kirkman, was called *The Counterfeit Lady Unveiled. Being a
Full Account of the Birth, Life, Most Remarkable Actions, and Untimely
Death of that Famous Cheat Mary Carleton, Known by the Name of the
German Princess* (1673). Richard Head and Kirkman collaborated on the
most extensive of these fictitious biographies—*The English Rogue Described
in the Life of Meriton Latroon.*[9] This is neither very English nor very
original; for the authors showed as much familiarity with their printed
predecessors as they did with actual rogues. The book is earthy and indecent,
but it lacks the satiric edge, the variety, and the lightness of touch that
characterize the best picaresque fiction; and its undoubted popularity must
have been among "non-literary" readers. A more interesting phenomenon

[7] Notable also are the uses of the letter form in the nondramatic writing of George Farquhar,
especially his *Love and Business in a Collection of Occasionary Verse and Epistolary Prose*
(1702).
[8] Ernest Bernbaum, *The Mary Carleton Narratives, 1663-1673* (Cambridge, Mass., 1914).
[9] Part I (the best part, 1665) is by Head; Part II (1668) is a continuation by Kirkman, and
Parts III and IV (1671) were done in collaboration; Part V, very brief, is of undetermined authorship.—*CBEL.* Very little is known about the lives of these men, who seem to have been
employed by booksellers or publishers. Kirkman did various translations, and Head did miscellaneous writing. Details about Kirkman have been deduced from his *Unlucky Citizen* (1673)
by R. C. Bald, "Francis Kirkman, Bookseller and Author," *MP,* XLI (1943). 17-32.

is Head's *Life and Death of Mother Shipton* (1667), which creates a biography for a presumably mythical prophetess or witch supposed to have lived in Yorkshire in the sixteenth century. Head did other books about rogues, and his *Floating Island* (1673) is an ingenious combination of the imaginary voyage with an exposé of London localities such as presently were to be associated with such writing as Ned Ward's *London Spy*.[10] Fictional counterparts of actual, if "tall," tales of voyages were frequent at the time. Henry Nevile's brief *Isle of Pines* (1668) anticipates the flat objectivity of *Crusoe* and *Gulliver,* and has its own philosophical view of man's natural ability to create both a population and an organized Christian society on a desert island.

The one man of high narrative genius to win permanent fame in this period was John Bunyan.[11] This enthusiastic tinker and "mechanick" preacher made certain proletarian narrative forms into vehicles for spiritual instruction. His first important work of this sort is *Grace Abounding* (1666), an autobiography focused on his conversion and early career as preacher. It is one of a common type of "fanatic" autobiographies,[12] and its chief interest lies in the fact that it concerns the author of more significant works. We learn from it that Bunyan came "of a low and inconsiderable generation," but yet that, as he says, "it pleased God to put it into their [his parents'] hearts to put me to school, to learn me both to read and write." All this small learning, however, he neglected and almost lost: his career, he insists, was "a miracle of precious grace," and no achievement is to be credited to man's instruction or ability. He became early "the very ringleader of all the youth

10 See below, Part I, ch. IX, n. 20.

11 John Bunyan (1628-1688) was born at Elstow, Bedfordshire, the son of a tinker. He attended school briefly either at the Bedford Grammar School or at Elstow. He was early set to learn his father's trade. Shortly after his mother's death in 1644 he was for two and a half years in the Parliamentary army, but probably saw no real action. He married about 1648 or 1649, and continued his work as a tinker. The next years were those of spiritual conflict. After the death of his wife (c. 1656), Bunyan began preaching throughout the region. He married again about 1659, and in the following year was imprisoned as an unlicensed preacher. Almost the whole of the next twelve years was spent in prison, where he continually reread and studied the Bible and Foxe's *Book of Martyrs,* as well as other Puritan literature. During his imprisonment he produced books and tracts with rapidity. He continued these labors in prison or out, and until his death preached widely, especially in or about London in his later years. — *Works of that Eminent Servant of Christ, Mr. John Bunyan* (Vol. 1 [all printed], 1692; 2v, 1736-7; 6v, Edinburgh, 1769); ed. George Offor (3v, 1852); ed. H. Stebbing (4v, 1859); *Some Gospel Truths Opened* (1656); *A Few Sighs from Hell* (1658); *Profitable Meditations* ([1661?]; 1862); *The Holy City* (1665); *Grace Abounding* (1666; 1680; 1879; 1888; 1897; Everyman's Library, 1928); *The Pilgrim's Progress* (Part I, 1678; Part II, 1684); ed. R. Southey (1830); ed. George Offor (1856); ed. Charles Kingsley (1860); ed. E. Venables (1866); ed. John Brown (1887); ed. C. H. Firth (1898); ed. James B. Wharey (Oxford, 1928); *The Life and Death of Mr. Badman* (1680); ed. J. A. Froude (1900); ed. John Brown (Cambridge, 1905); ed. G. B. Harrison (1928); *The Holy War* (1682); ed. John Brown (1887 and [Cambridge], 1905); ed. M. Peacock (Oxford, 1892); *A Discourse upon the Pharisee and the Publicane* (1685; 5th ed. 1703); *A Book for Boys and Girls* (1686); ed. E. S. Buchanan (1928); *The Heavenly Footman* (1698). — G. B. Cheever, *Lectures on the Pilgrim's Progress* (1828); Robert Southey, *Life of Bunyan* (1830); J. A. Froude, *Bunyan* (1880); John Brown, *John Bunyan: his Life, Times, and Work* (1885; revised by Frank M. Harrison, 1928—the standard life); James B. Wharey, *Sources of Bunyan's Allegories* (Baltimore, 1904); John Kelman, *The Road, a Study of Pilgrim's Progress* (2v, n.d. [1912?]); G. B. Harrison, *John Bunyan: A Study in Personality* (1928); William Y. Tindall, *John Bunyan, Mechanick Preacher* (1934). — Frank M. Harrison, *A Bibliography of the Works of John Bunyan* (Bibliographical Soc., 1932).

12 See Tindall, pp. 22-41.

John Bunyan

that kept me company, in all manner of vice and ungodliness." His worst specific vices were cursing, swearing, lying, dancing, and furtive ringing of the church bell. He married a poor but God-fearing wife—"not having so much household stuff as a dish or spoon between us both, yet she had for her part, *The Plain Man's Pathway to Heaven* and *The Practice of Piety,* which her father had left her when he died." These two books, especially the former, by Arthur Dent, proved a useful dowry. "The Plain Man's Pathway to Heaven" was clearly the ideal title for more than one work by Bunyan himself. His spiritual struggles now began, and as they protracted themselves, these pages of torment and ultimate triumph are studded with significant use of similitude and allegory.

And truly I did now feel myself to sink into a gulf, as a house whose foundation is destroyed: I did liken myself in this condition unto the case of a child that was fallen into a mill-pit, who, though it could make some shift to scramble and sprawl in the water, yet, because it could find hold neither for hand nor foot, therefore at last it must die in that condition.

Even earlier he had a vision of the good Christians of Bedford "as if they were on the sunny side of some high mountain, there refreshing themselves with the pleasant beams of the sun, while I was shivering and shrinking in the cold.... Methought also between me and them I saw a wall that did compass about this mountain. Now through this wall my soul did greatly desire to pass." After much search and effort he finds a straight and narrow passage in the wall "and so was comforted with the light and heat of their sun." Such passages are prophetic of better things in later works, especially in his *Pilgrim's Progress.*[13]

Pilgrim's
Progress

This great book is one of the several masterpieces by various authors written in prison. Bunyan's obstinate vocation to preach—by God's invitation but not by that of any bishop—had caused his arrest in 1660 and his imprisonment for almost twelve years thereafter. During this first imprisonment he wrote *Grace Abounding* and lesser works. For three years, 1672-5, he was "enlarged"; but for six months in 1675 he was again imprisoned for preaching, and during this six months in the bridge-house at Bedford, he composed *Pilgrim's Progress*—again a work about "The Plain Man's Pathway to Heaven"—here an "actual" but allegorical journey from the City of Destruction to the Heavenly Gates. He begins:

As I walk'd through the wilderness of this world, I lighted on a certain place, where was a Den; and I laid me down in that place to sleep: and as I slept I dreamed a Dream. I dreamed, and behold *I saw a man cloathed with Rags, standing in a certain place, with his face from his own House, a Book in his hand, and a great burden upon his back.* I looked, and saw him open the Book, and read therein; and as he read, he wept and trembled: and not being able longer to contain, he brake out with a lamentable cry; saying, *what shall I do?*

[13] The most scholarly text of *Pilgrim's Progress* is that of James B. Wharey (Oxford, 1928).

And when the reader hears this cry, he joins his lot with that of the man in rags, and begins the perilous journey.

For Bunyan, a born story-teller, takes us with him. At sight we learn to distrust Mr. Worldly Wiseman and any other who may "look like a Gentleman"; we rejoice when Christian loses his burden; we tremble as we pass the lions in the way; we suffer with Faithful; we are terrified by Giant Despair; we thank God for Hopeful as we swim the dark river, and are perhaps a trifle complacent in assuring ourselves that the fate of Ignorance will never be ours. The episodes are all naturally and thrillingly suspensive, and Bunyan makes them real for us by adding a very pretty sense of landscape surroundings. He is also a natural allegorist, as the "mechanick" preachers of his day were wont to be. We have seen some of his earlier similitudes in *Grace Abounding*. In his prefatory jolting couplets for *Pilgrim's Progress* he tells us

> By metaphors I speak; Was not Gods Laws,
> His Gospel-Laws, in older time held forth
> By Types, Shadows and Metaphors?

His defensive tone is interesting; his insistence on "my method" is natural. No writer of his sort has ever made abstractions live more readily. Christian himself is both universal and yet a peasant from Bedfordshire; Mr. Worldly Wiseman and Talkative we have often met, and Mrs. Diffidence's bolster lecture to her giant husband seems quite wifely and natural. The allegory is consistently ingenious but is not forced in its ingenuity, as is that at times in *The Holy War*. The real appeal of the allegory depends on our sympathy for Christian and on the weighty implications of each dramatic episode and of the action as a whole.

Ingenuity is frequently displayed in presenting doctrinal points. Bunyan tolerates no loose thinking or lack of thought about salvation. Doctrine explains the tragic fate of that "brisk lad Ignorance" (from the country of Conceit!), who is a "good liver," and advises his fellow travelers, "follow the Religion of your Country, and I will follow the Religion of mine." Such counsel will never do; and the last word of Christian's vision concerns the fate of Ignorance and makes the highly disquieting comment: "I saw that there was a way to Hell, even from the Gates of Heaven." Theology apart, the story introduces much deft social satire. "Vanity Fair" is the best known example of this, but it is pervasive. "Fine-spoken" men are reproved in Flatterer and Atheist, and above all in Mr. By-ends of the wealthy town of Fair-speech with his precious family connections—among whom one might expect to find the celebrated Vicar of Bray. His wife, "Lady Faining's daughter ... is arrived at such a pitch of Breeding, that she knows how to carry it to all, even to Prince and Peasant." This couple is "always most zealous when Religion goes in his Silver Slippers." By-ends has been thought a possible caricature of an opponent of Bunyan's, Edward Fowler, the latitudinarian Bishop of Gloucester; possibly also he is another victim of the author's prejudice against the world of fashion or of time-servers. These

The Doctrine Involved

are all minor merits in a story which is a masterpiece because of its gripping and basic character. We need not agree with Christian's theological technicalities; but we must share the acute agony expressed in his first lamentable cry in his search for peace and quiet of mind—*"What shall I do?"*

Mr. Badman

Bunyan's next important narrative is an example of aesthetic backsliding. *The Life and Death of Mr. Badman Presented to the World in a Familiar Dialogue between Mr. Wiseman and Mr. Attentive* (1680) is a warning "that wickedness like a flood is like to drown our English world." So Wiseman tells his friend the story of a reprobate child who became a bad apprentice, a fraudulent business man, a painted sepulchre as a husband, and a hypocrite as a Christian. At death "His sins and his hope went with him to the Gate, but there his hope left him, because it dyed there; but his sins went in with him, to be a worm to gnaw him in his conscience for ever and ever." Mr. Badman, though remotely allied to the rogues of the picar.-esque world,[14] is only a little more interesting as a rogue than as a subject for moralizing. The tedious dialogue, patterned after the method of *The Plain Man's Pathway to Heaven,* is drawn away from Mr. Badman by incessant preaching and by parallel episodic stories—borrowed at times from contemporary works such as Samuel Clarke's *Mirrour or Looking-Glass Both for Saints and Sinners* (1646). These stories are interesting, and they are surprising in that Bunyan superstitiously accepts them as veracious. One is the story of Dorothy Mately, "Swearer, and Curser, and Lier, and Thief," who on March 23, 1660, denied stealing twopence, and exclaimed *"That the ground might swallow her up if she had them."* The ground promptly obliged, and when later Dorothy was "digged up," she had the pennies in her pocket. One gets many details of local manners—including the fashion in which Dr. Freeman ("who was more than an ordinary Doctor") attempted to exorcise a possessed ale-house keeper. But more than once the reader agrees with Mr. Attentive, who says, "These are sad storyes, tell no more of them now." These sad stories, nevertheless, are now the most interesting bits in the book.

The Holy War

By the time Bunyan wrote his work that ranks highest after *Pilgrim's Progress,* namely *The Holy War* (1682), he was somewhat conscious of literary success among the faithful; and this book is definitely more complex and subtle in thought and allegory than any of his other works. It narrates the warfare "made by Shaddai upon Diabolus, for the regaining of the Metropolis of the World, or the losing and the taking again of Mansoul." Here again, remotely after the method of a narrated morality-play,[15] we have the theme of the salvation of the soul allegorically treated. But Bunyan's Mansoul is not a person but a town—so curious, so commodious, so advantageous that "there is not its equal under the whole Heaven." The allegory tends to be political rather than personal in emphasis, and we have

---

[14] Professor G. B. Harrison in his *John Bunyan: A Study in Personality,* pp. 161-162, suggests shrewdly that possibly Badman is allied to certain citizens of Bedford.

[15] The greatest indebtedness yet traced is to Richard Bernard's *Isle of Man* (1626). See James B. Wharey, *A Study of the Sources of Bunyan's Allegories* (Baltimore, 1904).

no such sympathy for this town divided against itself as we had for the torn mind of the man Christian. The story is one of kings, princes, and great leaders; it deals in technical and "ensnaring propositions." The posie for its title-page (as for that of *Pilgrim's Progress*) was the text from Hos. 12:10, "I have used similitudes"; and the critical reader is tempted to exclaim, "Too many of them!" Apart from the allegory of the psychology of conversion, we have the allied biblical account of man's fall and redemption. At times the political chicanery detailed shadows forth the evils of Bunyan's own days when nonconformist saints were persecuted.[16] There is also, it has been urged, a consciousness of the biblical story as reshaped by the millenarian Fifth Monarchy men in Bunyan's day. Sometimes these different levels of allegory clash, but not more commonly than is usual in such works.

If in general we have here the same bag of tricks that were so effective in *Pilgrim's Progress,* it is still a good bag, and the tricks still dazzle. One *Its In-* may weary slightly of the tumults of wars, the marshaling of forces, the *genuity* "ensnaring propositions" for armistices, and the trials of war criminals; one may feel that Bunyan should have stayed in Bedfordshire; but one must at least recognize that Bunyan knows "the methods of godliness" and is satirically caustic about those who do not. His daring directness is amazing. He lets that worthy gentleman Mr. Godlyfear remark of Emanuel, "If that is not a sign of his anger, I am not aquainted with the methods of Godliness"; and at the triumph after the first conquest of Mansoul from Diabolus, Bunyan tells us, "Now after the feast was over, *Emanuel* was for entertaining the Town of *Mansoul* with some curious riddles of secrets." This entertainment consisted of a reading and exegesis of the Holy Scriptures! Such passages are mildly breath-taking, and might lead one to doubt if a mind of such simple directness could be caustic. The careers of the "tatling Diabolonian gentleman" Mr. Carnal Security and of the devil's General, Incredulity, and also of the Election-doubters (the bodyguard of Diabolus) show that we need not fear for any naïveté in Bunyan's thinking. Places of residence are neatly devised: "In *All-base*-lane, at a house next door to the Sign of the *Conscience seared with an hot iron.*" The trial scenes are numerous; but many of them—for example, that of Mr. Falsepeace, who tries to deny his name—are masterly in execution. The vivid moral psychology is still excellent: "Now there was an old man in the Town, and his name was Mr. *Good-deed.* A man that bare only the name, but had nothing of the nature of the thing." (On this favorite theme the Arminian Henry Fielding was not more deft than the old Calvinist Bunyan.) Old Good-deed is no satisfactory petitioner for mercy: "nor can a thousand of old *Good-deeds* save *Mansoul.*" If *The Holy War* is nowadays less gripping than *Pilgrim's Progress* the explanation is probably that it is less psychological than social, that theological and political controversies intrude more obviously into the later book, and also that by the accident of history the application of military symbolism to religion is now definitely

---

[16] See ch. XIV of John Brown's *John Bunyan* on " 'Mansoul' and the Bedford Corporation." See also Tindall, *John Bunyan,* pp. 149-150.

out of vogue. But *The Holy War* is as typical of its age as is its remote cousin *Paradise Lost* or its nearer kin, Bunyan's greatest book.

Christiana's Pilgrimage   The same year *The Holy War* was published saw the appearance of an unauthorized continuation of *Pilgrim's Progress* by "T. S.," one Thomas Sherman. This event encouraged Bunyan to do his own continuing, and indeed it is clear from the early conversations of Christian with Mr. Worldly Wiseman and with Charity that something had to be done for Christian's wife and family. Hence in 1684 appeared the second part of *Pilgrim's Progress,* narrating the journey of the now aged Christiana and her children. The situation is a little awkward; for hardly have the pilgrims left the wicket gate behind before Christiana and her maid Mercy are attacked by two ruffians; and as their Reliever tells them, he marveled, "being ye knew that ye were but weak Women, that you petitioned not the Lord ... for a Conductor." Such a personage is presently forthcoming. He is Mr. Great-heart, and the pilgrimage speedily becomes his story. He kills giants, scoring a tremendous victory at Doubting Castle, and he offers much good counsel. In Bunyan's mind conversion for women and children apparently lacked the tense terrors that Christian experienced, but required rather more in the way of spiritual instruction. The result is the diminished interest that one normally finds in continuations; and yet this second part is very pleasant reading. There is more homeliness in it. Mercy picks up an unsatisfactory beau in Mr. Brisk, and young Matthew picks up the gripes and undergoes a symbolic purgation. Vanity Fair is reputedly "far more moderate" than in the good old days when Faithful fell its victim, and we are continually delighted to find reminiscences of Christian extant along the way. It is more placid than the first part of the story, but it is pleasingly placid.

Bunyan had no notable successors in his own kind. He was simply an outstanding narrative genius whose truest significance is spiritual rather than literary. The travel story, the rogue biography, the allegory will all find new life presently in the works of Defoe and Swift, among others; but the fervid spiritual glow will not be there. Bunyan made some use of proletarian or Puritan patterns in narrative, but he had far less influence on proletarian fiction than did even the French romances.

The Short Story or "Novel"   It remains to speak of one genre, the relatively short narrative called in Continental fashion, until well on in the eighteenth century, the novel. This type of short story had a steady continuing influence easily neglected.[17] That it was a recognized prose type is seen from the preface to Congreve's one attempt, *Incognita* (1692), where we are told, after an account of the nature of romances:

Novels are of a more familiar nature; Come near us, and represent to us Intrigues in practice, delight us with Accidents and odd Events, but not such as are wholly unusual or unprecedented, such which not being so distant from our Belief bring

[17] A few of these works are available for convenient reading in the Everyman's Library *Shorter Novels,* Volume II: *Jacobean and Restoration* [*Ornatus and Artesia, Oroonoko, The Isle of Pines,* and *Incognita*].

also the pleasure nearer us. Romances give more of Wonder, Novels more Delight.[18]

Pamela in its day was justly called "a dilated novel"; for it, like the genre Congreve describes, deals in "familiar matter" of its day. The short novel is the true source from which the later long novel emerges. In the Elizabethan period novels came chiefly from Italy; in the seventeenth century, England imported rather from Spain. The novels inserted in *Don Quixote* gave great pleasure and Cervantes' *Novelas Exemplares* were popularly known even before James Mabbe translated six of them in 1640. From Fletcher to Crowne many dramatists had taken plots from these stories. Mabbe's version was reissued in 1654, and in 1687 Sir Roger L'Estrange translated five of these tales with five others from Solorzano and called them *The Spanish Decameron*. There were many other "novels" also in vogue. Most prose stories in chapbook form would serve as novels even if they were merely unified episodes taken from the more fantastic romances. For Michaelmas Term, 1681, *The Term Catalogues* give a typical list of such publications:

The Fair Extravagant . . . . An English Novel.
The unequal Match, or The Life of Mary of Anjou, Queen of Majorca. An Historical Novel.
The Jealous Gentleman of Estramadure: out of Cervantes Saavedra his Novels.
The Lovely Polander. A Novel.[19]

At least a half dozen other novels were listed for the same Term, all of which sold for a shilling. Peter Motteux's periodical *The Gentleman's Journal* (1692-4) contained numerous excellent stories, and in 1700 appeared *A Collection of Pleasant Novels* (2v), which included the perennially popular "Secret History of Queen Elizabeth and the Earl of Essex," "The Happy Slave" (from the French of Brémond), and, among others, Congreve's *Incognita*.

The most praised and condemned single writer of such novels was doubtless Mrs. Aphra Behn,[20] who produced something less than a dozen of *Aphra Behn*

18 *Incognita: or, Love and Duty Reconcil'd. A Novel* (1692); ed. Bonamy Dobrée (Oxford, 1928). See ed. Dobrée, p. 5.
19 *The Term Catalogues* (ed. Edward Arber, 1903), I. 461. That these works had to compete with "truth" that was as thrilling as fiction can be seen by examining the next two items listed; (1) *The Life and Death of Capt. William Bedloe, one of the Chief Discoverers of the Horrid Popish Plot,* and (2) *Memoires of the Life and Death of Sir Edmond Bury Godfrey.* The mystery of the Godfrey murder (1678) was more thrilling than any novel could be—and still is! See Arthur Bryant, *Samuel Pepys,* Vol. II.
20 Aphra Behn (1640-1689), very likely the daughter of John Amis of Wye, near Canterbury, had a certainly obscure and probably indecorous early career. The most debated episodes are, first, her experiences in Surinam as (so she said) the daughter of the deputy-governor select who died on the voyage out and, secondly, the romantic aspects of her career in Antwerp in 1666. If she was ever in Surinam, it was not as the viceroy's daughter but in some dubious rôle such as that of mistress of William Scot, son of the regicide Thomas Scot. Her efforts in Antwerp in 1666 seem to have been directed towards selling information to the English government in the hope of making a livelihood and of getting a pardon for her lover, William Scot, from whom as an employee of the Dutch government at the Hague the information came. The spies and lovers in their correspondence signed themselves respectively Astrea and Celadon. Apparently they had used these names in Surinam. From Holland she returned to England, without her Scot, in 1667. Her literary career began thereafter, so far as we know. — *The*

these short stories as well as her *Love Letters between a Nobleman and his Sister*. She was even better known as a playwright. Ladies guilty of frailty sometimes enjoy narrating the adventures of others, and much perhaps must be forgiven Mrs. Behn. Her own "Life," as written soon after her death, is a highly interesting piece of fiction based on the speciously autobiographical passages in some of her stories, which, after the manner of her day, she desired to pass off as "true." "The History of the Life and Memoirs of Mrs. Behn, Written by one of the Fair Sex" was published by Charles Gildon in her *Histories and Novels* (1696). For over two centuries this life was generally accepted as sober truth, but recently, thanks to the studies of Professor Ernest Bernbaum,[21] it has come to be regarded as colored much by fiction. It romanticizes her supposed life in Surinam, where she associated on friendly terms, she says, with Oroonoko and Imoinda, who are immortalized in her most famous novel, *Oroonoko; or, The Royal Slave* (1688). About the same time that the "Life" takes Mrs. Behn to Surinam, it also places her in London where she marries a Dutch merchant, becomes a widow, and serves in Antwerp as a secret agent during the Dutch War. It is certain that in 1666 she performed something like this last function. Her career after 1670 was English and was notable as both amatory and literary.

Only the latter aspect concerns us here. Mrs. Behn had been publishing plays for about thirteen years before she is known to have printed any prose fiction. Her *Love Letters between a Nobleman and his Sister* (1684) was apparently very popular; but such work was not so lucrative as playwriting. In 1688 her best stories were published in a volume called *Three Histories, viz. Oroonoko, The Fair Jilt, and Agnes de Castro*. Some of her earliest written tales were apparently first printed in the second collected edition of her *Histories and Novels* (1697). In general her stories are marked by lively intrigues—chiefly amorous—handled without too much tact or care, but still lively and interesting. Action is delayed by slow, vague beginnings, and interest is not heightened by her lack of warm or incisive insight into motives. She makes a great display of casual devices to authenticate material; but it is wise to view such devices as art rather than truth. *The Fair Jilt* doubtless has a relation to her adventures as a spy in Holland, but it is unwise to assume much autobiography here: the story is ill-shaped and as usual combines realistic material with pure story-book stuff. Just

---

Histories and Novels... in one volume (1696); *Three Histories* (1688); *Plays, Histories, and Novels* (6v, 1871); *Works*, ed. Montague Summers (6v, 1915); *Novels*... with an introduction by Ernest A. Baker (1913). Concerning her plays, see above, ch. vi, n. 8.

[21] Ernest Bernbaum, "Mrs. Behn's *Oroonoko*," *Anniversary Papers by Colleagues and Pupils of George Lyman Kittredge* (1913), pp. 419-433; and by the same author, "Mrs. Behn's Biography a Fiction," *PMLA*, xxviii (1913). 432-453. Professor Bernbaum perhaps argued too strongly that Mrs. Behn never saw Surinam, but he made out a very plausible case. The only person to damage that case is Harrison Gray Platt, Jr., who in *PMLA*, xlix (1934). 544-559, gave evidence coupled with clever guessing that makes it possible that she was there as Scot's mistress. Montague Summers (*The Works of Aphra Behn* [1915], i, pp. xv-lxi) and V. Sackville-West (*Aphra Behn*, 1927) add little beyond their personal opinions concerning Mrs. Behn's life.

when one decides that Mrs. Behn must have witnessed the decapitation of some Dutch gentleman, the criminal in her story (*Prince Tarquin*), after having been struck a supposedly fatal blow by the sword of the headsman, makes an escape—and a recovery! Oroonoko also survives wounds that would have been fatal to anyone but that superman. Mrs. Behn, however, does frequently achieve an admirable illusion of reality, though she clearly has no high sense of duty to truthfulness or even to plausibility, unless one compares her work with the supernatural episodes of romance.

She treats her material usually in a somewhat hard mood that gives way at times to sentimentalism. One has little sympathy for most of her persons —Miranda "the fair jilt," Ardelia (in *The Nun: or, the Perjur'd Beauty*), or any of the people in *The King of Bantam*. We are eager for the success of few of her protagonists: we simply watch the puppets. This is, however, not always the case. *Agnes de Castro*, a translation from Mlle de Brillac, does have our sympathy; and it goes out even more strongly to the princely African lovers Oroonoko and Imoinda. As a brief and new romantic story *Oroonoko* is an astonishing masterpiece. For years, as in Davenant's *Cruelty of the Spaniards in Peru* (1658), there had been works idealizing aboriginal human nature as contrasted with gold-thirsty Christians. Mrs. Behn boldly takes as her hero a beautiful and powerful Negro slave whose mind is as noble as his body—and she makes and keeps him impressive to the end. It is easy to point out flaws in this brief tragic romance, but Mrs. Behn by some accident of genius has made real for us the noble aborigine as no one else had done. It is a great achievement in a period in which idealized persons are practically always artificial. It makes one realize that while the prose fiction of the Restoration is as a whole neither important nor greatly significant, a period that produced masterpieces as diverse as those of the righteous Bunyan and the unrighteous Mrs. Behn has much to its credit.

IX

The Essay and Allied Forms

Discursive-ness of the Essay

In the years 1660-1700 the essay developed slowly and chiefly in relation to allied types of writing.[1] Before *The Spectator,* and even afterwards, the term *essay* was so little defined that it might imply verse as well as prose, though prose was its normal vehicle. It was essentially tentative and discursive; and these qualities of mind were frequently inhibited in a period concerned, on the one hand, with dynamic thinking and controversial or hortatory writing and, on the other hand, with a realistic and scientific regard for definition as the objective in thought. Neither the neo-Augustan thirst for nobility of manner nor the scientific appetite for practical, rigid plainness of enunciation furthered the easy informality that is the soul of essay writing. The discursive play of reason—*discursive,* so their dictionaries said, meant "running to and fro"—was in this sensible era either somewhat neglected or was elevated by ingenious fancy into verse. The essay, furthermore, was hardly a classical form, though in Theophrastus, Cicero, Pliny the Younger, Lucian, and in the Socratic dialogue, one had allied forms that tempted imitators, and led Restoration authors somewhat out of the tradition of the essay if it be narrowly defined.

Essay Traditions

The essay, therefore, developed chiefly in relation to such types as the "character," the dialogue, the prose epistle, the pamphlet, and the "news-mongering" periodical—the last of which in the century to follow engrossed the form. The essay traditions established earlier in the seventeenth century were sound yet lacking in singleness. Authors with a passion for definition followed in the wake of Bacon and Feltham. That explicit schoolmaster Ralph Johnson, in his *Scholar's Guide from the Accidence to the University* (1665), described the essay as "a short discourse about any virtue, vice, or other commonplace." And the sixth and last of his "rules for making it" is: "In larger and compleat Essays (such as Bacon's, Feltham's, &c.) we must labour compendiously to express the whole nature of, with all observables about our subject." The Bacon-Feltham tradition (if it is a single tradition) with its emphasis on virtues, vices, and other truisms perpetuates itself best in the more limited "character," and less eminently in such essays as derive from accumulations in the author's commonplace-book. Outside

[1] In Hugh Walker's *The English Essay and Essayists* (1928) part of ch. IV deals with Restoration authors. For the end of the century Walter Graham's *English Literary Periodicals* (1930) is valuable in its more specialized field. The best survey of the essay for this whole period is E. N. S. Thompson's *Seventeenth-Century English Essay* (Iowa City, 1926; *Univ. of Iowa Humanistic Studies,* III, iii).

its allied type, the character, this Baconian essay tradition is less influential than the work of Montaigne.

The chief disciples of the great French father of the essay in this period were Abraham Cowley [2] (1618-1667) and Sir William Temple. In the last years of his life, Cowley, then in his middle forties, and somewhat disappointed with his lack of monetary success, withdrew himself from "the tumult and business of the world," and produced, among other works, eleven essays all in the personal vein of Montaigne, whom he quotes at least twice. He captures the truly discursive method of his master—frankly personal, frequently autobiographical, quoting aptly from the ancients as well as from the moderns, and making use of anecdote, witticism, and aphoristic moralizing. Called essays "in verse and prose," they embody considerable blocks of poetry translated or original. They deal with virtues and vices—liberty, solitude, obscurity, greatness, and avarice—but frequently from a definitely personal point of view. In the most prized of his essays, *Of Myself,* as well as in *The Danger of Procrastination* (significantly called "A Letter to Mr. S. L.") he is overtly autobiographical. In this last essay he speaks with frank informality concerning his design for a retired life:

Cowley's Essays

> But there's no fooling with life, when it is once turned beyond forty. The seeking for a fortune then, is but a desperate after-game; 'tis a hundred to one, if a man fling two sixes and recover all; especially if his hand be no luckier than mine.

Cowley's prose truly marks a development away from the somewhat cumbrous splendor of earlier rhetoric towards the simpler, plainer, and more exact manner which the Royal Society, with his aid, was formulating. We seem to hear Cowley *speaking* simply and directly in a fluid, not a rigid, style. Another more elaborate sentence, dating probably 1664, begins *The Garden,* which he addressed to Evelyn in return for the dedication to himself of Evelyn's *Kalendarium Hortense:*

> I never had any other desire so strong and so like to covetousness, as that one which I have had always, that I might be master at last of a small house and large garden, with very moderate conveniences joined to them, and there dedicate the remainder of my life only to the culture of them, and study of nature. . . . And there (with no design beyond my wall) whole and entire to lie in no unactive ease, and no unglorious poverty.

Here Cowley states as his own an ambition that was almost universal among Englishmen of his day, and does it in a style that is easy and far removed from the terse staccato that Bacon had fitted to the essay. Cowley is an independent artist, sensitive enough to stylistic values so that he is a natural eclectic as well as a literary proponent of the new "scientific" ideals in expression. One can make out a case for development in Cowley by going

[2] Cowley's poetry, largely antedating 1660, was very influential after that date, especially his imitations of Pindar, which encouraged poetic strivings after "the sublime." He was also admired for his Anacreontics and for the love poems in *The Mistress* (1647). See Arthur H. Nethercot, *Abraham Cowley. The Muse's Hannibal* (Oxford, 1931).

back to his *Discourse by Way of Vision concerning the Government of Oliver Cromwell* (1661) and citing the elaborate Ciceronian parallelisms put into the mouth of "the north west principality" in the character of Cromwell. The passage appealed to David Hume, who quoted it in his *History of England;* [3] but it is less Cowley's own voice than it is his notion of an idiom proper for the angel of destruction. Cowley wrote with flexibility, frankness, and ease; and his style, personal as it is, was an admirable example for such as could escape the formal and artificial nobility of the period or the terse, aphoristic manner that also claimed admirers. Cowley's prose, like Dryden's, is almost wholly "modern" in style.

Sir William Temple

The most approved essayist of these years was doubtless Sir William Temple,[4] who, both before and after his retirement (1681) from a distinguished political career, wrote with elegance, charm, factual negligence, and intellectual insight. His writings dealt either with affairs of state or with his personal reflections on the employments and delights of the contemplative life. To the first field are devoted his longer works, such as his *Observations upon the United Provinces of the Netherlands* (1673), his *Essay upon the Advancement of Trade in Ireland* (1673), his *Memoirs of what Past in Christendom from 1672 to 1679* (1692), and his *Introduction to the History of England* (1695), and, among his shorter works, such pieces as his essays *On the Original and Nature of Government* and *Of Popular Discontents.* His personal reflections or wisdom of life are expressed in such essays as those *Upon the Gardens of Epicurus* and *Of Health and Long Life;* but all his prose is marked strongly by his personality.

[3] Hume's *History of England,* ch. LXI, in ed. of 1786 and thereafter. Cf. Cowley's *Essays, Plays and Sundry Verses,* ed. A. R. Waller (Cambridge, 1906), pp. 347-348.

[4] Sir William Temple (1628-1699) was born in London, and at the age of sixteen he entered Emmanuel College, Cambridge, where he was for a time the pupil of Ralph Cudworth. He left without taking a degree, traveled abroad, and in France (1648) met Dorothy Osborne, her father, and her brother. A courtship began, but the Osbornes as ardent royalists opposed the match. The letters of Dorothy Osborne to Temple form one of the most famous Restoration correspondences. In 1654 the two were married. After eight years in Ireland, where Temple was prominent in the Irish parliament, they returned to England, and settled at Sheen. During the years following Temple served on diplomatic missions, drafted the Triple Alliance of 1668 between England, Holland, and Sweden, and became (1668) ambassador to the Hague. He returned to England in 1670, but was again at the Hague in 1674, where he brought about the marriage of William of Orange and the Princess Mary. Thereafter he twice declined to become Secretary of State, and in 1681 he retired from public life, and before 1689 removed from Sheen to his new home Moor Park (Surrey). — *Works* (2v, 1720; 4v, 1814); *Essays,* ed. J. A. Nicklin (1911); *Early Essays and Romances,* ed. G. C. Moore Smith (1930); *Poems* [1670]; *Observations upon the ... Netherlands* (1673); ed. G. N. Clarke (Cambridge, 1932); *Essay upon ... Trade in Ireland* (Dublin, 1673); *Miscellanea: the First Part* (1680); *Miscellanea: the Second Part* (1690); *Memoirs of ... 1672 to 1679* (1692); *An Essay upon Taxes* (1693); *An Introduction to the History of England* (1695); *Letters ... to the Earl of Arlington and Sir John Trevor* (1699); *Letters* (3v, published by Jonathan Swift, 1700-1703); *Select Letters* (1701); *Miscellanea: the Third Part* (published by Jonathan Swift, 1701); *Memoirs: Part Three* [1679-81] (published by Jonathan Swift, 1709). — Abel Boyer, *Memoirs* (1714); Martha (Lady) Giffard, *The Life and Character of Sir William Temple* (1728); Thomas P. Courtenay, *Memoirs of the Life, Works, and Correspondence of Sir William Temple* (2v, 1836); *Essays on Ancient and Modern Learning and on Poetry,* ed. Joel E. Spingarn (Oxford, 1909); Albert F. Sieveking, *Sir William Temple upon the Gardens of Epicurus, with Other XVII*th *Century Garden Essays* (1908); Dorothy Osborne Temple, *The Letters of ... to Sir William Temple,* ed. Edward A. Parry (1901); in Everyman's Library [1932]; ed. G. C. Moore Smith (Oxford, 1928); Clara Marburg, *Sir William Temple* (New Haven, 1932); Homer E. Woodbridge, *Sir William Temple* (1940).

His character, thus revealed, is that of a nobly self-indulgent Epicurean, too elegantly cool to be a lively partisan in the scurrilous politics of the eighties, too skeptical to believe in the scientific advances of the Royal Society or the intellectual subtleties of controversial divines such as the Cambridge Platonists, whom he had experienced as an undergraduate. Montaigne and such interpreters of Epicurus as Gassendi, Dr. Walter Charleton, and Saint-Évremond were his masters; his delight in his own reveries and in his modest possessions was his *summum bonum*. It is of course easy to exaggerate the completeness of his retirement. He declined public office after 1681; but King William evidently came to Sheen and to Moor Park for advice, and two of Temple's longer works, his *Memoirs ...from 1672 to 1679* and his *Introduction to the History of England,* were designed, so it has been shrewdly urged,[5] to increase the popularity of the Dutch King William. During most of the last decade of Temple's life Jonathan Swift was his secretary, and Swift's poem *To Congreve* as well as his mission from Temple to the King in 1693 shows that both secretary and patron had keen interest in what went on in London. But the rôle voluntarily assumed by Temple was sincerely motivated by his maxim that "A man, in public affairs, is like one at sea; never in his own disposal, but in that of winds and tides." Fundamentally Temple distrusted his own motive power and his ability to steer a course in a filthy sea. "Does anything," he asks, "look more desirable than to be able to go just one's own pace and way?" Once when young "and in some idle company," he and his friends all told their three dearest wishes. "Mine," he confides, "were health and peace, and fair weather." Such wishes sufficiently indicate the relaxed and pleasure-loving attitude of his later life as expressed in such typical essays as *Of Health and Long Life* and *Upon the Gardens of Epicurus.* In this gardening essay his description of Moor Park (Hertfordshire),[6] where he had spent his honeymoon long ago, is a typically attractive passage and one so famous in its day that it was echoed by Alexander Pope in his *Epistle to the Earl of Burlington* and so famous that for generations it influenced the development of the English garden.

Everyone from Swift and Pope to Goldsmith and Johnson commended Temple as a stylist. He "was the first writer who gave cadence to English prose," said Johnson, who professed to have formed his own style on Temple's. Certainly Temple had great significance as the leading exponent of easy dignity and rhythm: his influence here is undoubted. But in spite of the unkind remarks Macaulay and others have made about his intellectual *His Style* quality, it seems right to believe that Temple's highest function was to be, *and His* like Rousseau or H. G. Wells, a barometer and a weather vane. He was *Ideas* for the following age an intellectual nerve-center but by no means a storm-center. Not a powerful or original thinker and not a writer scrupulously

[5] By Professor H. E. Woodbridge, *Sir William Temple,* pp. 259-261.
[6] Not the seat in Surrey, where his later years were passed, and which he named Moor Park in memory of the earlier experience. The two places are often confused by writers about Temple.

accurate about his facts when he tried to display his learning, Temple nevertheless anticipated and contradicted by turns important tendencies in the
thought of his time. In his *Original and Nature of Government* and later
in essays such as *Of Health and Long Life* and *Upon the Gardens of
Epicurus,* he glorified the state of nature and "the first and most simple
ages" long before Rousseau was to do so. He enunciated well the patriarchal
origin of society, and was an early proponent in English of the notion that
climate determines national character; that artistic achievement may depend
on accidents of climate and cultural milieu. By now, let us hope, it is clear
that the important thing about his factually superficial essay *Upon Ancient
and Modern Learning* is not that it begot first a controversy with Wotton
and Bentley and finally occasioned Swift's *Tale of a Tub,* but rather that
it was a classical denial of the idea of progress at the very moment when
that idea was in England gaining its first momentum. Temple believed in
cyclic change but not in progress, and although his historical data were not
accurately presented in proof of his position (such "proof" would have been
difficult!), the position itself is still an inevitably recurrent classic attitude
towards the problem of change. So it is with many of his ideas: they may
be superficially stated but they are ingratiatingly stated, and they are ideas
that have haunted the mind of man in many ages. Temple's undoubted intellectual appeal was not due to his logic or to his learning, but rather to
his sensitiveness to human tendency in thinking. He is most influential,
perhaps, in *The Gardens of Epicurus* and elsewhere when stating his love
of retirement, his delight in his fruits, his flowers, and his bowling green
—all of which made evident the superiority of his manner of life to that
amidst the smell and smoke of the political battle. More than one disappointed statesman was to learn that lesson from him. It has universal
appeal. To sum up, his repute lies in his style, his gifts as literary critic,[7]
and his gracious and respectable Epicureanism. He is still the most readable
of the essayists of his age.

*Religious
and Philo-
sophical
Essays*

If Temple leaned to an Epicurean philosophy of life, there were other
writers who affected other schools of thought. Their courageous and dynamic
thinking usually promotes either of two interests, religion or politics. In
form their work overflows the limits proper for an essay and becomes more
like a moral monograph or treatise in size. In the case of Sir George Mackenzie[8] (1636-1691), for example, this is true not only of such youthful
pieces as his *Religio Stoici, the Virtuoso or Stoick* (Edinburgh, 1663) and
his *Moral Gallantry* (1667), but also of his last works, *The Moral History
of Frugality* (1691) and *Reason, an Essay* (1690). It is perhaps less characteristic of the Rev. Anthony Horneck's (1641-1697) *Happy Ascetick* (1681),
but only because he breaks up his exhortations into a score of pious "exercises." John Norris of Bemerton (1657-1711), called the last of the Cambridge

---

[7] For an account of Temple's critical essays see above, ch. II.
[8] Andrew Lang, *Sir George Mackenzie* (1909); F. S. Ferguson, "A Bibliography of the
Works of Sir George Mackenzie, Lord Advocate, Founder of the Advocates Library," *Edinburgh Bibl. Soc. Trans.,* 1 (1936). 1-60.

Platonists, in his *Miscellanies* (1687) shows more diversity, presenting in conventional form brief essays *Of the Advantages of Thinking* or *Of Solitude,* and other longer essays divided into sections, a series of *Contemplations,* and essays in the form of rather long letters to friends—on, for example, *An Idea of Happiness* or *An Account of Plato's Ideas, and of Platonic Love.* Since the days of James Howell many essays had assumed letter form. Jeremy Collier, remembered for his attack on the stage, brought out (1694-1709) four volumes of *Essays upon Several Moral Subjects* concerning the usual topics, most of which are treated in dialogues of varying lengths.

More important so far as substance goes were the works—treatises rather than essays—of Joseph Glanvill [9] (1636-1680) and Thomas Burnet of the Charterhouse (1635?-1715). Glanvill, in his *Vanity of Dogmatizing* (1661), which he recast once as *Scepsis Scientifica* (1665) and again as a part of his *Essays on Several Important Subjects in Philosophy and Religion* (1676), had influence in developing the doctrine of skepticism (or the open mind) as a method in thinking. The changes in style in the forms of this work, furthermore, indicate neatly the nature of the influences (the Royal Society and moral honesty among other things) that were modernizing English prose style. His *Plus Ultra* (1668) shows his belief in progress, and his *Essay concerning Preaching* (1678) had potency in reducing pulpit oratory to a sensible plainness and clarity. In structural form Glanvill's work is not a part of the essay tradition; his attitude towards style, however, may have helped prepare the way for the ease and informality of the essay. Burnet's *Telluris Theoria Sacra* (2 volumes, 1681-9), the first volume of which was made English as *A Sacred Theory of the Earth* (1684), is similarly a treatise, not an essay; but it is glowingly written, and with the Boyle lectures of men like John Ray (1627-1705) and William Derham (1657-1735) is an important influence in leading poets and essayists to describe and praise the works of the visible creation.

Glanvill and Thomas Burnet

These men represent the religious tradition behind the essay. Politics was hardly less favored as a subject for incisive prose. Somewhat like Temple in policy and temper and yet very different from him, was Sir George Savile,[10] who became the Marquis of Halifax and one of the chief counselors

---

[9] Ferris Greenslet, *Joseph Glanvill* (1900); Moody E. Prior, "Joseph Glanvill, Witchcraft, and Seventeenth-Century Science," *MP*, xxx (1932). 167-193; Hartwig Habicht, *Joseph Glanvill* (Zurich, 1936).

[10] Sir George Savile (1633-1695), created successively Viscount (1668), Earl (1679) and Marquis of Halifax (1682), was in his time a courtier of unsurpassed intellectual power and sharpness of wit. He served on many diplomatic missions and held many high offices. His caustic tongue made him enemies at court, but that fact did not silence him. He was a most able critic of the Cabal ministers, but when restored to the royal council in 1679 he tempered his wit in the King's presence and became a notable favorite. His reputation for moderate policies dates from the hysteria over the Popish Plot (1678). The defeat of the Exclusion Bill in 1680 was largely due to Halifax, who spoke sixteen times in the debate, answering Shaftesbury. At the end of 1680 he briefly withdrew from the battle; for while he had blocked the Monmouth faction, he had no enthusiasm for the succession of the Catholic Duke of York (James II). Within six months, however, he was back at court, where the rising influence of the Duke of York and his succession to the throne in 1685 reduced Halifax's influence, and caused him to turn hopefully towards William of Orange. In 1688 Halifax was a leading peer in the effort to secure the crown jointly to William and Mary. He was much attacked by extremists in policy, and, as his health failed, withdrew from public office, especially during his last

Politics and the Essay

of state after 1672. By temperament he was a mediator, an apostle of compromise; and when Sir Roger L'Estrange's periodical *The Observator* (December 3 and 4, 1684) attacked such moderation in a discourse on *The Character and Humour of a Trimmer,* Halifax wrote in reply his celebrated *Character of a Trimmer,* which circulated for some time in manuscript copies and was printed in 1688. It embodies with dignity and insight the essential spirit of the revolution of 1688. Shrewdly he says:

> This innocent word *Trimmer* signifieth no more than this, That if Men are together in a Boat, and one part of the Company would weigh it down on one side, another would make it lean as much to the contrary; it happeneth there is a third Opinion of those, who conceive it would do as well, if the Boat went even, without endangering the Passengers; now 'tis hard to imagin by what Figure in Language, or by what Rule in Sense this cometh to be a fault, and it is much more a wonder it should be thought a Heresy.

In this spirit Halifax promoted moderate ideas as to the necessity of law in the functioning of constitution, prince, and parliament. He was a firm Protestant and a reasonable opponent of the papists. He was an ardent nationalist; he adored, with unusually elevated rhetoric, "the Goddess Truth," and in a good-natured and witty conclusion expressed the opinion that from climate to laws England is by nature in all respects a Trimmer.

Shortly after the death of Charles II Halifax wrote his *Character of King Charles II.* This is less a pamphlet than is the *Trimmer,* and it is rather a series of essays on various aspects of the late monarch's personality—his religion, his dissimulation, his amours, his conduct to his ministers, his wit, his talents, and his disposition. It is a portrait etched with acid of deceptive strength, yet tempered finally with subservient kindliness. The writing here is more aphoristic, the style more terse and clipped; the weightiness of the work, however, as in the *Trimmer,* lies in its large yet acrid worldly wisdom. On the King's talent of "finding out other Men's weak sides" and neglecting his own faults, Halifax comments:

> Men love to see themselves in the false Looking-glass of other Mens Failings. It maketh a Man think well of himself at the time, and by sending his Thoughts abroad to get Food for Laughing, they are less at leisure to see Faults at home. Men choose rather to make War in another Country, than to keep all well at home.

Such moral commonplaces are perfect essay material. Halifax's other public pamphlets include two concerning the readiness of dissenters to club with

three years. — *Miscellanies* (1700, 1704, 1717); *The Life and Letters of ... Halifax, with a new Edition of his Works,* ed. H. C. Foxcroft (2v, 1898); *Complete Works,* ed. Walter Raleigh (Oxford, 1912); *A Letter to a Dissenter ... By T. W.* (1687, 6 eds.); *The Character of a Trimmer. By the Honorable Sir W. C.* (1688); *The Anatomy of an Equivalent* (1688); *The Lady's New-Year's-Gift* (1688); ed. Bonamy Dobrée (1927); *Maxims Found amongst the Papers of the Great Almanzor* (1693); *A Character of King Charles the Second* (1750); ed. Peter Davies (1927); *Savile Correspondence* (Camden Society, 1858). — H. C. Foxcroft, *Sir George Savile, Marquis of Halifax* (2v, 1898); G. P. Gooch, *Political Thought from Bacon to Halifax* (1914); A. W. Reed, "George Savile, Marquis of Halifax," in F. J. C. Hearnshaw, *The Social and Political Ideas ... of the Augustan Age* (1928).

the Catholics in the matter of toleration, and his *Maxims of State,* which illustrates his skill in turning out *pensées.*

Not excepting even the *Trimmer* his most popular work was the series Advice to a of essays written for his daughter Elizabeth (who later became the mother Daughter of the famous Earl of Chesterfield) and published under title of *The New-Year's-Gift: or, Advice to a Daughter* (1688). Written seriously and affectionately, these advices on such topics as religion, a husband, housekeeping and family, behavior, friendships, censoriousness, vanity, pride, and diversions, introduced the young lady to a rather melancholy social system in which women must study to protect their reputations and to manage patiently and tactfully "in case a *Drunken Husband* should fall to your share." These essays contain a great deal of long-refrigerated common sense, and were highly valued for a century or more by well-meaning parents. They reached at least a fifteenth edition by 1765. Halifax in a letter to Charles Cotton concerning Cotton's popular translation (1685) of Montaigne's *Essays* called the essays "the Book in the World that I am the best entertain'd with"; but in Halifax's own writing there is little of the discursiveness or of the geniality of Montaigne; he sticks to the point, illuminates his thinking with frequent brief similes but almost never by anecdote. His strength, as Dryden pointed out in *Absalom and Achitophel,* lay in "piercing wit and pregnant thought." Of these he is master. Apart from his *New-Year's-Gift* he is a pamphleteer rather than an essayist.

Lighter in tone and effect, though still didactic in avowed purpose, is *The Theo-* the type of essay that influenced Halifax, the "character."[11] This sort of *phrastan* writing had become well established early in the century by the work of *Character* such authors as Bishop Hall, Sir Thomas Overbury, and John Earle,[12] and it continued to be popular and fundamentally unchanged throughout the century. Upon the prose character the Restoration period patterned satirical portraits in verse as a popular extension of the type. Ralph Johnson in his *Scholar's Guide* defined the prose character as "a witty and facetious description of the nature and qualities of some person, or sort of people." In method it was analytical and abstractionist rather than concrete, dramatic, or vivid. It presented the traits essential to define a type or a quality, but did not strive to make the type live. In such variations from the norm as Richard Head's wheedling *Shopkeeper* there is attention to external objectivity; and in such other deviations as Halifax's *Charles II* or Richard

[11] On the "character" one may well consult: Gwendolen Murphy, *A Bibliography of English Character-Books* (The Bibliographical Society, Oxford, 1925); Henry Morley, *Character Writings of the Seventeenth Century* (1891); E. C. Baldwin, "The Relation of the English 'Character' to its Greek Prototype," *PMLA,* xviii (1903). 412-423; G. S. Gordon, "Theophrastus and his Imitators," in *English Literature and the Classics* (Oxford, 1912); Chester N. Greenough, "The 'Character' as a Source of Information for the Historian," in *Massachusetts Hist. Soc. Proc.,* liv (1922). 224-235; reprinted in *Collected Studies* (Cambridge, Mass., 1940), pp. 123-153; Gwendolen Murphy, *A Cabinet of Characters* (Oxford, 1925); E. N. S. Thompson, "Character Books and Familiar Letters," in *The Seventeenth-Century English Essay* (Iowa City, Ia., 1926); the late Chester N. Greenough's *Bibliography of the Theophrastan Character in English,* ed. J. Milton French (Cambridge, Mass., 1947).

[12] Concerning the early, formative period of the "Character" Professor Benjamin Boyce has in press an extensive study (Cambridge, Mass.).

Flecknoe's *Worthy Nobleman* (William, Duke of Newcastle), not types but individuals are represented, and this is usually the procedure in characters in satirical verse. Religious and political characters usually become controversial in tone and purpose, but the normal prose character remained in spite of variations a witty and facetious analysis of a type, a class, or an abstract moral quality.

Flecknoe and Butler   Its best practitioners in the Restoration period were Dryden's zany Richard Flecknoe and Samuel Butler, famous as the author of *Hudibras*. Flecknoe,[13] whose work is by no means so contemptible as Dryden reported, relies on wit for success in such pieces (from his total of 119 characters) as those about *A School-Boy, A Talkative Lady,* or *An Immitable Widdow.* A Catholic priest, he is habitually caustic when writing of religious sects and is severe also on the little hypocrisies that he detects among his own co-religionists. His passion for rewriting his characters is unusual: they appeared, many of them, in at least three different forms. Flecknoe recognized that "Wit ... is no solid food of life, but an excellent sawce or seasoning" to wisdom. As compared with the learned and subtle Butler[14] his wisdom is commonplace. Butler's scope and satiric edge are hardly paralleled among the writers of characters. Possibly because he was aware of his incautious savageness on political and religious topics, Butler never published his characters, which were first printed in 1759. In politics he gives us accounts of *A Modern Politician, A Republican, A Leader of a Faction,* that are so virulent as to imply perhaps a personal animus behind them. Both in these and in his diverse sketches of religious eccentricity—*An Hypocritical Nonconformist, A Fifth-Monarchy-Man, A Ranter, A Latitudinarian,* etc., he shows the biases one might expect from the author of *Hudibras.* On literary or antiquarian types he is also mordant: his accounts of *A Small Poet, An Imitater,* or *A Modern Critic* are important evidences of common literary predilections. The style is bluntly rough, terse, and spiced with what in an earlier age might have been called ale-house metaphors.

A Degenerate Noble: or, One that is proud of his Birth, Is like a Turnep, there is nothing good of him, but that which is under-ground, or Rhubarb a contemptible Shrub, that springs from a noble Root.

[13] Of the life of Richard Flecknoe (1620?-1678?) little is known. He was very likely not Irish, as Dryden led people to believe. He was a Roman secular priest, and he traveled perhaps as widely as his *Relation of Ten Years' Travels* asserted; that is, from England to Constantinople and the Greek islands; to the Cape Verde islands, Teneriffe, Funchal, and Brazil. He achieved posthumous notoriety when in 1682 Dryden entitled his attack on Shadwell *MacFlecknoe;* before this event his reputation had not been altogether contemptible. — Apart from five plays his chief works were *Miscellania* (1653); *A Relation of Ten Years' Travels* (1654?); *The Diarium, or Journal, in Burlesque Rhime* (1656); *Enigmatical Characters* (1658; rev. 1665); *Heroick Portraits* (1660); *A Farrago of Several Pieces* (1666); *The Life of Tomaso the Wanderer* (1667); ed. George Thorn-Drury (1925); *Epigrams* (1669, 1670, 1671, 1673, each ed. with additions). — Anton Lohr, *Richard Flecknoe, Eine Literarhistorische Untersuchung* (Leipzig, 1905); Paul H. Doney, *The Life and Works of Richard Flecknoe* (unpublished Harvard diss., 1928).

[14] On Samuel Butler's career and poems see above, ch. IV, n. 2.

A Republican . . . is so much a Fool, that, like the Dog in the Fable, he loses his real Liberty, to enjoy the Shadow of it.

A Leader of a Faction . . . is like a Figure in Arithmetic, the more Ciphers he stands before, the more his Value amounts to.

In pungency and satirical force Butler's characters are unsurpassed.

The character, as Halifax's *Trimmer* shows, tended at times to become a controversial pamphlet; and the pamphlet itself, as well as the essay, was closely bound up with journalism.[15] As early as 1621 Burton's *Anatomy* *The Rise of* had dolefully proclaimed that "If any read nowadays, it is a playbook or *Journalism* a pamphlet of news," and pamphlets that either reported events or (more frequently) expressed fierce opinions about events were common throughout the century. Early newspapers were too small to devote much space to editorial comment; and before 1695 when the Licensing Act finally lapsed, such comment was limited; after 1695 it was made at the peril of the author. The most meager news-sheets, however, tended to be violently partisan.[16] Just as the *Mercurius Britannicus* (No. 1: August 29, 1643) was founded as a counter to the royalist *Mercurius Aulicus* (January, 1643), so after 1695 George Ridpath's *Flying-Post* (1695-1731) was bitterly Whig while Abel Roper's *Post-Boy* (1695-1736) was a Tory organ. More closely related to intellectual and literary interests, and hence to essay writing, were journals which, instead of featuring news, disseminated opinion or information on popular subjects. Of these Sir Roger L'Estrange's *Observator* [17] (1681-87) devised a question and answer method of controversial exposition, which, however, speedily became a dialogue between the Observator and an op-

[15] Among many books that deal in part with early journalism may be noted the following: as bibliographies, "J. B. Williams" [i.e., J. G. Muddiman], *The Times Tercentenary Handlist of English and Welsh Newspapers, Magazines, and Reviews* (1920) [arranged chronologically]; Ronald S. Crane and Fred B. Kaye, *A Census of British Newspapers and Periodicals, 1620-1800* (Chapel Hill, N. C., 1927) [arranged alphabetically]; and *CBEL*, 11. 688-739; as histories, H. R. Fox Bourne, *English Newspapers* (2v, 1887); Stanley Morison, *The English Newspaper* (Cambridge, 1932); and Laurence Hanson, *Government and the Press, 1695-1763* (Oxford, 1936).

[16] The official government organ for the dissemination of news during this whole period was founded in 1665 at Oxford, and was called for 23 numbers *The Oxford Gazette*; in February 1666 it was transferred to London and became *The London Gazette*. It appeared twice a week normally, and has had a continuous existence since its founding. Its early specialty was foreign news, and the Gazetteer (its author) was attached to the office of the Secretary of State.

[17] Sir Roger L'Estrange (1616-1704) came of a loyalist family, and throughout a stormy career he was loyalist and Tory. After the Restoration he was appointed surveyor of printing presses and licenser of the press. In the ensuing struggle for freedom of the press he was powerfully active for government control and for censorship. He was knighted by James II in 1685, and, more or less by ministerial command, was returned M.P. for Winchester. The Whig triumphs in the Revolution of 1688 spelled ruin for Sir Roger, whom the Whigs regarded as a most notorious enemy to all liberty in England. He was thereafter imprisoned three separate times, and his writing after 1688 was practically all pot-boiling translation. He was earlier connected with two or three newspapers apart from his *Observator*, and he was the author of something like three score of political pamphlets. One of the earliest of these was a retort to John Milton called *No Blinde Guides* (1660). His most popular translations, often reprinted, were: *The Visions of Quevedo* (1667), *Five Love Letters from a Nun to a Cavalier* (1678), Seneca's *Morals* (1678), Tully's *Offices* (1680), *Twenty Select Colloquies out of Erasmus* (1680), *The Fables of Aesop*, et al. (1692), Terence's *Comedies* (1694), and *The Works of Flavius Josephus* (1702). For complete details with a bibliography, see George Kitchin, *Sir Roger L'Estrange* (1913).

posing straw-man—a Whig, or a Courantier, or a Trimmer. Less political and more intellectual was *The Athenian Gazette: or Casuistical Mercury* (1691-97), a project of the eccentric bookseller John Dunton,[18] whose staff for his periodical included Richard Sault, John Norris, Samuel Wesley (father of the founder of Methodism), and others. These men composed an "Athenian Society" and undertook to answer in the *Mercury* all questions on all topics. Most commonly questions related to matrimony or love, to theology or to ethical problems, to popular science or pseudo-science. Occasionally literary criticism had its day, as when the question appeared (January 16, 1692) "Whether Milton and Waller were not the best English poets? and which the better of the two?" Answers to a dozen or more questions in the space that a *Spectator* paper would fill (a folio half-sheet printed in two columns) produced paragraphs rather than essays; but the tendency towards essay writing is obvious. *The Athenian Mercury* was very popular in literary circles, and its editorial "Society" was praised in verses written by Nahum Tate (the poet laureate), Peter Motteux, Defoe, and Swift.

"Learned"   None of the periodicals so far named made a habit of reviewing con-
Journals   temporary belles-lettres. There had been in France and the Low Countries various periodicals that reviewed learned works, chiefly in the fields of theology, archaeology, or classical literature, and these began to be imitated in England. The Huguenot Jean de la Crose tried it in his *History of Learning* (1691-4) and his *Memoirs for the Ingenious* (1693), and at the end of the century was begun the more durable *History of the Works of the Learned* (1699-1712). There were several such "learned" journals. Apart from them stands the work of the Frenchman Peter Motteux (1663-1718) in a periodical that has obvious pioneering aspects in the field of belles-lettres, *The Gentleman's Journal* (1692-94). This is a periodical of miscellaneous contents, more like a modern magazine than any other periodical for years to come. It contained news, short stories, fables, poems, songs (with music), many essays, and comments on contemporary publications in the field of belles-lettres. Once or twice a whole number was the product of Motteux's sole pen, but generally contributors were numerous. Among them are named Congreve, Prior, Sedley, Tate, Tom Brown, Durfey, Southerne, Dennis, Crowne, Gildon, Oldmixon, and Tutchin. Motteux was that rare thing for his day, a kindly, commending critic; but either personal instability or lack of support made three volumes the extent of his *Journal's* life. Motteux is also known as the author of plays and operas and as the translator of Rabelais and Cervantes.[19]

---

[18] Dunton left an amusing life of himself, *The Life and Errors of John Dunton, late Citizen of London* (1705); ed. John Nichols (1818). In *Collected Studies* (Cambridge, Mass., 1940) of C. N. Greenough there are two essays on "John Dunton's ·*Letters from New England*" and Dunton's borrowings in his writing. See also Harrison R. Steeves, "The Athenian Virtuosi and the Athenian Society," *MLR*, VII (1912). 358-371.

[19] Robert N. Cunningham has done a biographical and critical study called *Peter Anthony Motteux* (Oxford, 1933), and also "A Bibliography of the Writings of Peter Anthony Motteux," *Proc. of the Oxford Bibl. Soc.*, III (1933). 317-337.

A more specialized periodical which had influence on later essay writing *Ned Ward* was Ned Ward's *London Spy* (1698-1700).[20] This was less an imitation of the popular *Turkish Spy* (1687, 1694) than it was a product of Ward's natural love for describing the low life of his day. In 18 monthly numbers of sixteen folio pages each the "Spy" and a friend visit such tourist spots as the tombs of Westminster Abbey, the law courts in Westminster Hall, St. James's Park, the zoo in the Tower as well as low-lived taverns, bagnios, and prisons of the city. For some years·Ward himself kept a public-house in Moorfields, and it was in such locales that his genius was most at home. His method is narrative interspersed with songs, characters, and other devices for variety. The language is frequently so much the slang of its day as to be somewhat difficult 250 years after the fact; but his diction normally is pungent and apt as are his vigorous but vulgar similes. The material often is shamelessly nasty and usually vividly detailed. In style the matter seems subjected to a definitely fluid and fluttering mind; and so the sentences float wittily onward in rather formless or casual fashion. As social documents the narratives are invaluable. The same comment may serve for Ward's satirical voyage pamphlets. His *Trip to Jamaica* (1698) gives a vivid picture of a transatlantic voyage in his day, and a most uncomplimentary account of the island itself. The chief pleasures of the voyage were lucrative backgammon and harmony made "in Lyricking over some *Antiquated Sonnets* and for varieties sake now and then a *Psalm*." In Jamaica he had difficulty with tropical dishes:

They make a rare *Soop* they call *Pepper-Pot;* its an excellent Breakfast for a *Salamander,* or a good preparative for a *Mountebanks Agent,* who Eats Fire one day, that he may get better Victuals the next. Three Spoonfuls so Inflam'd my Mouth, that had I devour'd a Peck of *Horse-Radish,* and Drank after it a Gallon of *Brandy* and *Gunpowder,* (*Dives* like) I could not have been more importunate for a Drop of Water to cool my Tongue.

His *Trip to New England* (1699) begins with the assertion that "Bishops, Bailiffs, and Bastards, were the three Terrible Persecutions which chiefly drove our unhappy Brethren to seek their Fortunes in our Forreign Colonies." Naturally he is caustic about the Boston blue laws—especially those against kissing; but he finds "one very wholesome Law"—that of punishing a scold by making her stand for a fixed period at her own door, gagged!

[20] Edward ("Ned") Ward (1667-1731), definitely a journalistic genius, wrote numerous pieces in Hudibrastic verse and much humorous prose. After his visits to America he settled in London and kept a tavern, to which men of High Church political sympathies were particularly welcomed. For the anti-Whig tendencies of his *Hudibras Redivivus* in 1705 he was condemned twice to stand in the pillory. He offended Alexander Pope in *The Poetical Entertainer* (1712-13), was put in *The Dunciad,* and retaliated in *Durgen* (1729) and *Apollo's Maggot in his Cups* (1729). His fame rested on *The London Spy.* — A list of his works may be found in CBEL, II, 596-599. *The London Spy* has been reprinted for the Casanova Society (1924) and has been edited by Arthur L. Hayward [1927]. *Five Travel Scripts Commonly Attributed to Edward Ward* have been reproduced by the Facsimile Text Society (1933) with a bibliographical note by Howard W. Troyer. Professor Troyer is the author of an excellent biographical and bibliographical study, *Ned Ward of Grubstreet* (Cambridge, Mass., 1946). See also Claude E. Jones, "A Short-title Checklist of Works Attributed to Edward Ward," *N&Q,* cxc (1946). 135-139.

Ward also seems to have had a hand in two related periodicals called *The Weekly Comedy as it is dayly acted at most Coffee Houses* (1699) and *The Humours of a Coffee-House, a Comedy* (1707-8), which are among the notable predecessors of *The Tatler*. Much of Ward's prose shows interests parallel but inferior to those of Richard Steele's work. His many verses—chiefly Hudibrastic—seem usually to lack the edged life of his prose.

Tom Brown   A somewhat similar writer, though one of more varied gifts, was Tom Brown,[21] whose prose illustrates most of the types popular in the period. His most remunerative work was probably translation; for through the years he was concerned, as collaborator at least, in translations of Mme D'Aulnoy, Saint-Évremond, LeClerc, Fontenelle, Scarron, Cicero, and Lucian. Early in his career he entered the lists against Dryden with three witty, satirical pamphlets in dialogue form: *The Reasons of Mr. Bays Changing his Religion* (1688), *The Late Converts Exposed* (1690), *The Reasons of Mr. Joseph Hains the Player's Conversion & Reconversion* (1690). These placed Brown at once high among the true blue Protestant wits approved by King William's court, and presently, after some more dialogues, some political poems, and a group of letters from the dead to the living, he attempted at the moment of the popularity of Dunton's *Athenian Mercury* a rival periodical, *The London Mercury* (32 numbers, 1692), which much annoyed Dunton. About the same time he made at least a small contribution to his friend Motteux's *Gentleman's Journal,* and had great success with his translation of Mme D'Aulnoy's letters, which he called *Memoirs of the Court of Spain* (1692). In 1700 his *Amusements Serious and Comical* were obviously in the tradition of *The London Spy,* though Brown, while by no means completely decent, is less crude than Ward. His *Laconics: or, New Maxims of State and Conversation* (1701) remind one of Halifax's *Maxims;* but these *New Maxims* deviate from aphoristic *pensées* in that they frequently illustrate a central point by facetious anecdote. From the Lucianic device of dialogues between famous dead celebrities Brown and some friends evolved, with an eye on recent French models, a considerable series of *Letters from the Dead to the Living* (1702-3; 1707). Neither so witty nor so intellectual as their greater predecessors, these letters are entertainingly scurrilous and topical. The deceased correspondents, writing from the lower regions, are less concerned with "the present state of the

---

[21] Thomas Brown (1663-1704), was born in Newport (Salop.), and was educated in the Grammar School there and in Christ Church, Oxford (1678-84), from which he was graduated B.A. in 1684. Probably while at Christ Church he composed out of disrespect to the famous Dean, Dr. Fell, his one "surviving" poem—an imitation of Martial, I. 32:

> I do not love you Dr. *Fell,*
> But why I cannot tell;
> But this I know full well,
> I do not love you, Dr. *Fell.*

For at least two or three years Brown taught school near London, and by 1688 he was established in the metropolis as a Grub-street Tory pamphleteer, which function was to occupy the rest of his grimy life. He was to suffer arrests for his scurrilities, and was to know debt as the driving force behind his pen. Much of his prose falls into letter form, dialogue, or allegorical fable. He campaigned against the "Pindarick way of preaching"—against an ornate or metaphorical pulpit style. An excellent account of Brown is given in Benjamin Boyce's *Tom Brown of Facetious Memory* (Cambridge, Mass., 1939), which includes a list of his works.

Plutonian kingdom" than they are with scandalous revelations which now they are able to make concerning the living. The device is made personal, topical, journalistic, and blithely shameless. In this journalistic tendency Brown had been somewhat anticipated by the *Dialogues of the Dead Relating to the Present Controversy concerning the Epistles of Phalaris* (1699) by William King of Christ Church—though King avoided the nastiness that Brown evidently loved. Apart from all this variety of journalistic prose Brown produced much negligible verse. It is dutiful to recall that *The Adventures of Lindamira* (1702) is perhaps the first real epistolary novel in English, and though possibly not altogether Brown's work,[22] is a work creditable to his eager pioneering spirit.

Most of the writers here surveyed tended to cultivate wit, ease, and plain- *Prose Style* ness—ideals that may suit a leisurely or a workaday world. The styles used range from the poised and measured elegance of Sir William Temple to the pert and nasty pungency of Ward and Brown. Among the scientists the ideals of exactness and functional plainness were cultivated with a persuasiveness that influenced literary circles also; but exactness outside of scientific circles was less sought than an elegant and conversational case. The style of Dryden's *Essay of Dramatic Poesie* illustrates this ease at its best. In this dialogue gentlemen and noblemen converse on dignified topics; in the dialogues and letters of Brown we may still be listening to gentlemen, but we hear them only in their tavern hours talking about tavern subjects. In the sermons of Archbishop Tillotson (whose style many, following Dryden's lead, strangely overpraised) and in the work of the philosopher Locke ideals of plainness were coupled with distinguished ability to marshal materials in orderly and effective fashion. By practically all of these writers the richness of imagery and the stately, somewhat cumbrous sentence structure of the early century had been discarded. They achieved familiarity and naturalness, but tended to lose individuality and subtlety. At worst their ease is that of negligent vulgarity; commonly it is that of casual and amiable informality. They lack finish and elegance in their commonplace "middle" style, to which presently Joseph Addison will add distinction by means of polish.

[22] The title-page reads: *The Adventures of Lindamira, a Lady of Quality. Written with her own Hand to her Friend in the Country; in Four Parts. Revised and Corrected by T. Brown.* These words have led careful students to doubt Brown's entire authorship, but a natural interpretation would be that the statements represent a typical attempt to authenticate the letters for an age that loved only "true stories." Internal evidence may cast doubt on Brown's authorship; but if one recalls that years later Richardson pretended in print to be only "the publisher" of Clarissa's letters, and that officially Rousseau was "editeur" of his *Nouvelle Héloïse*, the evidence of Brown's title-page against his authorship is weak.

BOOK III

The Restoration and Eighteenth Century (1660-1789)

PART II

Classicism and Journalism

Guide to reference marks

Throughout the text of this book, a point • set beside a page number indicates that references to new critical material will be found under an identical paragraph/page number (set in **boldface**) in the BIBLIOGRAPHICAL SUPPLEMENT.

In the Index, a number preceded by an S indicates a paragraph/page number in the BIBLIOGRAPHICAL SUPPLEMENT.

I

Eighteenth-Century Quality

Few centuries have with more facility been reduced to a formula than the *Labels* eighteenth; [1] and yet it has been questioned whether the century began *for the* "spiritually" with the days of John Locke and the glorious revolution of *Century* 1688 or whether it began with the accession of Queen Anne in 1702: it may also be questioned whether the century properly ended with the dawn of the French Revolution in 1789 or with the publication of the *Lyrical Ballads* in 1798. One can seldom date with exactitude the important turnings of history; but certainly to divide the Restoration period competely from the eighteenth century by stressing the numerical accident of 1700 is quite without logic. Few centuries, to be sure, have demonstrated more unity of

[1] In addition to the works cited in ch. 1 on the Restoration period, many of which are valuable also for later periods, the following titles are more specifically applicable to the first half of the eighteenth century. — For general or somewhat specialized histories of the literature of the time see Thomas S. Perry, *English Literature in the Eighteenth Century* (1883); Sir Edmund Gosse, *A History of Eighteenth Century Literature* (1889); Austin Dobson, *Eighteenth Century Vignettes* (Three Series, 1892-96: Dobson also published other volumes of delightful and valuable essays); John Dennis, *The Age of Pope* (1894); William Minto, *The Literature of the Georgian Era* (Edinburgh, 1894); Oliver Elton, *The Augustan Ages* (Edinburgh, 1899); David H. Stevens, *Party Politics and English Journalism, 1702-42* (Chicago, 1916); Oliver Elton, *A Survey of English Literature 1730-1780* (2v, 1928); Ray W. Frantz, *The English Traveller and the Movement of Ideas, 1660-1732* (Lincoln, Neb., 1934); F. C. Green, *Minuet: A Critical Survey of French and English Literary Ideas in the Eighteenth Century* (1935); Hoxie N. Fairchild, *Religious Trends in English Poetry, 1700-1780* (2v, 1939-42); Marjorie Plant, *The English Book Trade* (1939); Francis Gallaway, *Rule, Reason, and Revolt in English Classicism* (1940). — For political history see William E. H. Lecky, *A History of England in the Eighteenth Century* (8v, 1878-90; 7v, 1916-17); I. S. Leadam, *The History of England from the Accession of Anne to the Death of George II (1702-60)* (1909, 1921); *The Cambridge Modern History* (Vol. VI, by various authors, Cambridge, 1909); Charles Bechdolt Realey, *The Early Opposition to Sir Robert Walpole, 1720-27* (Lawrence, Kan., 1931); Keith G. Feiling, *A History of the Tory Party, 1640-1714* (Oxford, 1924); Keith G. Feiling, *The Second Tory Party (1714-1832)* (1938); George M. Trevelyan, *England under Queen Anne* (3v, 1930-34); Laurence Hanson, *Government and the Press, 1695-1763* (Oxford, 1936); William T. Laprade, *Public Opinion and Politics in Eighteenth Century England to the Fall of Walpole* (1936); Winston Spencer Churchill, *Marlborough, his Life and Times* (4v, 1933-38); Basil Williams, *The Whig Supremacy, 1714-1760* (Oxford, 1939); Basil Williams, *Carteret and Newcastle* (Cambridge, 1943); and William T. Morgan, *A Bibliography of British History, 1700-1715* (5v, Bloomington, Ind., 1935-42). — For ecclesiastical history see Charles J. Abbey, *The English Church and its Bishops, 1700-1800* (2v, 1887); John H. Overton and Frederic Relton, *The English Church, 1714-1800* (1906); N. Sykes, *Church and State in England in the Eighteenth Century* (1930). — For the intellectual background of the period see Sir Leslie Stephen, *History of English Thought in the Eighteenth Century* (2v, 1876); Carson S. Duncan, *The New Science and English Literature in the Classical Period* (Menasha, Wis., 1913); Fossey J. C. Hearnshaw (ed.), *The Social and Political Ideas of Some English Thinkers of the Augustan Age* (by various authors, 1928); Arthur O. Lovejoy, "The Parallel of Deism and Classicism," *MP*, XXIX (1932). 281-299; Preserved Smith, *A History of Modern Culture*, Vol. II (1934); Arthur O. Lovejoy, *The Great Chain of Being* (Cambridge, Mass., 1936); Richard F. Jones, *Ancients and Moderns: A Study of the Background of the Battle of the Books* (St. Louis, 1936); Basil Willey, *The Eighteenth Century Background* (1940). — For social life see Thomas Wright, *England under the House of Hanover* (2v, 1848); Thomas Wright, *Carica-*

character than, superficially considered, the eighteenth seems to have possessed. To the facile-minded it is composed merely of neo-classicism and a romantic revolt against that constricting tradition. The more careful historian, forgetting verbal labels, sees in it a unique fusion of ingenuity with traditionalism, of decorum with realism, of Stoic coolness with sentimental effusion, of simplicity with rococo ornamentation, and of aristocratic pomp with the manner of a "free" and hireling press. It preserves the Restoration love of rational simplification in life, thought, and art; it endorses the Restoration confidence in common sense as contrasted with logic-chopping; it trusts empirical thinking rather than the "high priori" road to metaphysical truth; and it sustains Restoration skepticism so far as the application of finite reason to problems of the infinite is concerned. The ideals of the later seventeenth century continue into the eighteenth.

Benevolism:
1. Collier

To anyone obsessed with the notion that all Restoration gentlemen were rakes at heart and libertines in conduct this last statement may be surprising; for the gentlemen of the early eighteenth century (Isaac Bickerstaff, for example, in his *Tatler*) looked upon their Restoration predecessors with self-respecting horror. Yet the Dorimants and Mirabels of comedy were less typical of their time than were the noble Clarendon, the industrious and life-loving Pepys, or the public-spirited Evelyn. Not all courtiers were rakes, nor did all the Puritans drop dead upon the coronation of Charles II. During the seventeenth century, as we have seen, there was a shift from the epic and Roman conception of "heroic virtue" as indispensable to the true gentleman, from ideals of composure, of *nil admirari,* and of Stoic restraint, to the ideal of the gentleman as a benevolent and Christian citizen of the world.[2] By 1700, certainly, the favored concept of the gentleman made him

---

ture History of the Georges [1868]; John Ashton, *Social Life in the Reign of Queen Anne* (2v, 1882; 1925); Henry B. Wheatley, *London Past and Present* (3v, 1891); H. D. Traill and J. S. Mann, *Social England* (6v, 1894-7; esp. Vol. IV [1663-1714] and Vol. V [1714-1815]); Sir Walter Besant, *London in the Eighteenth Century* (1903); William E. Mead, *The Grand Tour in the Eighteenth Century* (Boston, 1914); Myra Reynolds, *The Learned Lady in England, 1650-1760* (Boston, 1920); Edwin Beresford Chancellor, *The Eighteenth Century in London* (1920); Mary Dorothy George, *English Social Life in the Eighteenth Century* (1923) and *London Life in the XVIIIth Century* (1926); Dorothy Marshall, *The English Poor in the Eighteenth Century* (1926); A. S. Turberville, *English Men and Manners in the Eighteenth Century* (Oxford, 1926); R. B. Mowat, *England in the Eighteenth Century* (1932); Robert J. Allen, *Clubs of Augustan London* (Cambridge, Mass., 1933); John E. Mason, *Gentlefolk in the Making: Studies in the History of English Courtesy Literature from 1531 to 1774* (Philadelphia, 1934); Rosamond Bayne-Powell *English Country Life in the Eighteenth Century* (1935); Rosamond Bayne-Powell, *Eighteenth-Century London Life* (1937). — On the fine arts in this period see Sir Reginald Blomfield, *The Formal Garden in England* (1892); Sir Reginald Blomfield, *A History of Renaissance Architecture in England, 1500-1800* (2v, 1897); C. H. Collins Baker, *Lely and the Stuart Portrait Painters* (2v, 1913); Col. Maurice S. Grant, *Old Landscape Painters, Sixteenth to Nineteenth Centuries* (2v, 1925); William T. Whitley, *Artists and their Friends in England, 1700-1799* (2v, 1928); Albert R. Powys, *The English House* (1929); C. H. Collins Baker and Montague R. James, *British Painting* (1933); C. Reginald Grundy, *English Art in the Eighteenth Century* (1928); Beverley Sprague Allen, *Tides in English Taste, 1619-1800* (2v, Cambridge, Mass., 1937); Robert J. Allen, *Life in Eighteenth Century England* (Illustrative Set Number Four, The Boston Museum of Fine Arts, Boston, Mass., 1941).

[2] See the admirable studies of W. L. Ustick, "Changing Ideals of Aristocratic Character and Conduct in Seventeenth-Century England," *MP*, XXX (1932). 147-166; R. S. Crane, "Suggestions toward a Genealogy of the 'Man of Feeling,'" *ELH*, I (1934). 205-230; and W. E.

disinterestedly compassionate and moral, and useful rather than merely ornamental. In 1694 Jeremy Collier in a dialogue (*Of General Kindness*) between a benevolist and a disciple of Hobbes argues comprehensively in favor of "universal benevolence." He says:

My first Argument then shall be drawn from Community of Nature. We are all cast in the same *Mould,* allied in our Passions, and in our Faculties: We have the same Desires to satisfy, and generally the same Pleasure in satisfying of them. All Mankind is as it were one great *Being,* divided into several Parts; every Part having the same Properties and Affections with another. Now as we can't chuse but desire Accommodations for our own Support and Pleasure; so if we leave Nature to her Original Bias, if we hearken to the undepraved Suggestions of our Minds, we shall wish the same Conveniences to others.[3]

Along with Collier we find curiously different proponents of benevolism or "good nature." Among these the most influential was the third Earl of Shaftesbury[4] whose *Characteristicks* (1711) was widely read, much approved, and much attacked. Like the theodicies of his day Shaftesbury's work expounded the perfection of the universe, and particularly the naturalness of virtue in man. He believed it

2. Shaftesbury

impossible to conceive that a rational creature coming first to be tried by rational objects, and receiving into his mind the images or representations of justice, generosity, gratitude, or other virtue, should have no liking of these or dislike of their contraries. . . . Sense of right and wrong therefore being as natural to us as natural affection itself, and being a first principle in our constitution and make, there is no speculative opinion, persuasion, or belief, which is capable immediately or directly to exclude or destroy it.

His lordship thus concluded man to be endowed with a "Moral Sentiment" that instinctively instructed one in matters of right and wrong. The development of this faint non-rational monitor is the chief duty of man; and to this elegant peer perfect virtue is the result of an acquired perfect taste in morals. The relaxed and discursive suavity of Shaftesbury's style won

Houghton, "The English Virtuoso in the Seventeenth Century," *JHI,* iii (1942). 51-73; 190-219.

[3] *Essays upon Several Moral Subjects* (5ed., 1703), pp. 151-152. It is worth noting that here universal benevolence (sometimes regarded as a "romantic" notion) is based on the idea of the uniformity of mankind, commonly thought a "classical" concept. The classical-romantic dichotomy here, as frequently, is not merely useless but confusing.

[4] Anthony Ashley Cooper (1671-1713), third Earl of Shaftesbury, was the grandson of the first Earl, Dryden's Achitophel. The third Earl's education was supervised by his grandfather's protégé, John Locke, whose philosophy the third Earl disliked. He studied at Winchester and traveled on the Continent. For three years (1695-8) he sat in the House of Commons, and succeeded to the title in 1699. Bad health compelled him to withdraw from public life, and ultimately (1711) to retire to Italy. He died at Naples in 1713. — *Characteristicks of Men, Manners, Opinions, Times* (3v, 1711); ed. John M. Robertson (2v, 1900); *Life, Unpublished Letters, and Philosophical Regimen,* ed. Benj. Rand (1900); *Second Characters,* ed. Benj. Rand (Cambridge, 1914). — Thomas Fowler, *Shaftesbury* (1881); Cecil A. Moore, "Shaftesbury and the Ethical Poets in England, 1700-1760," *PMLA,* xxxi (1916). 264-325; W. E. Alderman, "Shaftesbury and the Doctrine of Moral Sense in the Eighteenth Century," *PMLA,* xlvi (1931). 1087-1094; and "Shaftesbury and the Doctrine of Optimism," *Trans. Wisconsin Acad.,* xxviii (1933). 297-305.

him friends and annoyed his enemies. In attacking the idealism of his lordship, Bernard Mandeville used in his *Fable of the Bees* (1714) a blunt, pungent, and earthy idiom.

3. Steele   Shaftesbury as a deist preached the natural beauty of virtue and benevolence. Richard Steele in his first work, *The Christian Hero* (1701), showed the superiority of Christian benevolence over Stoic arrogance of virtue. He formulates an answer to his own inquiry, "Why is it that the Heathen struts, and the Christian sneaks in our Imagination?" His conclusion, announced in his subtitle, is "No principles but those of religion [are] sufficient to make a Great Man." "Thus," he remarks, "are we fram'd for mutual Kindness, good Will and Service, and therefore our Blessed Saviour has been pleased to give us ... the Command of Loving one another." He thinks "the two great Springs of Human Actions are Fame and Conscience" (self-approbation?), and observes that Christianity, unlike Stoicism, does not require "an utter Extirpation, but the Direction only of our Passions." Under the Christian dispensation the passions are serviceable: love of fame stimulates us to great actions and conscience directs our acts to be useful to God and Man—all with the hope (and hope is a passion) of ultimate reward in heaven. Many another dogmatist in benevolence might be cited; but clearly Collier the non-juror, Shaftesbury the deist, and Steele the latitudinarian Captain of the Tower Guard approach the problem differently, yet all with strong emphasis on the emotional rather than the rational aspects of consciousness.

Practical   These are not matters merely speculative in the early days of the century.
Benevolence Both piety and morality were encouraged through practical, organized effort. Two important religious organizations, the Society for the Propagation of Christian Knowledge, founded in 1699, and the Society for the Propagation of the Gospel in Foreign Parts were in a flourishing state; equally significant at the time was the Society for the Reformation of Manners, founded shortly after the revolution of 1688 and patronized by Archbishop Tenison and other important clergymen as well as by the King and Queen. The reformation of manners in these hands was clearly on a neo-puritan basis, and the Society specialized, through a complex and far-flung organization, in punishing those guilty of lewdness, swearing, and profanation of the Lord's Day. It published pamphlets and books calculated to promote piety, and was behind attempts to purify the theatre as well as literature itself. One suspects, however, that whereas the sublime trait of benevolence was most commonly predicated of the upper classes, the need of reforming manners was viewed in relation to the lower ranks.[5]

If feeling, benevolism, or sentiment is so operative in the thought and good works of this era, what becomes of the notion that it was essentially

---

[5] See *An Account of the Societies for the Reformation of Manners* (1699); White Kennett, *A Complete History of England*, III (1706). 642-645; and John Strype, *Stowe's Survey of London* (1720), Book V, ch. III. A most important aspect of the social history of the century is the frequent founding of benevolent, charitable societies or institutions. See the careers of Thomas Coram, General James E. Oglethorpe, Henry Fielding, Sir John Fielding, Jonas Hanway, John Howard—and many others.

an Age of Reason? Man still, it must be avowed, finds himself described *Reason and* as *animal rationale:* it is still reason that differentiates him from the brutes.[6] *Common* Reason, furthermore, is uniform in all men who are uncorrupted by bad *Sense* education, false religion, or faulty social institutions; for "we are all cast in the same mould." Uniformity encourages individualism in that, being the rational equal of his fellowmen, the individual may trust his own powers —the light of reason should shine undiffracted within him. On the other hand, in case of doubt, there is appeal to the common sense *(consensus gentium)* of all men similarly endowed; one's ideas to be sound must accord with such common sense. To prefer one's "private" sense to common sense is irrational enthusiasm. To think in universal rather than parochial terms is an obvious duty; hence our rationalist may be a citizen of the world, a cosmopolitan. To prefer the Golden Age, untarnished by rational complexity or errors, over the corrupted present is also obvious good sense; hence the illuminated rationalist is frequently a primitivist, or at least regards the history of man since the patriarchal ages as a tragic record of rational defeat. Pierre Bayle in his *Dictionary* enjoyed repeating a sixteenth-century remark to the effect that the title of Orosius's history, *De miseria humana,* "was a very proper title, which well becomes history in general."

To these dogmas concerning reason, and to such corollaries as deism and neo-classicism, the uniformity of Nature led men. But the rationalism of the century has an inductive, a scientific and even journalistic, aspect that demands attention. In the period when Spinoza was exemplifying beautiful syllogistic argument, a great distrust of logic had developed. Divine truth, men said, should of its nature be clear and should need no intricate exegesis. This attitude is seen in one of the more extreme panegyrics to reason in the period, the fourth voyage of *Gulliver's Travels.* Here the Houyhnhnms represent "perfection of nature" (i.e., of reason), and, we are told,

their grand Maxim is, to cultivate *Reason,* and to be wholly governed by it. Neither is *Reason* among them a Point problematical as with us, where Men can argue with Plausibility on both Sides of a Question; but strikes you with immediate Conviction; as it needs must do where it is not mingled, obscured, or discoloured by Passion and Interest.

Obviously it is only a step from such a conception of reason to something very like common sense. Swift, though he praises reason, prefers common sense to intricate reasonings, and like the benevolists really exalts the non-reasoning aspects of the mind over logic. Ingenious and novel *imaginings* the author of *Gulliver,* like many others of his day, would be loath to decry; in his suspicion of ingenious and novel *reasonings* or opinions he is typical of his time.

The fact is that Reason, Nature, Truth, are ultimate norms not easily *"Nature"* capable of definition, especially if one begins and ends with the dogma of *as Norm*

[6] The rationalism of the time has been well analyzed and related to literary tradition by A. O. Lovejoy, "The Parallel of Deism and Classicism," *MP,* xxix (1932). 281-299.

uniformity. A disputatious, and hence ungenteel, love of logic had little affinity with these undefined ultimates. Men agreed with Aristotle that art was to imitate Nature; and obviously such imitation was not to be photographic or realistic, but was to attend to essential meanings or principles. When the young Cicero applied to the Delphic Oracle for counsel in his ambition to become a great orator, he heard the portentous injunction: "Follow Nature!" These two words were doubtless the categorical imperative of the neo-classical period. "Nature" was the complex system or set of principles divinely ordained and manifested in the Creation. To this system man should conform; of this system the moralist and the poet were the interpreters; by this system the critical intelligence could evaluate either life or letters. So Pope enthusiastically voiced the view of his day when he affirmed that

> Unerring nature, still divinely bright,
> One clear, unchanged, and universal light,
> Life, force, and beauty, must to all impart,
> At once the source, and end, and test of art.

*George
Berkeley*

To such views led the widely diffused principles of uniformity and universality, the sense of allegiance to the whole system. Such untechnical thinking on the part of literary men was balanced by more elaborate works of technical philosophers. John Locke had stimulated "practical" ideas about government and society, but he had also promoted speculations in the field of the theory of knowledge—as to *how* we know and *what* we know. This type of theorizing was continued by the greatest thinker of the first third of the century, George Berkeley [7] (1685-1753), who in his *Treatise concerning the Principles of Human Knowledge* (1710) expounded a theory of immaterialism based on the proposition *esse est percipi*: to be is to be perceived. Material objects do not exist except in our minds, or if they do we can know them only in our minds. Such limitation of our knowledge, which Berkeley defended adroitly in his *Three Dialogues between Hylas and Philonous* (1713), inadvertently opened the way to David Hume's cogent skepticism. In 1713 and later Berkeley, who was a man of great personal charm and who commanded an English style few philosophers, if any, have surpassed, was on friendly terms with the leading literary men of London. Swift introduced him everywhere; he was Pope's friend; he wrote several essays for Steele's *Guardian,* and achieved a just and considerable reputation as a writer. In 1728 he went to America with the project of founding a college for the education of both the Indians and the colonists. The project was not realized, but while living at Newport, Rhode Island, he wrote his popular dialogues, *Alciphron: or, The Minute Philosopher*

[7] Berkeley's *Works* have been edited by Alexander C. Fraser (4v, Oxford, 1871; rev., 1901) and by George Sampson (3v, 1897-8). — Joseph M. Hone and Mario M. Rossi, *Bishop Berkeley: His Life, Writings and Philosophy* (1931); John Wild, *George Berkeley: A Study of his Life and Philosophy* (Cambridge, Mass., 1936); T. E. Jessop, *A Bibliography of George Berkeley* (Oxford, 1934).

(1732). In America he also acquired a great faith in the medicinal uses of tar-water, which became for him almost a panacea. Historically, Berkeley is known for his doctrines of philosophical immaterialism: in his own day he was most favorably known for his *Alciphron* and for his *Siris: A Chain of Philosophical Reflections and Inquiries concerning the Virtues of Tar-Water* (1744). Men of his day could be both extremely theoretical and extremely practical in their thinking.

Although he was a good servant of his Church, and rose to be a bishop, Berkeley's writings were less ecclesiastical or spiritual than the writings of two other men. The first was Bishop Joseph Butler (1692-1752). No man of the moment was comparable to Berkeley in speculative skill, but Butler acquired permanent fame as author of one of the most impressive attempts in English to construct a rationalist demonstration of the existence of the deity.[8] This attempt, his masterly *Analogy of Religion, Natural and Revealed, to the Constitution and Course of Nature* (1736), undermined most of the argumentative positions taken by the deists of the period and either terminated the controversies they had for a generation maintained or at least caused a considerable shift of ground. Faith less dependent than Butler's on man's philosophizings was alive at this time, but not common. Its great exemplar was William Law (1686-1761), who in his *Serious Call to a Devout and Holy Life* (1728) produced a work of permanent and compelling power, expressive of fervent spirituality and consecration in the highest degree.[9] In the early thirties John and Charles Wesley were briefly Law's disciples, and later at King's Cliffe, Northamptonshire, his home, the aunt of the historian Gibbon and a wealthy friend of hers were devoted followers of his systematic spirituality. In London he had been sought after by John Byrom (1692-1763), eccentric poet and religious writer. Law had no large following.

Bishop Butler and William Law

Unlike Butler, Law engaged in controversies: he took part in the Bangorian controversy (1717) by attacking Bishop Hoadly; he answered Mandeville's *Fable of the Bees,* and his opinion of the theatre of the time was more condemnatory than that of his fellow non-juror, Jeremy Collier. Law was a mystic, but he was also a practical reformer—and many men in his day assumed this latter rôle. The empirical method led men to accumulate, abstract, and generalize the experience of the day; and this led them to be critical of experience, for their task was to relate the truth of the moment to the whole system of things, to evaluate the detail as a part of "unerring

The Criticism of Experience: Reform and Satire

---

[8] Apart from the *Analogy* Butler's reputation rests upon his *Fifteen Sermons Preached at the Chapel of the Rolls Court* (1726). Butler's *Works* are edited by John H. Bernard (2v, 1900). The *Analogy* has been often edited and is available in the Everyman's Library (ed. Ronald Bayne) and in the Oxford World's Classics (ed. William E. Gladstone). See Frederick D. Maurice, *The Conscience* (1872); W. M. Egglestone, *Stanhope Memorials of Bishop Butler* (1878); Ernest C. Mossner, *Bishop Butler and the Age of Reason* (1936); William J. Norton, *Bishop Butler, Moralist and Divine* (New Brunswick, N. J., 1940).

[9] Law's *Works* (9v, 1753-76); ed. G. B. Morgan (Brockenhurst, 1892-3, privately printed); *A Serious Call* is edited by John H. Overton (1898) and C. Bigg (1899). — John H. Overton, *William Law, Nonjuror and Mystic* (1881); G. Moreton, *Memorials of the Birthplace and Residence of Law at King's Cliffe* (Guildford, 1895).

Nature." Otherwise "the truth of today" remained unstable and perhaps trivial. Increasingly, through distrust of present achievement, the century looked before and after, and became either primitivist or perfectionist. The critical attitude towards the diversity of present experience borrowed warrant from the classical traditions of satire, chiefly from Horace, but also from Juvenal, Martial, and Persius, and gave the early eighteenth century its most typical literature, a literature that castigated the follies of fashionable life (particularly feminine foibles), the corruptions of political and commercial affairs, the vulgar taste of the numerous *nouveaux riches,* and even the petty jealousies of literary men towards rivals.

Peace and Controversy   The age has been praised for its love of peace, and, considering the fact that between the accession of William and Mary (1688) and the Peace of Utrecht (1713) England had been at war for all but four of twenty-five years, one can understand a frequent outcry for peace. But it is mere Whiggery to assume that the Revolution of 1688 had solved all problems in church and state, and had secured peace—whether political or spiritual. The Church was beset by lassitude within and by Catholics, sectaries, and deists from without. One has only to recall the lot of non-jurors, or to compare the fictitious Big-Endians and Little-Endians in *Gulliver* with the actual if grotesque indecorums of the Bangorian controversy, to see that the Church was hardly at peace. In politics things were no better. "One half the Nation," Voltaire remarked, "is always at Variance with the other half. I have met People who assur'd me that the Duke of *Marlborough* was a Coward, and that Mr. *Pope* was a Fool." [10] Even the succession to the throne was threatened at least slightly by the death of Queen Anne (1714), by the Atterbury plot of 1723, and by the Jacobite invasion of 1745. The burdensome national debt resulting from the long wars drove England to lotteries and to experimentation in stock companies, many of which were formed at this time, frequently on the pattern of the long-established East India Company. Of these imitations the South Sea Company was the most notable. Incorporated in 1711, and possibly a project from the mind of the ingenious Daniel Defoe, this company was accorded an extensive trade monopoly in return for taking over a sizable part of the national debt. The Company at times rivaled in influence even the Bank of England (incorporated in 1694); but the highly inflated value of its stock caused in 1720 England's first great panic in the stock market. Of the immediate effects of this panic, Dr. Arbuthnot wittily remarked that "the Government and South Sea Company have only locked up the money of the people upon conviction of their lunacy, as is usual in the case of lunatics, and intend to restore them as much as is fit for such people, as they see them return more and more to their senses." Of the long-term chastening effects of the bursting of this bubble there is much evidence, which includes even a revulsion from the mercantilist worship of Commerce to the physiocratic idea that wealth comes basically from the soil.

[10] In his *Letters concerning the English Nation* (1733) as translated by John Lockman (ed. Charles Whibley, 1926), p. 162.

If a widespread preoccupation with one's chances in lotteries and in the *Utilitarian* stocks did not make for peaceful relaxation, it may perhaps account in part *Values in* for the insistence on utilitarian values. Literature, with its unparalleled *the Arts* development of journalism and with its preoccupation with daily life and how best to lead it, had obviously "useful" ideals to accord with its Roman traditions. In the other fine arts a similar attention to pragmatic needs was apparent. Although Sir Christopher Wren's masterpiece was St. Paul's Cathedral (built 1675-1710), the great achievement in the architecture of his day was not in public buildings but in the transformation of domestic architecture from the frequently gloomy Tudor Gothic to the lighter, more spacious and definitely more comfortable "Queen Anne" mansion of Italian origin. Under the patronage of Pope's friend the third Earl of Burlington (1695-1753) various architects developed a style for small houses that was severely neo-Palladian and chastely elegant: they saved England, largely, from the excesses of the Continental rococo.[11] Such residences demanded landscaping, and the shift from the rigidly formal gardens, produced by Dutch designers brought over by William III, to a more "natural" and "picturesque" system was early urged by Addison and Pope, as well as by Pope's influential professional friends Charles Bridgman and William Kent, and by "Capability" Brown. Proper settings for stately homes were effectively devised by such men. Interiors in some sense were improved—at least lightened—by the substitution of paint or of the increasingly fashionable and artistic wallpapers for dark oak paneling or tapestry hangings. Domestic furniture of the day was assuming new patterns of elegance and delicacy as oak gave way to the mahogany of Central America; the great designers, however—Chippendale, Hepplewhite, Sheraton, and the Adam brothers— belong to the middle and later part of the century. New paintings for the walls were of less distinction than they had been in the days of Van Dyck, since the visiting Continental artists were less eminent. Sir Godfrey Kneller was perhaps the best of these. Of native English painters William Hogarth (1697-1764) was easily the greatest. The authentic, journalistic realism of his numerous conversation pieces, designed frankly to correct the manners of the time, was so finely detailed that its lack of elegance proved no barrier to popularity. Since Hogarth began as an engraver, his paintings were commonly popularized by engraving. In general the best work of this kind at this time was done by imported French artists; but the English practitioners of the mezzotint method were producing by the beginning of the century brilliant and delicately shaded portraits. John Smith (1652?- 1742) was perhaps the most eminent early artist in this method, which was to become famous as *la manière anglaise*. Smith's mezzotint (1703) of Lely's portrait of Wycherley is a well-known specimen.

[11] Fiske Kimball, "The Creation of the Rococo," *Jour. Warburg and Courtauld Institutes*, IV (1941). 119-123; "Burlington Architectus," *Jour. Royal Institute of British Architects*, October 15, 1927, pp. 675-693 [cf. George Sherburn, "'Timon's Villa' and Cannons," *Huntington Library Bull.*, No. 8 (1935). 132n]; "Les influences anglaises dans la formation du style Louis XVI," *Gazette des Beaux-Arts*, V (1931). 29-44; 231-255; and *The Creation of the Rococo* (Philadelphia, 1943).

Opera

In the early century, music, which had long been among the most favored of English arts, was hardly regarded as a "useful" art; for the time was torn with arguments concerning the "absurdities" of Italian opera. With the passing of the great English musical tradition of the sixteenth and seventeenth centuries, the arrival (1710) of George Frederick Handel [12] (1685-1759) in London gave impetus to the fashionable amusement of opera, and for half a century English music was Handel and opera. The overelaborate scenic effects and the supposed absurdity of dialogue sung in an unintelligible foreign language caused the *Tatler* and *Spectator,* among others, to attack opera as completely non-intellectual and hence contemptible. John Dennis (doubtless intended in *Tatler* No. 4 as the "great critic" who "fell into fits in the gallery, at feeling, not only time and place, but language and nations confused in the most incorrigible manner"), like Mme Dacier in France, regarded opera as coöperating perfectly with evil manners to corrupt the taste of the time. To many a critic or supporter of the drama, opera was as sinister in the early eighteenth century as the cinema has seemed in the twentieth. The English were still great music-lovers, but as the century advanced their music was with growing frequency produced for them by imported composers and performers.

Formalism in Art

Italian opera, like the other arts of the period, was marked by extreme formalism—even more extreme than in the dramas of the century. Popularity of arts so rigidly controlled by tradition naturally has led critics to label the period "artificial." The term, of course, is always equivocal and relative. Clearly the period frequently regarded technical ingenuity as highly as it did substance. The very formality of the Roman, Italian, or French traditions imposed ingenuity as the *sine qua non* of novelty, and novelty is insisted on by all traditionalist critics. (Dulness, as Pope was to say in so many ingenious ways, is the worst of aesthetic crimes.) Artificiality and frivolity can easily be asserted of a century, the arts of which were dominated by a regard almost exclusively directed to the upper classes and to luxurious amusement. But one must remember that behind this superficial gaiety England was in the eighteenth century building a far-flung empire by means of a reputation for commercial honesty that was world-wide except in England itself—where one thought every man had his price. It was an age of crudely robust aspects, in which a Richard Savage, a James Annesley, an Elizabeth Canning could look Defoe's personages—Moll Flanders or Colonel Jacque—in the eye and remind them that real life is stranger than fiction. One must remember this fact when faced with the facile generalizations that stress the peace and nobility of these second-generation Augustans and neglect the more or less honest rough and tumble of their daily life. Along with their devotion to the Roman tradition they developed a sentimental cast of thought and at the same time a libelous journalism that should not be forgotten.

[12] He was born, of course, Georg Friedrich Händel in Halle (Saxony) and received much of his musical training in Italy.

II

The Critical Temper and Doctrine, 1700-1750

The unpeaceful nature of the early eighteenth century can be seen *The Dis-* nowhere more clearly than in literary criticism. Much of this sort of writing *repute of* was not of permanent eminence, but it does illuminate both the mood and *Criticism* the intellectual quality of the period.[1] The critical function and tempera- ment were freely disparaged on a variety of grounds. One of these was the quarrel over the relative merits of ancient and modern writers—a quarrel long current in both France and England. In the preface to his edition of Sir Charles Sedley's *Miscellaneous Works* (1702) Captain William Ayloffe bursts out:

Parnassus is in Arms against it self, and the Daughters of *Helicon* as mutinous, as the execrable Sons of the Earth. The Factious Ensigns are every where dis- play'd, and the Various Wits rank'd in formidable Batallions. If a Man sets up for a Poet he is immediately attacqu'd by a Satyrical Party; Destruction is the Word; and, as for Quarter, they give none; these are the blood-thirsty Hussars of *Parnassus,* cut out for the ruine of others, tho' rarely with any great Honour to themselves.

Politics also muddied the springs of criticism. In 1705 Ned Ward in his *Hudibras Redivivus,* No. 1, gave writers advice from the gutter:

> For he that writes in such an Age,
> When Parties do for Pow'r engage,
> Ought to chuse one Side for the Right,
> And then, with all his Wit and Spite,
> Blacken and vex the Opposite.

[1] Important further aid in the study of the criticism of this period will be found in the following: P. Hamelius, *Die Kritik in der englischen Literatur des 17. und 18. Jahrhunderts* (Leipzig, 1897); George Saintsbury, *A History of Criticism and Literary Taste in Europe* (3v, Edinburgh, 1900-4); Louis Charlanne, *L'Influence française en Angleterre au XVIIᵉ siècle* (Paris, 1906); G. M. Miller's *The Historical Point of View in English Literary Criticism from 1570-1770* (Heidelberg, 1913); *Critical Essays of the Eighteenth Century 1700-1725,* ed. Willard H. Durham, [introduction] (New Haven, 1915); Caroline M. Goad, *Horace in the English Litera- ture of the Eighteenth Century* (New Haven, 1918); John W. Draper, "Aristotelian Mimesis in Eighteenth-Century England," *PMLA,* xxxvi (1921). 372-400; Raymond D. Havens, *The In- fluence of Milton on English Poetry* (Cambridge, Mass., 1922); A. F. B. Clark, *Boileau and the French Classical Critics in England, 1660-1830* (Paris, 1925); Marvin T. Herrick, *The Poetics of Aristotle in England* (New Haven, 1930); John W. Draper, *Eighteenth Century English Aesthetics: A Bibliography* (Heidelberg, 1931); Samuel H. Monk, *The Sublime: A Study of Critical Theories in XVIII-Century England* (1935); Beverley S. Allen, *Tides in English Taste, 1619-1800* (Cambridge, Mass., 1937); Ronald S. Crane, "Neo-classical Criticism," in *Dictionary of World Literature,* ed. Joseph T. Shipley (1943), pp. 193-203.

> Scurrility's a useful Trick,
> Approv'd by the most Politic;
> Fling Dirt enough, and some will Stick.

As for the manners and morals of criticism—on that subject Jonathan Swift was superlatively opprobrious. In his *Battle of the Books* he describes Criticism as

a malignant Deity . . . extended in her Den, upon the Spoils of numberless Volumes half devoured. At her right Hand sat *Ignorance,* her Father and Husband, blind with Age; at her left, *Pride* her Mother, dressing her up in the Scraps of Paper herself had torn. There, was *Opinion* her Sister, light of Foot, hoodwinkt, and headstrong, yet giddy and perpetually turning. About her play'd her Children, *Noise* and *Impudence, Dullness* and *Vanity, Positiveness, Pedantry,* and *Ill-Manners.* The Goddess herself had Claws like a Cat: Her Head, and Ears, and Voice, resembled those of an *Ass. . . .*

In his "Digression concerning Criticks" in *A Tale of a Tub* Swift is equally caustic, and more personal:

Every *True Critick* is a Hero born, descending in a direct Line from a Celestial Stem, by *Momus* and *Hybris,* who begat *Zoilus,* who begat *Tigellius,* who begat *Etcætera* the Elder, who begat *B—tly,* and *Rym—r,* and *W—tton,* and *Perrault,* and *Dennis,* who begat *Etcætera* the Younger.

Abuse of the critical function was often blamed on antiquarian specialization such as that of Bentley, Rymer, Tom Hearne, and Lewis Theobald. Verbal criticism, as textual emendation was called, was abused as pedantry. Even before Swift wrote, Dennis, for example, had a reputation as an ill-natured critic. He at one extreme was frequently castigated for subservience to rules, and at the other extreme blows fell upon sprightly authors who defended irregularities by remarking pertly, "Shakespear writ without rules."

John Dennis

　　Most notable among the so-called "rules" critics of the period was doubtless John Dennis,[2] who, like Dryden, struggled intermittently to reconcile divergent critical traditions, and who, like Rymer, ultimately tended to rely on rules and common sense. Dennis began in the last decade of the seventeenth century as a poet, dramatist, pamphleteer, and critic. In the last capacity

---

[2] John Dennis (1657-1734), born in London, educated at Harrow and Cambridge (M.A., 1683) made the grand tour in 1688, and upon his return became a frequenter of Will's and other London coffee-houses and a valued, if at times eccentric, member of the literary circle whose center was John Dryden. "Before 1706," Mr. Hooker tells us, "he had produced six plays, seven critical treatises, four long poems, at least three political treatises, a collection of letters together with a translation of Voiture, a translation of part of Tacitus, and various shorter items of a miscellaneous nature." His later years were marred by poverty, ill health, and controversy; but his pen kept busy. Apart from his unfortunate attacks on Pope and other literary men his later works dealt with attacks on Tories, with the theatre, or with religion. His publication of *Letters upon Several Occasions* (1696) and *Original Letters, Familiar, Moral and Critical* (2v, 1721) marks a departure that Pope and many another literary man were to follow. His plays and poems are at this distance negligible. His *Critical Works* have been admirably edited by Edward N. Hooker (2v, Baltimore, 1939-43) with a long introduction in Vol. II; and his life is well treated by H. G. Paul, *John Dennis* (1911). See also Fred Tupper, "Notes on the Life of John Dennis," *ELH,* v (1938). 211-217; and Hoxie N. Fairchild, *Religious Trends in English Poetry,* I (1939). 183-189, *et passim.*

he achieved a considerable reputation. His critical writing appeared in about a dozen longer pieces as well as in shorter prefaces, dedications, and letters. His views derived, on the one hand, from the traditions of Aristotle, Horace, Boileau, Bossu (whose treatise on the epic was standard), Rapin (who was the favorite commentator on Aristotle), St. Évremond, and Dryden. On the other hand, he owed much to his strong admiration for Shakespeare and Longinus and to his worship of John Milton. He is the first admirer of Milton to put himself extensively in print. Dennis thus combines a rationalist tradition with an unbounded love of sublimity and enthusiastic passion. He was ridiculed often for his love of such words as "furious" and "tremendous."

Like Dryden his difficulty in reconciling his diversities was augmented *Dennis on* by accidental circumstance. Himself an unsuccessful playwright, he believed *the Drama* wholeheartedly in the stage as an instrument in reforming manners, and defended the theatre as an institution even though vehement in condemning its increasing decadence in his time. He replied to Collier's attack caustically in his *Usefulness of the Stage* (1698) and again in *The Person of Quality's Answer to Mr. Collier's . . . Disswasive from the Play-house* (1704). He replied to William Law's *Absolute Unlawfulness of the Stage-Entertainment* (1726) in his *Stage Defended* (1726). In *An Essay on the Operas* he had in 1706 attacked Italian opera, which he regarded as both aesthetically and morally corrupting. He ably defended Etherege's *Sir Fopling Flutter* in 1722, and more than once attacked plays and playwrights (notably Richard Steele) of the rising sentimental school.

His more important early critical treatises were his *Impartial Critick* *His Major* (1693), a reply to Rymer's *Short View of Tragedy; The Advancement and* *Treatises* *Reformation of Modern Poetry* (1701), which states his central critical positions, and the similar *Grounds of Criticism in Poetry* (1704). His attack on Rymer, concerned with the attempt to force a chorus on modern tragedy, states a position of relativity with regard to the rules that would have been of great importance if Dennis had firmly adhered to it. He here holds that devices, such as a chorus, "adapted to the Religion and Temper" of the Greeks, may not be at all effective in a nation of different religion, climate, and customs. In general, however, Dennis firmly supports the "ancient" rules as the established guides to good writing, though they must be intelligently used. He praises Milton for rising above the rules in *Paradise Lost,* and blames Addison for slavish and ineffectual following of them in *Cato.* His handling of the last act of Addison's tragedy has much of the prosaic common-sense method that Rymer used on *Othello.* Later in his unpublished attack on Welsted, *The Causes of the Decay and Defects of Dramatick Poetry,* he depends on the rules unquestioningly, and in his *Essay on the Genius and Writings of Shakespear* (1712) he regrets that Shakespeare, "one of the greatest Genius's that the World e'er saw for the Tragick Stage," could not have "join'd to so happy a Genius Learning and the Poetical Art." Poetical Art means the rules! It is, however, the general rule of decorum and regularity rather than the more mechanical rules of the unities that Dennis cherishes.

Passion and Enthusiasm

More interesting to post-romantic students is Dennis's theory of the relation of religion and passion to poetry. Historically, Dennis here has great importance in showing that sound neo-classicism held no brief for poetic frigidity. To Dennis, as well as to Milton and other neo-classicists, passion is a chief element in poetry; but no other critic of the time has so explicitly expounded this view. Poetry must please in order to instruct: there is no pleasure without passion; there is no religion without passion. Passions are in Dennis's system of two kinds: ordinary, which arise from known, objective causes, and enthusiastic, which arise from unknown causes, in contemplation. The chief enthusiastic passions are admiration and terror; horror, joy, sadness, and desire are also mentioned. In his love of passionate sublimity he clearly owes much to both Longinus and Milton. Enthusiasm, condemned by Dennis and all other churchmen when it means non-rational religion, is praised as a divinely given element in poetic pleasure. This view, stated by Dennis in his *Advancement and Reformation of Poetry* and in *The Grounds of Criticism in Poetry,* was to be popularized, as we shall see, in Shaftesbury's *Moralists.* Divinely given enthusiasm or passion joins poetry and religion, and Dennis's notion of "advancement and reformation" depends upon his belief that the ancients, where they have excelled the moderns, have relied upon their religion for material; but since the moderns have a true religion, they may, if they will infuse their poetry with divine spirit, as Milton has done, easily surpass the ancients. This sort of reasoning frequently misleads Dennis. Of all the defenders of passion that criticism has produced surely he is the most devoted to categories and to "logic."

His Conditioned Perceptions

One wonders how far Dennis's precepts conditioned his perceptions. He has a glowing admiration for Milton and a great, if qualified, admiration for Shakespeare. He is capable of feeling "a delightful Horrour, a terrible Joy" over Alpine scenery that made him lyrical; and he felt strongly impressed by that "incomparable Statue of *Laocoon,* which," he says, "I saw at *Rome,* in the Gardens of *Belvidere,* and which is so astonishing, that it does not appear to be the Work of Art, but the miserable Creature himself, like *Niobe,* benumm'd and petrify'd with Grief and Horror." Perception could move him: precept by contrast frequently made him a victim. His least happy *idée fixe* was the depravity of the taste of his day. The corollary was that if a new piece of writing was popular, it was bad, and duty required him to attack it. So in his later days he attacked many of Pope's works as well as *The Tatler, The Spectator, Cato,* and *The Conscious Lovers.* Criticism, as we have seen, had in general a bad reputation, and as early as 1696 in his *Remarks* on Blackmore's *Prince Arthur,* Dennis found it advisable to protest against the charge of ill nature. After 1705, when he began to "retire from the world," and particularly after 1711, when he became embroiled with Pope and Steele, his fame for ill nature increased. But there was an honest directness and vigor about Dennis's thought and insight into poetic problems that continued to command respect. His rages were obvious and amazing; his calmer thought was commonly of obvious value. The frequent disparagement that he and Pope bestowed on each other in their writings is one of the more disgraceful episodes of the period, but in spite of what they printed it is probable that each respected the other's abilities. In fact, Pope advertised in 1730 that he would take any victim out of his *Dunciad* if the man would present a certificate of his being a wit or a poet "from any *three of his companions* in the Dunciad, or from Mr. *Dennis singly,* who is esteemed equal to any three of the number." Not a high compliment perhaps; for Pope knew Dennis's habitual scorn for most of his contemporaries; but still it represents an official opinion. If Dennis's views on passion had been more widely heeded, later Augustan poetry would certainly have been more declamatory: conceivably it might have been more truly moving.

Contrasting with Dennis in many ways and yet often agreeing with *Shaftesbury* him stood the famous philosopher, the third Earl of Shaftesbury.[3] His lord- *as Critic* ship was perhaps hardly a critic at all. He theorizes about the art of poetry interestingly, but his applied criticisms are hardly reputable. He had less taste than Dennis for "our old dramatic poet" Shakespeare, but allowing for the dramatist's "natural rudeness, his unpolished style, and antiquated phrase and wit, his want of method and coherence, and his deficiency in almost all the graces and ornaments...yet by the justness of his moral, the aptness of many of his descriptions, and the plain and natural turn of several of his characters, he pleases the audience, and often gains their ear without a single bribe from Luxury or Vice." *Hamlet* is called "that piece of his which appears to have most affected English hearts," and is praised as being "almost one continued moral." In general, the English muse is regarded by his lordship as not yet out of swaddling clothes. Many of his judgments—those on Dryden and Sir Christopher Wren's new St. Paul's notably—must have been colored by personal prejudice. He believes in ridicule as a test of truth, but no words are too harsh to express his de-testation of the ridicule found in Swift's *Tale of a Tub.* On the other hand, he praises the Duke of Buckinghamshire's *Essay on Poetry* (after all—*a duke!*), admires French tragedy and its rules, and so naturally thinks well of Rymer as a critic.

His theories spring from his belief that harmony with Nature leads to that *On Taste* *summum bonum,* serenity; that the three major aspects of Nature, the Good, the Beautiful, and the True, are at bottom one. A difficulty in his philosophizings was to reconcile *(a)* the idea that this is a divinely created and ordered, a perfect, world, and *(b)* the idea that man should strive to improve his world. Shaftesbury, then, stresses man's *natural appetite* for these ultimates of Goodness, Beauty, and Truth, which drives man towards

---

[3] On Shaftesbury's philosophy and life see above, Part II, ch. I, n. 4. On his criticism see two papers by Alfred O. Aldridge, "Lord Shaftesbury's Literary Theories," *PQ,* xxIV (1945). 46-64, and "Shaftesbury and the Test of Truth," *PMLA,* LX (1945). 129-156.

an ideal quasi-Platonic goal. He endows man with a "moral sentiment," a natural faculty or internal sense which enables one to distinguish deformity from beauty and vice from virtue. This faculty is at times called *taste*. The seeds of taste exist naturally in man's mind; but they must be cultivated: taste is by no means subjective or even easy to attain. In the *Advice to an Author* he exclaims, " 'Tis not by wantonness and humour that I shall attain my end and arrive at the enjoyment I propose. The art itself is severe, the rules rigid." And again, in his *Miscellanies* (III, ii): "A legitimate and just taste can neither be begotten, made, conceived, or produced without the antecedent labour and pains of criticism."

Thus he resents the facility of the young coffee-house wit who alleges "that we Englishmen are not tied up to such rigid rules as those of the ancient Grecian or modern French critics." In his opinion "there is nothing more certain than that a real genius and thorough artist in whatever kind can never, without the greatest unwillingness and shame...be prevailed with to prostitute his art or science by performing contrary to its known rules." It is then natural that he condemns tragicomedy, and in general follows Continental traditions of art and opinions of the English genius.

On the Imagination   He is aware of the difference between imaginative delusion and imaginative illusion, and endorses the latter highly.

We may...presume to infer from the coolest of all studies, even from criticism itself... "that there is a power in numbers, harmony, proportion, and beauty of every kind, which naturally captivates the heart, and raises the imagination to an opinion or conceit of something majestic and divine." ... Without this imagination or conceit the world would be but a dull circumstance, and life a sorry pastime. Scarce could we be said to live.

But the trained imagination abominates the particular image. It could easily make every subject "appear unlike anything extant in the world besides. But this effect the good poet and painter seek industriously to prevent. They hate minuteness, and are afraid of singularity."

On Enthusiasm   In the first treatise in his *Characteristicks,* "A Letter concerning Enthusiasm," Shaftesbury had attacked religious enthusiasm (that is, irrationality), and had stated the notion "that provided we treat religion with good manners, we can never use too much good-humor, or examine it with too much freedom and familiarity." From this and other dangerous positions he evolved the notion that ridicule is admirable as a test of truth—a view that may have stimulated writers to use ridicule in satire. His attitude towards enthusiasm, however, cannot be taken from a reading of this first treatise alone, though even here he asserted that enthusiasm sits "gracefully with an ancient," and again that "No poet...can do anything great in his own way without the imagination or supposition of a divine presence, which may raise him to some degree of this passion [enthusiasm] we are speaking of." [4] The fifth treatise in his *Characteristicks,* "The Moralists, a Philosophical

[4] On the "rationalist" or scientific attitude towards enthusiasm see George Williamson's excellent article on "The Restoration Revolt against Enthusiasm," *SP,* xxx (1933). 571-603.

Rhapsody," was largely devoted to an exposition of the approved or "sweet" enthusiasm. Shaftesbury called this treatise his "principal performance." In it Theocles, a lover of nature and romantic solitude, converts Philocles by showing him the transcendent beauty of the landscape at dawn. The scene reaches its climax in the famous apostrophe to Nature ("Moralists," III, i), after which Philocles concludes,

> "The transports of poets, the sublime of orators, the rapture of musicians, the high strains of the virtuosi—all mere enthusiasm! Even learning itself, the love of arts and curiosities, the spirit of travelers and adventurers, gallantry, war, heroism—all, all enthusiasm!" 'Tis enough; I am content to be this new enthusiast in a way unknown to me before. . . . For is there a fair and plausible enthusiasm, a reasonable ecstasy and transport allowed to other subjects, such as architecture, painting, music; and shall it be exploded here?

Such passages in Shaftesbury certainly helped to turn poets to a new enthusiasm for nature—to be seen later in James Thomson, Joseph Warton, William Whitehead (his *Enthusiast*), and many another.[5] Enthusiasm as related to religion was still deplorable, but as applied to the arts it was more than desirable. It is his moral philosophy and such incidental passages scattered through his other writings that made Shaftesbury an influence in shaping literary ideals. In his third treatise, "Advice to an Author," he devoted a section (II, ii) to a defense of criticism. His consistent *politesse*, dignity, and serenity all served as examples to turbulent commoner critics.

Less ostentatiously noble than his lordship but equally devoted to high moral ideals for criticism and poetry was Richard Steele's collaborator in *The Spectator*, Joseph Addison.[6] More widely and more intelligently read than his lordship, Addison seems (though by no means a critic greatly daring) far more modern than either Dennis or Shaftesbury. After several years at Oxford and a residence of four years on the Continent, including a scholarly tour of classic Italy, Addison could still live with the coffee-house wits as a *bon vivant*—he drank copiously and soberly—and as a scholar who was no pedant. He seemed to Pope in days of hostility— *Addison as Critic*

> born to write, converse, and live with ease.

Thus to him as to Shaftesbury the critic was at best the ideal fine gentleman. In *Spectator* No. 291, where he lays down qualifications for the true critic, he remarks contemptuously, "A few general rules extracted out of the French authors, with a certain cant of words, has sometimes set up an illiterate heavy writer for a most judicious and formidable critic." Addison doubtless believed in the rules; but he more than once disparaged them casually, and he commonly found other things to talk about. With him perception outweighed precept in importance. The true critic essentially *On the Character and Training of a Critic*

[5] See two notable articles by Cecil A. Moore: "Shaftesbury and the Ethical Poets in England, 1700-1760," *PMLA*, XXXI (1916). 264-325, and "The Return to Nature in English Poetry of the Eighteenth Century," *SP*, XIV (1917). 243-291.

[6] On Addison's career and writings apart from criticism see Part II, ch. v.

was the man of taste, and a fine taste seemed "the utmost perfection of an accomplished man." To test one's taste he advised in *Spectator* No. 409 three procedures: (1) see if the generally approved classics afford delight; (2) see if the individual quality of different authors is felt; and (3) see if disparate statements of the same thought by a great author and an ordinary writer produce different effects. Psychological response rather than correspondence with precedent was stressed. Taste depended on training, which included reading the best authors, conversation with men of politeness, familiarity with the best critics ancient and modern, a love of simplicity rather than of artificial ingenuity, and development of one's imagination.

On Genius   Possibly Addison's eleven *Spectator* papers on the Pleasures of the Imagination (Nos. 411-21) are his most original contributions to the theory of criticism.[7] A rival for this honor would be *Spectator* No. 160, which gives account of two types of geniuses—the natural, "who by the mere strength of natural parts, and without any assistance of art or learning" have delighted readers, geniuses like Shakespeare and Pindar; and, secondly, the trained geniuses, "that have formed themselves by rules, and submitted the greatness of their natural talents to the corrections and restraints of art"—men like Plato, Aristotle, Virgil, Tully, and Milton. This dual concept of genius had enormous influence; but it is perhaps less important than Addison's papers on imagination.

On the   Dennis, Shaftesbury, and Addison differed notably in their accounts of
Imagination the imagination. To Dennis its function was to vivify, to present absent objects to the mind as if present. Images of "absent terrible objects" move one violently, and for him constitute the source of enthusiasm in poetry. Like Hobbes and Locke, Dennis stresses the importance of judgment as a control over the imagination. To Shaftesbury imagination is primarily the force that elevates the mind, not to passion, but to the lofty serenity that his admiration for Plato led him to love. Addison is less philosophic and more scientific. He is the empiricist who, somewhat after the manner of Hobbes and Locke, wishes to examine into the workings of the imagination and its effects on the mind. These last are pleasurable, and he finds (in No. 412) that such pleasures coming from outward objects arise from "what is great, uncommon, or beautiful." [8] The general effect of these pleasures is refining: "A man of polite imagination is let into a great many pleasures, that the vulgar are not capable of receiving." A more specialized effect is felt by the imaginative writer:

[7] In recent times there has been controversy over these essays. W. B. Worsfold's *Principles of Criticism* (1897), chs. III-V, exaggerated and mistook their importance; others have denied them any importance. Beyond doubt they meant much to the eighteenth century. See C. D. Thorpe, "Addison's Theory of Imagination as 'Perceptive Response'," *Papers of the Michigan Academy*, XXI (1936). 509-530. On Addison's predecessors in this field see Donald F. Bond, "The Neo-Classical Psychology of the Imagination," *ELH*, IV (1937). 245-264. Also D. F. Bond's "'Distrust' of Imagination in English Neo-Classicism," *PQ*, XIV (1935). 54-69.

[8] By this statement he encouraged a host of succeeding theorists to analyze sublimity, beauty, the picturesque, and other types of imaginative stimuli. Francis Hutcheson (1694-1746) in his *Inquiry into the Original of our Ideas of Beauty and Virtue* (1725) and in his *Essay on ... the Passions* (1728) was an early disciple. See Clarence D. Thorpe, "Addison and Hutcheson on the Imagination," *ELH*, II (1935). 215-234.

It would be in vain to enquire, whether the Power of imagining Things strongly proceeds from any greater Perfection in the Soul, or from any nicer Texture in the Brain of one Man than of another. But this is certain, that a noble Writer should be born with this Faculty in its full Strength and Vigour, so as to be able to receive lively Ideas from outward Objects, to retain them long, and to range them together, upon occasion, in such Figures and Representations as are most likely to hit the Fancy of the Reader. A Poet should take as much Pains in forming his Imagination, as a Philosopher in cultivating his Understanding. He must gain a due Relish of the Works of Nature, and be throughly conversant in the various Scenery of a Country Life.

Such forming of the poet's mind results in the forming of pleasing images in his poetry, in that final "Embellishment to good Sense" that "makes one Man's Compositions more agreeable than another's." Judgment, Addison thinks, must operate along with imagination (No. 416); but he talks much less of the necessity of control than had the critics of Dryden's day—including Dennis. Addison also is less worried by the possibility of the imagination's overwhelming the understanding. He is less concerned with the confusion between illusion in practical matters (which is delusion) and that in poetical matters, where illusion, provided it is an embellishment to *good sense,* cannot be dangerous.

By nature Addison loved the simple and the direct rather than the complex *On Classical* and the fanciful, but he had commendation for all these qualities. His *Simplicity* mind shows a delicate balance between an easy-going common sense that could in *Spectator* No. 40 condemn poetic justice as unnatural and a somewhat rigid rationalism that in the same essay could also condemn tragicomedy as unnatural. Although he follows the French classical critics in his method of praising the ballad of *Chevy Chase* (*Spectator* No. 70), his love of sensible simplicity is here admirably expressed:

I know nothing which more shews the essential and inherent Perfection of Simplicity of Thought, above that which I call the Gothick Manner in Writing, than this, that the first pleases all Kinds of Palates, and the latter only such as have formed to themselves a wrong artificial Taste upon little fanciful Authors and Writers of Epigram.

Trivial ornament, often called "Gothick" at this time, he opposed to the universality of simplicity.

If he was bold in this admiration of ballads,[9] he was also outspoken in his admiration of the complex art of John Milton. After Dennis he is one *On Milton* of the very first to praise Milton extensively. In method, the eighteen papers in his series on *Paradise Lost* (*Spectator,* No. 267, and thereafter on Saturdays until No. 369) are most revealing. The first four are, in his phrase, done "according to Aristotle's method." That is, they deal with the topics treated in the *Poetics* in connection with the epic. Here the rules become principles

---

[9] See S. B. Hustvedt, *Ballad Criticism . . . during the Eighteenth Century* (1916), pp. 65-78; E. B. Reed, "Two Notes on Addison" [one on ballads], *MP,* VI (1908). 186-189; and E. K. Broadus, "Addison's Influence on the Development of Interest in Folk-Poetry in the Eighteenth Century," *MP,* VIII (1910). 123-134.

of criticism, and the critic's observations are conventional. In No. 291 he in a sense defines the function of criticism so as to defend the next paper (No. 297) on the imperfections of the poem. Thereafter (Nos. 303 to 369) he devotes one paper to the beauties of each of the twelve books. Evidently it is twelve times as important to point out beauties as it is to find faults. It is possible that in these papers, which quote Milton with exquisite taste but comment somewhat perfunctorily upon the quotations made, Addison more or less founds a school of "beauties" criticism; for throughout the ensuing century almost every important author has his merits displayed in a volume (sometimes two), the title of which begins "The Beauties of ——." In any case Addison exhibits the sensitiveness that results from genteel training of imagination reinforced by good sense. Occasionally—for instance in his praise of *Chevy Chase* or in his opinion that Caliban, as a product of sheer imagination, is a greater effect of genius than Hotspur or Julius Caesar—Addison surprises one by his independent insight.[10] Usually, however, as in his dispraise of Italian opera as non-intellectual, he spoke for better or worse the wisdom of his time. The fact that he spoke it unassumingly and elegantly and in the highly popular *Spectator* gave it enormous vogue and influence.

Pope as Critic

In similar fashion poetic eminence gave vogue to the critical writing of Alexander Pope.[11] His almost juvenile *Essay on Criticism* was, to be sure, published before he was eminent, and it speedily became a bible for neo-classicists. The rest of Pope's output in criticism, except for *The Dunciad* and for fairly brief passages in other poems, was in prose. Most notable are the prefaces to his *Iliad* (1715), to his edition of Shakespeare (1725), and to his collected *Works* (1717). His general position as a critic has been too frequently deduced only from his early writing, such as the *Essay on Criticism,* a poem published before he was twenty-three and perhaps written before he was twenty-one. His *Discourse on Pastoral Poetry* was apparently written before 1709, though published in 1717. In these works Pope is the elegant amateur and the complete traditionalist. In the preface to his *Works* (1717) he affectedly remarks that poetry and criticism are "only the affair of idle men who write in their closets, and of idle men who read there"; and with equal self-depreciation he remarks as a traditionalist, "All that is left us is to recommend our productions by the imitation of the Ancients." But no one should imagine those were his permanent views. At the end of the noble account of the evolution of Society in Epistle III of the *Essay on Man,* at the point where tyranny and superstition have enslaved man, appears the poet as reformer:

> 'Twas then the studious head or gen'rous mind,
> Follow'r of God, or friend of human-kind,

[10] Both Addison and Steele make admirable comments on Shakespeare. See J. H. Neumann, "Shakespearean Criticism in *The Tatler* and *The Spectator,*" *PMLA,* XXXIX (1924). 612-623.
[11] On Pope's criticism see Austin Warren, *Alexander Pope as Critic and Humanist* (Princeton, 1929), and John E. Butt, *Pope's Taste in Shakespeare* (a paper read before the Shakespeare Association, 1936). On Pope's poetry see Part II, ch. VIII.

> Poet or patriot, rose but to restore
> The faith and moral Nature gave before. . . .

To Pope as, later, to Johnson evidently the poet might be "the interpreter of nature and the legislator of mankind."

His theory of poetry and criticism is usually, however, deduced from the *Essay on Criticism*. This poem has as its general office the same function Shaftesbury performed in Part II, Section ii, of his "Advice to an Author"; namely, the rehabilitation of the critic in good nature and good manners. Only the first 200 lines of the poem concern the theory of the art of letters; the rest deals with the manners appropriate to a polite critic. In the first section Pope starts with the view that as poets must by natural endowment have genius, so critics must have taste; that most men "have the seeds of judgment in their mind," and that this natural taste must be developed by a study of Nature (that is, of the moral system of the universe together with its manifestations) and a study of the ancients and of ancient rules. One may, he suggests, rise above the rules, but that way danger lies. The rules have authority, not because they are ancient or Aristotelian, but because they are "nature methodised"—are based in reason. Pope, like Addison, Hobbes, and Locke, stands in the empirical tradition: the rules are simply the procedure of ancient authors codified. In all this there is nothing new, and Pope intended there should be nothing new: he was stating only the accepted wisdom of his day. But the brilliance of the statement kept his precepts in vogue long after their early vitality had evaporated. It was this vogue fully as much as any essential falseness of doctrine that later enraged romantic critics—De Quincey, for example.

Pope in his satirical writing is rationalist in temper, and even has much of the common-sensical attitude towards the handling of material. In his *Bathos (The Art of Sinking in Poetry)* (1728) he ridicules the affected diction of many contemporaries, and in *The Dunciad,* a poem devoted to good common sense as well as to virulent personal satire, he attacks pretentiousness in scholarship, criticism, and editing. In various critical passages found in his letters he writes in a similar tone. His attack, in one letter, on the poetry of Crashaw foreshadows remotely that of Johnson on the metaphysical poets.

In the prefaces to the *Iliad* and to his edition of Shakespeare Pope is somewhat more incisive. He glories in Homer's "invention," and while he analyzes the poem according to Aristotle's method, he uses the theme of invention to unify the analysis. He gives a striking comparison of Homer and Virgil, from which dates the unexpected eighteenth-century preference of Homer, the poet of nature, to Virgil, the poet of art. In his account of Homer's imperfections he adopts the typical idea of his day that progress has improved manners. His successors argued long over the question of the purity or the corruptness of manners in Homer's pristine time. Pope's account of his own attempts to preserve in English Homer's fire and sim-

An Essay on Criticism

Pope on Homer and Shakespeare

plicity shows insight into problems that were perhaps beyond him to solve. The preface to Shakespeare is less notable. Pope neatly tries to throw the blame for imperfections on Shakespeare's first publishers, who were, he thought, ignorant actors. His appreciation of Shakespeare's characters and of his power over the passions is admirable. His bold opinion that "To judge . . . of Shakespear by Aristotle's rules, is like trying a man by laws of one country, who acted under those of another" is creditable and on the whole typical of the time: but it was an opinion that neither the time nor Mr. Pope could consistently cling to.

His Notes on Homer

Pope's method is very like Addison's in applied criticism. This can best be seen in the notes to the *Iliad* and *Odyssey,* which were widely studied during the whole century. Some notes are almost little essays in themselves. The character of Axylus, "a friend to mankind," inserted as a note to *Iliad* vi, 16, is a striking portrait of "the good man" as drawn after Homer. More literary in content are notes to such lines as vi, 595, on the domestic scene between Hector and his infant son. Here, typically, Pope uses the analogy of poetry with painting; he concludes with the important comment that *"Longinus* indeed blames an author's insisting too much on trivial Circumstances," but Pope holds "There is a vast difference betwixt a *small* Circumstance and a *trivial* one, and the smallest become important if they are well chosen, and not confused." More conventional seems the note to Book xi, line 669, on "low" words in poetry—with the influential passage from Boileau quoted. Pope's method in all these notes, however antiquarian some may be, is to exhibit the beauties of the poetry. This purpose he asserts at the beginning of the notes to both the *Iliad* and the *Odyssey.* He goes further in defining his purpose by being depreciatory of commentators who are always giving us exclamations instead of criticisms. This is the fault of his French predecessor, Mme Dacier: she often gives only "general Praises and Exclamations instead of Reasons." Criticism to Pope is a reasoned discourse about art: in his mature criticism he seldom indulges in stale or unintelligent thinking, though he does not escape the prejudices that were traditional in his day.

Lesser Critics: Textual Criticism

The numerous lesser critics of the period resemble in many ways these four critics just considered. Their vehicles were pamphlets, prefaces, and, increasingly, the periodical essay. There was also a weighty amount of textual criticism done in editions of ancient or modern authors. Shakespeare found in the period 1709-47 five different editors, of whom Pope and Lewis Theobald (1688-1744) are most often recalled. Theobald in his periodical *The Censor* (1715-17) published some brief essays about Shakespeare; and his later remarks on Pope's negligent editing won for him the distinction of being Prince of Dulness in *The Dunciad.* None of Shakespeare's editors before Edmond Malone equaled in editorial care or scholarship the work of Richard Bentley (1662-1742) on Horace (1711), though Bentley lost much of his reputation in 1732 by his tinkerings with the text of *Paradise Lost.* The most scrupulous editing in the period was the work of Thomas

Hearne (1678-1735), the greatest medievalist of the century,[12] and the scholarly edition of Thuanus (7 volumes, folio, 1733) produced by Samuel Buckley (1673-1741) with the aid of the Jacobite historian Thomas Carte (1686-1754) and the wealthy and learned physician Dr. Richard Mead (1673-1754). In comparison with the volumes of these competent editors, the textual work of purely literary men, like Pope and (later) Bishop Percy, is inferior. The relatively amateurish editing of Shakespeare, however, together with the increase of dramatic criticism in the periodical essays augmented the popularity of that great dramatist. By 1737 Pope could write of him as "the divine, the matchless, what you will"; and a torment of "rules" critics was the unblinkable fact that "Shakespear writ without rules."

In the less technical sorts of criticism the minor men followed the methods *Gildon* of the greater critics. Charles Gildon [13] (1665-1724), an admirer of Dryden, *and Others* Congreve, and Dennis, was avowedly a "modern," but a modern who was obsessed by the practices of the ancients—and by rules. Lewis Theobald in his edition of Shakespeare curiously remarked that Gildon was "one attached to Rymer by a similar way of thinking and studies." He certainly was a "rules" critic, but in his early *Miscellaneous Letters and Essays* (1694) he was strong on the side of Shakespeare and opposed to Rymer. His last critical work of note was *The Laws of Poetry ... Explain'd and Illustrated* (1721) in commentaries on the critical poems of three noble lords—Buckinghamshire, Roscommon, and Lansdowne: like much of Gildon's hack work it was obviously a bid for patronage in days when he was both poor and blind. In his *Complete Art of Poetry* (1718) and elsewhere he showed an admiration for Shakespeare but no really stimulating thought. The *Art of Poetry* was for a time kept in memory by a couplet in *The Spleen* by Matthew Green, who asserts of his Muse that she

> Draws from the spring she finds within;
> Nor vainly buys what Gildon sells,
> Poetic buckets for dry wells.

Such buckets, however, had a market; for one Edward Bysshe had brought out *The Art of English Poetry* in 1702, which ran to ten editions by 1739. More interesting than these men was Leonard Welsted (1688-1747), who in addition to poems of some slight repute brought out a translation of Longinus in 1712 with "Remarks" added "on the English Poets" (chiefly Shakespeare and Milton); and in 1724 his prefatory "Dissertation concerning the Perfection of the English Language, the State of Poetry, etc." appeared in a volume of his *Epistles, Odes, etc.* These two essays illustrate the average

---

[12] When Hearne's library was to be sold the *London Daily Post* (February 21, 1736) printed an epigram that exhibits the gift of the time for such witticism as well as Hearne's high reputation as a scholar:
> "Pox on't, quoth Time, to Thomas Hearne,
> Whatever I forget, you learn!"

[13] On Gildon's career see Paul Dottin, "An Essay on Gildon's Life," in Gildon's *Robinson Crusoe Examin'd and Criticis'd* (1923).

taste of the time rather than independent thinking. A work of like interest is *The Arts of Logick and Rhetorick* (1728) which John Oldmixon (1673-1742) based upon *La Manière de Bien Penser* (1687) of Father Dominique Bouhours, a highly valued French critic and essayist. Oldmixon, like most of these minor critics, had found himself placed among Pope's dunces, and this book contains personal retorts of stale virulence. Among the few critics to defend Pope in print was Joseph Spence (1699-1768), who won affection by *An Essay on Pope's Odyssey: in which Some Particular Beauties and Blemishes ... are Consider'd* (1726-7). The display of his beauties led Pope to forgive the blemishes, which Spence pointed out chiefly as faults in over-decorative style. Spence's collections of important literary *ana,* mostly about Pope, were published long after his death as *Anecdotes* (1820). His largest work was a tall folio called *Polymetis* (1747), which was a popular classical handbook for the later century.

Critical Agreements and Dis-agreements   Criticism in the early eighteenth century had a small core of generally accepted doctrine, including beliefs in the moral function of poetry, the value of the ancients as guides or models, the necessity of probability in one's poetic fictions, and the necessity of art to correct nature and to give to form a desirable directness and clarity. There was, however, no agreement on such matters as tragicomedy and poetic justice, and the three unities were in general respected but not carefully observed.[14] There were differences of opinion on the matter of rime vs. blank verse, and, more significant, about the function—but not the importance—of the imagination. Simplicity, sublimity, elegance, and ease were differently, if highly, valued. Even where there was basic agreement, there was likely to be difference in emphasis. The rules of Nature must be observed; the rules of France might be slighted, at the cost of elegance, for the sake of vigor, variety, and richness. As Pope himself put it:

> The rules a nation, born to serve, obeys;
> And Boileau still in right of Horace sways.
> But we, brave Britons, foreign laws despised,
> And kept unconquered, and uncivilized.

But, as he continued in his *Essay on Criticism,* some among "the sounder few" had labored to restore "wit's fundamental laws," and laws were essential. There was, finally, a faint awareness that while the Greco-Roman tradition was dominant, China and Peru and all sorts of other sources of law were waiting to be heard from.

[14] Clarence C. Green's *Neo-Classic Theory of Tragedy in England during the Eighteenth Century* (Cambridge, Mass., 1934) gives a good account of divergences of opinion over dramatic rules.

III
Defoe and Journalism

The art of pamphleteering throve mightily in the seventeenth and eighteenth centuries. Essentially it had little in common with the classical dignity
and magnificence that characterized nobler forms of writing: it was perhaps
the reverse side of the tapestry. In the eighteenth century the pamphlet
supplemented the newspaper; arguments, that is, that were too long for the
single folio sheets or half-sheets that then constituted newspapers, dilated
in independent publications of moderate size. The newspaper itself took
on life after 1695 when the Licensing Act lapsed.[1] Not that the lapsing of
this act made journalism a safe profession: it long remained an anonymous
and furtive employment. Immediately in 1695 the Tories founded an "organ,"
The Post-Boy (1695-1735), edited at first by Abel Roper; and the Whigs
countered with their *Flying-Post* (1695-1731), long presided over by George
Ridpath. *The Post-Man* (1695-1730) was also Whig in bias. Few newspapers
of the day lived as long as these; journals were born to argue over a crisis,
and they ceased when new topics came into play. The first successful daily,
The Daily Courant (1702-35), published by Samuel Buckley, was during
its early and prosperous existence a commercial sheet of Whig tendencies
that grew violent later.

Certain periodicals specialized in comment on news or in essay material
rather than in printing news itself. L'Estrange's *Observator* and Dunton's
Athenian Gazette[2] had ceased publication before 1700, but their formerly
popular methods of dialogue or question and answer still occasionally
found able if vituperative imitators. In 1702 John Tutchin (d. 1707), whose
poem *The Foreigners* had provoked Defoe's *True-Born Englishman,*
founded a Whig *Observator* (1702-12), borrowing the title from Sir Roger
L'Estrange's earlier success. This, in turn, inspired the non-juring Tory,

---

[1] The best bibliographies concerning the history of English periodical publications—essays,
reviews, newspapers—are those made by H. G. Pollard for the *Cambridge Bibliography of
English Literature* (Cambridge, 1940), II. 656-739. The section dealing with "The Periodical
Essay" (pp. 660-668) is by Walter Graham. For newspapers see II. 688-739. Useful among
histories of journalism for this period are the following: H. R. Fox Bourne, *English Newspapers*
(2v, 1887); Edwin B. Chancellor, *The Annals of Fleet Street* (1912); David H. Stevens,
Party Politics and English Journalism, 1702-1742 (Chicago, 1916); Walter Graham, *English
Literary Periodicals* (1930); Stanley Morison, *The English Newspaper* (Cambridge, 1932);
David Nichol Smith, "The Newspaper," *Johnson's England,* ed. A. S. Turberville (Oxford,
1933), II. 331-367 (dealing in part with this period); James R. Sutherland, "The Circulation
of Newspapers and Literary Periodicals, 1700-1730," *Library,* xv (1934). 110-124; Laurence
Hanson, *Government and the Press* (Oxford, 1936). The *Census of British Newspapers and
Periodicals, 1620-1800* made by Ronald S. Crane, F. B. Kaye, and M. E. Prior (Chapel Hill,
1927) is useful both as a bibliography and as a finding-list for American holdings.
[2] See above, Part I, ch. IX, n. 18.

Charles Leslie, to start *The Rehearsal* (1704-9), which attacked Tutchin's *Observator*, Defoe's *Review*, and other Whig utterances.

Politics and Journalism   By 1709 London had at least eighteen separate papers, issuing in all about fifty numbers a week;[3] and the power of the newspaper as a political influence was becoming such that in 1712 the Tory ministry evolved a clever scheme of a stamp tax of a halfpenny per issue on each paper, and the added cost to the buyer crushed Whig journals: Tory papers perhaps were secretly subsidized. Any setback to "Grub-street," as the press was now called, was temporary. Upon the death of Queen Anne the Tories went out of power, and then new Whig journals appeared. Every crisis brought out new papers: Addison and Steele argued on opposite sides of the Peerage Bill in 1719 in their serial pamphlets *The Plebeian* (Steele) and *The Old Whig* (Addison). In the same year John Trenchard (1662-1723) founded, with the able aid of Thomas Gordon (d. 1750), *The London Journal,* in which they published a notable series of essays, collected in 1724 into four volumes called *Cato's Letters*. These argued for punishment of South Sea directors after their "bubble" burst, and for various other good Whig causes. Gordon became one of Sir Robert Walpole's writers, and, apart from politics, published in 1728-31 a valued translation of Tacitus. During Walpole's term of office (1721-42) as prime minister the press became more violent than it had been, but no more soundly intellectual.[4] Attacks on his ministry were led by a coalition of "Patriots," who under the guidance of Viscount Bolingbroke sponsored *The Craftsman* (1726-47). Walpole's most annoying organ was *The Daily Gazetteer* (1735-48), which absorbed three government papers, and was said to be delivered gratis throughout the land in support of the minister. Walpole habitually employed untalented but obedient hacks for his journals, men who could be bought and controlled. Throughout the first half of the century, however, almost all writers from Defoe to the Earl of Chesterfield dabbled overtly or secretly in journalism. Henry Fielding, for example, was intermittently concerned with at least four or five newspapers. Like most of the abler literary personalities of the early forties, he wrote against Walpole.

News Pamphlets   Many newspapers featured the leading article or essay, and when space did not permit long accounts, or when the proprietor of the journal did not wish to risk suppression, a pamphlet was the normal result. In form the pamphlet was most diverse: it might be narrative—realistic or allegorical— it might be argumentative, it might be dialogue, and it was very likely to be cast in the form of a letter. It might be a "feature story," as was Defoe's brilliant *True Relation of the Apparition of one Mrs. Veal*[5] (1706); it

---

[3] See Stanley Morison, *op. cit.,* p. 84.

[4] On the literary opposition to Walpole see Charles B. Realey, *The Early Opposition to Sir Robert Walpole, 1720-1727* (Lawrence, Kan., and Philadelphia, 1931); William T. Laprade, *Public Opinion and Politics . . . to the Fall of Walpole* (1936); and Keith G. Feiling, *The Second Tory Party, 1714-1832* (1938), as well as the works already cited, especially Hanson.

[5] On this clear case of actual journalistic reporting see Sir Charles H. Firth, "Defoe's *True Relation of the Apparition of Mrs. Veal,"* RES, vii (1931). 1-6; and Dorothy Gardiner's "What Canterbury knew of Mrs. Veal and her Friends," RES, vii (1931). 188-197.

might be a practical joke as were the numerous Bickerstaff-Partridge pamphlets of 1708-9, which prophesied the death of the Tory almanac-maker Partridge, and after the fatal evening jeered at him for not admitting his decease.[6] It loved ingenuity, and rose to allegorical excellence in the master-piece of Dr. John Arbuthnot [7] (1667-1735), now known as *The History of John Bull* (1712), in which the whole futility of the War of the Spanish Succession was displayed from the point of view of an English Tory under guise of a lawsuit between Lord Strutt (Spain) and Lewis Baboon (Louis XIV of France) and John Bull (England). "John Bull" as symbolizing England is Arbuthnot's invention. Pamphleteers loved irony, and achieved their most incisive and dangerous appeal through this device. Defoe suffered in the pillory for his ironic *Shortest Way with the Dissenters* (1702); Swift has been castigated for his ironic pre-Malthusian *Modest Proposal for Pre-venting the Children of Poor People from being a Burthen to Their Parents* (1729); and Fielding's burlesque biography of *Jonathan Wild* (1743) used irony to cover a shrewd attack on party politics if not on Walpole himself. Pamphleteering might be dangerous if directed against the ministry (such attacks were frequently ruled seditious) or in favor of the Pretender—such writing was high treason. In 1719 an unfortunate eighteen-year-old printer, John Matthews, was hanged, drawn, and quartered for aiding the publica-tion of a Jacobitical pamphlet called *Vox Populi, Vox Dei*. Such grim facts darkened the careers of even the masters of this type of writing, and dark-ened few careers more than they did that of Daniel Defoe.

No writer of the whole century had a life more full of strange surprising adventures than did Defoe [8] (1660-1731). Son of a dissenting tallow-chandler of London named James Foe (Daniel added the genteel "De" when over forty years of age), he rebelled with Monmouth in 1685 and escaped without punishment. Already well married (1684), he for some years prospered by trading in hosiery, though various lawsuits indicate that his reputation for honesty was sadly tarnished even before 1692, when war ruined his export trade and caused his failure for the sum of £17,000. One way or another

Daniel Defoe

---

[6] William A. Eddy, "Tom Brown and Partridge the Astrologer," *MP*, XXVIII (1930). 163-168.

[7] Arbuthnot, a royal physician and popular wit, with his close friends Swift, Pope, Gay, and Parnell, constituted the Scriblerus Club, and was largely concerned in the "Memoirs of Martinus Scriblerus," published by Pope in 1741. His *Life and Works*, ed. George A. Aitken (Oxford, 1892) is the only modern edition of his writings. An excellent study of his mind and genius is found in Lester M. Beattie's *John Arbuthnot Mathematician and Satirist* (Cambridge, Mass., 1935). Herman Teerink's edition of *John Bull* (Amsterdam, 1925) has textual usefulness: his ascription of the work to Swift lacks proof.

[8] There is no complete edition of Defoe's works, which run to over 400 titles. The titles are best listed in *CBEL*, II. 495-514. Collected editions—chiefly of the novels—have been made; see *Romances and Narratives*, ed. George A. Aitken (16v, 1895) and *Works*, ed. Gustavus H. Maynadier (16v, 1903-4), and *Novels and Selected Writings*, 1719-29 (3v, 1869). For biographies see William Lee, *Life and Recently Discovered Writings*, 1719-29 (3v, 1869); Thomas Wright, *Life* (1894; rev. ed., 1931); William P. Trent, *Daniel Defoe: How to Know Him* (Indianapolis, 1916); Paul Dottin, *Daniel De Foe et ses romans* (3v, Paris, 1924), cheapened in an English translation of Vol. 1 (1929); James R. Sutherland, *Defoe* (1937: the best one-volume life); John R. Moore, *Defoe in the Pillory and Other Studies* (Bloomington, Ind., 1939). For criticism see Arthur W. Secord, *Studies in the Narrative Method of Defoe* (Urbana, Ill., 1924).

much of this indebtedness was later paid off; but for the rest of his career Defoe had in his heart the strong dread of the law and the fear of a debtor's prison. He learned the trick of quiet disappearance, and practised it often when legal danger threatened—and more than once it threatened because of his career as a writer, which he undertook when his chosen function of "true-born merchant" was closed to him. Practically all of his writing was done after he was thirty-five, and the first of his famous stories, *Robinson Crusoe,* was the work of his sixtieth year.

Defoe's Personal Character

His personal character as seen in his writings is worth considering.[9] As seen in real life it was none too favorably regarded by his critics. In the bitter days of 1713 when his *Mercator* was supporting Tory ideas of trade, that firm Whig Joseph Addison, in his *Tryal of Count Tariff,* spoke of Defoe as "a false, shuffling, prevaricating rascal . . . unqualified to give his testimony in a Court of Justice." This from one who at times tactfully hinted faults and hesitated dislikes, is unduly severe; one must at least allow that when Defoe's own fortunes were not at stake, he had frequently a disinterested and highly intelligent attitude towards the public welfare. Like Robinson Crusoe and all his fictitious heroes, he was suspiciously shrewd and excessively ingenious; he was as a partisan or a businessman slippery and changeable: one could not tell which side he was on or even which side he thought he was writing on—such was his gift of irony. But in his more disinterested moments his ingenuity is amusingly canny. His first real book, for example, called *An Essay upon Projects* (1697), is significantly public spirited. Some of his projects, here presented,·with regard to reforms in legal procedure are doubtless the result of his own sad experiences; but his desire to see the highways of England improved (by means of humanely directed slave labor!), his plan for an asylum for idiots and, at the other extreme, for an academy to correct and stabilize the English language, and, above all, his projected "academy for women," which shows his confidence in the capabilities of women along with suspicions of their discretion—all these projects display the desire of his time to improve practical conditions of life. Such desires never left Defoe, and they operate in very diverse fields. In 1724-7, for example, appeared one of his most popular and useful works, *A Tour thro' the Whole Island of Great Britain* (three volumes),[10] which was important for fifty years as a guidebook and even longer as a document in the economic history of England. It is by a tradesman, and is about trade for the most part; but when he reaches Windsor Castle, he remarks, "I must leave talking of Trade, River, Navigation, Meal, and Malt, and describe the most beautiful, and most pleasantly situated Castle, and Royal Palace, in the whole Isle of Britain." And when he describes the paintings in St. George's Hall and tells us, "I had some Pretensions to Judgment of pictures," the reader may recall that in 1720 he had

[9] On this difficult subject see Hans H. Andersen, "The Paradox of Trade and Morality in Defoe," *MP,* xxxix (1941). 23-46, and John R. Moore, "The Character of Daniel Defoe," *RES,* xiv (1938). 68-71.

[10] Edited by George D. H. Cole (2v, 1927, and also for Everyman's Library).

published a translation of Du Fresnoy's *Compleat Art of Painting*. He was furthermore well informed in the history of modern Europe, and his geographical knowledge was far from contemptible. His intellect was eager, retentive, far-ranging, shrewd, and ingenious: what he lacked was a just and tenacious adherence to honest dealing in practical matters.

Any career as political writer was dangerous; and Defoe, as a dissenter, a writer for hire, and an ironist, seems usually to have been in danger. He began as a satirical political poet; and by the time (1703) when he first collected his works, he had produced several poems of this kind. His most effective and popular verse was doubtless the *True-Born Englishman* (1701), which defended William III against the prejudices of such subjects as disliked the King's Dutch origin or Dutch advisers. He begins briskly— *Defoe's Adventurous Career*

> Where-ever God erects a House of Prayer,
> The Devil always builds a Chapel there:
> And 'twill be found upon Examination,
> The latter has the largest Congregation.

And he concludes in a rugged fashion natural to a bourgeois—

> Fame of Families is all a Cheat,
> *'Tis Personal Virtue only makes us Great.*

In 1706 he published an almost epic satirical attack (in twelve books) on divine right, called *Jure Divino*. But prose was his trade—even when he used metre and rime; and his crucial writings were prose pamphlets. As a dissenter he early engaged, somewhat equivocally at times, in the arguments over "occasional conformity," by which practice of occasionally taking the Anglican communion—a practice which Defoe called "playing-Bopeep with God Almighty"—dissenters might qualify for public office. In his *Enquiry into the Occasional Conformity of Dissenters* (1698) he remarks of such fellow dissenters as thus conformed, "These are Patriots indeed, that will damn their Souls to save their Countrey." In 1701, according to his own boast, "guarded with about sixteen gentlemen of quality," he entered the House of Commons and presented Mr. Speaker with *Legion's Memorial to the House of Commons*. The foolhardiness of this act at such a moment can be guessed if one reads the threatening end of the pamphlet, which told Mr. Speaker that "Englishmen are no more to be slaves to Parliaments than to a King. Our name is LEGION, and we are many." The pamphlet succeeded in its aims; but the next year its author had no such luck. His *Shortest Way with the Dissenters* (1702) he had conceived as a playful ironic attack on the extreme High Church people who believed that "if the Gallows instead of the Counter, and the Gallies instead of the Fines, were the Reward of going to a Conventicle, to preach or hear, there wou'd not be so many Sufferers." Defoe's irony here backfired: both dissenters and churchmen were offended, and the government ordered his arrest. After successfully hiding for over four months, he was taken, tried, and condemned to pay a heavy fine and to stand in the pillory three times. A sentence of such severity was a thunderbolt: in Defoe's time more than one sinner died from the effects of missiles hurled at pilloried heads. But our hero's ingenuity was equal to the occasion: his friends were rallied about him; he composed a *Hymn to the Pillory,* which sold well during his exposure; and when he came down "from his Wooden Punishment" the crowd treated him, so a Tory journalist complained, "as if he had been a Cicero that had made an excellent oration in it." [11] After this uncomfort-able triumph Defoe was returned to Newgate for an indeterminate sentence, totally unable to pay the large fine that had been imposed along with the pillory. His tile works at Tilbury were gone; he was now irretrievably bankrupt a second time, with no prospect of release from prison. Late in 1703, however, his fine was suddenly paid by the Crown, and Defoe, bound over to good behavior, was released. Good behavior apparently meant be-coming the man Friday of Robert Harley, a rising politician soon (1704) to be Secretary of State and later (1710-14) to be a Tory prime minister.[12]

Defoe's Review

During the first decade of the century Defoe's important achievements were to aid, by journalism or by pamphlet or by confidential personal work, the Union with Scotland (1707) and to further the Whig cause and English trade in his extensive journal, *A Review of the Affairs of France* (1704-13).[13] It will be remembered that during these years England and France were at war. Defoe's *Review* was actually a political or economic serial pamphlet that appeared, during most of its run, in four quarto pages three times a week. So far as is known, Defoe wrote its nine volumes singlehanded—an almost unparalleled feat in the journalism of the day, all the more surprising because some of the time Defoe was out of London—even as far away as Scotland, where he was serving as confidential agent of the government. The *Review* has not much in common with the lighter periodical essay of the type of *The Tatler;* but Defoe and others have thought that his moral-izings and the amusing sections captioned as "Advice from the Scandalous Club" were among the formative influences of *The Tatler.* When Harley and the Tories came into power in 1710 the influence of the Whig *Review* de-clined, and presently in its place Defoe was writing for the Tories a new trade journal called *Mercator, or Commerce Retriev'd* (1713-14).

Other Newspaper Connections

After 1715 he was connected with various papers, among which *Mercurius Politicus* (1716-20), *The Daily Post* (1719-25), Applebee's *Weekly Journal* (1720-26), and Dormer's *News-Letter* (1716-18) mark, with one exception, his principal periods and places of journalistic employment. The exception is significant. In 1717 he was as a reputed Tory secretly placed by the Whig

[11] Theodore F. M. Newton, "William Pittis and Queen Anne Journalism," *MP,* xxxiii (1935-6). 169-186; 279-302. The quotation is from p. 181.

[12] David H. Stevens, "Defoe and the Earl of Oxford," *Party Politics and English Journalism* (Chicago, 1916), pp. 47-60.

[13] Recently the *Review* has been made available for study in a beautiful facsimile edition made by the Facsimile Text Society—with an excellent introduction by Arthur W. Secord. The *Review* shows Defoe's ability as a social and economic thinker at his best. See A. E. Levett, "Daniel Defoe," *The Social and Political Ideas . . . of the Augustan Age,* ed. F. J. C. Hearn-shaw (1928), and John R. Moore, "Daniel Defoe and Modern Economic Theory," *Indiana Univ. Studies,* xxi (1934). 1-28.

ministry on the staff of the Tory-Jacobite *Weekly Journal; or, Saturday's Post*, published by Nathaniel Mist. It was his task to moderate the fury of this journalistic storm-center, and until 1724 he had some success in the attempt: in all such government jobs he was likely to be acting a part— and not too sincerely. More than once he was writing for both Whig and Tory journals at the same time. Just after *Robinson Crusoe* (1719), he began work on Applebee's *Journal*, writing stories about Jack Sheppard and other criminals, which led him into the genre of criminal biography.

Most of Defoe's longer works were in part related to his journalism or to his love of "projects." That he wrote his longer stories at all was probably due to the unexpectedly great success of *Robinson Crusoe*,[14] the first part of which was a fictional grafting upon the story of Alexander Selkirk, who had lived alone on Juan Fernandez from 1704-9, and whose return to England in 1711 had caused the publication of many narratives of his history. Defoe's masterpiece was acclaimed at once, and when four editions were called for within four months, he followed it with a second volume of *Farther Adventures of Robinson Crusoe*, which was not worthy of the first. In 1720 a moralizing treatise was added as a third volume; it was entitled *Serious Reflections ... of Robinson Crusoe*. Only the first *Strange Surprising Adventures of Robinson Crusoe* won fame, and its popularity was and remains enormous.[15] "There is not an old Woman," wrote Gildon, enviously attacking, "that can go to the Price of it, but buys ... and leaves it as a Legacy, with the *Pilgrim's Progress*, the *Practice of Piety*, and *God's Revenge against Murther*, to her Posterity." It was, however, to be more than a middle-class masterpiece: though sprawling in structure and careless in detail, it expressed the eighteenth-century epic theme of the power of the average man to preserve life and to organize an economy in the face of the most unpromising environment. A modern novelist would focus on the horrors of isolation, the loneliness of Crusoe's island; for Defoe these things hardly existed: his mind, as always, was on the God-given power of sinful man to win through—and on the human ingenuity that embellishes the effort.

His Longer Works: Robinson Crusoe

This success led rapidly to other long narratives, produced with a speed almost unaccountable if we consider that in addition to books he was turning out newspaper leaders and pamphlets in quantity. Within twelve weeks in the summer of 1720 he published his historical romance *The Memoirs of a Cavalier*, his *Captain Singleton*, which was another voyage story with pirates featured, and his *Serious Reflections* of Crusoe. During the year 1722 his longer books included *Moll Flanders, Due Preparations for the Plague, Religious Courtship, A Journal of the Plague Year*, and his *Colonel Jacque. Roxana* appeared in 1724, *Capt. George Carleton* in 1728, and in

His Facility in Writing

---

[14] Henry C. Hutchins, *Robinson Crusoe and its Printing, 1719-31* (1925), gives a thorough account of the early editions.

[15] The story even created in Germany a literary type known as *Robinsonaden*. See H. Ullrich, *Robinson und Robinsonaden* (Weimar, 1898), and the learned work of Philip B. Gove, *The Imaginary Voyage in Prose Fiction* (1941), pp. 122-154.

1729 *Robert Drury's Journal,* a work about Madagascar that seems at least in part Defoe's. His *Compleat English Gentleman,* incomplete at his death, was published in 1890. Not all of these works are certainly the exclusive creations of Defoe; but on the other hand it is probable that other books unidentified, especially translations, were made by him.

The Vivid-ness of His Plague Year   Obviously his pen was indefatigable; equally obvious is the fact that his art was chiefly nature: he wrote rapidly, revised seldom,[16] and succeeded through a natural gift for ingenious episode and specific detail. Some of the details in his *Journal of the Plague Year* are so living and horrible as to seem the plausible memories of an eye-witness rather than the work of an author who was only five years old when in 1665 the plague ravaged London.[17] The bellman walking by night in front of the dead-cart, ringing his bell and calling "Bring out your dead!" appalls the memory. The "agony and excess of sorrow" of the pitiful stranger "muffled up in a brown cloak" and come to the great pit to see the body of some one dear to him buried is communicated to us with the full horror of the scene. For sheer grimness this book is Defoe's masterpiece; but all his stories are full of what he calls "speaking sights."

His Charac-terizations   His gifts in characterization can easily be underrated. The spiritually gaunt and awesome figure of Moll Flanders, victim of society and of the Devil, born in Newgate of bad blood that could come to no good, and the more gracious figure of Colonel Jacque—born with genteel blood in him, fortunately—form two of the best contrasting genre pictures of the century. Crusoe and Friday, Singleton and his Quaker William are as authentic as they are casual in portrayal. More than one of these characters illustrates some editorial point. William dramatizes Defoe's prejudice against Quakers [18] —together with his admiration for their shrewdness; Moll Flanders illus-trates the techniques of thieves and adventuresses; Colonel Jacque illustrates the inequity of Spanish trade barriers. Defoe always admires the merchant, and his heroes are always adding up their financial profits, frequently for Defoe's delight rather than for the reader's pleasure.

Lack of Structure   He lacks well-knit structure; several of his stories show a break near the middle which might suggest that Defoe has for the moment run out of adventures, and presently must open a new vein. When Crusoe has estab-lished his economy, there is a pause; then the footprint is seen, Friday is introduced, and we can observe education impressing the blank sheet which is the mind of the man of Nature. *Captain Singleton* is half devoted to a trip across central Africa and half devoted to pirate adventures. *The Memoirs of a Cavalier* divides interest between Continental wars of the seventeenth century and the Cavalier's services to King Charles I in the English Civil

---

[16] William T. Hastings, in "Errors and Inconsistencies in Defoe's *Robinson Crusoe,*" *MLN,* XXVII (1912). 161-166, points out amusing bits of carelessness.

[17] Watson Nicholson's *Historical Sources of Defoe's Journal of the Plague Year* (Boston, 1919) is valuable as a study of Defoe's factual sources: the book fails in the author's purpose to depreciate Defoe's imaginative gifts.

[18] Ezra K. Maxfield, "Daniel Defoe and the Quakers," *PMLA,* XLVII (1932). 179-190.

Wars. *Moll Flanders*, in many ways his most naturally constructed work, deals first with her amorous adventures and in middle age her adventures as a thief. *Moll* comes closer to standard technique in novel writing in that a nucleus of a social group is reunited at the end of the story. Normally only the central character continues throughout the whole story. Defoe seldom uses chapter divisions, and thus lacks an easy mechanical aid in emphasizing dramatic moments as well as preparation for and punctuation of minor climaxes.

In pattern, his narratives are fictional autobiographies always pretending to be "true" stories, and so cleverly authenticated with fictional detail that it is at times difficult to believe that they have no basis in actuality. *The Memoirs of a Cavalier* has been the object of several attempts—all fruitless —to identify the hero with an actual cavalier. *Moll Flanders* ends with the gratuitous note, "Written in the year 1683"; but the date is obviously impossible. In general Defoe's sense of the passing of time in a story is vague and poor. Crusoe's adventures and Moll Flanders' love affairs drift on through an excessive number of years. Lacking neat arts of construction, Defoe excelled in rich variety of superbly devised episode. An adventure to Defoe was not so much a hairbreadth escape as it was an exercise of human ingenuity or a piece of surprising and delightful good luck. The bit about the small Jacque's hiding his money in the hollow tree is a perfect synthesis of Defoe elements: Jacque's vanishing sense of wrong-doing, his fear of being done out of his stolen prize, his sense of his own incompetence, his grief at his supposed loss when the money falls down inside the tree, and, above all, the final "revolution and discovery" that terminates this little financial tragicomedy, are all essential Defoe. By turns he is to be seen counting his profits, or listening to the voice of a very circuitous and personal Devil, or considering the moral or social implications of his episodes.

"Truth" in His Fiction

The relation of Defoe's longer narratives to the tradition of the English novel has been debated.[19] He has been regarded as following the picaresque type of fiction, and if the word *picaresque* is loosely used—as it certainly is by critics—one understands what is meant. But actually Defoe wrote rogue biography rather than the true picaresque. The eighteenth century was to conceive the picaresque in the light of René LeSage's masterpiece, *Gil Blas* (1715-35). There the tradition as formulated required biographical pattern, episodic structure with the protagonist living by his wits and passing from one social stratum to another or from one professional class to another, the object of the change being diversified social exposé or satire. This tradition is common in eighteenth-century novels, and is seen in Sarah Fielding's *David Simple* (1744-53), Francis Coventry's *Pompey the Little* (1751), Charles Johnstone's *Chrysal* (1760-65), Smollett's *Adventures of an Atom* (1769), and many other minor masterpieces; but with this

The Picaresque Tradition

[19] It is shrewdly argued in Arthur W. Secord, *Studies in the Narrative Method of Defoe* (Urbana, Ill., 1924).

tradition, so far as conscious social exposé is concerned, Defoe has little in common. His traditions are clearly those of biography, voyage literature, and the moral treatise—of which last he himself produced various examples.[20] It is from the manual of piety that Defoe acquired his moralizing tone— which is hortatory rather than satirical. With the types of novel destined to be popular later in the century Defoe has less in common than one might think; but, on the other hand, with the spontaneous, unsophisticated methods of narration, far more fundamental than the temporary fashions that shaped the novel ten years or more after his death, Defoe has a great deal in common. He lacks power over domestic emotions, and these were to be the stock in trade of the sentimentalists; but his gifts are more basically sound than theirs, and his influence will endure as long as theirs. He is perhaps more realistic than many of them are; but he never seems to worry about conscientious fabrication of real life: he is, like the truly natural storyteller, content to create elaborate illusions of reality, and makes no attempt to build up a complete and authentic picture of Life for us. His stimulus— monetary returns apart—is that of his century: appetite for reflection upon the duty of man to man in a social world. The moral treatise thus becomes the positive pole in his fictional creations; adventure becomes the negative pole.

Preacher and Commentator

From first to last we may call him the preacher or editorial commentator. Crusoe is disobedient to his parents and to the God who had appropriately placed him in the scale of being; as a consequence of sin in leaving his proper station he is thereafter to feel frequently that he was "the most miserable wretch that ever was born." In *Moll Flanders* Defoe glides easily and briefly into editorial comments on the advantages of a foundling asylum, and *A Journal of the Plague Year,* written when a recurrence of the plague was feared in London, takes time to argue the inhumanity of so vital a matter as quarantine. His voyage stories like to expose the unfair trading practices of low foreigners, who—to make matters worse in his extreme Protestant mind—are Catholics as well as foreigners. His historical romances at times reflect the ideas of the Good Old Cause of the sixteen-forties. His geographical and historical detail is the product of much journalistic reading, and it is this reading, together with his shrewd observation of contemporary life, that gave both the rich variety and the vivid detail of his narratives. The vitality and fecundity of genius shown by Defoe after he was sixty years old remain as astonishing as are the earlier wily arts of the ablest journalist and pamphleteer of his time.

---

[20] His *Family Instructor* (1715) was frequently reprinted and so was his *Religious Courtship* (1722).

IV

Jonathan Swift

In some ways Jonathan Swift's career [1] parallels that of Daniel Defoe.[2] Both were considerably occupied in the dangerous career of political writer, and both were energetic supporters of Robert Harley, Earl of Oxford. The contrast between the two has been symbolized by the supposition that *Swift and* Swift was received by the front door whereas Defoe waited on the back *Defoe: a* stairs. Defoe was, to be sure, a tradesman, and Swift came of somewhat *Contrast* more genteel stock; but the real difference in the men lies in the fact that Defoe was a dissenter and had a middle-class practical education. Swift was a churchman, and *speciali gratia* a university graduate. An independent neo-classicist, Swift had and knew how to use brilliantly a "good classical training." Defoe was hardly conscious of the classics as patterns for writing. Both men were endowed with a strong common sense; both viewed mankind with curiosity—and suspicion. Defoe possessed a wide factual knowledge of the political, social, and economic conditions of England, whereas Swift was content to condemn "conditions"—rashly at times—because he found them abysmally divorced from his ideals. He viewed conditions with

[1] The *Works* of Swift, collectively published by George Faulkner in 1735 (4v, Dublin), *et seq.*, have been edited as follows: by John Hawkesworth (12v, 1755; 20v, 1764-79), Thomas Sheridan (17v, 1784), Sir Walter Scott (19v, Edinburgh, 1814, 1824), Temple Scott (Bohn Library, 12v, 1897-1908), and Herbert Davis (1939 ff., in progress). The *Poems* have been superbly edited by Harold Williams (3v, Oxford, 1937) and the *Correspondence* by F. Elrington Ball (6v, 1910-14). See also *Vanessa and her Correspondence with Jonathan Swift*, ed. Alexander M. Freeman (1921); and *The Letters of Swift to Charles Ford*, ed. David Nichol Smith (1935); *A Tale of a Tub* (1704, 1710); ed. A. C. Guthkelch and David Nichol Smith (Oxford, 1920); *Gulliver's Travels* (1726, 1735 [in *Works*]); ed. G. Ravenscroft Dennis (Bohn Library *Works*, Vol. VIII, 1899); Harold Williams (1926); Arthur E. Case (1938); Herbert Davis and Harold Williams (Oxford, 1941). — Among the many biographies may be mentioned those of John, fifth Earl of Orrery (*Remarks*, 1752); John Hawkesworth (1755); Deane Swift (1755); Samuel Johnson (*Lives of the Poets*, 1781); Thomas Sheridan (1784); John Forster (1875); Sir Henry Craik (1882; 2v, 1894); John Churton Collins (1893); Carl Van Doren (1930); Bertram Newman (1937); and Robert W. Jackson (1939). — The best commentaries are William A. Eddy, *A Critical Study of Gulliver's Travels* (Princeton, 1923); Sybil Goulding, *Swift en France* (Paris, 1924); Emile Pons, *Swift: Les années de jeunesse et le Conte du Tonneau* (Strasbourg, 1925); F. Elrington Ball, *Swift's Verse* (1928); Herbert Davis, "Swift's View of Poetry," *Studies in English* (Toronto, 1931); Harold Williams, *Dean Swift's Library* (1932); Marjorie Nicolson, *The Microscope and English Imagination* (Northampton, Mass., 1935); Richard F. Jones, *Ancients and Moderns: A Study of the Background of the Battle of the Books* (St. Louis, 1936); Ricardo Quintana, *The Mind and Art of Jonathan Swift* (1936). — Bibliographies of Swift have been published by W. Spencer Jackson in Vol. XII of the Bohn Library (Temple Scott) ed. of Swift's *Prose Works* (1908), by Dr. H. Teerink (Hague, 1937), by Harold Williams in *CBEL*, II. 581-596, and by Louis A. Landa and James E. Tobin, *Jonathan Swift, A List of Critical Studies Published from 1895 to 1945* (1945). More specialized aids are cited below in footnotes.

[2] See John F. Ross, *Swift and Defoe: a Study in Relationship* (Berkeley and Los Angeles, 1941); ably reviewed by Louis A. Landa in *PQ*, XXI (1942). 221-223.

contempt, and hence has been called a cynic; but if a cynic is one who denies the existence of humane values, the term cannot be applied to him; for his excellent sense of values is implicit in all that he wrote. He wrote contemptuously and vexatiously, if you like, yet always for the good of mankind. Curiously enough, like Defoe, when he was sure a public measure was right—and, when sure, he was likely to be very sure—he was sometimes unscrupulous in his means of supporting that measure. The personal reputations of Defoe and Pope have suffered because critics have known them only partially. Swift, more than any man of his day, has suffered from deliberate romanticizing of his career. It is true that he, more than most geniuses, fancied himself in the rôle of merit unrewarded; it is true that he writes frequently in an emotionally intense manner: his external frigidity indicates ardor within; but it is also true that he writes with exquisite playfulness. The romantics exaggerated the blackness of his grumblings and intensities, and forgot his gifts for sheer fun.

Aspects of Swift's Career

Intellectually his career has ecclesiastical, political, social, and even philosophical aspects: chronologically it has four or five phases that must be surveyed if we are to understand him. He was born (1667) of English parents living in Ireland; and there he was educated. He was graduated from Trinity College, Dublin, with some difficulty because of his refusal to study logic, and he left Ireland for England at the time of the Revolution (1688). This first phase of his career, in which his rôle had been that of dependent poor relation, had unfortunately built up in the young man an inordinate and overbearing pride.

Swift at Moor Park

His second rôle was that of secretary to Sir William Temple, then living in retirement chiefly at Moor Park, Surrey. While Swift languished here, his former schoolmate and friend, William Congreve, was winning fame in London. Eyeing, therefore, the metropolis, Swift was discontented at Moor Park. There were compensations—some perhaps unappreciated. He there met distinguished guests—among them King William himself; and he learned from Temple much about politics [3] and absorbed Temple's disbelief in the idea of progress, his belief in cycles of change whereby civilization graced now China, now Peru, now Greece and Rome. Clearly he must have enjoyed his duty of supervising the education of the eight-year-old child, Esther Johnson, who perhaps was Sir William's natural daughter. Swift later developed an appetite for improving the minds of ladies whom he knew: Stella (as he later called Esther Johnson, after she had gone to live in Ireland) was his first and his only "perfect" pupil. In her, mind predominated, as he thought it should, over emotion.

His Early Odes

During his periods of service at Moor Park, ending with Sir William's death in 1699, Swift read and thought much, and wrote. His writing rather strangely began with a group of Pindaric odes, of which he published only one. This *Ode to the Athenian Society,* printed in *The Athenian Gazette*

---

[3] Robert J. Allen, "Swift's Earliest Political Tract and Sir William Temple's Essays," *Harvard Studies & Notes in Phil. & Lit.,* xix (1937). 3-12.

(1692), is like the odes which he did not publish, turgid, lofty, and obscure: not at all like Swift! If Dryden ever made the alleged remark, "Cousin Swift, you will never be a poet," it may well have been made as a critique on this ode. His unpublished epistles to Congreve and to Sir William are similarly involved and artificial: being in couplets they have no duty to rise to Cowleyan ecstasy. Never again was Swift to try lofty flights except to burlesque them. He evidently decided that thereafter any verse of his must be natural in a realistic, functionalist sense: his poetry was to be as "unpoetical" as possible, without ornament or high emotional glow.

At Moor Park also he wrote (1696-8) his first and very important prose, *A Tale of a Tub* and *The Battle of the Books,* which he published in 1704. Infinitely superior to his odes, these pieces are, nevertheless, akin to the *Early Prose* method of those early poems in their effervescence, in the way his fancy *Masterpieces* coruscates around the ideas it wishes to express or to discredit: there is no urge to forward-moving, direct structure here in his thought. These works had their origin in the so-called quarrel between the ancients and the moderns, which Temple's essay *Of Ancient and Modern Learning* (1690) had fanned into flame. William Wotton, a Cambridge don, in his *Reflections upon Ancient and Modern Learning* (1694), patiently explained to Temple and the world the real advances of modern science, and attacked Temple's ignorance as shown in his remarks about the antiquity of Aesop and the *Epistles* of Phalaris. In 1693 the Christ Church wits of Oxford set on young Charles Boyle, later Earl of Orrery, to edit the *Epistles* of Phalaris and thus exhibit their true quality—without repeating Temple's errors. The edition (1695) attacked Richard Bentley, then royal librarian at St. James's, for alleged discourtesy. Bentley, ever a fighter, had aided Wotton with a "Dissertation" appended to his *Reflections* in 1697, and retorted also in a second *Dissertation.* Swift, doubtless perceiving the impossibility of a crushing answer, began his part in the struggle, which was to pour out his already copious supply of contempt upon the whole silly controversy, and, more broadly, upon the conceited complacency of modern scholarship, criticism, and poetry. His vehicle in the simpler *Battle of the Books* (out of respect to Bentley the battle took place in the royal library) is the prose mock-heroic, and here Swift exhibits at its best the love of classical epic techniques that marked his period. The mock epic simile in which Bentley and Wotton are spitted on a single spear and the episode of the spider and the bee, with the fine moral by Aesop, constitute perfection in neo-classical writing. *A Tale of a Tub* is of wider scope and less unified structure. In the narrative sections about the three brothers, Peter (the Roman Church), Martin (the Lutheran or Anglican Church), and Jack (the English dissenters or extreme Protestants), he burlesques church history and dogma in a rash and, so others felt, sacrilegious fashion.[4] In the Digressions of the *Tale* he satirizes modern learning, criticism, and the general self-sufficiency of "moderns."

---

[4] On Swift's attitude towards religion, learning, and pedantry see David Nichol Smith, "Jonathan Swift, Some Observations." *Trans. Royal Soc. of Lit.,* XIV (1935). 29-48.

Here also, as in the section on "The Mechanical Operation of the Spirit," there are philosophical implications as to the methods of knowledge that have significance in the period. Practically no political issues are raised in this book.

In 1694, ambitious of a more independent career than Moor Park promised, Swift had returned to Ireland and become an ordained Anglican priest.[5] During a dull year in an Irish parish he found time to fall in love with a Belfast heiress, who regarded her ill health and his meager income as barriers to the marriage which in 1696 he much desired. Disappointed, he returned to Moor Park, and when, after Temple's death, he was back in Ireland as chaplain to the Earl of Berkeley and the heiress tried to reopen negotiations for a match, he concluded the affair with chilly regrets that neither his fortune nor her health had greatly improved. His reputation in the first decade of the new century doubtless depended on *A Tale of a Tub,* which was a sensation if not altogether a success, and on his position as editor of Temple's *Letters* and *Memoirs.* In the Berkeley household he produced certain literary witticisms that are typical of his playfulness—the best of these in verse is the burlesque *Petition of Frances Harris,* the maidservant who lost her purse and so her parson too. In prose his solemn banter of Lady Berkeley's fondness for the Hon. Robert Boyle's pious *Meditations* produced a delightful trifle, his *Meditation upon a Broomstick,* with its pontifical conclusion, "Surely Man is a Broomstick." Grave buffoonery was already his forte.

His London Years   From 1708 to 1714 Swift was chiefly in London, and these years, especially those after 1710, represent his period of triumph and disillusionment in public affairs. Some of his innocent playfulness persists in the early works of this period. *The Predictions for the Year 1708 ... by Isaac Bickerstaff, Esq.,* for example, and its succeeding pamphlets, in which the pseudonymous author (Bickerstaff) [6] of the later *Tatler* is created, are a real contribution to the literature of laughter, and the poetic rendering, new style, of Ovid's *Baucis and Philemon* shows Swift's gift of visual myth-making. In *Baucis and Philemon,* however, there is a savage undertone in the poet's attitude towards the village "Pack of churlish Boors," who may be thought to represent average mankind.

But by 1708 Swift had more serious work to do—though always he would do it with a mixture of savagery and mirth. His duty in London was to serve as a sort of representative of his Archbishop in attempting to regain for the Irish church certain tithes, which Queen Anne had remitted to English parishes but not to those in Ireland. He is consequently involved

<hr/>

[5] On the much disputed problems concerning Swift's religion see C. Looten, *La Pensée religieuse de Swift et ses antinomies* (Lille and Paris, 1935); Hans Reimers, *Jonathan Swift: Gedanken und Schriften über Religion und Kirche* (Hamburg, 1935); see also F. M. Darnall, "Swift's Religion," *JEGP,* xxx (1931). 379-382; and especially Louis A. Landa, "Swift, the Mysteries, and Deism," *Studies in English, University of Texas* (Austin, 1945; dated 1944). pp. 239-256.

[6] W. A. Eddy, "Tom Brown and Partridge the Astrologer," *MP,* xxviii (1930). 163-168, illuminates this procedure.

in ecclesiastical politics, and these concerned the Bill for Occasional Con- *Ecclesiasti-*
formity. As early as Section xi of *A Tale of a Tub* Swift had disapproved *cal Politics*
of the occasional conformity [7] of the Lord Mayor of 1697, as Defoe had
done in his *Enquiry into the Occasional Conformity of Dissenters;* and now
Swift in his *Letter...concerning the Sacramental Test* (1709) opposed
repeal of the Test, even for Ireland. The Letter is supposedly by a member
of the Irish Parliament, who assures his English cousins: "If your little
finger be sore, and you think a poultice made of our vitals will give it any
ease, speak the word and it shall be done." The argument and tone of the
Letter, typical of Swift's method of inflaming rather than convincing,
estranged him from the government of Godolphin and Sunderland, whose
price for the desired tithes was repeal of the Test in Ireland. Consequently
when in 1710 these Whigs went out of office and Swift's personal friend
Robert Harley, a moderate Tory, became Lord Treasurer, it was easy for
Swift to shift allegiance in party alignments that meant little at the time.
In ecclesiastical issues he made no change: his brilliantly ironical *Argument
to prove that the Abolishing of Christianity in England, may ... be Attended with some Inconveniences* (1711) continues his bitter attack upon
those who would abolish the Test. It is one of his best ironical pieces.

For nearly four years (1710-14) he supported Robert Harley and Henry *His Services*
St. John, each ennobled presently, the former as Earl of Oxford and the *to Robert*
latter as Viscount Bolingbroke. Support of these moderate Tories cost *Harley*
him the friendship of Addison and Steele, and doubtless of many others. The
new ministry had started a paper called *The Examiner* (August 3, 1710 to
July 26, 1714). It had not gone too well, but when Swift briefly took charge
in October, 1710 (Nos. 14-46), it became a powerful aid to the ministry.
Among its writers were Dr. William King (1663-1712), Mrs. Mary Manley,
the novelist, and others—notably William Oldisworth (1680-1734), who
was editor after the first volume, which ended in July, 1711. Before *The
Examiner* Swift had had experience in writing for Steele's *Tatler* and later
for his friend Harrison's continuation of *The Tatler.* Both in *The Examiner*
and in his pamphlets Swift's function was to aid the ministry by discrediting
the war party, especially the great general, John Churchill, Duke of Marlborough, and to persuade the public that the war was being prolonged
because there was money in it for such men as the general, and James
Brydges as paymaster and Robert Walpole as Secretary at War. The first
step was to urge the selfishness of England's allies, to persuade readers that
this had become a Continental, not an English fight. In his great pamphlet,
The Conduct of the Allies (1711) and in its pendant *Some Remarks on
the Barrier Treaty* (1712) Swift did these things effectively and perhaps

[7] The Corporation Act of 1661 and the Test Act of 1672 had required all officers of the
Crown to take oaths of allegiance and to receive the sacrament of the Lord's Supper in the
established church. These acts excluded Catholics from public office, but dissenters frequently
did not scruple to take the Anglican communion occasionally, and thus qualify for office.
Extreme high-churchmen were eager to promote bills forbidding this Occasional Conformity.
To abolish "the Test," Swift says with supreme hyperbole, would be to abolish Christianity;
but he is not sure that prohibiting Occasional Conformity is expedient.

sincerely: in politics it was easy for him to believe as he chose to believe. Among several other pamphlets in this process his *Public Spirit of the Whigs* (1714) was dangerously successful. It was a blistering reply to Steele's *Crisis* (1713), and it led the House of Lords to vote Swift's piece "a false, malicious, and factious libel" and to offer a reward of £300 for the discovery of the author. The Lord Treasurer reassured the author privately with a gift of £100, and when the new Parliament met, Steele, because of *The Crisis* and other impudent behavior, was expelled from the House of Commons. For all these trying and dangerous labors Swift naturally hoped for public rewards. More than once when opportunities for ecclesiastical preferment seemed promising he jogged the memory of the Lord Treasurer, and so did his friends. In April, 1713, he was finally made Dean of St. Patrick's Cathedral, Dublin—a place that paid better than some English bishoprics, but still it was in a sense exile, and he was not a bishop! Although he spoke often of the ingratitude of ministers, Swift continued to esteem and to correspond with both Harley and St. John. These two ministers had not well coöperated, and their ministry was a failure before the Queen died in August, 1714. The Tory party then totally disintegrated. Wittily perverting the posy from Virgil, famous as the motto of the East India Company, Dr. Arbuthnot, physician to her late Majesty, wrote, "Fuimus Tories." The *ingens gloria* of Swift was also eclipsed.

Non-political Writing   A gentleman's pen is by no means so tireless as a hack writer's; hence during his period of party politics Swift produced no works of imaginative importance. He had written admirable *Tatlers,* and deserves credit for formulating some methods of that periodical. He had written only one pamphlet with his name signed to it. Early in 1712 he had addressed to Lord Oxford *A Proposal for Correcting, Improving and Ascertaining the English Tongue,* in which he advocated the establishment of an English Academy, but without success: "precision and perspicuity," as the Earl of Chesterfield was later to remark, "not being in general the favourite objects of ministers." Swift at various times in his career exhibits an amateur interest in purity and decorum of language. In his *Proposal* he praises notably the simplicity, beauty, and strength of the King James version of the Bible and the "true sublime eloquence" of the English liturgy. His wish to reform speech and style appears again most favorably in his *Letter to a Young Clergyman* (1721), where he defines a true style as "Proper words in proper places." His insistence on elegance in conversation is seen also in his essays on education and in his masterly satire on trite diction in his *Complete Collection of Genteel and Ingenious Conversation,* published in 1738 but probably written some years earlier.

The Journal to Stella   To posterity the most attractive of Swift's writings during his political activities in London is probably the volume that contains his letters to Esther Johnson and her duenna Rebecca Dingley. These were first published in 1766-8, and since 1784 have been printed under the title of *Journal to Stella*—though the name Stella was apparently not used by Swift for Esther

Johnson at that period (1710-13) or in the correspondence. The letters give a most vivid picture of daily life in London and a behind-the-scenes account of the politics of the day, detailed if not altogether unprejudiced. But because of the title, *Journal to Stella,* interest has fallen upon the display and the nature of the affection Swift so obviously felt for these ladies, particularly for Stella. His somewhat crudely jocose attitude towards the duenna "Bec" is not without affection or respect; but for her he would not indulge, as he does for Stella, in the baby-talk language that sprinkles the correspondence. Some of Swift's acquaintance believed that in 1716 he was secretly married to Stella: such gossip was common about other men of Swift's day, and the evidence in his case, in some ways plausible, is not perfectly convincing in view of the unaccountable fact that Swift and Stella never lived under the same roof or met in private.[8] The *Journal,* however, is a most delightful document, and shows Swift at his playful best, whether in giving accounts of his drunken servant Patrick, who liked to read Congreve's plays, or in apostrophizing an unanswered letter from Stella:

And now let us come and see what this saucy dear letter of MD says. Come out, letter, come out from between the sheets; here it is underneath, and it won't come out. Come out again, I say; so there. Here it is. What says Presto [Swift] to me, pray? says it. Come, and let me answer for you to your ladies. Hold up your head then, like a good letter. There.

After his retirement to Dublin in 1714 Swift spent several doleful years. *The Irish* Always an insatiate and witty grumbler, he uses expressions in letters to his *Patriot* English friends that can be much discounted and yet still convey deep depression. "You are to understand," he writes to Pope, "that I live in the corner of a vast unfurnished house ... and when I do not dine abroad, or make an entertainment, which last is very rare, I eat a mutton-pie, and drink half a pint of wine. My amusements are defending my small dominions against the archbishop, and endeavouring to reduce my rebellious choir. *Perditur haec inter misero lux."* For a time he wrote little; but after a few years he began, either out of sense of the injustices that Ireland suffered or out of his desire to vex the English ministry, to write pamphlets like the *Letter to a Young Clergyman,* which was designed to improve the Irish priesthood, or like his vexatious *Proposal for the Universal Use of Irish Manufacture* (1720), which urged a complete boycott of English imports.

---

[8] In view of this last fact the relevance of the marriage ceremony to any understanding of Swift's work is hard to see. Yet much ink has been shed on this subject. In his *Jonathan Swift* (1893) J. Churton Collins argued against the ceremony. In the Temple Scott edition of Swift's *Works,* XII (1908). 83-106, the Rev. J. H. Bernard summarized the evidence and believed in the marriage. In *PMLA,* XLII (1927). 157-161, Marguerite Hearsey presented "New Light on the Evidence for Swift's Marriage," and the whole controversy is summarized by Maxwell B. Gold, *Swift's Marriage to Stella* (Cambridge, Mass., 1937). Mr. Gold is convinced that there was a marriage ceremony, that Swift offered to announce the marriage publicly, and that his (alleged) impotence precluded consummation. For this somewhat curious position Mr. Gold has less new evidence of importance than he imagines; and without further new evidence the marriage ceremony can neither be proved nor disproved. R. K. Root has admirably reviewed Gold's book in *PQ,* XVII (1938). 205-206. A general view of "Swift and Marriage" is given by George Hand in *Essays and Studies by Members of the Department of English of the University of California,* XIV (1943). 73-92.

His position among the Irish was completely changed by the appearance of a series of pamphlets published in 1724, and commonly known as *Drapier's Letters*. Like all pamphleteers Swift liked to write in an assumed character, and here he signed his letters "M. B. Drapier." He was taking occasion again to inflame passions rather than to calm the minds of such people as believed that a patent granted to one William Wood to coin halfpence for Irish use was a "vile job" designed to cheat impoverished Irish subjects by false or debased coinage. Wood's halfpence were, as the Master of the Mint—Sir Isaac Newton himself!—certified, a sound coinage; but throughout most of 1724 Dublin was in a tumult, and Swift was fanning the flames. In October, after his fourth letter had breathed defiance and urged a boycott of the coinage, a reward of £300 was offered for discovering the author: the printer was already in confinement. The authorship was no secret, but *proof* of authorship was not to be bought. With fervor Irish mouths were quoting I Sam. 14: 45: "Shall *Jonathan* die, who hath wrought this great salvation in Israel? God forbid: as the Lord liveth, there shall not one hair of his head fall to the ground; for he hath wrought with God this day." It was one of Swift's greatest triumphs, and Pope's lines upon the affair were, Swift thought, "the greatest honor I shall ever receive from posterity." Pope wrote:

> Let Ireland tell, how Wit upheld her cause,
> Her Trade supported, and supply'd her Laws;
> And leave on SWIFT this grateful verse ingrav'd,
> The Rights a Court attack'd, a Poet sav'd.

After 1724 Swift was not merely the "Hibernian Patriot"; he was the best loved man in Dublin, far more of a personage than he could ever be anywhere in England. In 1726 when he landed in Dublin after a sojourn of over four months in England, upon his arrival all the church bells were rung and bonfires blazed at night. A hostile English newspaper commented, "There's scarce a Street in Town without a Representation of him for a Sign." On his birthday (November 30) thereafter Dublin celebrated frequently with peals of bells, bonfires, and illuminations; and on July 1, 1740, in celebration of the fiftieth anniversary of King William's victory at the Boyne, the Dean, in turn, gratified the populace with "the largest bonfire ever seen" in Dublin. Building bonfires of one sort or another had long been his sport.

Gulliver's Travels   Before he undertook the rôle of Drapier, Swift had already completed much of his masterpiece, *Travels into Several Remote Nations of the World,*[9]

[9] For editions of *Gulliver* see n. 1 of this chapter. For commentaries, not in editions, see Henry M. Dargan, "The Nature of Allegory as Used by Swift," *SP*, XIII (1916). 159-179; Sir Charles H. Firth, "The Political Significance of *Gulliver's Travels*," *Proc. of the British Academy*, IX (1920), reprinted in Firth's *Essays Historical and Literary* (Oxford, 1938); Lucius L. Hubbard, *Contributions toward a Bibliography of Gulliver's Travels* (Chicago, 1922); William A. Eddy, *A Critical Study of Gulliver's Travels* (Princeton, 1923); Marjorie Nicolson and Nora M. Mohler, "The Scientific Background of Swift's 'Voyage to Laputa'," *Annals of Science*, II (1937). 299-334, and by the same authors, "Swift's Flying Island in the 'Voyage to Laputa'," *Annals of Science*, II (1937). 405-430; R. W. Frantz, "Gulliver's 'Cousin Sympson',"

which was printed in London in 1726. Though some parts may have been devised in the days of the Scriblerus Club (c. 1713-14), most of it was certainly written in the years 1721-5. Of all Swift's writings it best shows the merits of his mind and his gifts of expression. The voyages to Lilliput and to Brobdingnag illustrate the increasing tendency of the day to see truth in relative terms: as Gulliver is to the Lilliputians, so are the Brobdingnagians to him. Under the microscope truths assume different shapes. These first two voyages focus attention on the corruptions of court life; but Lilliput had had a noble past (chapter VI) before sophistication and chicanery had corrupted "original institutions," and the Brobdingnagians are for the most part large of mind as well as of body. Both of these nations, pictured with richly ingenious and delightful surface detail, have lessons for Gulliver, and throughout these two voyages Swift's playfulness is dazzling. The next voyage to be written was the fourth, to Houyhnhnmland, where animal man, the Yahoo, is contrasted with the "perfection of nature" seen in the Houyhnhnms—who are figured as horses. Again Swift gives childlike play to surface ingenuity in his depiction of the human habits of these "horses"—their weaving of mats, threading of needles, etc. Gulliver is not quite identified with the loathsome Yahoos, but his kinship is as unquestionable as is his admiration for Houyhnhnm virtues. Although this voyage is Swift's most misanthropic writing, yet he makes Gulliver profit in truthfulness, cleanliness, and devotion to the life of reason, from his association with these ideal people. His unsociability upon his return to human society is doubtless misanthropic: it illustrates Swift's fundamental horror of the gulf between the actual and the ideal. The fourth voyage, with the third, which was the last to be written, deals with corruptions of theoretical reason, while the first two voyages had dealt with matters of practical reason. Gulliver's Houyhnhnm master "dreaded lest the corruption of 'reason' might be worse than brutality itself," and in the third voyage Gulliver met men whose thirst for theory and for novelty in technical method—whether in the writing of books, in the manufacture of sunbeams, or the making of clothes—made them to him more dreadful than brutes. Technical knowledge had been disparaged in the first two voyages in brief passages where the educational methods of the nations visited were described. In this third voyage technical knowledge is extensively derided: he regards its ingenuity as misplaced, its passion for novelty as unnatural, and its preoccupations in general as unfitting man for society. And the chief function of reason, according to eighteenth-century views, was to fit man for a happy life among his fellows. As a whole *Gulliver's Travels* has the multiple intentions of a masterpiece: it can be read by children for its narrative and descriptive charm; it can be read by learned historians as an allegory of the political life of Swift's time; it can be read as a burlesque

HLQ, I (1938). 329-334; John R. Moore, "The Geography of *Gulliver's Travels*," *JEGP*, XL (1941). 214-228; Merrel D. Clubb, "The Criticism of Gulliver's 'Voyage to the Houyhnhnms,' 1726-1914," *Stanford Stud. in Lang. and Lit.* (1941), pp. 203-232; Arthur E. Case, *Four Essays on Gulliver's Travels* (Princeton, 1945).

of voyage literature; it can be read (at least it has been read) as a master-piece of misanthropy; it is perhaps best read as the ingenious reflections of a thoughtful man on the abuses of human reason. It fascinates the reader by the seemingly unaffected directness and simplicity of its manner or by the subtlety of its reflections on man and his corrupt behavior at court, at home, or in his study. It is important to realize that it could be written only by one who had the highest ideals for human achievement and who despaired of the achieving.

*Later
Occasional
Pieces*

After his exploits as Drapier Swift wrote less and less, and what he wrote tended to be *jeux d'esprit* merely. One of his best poems, *Cadenus and Vanessa,* which had been written in 1712 or 1713 to cure Esther Van-homrigh of a passion for Swift, appeared in 1726, three years after the lady's death. On one level it is a piece of autobiography; on a higher level it is again Swift's program for the improvement of the feminine mind. It was in this latter fashion that contemporaries took it, without looking for scandal. It thus finds a less imaginative equivalent in his prose *Letter to a very Young Lady on her Marriage.* In more savage tone appeared in 1729 his *Modest Proposal for Preventing the Children of Poor People from Being a Burthen to their Parents or Country.* By this proposal that the starving Irish should sell their own infants as food and thus make a modest, inoffensive livelihood, Swift is again charging the British Parliament with gross injustice to Ireland,[10] and is, at least in method, mimicking the "political arithmeticians" who held that people are "a most precious *commodity,*" as one of them said. The Laputanlike "systems" of such projectors as continually sent the ministry wild projects for raising money must have irked Swift, who, with his Brobdingnagians, derided the mystery of politics and preferred a modicum of moral common sense. Thus he rises to an ironic climax when he exclaims, "Let no man talk to me of other expedients," such as—and he enumerates several devices agreeable to justice and good sense that might serve rulers actuated by morality and benevolence. Unlike Burke at the other end of the century, he does not *seem* to rail at the rising influence of "sophisters, economists, and calculators" who were thought to subvert political honor. Swift assumes the quiet tone of a humble projector, who, weary of visionary schemes, has fortunately fallen upon this proposal, "which as it is wholly new, so it hath something solid and real, of no expense and little trouble, full in our power, and whereby we can incur no danger in *disobliging* ENGLAND." And, like a good scientist, he is willing to consider any other project "equally innocent, cheap, easy, and effectual." Irony can go no further than in this pamphlet.

The publication of many of Swift's small things was left to his friend Pope, who in four volumes of *Miscellanies* (1727-32) grouped together pieces by members of the Scriblerus Club. Swift here made a dominant showing. In 1735, as we now know, he coöperated with his Dublin publisher in

---

[10] See Louis A. Landa's two articles: *"A Modest Proposal* and Populousness," *MP,* XL (1942). 161-170; "Swift's Economic Views and Mercantilism," *ELH.* X (1943). 310-335.

bringing out his *Works,* and almost his last literary labors must have been the revision of his letters to Pope, which Pope had sent him, already printed in a volume, with an anonymous letter suggesting publication. All of Swift's major works were published with some background of mystification, and he evidently understood and abetted Pope's schemes. The letters appeared in the early summer of 1741: Pope in London published the text he had prepared; Faulkner in Dublin used the text Swift had revised for him. Pope protested hypocritically at the "tricks" of publishers; the Dean, so far as we know, said nothing.[11]

Swift had from his early years suffered from labyrinthine vertigo; before *His Mental* he was sixty he was very deaf; and in his seventy-fifth year (March, 1742) *Decay* guardians were appointed, since his mind—said in the application for the appointment of guardians to have been failing for eighteen months—was then much decayed. He had long been socially difficult, what with his quick temper, his pride, and his love of practical jokes; and his relatives tended to stress his violence of mood. He himself had long complained of loss of memory, and such complaints increased, justifiably, in the last years. It is doubtfully accurate, however, to say that Swift went mad. Old age, aggravated by vertigo and deafness, caused the decay of his faculties. Violence there doubtless was: there had always been a tendency to violence in Swift, and with the restraining power of reason weakened, childish indulgence of wrath developed. It is said that when his mind was quite gone, his servants used to take money for allowing people to come in and stare at him. He died thus "a driveler and a show" in 1745.

In the case of more than one great writer a single phrase seems to sum *Indignation* up the characteristic quality of the man. Thus *saeva indignatio* has been *and a Sense* the fixed label for Swift's dominant mood. Such a summation is dangerous, *of Values* since, for example, it excludes totally the quality of effervescent playfulness that is almost equally important; but a mordant indignation certainly explains much of Swift. His lack of peace within himself was due to many things, but certainly was in large part due to the abysmal gulf between his ideals for human nature and human nature as he found it. He called himself a misanthrope, and it is clear that for human nature as found in the mass he had unlimited contempt. But he had also a high and clear sense of values, and this caused his contempt to tear his heart with an anxiety to improve humanity. His passion for improving women is obvious: not merely little Stella, the heiress Varina, and the passionate Vanessa were subjected to his instruction: the Countess of Burlington, Lady Betty Germain, Lady Acheson, and even the ineffable Letitia Pilkington, were all his pupils. He might occasionally make them cry, but they all loved and respected their "teacher." (One must never forget that most people found Swift a very companionable person.) He was constantly trying to improve the government, the English language, the Irish clergy, Trinity College Dublin,

[11] Maynard Mack, "The First Printing of the Letters of Pope and Swift," *Library,* xix (1939). 465-485; and Capt. Vinton A. Dearing, "New Light on the First Printing of the Letters of Pope and Swift," *Library,* xxiv (1943). 74-80.

and all the world besides, for he wrote chiefly for the mankind that he despised. A man so devoted to human uplift is a strange sort of misanthrope —one who despairs and believes at once.

Reason and
Dogmatism

To Swift "reason" was the good word. His most significant comments on reason are to be found in the Digression ix "On Madness" in *A Tale of a Tub*, in *The Mechanical Operation of the Spirit*, published with the *Tale*, and in the last two voyages of *Gulliver*. In his discourse "On Madness" he applies a highly skeptical analysis to the act of intellectual conviction, to the problem of just what happens in the mind when we are "convinced." To him it seems not to be a rational process but rather a matter of two minds vibrating in unison, or some such thing. The proselytizer or the conqueror, who wishes to make men agree with *him,* is mad. So are the enthusiasts who imagine they have private revelations or inspirations about spiritual truths. He holds that the more a man "shapes his understanding by the pattern of human learning, the less he is inclined to form parties after his particular notions." Swift is a conservative, believing in common sense, not in private notions, but in the uniformity of nature. One should accept things as they are, to be happy; one should (ironically) "content his ideas with the films and images that fly off upon his senses from the superficies of things.... This is the sublime and refined point of felicity, called, the possession of being well deceived; the serene peaceful state, of being a fool among knaves." In less ironical vein another might have said: "Be content with what the physical senses offer, and know that The Whole is designed and governed by the All-wise Creator." That was the road many of his generation took; but Swift was no optimist. He assented to orthodox Anglican doctrine dogmatically; he tolerated no argument about such matters: they were settled. But he was at the same time temperamentally despondent and even skeptical: only dogmatism could keep the peace. He came to attach almost a transcendent meaning to reason, but what he really valued was the concept of the "light of reason" as opposed to any logical argumentative faculty. Hence Swift is an anti-rationalist and almost an enthusiast when he praises reason in its perfection. He is normally a common-sense rationalist, and despises strange new doctrines: his contempt for the Laputan thirst for novelty in practical matters is paralleled by his hatred of new theories in religion, statecraft, or in society. "Common sense suffices," might almost have been his remark. In the Digression on Madness he exclaims: "But when a man's fancy gets astride on his reason, when imagination is at cuffs with the senses, and common understanding, as well as common sense, is kicked out of doors; the first proselyte he makes, is himself, and when that is once compassed, the difficulty is not so great in bringing over others; a strong delusion always operating from without as vigorously as from within." That sentence contains by implication Swift's basic theory of writing: it is useless to argue with Men; the thing to do is to warm and dazzle them with a bonfire.

Swift's art, then, is as significant as his intellectual content. But it is not so much the structural or architectural design of his greater works that is impressive. The alternating narrative (*dulce*) and digression (*utile*) of *A Tale of a Tub* have been rhapsodically praised, though that method seems to be a novelty that Swift himself should have seen as confusing and ineffectual. Likewise the multiplication of preliminaries to the *Tale,* though each is in itself a gem, is excessive. In *Gulliver* he has more control, and shapes his materials more easily than he did in the *Tale.* But there is still a curious duality, which makes easy contrasts in relative values, but is essentially, and quite satisfactorily, episodic. Like the other writers of his day Swift achieves highest excellence in the invention of detail. In his gift for allegory and for myth-making he certainly surpasses all others of his time. Here he is supreme, ranging from the spider and the bee to Lilliput and Brobdingnag. One may note also such typical small bits as the incisively casual ending of his *Seasonable Advice* [as Drapier] *to the Grand Jury,* which might be forced into indicting him:

Once upon a time the *Wolves* desired a League with the *Sheep,* upon this Condition; that the Cause of strife might be taken away, which was the Shepherds and *Mastiffs;* this being granted, the *Wolves* without all Fear made Havock of the Sheep.

This ability to strike out analogies that are simple-appearing but serpentlike in implication marks one of Swift's great merits—perhaps his greatest. He is constantly praised for his precision, plainness, and purity of language. (Purity is here used in its rhetorical sense: his passion for arousing disgust by the frank use of foul words and images is of course one of his abnormalities.) He knows how to make words do what he wants them to do as well as any man who ever wrote English; but sometimes he is not clear as to just what he wants to do, and allows himself a virtuosity of witty effervescence that delights or wounds by turns: it consistently dazzles. Sensitive minds find a lack of shading in his images, which do come forth with tense explicitness usually, with every phrase in perfect individual focus. He represents at its best the eighteenth-century ambition to combine clarity and strength of style. He and Defoe together represent two different approaches to problems of life, the aristocratic classicist and the middleclass economist. The writings of both, though aiming to reform, call attention to the numerous abuses of the *ancien régime,* and so become an important part of the movement of illumination that led to the abolition of this regime that they merely wished to reform.

V

Addison, Steele, and the Periodical Essay

The Nature
of the
Periodical
Essay

The periodical essay, "invented" towards the very end of the seventeenth century, reached its acme of achievement early in the eighteenth in the work of Richard Steele (1672-1729) and Joseph Addison (1672-1719). It maintained a great popularity throughout the century, and disappeared about 1800.[1] Rigorous definition of this peculiarly eighteenth-century type of publication is not very helpful. The "dialogue" papers, such as Sir Roger L'Estrange's *Observator* (1681-7), *The Athenian Gazette* (1690-97), Tutchin's *Observator* (1705-6), and Charles Leslie's *Rehearsal* (1704-9), as well as others of the same type, used material similar to that embodied in the periodical essay, but, because of their mechanical dialogue form, never achieved essay structure. "Learned" periodicals were more technical and bookish in substance than essays should be, and hence most of the work of Jean de la Crose in his various periodicals or of such writers as Richard Willis in his *Occasional Paper* (1697-8) fell into the class of book-reviewing. Popular monthly reviews we shall find established in the second half of the eighteenth century; and the magazine, as they knew it—a storehouse for fugitive reprints from weekly newspapers,—has been regarded as beginning in 1731 with *The Gentleman's Magazine.* The periodical essay has been aptly described as dealing with morals and manners, but it might in fact deal with anything that pleased its author. It covered usually not more than the two sides (in two columns) of a folio half-sheet: normally it was shorter than that. It might be published independently of other material, as was *The Spectator,* except for advertising; or it might be the leading article in a newspaper.

Formative
Influences

The shaping influences of this essay were journalistic rather than the traditions of Montaigne, Bacon, or Cowley. There is a considerable influence of the seventeenth-century "character"; [2] and such pictures of daily life as

---

[1] For a bibliography of the periodical essay see Ronald S. Crane and F. B. Kaye, *A Census of British Newspapers and Periodicals, 1620-1800* (Chapel Hill, 1927) or Walter Graham in *CBEL,* II. 660-668. For historics and criticism see Nathan Drake, *Essays . . . Illustrative of the Tatler, Spectator, and Guardian* (3v, 1805); John Nichols, *Literary Anecdotes of the Eighteenth Century* (9v, 1812-15. Index in Vol. VII); H. R. Fox Bourne, *English Newspapers* (2v, 1887); Lawrence Lewis, *The Advertisements of the Spectator* (1909); Hugh Walker, *The English Essay and Essayists* (1915); George S. Marr, *The Periodical Essayists of the Eighteenth Century* (1924); Walter Graham, *English Literary Periodicals* (1930); James R. Sutherland, "The Circulation of Newspapers and Literary Periodicals, 1700-1730," *Library,* xv (1934). 110-124.
[2] Walter Graham, "Some Predecessors of the *Tatler,*" *JEGP,* xxiv (1925). 548-554; and "Defoe's *Review* and Steele's *Tatler*—the Question of Influence," *JEGP,* xxxiii (1934). 250-254; Edward C. Baldwin, "The Relation of the Seventeenth-Century Character to the Periodical Essay," *PMLA,* xix (1904). 75-114.

those in Ned Ward's *London Spy* (1698-1700)—supposedly descended from G. P. Marana's *Turkish Spy* (which was not a periodical)—clearly had influence also. The periodical or pamphlet cast in the form of a letter, like Willis's *Occasional Paper* or the anonymous *Miscellaneous Letters* (1694-6), helped to popularize the use of the letter as an essay device. The periodical essay usually had a dual aim: to amuse and to improve. It was through deft management of the second of these, while not neglecting the first, that Steele and Addison achieved their great success. The editorial devices that they adopted—the single editor, aided by relatives or friends, or the club of editors—had existed before them. The Observator was the best known type of editorial personality of earlier times, and *The Weekly Comedy* (12 numbers, 1699) and *The Humours of a Coffee-House* (1707-8), both probably by Ned Ward, who had the assistance of William Oldisworth in the second, showed how use could be made of a club or of a group of persons that parallels noticeably the club of *The Spectator*. Editorial personalities were not very carefully delineated at best. The Tatler, Isaac Bickerstaff, frequently forgets his age of sixty-four and his profession as astrologer. The Spectator is supposed to be a very taciturn man; but he gossips with all the garrulity of his tattling predecessor. Serial publication fully as much as collaboration is probably responsible for the inconsistencies of age and behavior seen in the portraiture of both the Spectator and his friend Sir Roger de Coverley.

One must conclude that the superiority of *The Tatler* and *The Spectator* [3] over all other such periodicals—even those done separately by Steele and Addison—is in part due to the happy combination of these two authors. *The Early* In literary reputation Addison [4] far surpasses Steele, but in his prose he is *Careers of* never at his best except when working beside Steele.[5] Steele may have done *Addison* his most agreeable writing in the periodical essay, but as a pamphleteer *and Steele* he was more stirring than Addison, and as a playwright he had more influence than Addison—though he never produced a tragedy. The two

[3] The first collected edition of *The Tatler* was in four volumes, 1710-11. There were at least 25 editions reprinted before 1800. It has been edited notably by John Nichols (6v, 1786), Robert Bisset (4v, 1797), Alex. Chalmers (4v, 1803), George A. Aitken (4v, 1898-9). The first collected edition of *The Spectator* was the small octavo (8v, 1712-15). It has been edited by John Nichols (8v, 1789), Robert Bisset (8v, 1793-4), Alex. Chalmers, (8v, 1806), G. Gregory Smith (8v, 1897-8; 1907 in Everyman's Library), George A. Aitken (8v, 1898).

[4] Addison's collected *Works* (with or without the periodical essays) have been edited by Thomas Tickell (4v, 1721; 3v, 1726); Richard Hurd (6v, 1811); George W. Greene (6v, 1856); A. C. Guthkelch (2v, 1914). His *Letters* have been edited as a part of the *Works* by Hurd, and separately by Walter Graham (Oxford, 1941). There is no first-rate life of Addison, but lives have been written by Samuel Johnson (*Lives of the Poets,* ed. G. B. Hill, Oxford, 1905, II. 79-158); Lucy Aiken (2v, 1843); William J. Courthope (1884). Bonamy Dobrée in his *Essays in Biography* (Oxford, 1925) gives an interesting but somewhat prejudicial account of Addison.

[5] Steele's *Dramatic Works* were collected in 1723, 1734, etc. They have been edited by George A. Aitken (1894, 1903). French translations of his political pamphlets were collected as *Œuvres diverses sur les affaires de la Grande Bretagne traduit de l'Anglois* (Amsterdam, 1715). His miscellaneous prose is well edited by Rae Blanchard as *Tracts and Pamphlets* (Baltimore, 1944). Steele's *Correspondence* is edited by John Nichols (1787, 1809) and by Rae Blanchard (Oxford, 1941). The best biographies are those by Austin Dobson (1886), George A. Aitken (2v, 1889), and Willard Connely (1934). That by Aitken contains an excellent bibliography, as does the *CBEL*.

men had been schoolmates in the Charterhouse, and had been at Oxford together, though not in the same college. From the University their paths seemed to diverge: Steele went into the army, became a captain of the Tower Guard, definitely a "city captain's" job, and there wrote his first book, *The Christian Hero* (1701), a pamphlet in commendation of King William III and of Christian as opposed to Stoic morals.[6] After producing three "reformed" comedies, and contributing verses to a monthly miscellany called *The Muses Mercury* (1707), he went into politics, and became the writer of the official *Gazette,* a periodical which he wrote from 1707 to 1710 "without ever erring against the rule observed by all Ministries, to keep that paper very innocent and very insipid." *The Tatler,* which he began April 12, 1709, and which appeared three times a week, until he suddenly dropped it with No. 271 (January 2, 1711), gave some release from this enforced tameness as Gazetteer.

Addison's Early Works

When Steele left Merton College, Oxford (1694), without a degree, to enlist in the Duke of Ormonde's regiment of horse guards, his friend Addison, already an M.A., stayed on in various capacities, attaining in 1698 a fellowship in Magdalen College, which, though most of the time out of residence, he held until 1711. At Oxford he won some reputation for his verses, especially for those in Latin, which are still regarded as among the most correctly elegant to come from an English pen.[7] Among these his *Pygmaio-geranomachia* (1698) ("The Battle of the Pigmies and the Cranes") has been especially praised as inaugurating the typical eighteenth-century mock-heroic tradition and as demonstrating better than other poems by Addison his imaginative deftness. Deciding to make diplomacy his career, he spent the years 1699-1703 in a leisurely grand tour that enabled him to acquire the necessary languages and acquaintance with the courts of France, Italy, Germany, and Holland. During the years after his return he published certain classical translations; a poetical *Letter from Italy* to his patron Charles Montagu, Earl of Halifax; and, his great success, *The Campaign* (1705), a patriotic celebration of the Duke of Marlborough's victories. This poem was his best liked work before *The Spectator,* and in some sense it made his reputation. Most of his English poems, except his hymns, *Milton's Stile Imitated in a Translation out of . . .the Third Aeneid* (1704), and his *Song for St. Cecilia's Day* (1694), are in the heroic couplet. His opera *Rosamond* (1707) pleased the Marlboroughs, who now owned Fair Rosamond's manor of Woodstock, but to the general public it seemed dismal. *The Campaign,* more successful as a party pamphlet perhaps than as a poem, procured its author's advancement to be Under-Secretary of State (1706-8). In 1709 his brother died in India, and shortly thereafter Addison is evidently, in contrast to Steele, a comparatively rich man. His career had none of the

---

[6] Ed. Rae Blanchard, with an Introduction (Oxford, 1932).
[7] Leicester Bradner, "The Composition and Publication of Addison's Latin Poems," *MP,* xxxv (1938). 359-367.

happy-go-lucky character of Steele's, and his position among men of letters and among statesmen was assured.

When Steele began *The Tatler,* Addison was in Ireland as Secretary to the Lord Lieutenant of that realm. To Steele, consequently, belongs all the credit for the initiation of *The Tatler,* though he had some help from Swift, with whom he was then on terms of intimacy. The first four numbers were distributed gratis; thereafter it sold for a penny. It consisted of a folio half-sheet, and it was published on the days the London post went to the country, Tuesdays, Thursdays, and Saturdays. In the dedication to the first collected volume Steele wrote: "The general purpose of this paper, is to expose the false arts of life, to pull off the disguises of cunning, vanity, and affectation, and to recommend a general simplicity in our dress, our discourse, and our behavior." But with this attention to the *utile* Steele wisely heeded the appetite for the *dulce,* for amusement. Diversity was the great need, and so at the start he divided each paper into contrasting sections that derived from various sources, chiefly coffee-houses, in which he had (so he jokingly said) agents. "All accounts of gallantry, pleasure, and entertainment" were to come from the fashionable White's Chocolate-house—near St. James's Palace. Swift got his letters at White's, which became increasingly notorious for its gaming for high stakes. Poetry was to be reported from Will's Coffee-house, already made famous by Dryden, Wycherley, Congreve, and others, and the meeting place of Addison and his little coterie until they moved to Button's—founded apparently for their use. "Learning" was reported from the Grecian, near the Inns of Court, and "foreign and domestic news" came from St. James's Coffee-house, again near the palace. All other subjects, he concludes, "shall be dated from my own apartment." In No. 18 Steele remarked that his "chief scenes of action" were "coffee-houses, play-houses, and my own apartment"; that, consequently, he should find a public "as long as there are men or women, or politicians, or lovers, or poets, or nymphs, or swains, or cits, or courtiers in being." The days of publication show that he aimed to reach the country as well as "the cits"; this account of his audience again shows his breadth of intended appeal. For the first forty numbers his motto was Juvenal's *Quicquid agunt homines . . . nostri farrago libelli,* and his other favorite was the Horatian *Celebrare domestica facta.* As time went on and his success was quite assured, the number of sections in a given issue began to decline, until seldom more than two sections appeared, and "From my Own Apartment" became by all odds the favorite source of writing.[8] The precedent of division, however, enabled Steele, even in *The Spectator,* when time pressed and he was lazy, to slap together three letters that correspondents had sent in (and which he usually seems to have revised or rewritten), and call the three letters an essay.[9]

[8] Chester N. Greenough, "The Development of the Tatler," *PMLA,* xxxi (1916). 633-663.
[9] In 1725 Charles Lillie, the perfumer, to whose shop Tatler-Spectator correspondence had been addressed, was allowed to publish two volumes entitled *Original and Genuine Letters Sent to the Tatler and Spectator.* These volumes show the quantity and diversity of letters sent in. A few here printed had been used actually in the periodicals, but in a revised form.

Out of the 271 numbers of *The Tatler* Steele wrote 188, and Addison only 42; together they did 36 others.[10] Steele's prose never attained the elegant ease and correctness of Addison's, and yet it is probable that his tendency to warm to a subject and to write intimately and personally, as the reader's friend, contributed much to the success of the paper. Addison's best essays here are the result of his slightly chilly insight into the typical mental attitudes of his day. His portraiture of Ned Softly (No. 163), the pest who insisted on reading his verses aloud to the frequenters of Will's, exhibits a mastery of good-natured satire; and his Tom Folio (No. 158) is highly typical of the day in its laughter at pedantry. Much used by later writers was his depiction of the Political Upholsterer (Nos. 155, 160, etc.), an ignorant reader of news comically eager to know what the Czar of Muscovy was about but unregardful of the doings of his own family. His device in narrating the adventures of a shilling (No. 249) was also much imitated. These are papers of ingenious insight. Steele had the more pedestrian sections to do—the news, the theatre, and all that. But Steele had an interest in family affairs and a kindly way of writing about "the fair sex"[11] that won him friends and readers. Bickerstaff writes about his nephews (Nos. 30, 207), about the relations of parents and children (Nos. 235, 263),[12] and about the death of his father (No. 181)—surely Steele's own memories here—in an autobiographical intimacy exceedingly rare in that or any day. In view of the frequent essays on love and marriage, and also in view of the attitude of the Restoration period towards matrimony, it is interesting to read the comments of John Gay in his *Present State of Wit* (1711),[13] and see that he regards the Steele type of paper as giving *The Tatler* its peculiar appeal. He is enthusiastic in his praise, and remarks:

It would have been a jest some time since, for a man to have asserted that any thing witty could be said in praise of a married state; or that devotion and virtue were any way necessary to the character of a fine gentleman.... [Bickerstaff's] writings have set all our wits and men of letters upon a new way of thinking, of which they had little or no notion before; and though we cannot yet say that any of them have come up to the beauties of the original, I think we may venture to affirm, that every one of them writes and thinks much more justly than they did some time since.

"It is no small thing," wrote Taine, "to make morality fashionable";[14] and Steele and Addison between them did more to rehabilitate English

---

[10] These are the figures of Nathan Drake, *Essays . . . Illustrative of the Tatler, Spectator, and Guardian*, III (1805). 376. The figures are very likely not too exact.

[11] Rae Blanchard, "Richard Steele and the Status of Women," *SP*, XXVI (1929). 325-355; also Joachim Heinrich, *Die Frauenfrage bei Steele und Addison* (Leipzig, 1930).

[12] No. 189, one of the best of these family papers, shows Steele's technique of using material from real life: here from the Molesworth family. See Robert J. Allen, "Steele and the Molesworth Family," *RES*, XII (1936). 449-454.

[13] Gay's remarkably good-natured pamphlet is reprinted in Edward Arber's *English Garner*, VI, (1883). 503-512, and from there in John Churton Collins, *An English Garner: Critical Essays and Fragments* [n.d.], pp. 201-210.

[14] Hippolyte A. Taine, *History of English Literature* (trans. by H. Van Laun, 1871), II. 103.

manners after the Restoration excesses than any other two men—not excepting the clergy.

The Spectator is of course by far the best of all periodical essays.[15] It also **The**
was a folio half-sheet, but unlike *The Tatler* it appeared daily—a severe **Spectator**
strain on the versatility and industry of its authors. It began two months
after Steele had suddenly abandoned *The Tatler,* and it ran from March
1, 1711 to December 6, 1712 (555 numbers) as a collaborative project. It
was then discontinued; but in June 1714 Addison, without Steele's aid, revived it, and saw it through another volume, somewhat more staid than
earlier volumes had been. Steele probably had wished to attend to other
matters—politics in particular. The paper had by no means abated in popularity, so far as one can observe. When, on August 1, 1712, Bolingbroke's
halfpenny tax was levied and many newspapers immediately disappeared,
The Spectator had doubled its price to twopence, and gone bravely on its
way. But soon thereafter the members of the Spectator's Club began to
die or to get married and go to live in the country. Clearly Steele foresaw
an end to *The Spectator,* and he did not wish piratical successors to plagi-
arize the personalities Addison and he had created.

In *The Spectator* Addison did by all odds his best writing—writing so
polished and easy that it makes his other works seem cold and formal.
Here he wrote rather more papers than Steele did,[16] and almost fifty were
contributed by such men as Eustace Budgell (1686-1737), John Hughes
(1677-1720), Alexander Pope, and others. At the time Steele was commonly
regarded as "Mr. Spectator," and he doubtless had the editorial responsibility.
The first essay, by Addison, gave a sketch of Mr. Spectator's character, and
in the second Steele introduced the famous Club. Of its members the
Templar (student of law), the Clergyman, and Captain Sentry (reporting
on military affairs) showed again the desire for diversity in point of view;
but neither they nor the slightly more useful Will Honeycomb ("the man
about town") and Sir Andrew Freeport (the merchant) are prominent
in many papers. Sir Roger de Coverley, however, appeared in many of the
most delightful essays. At first he was designed to be the survival of a
Restoration rake, but by an inconsistent transformation he became the Tory
country squire, aged and lovable, but politically incompetent.[17] As an

---

[15] The collected sets were in eight volumes. Addison's revival ran from No. 556 to 635
(June 18, 1714 to December 20, 1714). A ninth volume, by William Bond, Nos. 636-695
(January 3, 1715 to August 3, 1715), had of course no real relationship to its distinguished
predecessors. Bond was a writer "of very little genius" who later assisted Aaron Hill in his
Plain Dealer (1724-5). Bond died in 1735.

[16] N. Drake, *Essays . . . Illustrative of the Tatler,* etc. (1805), III. 377-379, reports that Addison wrote 274 complete papers; Steele 240; Budgell 37; John Hughes 11, etc. Fifty-three are left
anonymous. It is difficult to be exact in this matter. Addison began signing his essays with
one of the four letters *C, L, I, O*; Steele thereupon began using *R* and *T*. Budgell used *X,*
and *Z* stands for Hughes or some unknown person. In the original sheets these isolated letters
were at times badly placed, and they sometimes omitted or changed in the collected
editions. The first collected edition changed or dropped 18 of these signatures from the
original sheets, and later changes have been made. Almost no two editions seem to agree in
their uses of these letters.

[17] Émile Legouis, "Les deux Sir Roger de Coverley," *Revue Germanique,* II (1906). 453-471·

outmoded figure he was once or twice contrasted with the Whiggish Sir Andrew Freeport in a manner prophetic of the social and economic revolution that was to occur in England at the end of the century.

Its Moral Purpose

The purpose of the papers, well announced in No. 10, was "to enliven morality with wit, and to temper wit with morality." Addison continued: "It was said of Socrates, that he brought philosophy down from Heaven to inhabit among men; and I shall be ambitious to have it said of me, that I have brought philosophy out of closets, and libraries, schools, and colleges, to dwell in clubs and assemblies, at tea-tables and in coffee-houses." The success of the essays depended precisely on the ability of the two authors to do just this—to popularize moralizing. Steele, more than any man of equal literary ability in his day, reacted against the immorality of the Restoration. His dramatic criticism in both *The Tatler* and *The Spectator* is filled with this animus. His attacks on Etherege in Nos. 51 and 65 of *The Spectator* are significant of the changed taste. Steele is quite conscious of his bias, and comments on it in a letter supposedly from a gentleman aged "between fifty and sixty" who had enjoyed the best company in "the joyous reign of Charles the Second." He writes to Steele in No. 158:

I have observed through the whole Course of your Rhapsodies, (as you once very well called them) you are very industrious to overthrow all that many your Superiors who have gone before you have made their Rule of writing....It is monstrous to set up for a Man of Wit, and yet deny that Honour in a Woman is anything else but Peevishness, that Inclination is the best Rule of Life, or Virtue and Vice any thing else but Health and Disease. We had no more to do but to put a Lady in good Humour, and all we could wish followed of Course. Then again, your *Tully,* and your Discourses of another Life, are the very Bane of Mirth and good Humour. Prithee don't value thy self on thy Reason at that exorbitant rate, and the Dignity of humane Nature; take my Word for it, a Setting-dog has as good Reason as any Man in *England....* I shall sum it up all in this one Remark, In short, Sir, you do not write like a Gentleman.

Mr. Spectator might have replied (had reply been necessary) that the character of the gentleman, *si quid mea carmina possunt,* was being reformed.

Its Social Criticism

Social comment in the essays was, then, diverse both in matter and in tone. Many papers laughed at the follies and foibles of the ladies: the periodical was a tea-table companion. Problems regarding love and marriage appear continually. Wifely extravagances are chided (328); giggling damsels in church are reproved (158); the feminine violence in party politics is gently ridiculed in the famous paper about party patches (81). There is much puffing of favorite plays or actors, much ridicule of Italian opera as non-rational pleasure; there are amusing skits on the fashionable puppet-show (then in its Golden Age in England) and on the more robust inelegant athletic combats of Hockley-in-the-Hole. There are sobering narratives such as Steele's famous retelling of the tale of Inkle and Yarico (11),[18] Addison's

[18] Lawrence M. Price, *Inkle and Yarico Album* (Berkeley, 1937).

Vision of Mirza (159), the account of the career of that typically prosperous "cit," Sir John Anvil (299), or of the weaver's unhappy wife who lost her benefit in the lottery (242). From these the material ranges to philosophical or moral disquisitions on benevolence (Nos. 27, 169, 177, 181, etc.) or on courage (350), on tranquillity (196), or even on immortality (111); to dissertations upon instincts in brutes (Nos. 120, 121, 128), to exhortations against "the two great errors into which a mistaken devotion may betray us"—enthusiasm and superstition; or, finally, to the popular doctrines about self-love, expounded by Henry Grove in No. 588. Steele's essay for Good Friday, 1712 (No. 356), well illustrates the suiting of material to occasion, certainly a part of the journalistic art here required.

Its Pictures of Daily Life

Many of the best papers rely for interest on descriptions of everyday life. In No. 454 Mr. Spec. rises at 4 A.M. at Richmond and takes boat for London and Covent Garden Market. Similarly Sir Roger's visits to Westminster Abbey (329) and to Vauxhall (383) are vivid reflections of London, as, on another level, is Tom Trusty's story of his life as a servant (96). Probably the best descriptive papers, however, are those dealing with country life. Budgell's account of a country wake (161), Addison's pictures of Sir Roger at the assizes (122), of the fashions of the Western Circuit (129), and Steele on the pains and pleasures of married life in the country (254) are all good documentary records of their day. For real charm the sketches of life in Coverley Hall, with Will Wimble (a younger son), Moll White the witch, the family portraits, Mr. Spectator philosophizing amongst the poultry, and Sir Roger at church—these are among the best the essays offer in this kind.

Its Avoidance of Politics

Almost any subject might be treated in these essays. We have seen how excellent Addison was in criticism, and on the drama Steele certainly was both wise and influential: as bookish men they might be expected to write about books. One topic that might be expected, however, they firmly banned. "I never espoused any Party with Violence, and am resolved to observe an exact Neutrality between the Whigs and Tories, unless I shall be forced to declare myself by the Hostilities of either Side." This stand in No. 1 is reiterated in No. 262 and elsewhere. Probably what was intended was a promise to avoid attacks on ministers of state as well as to avoid the extreme party spirit then prevalent. The Tories were in power; Addison and Steele were out of office, and *The Spectator* papers were a sort of holiday exercise: it was a pleasure to avoid acrimony—and perhaps to feel superior to it all. Later in his satirical portrait of Addison, Pope, as will be remembered, applied to him, in partial compliment, the name of Cicero's non-partisan friend, Atticus. Addison was born "to converse with ease," [19] and not to write political pamphlets. The non-partisan promise in *The Spectator* by and large was kept. There were, to be sure, moments when

---

[19] To Joseph Spence (*Anecdotes*, 1820, p. 50) Pope remarked that with intimates Addison "had something more charming in his conversation than I ever knew in any other man: but with any mixture of strangers, and sometimes only with one, he seemed to preserve his dignity much."

they came close to the line—when they printed the suppressed preface to the Bishop of St. Asaph's *Four Sermons* (384), a procedure which as a party stroke contravened all their nobly protested principles, and when they praised Prince Eugene (340) and the Duke of Marlborough (139 and in the dedication to Volume iv of the collected editions). But consistently their attitude was cool and dignified: they were never rabid partisans in *The Spectator*.

Its Interest in Trade

Addison at least was so filled with a healthy interest in trade that his Whig instincts could not be suppressed there. They were not, however, argumentatively presented. Probably no one—least of all Addison himself —realized the possible party bias of his ideas. He was one among the nation of traders that was bestirring itself in this century. Like Defoe, he praises the merchant frequently and highly. The merchant is the true internationalist: he brings the culture of all the world to the Thames, and makes mankind one. In the Royal Exchange (and Mr. Spectator was on 'Change far more often than most readers realize) Addison is nobly moved: "I am a Dane, Swede, or Frenchman at different times, or rather fancy my self like the old Philosopher, who upon being asked what Country-man he was, replied, That he was a Citizen of the World. . . . As I am a great Lover of Mankind, my Heart naturally overflows with Pleasure at the sight of a prosperous and happy Multitude, insomuch that at many publick Solemnities I cannot forbear expressing my Joy with Tears that have stolen down my Cheeks." Addison's sound mercantilism does not normally give way to emotion so extremely, but in his day many an English heart was being warmed by prosperity.

Its Vogue and Influence

If one wishes to know what the eighteenth-century Londoner and his environment looked like, the best source of information is the paintings and engravings of William Hogarth; if one wishes to know what the eighteenth-century Londoner thought about, one can do no better than to read *The Spectator:* it both conditioned and freshened the minds of its readers, and it was read throughout the century. The collected editions sold far better than did the original sheets. The influence of these essays is not due to any great mental power of their authors. It is due rather to their natural journalistic sympathy with their environment and the people in it; it is due above all to charm of style. It is well known how Benjamin Franklin in far-off Boston as a boy taught himself to write by imitating *The Spectator* and how Hugh Blair in 1760 and for more than a score of years thereafter, in reading his Lecture xix [20] and there giving "directions concerning the proper method of attaining a good style in general," approved a process with regard to imitating *The Spectator* that was substantially the one Franklin, and doubtless many another, had followed. Addison's style was the model for simplicity, plainness, and elegance during more than a century. Its best praise and shrewdest criticism came perhaps from Dr. Johnson at the very end of his *Life* of Addison:

[20] Hugh Blair, *Lectures on Rhetoric and Belles Lettres* (2v, 1783).

His prose is the model of the middle style; on grave subjects not formal, on light occasions not groveling; pure without scrupulosity, and exact without apparent elaboration; always equable, and always easy, without glowing words or pointed sentences. Addison never deviates from his track to snatch a grace; he seeks no ambitious ornaments, and tries no hazardous innovations. His page is always luminous, but never blazes in unexpected splendour.

It was apparently his principal endeavour to avoid all harshness and severity of diction; he is therefore sometimes verbose in his transitions and connections, and sometimes descends too much to the language of conversation: yet if his language had been less idiomatical it might have lost somewhat of its genuine Anglicism. What he attempted, he performed; he is never feeble, and he did not wish to be energetick; he is never rapid, and he never stagnates. His sentences have neither studied amplitude, nor affected brevity; his periods, though not diligently rounded, are voluble and easy. Whoever wishes to attain an English style, familiar but not coarse, and elegant but not ostentatious, must give his days and nights to the volumes of Addison.

Both *The Tatler* and *The Spectator* had immediate imitators. In *Tatler* No. 229 Addison mentioned *Tit for Tatt* (5 numbers, 1710), *The Whisperer* (1709), and *The Female Tatler* as rivals or critics. The last of these ran to 115 numbers (July, 1709-March, 1710), and hence it may be thought abler than the others. There were also *The North Tatler, The Tory Tatler,* etc. When Steele suddenly stopped *The Tatler* it was continued by at least three would-be successors. One of these, William Harrison, whom Swift aided, continued his essays through one volume (52 numbers) rather wearily. Of the continuations of *The Spectator* by Addison and, *longo intervallo,* by William Bond, mention has already been made. The best successor was Steele's own *Guardian,* which ran daily for 175 numbers in 1713 (March 12 to October 1) under the editorship of "Mr. Nestor Ironside," whose relations in the Lizard family aided him.

Imitators

If *The Spectator* had not existed, *The Guardian* might outrank all periodicals of this kind; but it is shaded by its predecessor, and the fact that Addison—busy with his tragedy, *Cato*—had no part in the early numbers certainly diminished its interest. In No. 98 Addison considers the imitators who have tried the "diurnal" essay and justly finds them deficient. Some *Guardians* concern the lion's mouth erected for a post-box at Button's Coffee-house and are triflingly amusing; another series concerns the absence of a "tucker" from the latest fashions in ladies' dress—a change that left their bosoms less covered than heretofore. "Let him 'fair sex' it to the world's end," might have been the reaction of Steele's now estranged friend Swift, whom Steele had attacked rashly in *Guardian* No. 53. There was a great deal of politics and of piety in *The Guardian* and relatively less light and effective satire. There was little literary criticism of first interest. A series of papers on the pastoral (Nos. 22, 23, 28, 30, and 32), probably by Thomas Tickell,[21] had praised the pastorals of Ambrose Philips, and

The Guardian

---

[21] Richard Eustace Tickell, *Thomas Tickell* (1931), p. 26; and John E. Butt in *Bodleian Quar. Rec.,* v (1928). 299.

led Pope, whose jealousy was aroused because of lack of mention of his own pastorals, to submit anonymously an attack on Philips in No. 40. Such procedure caused difficulties among the staff contributors. Pope wrote at least eight papers for Steele, of which No. 78 ("A Receit to Make an Epick Poem") and No. 173 ("On Gardens") are notable. In general *The Guardian* has the diversity of its great predecessors, but not their distinction.

Addison and Steele in Politics

The Guardian found its writers in a bitter season of politics. The Tory peace of Utrecht was signed in April, 1713, and all poets, Whig and Tory alike, burst into early songs thereupon. The Pretender, the Whigs were certain, would be brought in if the Tories and the Catholics could do it. New peers, it was rumored, were to be created to support a Tory majority, and Steele protested in a pamphlet *Letter to Sir M[iles] W[arton] Concerning Occasional Peers* (March 5, 1713). In April Addison's *Cato* had a great welcome as a political document from both Whigs and Tories; but more typical of the moment was his partisan pamphlet *The Tryal of Count Tariff*. Religion got sadly mixed with politics. A Tory parson at Putney preached a sermon *Whigs no Christians,* and Whig retorts were as numerous as they were Christian. *The Guardian* itself was often attacked for its politics, especially by the Tory *Post Boy,* probably because at the moment Steele was the most vigorous of Whig writers. Defoe was working for Harley and the Tories. Parliament was dissolved, but both Steele and Addison were reëlected—Steele with some difficulty. In the late summer he began his attacks on the ministry for not compelling the French to destroy the harbor at Dunkirk, as the late treaty required, and on this subject he wrote often, most effectively perhaps in *The Importance of Dunkirk Consider'd* (September, 1713). He dropped *The Guardian,* and within the week began the more partisan *Englishman* (57 numbers: October 6, 1713 to February 15, 1714). In his fiery pamphlet *The Crisis* (January, 1714) he turned to attack the Tories on the prejudicial grounds that they were at heart Catholics and Jacobites, and during the months to follow he and his fellow Whig writers repeated these unjust charges. A solid Tory vote speedily expelled him from the House of Commons, but that did not quiet his pen. He continued to harp upon Dunkirk, religion, and the succession, and in *Mr. Steele's Apology for Himself and his Writings* (October, 1714) made an able defense of his career. There was scant application of reason to politics while the succession was in doubt. The Hanoverian Prince George was not popular: he was a German. The Jacobite Pretender ("James III") was unpopular: he was a Catholic. Religion settled the matter, and when the Queen died (August 1, 1714), the Protestant succession was readily secured, and in spite of the Jacobite invasion of the North in 1715, George I was King of England.[22]

The remaining periodicals published by Steele and Addison are of slight

---

22 The new King's mother, Sophia, Electress of Hanover, was granddaughter of King James I of England. The Electress Sophia had longed to be Queen; but she died, aged 83, less than two months before Queen Anne. Soon after King George the First's arrival in England Steele was made governor of Drury Lane Theatre and in April, 1715, he was knighted.

literary influence. Steele's *Lover* (40 numbers: February 25 to May 27, 1714) was an attempt to recapture the playful attention of the fair sex; Addison's *Freeholder* (55 numbers: December 23, 1715 to June 29, 1716) *Their Later* was a combination of polite small talk with politics and trade. Steele's lesser *Periodicals* efforts, *The Reader* (1714), *Town Talk* (1715-16), *The Tea Table* (1715-16), and *Chit Chat* (1716) were all short lived. In 1719 he and Addison found themselves, with only temporary acrimony, on opposite sides in the debate concerning the proposal of the Whig ministers to limit the size of the peerage. Steele in *The Plebeian* (4 numbers, March and April, 1719) opposed his party chiefs, and lost standing in consequence. Addison, more conservative, supported the limitation, like the reliable party man that he was, in his *Old Whig* (2 numbers, March and April, 1719) Addison died within two months after this final effort.[23] Steele's stand cost him his place as governor of Drury Lane Theatre, and turned his writing into theatrical channels for most of the rest of his career. His projected "fishpool"—a vessel to bring fish alive from the sea by means of allowing salt water to flow through the ship's bottom—was a characteristic and ineffective attempt to get rich through inventive ingenuity.[24]

The more successful minor writers of periodical essays must be men- *Lesser* tioned briefly. During the first half-century notable political-literary period- *Essayists* icals were John Trenchard's and Thomas Gordon's *Independent Whig* (1720-21) and their *Cato's Letters,* collected from *The London Journal* [25] (1720-23); *Pasquin* (1722-4) by George Duckett, Nicholas Amhurst, and Steele; *The Craftsman* (1726-47); and *Common Sense* (1737-43), a paper in opposition to Walpole, managed by Charles Molloy for the Earl of Chesterfield, George Lyttelton, and others. Henry Fielding combined literature and politics in his *Champion* (written with James Ralph, 1739-44), in *The True Patriot* (1745-6), *The Jacobite's Journal* (1747-8), and *The Covent-Garden Journal* (1752).[26] This last periodical conducted a "paper war" with Sir John Hill's *Inspector,* a newspaper essay that ran to 152 numbers (1751-3). More definitely literary and moralistic was *The Lay Monk* (40 numbers, 1713-14) by Sir Richard Blackmore and John Hughes; Ambrose Philips's *Freethinker* (350 numbers, 1718-21) was one of the ablest in this kind; Eustace Budgell, Addison's eccentric cousin, conducted *The Bee* (118 numbers, 1733-5); and Aaron Hill's *Plain Dealer* (117 numbers, 1724-5) and his *Prompter* (173 numbers, 1734-6) are interesting for their attention to the theatre. Eliza Haywood, the novelist, wrote for more than one periodical: her slight success is best seen in *The Female Spectator*

---

[23] Steele was distressed that Addison made Thomas Tickell his literary executor. When Tickell published Addison's *Works* (4v, 1721) Addison's unsuccessful and unacknowledged play *The Drummer* (1716) was omitted. Because of Steele's protest in the dedication (to Congreve) which he prefixed to an edition of the play (1722), Tickell included it in the smaller trade edition of Addison's *Miscellaneous Works* (3v, 1726).

[24] In November, 1718, Steele published *An Account of the Fish-pool* in the hope of attracting investors.

[25] Charles B. Realey, *The London Journal and its Authors, 1720-1723* (Lawrence, Kansas, 1935; *Bull. Univ. of Kansas*, XXXVI).

[26] Ed. Gerard E. Jensen, with introduction (2v, New Haven, 1915).

(24 numbers, 1744-6). There were two interesting "literary" newspapers of the time that featured leading essays: *The Universal Spectator* (907 numbers, 1728-46), written by Defoe's son-in-law, Henry Baker, with help from James Ralph, and *The Grub-street Journal* (418 numbers, 1730-37), written by the non-juror, Richard Russel, and the Cambridge botanist, John Martyn.[27] Clinging for a while to Alexander Pope's coat-tails, this paper threw mud at his enemies—and sometimes at his friends. Their most independent policy was to oppose deism and support Jeremy Collier's attacks on the theatre. This last aim involved Russel unpleasantly with Henry Fielding. By the middle of the century periodical essays might deal with any subject in any.tone; and their subjects and tones might vary from day to day: they were personal organs unless guided by party politics; and as personal organs, their interest depended on the compelling power of the author's personality and style. None of them approached with any consistency the excellence of those produced by Steele and Addison.

[27] James T. Hillhouse, *The Grub-street Journal* (Durham, N. C., 1928) gives an excellent account of this journal. Professor Hillhouse is one of many who think that Pope was actually—as Russel wished them to think—the manager or editor of the *Journal*.

VI

The Drama, 1700-1740

Although the eighteenth century is not a brilliant period in English drama, the first half of it saw two developments of historical importance in the theatre. The one was a change in the quality of the managers of the playhouses, and the other was the moral reform (accompanied by increasing sentimentality) in comedy.[1]

In the days of Charles II the licensed theatres were managed by courtiers, *Theatres* friends of the King. In the early eighteenth century the management passed *and Play-* for the most part into the hands of professional theatrical people, usually *wrights* actors. The normal number of major theatres in London during the first half of the century was two—Drury Lane and Lincoln's Inn Fields, or after 1732 Covent Garden; while a third house in the Haymarket, designed by Sir John Vanbrugh,[2] was acoustically suited only for opera. Of the lesser theatres the so-called Little Theatre in the Haymarket is of peculiar interest as showing the farces of the mad Samuel Johnson of Cheshire, of Henry Fielding, and later of Foote. The change in the social and, perhaps, intellectual class of managers in these theatres brought a different type of author to write for the stage. Restoration comedies were likely to be written by gentlemen and about people who imagined themselves to be gentlemen and ladies. The comedy of the eighteenth century was written by authors who would stoop to allow mere actors to revise and reshape their work;

[1] For large collections of eighteenth-century plays see *Bell's British Theatre, Consisting of the Most Esteemed English Plays* (21v, 1776-81; 36v, 1791-1802); *The British Theatre; or, a Collection of Plays*, ed. Eliz. Inchbald (25v, 1809; 20v, 1824); *A Collection of Farces and other Afterpieces Selected by Mrs. Inchbald* (7v, 1809, 1815). — For smaller anthologies one may mention David H. Stevens, *Types of English Drama, 1660 to 1780* (Boston, 1923); Dougald MacMillan and Howard M. Jones, *Plays of the Restoration and Eighteenth Century* (1931); and George H. Nettleton and Arthur E. Case, *British Dramatists from Dryden to Sheridan* (Boston, 1939). — For general histories of the drama of the period the following are useful: Colley Cibber, *An Apology for the Life of . . . Written by Himself* (1740); ed. Robert W. Lowe (2v, 1889); David E. Baker, *The Companion to the Playhouse* (2v, 1764; reworked and enlarged by Isaac Reed and Stephen Jones under the title of *Biographia Dramatica*, 3v, 1812); John Genest, *Some Account of the English Stage from 1660 to 1830* (10v, Bath, 1832); Percy Fitzgerald, *A New History of the English Stage* (2v, 1882); Ashley H. Thorndike, *Tragedy* (Boston, 1908), and *English Comedy* (1929); George H. Nettleton, *English Drama . . . 1642-1780* (1914); George C. D. Odell, *Shakespeare from Betterton to Irving* (2v, 1920); Joseph W. Krutch, *Comedy and Conscience after the Restoration* (1924); Allardyce Nicoll, *A History of Early Eighteenth Century Drama* (Cambridge, 1925) [very valuable for its play lists with dates of performances]; Hazelton Spencer, *Shakespeare Improved* (Cambridge, Mass., 1927); Frederick W. Bateson, *English Comic Drama, 1700-1750* (Oxford, 1929); Charles H. Gray, *Theatrical Criticism in London to 1795* (1931); Clarence C. Green, *The Neo-Classic Theory of Tragedy in England during the Eighteenth Century* (Cambridge, Mass., 1934).

[2] Robert J. Allen, "The Kit-Cat Club and the Theatre," *RES*, VII (1931). 56-61. The building of this house makes an interesting story.

and that meant that frequently it was by men and women writing for money and taking an attitude towards human nature and genteel manners not unlike that found among the citizens who had been the objects of satire in Restoration comedy. Playwrights like Susanna Centlivre and Henry Fielding complained loudly of the difficulty of pleasing the whims of uneducated managers; and the audiences, frequently disorderly if not actually riotous, were also difficult.[3] The net result was a period of confused and mediocre writing, which did not entirely cease when in 1747 Garrick took over the management of Drury Lane.

New Tendencies in Plays   The plays were marked by an increased avoidance of both bawdiness and wit, though neither was usually quite absent from a successful play. There was, as we shall see, a considerable accession of sentimentality. The stage at times became a part of the political battleground of the period. *The Beggar's Opera* (1728) stimulated the development of a type of musical show that was part farce and part political propaganda. Henry Fielding wrote political farces of such brilliance and virulence that Parliament passed in 1737 the Licensing Act, by which all plays had to be read and approved by deputy licensers appointed by the Lord Chamberlain before they could be performed on the stage. Unless made topical, farcical, or sentimental, comedy could hardly hold the stage—so little salt of true wit did new plays have. As a result there arose a variety of dramatic "entertainments" incidental to the legitimate types of plays, the chief of which was the completely non-literary pantomime.[4]

The witty comedy of manners fared badly. Not that Jeremy Collier drove either immorality or profaneness completely from the stage: the very plays that he condemned, in fact, still held the boards moderately well. Playwrights continued also to rework Elizabethan plays or French plays; but the really new thing was the "reformed" or "genteel" or "sentimental" comedy. Based partly upon the honest habit of audiences in all ages to glow emotionally over happy or distressful domestic scenes and partly upon the benevolist view of human nature that Hobbes had provoked in the clergy, in the Cambridge Platonists, and in deists of the type of Lord Shaftesbury, the sentimental view of man was so common that inevitably it appeared on the stage.[5] The passion to reform, to set the human heart in harmony with those principles of virtue that are Nature, produced moral plays as readily as it did moral periodical essays.

[3] Julian L. Ross, "Dramatist versus Audience in the Early Eighteenth Century," *PQ*, XII (1933). 73-81.

[4] See three articles by Emmett L. Avery: "Dancing and Pantomime on the English Stage, 1700-1737," *SP*, XXXI (1934). 417-452; "Vaudeville on the London Stage, 1700-1737," *Research Studies of the State College of Washington*, V (1937). 65-77; and "The Defense and Criticism of Pantomimic Entertainments in the Early Eighteenth Century," *ELH*, V (1938). 127-145. See also Charles R. Baskervill, "Playlists and Afterpieces of the Mid-Eighteenth Century," *MP*, XXIII (1926). 445-464.

[5] See Ronald S. Crane, "Suggestions toward a Genealogy of the 'Man of Feeling'," *ELH* I (1934). 205-230. For special histories of sentimental comedy see Arthur Eloesser, *Das bürgerliche Drama. . . . im 18. und 19. Jahrhundert* (Berlin, 1898); Osborn Waterhouse, "The Development of English Sentimental Comedy in the Eighteenth Century," *Anglia*, XXX (1907). 137-172; 269-305; and Ernest Bernbaum, *The Drama of Sensibility* (Boston, 1915).

It is no longer possible to say that sentimental comedy began with Cibber's *Love's Last Shift* (1696); [6] but since Cibber was the most influential theatrical personage during much of the half-century, it will be convenient to treat him as our first nexus of dramatic sentimentalism. Son of a Danish sculptor whose career had been English, Colley Cibber (1671-1757) achieved notable success as an actor and as a comic playwright; he was also from about 1710 to 1733 the dominant force in the management of Drury Lane.[7] It is important to remember that Cibber's characteristic rôles throughout his career were those of fops, and that in his first play, *Love's Last Shift*, he created a somewhat new type of fop for himself in his Sir Novelty Fashion, a rôle perfected in Vanbrugh's continuation of Cibber's plot, *The Relapse* (1696), where Sir Novelty was ennobled as Baron Foppington. Cibber's fops were not merely overdressed effeminates; rather they were ostentatiously simple-minded or vapid. He acted these rôles so well that in the eyes of his public he *was* the vapidity that he counterfeited. Thus it was easy for his critics (whom Pope led) to regard him as a dunce. From school days, Cibber tells us, "A giddy negligence always possess'd me." In large part, however, this may have been pose; for Cibber was a shrewd and even courageous manager of Drury Lane. His intriguing personality conditioned his contemporary reputation as manager, actor, playwright, and heir apparent to the throne of Dulness in Pope's *Dunciad*.

During almost fifty years' work as playwright he produced over a score of plays, afterpieces, or ballad operas, most of which were well received. But a giddy negligence certainly possessed him when it came to the apt use of words, and he failed in several attempts to write tragedy. As a writer of comedy he realized that he was no wit, and he depended on story and situation rather than on well-written dialogue. His favorite early trick of situation was to reform an erring male suddenly—almost accidentally—in the last act. So Loveless in *Love's Last Shift* is restored to conjugal fidelity when his forsaken wife masquerades as a prostitute to win him back. Again in *The Careless Husband* (1704) a wife, through a casual act of kindness, shames the heart of a moderately shameless husband. At these

Colley Cibber (margin note)

---

[6] DeWitt C. Croissant, "Early Sentimental Comedy," *Parrott Presentation Volume* (Princeton, 1935), pp. 47-71; Kathleen M. Lynch, "Thomas D'Urfey's Contribution to Sentimental Comedy," *PQ*, ix (1930). 249-259.

[7] The small events of Cibber's life are too complex for brief recording. His distinguished theatrical career was eclipsed by the subsequent phase as poet laureate (1730 ff.). His odes for the New Year and for the King's birthday justly occasioned much ridicule. Pope had disliked him from about 1717, and after 1730 Fielding continually ridiculed him. In 1743 Pope made Cibber the hero of his revised *Dunciad*. That Cibber had an ambitious genius may be seen from his autobiography (his *Apology*—by all odds his most valued work) and also from his boldness in publishing a quarto volume of nearly 300 pages called *The Character and Conduct of Cicero Considered* (1747) and a poetical *Rhapsody upon the Marvellous: Arising from the First Odes of Horace and Pindar* (1751). His *Letter from Mr. Cibber to Mr. Pope* (1742) had a considerable success in its jocular attack on the poet. — Only his *Plays* have been collected (2v, 1721; 4v, 1760; 5v, 1777). By writing his own life in his *Apology* (1740) Cibber made it difficult for modern biographers. Richard H. Barker's *Mr. Cibber of Drury Lane* (1939) may be recommended, as, for commentary on his plays, may be DeWitt C. Croissant's *Studies in the Work of Colley Cibber* (Lawrence, Kan., 1912). On Fielding's criticism of Cibber see Houghton W. Taylor, "Fielding upon Cibber," *MP*, xxix (1931). 73-90.

facile redemptions the audience shed honest tears, and the historians have since hailed Cibber as a reformer of comedy. Shamelessness for four acts he counterbalanced by an artificial and sudden triumph of virtue in the last. Cibber was no moral reformer: he realized that a new tone would please, and he hit upon the one most likely to please. His cleverness as a playwright lay in devising situations and stage business and in the rapid movement of his plots. Typical in these matters are two notable successes, *Love Makes a Man* (1700) and *She Wou'd and She Wou'd Not* (1702). Like most practical playwrights he did not disdain topical aids to success: his *Non-Juror* (1717) is a clumsy secondhand adaptation of Molière's *Tartuffe* to the anti-Catholic fervor of the time [8] (heated by the Bangorian controversy just then), and his *Refusal* (1721) attempted to capitalize on the furor over the South Sea Bubble. His service to patriotism and the Whigs in *The Non-Juror* was rewarded in 1730 when he was made poet laureate. His best play was probably *The Careless Husband,* of which in 1764 David Erskine Baker could write extravagantly:

This comedy contains, perhaps, the most elegant dialogue, and the most perfect knowledge of the manners of persons in real high life, extant in any dramatic piece that has yet appeared in any language whatever.

Though the play was extremely popular, these judgments were most absurd. Cibber's writing was at times effective but never subtle. His early critics, John Dennis, Pope, and Fielding, for example, thought Cibber a most egregious murderer of the King's English. While the absurdities of his plays were obvious, the sprightliness, variety, and individuality of his work, aided by his ability to create effective rôles for leading members of the Drury Lane company, made many, if not most, of his comedies consistently "good theatre."

Sir Richard
Steele

Cibber's friend Richard Steele was a different sort.[9] "At the Restoration," Dennis said scornfully, "the Theaters were in the Hands of Gentlemen." In some moods he did not allow this quality (except by birth) to Steele, who nevertheless was the chief instrument in the attempt to get the theatre back into genteel hands. At the beginning of 1715, already a licensed partner in Drury Lane, Steele petitioned (successfully) the King for a life-patent to the theatre, urging "That the use of the Theatre has for many years last past been much perverted to the great Scandal of Religion and Good Government." From 1715 to 1719 Steele apparently was in close contact with other licensees; but after the presentation of *The Conscious Lovers* (1722) there is little evidence of his active participation in anything except the profits from the theatre. During the first years of his connection with Drury Lane he probably exercised a strong informal influence, but this is difficult to define or to establish except through his essays.

[8] See three articles by Dudley H. Miles: "The Original of *The Non-Juror,*" *PMLA*, xxx (1915). 195-214; "The Political Satire of *The Non-Juror,*" *MP*, xiii (1915). 281-304; "A Forgotten Hit: *The Non-Juror,*" *SP*, xvi (1919). 67-77.

[9] On Steele's career see Part ii, ch. v. Even on his plays the best factual commentary is in George A. Aitken's *Life of Richard Steele* (2v, 1889).

His plays are definitely on the side of gentility and bourgeois respectability. Three came out early in the century, before he was engrossed in politics. *The Funeral: or Grief a-la-Mode* (1701) was a comedy of manners and intrigue in which Lord Brumpton feigns death in order to test the affection of his wife as well as that of his son, whom the villainous and actually bigamous wife has persuaded him to disinherit. The hypocrisy of the "widow's" grief and the moral prating of the vulturous undertaker afford some comedy here, as do two pairs of lovers—the one coyly hesitant, the other somewhat more boisterously active. Both of the young gentlemen are officers in the army (like Steele), and both are far more reputable and more human than their immediate predecessors in comedy. Steele boasted of the innocence of the play in his preface. This success encouraged performance of *The Lying Lover* (1703), a play of much the same sort, but too serious in tone for its time. It was, as Steele himself confessed, "dam'd for its piety." His object in the play was, he said, to promote "Simplicity of Mind, Good-nature, Friendship, and Honour" and "to attempt a Comedy, which might be no improper Entertainment in a Christian Commonwealth." Steele here took occasion to demonstrate, as throughout his career he liked to do, the evils of dueling. None of these objectives, obviously, was generative of true comedy. He had better luck with his next, *The Tender Husband* (1705), which is again in the sentimental moralizing mood, but has a better story, one dealing, as we are told in conclusion, with "A Son too much confin'd—too free a Wife." The "free" wife, Mrs. Clerimont, is scared into virtue by a device worthy of Cibber: her husband disguises his mistress Fainlove as a man, who is to be compromisingly discovered with Mrs. Clerimont, who in turn is unaware of the trick. Young Clerimont has the more rational design of marrying an heiress, and since he has been "a great Traveller in Fairy-land," and knows "Oroondates, Cassandra, Astraea, and Clelia" as "intimate Acquaintance," he easily impresses the romance-reading city heiress, Biddy Tipkin, and saves her from a hateful marriage to a country lumpkin named Gubbin—who ultimately marries Fainlove. This seems a more normal play for the time, with an artificial intrigue, with scenes in the Park rather than in Newgate, as in *The Lying Lover*. But it is still a play stressing serious and domestic rather than frivolous and elegant problems.

For years thereafter Steele in his periodical essays preached the gospel of reformed gentility, of the true gentleman as compared with Etherege's Dorimant. Finally in 1722 he brought out his best play, which he once intended to call "The Fine Gentleman," but actually called *The Conscious Lovers*. The contrast with the Restoration is here complete—as it was not in *The Tender Husband*. The characters are frankly middle-class; the lovers are not in doubt about each other's affection, though no word of affection has passed between them: their love is "conscious," i.e., mutually understood. The character of young Bevil is thoroughly upright and worthy; his sense of filial duty (derived in part from Terence's *Andria*) is extreme

The Conscious Lovers

for anything except a sentimental comedy, and his attitude towards Indiana is so excessively idealized as to be unrealistic but still commendable. The treatment of marriage as properly an affair of love rather than of marriage settlements is typically sentimental, and still another mark of the type is the reiterated prejudice against dueling. The piece is not only, however, a storehouse of sentimental clichés, but also a play of well-knit structure. The dénouement—the discovery that Indiana is Sealand's daughter—is certainly conventional; but it is here handled with a sure and restrained touch. The neatness of plotting and the naturalness of expression make the play the best sentimental comedy before Hugh Kelly's *False Delicacy* (1768). But in its moral intention it is in no wise truly comic. Fielding ironically made worthy Parson Adams characterize the superiority of its morals: "'Aye, there is nothing but heathenism to be learned from plays,' replied he, 'I never heard of any plays fit for a Christian to read, but *Cato* and the *Conscious Lovers;* and, I must own, in the latter there are some things almost solemn enough for a sermon.'" John Dennis, again, summed up clearly Steele's divergence from the classical theory of comedy as curative of men's follies through ridicule. In comedy ideal patterns of conduct tend to be implicit, not explicit, as in Steele. So Dennis tells us:

How little do they know of the Nature of true Comedy, who believe that its proper Business is to set us Patterns for Imitation: For all such Patterns are serious Things, and Laughter is the Life, and the very Soul of Comedy. 'Tis its proper Business to expose Persons to our View, whose Views we may shun, and whose Follies we may despise; and by shewing us what is done upon the Comick Stage, to shew us what ought never to be done upon the Stage of the World.

Dennis's theories were sound, but the difficulty in an increasingly prudish and genteel age was to find respectable and interesting follies of any variety *Other* to dramatize. After *The Conscious Lovers* many a play was written with *"Reformed"* the polite intention, as the Rev. James Miller remarked in the Dedication *Comedies* to his comedy *The Man of Taste* (1735), "to entertain the Town, without giving Offence, either to Virtue, Decency, or Good Manners." In general these plays are comedies of manners or of intrigue with sentimental elements added. Such had been the character of the plays of Thomas Baker, Charles Burnaby, Charles Johnson, and even of Addison's neglected comedy *The Drummer* (1716); it was to be the nature of the plays of James Miller and Robert Dodsley, the latter of whom as an ex-footman naturally and effectively featured somewhat proletarian emotions. Perhaps the best of the more sentimental mid-century plays was *The Foundling* (1748) by Fielding's friend Edward Moore [10] (1712-1757), whose masterpiece, however, was his bourgeois tragedy, *The Gamester* (1753).

Susanna   Among comic writers depending less on these sentimental motivations of
Centlivre   action one must consider Mrs. Susanna Centlivre and Henry Fielding. After a picturesque early life Mrs. Centlivre turned to the exasperating

[10] John H. Caskey, *The Life and Works of Edward Moore* (New Haven, 1927). Moore's collected *Poems, Fables, and Plays* were published in 1756.

career of playwright.[11] She wrote fourteen comedies, two tragedies, and three farces, and of the comedies at least four achieved and deserved great success, not so much for their literary quality as for their brisk movement of intrigue and easy flow of incident. Her fourth comedy, *The Gamester* (1705), builds in the fourth act to a thrilling scene in which the gaming lover first sweeps the boards, and then loses all to his lady (disguised as a man), including, finally, her own picture set in diamonds. His cure from gaming—and his marriage to the lady—result. In *The Busie Body* (1709) there is even livelier intrigue, and the rôle of Marplot was long a favorite with many comic actors. *The Wonder: A Woman Keeps a Secret* (1714), a similar triumph of theatrical instinct and sound plot construction, kept the stage for well over a century, and in Don Felix furnished Garrick with one of his best rôles. More wit and perhaps even hardness of style is seen in her last great success, *A Bold Stroke for a Wife* (1718). Here and in her other late plays Mrs. Centlivre has been thought to imitate Congreve; but marriage is her theme, and in these plays as in sentimental comedies (unlike the Restoration plays), there is little or no aversion to matrimony or coyness in confessing a passion.

Henry Fielding's abilities as playwright are so greatly overshadowed by his fame as novelist that they have hardly been properly recognized.[12] Although he was not at his best in comedy, he at least illustrates the difficulty of writing comedy of manners in his day. He has been thought too imitative of Congreve and Wycherley; actually the trouble was that comedy of manners was a constricted genre, and that the life had gone out of it. Other difficulties arose from his ideas that "the highest life is much the dullest," and that London high society was incorrigibly shameless. He saw

Fielding's Comedies

---

[11] Mrs. Centlivre's *Works* have been collected (3v, 1760-61; 3v, 1872). There is no good biography. See John W. Bowyer, "Susanna Freeman Centlivre," *MLN*, XLIII (1928). 78-80; James R. Sutherland, "The Progress of Error: The Biographers of Mrs. Centlivre," *RES*, XVIII (1942). 167-182. For critical commentary see R. Seibt, "Die Komödien der Mrs. Centlivre," *Anglia*, XXXII (1909). 434-480; XXXIII (1910). 77-119; and also Ezra K. Maxfield, "The Quakers in English Stage Plays Before 1800," *PMLA*, XLV (1930). 256-273. Paul B. Anderson, in his "Innocence and Artifice: or, Mrs. Centlivre and *The Female Tatler*," *PQ*, XVI (1937). 358-375, gives some reasons for thinking Mrs. Centlivre a writer of *The Female Tatler*. The real contribution of his article, however, is to show the hard life of the female author. Walter Graham in his "Thomas Baker, Mrs. Manley, and *The Female Tatler*," *MP*, XXXIV (1937). 267-272, leads one to doubt the validity of Professor Anderson's tests for authorship.

[12] On Henry Fielding see Part II, ch. x. His dramatic career lasted from 1728 to 1737, though three of his plays were first performed later than 1737. His plays have been collectively published in his *Works* since 1762. The most complete collection of them appears in the *Works* as edited by William E. Henley (16v, 1903). [The plays are in Vols. VIII-XII.] James T. Hillhouse has admirably edited *The Tragedy of Tragedies* (New Haven, 1918). For the history of Fielding's theatrical career see Wilbur L. Cross, *The History of Henry Fielding* (3v, New Haven, 1918)—to be supplemented by later studies such as Emmett L. Avery's article, "Fielding's Last Season with the Haymarket Theatre," *MP*, XXXVI (1939). 283-292. See also Helen S. Hughes, "Fielding's Indebtedness to James Ralph" [for stimulus to burlesque the amusements of the town], *MP*, XX (1922). 19-34; Charles W. Nichols, "Social Satire in Fielding's *Pasquin* and *The Historical Register*," *PQ*, III (1924). 309-317, and "Fielding's Satire on Pantomime," *PMLA*, XLVI (1931). 1107-1112; G-E. Parfitt, *L'Influence française dans les œuvres de Fielding et dans le théâtre* (Paris, 1928); Charles B. Woods, "Notes on Three of Fielding's Plays" [*The Letter-Writers, The Modern Husband, Eurydice Hiss'd*], *PMLA*, LII (1937). 359-373; Winfield H. Rogers, "Fielding's Early Aesthetic and Technique," *SP*, XL (1943). 529-551.

nothing comic about it. His first play, *Love in Several Masques* (1728), staged before he was twenty-one, could not equal *The Beggar's Opera*, with which it tried to compete, but it was a lively, light comedy. *The Temple Beau* (1730) shows more firmness of character-drawing, but, except for touches of realism in his handling of the life of law students, it is not of vivid interest. In *The Modern Husband* (1732) and *The Universal Gallant* (1735) Fielding presented his frank condemnation of London high life— later to be elaborated in Tom Jones's Lady Bellaston and in the noble lords and colonels in *Amelia*. "The decency of polite life" was not here preserved, and the audience was not amused. On the other hand, in a completely unlocalized play like his *Miser* (1733), which is the best English version of Molière's *L'Avare*, he maintained both decency and lightness of touch. Of his five-act comedies this adaptation alone kept the stage with a long and distinguished history.

His Predecessors in Farce   But comedy was not Fielding's true *métier*: he was really at home in his farces, which have hardly been surpassed in English. He had some notable predecessors, but only John Gay [13] in his *Beggar's Opera* (1728) compares with Fielding. Gay's sense of absurdity in dramatic situations or verbal idioms was early well displayed in his afterpiece *The What D'Ye Call It* (1715), which burlesqued *Cato* and other toplofty plays. The excessive dependence on the absurd limited Gay's success in some plays. In *Achilles* (1733), for example, the Greek slacker-hero appeared among the spinning maidens wearing women's clothes *over his armor*. In his great success, *The Beggar's Opera*, which had an unparalleled run, he burlesqued Italian opera, satirized aristocratic marriage customs, and brought on the stage a symbolic representation of the famous fight Walpole had had with his brother-in-law and fellow minister, Lord Townshend, a representation which coupled farce with political satire. The biting irony and not too bitter cynicism of Gay's lines and his exquisitely turned lyrics gave him preëminence in the tradition that he more or less began. Another predecessor of Fielding's wrote a quite unintentional burlesque of the heroic plays of the day. This was the mad Samuel Johnson of Cheshire—not the Doctor—who in 1729 got produced in the Little Theatre in the Haymarket his very "poetic" drama *Hurlothrumbo: or, the Super-Natural*, which was downright insanity with hardly a lucid interval, but which in its mad imagery and diction is as good a burlesque of dramatic fustian as was ever penned.

Fielding's farces made much use of these ingredients just indicated: po-

[13] On John Gay see Part II, ch. VIII. His plays have been collectively printed as *Plays* (1760; 2v, 1923), and in his *Works* (4v, Dublin, 1770, 1772, 1773). His *Poetical Works*, ed. G. C. Faber (Oxford, 1926) contains the major plays and fragments of the others. *The Beggar's Opera* has been edited by Oswald Doughty (1923) and Frederick W. Bateson (1934). For comment on his dramatic work see Lewis Melville, *Life and Letters of John Gay* (1921); A. E. H. Swaen, "The Airs and Tunes of John Gay's *Beggar's Opera*," *Anglia*, XLIII (1919), 152-190; William E. Schultz, *Gay's Beggar's Opera: Its Content, History, Influence* (New Haven, 1923); Frank Kidson, *The Beggar's Opera: Its Predecessors and Successors* (1922); George Sherburn, "The Fortunes and Misfortunes of *Three Hours after Marriage*," *MP*, XXIV (1926). 91-109; Edmond M. Gagey, *Ballad Opera* (1937); William H. Irving, *John Gay* (Durham, N. C., 1940); Bertrand H. Bronson, "The Beggar's Opera," *Studies in the Comic* (*Univ. of California Pub. in English*, 1941), pp. 197-231.

litical satire, satire on the absurd manners of "high" people, satire on the irrational amusements of the town, and satire on the irrationally inflated diction of supposedly rational dramas. His farces varied in length according *Fielding's* to their function as brief afterpieces or as half of an evening's entertainment. *Farces* He apparently liked the idea of the "double feature," an equal division of the evening between two pieces. The afterpiece is represented by his *Mock Doctor* (1732), based on Molière; by *Tumble-Down Dick* (1736), a screaming vulgarization of the Phaeton story; and by *Eurydice* (1737), a burlesque that involved giving the lady of Orpheus the psychology of a prudish "fine lady." In his longer farces we find him successful in reviewing episodically the topical follies of his day. *The Author's Farce* (1730) burlesqued the amusements of the town; and *Pasquin* (1736) and *The Historical Register for 1736* (1737) continued this theme, adding savage attacks on the political corruption of the day. These last two plays largely provoked the Licensing Act of 1737 [14] that shut Fielding off the stage. These two, it may be noted, were of the "Rehearsal" pattern, in which Fielding excelled. His *Welsh Opera* (1731) was a ballad opera burlesquing the royal family, and *Don Quixote in England* (1733) had attacked corruption in elections: such satire was permitted, but the Walpole ministry was dangerous to satirists. *The Letter-Writers* (1731) and *The Lottery* (1732) were topical skits—as indeed all his farces are. With slight annotation they come to life, and display all the incongruous disparity that marked society during the reign of Sir Robert Walpole.

The *Tragedy of Tragedies; or, the Life and Death of Tom Thumb the Great* (1730), as his best farce was called in its last form, stands somewhat apart. It is a literary burlesque surpassing even Buckingham's *Rehearsal* by its incisive exposé of rhetorical absurdity in the heroic tragedy of the seventeenth and eighteenth centuries. It is, of course, also a satire on courtly "greatness," but its chief merit lies in the skill with which he parodies or quotes verbal absurdity; no one has ever doubted Fielding's sense of excellence or bathos in diction. This farce, he pretended, was a newly discovered Elizabethan play of great influence, a device which enabled him to display the "influence" in footnotes showing parallels, which he was burlesquing. *Tom Thumb*, as well as one or two others of Fielding's farces, broke all records of the time for long runs. Their topical nature, however, made all except *Tom Thumb* relatively short lived; while they lived, they enjoyed all the triumphs of boisterous journalism dramatized.

Contemporary with Fielding's plays in the thirties and stimulated by much the same influences, were the theatrical pieces produced by Henry Carey (1687?-1743). After two farces, one of which, *The Contrivances* *Henry* (1715), he remade in 1729 into a ballad opera, Carey as dramatist—he *Carey* was also a nondramatic poet of ability—concentrated on operas and burlesques. His productions *Amelia* and *Teraminta* (both 1732) were

[14] For other influences as well, see P. J. Crean, "The Stage Licensing Act of 1737," *MP*, xxxv (1938). 239-255.

English operas after the Italian manner, and were only moderately successful as poetic operas. But his burlesque tragedy *Chrononhotonthologos*
(1734), "Being the Most Tragical Tragedy, that ever was Tragediz'd,"
fared better as a Fielding-like criticism of the amusements of the town. It
was staged at the Little Theatre in the Haymarket, and its frank criticism
of the theatre of its day may have caused Drury Lane to decline his next
ballad farce, *The Honest Yorkshire-Man* (1735), which, however, proved
a great success. So did his next piece, a burlesque opera, *The Dragon of
Wantley* (1737), with a story as grotesque as Gay's *Acis and Galatea,* taken
from a ballad that told how Moor of Moor Hall slew a terrible dragon
and thus won Margery for his bride. The inevitable sequel pictured Margery
as a shrew. The title *Margery: or, A Worse Plague than the Dragon* (1738)
indicates the tone. Carey was a clever lyrist, and his inventions caught the
mood of his decade ably.

*The Weak-
ness of
Tragedy*
Turning now from low farce to lofty tragedy we find ourselves in a
period, as Dr. Johnson admirably put it, when

> crush'd by Rules, and weaken'd as refin'd,
> For Years the Pow'r of Tragedy declin'd;
> From Bard, to Bard, the frigid Caution crept,
> Till Declamation roar'd, while Passion slept.
> Yet still did Virtue deign the Stage to tread,
> Philosophy remain'd, though Nature fled.

It is not true that there was no passion in the tragedies of the time; but the
passion was falsified by sentimentality or weakened by flat details of middle-
class life. There was a considerable amount of domestic pathos, but the
tones of noble Roman declamation were more artificially valued. Limited
in literary ability, tragic writers took refuge in gloomy stage settings such
as Congreve used in *The Mourning Bride*—settings which, it will be remembered, evoked the high admiration of Dr. Johnson. Rowe was more
melodramatic than Congreve, and he set the last act of his *Fair Penitent* in

A Room hung with Black; on one Side, Lothario's Body on a Bier; on the other,
a Table, with a Scull and other Bones, a Book and a Lamp on it. Calista is
discovered on a Couch, in Black; her Hair hanging loose and disordered. After
soft Music, she rises and comes forward.

Daggers, bones, tolling bells, and corpse-laden biers were easy supports for
deficient imaginative power and stylistic frigidity.

*Nicholas
Rowe*
Of the tragic writers Nicholas Rowe [15] (1674-1718) was probably the

[15] Rowe was a native of Bedfordshire, the son of a barrister. In 1688 he entered Westminster School, but soon left, entered the Middle Temple, was called to the bar, but abandoned
the law for literature. As a writer of tragedies he came to know all the literary men of his
day, especially Addison and Pope. In 1709 he published an edition of Shakespeare's *Works*
(6v; 9v, 1714), and became in a sense the first editor of the plays. In 1715 he succeeded
Nahum Tate as poet laureate, and as an ardent Whig received other small rewards. — His
plays have been collected in various editions (2v, 1720; in *Works*, 3v, 1728; 2v, 1736). For
commentary see Edmund K. Broadus, *The Laureateship* (Oxford, 1921); Alfred Jackson,
"Rowe's Historical Tragedies," *Anglia*, LIV (1930). 307-330; James R. Sutherland, *Three Plays*
[and introduction] (1929).

ablest: his plays at least were most often acted.[16] Practically all of his seven tragedies were successes, and he was obviously less "crush'd by rules" than others of his day, since he harked back to various English traditions. His first tragedy, *The Ambitious Stepmother* (1700), is a play of palace intrigue with echoes of Restoration heroic plays; but the rants have been cut in favor of pathos in Otway's manner, which is what Rowe admired. *Tamerlane* (1701), his most frequently performed play, was a part of the chorus of commendation of King William III, in which we have seen Defoe, Swift, and Steele also joining in this same year. Tamerlane stands for King William and Bajazet for his base opposite, Louis XIV. The play showed what could be done with political tragedy; for it was regularly acted throughout most of the century on King William's birthday (November 4) and frequently also on November 5, the anniversary of his landing in England in 1688. *The Fair Penitent* (1703) had a more genuine popularity: the "gay Lothario" and the "fair Calista" became patterns for later characterizations, such as Richardson's Lovelace in *Clarissa* and Fielding's Miss Matthews in *Amelia*. The play, though perhaps melodrama rather than true tragedy, must nevertheless have been thrilling theatre. For diversity Rowe then turned to classical and heroic rant in his *Ulysses* (1705) and to the days of Hengist in medieval Kent for his pathetic *Royal Convert* (1707)—which was not one of his most popular plays. *Jane Shore* (1714), which, so Rowe fondly imagined and even stated on the title-page, was "written in imitation of Shakespear's style," was another success of pathos and feminine distress. Shakespeare apart, Rowe here created a magnificent rôle for an emotional actress. His last play, *Lady Jane Grey* (1715), again focused attention on the distress of a lady. This tradition of "she-tragedies," as they were called, derived from Otway and perhaps Racine. Clearly Rowe ranged widely for materials; he observed the rules loosely; he concentrated his powers on depicting distress. The woes depicted are more likely, even in the historical plays, to arise from domestic rather than from national situations. Thus he works in the same vein as the sentimental playwrights who were producing lachrymose comedies.

Many of the tragedies of the time were less in the English tradition than in the Franco-Roman. One such play, Addison's *Cato,* was perhaps the most esteemed tragedy of the half-century, and one of the most frequently performed. *Cato* by any other author than Addison,[17] however, might have been less regarded. It is the product of a formally correct rather than a nobly sympathetic mind, and it owed its first popularity (as did

Addison's Cato

---

[16] In *Research Studies, State College of Washington,* IX (1941), 115-116, Professor Emmett L. Avery has a note on "The Popularity of *The Mourning Bride*," in which he lists the number of performances given to the most frequently acted tragedies during the period 1702-76. They are in part as follows:

Otway, *The Orphan*	314	Otway, *Venice Preserved*	269
Rowe, *Tamerlane*	282	Rowe, *The Fair Penitent*	261
Rowe, *Jane Shore*	279	Addison, *Cato*	226
Southerne, *Oroonoko*	272	Congreve, *The Mourning Bride*	205.

[17] On Addison see Part II, ch. v.

Rowe's *Tamerlane*) to a political situation. Written for the most part ten years before it was performed, it was staged in 1713, pretty surely as a political document. The Whigs identified Cato with the Duke of Marlborough; the Tories identified Marlborough with Caesar, the would-be dictator. Each party presented Barton Booth (who made his reputation as Cato) with a purse of fifty guineas, and both parties were loud in their applause of the play. Addison, of course, protested his innocence of any political intention. After Rowe's warm scenes the love dialogue in *Cato*—there is not much of it—is positively frigid; but the play is full of noble Roman sentiments that were cherished by patriots for a century or more. Americans will remember Nathan Hale when they hear Cato saying:

> What pity is it
> That we can die but once to serve our country!

Somewhat more aptly English and rational is Cato's noble injunction:

> Remember, O my friends, the laws, the rights,
> The gen'rous plan of power delivered down,
> From age to age, by your renowned forefathers,
> (So dearly bought, the price of so much blood)
> O let it never perish in your hands!
> But piously transmit it to your children.
> Do thou, great Liberty, inspire our souls,
> And make our lives in thy possession happy,
> Or our deaths glorious in thy just defense. (III, v)

Such eloquence, one hopes, is not merely a sublimation of anti-Jacobitical emotions.

Other Tragedies

Cato is the zenith in English neo-classical tragedy. Before Addison, Dennis had also used the patriotism resulting from victories over the French to create interest in his *Appius and Virginia* (1709), which was not a success, though it was less criticized than his later reworking of *Coriolanus* as *The Invader of his Country* (1719).[18] *Cato's* chief rival was its immediate predecessor, Ambrose Philips's adaptation from Racine's *Andromaque* (1667), called *The Distrest Mother* (1712). The wits of Button's coffee-house formed more or less a claque for this play, which, however, deserved the aid. Other classical stories were handled by many authors, of whom the most eminent (but not for tragedy) was James Thomson,[19] author of *The Seasons* and of five not very notable tragedies. As Dr. Johnson said so often, classical stories were becoming trite and stale in the hands of second-rate writers.

Oriental and English Plots

Other sources of story for tragedy were chiefly two: Oriental tales and English history, frequently medieval. The best Oriental tragedies were attractive in part for their deistic tendency to contrast Mohammedan virtue with Christian, with the preference going frequently to the former; for

---

[18] On Dennis see Part II, ch. II. The best discussion of his plays and the pamphlets they provoked will be found in his *Critical Works* as edited with introduction by Edward N. Hooker, Vol. II (Baltimore, 1943).
[19] On James Thomson (1700-1748) see Part II, ch. IX.

virtue like all else of value was universal. Among these Oriental plays were *Busiris* (1719) and *The Revenge* (1721), both by Edward Young,[20] author later of the *Night Thoughts;* John Hughes's *Siege of Damascus* (1720), and Aaron Hill's [21] adaptations from Voltaire, the tragedies *Zara* (1735) and *Meropé* (1749). Hill also sought variety, as Rowe had done, by going to English history for tragic story, as one sees in his *Elfrid* (1710), which he reworked in 1731 as *Athelwold*. The egregious novelist and journalist, Mrs. Mary Manley, used history for the story of her tragedy *Lucius, the First Christian King of Britain* (1717), and Ambrose Philips also tried his hand at English historical material in his tragedies *The Briton* (1722) and *Humfrey, Duke of Gloucester* (1723). Of all these attempts Philips's were the best written, but neither his nor the others met success comparable to that of Rowe. Such plays, however, show a tendency to depart from classical material to a "medieval revival" that undermines classicism in matter but not in manner: the new material is still poured into the same traditional Franco-Roman forms.

All these tragic writers were conscious of the rules; but usually they *Tragedy* departed in some respects from strict observance of dictated procedure. *and the* Naturally in adapting Racine, Philips tried, as Steele in his prologue for *Rules* *The Distrest Mother* says, to observe the rules duly. "Our author," Steele says,

> Not only rules of time and place preserves,
> But strives to keep his characters intire,
> With French correctness, and with British fire.

The spirit of such "brave Britons" who studied "wit's fundamental laws" as set down by the French, normally infused a certain independence into the traditionalism that dominated tragedy more than any other genre. To modern readers, and even to Dr. Johnson, these tragic poets seemed "crush'd by rules"; but foreign eyes saw the matter quite differently. The master of the Italian comedians in Paris, Luigi Riccoboni, an authority on all the theatres of Europe, in his *Historical and Critical Account of the Theatres in Europe* (1741) gives his reactions to English tragedy, formed in 1727, when he visited England. The English theatre is highly praised. He writes as follows:

Reason alone sketched out the first Rules of the Theatre in the *Grecian* Tragedies: *Aristotle* established an Art, and made the Laws for us; the *Latins*

---

20 On Young see Part II, ch. IX.

21 Aaron Hill (1685-1750) was educated at Barnstaple with John Gay, and later at Westminster. When young he traveled much, and in 1710 and thereafter he was intermittently concerned with writing for the stage or managing theatrical or operatic companies. In addition to seven tragedies he produced a very successful farce, *The Walking Statue* (1710). He wrote much about the theatre in his periodicals *The Plain Dealer* (1724-5) and *The Prompter* (1734-6). His *Collection of Letters between Mr. Aaron Hill, Mr. Pope, and Others* (1751) have theatrical interest also. Hill and Pope were alternately friends and enemies, and kept the public informed (at least Hill did) of their attitudes. — Hill's *Works* (4v, 1753), published for the benefit of his family, include letters, plays, poems, and some prose. There is a good biography by Dorothy Brewster (1913). Some of his plays are treated by Harold L. Bruce, *Voltaire on the English Stage* (Berkeley, Calif., 1918).

adopted them, and Moderns have confirmed them by the Heaps of Poems, by the so great Number of Dramas, which the *Italians,* and, still more, the *French* have already, and yet continue to supply us incessantly with. One therefore can't step aside from these Rules without incurring the Censure of the whole World. Otherwise nothing can be objected to the *English* Poets, but their having received a particular Maxim, which differs from those of other Countries, and which does not want its Defenders to support it. In such a general Agreement of Opinions authorized by Good-Sense, I am persuaded that the Men of Learning in *England* are sensible of the Irregularity of their Stage, and that (like the *Spaniards*) they are the first who take Notice of it. Were it permitted to depart from these Rules, which Reason itself hath dictated, the *English* Theatre would be able to balance in Reputation both the Ancient and the Modern. The Excellence of the English excels all the Beauties which the other Theatres in *Europe* can shew us; and if some time or other the *English* Poets would submit themselves to the three Unities of the Theatre, and not expose Blood and Murder before the Eyes of the Audience, they would at least partake of that Glory which the other more perfect modern Theatres enjoy.

Present-day students of these tragedies are likely to feel that more than a respect for rule was needed to vivify and make natural the materials that went into these plays, whether classical, Oriental, or medieval English.

Lillo's Innovation
Truly fresh substance, however, is seen in the two successful tragedies of George Lillo [22] (1693-1739), author of at least five. In the first of these, *The London Merchant: or, The History of George Barnwell* (1731), Lillo flung a challenge in the face of neo-classical tragedy. His hero was an apprentice, who, corrupted by the siren Millwood (the only really authentic characterization in the play), murdered his wealthy benefactor. This plot discards all theory as to "greatness" in a tragic hero: the story comes from an Elizabethan ballad, and deals with middle-class people only. And it is written in plain prose, though the ends of scenes may be tagged with couplets. It is the stark honesty of the grim bare presentation of a type story, together with the freshness of the theme, that gave the play its initial success. So sound a neo-classicist as Alexander Pope attended and approved the first performance. Lillo evidently knew he had not invented a genre but was simply reviving an Elizabethan tradition; for he made a version of *Arden of Feversham* (performed 27 May 1736), and he definitely associated George Barnwell with the Elizabethan, not the Georgian, period. In spite of the reputation of his play for moral power (until the middle of the nineteenth century it was regarded as an "improving" holiday amusement

---

[22] Concerning Lillo's life little is known. See Drew B. Pallette, "Notes for a Biography of George Lillo," *PQ*, XIX (1940). 261-267. His *Works* were collectively published after his death, in 1740, and were republished with a life by Thomas Davies (2v, 1775, 1810). The best account of Lillo and his plays is found in Sir Adolphus W. Ward's edition [with introduction] of *The London Merchant* and *Fatal Curiosity* (Boston, 1906). On Lillo's influence see Jacob Minor, *Die Schicksalsdrama* (1884); H. W. Singer, *Das Bürgerliche Trauerspiel in England* (1891); A. Kunze, *Lillos Einfluss auf die Englische und die Deutsche Literatur* (Magdeburg, 1911); William P. Harbeson, *The Elizabethan Influence on the Tragedy of the Late Eighteenth and the Early Nineteenth Centuries* (Lancaster, Pa., 1921); Fred O. Nolte, *Early Middle Class Drama, 1696-1774* (Lancaster, Pa., 1935); T. Vincent Benn, "Notes sur la fortune du *George Barnwell* de Lillo en France," *RLC*, VI (1926). 682-687.

for apprentices), Lillo stimulated practically no disciples in England. In France and Germany, however, the play caused the production of Lessing's *Miss Sara Sampson* (1755), the initial example of *bürgerliches Trauerspiel,* and in France Diderot's *Le Fils Naturel* (1757) had a deliberate intention of revolutionizing French tragedy. When these Continental influences re-acted on England at the beginning of the nineteenth century, the result was melodrama rather than new tragedies. In 1736 Henry Fielding, a close friend of Lillo's, brought out Lillo's second success, *Fatal Curiosity,* as half of the evening's bill in the Little Theatre in the Haymarket—the other half being a Fielding farce (*Tumble-Down Dick*). *Fatal Curiosity,* in honestly plain blank verse, was a short tragedy in three acts—again a family tragedy. Its length fitted it for Fielding's purpose of half an evening's enter-tainment, but made it less useful for ordinary performance. It had less vogue in England than in Germany, where it stimulated the writing of tragedies of fate. Thus Lillo became more important as an influence than for absolute achievement. He illustrates well, however, the feeling of a need for novelty in dramatic method and the turning from aristocratic to middle-class ma-terial. It was, for the most part, unorthodox people like Fielding and Lillo who, writing somewhat eccentrically, kept alive true theatrical instincts in the face of a crushing traditionalism, more powerful in the drama than elsewhere in literature.

VII

Traditions in Early Eighteenth-Century Poetry

The Concept of Genres

Poets and critics in the early eighteenth century thought of poetry as consisting of various specialized traditions called *genres*.[1] The classical traditionalist did not sit down to write a poem; he attempted a certain kind of poem—an epic, a great ode, a satire, an elegy, an epistle, a song, or a pastoral. And he had precedent for the general procedure that each tradition or genre entailed and even for various minutiae within the general pattern; he had in addition a storehouse of apt phrases that had accumulated in the previous masterpieces of the genre chosen, and these phrases were to be treated at will as heirloom jewels to be reset and effectively used again and again. With these definitely constricting influences of tradition it was the fate of the eighteenth century to struggle. The poets whom we are now to consider believed in liberty, but in liberty within the law—and they stressed law. But they were not slaves to one tradition, and in addition to the classical genres they built for themselves various non-classical traditions, such as the burlesque (which they thought had classical warrant and which usually depended on a classical generic pattern), narratives in the manner of fabliaux, ballads, biblical narratives, hymns, descriptive topographical poems, and many others. Even in this period the classical genre was not the sole possible precedent.

Decay of the Genres

In fact, the classical genres had seen their best days before 1700. Milton had achieved greatness in the epic, but Sir Richard Blackmore in his repeated attempts showed piety, patriotism, and the desire to achieve greatness—but never true epic quality itself.[2] The Miltonic influence led to a lamentable number of biblical epics of no distinction. *The Life of Our Blessed Lord* (1693) by the elder Samuel Wesley (1662-1735) and Aaron Hill's Pindaric *Gideon* (1749) may serve as examples. The most discussed epic of the half-century was doubtless Richard Glover's *Leonidas* (1737), which enjoyed approval or disparagement according to one's attitude towards the ministry of Sir Robert Walpole; for *Leonidas* was

---

[1] In addition to the general histories of the period it is helpful to consult on poetry William J. Courthope, *A History of English Poetry*, Vol. v (1905); and, as always, Samuel Johnson's *Lives of the English Poets* (1779-81); ed. George Birkbeck Hill (3v, Oxford, 1905); William J. Courthope, *Life in Poetry and Law in Taste* (1901); Raymond D. Havens, *The Influence of Milton on English Poetry* (Cambridge, Mass., 1922); and Hoxie N. Fairchild, *Religious Trends in English Poetry, 1700-1780* (2v, 1939-42).

[2] On the epic see René Le Bossu, *Traité du poème épique* (1675; in English 1695, 1719); Alexander Pope, "A General View of the Epic Poem ... extracted from Bossu," in Pope's *Odyssey* (1725); Elizabeth Nitchie, *Vergil and the English Poets* (1919); Hugh T. Swedenberg, Jr., *The Theory of the Epic in England, 1650-1800* (Berkeley, Calif., 1944).

written in support of that oppositional "patriotism" that Dr. Johnson came to regard as "the last refuge of a scoundrel." The reputation of *Leonidas,* however, was such that its original nine books in blank verse were in 1770 enlarged to twelve, and the poem was translated into French and German.[3] Epics were essential to poetic respectability, but they were relatively few in number and feeble in merit. Odes, on the other hand, were numerous but undistinguished.[4] From the time of Congreve's *Ode to the Queen* (1706), with its important Discourse in protest against the "irregular" odes of Cowley, poets knew the duty of Pindaric regularity, but preferred the laxness of Cowley's form. This laxness led only to mediocrity, and while practically every poet from 1700 to 1750 attempted a Cowleyan ode, even Pope himself failed in his *Ode for Music*—though it may be noted that Pope, like many such ode writers, was attempting only a libretto. In the forties Collins, Warton, and Gray showed how odes might be written well. In satire during the first quarter of the century success depended on more than adherence to the Horatian or Juvenalian tradition:[5] Samuel Wesley (1662-1735) in 1700 produced a satirical epistle *On Poetry* and his friend Blackmore in the same year published his *Satyr against Wit;* but pious railing alone availed little. Sir Samuel Garth found a way more pleasing to the time in his satirical mock-epic, *The Dispensary* (1699), which in its day made exciting reading, but is so topical that it is now unreadable. Its wealth of satire on individual physicians and apothecaries of the time followed the tradition of personal satire that Dryden and Boileau had sponsored, and that Pope was to follow. The first Horatian satires to achieve real success were the seven that Edward Young published in 1725-8 as *Love of Fame, the Universal Passion.* Practically all of Pope's satires postdated these of Young, which were highly praised. Among the numberless imitators of Horace Pope alone in this period won permanent reputation. The same limited success could be pointed out for other classical genres. The pastoral, attempted with credit by Ambrose Philips and Pope,[6] was

[3] Richard Glover (1712-1785), one of the relatively few poets frankly and profitably engaged in trade, published in 1739 *London; or, The Progress of Commerce,* in blank verse, and also a very popular ballad, *Admiral Hosier's Ghost,* on naval events in 1726. He wrote three tragedies, *Boadicea* (1753), *Medea* (1761), and *Jason* (1799). After his death the publication of a second long epic, *Athenaid* (1787), aroused no interest. He was an amateur Greek scholar, and his *Medea,* in form a Greek tragedy, was a part of the "Greek revival" in the mid-century. See J. G. Schaaf, *Richard Glover, Leben und Werke* (Leipzig, 1900).

[4] On the ode see George N. Shuster, *The English Ode from Milton to Keats* (1940); also Oswald Doughty, *English Lyric in the Age of Reason* (1922).

[5] On satire see C. W. Previté-Orton, *Political Satire in English Poetry* (Cambridge, 1910); Caroline M. Goad, *Horace in the English Literature of the Eighteenth Century* (New Haven, 1918); Hugh Walker, *English Satire and Satirists* (1925); David Worcester, *The Art of Satire* (Cambridge, Mass., 1940); Mary Claire Randolph, " 'Hide and Seek' Satires of the Restoration and XVIII-Century," *N&Q,* CLXXXIII (1942). 213-216; and "The Structural Design of the Formal Verse Satire," *PQ,* XXI (1942). 368-384.

[6] On the pastoral see Fontenelle, *Poésies pastorales, avec un discours sur la nature de l'eclogue* (1688, translated into English, 1695); *The Guardian,* Nos. 22, 23, 28, 30, 32 [by Thomas Tickell], and No. 40 [by Pope] (all in April, 1713); Harold E. Mantz, "Non-Dramatic Pastoral in Europe in the Eighteenth Century," *PMLA,* XXXI (1916). 421-447; Richard F. Jones, "Eclogue Types in English Poetry of the Eighteenth Century," *JEGP,* XXIV (1925). 33-60; Marion K. Bragg, *The Formal Eclogue in Eighteenth-Century England* (Orono,

better done either in John Gay's burlesques of the genre or in the type of descriptive writing that is either topographical, in the manner of Sir John Denham's *Cooper's Hill,* or philosophical, in the manner of Thomson's *Seasons.* Early in the century there developed in the pastoral, as in the epic, a burlesque tradition of "town eclogue" which Swift, Gay, and Lady Mary Wortley Montagu tried successfully. Burlesques, it may be remarked, may serve as playful expressions of affection for a genre: they do not necessarily imply contempt for it.[7]

Modified Patterns in Poetry

But the constricting rigidity of the classical genres easily drove poets to experiment with other patterns of writing. Some poets could dominate a tradition; most preferred to follow tradition loosely or to follow new or blurred patterns. They were encouraged in departures from the classical by their great admiration for earlier English poets. Shakespeare, whom a wit from Button's coffee-house could call "perhaps the greatest Genius the World ever saw in the Dramatick way" in a newspaper article of 1722, and whom according to Pope in 1737 every playhouse bill styled "the divine," had a general influence, which became specific at times in the drama.[8] Spenser, still called "our arch-poet," was imitated, though feebly, by several poets,[9] among them, Samuel Croxall (d. 1752) and Thomas Purney[10] (c. 1717) the riming chaplain in ordinary to Newgate Prison, and more reputably by Prior and James Thomson. John Hughes edited Spenser (1715) with interesting critical essays. Lesser poets claimed disciples also. Ned Ward and the other numerous followers of *Hudibras* were naturally not regardful of classical tradition. Defoe, whose rough-hewn couplets in his early satires constitute some of the most respectable if least attractive verse of the first decade of the century, could simply write an argument in verse as a more effectual and dignified vehicle than prose, and could write with little or no attention to what classical satirists had done. Narrative poets liked to versify Bible stories—frequently in the Cowleyan form of the ode, which was thought appropriate to the enthusiastic Oriental style—or to invent fables in the manner of Aesop, or fabliaux in the manner of Chaucer, or simply in the manner of one retelling a practical joke. Swift's *Baucis and Philemon* has a relationship to Ovid, but it has an equally close relationship to English village life. Hardly a volume of miscellanies appeared in the years 1700-1750 that did not contain jocose narratives of rural life.

Me., 1926); J. E. Congleton, "Theories of Pastoral Poetry in England, 1684-1717," *SP,* XLI (1944). 544-575. On the Georgic see Marie L. Lilly, *The Georgic* (Baltimore, 1919); Dwight L. Durling, *Georgic Tradition in English Poetry* (1935).

[7] On burlesque see Albert H. West, *L'Influence française dans la poésie burlesque en Angleterre entre 1660 et 1700* (Paris, 1931); Richmond P. Bond, *English Burlesque Poetry, 1700-1750* (Cambridge, Mass., 1932).

[8] We need a thorough study of Shakespeare's reputation for the years 1700-1750. See George C. D. Odell, *Shakespeare from Betterton to Irving* (2v, 1920); Hazelton Spencer, *Shakespeare Improved* (Cambridge, Mass., 1927); James R. Sutherland, "Shakespeare's Imitators in the Eighteenth Century," *MLR,* XXVIII (1933). 21-36.

[9] See Herbert E. Cory, *The Critics of Spenser* (Berkeley, Calif., 1911); and Harko G. de Maar, *A History of Modern English Romanticism,* I (1924).

[10] Thomas Purney's *Works,* ed. H. O. White (Oxford, 1933). Also H. O. White, "Thomas Purney, a Forgotten Poet and Critic," *E&S,* XV (1929). 67-97.

Reflective or discursive poetry, fairly independent of Horace, had been stimulated by Dryden as well as by the philosophic tendencies of the time. Bernard Mandeville's *Grumbling Hive* (1705) was destined to have fame when made a part of *The Fable of the Bees:* such a poem carries more weight of thought than an Aesopian fable. Blackmore's *Nature of Man* (1711), his *Creation* (1712), and *Redemption* (1722) are all works that regard very little classical forms while faithfully versifying rationalist doctrines about the duties of man and about the superiority of religious to philosophical solutions of moral problems as then seen. Without denying revelation Blackmore in *Creation* tries to support religion on the grounds of natural reason. Similar poems appear throughout the century: the most read were Pope's *Essay on Man* and Young's *Night Thoughts.* Less known was Aaron Hill's Pindaric *Creation* (1720) with its long preface in praise of the "terrible simplicity" and "magnificent plainness" of Hebrew poetry.

Various patterns more or less new were used also for descriptive poems.[11]   *Descriptive-*
Parks and estates were described, partly because of their beauties and partly   *reflective*
because praise might open the door to patronage. Denham's *Cooper's Hill*   *Patterns*
and Waller's *Poem on St. James's Park* (1661) were forerunners of much of this writing; the one glorifying picturesque "prospects" from a hill-top and the other praising the beauties of the gardener's art. All these descriptive types are likely to be as much interested in moral reflections as in description; but the description aided readability. Addison's disciple Thomas Tickell (1685-1740) in 1707 brought out a poem on *Oxford* and later one describing *Kensington Garden;* Pope's *Windsor Forest,* with reflections about civic glory and the pleasures of peace, succeeded so well that two years later his friend Sir Samuel Garth[12] printed his *Claremont* (1715) in praise of the beautiful villa of the Earl of Clare. Dozens of such poems appeared, the best of which were by John Dyer. Thomson's *Seasons* belong rather outside this topographical tradition since they are, as we shall see, less focused on description and more philosophical in intention.

The tendency to grandiose ideals led poets who might have written what we now call lyrics to express their emotions in Pindarics rather than in less swollen lyric forms. There are, however, two commendable developments   *Songs and*
in the shorter forms that call for mention: the development of hymn writing,   *Ballads*
and the awakening of literary interest in ballads. What we now call lyrics they called songs, and the tradition of the cavalier lyrists persisted in song, with no access of merit except when the singer took on a witty or satiric tone. That there was a strong tradition of song in the century, leading straight to Robert Burns, will be seen if one recalls the fact that in 1688 *Lillibulero* "sang James II off his throne," that *Rule Britannia* was first

11 Robert A. Aubin, *Topographical Poetry in XVIII-Century England* (1936).
12 Sir Samuel Garth (1661-1719), born a Yorkshireman, educated at Cambridge and Leyden, became a well-known London physician and wit in the nineties. He was also known as a religious freethinker. An ardent Whig, he was knighted in 1714 and appointed a royal physician. *The Dispensary* is said to have achieved ten editions by 1741. His other poems are chiefly political in stimulus, but a notable achievement was the translation of Ovid's *Metamorphoses* (1717) "by several hands," which he supervised and in part translated.

sung in 1740, and that succeeding generations have delighted in Henry Carey's *Sally in our Alley,* Gay's *'Twas When the Seas Were Roaring* (not to mention the ever-delightful songs of his *Beggar's Opera*), and Fielding's *Roast Beef of Old England.*

Songs and ballads were hardly differentiated in this period, which nevertheless saw the emergence of an interest in balladry that was to become important later.[13] The ballad was a song of narrative nature. Swift's two saints found the cottage walls of Baucis and Philemon plastered with broadside ballads, and aesthetic judgments of such poems are usually biased by their social humility. The dean of ballad writers was Tom D'Urfey, who published many songbooks before his death in 1723, but few poets failed to write ballads, and none lived without knowing well ballads that as yet had hardly got into reputable print in spite of a long traditional existence. Addison's praise of *Chevy Chase* we have seen; and though greeted jocosely, it doubtless promoted genteel interest in ballads. Prior based his *Henry and Emma* upon *The Nut-brown Maid;* Thomas Tickell produced a tragic love ballad in his *Colin and Lucy,* which had enduring popularity; in 1719 appeared Lady Wardlaw's *Hardyknute,* long supposed to be a genuine piece of antiquity and admired as such by all the ballad scholars of the century; in the same year Thomas Hearne in the preface to his edition of William of Newburgh's *Historia* quoted from the *"Cantilena celebratissima...volgo vocata* Chevy-chase"; and in 1723 David Mallet brought out his imitation ballad *William and Margaret,* which was at once popular. Collections of ballads began to appear. In 1723-5 were published three volumes called *A Collection of Old Ballads,* the first collection of such materials. Though the collection was too miscellaneous to accord with later tastes in ballads, it did pioneer work, and had at least the success of a third edition (1727). On slight evidence the editor has been thought to have been Ambrose Philips, who certainly had a connection with a songbook called *The Hive* (1724; fourth edition, 1732-3). This, however, contained little ballad material.[14]

Allan Ramsay

The work of Allan Ramsay (1686-1758) [15] in editing from the Bannatyne

[13] Sigurd B. Hustvedt, *Ballad Criticism ... during the Eighteenth Century* (Cambridge, Mass., 1916).

[14] Mary G. Segar in *LTLS,* Dec. 6 and 13, 1923 and also March 3, 1932, gives the slight evidence for Philips's editing. Lillian de la Torre Bueno, "Was Ambrose Philips a Ballad Editor?" *Anglia,* LIX (1935). 252-270, argues against Philips's connection with the work. *The Monthly Chronicle,* I (1728). 239, lists the third edition of *The Hive,* "To which is prefix'd a Criticism on Song-Writing. By Mr. Philips." *The Daily Journal,* May 5, 1735, in advertising the fourth edition, ascribes the prefatory essay to "A. Philips." Has the *Collection of Old Ballads* become confused with *The Hive?*

[15] Ramsay, born in Lanarkshire, passed most of his life in Edinburgh, where he was socially an important literary figure early in the century. He kept a bookshop, and about 1725 there started one of the first circulating libraries in Great Britain. The Scottish songs and poems that he printed from the MS collection (1568) of George Bannatyne were not traditional poems, but Ramsay's public was not discriminating in such matters. Their appetites had been stimulated by the *Choice Collection of Comic and Serious Scots Poems* (1705-11 and several reprints) published by James Watson (d. 1722). Ramsay himself was a popular song writer (*The Lass o' Patie's Mill, Lochaber no More,* etc.), and he delighted in the pastoral also. His most popular success was his pastoral drama *The Gentle Shepherd* (Edinburgh, 1725).

MS *Christ's Kirk on the Green* (1718) and a volume of *Scots Songs* (1718, 1720), and in his miscellanies *The Ever-Green* and *The Tea-Table Miscellany* (both 1724) was also important, if only for his known influence on Robert Burns. Ramsay did not hesitate to modernize or "improve" texts of the ballads he printed, but he included an increasing number of traditional folk ballads as new editions of *The Tea-Table* were called for. The popularity of the work is seen in the numerous editions that appeared throughout the century. Ramsay had no definite concept of true balladry. He regards *Hero and Leander* as a ballad, and evidently values ballads for their "merry images of low character." The tradition of the ballad, in any case, was purely native and throve alongside of more sophisticated genres.

The English hymn is a similar phenomenon. While the great honors in hymnology are given to the Wesleys, who are treated later in this volume, the early eighteenth century produced at least one great writer of hymns. *English* Isaac Watts (1674-1748), one of the most scholarly and talented writers *Hymns* among the dissenters of the time,[16] wrote spiritual manuals, a much-used *Logic* (1725), and various theological works. More permanently important were his volume of *Hymns* (1707) and his *Psalms of David* (1719)—a total of several hundreds of songs designed for dissenting congregations. Of these about a dozen are among the finest of English hymns. The poetic art of the day excelled in expressing public rather than private emotion, and its sense of the metrical line fitted the quaint necessity of Watts's school of worship—the giving out the hymn line by line for singing. Thus Watts's magnificent "Our God, our help in ages past" has the dignity of established tradition coupled with the fervor of dissenting piety. Watts's diction and imagery are by no means always so august as in this hymn or so easy as in his well-known "Jesus shall reign where'er the sun" and "When I survey the wondrous cross." Among other writers of hymns must be named the saintly non-juring bishop Thomas Ken (1637-1711) whose morning and evening hymns, ending with the doxology, "Praise God from Whom all blessings flow," have remained in widespread use. Bishop Ken during his residence at Longleat exercised a spiritual influence on Mrs. Elizabeth Singer

After 1730, though he continued to write, he ceased publishing. His son Allan (1713-84) was a celebrated painter. — *Poems* (1720 ff.); *Poetical Works*, ed. Charles Mackay (2v, 1866-8); *Burns, Ramsay, and the Earlier Poets of Scotland*, ed. Allan Cunningham and Charles Mackay (2v, 1878). — Leigh Hunt, *A Jar of Honey from Mt. Hybla* (1848), ch. viii; Daniel T. Holmes, *Lectures on Scottish Literature* (1904); John W. Mackail, "Allan Ramsay and the Romantic Revival," *E&S*, x (1924). 137-144; Burns Martin, *Allan Ramsay, a Study of his Life and Works* (Cambridge, Mass., 1931). — *Bibliography of Allan Ramsay* (Glasgow Bibliographical Society, 1931).

[16] Watts's father kept a boarding school at Southampton, and saw that his son had a good education in dissenting schools. Intellectually very able, young Watts became the preacher of a London congregation; but, his health breaking, he passed the last thirty-six years of his life quietly in the house of friends at Theobalds, or at Stoke Newington. — His collected works are edited by D. Jennings and P. Doddridge (6v, 1753), G. Burder (6v, 1810-11; 9v, Leeds, 1812-13). See Thomas Milner, *The Life and Times, and Correspondence of I. Watts* (1834); Edwin Paxton Hood, *Isaac Watts, His Life and Writings* (1875); Thomas Wright, *Isaac Watts and Contemporary Hymn-Writers* (1914); Wilbur M. Stone, *The Divine and Moral Songs of Isaac Watts: An Essay thereon and a Tentative List of Editions* (1918); Vivian de Sola Pinto, "Isaac Watts and the Adventurous Muse," *E&S*, xx (1935). 86-107; Arthur P. Davis, *Isaac Watts, His Life and Works* [1943].

Rowe—also a hymn-writer. Joseph Addison also should be here named for two small poems which he published in the *Spectator*. The first, found in No. 453, is the well-known stanzas beginning "When all thy mercies, O my God"; and the second, published a fortnight later in No. 465, is the "Ode" as he called it, the first stanza of which is so typical of the physico-theological view of the universe popular at the time:

> The spacious firmament on high,
> With all the blue etherial sky,
> And spangled heav'ns, a shining frame,
> Their great Original proclaim:
> Th' unwearied Sun, from day to day,
> Does his Creator's power display,
> And publishes to every land
> The work of an Almighty hand.

Watts as Critic and Secular Poet   Like Addison, Watts had literary interests outside of hymn-writing. His critical ideas were fresh and independent. Like Dennis he believed that modern poetry can be elevated only by avoiding profaneness and cultivating a fervor of faith. Like Dennis he believed in Longinus and the sublime; but his idea of sublimity was less rhetorical than that of Dennis and most writers of the century. Like the French critic Rapin he preferred incessant study of the true eloquence of the biblical prophets to the daily and nightly reading of the *exemplaria Graeca* recommended by Horace. Concerning his handling of the couplet he says:

In the poems of heroic measure, I have attempted in rhyme the same variety of cadence, comma, and period, which blank verse glories in as its peculiar elegance and ornament. It degrades the excellency of the best versification when the lines run on by couplets, twenty together, just in the same pace, and with the same pauses. It spoils the noblest pleasure of the sound: the reader is tired with the tedious uniformity, or charmed to sleep with the unmanly softness of the numbers, and the perpetual chime of even cadences.

It is a pity such sense on the technique of the couplet, published in 1706, could not have prevented more often the faults thus early proscribed. Watts's independence is further seen when he passes to the subject of blank verse, which he highly approved. His translation of Casimir's *Dacian Battle* into blank verse has a dignity and strength worthy of Dr. Johnson's praise. The Doctor liked its imagination, and possibly he could the more easily praise this poem because the blank verse was avowedly not Miltonic. In his preface Watts says:

In the essays without rhyme, I have not set up Milton for a perfect pattern; though he shall be for ever honoured as our deliverer from the bondage. His works contain admirable and unequalled instances of bright and beautiful diction, as well as majesty and sereneness of thought ... yet all that vast reverence ... cannot persuade me to be charmed with every page of it. The length of his periods, and sometimes of his parentheses, runs me out of breath: some of his numbers seem too harsh and uneasy. I could never believe, that roughness and obscurity added anything to the true grandeur of a poem; nor will I ever affect archaisms, exoticisms, and a quaint uncouthness of speech, in order to become perfectly Miltonian. It is my opinion, that blank verse may be written with all due elevation of thought in a modern style.

Again one wishes that James Thomson, for example, might have profited by this lesson—which Dr. Johnson, the purist, would certainly approve, though regretting Watts's too frequent avoidance of rime. Johnson regrets also that some of Watts's odes were "deformed by the Pindaric folly then prevailing." In some of these Pindarics Watts talks of his muse in a manner anticipatory of Collins. In three poems—*Two Happy Rivals (Devotion and the Muse), Free Philosophy,* and *The Adventurous Muse*—he shows this attitude:

> I hate these shackles of the mind
> > Forged by the haughty wise;
> Souls were not born to be confin'd,
> And led, like Samson, blind and bound....

Such a passage of antinomianism may bring us to a last trait in Watts's genius—his childlikeness. His volume of *Divine Songs Attempted in Easy Language for the Use of Children* (1715) is an early volume of children's verses, many of them hymns and all of them very moral. The tradition of English-speaking dissent, at least, absorbed, almost as folklore, his stanzas beginning "Let dogs delight to bark and bite," "Birds in their little nests agree," and "How doth the little busy bee." For at least two centuries, also, his *Cradle Hymn* ("Hush, my dear, lie still and slumber") was the lullaby most familiar in many a humble home. In several respects his verses for children anticipate no less a person than William Blake. Watts's contrasts—*Against Quarrelling and Fighting* and *Love between Brothers and Sisters,* his busy bee and his sluggard—show something of Blake's tone, purpose, and symbolic imagery. So does the following passage, among others, which comes from *Innocent Play:*

> Abroad in the meadows to see the young lambs
> Run sporting about by the side of their dams,
> > With fleeces so clean and so white;
> Or a nest of young doves in a large open cage,
> When they play all in love, without anger or rage,
> > How much may we learn from the sight.

Watts does interestingly what Blake was later to do superlatively.[17]

It becomes clear that patterns of poetry varied considerably in the early eighteenth century, and the work of Watts shows that the variation was not altogether due to different attitudes towards classical genres but in many cases was due rather to bias in the individual poet or to his accidental

17 V. de S. Pinto, "Isaac Watts and William Blake," *RES,* xx (1944). 214-223.

*The
Countess of
Winchilsea*

status in society. It may be well to examine the work of certain authors who illustrate personal influences in their writing. The slight fame of Anne Finch, Countess of Winchilsea,[18] as poet derives in part from the passing mention that Wordsworth gave her in his "Essay Supplementary to the Preface" (1815). He thought her *Nocturnal Reverie* and Pope's *Windsor Forest* the only poems between *Paradise Lost* and *The Seasons* that contained "a single new image of external nature." Those who have echoed Wordsworth's rash praise have probably imitated him in forgetting the stilted and conventional opening lines of this admirably descriptive poem. In her own day Lady Winchilsea had modest and deserved repute; on her contemporaries the effect of a countess poetizing paralleled the later effect on Dr. Johnson of a woman preaching. Ardelia (as her ladyship called herself in print) did it surprisingly well. Her work is characteristic of the late seventeenth century, in which most of it was written. She published in two or three miscellanies and in a volume called *Miscellany Poems on Several Occasions, Written by a Lady* (1713). She wrote two plays (not intended for the stage); several fables from La Fontaine, among which *The Atheist and the Acorn* is admirable; various Pindarics of a tame sort; satires; religious poems, and several songs. In *Fanscomb Barn* she imitates Milton in a plain blank verse, used, perhaps in burlesque, to present the antics of vagrants frequenting the barn. Burns's *Jolly Beggars* was in spirit more than a century distant from this only moderately amusing attempt. In her *Petition for an Absolute Retreat* there is none of the enthusiasm of Shaftesbury's praise of solitude and nature; we have rather the celebration of the classic theme of the golden mean, much in the fashion of the popular *Choice* by John Pomfret (1667-1702), which in 1700 and 1701 had gone through several editions, won instant fame, and was long regarded as perhaps the most read of English poems.[19] Her simple honesty of description is seen at its best in such poems as *The Nightingale, To the Eccho,* and *A Nocturnal Reverie.* In contrast with the female dramatists and novelists of the time the Countess and her very religious friend Elizabeth Singer Rowe (1674-1737) illustrate the improvement of the times in decorum and virtue.[20] Mrs. Rowe (whose husband's uncle was the schoolmaster of Isaac Watts) wrote numerous pastorals, hymns, "devout soliloquies," Pindarics,

*Elizabeth
Singer
Rowe*

[18] Anne Kingsmill Finch (1661-1720), of an ancient Hampshire family, served as Maid of Honor to Mary of Modena (queen of James II) in 1683, with Catherine Sedley and with Anne Killigrew, to whom Dryden addressed his famous ode. In 1684 Anne Kingsmill married Heneage Finch and withdrew from court. Mr. Finch was in the service of James II, and after 1689 he and Anne lived at Eastwell Park (Kent) with the fourth Earl of Winchilsea, to whose title the non-juring Heneage succeeded in 1712. Most of her ladyship's poems were probably written before 1712, and many of them she left in MS unpublished. — *Poems,* ed. Myra Reynolds (Chicago, 1903) [introduction]; John M. Murry, "Anne Finch, Countess of Winchilsea," *New Adelphi,* I (1927). 145-153; Helen S. Hughes, "Lady Winchilsea and her Friends," *London Mercury,* XIX (1929). 624-635; Reuben A. Brower, "Lady Winchilsea and the Poetic Tradition of the Seventeenth Century," *SP,* XLII (1945). 61-80.

[19] E. E. Kellett, "Pomfret's 'Choice,' " *Reconsiderations* (Cambridge, 1928), pp. 163-181.

[20] Helen Sard Hughes, *The Gentle Hertford, Her Life and Letters* (1940), presents an illuminating account of the social background of Mrs. Rowe. The "gentle Hertford" is, of course, Frances Thynne (1699-1754) for years a patroness of letters when she was Countess of Hertford and, more briefly, Duchess of Somerset.

and paraphrases of Scripture stories; but her literary merits were somewhat inferior to her piety. Dr. Johnson was sure that Isaac Watts and Mrs. Rowe were "applauded by angels and numbered with the just." Beautiful as well as pious, it was the lot of this young woman to have two poets as diverse as Watts and rakish Matt Prior in love with her:[21] at thirty-five she married tuberculous young Mr. Rowe, aged twenty-two.

Lady Winchilsea and her applauded friend may be balanced as personal exhibits in poetry by two men of Oxford, Christ Church wits, who achieved fame with less of gravity in it. John Philips (1676-1709) and Edmund Smith (1672-1710) were more than typically brilliant students and more than usually lax with regard to college regulations. Smith had written Latin Alcaics on the death of Dr. Pocock (1691), which Dr. Johnson found not "equalled among modern writers"; yet Smith, called "Captain Rag" and "the handsome sloven," after several years of exasperating conduct in the University, was expelled. "At Oxford, as we all know," remarks Dr. Johnson, "much will be forgiven to literary merit"; and Smith's youthful promise had been brilliant.[22] When Swift's anonymous *Tale of a Tub* appeared in 1704, Atterbury thought Smith and Philips were the authors of it. At Christ Church Philips also was "eminent among the eminent." [23] Though a less witty tavern-companion than Smith, he was still convivial, and the opening lines of his first poem, *The Splendid Shilling* (1701), indicate the carefree nature of his Oxford existence:

"Rag" Smith and John Philips

> Happy the Man, who void of Cares and Strife,
> In Silken, or in Leathern Purse retains
> A *Splendid Shilling:* He nor hears with Pain
> New Oysters cry'd, nor sighs for chearful Ale;
> But with his Friends, when nightly Mists arise,
> To *Juniper's, Magpie,* or *Town-Hall* repairs:
> Where, mindful of the Nymph, whose wanton Eye
> Transfix'd his Soul, and kindled Amorous Flames,
> *Chloe,* or *Phillis;* he each Circling Glass
> Wisheth her Health, and Joy, and equal Love.
> Mean while he smoaks, and laughs at merry Tale,
> Or *Pun* ambiguous, or *Conundrum* quaint.

All Philips's English poems are in blank verse, and on relatively prosaic subjects all make either serious or jocose use of Milton's lofty manner. For facetious effect the device soon wears thin, and the author's one serious use of it in praise of Marlborough, *Blenheim* (1705), was rough in rhythm and

---

[21] H. B. Wright, "Matthew Prior and Elizabeth Singer," *PQ,* xxiv (1945). 71-82, prints very interesting letters from Prior to Miss Singer, and concludes that the friendship was literary rather than amorous.

[22] Smith's *Works* were edited by Oldisworth in 1714 and were reprinted in 1719 and 1729. — Johnson's *Lives of the Poets* (Oxford, 1905), II. 1-23. Elizabeth M. Geffen's two biographical articles support Johnson's account. See *N&Q,* June 6, 1936, pp. 398-401 and *RES,* xiv (1938). 72-78. Smith's best work was his tragedy, *Phaedra and Hippolitus* (1707), based on Racine's *Phèdre.*

[23] John Philips, *Poems,* ed. M. G. Lloyd Thomas (1927) [introduction].

disparate in imagery and diction. *Cyder* (1708), one of the happiest frivolous imitations of the *Georgics,* was his most approved work. After Philips's death, Edmund Smith wrote in heroic couplets an epistolary elegy in his memory, which consists in part of a defense of blank verse for "lower themes." Philips's genius was essentially realistic, and his use of Miltonic verse in such case becomes an interesting and not too fortunate accident. There is some slight reason for thinking that blank verse had influential supporters at Christ Church. In view of the complete devotion of these two university wits to classical patterns one may surely assume that Philips's desire to free himself from the bondage of "Gothic rhyme" was due to the lack of rime in classical poetry.

Poets of the "Little Senate"

Ambrose Philips [24] (1674-1749), not a relative of John Philips, belongs with Thomas Tickell [25] (1685-1740), Leonard Welsted [26] (1688-1747), and others in the little senate that was attentive at Button's coffee-house to Joseph Addison. In his own day Ambrose acquired some fame both for his *Pastorals,* which exceeded Pope's in popularity and showed a discipleship of Spenser, and also for his infantile trochaics addressed to children. "To Miss Margaret Pulteney" he wrote on April 27, 1727:

> Dimply damsel, sweetly smiling,
> All caressing, none beguiling,
> Bud of beauty, fairly blowing,
> Every charm to nature owing,
> This and that new thing admiring,
> Much of this and that enquiring. . . .

And so forth. It was these or similar verses that led the wits to describe the style as "namby-pamby," which became a derogatory nickname for "Amby" Philips. A certain personal pomposity that ill accorded with this infantile style doubtless aggravated the mirth; for Philips was not without ability. His translations of Pindar are undistinguished, but his stanzas from Sappho ("Bless'd as the immortal gods is he") have sure and lovely rhythms and apt diction. His *Winter Piece,* sent from Copenhagen in 1709, is an attempt at descriptive writing, which, however, fails really to bring before us either a definite picture or the moods of winter.

Ten years older than most of the poets we have been considering, and far abler, was Matthew Prior [27] (1664-1721), who was, however, their con-

---

[24] Ambrose Philips, born in Shropshire and educated at St. John's College, Cambridge (1693-6), spent the decade 1696-1706 as a fellow of St. John's, visited Denmark, became a member of the Addison circle, and was in 1713 involved in a literary quarrel with Pope over his *Pastorals.* With the accession of George I, he was made justice of the peace for Westminster, was given the commissionership of the lottery (1714), became a member of the Irish Parliament (1727) and Registrar of the prerogative court (1734). His *Poems* are edited by Mary G. Segar (1937) [introduction].

[25] John E. Butt, "Notes for a Bibliography of Thomas Tickell," *Bodleian Quar. Rec.,* v (1928). 299-302; R. Eustace Tickell, *Thomas Tickell and the Eighteenth Century Poets* (1931).

[26] Welsted's *Works* were edited by John Nichols (1787) with a memoir.

[27] For Prior's collected works see *Poems on Several Occasions* (1707, 1709, 1718, etc.); *Miscellaneous Works* (2v, 1740); *Writings,* ed. A. R. Waller (2v, 1905-7). — Francis Bickley, *Life of Matthew Prior* (1914); L. G. Wickham Legg, *Matthew Prior* (1921); Oswald Doughty,

temporary and superior in repute. Like many poets Prior came of a good *Matthew* family much reduced in circumstances. As a boy he worked in his uncle's *Prior: His* tavern in Charing Cross and attended Westminster School. His skill at *Education* Latin verses was discovered by the poetic Earl of Dorset, who became his patron and ultimately sent him to Cambridge. The influence of the witty Dorset and his friends Sir Charles Sedley and Fleetwood Shepherd on the budding poet was ineradicable. He became perhaps the ideal neo-classicist, writing with both lightness and a noble urbanity, with elegant ease and a deft and imaginative use of classical mythology unequaled in the century. He avoided the pedantry involved in minute attention to classical patterns, yet he captured the mood and felicity of both Horace and Anacreon. His favorite English poet was Edmund Spenser, at whose feet in Westminster Abbey he was at his own desire buried.

> I'll follow Horace with impetuous Heat,
> And cloath the Verse in Spenser's Native Style,

he says in an ode on *The Glorious Success of Her Majesty's Arms* (1706), written in a modified Spenserian stanza.

From boyhood Prior wrote verses, and at Cambridge he acquired a local reputation, which became national when he and his friend Charles Montagu (later Earl of Halifax) burlesqued Dryden's *Hind and the Panther* in their *Story of the Country-Mouse and the City-Mouse* (1687). Poetry was Prior's *Autobio-* acknowledged vocation, but he was ambitious to advance his fortunes, and *graphical* his friends aided his start in the world of politics and particularly of diplo- *Elements* macy. Poetry became during the many busy years that followed either a *in His* relaxation or a device for flattering patrons into attention or a vehicle for *Poetry* serious philosophizing. Much of his verse, like his early epistles to Fleetwood Shepherd, is definitely and intimately autobiographical, so intimately that at times the personal references are not too illuminating. His career as diplomat in Holland or France was crowned by his acting as plenipotentiary in negotiating the peace of Utrecht (1713), known derisively as "Matt's peace." As a result the Whigs, when again in power, kept him in confined arrest for over a year (1715-16). He had been a protégé of Robert Harley—as Defoe, Swift, and Pope were also. Harley (in 1711 created Earl of Oxford) remained Prior's good friend in the last years, after both were released from their Whiggish imprisonments, and he provided the poet with a country residence, Down Hall, about one visit to which Prior wrote some of his most amusing "cantering anapestics." Harley assisted Prior also in arrangements for the magnificent subscription edition of his *Poems* (1718), which is said to have netted the author something like four thousand guineas. It was a moment when society was being kind to

---

"The Poet of the 'Familiar Style'" *English Studies*, VII (1925). 5-10; W. Knox Chandler, "Prior's *Poems*, 1718: a Duplicate Printing," *MP*, XXXII (1935). 383-390; Charles K. Eves, *Matthew Prior, Poet and Diplomatist* (1939). Professor H. Bunker Wright and Henry C. Montgomery have recently illuminated a little-known aspect of Prior's career—his collection of paintings—in their article on "The Art Collection of a Virtuoso in Eighteenth-Century England," *Art Bulletin*, XXVII (1945). 195-204.

poets: Pope was getting a modest fortune for his *Iliad;* Addison was retiring as Secretary of State with a generous pension; even Dick Steele had his sinecures.

Types of His Poetry   Prior's volume was called *Poems on Several Occasions,* and the best pieces here collected were personal, if not autobiographical. Three types of poem, however, lie outside this personal field: his verse narratives, his Anacreontics, and his philosophical poems. The narratives—*The Ladle, Paulo Purganti,* and *Hans Carvel,* are deftly handled, and are the best of a type popular at the time but not too creditable to it. They parallel the century's love of practical jokes, preferably crude ones. The Anacreontics are elegantly frivolous and excel in the lightness of touch that characterizes Prior's work to a rare degree. *Cupid Turned Stroller* is a good example. The philosophical poems, which he thought his important works in verse, are now hardly readable except as intellectual documents for the time. The first poem in all his collections was the college Pindaric *On Exodus iii:14. I Am that I Am,* which avows the limitations of human reason in what might be skeptical fashion except for a bow to Faith in the last lines. *Solomon on the Vanity of the World,* published in 1718 but written earlier, is a dignified soliloquy in three books of despondent heroic couplets, in which Prior expresses the Christian pessimism common to his century and to his race. Neither knowledge, pleasure, nor power avails in the face of human vanity of reason and effort. "The Pleasures of Life do not compensate the Miseries."

> Alas! We grasp at Clouds and beat the Air,
> Vexing that Spirit We intend to clear.
> Can Thought beyond the Bounds of Matter climb?
> Or who shall tell Me, what is Space or Time?
> In vain We lift up our presumptuous Eyes
> To what our Maker to their Ken denies:
> The Searcher follows fast; the Object faster flies.
> The little which imperfectly We find,
> Seduces only the bewilder'd Mind
> To fruitless Search of 'Something yet behind.

Prior, having an unusually fine library, was widely read, and this poem, the product of his great reading and reflection, he regarded as his masterpiece. While under arrest in 1716, he wrote—hastily and carelessly, so he said—*Alma: or, the Progress of the Mind,* which manifests again his skeptical tendency by ridiculing all systems of philosophy. It is supposedly a dialogue between Prior and his friend Richard Shelton, and its burlesque is neatly cast in the tetrameter couplet, in which Prior wrote both frequently and excellently.

His Playfulness   These poems illuminate their age and Prior's mind; but they are relatively impersonal; Prior is more pleasing when he is easily and elegantly familiar and facetious or when sentimentally melancholy. Love and poetry were his favorite relaxations, and he mingled the two in the eighteenth-century manner that employed a touch of acid cynicism, a touch of affectionate playfulness, and a great deal of implicit physical desire. In his tradition, as in Restoration comedy, love was a game in which one's emotions should not become too much involved. Contrary to the decorum of the time Prior's loves were seldom bestowed upon ladies but rather upon barmaids of wit and willingness.[28] *The Secretary* (1696) gives the tone for a week-end relaxation from his diplomatic activities at the Hague:

> While with labour assid'ous due pleasure I mix,
> And in one day atone for the bus'ness of six,
> In a little Dutch-chaise on a Saturday night,
> On my left hand my Horace, a Nymph on my right.
> No Memoire to compose, and no Post-Boy to move,
> That on Sunday may hinder the softness of love;
> For her, neither visits, nor parties of tea,
> Nor the long-winded cant of a dull refugée.
> This night and the next shall be her's, shall be mine,
> To good or ill fortune the third we resign:
> Thus scorning the world, and superior to fate,
> I drive on my car in processional state.

His various poems to Cloe are happy descendants of Horace, and might well as graphic portrayal have been "painted" by Watteau, Fragonard, or Boucher. Their bouquet is unique in eighteenth-century England. The acidulated seriousness of the quatrain *The Lady who offers her Looking-Glass to Venus* (an episode in his "pastoral war" with Cloe) is quintessential Prior:

> Venus, take my Votive Glass:
> Since I am not what I was;
> What from this Day I shall be,
> Venus, let Me never see.

Thus love and beauty are reduced to ingenious tragicomical wit.

Prior's mock seriousness enables him to do admirably what Ambrose *His Poems* Philips did intolerably: write verses to and about children. *To a Child of* *to Children* *Quality Five Years Old (The Author Suppos'd Forty)* is sheer wit, but his grown-up tone in his brief *Letter to the Honourable Lady Miss Margaret Cavendish-Holles-Harley* is equally deft and more substantial. In *Cupid Turned Stroller* we see again his ability to grasp and sophisticate a small child's point of view. For the debutante age we have his account in *The Female Phaeton* of how Lady Catherine Hyde ("Kitty"), who later became perhaps the most beautiful woman of her age and, as Duchess of Queensberry, patroness to John Gay, persuaded the Countess her mother (as Phaeton had persuaded Apollo his father) to lend her the family car:

---

[28] On two such that appear in his poems see H. B. Wright, "Matthew Prior: A Supplement to his Biography," *Northwestern University Summaries of Doctoral Dissertations,* v (1937). 34-38; and by the same author, "Matthew Prior's Cloe and Lisetta," *MP,* xxxvi (1938). 9-23.

> Fondness prevail'd, Mamma gave way;
>   Kitty, at heart's desire,
> Obtained the chariot for a day,
>   And set the world on fire.

In these last two poems the poet shows what genius can do with classical mythology in days when such tricks were hackneyed.

Prior's wit from early manhood was cut by a constitutional melancholy, the result perhaps of early dissipations and disappointments. In all his reflective poems this tone crops out, and phrases like "this cheat of life" are common. His sense of history as tragedy, expressed in the lines *Written in the Beginning of Mezeray's History of France,* is but the public aspect of "the cheat of life," and his *Epitaph* for Saunt'ring Jack and Idle Joan expresses the same feeling for private life. Such melancholy is the moving element in his masterly epitaph for *Jinny the Just*—published only in 1907 —and is seen also in the words of the landlady in *Down-Hall:*

> Why Things since I saw you, most strangely have vary'd,
> And the Hostler is Hang'd, and the Widow is Marry'd.

> And Prue left a Child for the Parish to Nurse;
> And Sisley went off with a Gentleman's Purse;
> And as to my Sister so mild and so dear,
> She has lain in the Church-yard full many a Year.

> Well, Peace to her Ashes; what signifies Grief:
> She Roasted red-*Veal,* and she Powder'd lean-*Beef:*
> Full nicely she knew to Cook up a fine Dish;
> For tough was her *Pullets,* and tender her *Fish.*

This tone of realistic and melancholy frivolity is pervasive in Prior: it may be the mark of a superficial nature, but his frivolities are universally moving. The lesson of life possibly may be, as he says at the start of *Solomon* "That We pursue false Joy, and suffer real Woe"; but it seems rather to be that since real woe is our lot, all transitory joys are to be cherished. He was essentially Epicurean.

His Artistic Conscience

Much of Prior's conscience was aesthetic: elegance and finish and neat ingenuity were the things that mattered most to him in art and life, and he had the gift of finding these traits where others could and can see chiefly vulgarity; but however Hogarthian his landladies and barmaids were in real life, in his poems they are refined into figures by Boucher. Not content with refining such dross into gold, he further worked the gold into exquisite filigree marked by delicacy and sure firmness of form. His rhythms and metres are tactfully chosen and lightly manipulated. In his preface to *Solomon* he expresses a feeling, more common in his age than one is likely to think, that the heroic couplet is far from a perfect vehicle. Donne and his contemporaries had so blurred it with enjambement that it "was found too dissolute and wild, and came very often near Prose." As "corrected" by Davenant, Waller, and Dryden, "It is too Confined":

It cuts off the Sense at the end of every first Line, which must always rhime to the next following; and consequently produces too frequent an Identity in the Sound, and brings every Couplet to the Point of an Epigram. It is indeed too broken and weak, to convey the Sentiments and represent the Images proper for Epic. And as it tires the Writer while he composes, it must do the same to the Reader while he repeats; especially in a Poem of any considerable length.

Prior was at his best in the tetrameter couplet, which certainly avoids the sedateness and heaviness of the longer line.

Having seen how these various poets differ in their bias of literary or *Metrical* personal tradition, we may profitably summarize their more technical biases *Tendencies* in metrics. Obviously the romantic notion that they could excel in only one metre—that of Dryden and Pope—is untenable. It is true that the numerous imitators of Milton's blank verse, being otherwise realists in attitude towards poetry, were unhappy in their attempts to marry his exotic idiom to everyday detail; but their attempts show that they valued blank verse. Not all blank verse, as we have seen, is Miltonic in pattern. Various quaint habits contrived to undermine the repute of the measure: Dr. Fell preached at Christ Church, Oxford, *in blank verse,* and in 1712 John Ozell (d. 1743), a hack translator, brought out a version of the *Iliad* in blank verse, but printed as prose. The fact that such men confused unrimed verse with prose does not mean that all men did: there are plenty of witnesses to the contrary. Even Pope with patience heard Bishop Atterbury frequently condemn rime, and promised, evidently without seriousness, "to allow it unfit for long works...as soon as Homer is translated." It was post-Miltonic performance fully as much as prejudice that limited the repute of blank verse.

Apart from the heroic couplet and blank verse the favorite metres were chiefly two. The tetrameter couplet, as practised by Swift and Prior, is handled with admirable individuality: the use of feminine rimes is not too frequent, and Prior, unlike Swift, avoids both the cleverness and the grotesqueness of Hudibrastic rime. There is more tendency to stop the lines than in *L'Allegro* and *Il Penseroso,* and variety is secured rather by change of tone and by varying light stresses. After the heroic couplet that with four stresses is the best metre of the period. The Pindaric, in Cowley's manner, is frequently used, but almost invariably is flawed by an elaborate tumidity or a prosaic bathos or—which is worse—by both together jostling each other in the same passage; but somehow the metre maintained popularity. The thirst for regularity crept in upon the Pindaric, and Congreve's prefatory Discourse to his *Ode to the Queen* marks a terminal point in the definition of this form. Like octosyllabics and Pindarics the measures used in songs were less varied and more regular than formerly; but it would be easy to exaggerate the regularity here. Trisyllabic measures in song decrease, although Prior in *Down Hall* and *Jinny the Just* had used anapestics with rollicking charm. That this rhythm could be used in song is seen in the popular lines addressed to Mrs. Howard (Countess of Suffolk), supposedly by the Earl of Peterborow (1658-1735):

> I said to my heart, between sleeping and waking,
> "Thou wild thing! that always art leaping or aching,
> What Black, Brown, or Fair, in what clime, in what nation,
> By turns has not taught thee a pit-a-pat-ation?"

Such "society verse" had its obvious usefulness, but short poems and irregular metres, though they existed, were not highly valued. The stage was set for Pope and regularity.

VIII

Pope and His Group

The masters whom Pope followed most consistently in his career were *Pope's* Horace and Boileau. His *Pastorals* were, to be sure, of Virgilian derivation, *Masters* but if he wrote a little "Ode to Solitude," it was perfect Horace; his *Essay in Poetry* *on Criticism* was formed after both Horace and Boileau, and his satires and epistles show the same discipleship.[1] Nevertheless, Pope owed much to native English writers: he is "discovered" at three different periods of his career reading the *Faerie Queene;* investigation has brought to light as many echoes of Miltonic phrases in his work as any other poet of the century can show;[2] his versification was a development from the techniques of Dryden. In him, without animosity, diverse traditions meet. To both Pope and his school true poetry was universal, and on such principle one should admire both Horace and Spenser, both Boileau and his greater contemporary, John Milton. The antagonisms later premised between classic and romantic were non-existent in his day: one was both—though doubtless Horace and Boileau were the dominant influences.

Although Pope was frequently annoyed—to put it mildly—by criticisms of his own work, he was tolerant of various traditions in poetry. This fact is evident if we consider the sort of poetry written by some of his closest friends, whom it may be well to consider briefly before passing to Pope's own writing. These friends may be divided into several groups: his early *His Friends* friends included William Walsh, Wycherley, Garth, Granville, Southerne, and Congreve; his next close friends and associates were Rowe, Swift, Gay, Arbuthnot, and Parnell, and his assistants on the *Odyssey,* Fenton and Broome. Here also may come Lady Mary Wortley Montagu, who about the time of *The Dunciad* became Pope's bitter enemy. His friends who were in part disciples—his imitators speedily were innumerable—would include Aaron Hill (1685-1750), Samuel Wesley the younger (1691-1739), Joseph Spence (1699-1768), Robert Dodsley (1703-1764), David Mallet (1705?-1765), George, Lord Lyttelton (1709-1773), and the Rev. Walter Harte (1709-1774). His champion in later years and literary executor, William Warburton (1698-1779), though not among the poets, deserves mention as an example of how Pope's prestige could be imparted posthumously to a

[1] W. H. Williams, "Pope and Horace," *Temple Bar,* cxv (1898). 87 ff.; James W. Tupper, "Pope's Imitations of Horace," *PMLA,* xv (1900). 181-215; A. F. B. Clark, *Boileau and the French Classical Critics in England* (Paris, 1925); Émile Audra, *L'Influence française dans l'œuvre de Pope* (Paris, 1931). For further works about Pope see below, note 12.
[2] Raymond D. Havens, *The Influence of Milton on English Poetry* (Cambridge, Mass., 1922), pp. 573-583.

brash and inferior personage. His other friends included the most interesting men of his day—George Berkeley (1685-1753) the philosopher; the architectural Earl of Burlington (1695-1753), who with Pope and others fought to preserve classicism from the rococo; William Kent (1684-1748), who as painter, architect, and landscape gardener worked out new ideas—perhaps Pope's —in landscaping; Charles Jervas [3] (1675?-1739), who taught Pope painting and in whose London house Pope frequently stayed; Sir Godfrey Kneller (1646-1723), and the two Jonathan Richardsons, who were later to be his chief painting friends. With musicians he was less intimate perhaps, but he evidently had some acquaintance and friendly relations with both Buononcini and Handel. The friendly Countesses of Burlington and Peterborow were both musical. The list might be expanded indefinitely. When Pope wrote, "Envy must own, I live among the great," it is to be feared that he was not thinking of the famous persons just enumerated but rather of the various and numerous noble lords and ministers of state with whom he was on intimate terms. He numbered dukes among his friends, though not among his closest friends; and duchesses and countesses were his humble servants. At the other end of his scale, writers like Mrs. Catharine Cockburn and Defoe's son-in-law Henry Baker apparently pined in vain for his acquaintance. He was much sought after socially, a fact that gives the lie to the sentimental notion that a keen satirist must be fundamentally an ill-natured man. Such an idea was the product of a romantic sentimental period, and not of the late seventeenth-century tradition in which Pope was reared.

His early friends were men older than himself and not of the rising sentimental group. The literary work of Wycherley, Southerne, Congreve, Garth, and Rowe, has been at least briefly treated elsewhere in this volume. *William Walsh*, more notable as a courtier than as a poet, had in his own day excessive reputation. Dryden had called him "the best critic of our nation"—meaning doubtless of our coffee-house society. His poems consist of pastorals, elegies, songs, and love lyrics, all of which express tender conventional images in smooth verse.[4] His personal charm and magnificence— he was tall and, as Dennis tells us, "loved to be well dressed"—dazzled the young Pope, and his chief title to fame is the fact that in some measure he formed Pope's genius. To Spence Pope said:

> About fifteen, I got acquainted with Mr. Walsh. He used to encourage me much, and used to tell me, that there was one way left of excelling: for though we had several great poets, we never had any one great poet that was correct; and he desired me to make that my study and aim.

In 1707 the youthful poet journeyed to Worcestershire and spent several weeks there with Walsh. Some of his early poems were submitted to Walsh

William Walsh

---

[3] Jervas has claim to literary reputation through his admirable translation of *Don Quixote*, published in 1742 after his death.

[4] Walsh's *Works in Prose and Verse* were published by Pope's enemy Edmund Curll in 1736. His poems are in Samuel Johnson's collection (Vol. xii); in R. Anderson (Vol. vi), and in Alex. Chalmers (Vol. viii). For his biography see *DNB*.

for correction, and it is probable that under his influence the *Essay on Criticism* was conceived. To Walsh's memory, in effect, the poem is in its conclusion dedicated, and there can be no doubt that his influence on Pope was considerable.

Another elderly wit and man of the world who was Pope's early friend was George Granville, Baron Lansdowne (1666-1735). The poetical son of Waller, Granville as a young man wrote songs to a cruel north-country beauty whom he called Myra. In the didactic couplet tradition his chief performance was his *Essay on Unnatural Flights in Poetry,* which was among the forerunners of Pope's *Essay on Criticism.* He wrote four plays, some of which enjoyed a considerable success in their seasons.[5] In the Tory régime of 1710-14 he was Secretary at War, was created a peer in 1712, was sent to the Tower in 1714, and in 1720 began nine years of discreetly self-imposed exile as a debtor and a Jacobite. To Granville, Pope had addressed his *Windsor Forest,* and in a later poem, published within a month after Lord Lansdowne's death, Pope admirably summed up his lordship's character in the phrase, "Granville the polite." The early commendation of distinguished elderly courtiers like Wycherley, Walsh, and Granville, left Pope somewhat unprepared for the distinctly smaller enthusiasm that writers of his own age felt for his youthful poems, and led to a certain, perhaps natural, irritation.

In 1713, if not before, Swift, Gay, Parnell, and Pope were occasionally meeting with Dr. Arbuthnot in his apartments in St. James's Palace as members of what has been called "The Scriblerus Club."[6] The Club was informally under the patronage of the Prime Minister (the Earl of Oxford); but it was not political in purpose. Arbuthnot,[7] a court physician, an amateur in music, an expert card-player, and a supreme wit, was probably the center of this group, who were inventing "The Memoirs of Martinus Scriblerus" as a burlesque on the various sorts of pedantry rampant in their day. The *Memoirs* were ultimately published by Pope in 1741 long after the deaths of all the group except Pope and Swift. The satiric impulse of the Club, however, bore minor fruit much earlier. The wit of Arbuthnot had been shown in his *John Bull* and his *Art of Political Lying* (1712). His verses, of which his philosophical poem *Know Yourself* (1734) was the most ambitious example, were never notable except for small bits of epigrammatic wit. Of Swift's poetry, already mentioned, hardly more need be said, except that unlike Pope he seldom uses the heroic couplet and is normally a realist with small traces of the noble Roman in his verse. Thomas Parnell (1679-1718), a protégé of Swift's from Ireland, was less interested in satire than his fellow Scriblerians; but he doubtless enjoyed the conviviality of their

"Granville the Polite"

The Scriblerus Club

---

[5] Granville's *Poems upon Several Occasions* (1712) went through at least four editions during his lifetime. Elizabeth Handasyde, *Granville the Polite* (Oxford, 1933), stresses properly his public career but gives a full account of his writings.

[6] On the Scriblerus Club and its productions see Robert J. Allen, *The Clubs of Augustan London* (Cambridge, Mass., 1933), pp. 260-283, and George Sherburn, *The Early Career of Alexander Pope* (Oxford, 1934), pp. 69-82.

[7] On Arbuthnot see Part II, ch. III, n. 7, and on Swift Part II, ch. IV.

meetings.[8] He published little in his lifetime, and that little chiefly in miscellanies. Much of the summer of 1714 he spent at Binfield with Pope, and for a time aided in the preparation of notes for Pope's *Iliad* and of a prefatory discourse on "The Life, Writings, and Learning of Homer." He was an admirer of Milton, and his best poems, like Pope's, are full of Miltonic echoes. His *Hermit* is a retelling of an ancient story designed to illustrate the ease with which the limited human mind mistakes the ways of Providence. *A Night-Piece on Death* is an obvious forerunner of the "graveyard" school: Goldsmith rashly preferred it to Gray's *Churchyard*. Among his other pieces *A Fairy Tale* and the *Hymn to Contentment* are admirable. His less distinguished work consists of numerous "divine poems" based on Bible stories: these are in the heroic couplet. Some of his better poems use the tetrameter in the manner of *Il Penseroso,* and his Arthurian *Fairy Tale* is in somewhat too regular *rime couée*. Parnell should have had a more productive career, but he was naturally idle, and sorrow over the death of his wife drove him to intemperance and away from poetry.

John Gay   Like Parnell, John Gay [9] (1685-1732) worked closely with Pope but independently. Contemporaries at times gave Pope partial credit for some of Gay's successes; but the twentieth century has more justly recognized Gay as a genius in his own right, whose reputation suffered unduly in being shadowed by Pope's supposed aid. Gay's first printed piece apparently was *Wine* (1708), an imitation of Milton and of the latest poetic hit, Philips's *Cyder.* Gay evidently had read *Paradise Lost* with keen attention to mannerisms of style, and it is interesting to see him copying Milton's stateliness rather than attempting the elegant informality that Philips coupled with the great master's idiom. Gay never again seems to have tried nondramatic blank verse, and one suspects that *Wine* was an opportunist attempt to score in the vein in which, four months previously, the Oxonian Philips had won success. It must have been a hasty piece of work, and Gay did not include it in his *Poems* (1720).

Wine was a burlesque, and this type of writing was to be Gay's favored province. Four of Ambrose Philips's *Pastorals* had been printed in 1708, and all six were printed at the beginning of Tonson's *Poetical Miscellanies* (1709). Pope's *Pastorals,* which had perhaps been in Tonson's hands since

---

[8] Parnell's *Poems on Several Occasions* (1722) were published by Pope, and his enlarged *Works in Verse and Prose* (1755) include hitherto unpublished pieces. *Poems,* ed. George A. Aitken (1894); *Minor Poets of the Eighteenth Century* (Everyman's Library, 1930). Parnell's life has been written by Oliver Goldsmith (1770; in Goldsmith's *Works,* ed. J. W. M. Gibbs, IV (1885). 155-178), and by Samuel Johnson, *Lives of the Poets,* ed. Hill, II (1905). 49-56.

[9] Gay's formal education took place in the Grammar School of Barnstaple (Devon), his native town, where the schoolmaster (Robert Luck) was a poet and where Aaron Hill and William Fortescue (later Master of the Rolls and lifelong friend of Gay and of Pope) were schoolmates. Of a moderately well-to-do family Gay became at about the age of seventeen apprentice to a London silk mercer. This apprenticeship he quit in 1706, and presently seems to have started a career as writer with the aid of Aaron Hill. In 1713 he served as secretary to the Duchess of Monmouth, widow of the rebel son of King Charles II. Thereafter he was usually in minor public employments, and was the protégé of the Earl of Burlington, William Pulteney (later Earl of Bath), and the Duke and Duchess of Queensberry. — For his bibliography see Part II, ch. VI, n. 13. His *Poems,* first collected in 1720, are edited by John Underhill (2v, 1893), Francis Bickley (1923), and G. C. Faber (Oxford, 1926).

1706, and had been highly praised when in manuscript by Pope's elderly admirers, were first printed at the end of this miscellany. Philips's poems seem to have been preferred to Pope's by the writers of periodicals, and such preference came to annoy Pope. It was partly a matter of Whig prejudice against him among the wits at Button's coffee-house. In 1713, in *Guardian* No. 40, he provoked a pastoral war by ironically praising Philips highly— for his faults, which were made evident! In this war Gay was Pope's chief ally. Philips, following Spenser distantly, had endeavored to strike out a pastoral manner both English and "different": Pope had composed in the French-Roman tradition relying, with warrant, on his melodic lines for whatever distinction he might have. Gay, and in 1717 Thomas Purney, really struck out new lines in rural poetry, not so much through the burlesque of pastoral artificiality as through particularity in rural details. Pope, and even Gay himself, pretended at times that Gay had no knowledge of the country; but in his *Rural Sports*—where he addresses Pope as "You, who the sweets of rural life have known" and paints himself as one who never "brightened plough-shares in paternal land"—and especially in his *Shepherd's Week* (written in part to discredit Philips),[10] Gay gave readers more of country sights, sounds, and folklore than any poet of the half-century if we except Thomson—and even Thomson did not use folklore as did Gay. The details are never sentimentalized, and for that reason are neglected by romantic critics who love sentimental rustic details. The influence of this pastoral war and of Gay's poems in it would be hard to trace. Clearly there existed along-side the neo-classical "elegant" rural tradition a jocose rural type of poem; and of this type such poems as these by Gay and later Shenstone's *School-mistress* (1737-42) are important.

In most of his poems in the pentameter couplet Gay preserved an *Trivia* informal if not a burlesque tone. *Trivia; or, The Art of Walking the Streets of London* (1716) is the most admired of the longer "town eclogues" or burlesque Georgics such as Swift, Lady Mary Wortley Montagu, and others were popularizing. In this imitation of Virgil's *Georgics,* Gay, like many realists, stressed the gutter to the neglect of more pleasant prospects; but for the foot passenger his warnings were vivid and sage. Like Hogarth he paints the grotesque reality of London life for purposes of not too serious instruction. *Trivia* shows his most mature and careful use of the couplet, and while many passages are quite in accord with Pope's rhythms, many are not. Witness the enjambement of the following somewhat Swiftian passage:

> The man had sure a palate cover'd o'er
> With brass or steel, that on the rocky shore
> First broke the oozy oyster's pearly coat,
> And risqu'd the living morsel down his throat.
> What will not lux'ry taste? Earth, sea, and air
> Are daily ransack'd for the bill of fare.

[10] Hoyt Trowbridge, "Pope, Gay, and *The Shepherd's Week,*" MLQ, v (1944). 79-88.

In his later epistles—the one to the Earl of Burlington (*A Journey to Exeter*) or the one to Pulteney from Paris—Gay is less studied than in *Trivia,* and allows metrical substitutions that Pope would have balked at.

Gay's Love of Burlesque

Informality and burlesque permeated most of Gay's work. In his *Letter to a Lady* (1714), really to the Princess of Wales newly arrived from Germany, he practically burlesqued the congratulatory epistle, and his libretto for *Acis and Galatea* (set by Handel) was a delightfully spirited burlesque of one of Ovid's *Metamorphoses.* He carried the spirit of burlesque, or at least of satire, even into his songs, which are among his finest achievements. Apart from *Black-ey'd Susan,* which is in the true spirit of balladry, his best songs are in his plays. In *Acis and Galatea* occur the robust lines:

> O ruddier than the cherry,
> O sweeter than the berry—

which owe much of their fame doubtless to Handel's setting. In *The Beggar's Opera* we have his most finished lyrics—and there is no really good reason for thinking that he did not write every one of them himself. Peachum's opening song is the key to the whole vein of political satire in the play:

> Through all the employments of life
>   Each neighbour abuses his brother;
> Whore and Rogue they call Husband and Wife:
>   All professions be-rogue one another.
> The Priest calls the Lawyer a cheat,
>   The Lawyer be-knaves the Divine;
> And the Statesman, because he's so great,
>   Thinks his trade as honest as mine.

Such political lyrics satirize cuttingly and cynically the modes of the court, and in this dangerous kind Gay set an example for Fielding and many another lyrical critic of the Walpole régime. Gay's range is seen in his love songs, which vary from "The Turtle thus with plaintive crying" to the amusing duet between mother and daughter, "O Polly, you might have toy'd and kist," and the famous masculine protest of Macheath, "How happy could I be with either." Similarly the drinking songs range from the boisterous chorus of highwaymen, "Fill every glass," to Lucy's more seductive, "Come, sweet lass."

In the twentieth century *The Beggar's Opera* has surpassed all Gay's other writing in popularity, but in his own century, and even into the nineteenth, his *Fables* (1727-38) had rivaling vogue.[11] The first fifty of these, addressed to the small but royal Duke of Cumberland, made, with its engravings, a charming book, though the wisdom inculcated was far from being weakly sentimental or childlike. Sixteen additional fables were published in 1738, six years after Gay's death, and this second group is frankly addressed to adults, as indeed the first might well have been. Story element

---

11 The *CBEL* tells us that there were more than sixty editions of the *Fables* before 1800.

is neglected in all these fables in favor of a worldly wisdom that is often bitterly caustic. *The Hare and Many Friends* has thus been interpreted as an autobiographical reproach to Gay's friends, but there is no reason for such an interpretation. The *Fables* prepare one somewhat for the epitaph which Gay composed for himself and which somewhat strangely stares at the tourist in Westminster Abbey from Gay's tomb:

> Life is a jest; and all things show it.
> I thought so once; but now I know it.

So spoke the spirit of the age through a genius that was essentially good-natured and very highly talented.

We come finally to the greatest poet of this group—and of the century— Alexander Pope.[12] Born of Catholic parents six months before the glorious and Protestant Revolution of 1688 and dying in 1744 when the last attempt at a Catholic and Jacobite invasion was imminent, he proudly suffered throughout his life minor disabilities for a religion regarded as almost treasonable; and he perhaps unconsciously fostered instincts of furtiveness that adherence to a proscribed cult entailed. He was debarred from a university training, but from tutors at home in Windsor Forest or from friends he acquired and indulged a great appetite for reading and at least superficial learning. From childhood he composed verses, and while Pope was still seventeen, Jacob Tonson, the leading publisher of poetry at the time, a publisher who owned—or thought he owned—the copyrights in Shakespeare

Alexander Pope: His Early Life

---

[12] Pope's life, except for literary quarrels, was uneventful. Shortly after his birth in London, the family left the City, and most of the years between 1700 and 1716 were passed at Binfield in Windsor Forest. After perhaps two years' residence at Chiswick he and his mother moved to Twickenham, his home for the rest of his life. His career as writer is easily divided into three periods: 1709-17 (early works), 1715-26 (translating and editing), 1728-44 (satires and epistles). — His *Works*, collected in several editions in his lifetime, were edited by his literary executor and friend, William Warburton (9v, 1751—often reprinted in the eighteenth century); by Joseph Warton (9v, 1797, 1803, 1822); by William Lisle Bowles (10v, 1806; 8v, 1812); by William Roscoe (10v, 1824; 8v, 1847); by Whitwell Elwin and William J. Courthope (10v, 1871-89). The Twickenham Edition (ed. John Butt, Geoffrey Tillotson, James R. Sutherland, and others, 1939—) is in progress: three volumes of six have appeared; *The Prose Works*, Vol. I, ed. Norman Ault (Oxford, 1936). — *The Iliad of Homer Translated* (6v, 1715-20); ed. Gilbert Wakefield (5v, 1806; 3v, 1817); *The Odyssey of Homer* (5v, 1725-6); ed. Gilbert Wakefield (4v, 1806; 2v, 1817); *The Works of Shakespear* edited (i.e., the plays only, 6v, 1725; 8v, 1728; 10v, 1728; 9v, 1731, 1735; 8v, 1734-6, etc.). — Thomas J. Wise, *A Pope Library* (1931); Reginald H. Griffith, *Alexander Pope: A Bibliography* (2v, Austin, Texas, 1922-7); James E. Tobin, *Alexander Pope: A List of Critical Studies from 1895-1944* (1945). — Edwin Abbott, *A Concordance to Pope* (1875). There are biographies by Samuel Johnson, *Lives of the English Poets*, ed. G. B. Hill, III. 82-276; Robert Carruthers (1853; improved ed., 1857); Sir Leslie Stephen (1880); William J. Courthope (1889, Vol. v of the *Works*); "George Paston" [Miss E. M. Symonds], *Mr. Pope* (2v, 1909); George Sherburn, *Early Career* (Oxford, 1934). For criticism see Joseph Spence, *An Essay on Pope's Odyssey* (1726-7); Jean Pierre de Crousaz, *Examen de l'Essai ... sur l'Homme* (Lausanne, 1737; Paris, 1748, 1766), Crousaz, *Commentaire sur ... l'Essai sur l'Homme* (Paris, 1738); Joseph Warton, *Essay on the Genius and Writings of Pope* (2v, 1756, 1782; 1806); Joseph Spence, *Anecdotes*, ed. Samuel W. Singer (1820); Matthew Arnold, *On Translating Homer* (1861); Charles W. Dilke, *Papers of a Critic* (2v, 1875); Émile Montégut, *Heures de lecture d'un critique* (1891); William E. Mead, *The Versification of Pope* (Leipzig, 1889); James T. Hillhouse, *The Grub-street Journal* (Durham, N. C., 1928); Austin Warren, *Pope as Critic and Humanist* (Princeton, 1929); Edith Sitwell, *Alexander Pope* (1930); Willard H. Durham, "Pope as Poet," *Essays in Criticism, Second Series* (University of California, 1934), pp. 93-110; Geoffrey Tillotson, *On the Poetry of Pope* (Oxford, 1938); Robert K. Root, *The Poetical Career of Alexander Pope* (Princeton, 1938).

and Milton, solicited the privilege of publishing Pope's *Pastorals* for him. By 1709, when these poems appeared, the young poet had been introduced to the London coffee-house circles by his elderly sponsors, and was launched on a career at twenty-one. His *Essay on Criticism* [13] (1711) gained him a considerable fame, as did *Messiah,* first published by Steele in *The Spectator* for May 14, 1712, where the unnamed author was called "a great genius." When in 1713 he announced a subscription for a translation of the *Iliad,* his friends were enthusiastic, and his acquaintances were inclined to lift eyebrows over the idea that a young man without academic training should try to translate the greatest of all poets. The moment was tense and violently partisan so far as politics and religion were concerned; Pope furthermore had estranged the wits at Button's (good Whigs!) by his war with Philips and by his friendship with the "turncoat" Swift. While he was translating the *Iliad* (1713-20), Pope was frequently attacked in print, chiefly for his religion and for his alleged incompetence in Greek. The attacks were the more annoying because the *Iliad* was most cordially received practically everywhere except at Button's. Two days after Pope's first volume of Homer appeared, Thomas Tickell published a translation of *Iliad* i, said privately to have been done with the aid of Addison. The attempt, if it was one, to show how superior a translation an Oxonian poet could produce, was a failure—but it did not fail to irritate Pope. It was in part the attacks on his work during the nine long years of translation (for when the *Iliad* was completed, he presently went on with the *Odyssey*) that changed Pope into a satirist.

Pope's Poems (1717)   In 1717 he collected his *Poems* in a volume that marks the end of his early experimental period. Associated with the *Pastorals* in this volume was *Windsor Forest,* a poem devoted to praise of the retired life and of the peace of Utrecht. It is not in intention a descriptive poem [14] so much as a meditation on court life, retirement, peace, prosperity, and other topics. There were descriptive details, but they in no way surpass the best passages of his *Pastorals,* with which also his *Messiah* (an imitation of Virgil's fourth Eclogue) is usually associated. Less important were certain poems collected from various miscellanies: his first epistle in verse (1712) addressed *To a Young Lady with the Works of Voiture,* several versions of Ovid and other ancients, two modernizations from Chaucer, and various small pieces. *The Temple of Fame* had been published separately in 1715, and his *Epistle to Charles Jervas,* significant as showing Pope's interest in his other art of painting, had been prefixed to Dryden's translation of Du Fresnoy in 1716.

Two Poems of Pathos   Two poems first printed in this volume have unusual interest as being studies in highly emotional expression: the *Verses to the Memory of an Unfortunate Lady* and *Eloisa to Abelard.* The *Unfortunate Lady* is confused and somewhat theatrical—possibly it is emulous of the manner of his friend

---

[13] On this poem see Part ii, ch. ii, n. 11.
[14] On the arguable matter of Pope's descriptive powers see the incisive remarks of Ann Winslow, "Re-evaluation of Pope's Treatment of Nature," *Univ. of Wyoming Pub.,* iv (1938). 21-43.

Rowe.[15] The confusion is curiously evident in Dr. Johnson's violent common-sensical comment on the poem, which he summarizes in favor of the
harsh uncle and characterizes the whole as "the amorous fury of a raving
girl." But since the girl has committed suicide, clearly it is not *her* raving,
though it at times might seem to be. *Eloisa to Abelard,* based on John
Hughes's translation of the famous love letters, is a greater work. Like the
Unfortunate Lady it is a tragic monologue, but the "raving" of Eloisa has a
definite and powerful story behind it, which makes the tragedy moving. As
eloquent Roman pathos the poem is not surpassed in English. It is also
tensely dramatic—witness Eloisa's sense of sacrilege as she takes her vows
as nun with her thoughts and eyes all on Abelard:

> As with cold lips I kiss'd the sacred veil,
> The shrines all trembled, and the lamps grew pale:
> Heav'n scarce believ'd the conquest it survey'd,
> And Saints with wonder heard the vows I made.
> Yet then, to those dread altars as I drew,
> Not on the Cross my eyes were fix'd, but you....

The poem is a fusion of medieval and Ovidian material. In the volume we
have evidence of Pope's love of Chaucer, and about this time he was doing
verses for the Rev. Aaron Thompson's translation of Geoffrey of Monmouth
(1718), which in turn probably stimulated the project of an epic in blank
verse on the story of Brutus, supposed founder of the British empire.[16]
This project was never completed. The casting of *Brutus* into the form of
a classical epic and *Eloisa* into the form of Ovid's *Heroides* shows the spirit
of Pope's work: there is no feeling on his part that traditions should be kept
"pure"; romantic medieval material is recast in preferred classical forms.

But even *Eloisa* is of less interest than the gem of the 1717 volume— **The Rape**
The Rape of the Lock.[17] Published in a brief form in 1712 the poem was **of the Lock**
enlarged in 1714 most advantageously by adding the "machines"—sylphs,
gnomes, etc.—and other important details. Thus executed, the poem was at
once recognized as a masterpiece; it remains for many Pope's most delightful
poem, and for all, the best mock-heroic poem in the language. It may then
be read as a burlesque of classical epic devices—the proposition, the invoca-
tion, the epic speeches, the episodes of games or of the descent to the lower
regions are all delightfully depreciated here without being vulgarized—and
vulgarization was usual in these mock-heroics. Pope's elegance as compared
with the realism of Swift or even of Gay is characteristic. *The Rape* may
also be read as a poem on an occasion, as designed to reconcile Arabella
Fermor (Belinda) and her family with the family of Lord Petre, he being

[15] Geoffrey Tillotson, "Lady Mary Wortley Montagu and Pope's ... *Unfortunate Lady,*"
RES, XII (1936). 401-412.
[16] Pope's prose summary of his projected *Brutus* was printed in Owen Ruffhead's *Life of
Pope* (8vo, 1769), pp. 410-424. See also Friedrich Brie, "Popes *Brutus,*" *Anglia,* LXIII (1939).
144-185.
[17] The best commentary on this poem is that of Geoffrey Tillotson in Pope's *Poems* Twickenham ed. (1940), Vol. II.

the baron who in real life had cut the lock. As such the poem is enormously clever in making Belinda charming (though her bereaved screams were excessive in a decorous age) and in making the lock ultimately immortal and, meanwhile, trivial. As "society verse" it takes superlative rank, and is comparable with Sheridan's later *School for Scandal* as a completely satisfying depiction, in laughing satire, of the frivolities of a polite age. Considered as a work of imagination the poem is perhaps Pope's highest achievement. It has been urged that Ariel is borrowed from *The Tempest* and that the sylphs and gnomes come from the Rosicrucian *Comte de Gabalis* by Montfaucon de Villars. But both Ariel and the sylphs are handled with originality. The sylphs in particular are purified of the dross of sex that Rosicrucians imputed to them. The best imaginative achievement in the poem lies in the element of burlesque. "Burlesque," Addison had said in *Spectator* No. 249, "is ... of two kinds, the first represents mean persons in the accoutrements of heroes; the other describes great persons acting and speaking, like the basest among the people." Pope's talent is exercised both in diminution and in aggrandizement: Agamemnon's scepter dwindles to become Belinda's bodkin; Clarissa swells and talks like a Homeric sage. Finely turned are the passages where Belinda's dressing-table becomes an altar, Belinda's mirrored image becomes the goddess, and her maid "the inferior priestess." More ingeniously sustained is the heroic battle of ombre in Canto III, but skilful ingenuity is present in every exquisite page of the work.

Pope's Homer

For a decade or more Pope was engrossed in translating the *Iliad* and the *Odyssey,* and editing Shakespeare's plays. From translation in Pope's day one could acquire both fame and fortune; from editing less could be expected. Pope's gains from Homer have been variously estimated: all one can do is to guess at them, but he may have got as much as £9000, which seems to be an unparalleled return for such labors. In spite of Pope's obvious deficiencies in academic training and in spite of many attacks by envious minor authors, the translation was well received, and it deserved to be. Unfortunately the synchronized publication of his first volume of the *Iliad* (June 6, 1715) and Tickell's translation of Book 1 (June 8, 1715) caused a sharp breach in his relations with Addison,[18] to whom Pope forthwith addressed the satirical portrait (published about six years later), which in its final form was to appear in the *Epistle to Dr. Arbuthnot* (1735) as the portrait of "Atticus." Pope's performance in the *Odyssey* brought less fame and more obloquy because while he announced himself as "undertaking" the translation, that ambiguous word concealed the fact that his friends Elijah Fenton [19] (1683-1730) and William Broome (1689-1745) were to translate half the poem. Pope was unjustly accused of underpaying his assistants: what they chiefly complained of was that concealment of their

18 Arthur E. Case, "Pope, Addison, and the Atticus Lines," *MP,* XXXIII (1935). 187-193; Norman Ault, "Pope and Addison," *RES,* XVII (1941). 428-451.

19 For Fenton's poems see the collections of Samuel Johnson, Robert Anderson, and Alexander Chalmers. His letters to and from Pope and Broome are in Pope's *Correspondence,* ed. Sherburn (Oxford, 1956).—W. W. Lloyd, *Elijah Fenton* (1894); Earl Harlan, *Elijah Fenton* (Philadelphia, 1937).

part in the matter robbed them of just fame. It is probable that, as Broome said, Pope revised every page of their work to give integrity of style to the whole.

Pope's success with Homer, though thus qualified, was great. He made the father of all poetry live for those of his day who were not scholars, and though he wrote for his day, his translation still remains about the most lively and readable of poetic translations. Less encrusted with magnificent imagination than Chapman's version, it has more, and more varied, narrative movement; not so simple or plain as Cowper's version, it has more nervous power and is less relaxed. It is naturally not a very faithful translation, if by that adjective one means *literal*. Pope follows the ideals in translation stated by his French contemporary Houdar de la Motte, who in his *Iliade* (1714) tried to make Homer write like an eighteenth-century poet. So Pope omits or multiplies lines as he pleases in order to make Homer more vivid for readers of 1715. The diction of his translation has been criticized perhaps severely, but there is ground for criticism. He is timid about everyday words that might seem "low." In his day English was regarded as both an inferior and a "failing" language. Pope himself had written, "And such as Chaucer is, shall Dryden be," and the line was quite in keeping with the ideas of his day. The Greek of Homer was regarded as changelessly and supremely poetic, and the consequent problem was to bridge the linguistic abyss between the two tongues. Pope was much influenced by the success of Milton in giving to English an epic dignity, but the influence did not operate happily. It resulted frequently in an inflated phrasing stiffened with Latinity that was neither felicitous nor Miltonic. Even in other poems Pope was capable—for the sake of rime—of using heavy Latin derivatives: his "lab'ring oxen ... from the field *retreat*." Another false taste of his day was for terse epigram or moral commonplace as well as for elegant periphrasis. "Glitt'ring forfex" is admirable as witty periphrasis for Lord Petre's scissors; but there is obvious affectation in "finny prey" for fish and "fleecy care" for sheep. It is unjust to represent Pope as inventing any of these mannerisms, but his Homer, remarkable in general for its eloquent dignity and its nervous speed, did at times propagate such heresies. In spite of these faults his translation is far more readable than some critics would have one believe.

His edition of Shakespeare was again a qualified success.[20] Like the *Iliad* and the *Odyssey* the bulky quarto volumes of these plays were published by subscription—for the benefit in this case of Jacob Tonson the bookseller, not for Pope's benefit. Pope was paid only moderately for this enterprise; but he was given paid helpers—Gay, Fenton, and possibly others. The edition was at first unpopular because expensive. Cheaper reprints in smaller format (of which there were at least four in Pope's lifetime) were better

His Edition of Shakespeare

---

[20] On the history of this edition see Thomas R. Lounsbury, *The First Editors of Shakespeare* (London, 1906) or *The Text of Shakespeare* (New York, 1908). The two titles are for a single work. Also David Nichol Smith, *Shakespeare in the Eighteenth Century* (Oxford, 1928); Ronald B. McKerrow, *The Treatment of Shakespeare's Text by his Earlier Editors, 1709-1768* (British Academy Lecture, 1933).

liked. Pope's preface indicated an understanding of the nature of an editor's textual duty and an appreciation of the excellences of Shakespeare's genius and style, though the great bard's defects were allowed to loom large. Pope indicated the "best" passages in the plays, in a somewhat casual fashion,[21] by placing inverted commas in the margins opposite choice bits. In making his text he had a fairly good collection of early folios and quartos to work from, but the tediousness of the labor was too much for him. His chief improvements in the text lie in his restoring "prose" passages to their original blank-verse form, in the addition of passages from the quartos hitherto omitted in folio reprints, and in his occasionally happy textual emendations. In days when clarity of style was a cult and when textual emendation à la Richard Bentley was a mania, it was inevitable that Shakespeare's complex language should be tinkered with inexpertly; but while Pope's ignorance of the meanings of words in Elizabethan English (for which dictionaries were quite inadequate) led him to grotesque definitions, it also probably restrained him from lavish emendation. It was his failure to do an all-out job on the text that Lewis Theobald [22] (1688-1744) reproached Pope for in his two-hundred page review of Pope's work on *Hamlet*, published in 1726 as *Shakespeare Restored: or, a Specimen of the Many Errors, as well Committed, as Unamended, by Mr. Pope*. Theobald had read much more Elizabethan English than had Pope, and many of his criticisms were just; almost an equal number, however, were either wrong or petty. When in 1734 Theobald published his own edition of Shakespeare (dated 1733) it was a considerable advance upon Pope's, but it was not then generally so regarded—perhaps because meanwhile, as a reward for *Shakespeare Restored*, Pope had made Theobald the "hero" of his *Dunciad*.

The Dunciad

In Pope's later career, chiefly that of satirist, three important works or groups of works appear: *The Dunciad*, the "Moral Essays" (including the *Essay on Man*), and his imitations of Horace and similar epistles or satires. For many critics *The Dunciad* is the climax of Pope's achievement. There are, however, certainly two and possibly three *Dunciads*. The first,[23] composed in part under the influence of Swift, appeared in three books (1728) as a counterblast to all critics of Pope's works, to all bad poets, to publishers,[24] and to all professors of pedantry such as Theobald, who is now the hero, and thus expresses his ardent devotion to the Goddess, Dulness:

> For thee I dim these eyes, and stuff this head,
> With all such reading as was never read;
> For thee supplying, in the worst of days,
> Notes to dull books, and prologues to dull plays;

---

[21] John E. Butt, *Pope's Taste in Shakespeare* (Shakespeare Assoc., 1936); James R. Sutherland, " 'The Dull Duty of an Editor,' " *RES*, xxi (1945). 202-215.

[22] Richard F. Jones, *Lewis Theobald* (1919).

[23] R. H. Griffith, "The *Dunciad* of 1728," *MP*, xiii (1915). 1-18; cf. *Colophon*, iii (1938). 569-586.

[24] The most poisonous of the publishers of the day was Edmund Curll (1675-1747). See Ralph Straus, *The Unspeakable Curll* (1927). The first modern copyright law was passed in 1709, and the ensuing years of confusion and of piracies agonized marketable authors.

For thee explain a thing till all men doubt it,
And write about it, Goddess, and about it;
So spins the silkworm small its slender store,
And labours, 'till it clouds itself all o'er.

In 1729 Pope reissued this version with changes and elaborate burlesque apparatus as *The Dunciad Variorum*.[25] The poem was still a satire on pedantry: *dunce* is derived from Duns Scotus. But the modern meaning of *dunce* opened the way for a shift in emphasis, when in 1742, probably at the suggestion of William Warburton (like Theobald an editor), the poem was in part recast to make Colley Cibber the hero and vapidity the essential quality of dulness. A fourth book, published as *The New Dunciad* (1742) advertised the coming change, and *The Dunciad in Four Books* appeared [26] late in 1743. The very conclusion of the fourth Book rises to something like nobility in expressing scorn of cheap, dull art, and this Book as a whole is one of Pope's most richly imaginative and wise pieces. The merit of the poem as a whole lies in its generalized satirical insight expressed in barbed couplets; the personal spites of the author may be set down as defects for the most part. Even these personal stimuli, however, can be generalized. Whether Pope succeeded, however, in emancipating himself from personal spite and in generalizing his dislikes has been doubted. Theory and practice do not always accord. Certainly there is more of personal animus in *The Dunciad* than in any other great English satire; but there is also a universal lesson for humanists which textual critics and professors of literary pedantry would do well to keep always in mind.

By 1730, if not earlier, Pope was at work on his "ethic epistles," which he projected in several parts. Two parts were actually written: the "Moral Essays" and the *Essay on Man*. The first of the "Moral Essays" to appear (1731) is now number four. It was addressed to the Earl of Burlington, an architect and an important patron of architecture. It was called "Of Taste," "Of False Taste," and finally "Of the Use of Riches." It was Pope's first publication after *The Dunciad,* and it turned his satirical shafts away from Grub-street scribblers towards the palatial and tasteless lavishness of *nouveaux riches,* whose new mansions lay heavy on the earth. The dunces waiting their chance, insisted, without much ground, that the satire was largely directed through "Timon" against the Duke of Chandos, who had subscribed generously to Pope's *Iliad*.[27] Thus from his alleged treatment of Addison and the Duke, Pope's enemies built up the legend of his constitutional ingratitude. The real importance of the poem is its aid in promoting plainer tastes in architecture and more natural and picturesque methods of landscaping one's garden and park. Among the other "Moral Essays" the

The "Moral Essays"

25 James R. Sutherland, "The *Dunciad* of 1729," *MLR*, xxxi (1936). 347-353. See also the introductory essay by Robert K. Root to his facsimile edition of *The Dunciad Variorum* (Princeton, 1929).

26 Its appearance was probably delayed by litigation over the copyright, which Pope had sold in 1729. See Howard P. Vincent, "Some *Dunciad* Litigation," *PQ*, xviii (1939). 285-289.

27 George Sherburn, "'Timon's Villa' and Cannons," *Huntington Library Bull.*, No. 8 (1935). 131-152.

third, to Lord Bathurst, attacks avarice and allied vices. It ends with the brilliant story of the career of Balaam the India merchant, a shrewd piece of apparently impersonal satire. The essay addressed "To a Lady" (Pope's lifelong friend, Martha Blount) "Of the Characters of Women" is an elaborate compliment to Miss Blount, who amidst the *varium et mutabile* of her sex is said to be *semper eadem*. The famous character of Atossa, probably originating in that of Katherine, Duchess of Buckinghamshire, was added to the poem only after the Duchess's death and just before Pope died. The first of these "Moral Essays," addressed to Lord Cobham, "Of the Knowledge and Characters of Men," is Pope's best statement of the favorite theme of his day, the fallible limitations of human reason. Brilliantly written, it is in doctrine closely related to the *Essay on Man*.

An Essay on Man: *Its History and Doctrine*

This "philosophical poem," which along with the *Essay on Criticism* became an integral part of the eighteenth-century intellectual tradition, was published in four epistles during twelve months of 1733-4. Pope's ingenuity was again active. Realizing that his dunces would attack whatever he printed as his, he planned to publish this poem anonymously and at the same time to publish other poems over his own name, so that his authorship of the *Essay* might be unsuspected and the unknown "new" author of the *Essay* be praised. The scheme worked, and the poem, soon acknowledged by Pope, attained even international fame. Presently a Swiss professor of logic named Crousaz attacked the poem as heterodox and Leibnitzian. Although William Warburton came forward as Pope's defender, lovers of orthodoxy began to waver in their admiration, and by 1781 Dr. Johnson,[28] who earlier had defended the poem, attacked its doctrines strongly. It was admired by many, however, including Immanuel Kant, and has frequently been a favorite literary document with scientists and philosophers, though not a favorite piece of philosophizing with Anglican literary critics. No idea in the poem is new or peculiar to Pope or to Lord Bolingbroke, who had encouraged and greatly influenced Pope in writing the *Essay*. The first epistle discusses the relation of man to God, and presents an exposition of the idea of the universe as a "great chain of being," a rising continuous scale, ideally perfect in its completeness, its order, and its unity.[29] As corollary to this notion of divine design permeating the whole universe, Pope concludes, "Whatever is, is right." In so concluding he does not deny the existence of evil, but asserts that ultimately evil works God's will. He essayed the impossible task of reconciling these views with the doctrine of free will and the obligation to moral effort. The second epistle discusses man's psychological nature, and

[28] See Allen T. Hazen and E. L. McAdam, Jr. in the *Yale Univ. Library Gazette,* x (1936). 45-51; and Georges A. Bonnard, "Note on the English Translations of Crousaz' Two Books on Pope's *Essay on Man,*" *Recueil de Travaux* (Université de Lausanne, vii (1937). 175-184. Hazen and McAdam established finally the fact that Dr. Johnson translated Crousaz's *Commentary* in 1739. The footnotes of Johnson show less hostility to Pope than does Johnson's *Life* (1781). See also A. W. Evans, *Warburton and the Warburtonians* (1932) for Warburton's entrance into the controversy.

[29] The classic treatment of this idea so fundamental in the thought of the early eighteenth century is Professor Arthur O. Lovejoy's *Great Chain of Being* (Cambridge, Mass., 1936).

while stressing the dichotomy of passion and reason, tries to reconcile the two. The third presents a sentimental picture of man's social coöperativeness and an account of the evolution of society from a primitive state to its present decadent condition. Some months after these three Pope published the fourth epistle, "Of Happiness." One may justly question whether Pope or many of his orthodox readers realized the essential, but not quite inevitable, deistic bias of these epistles: Pope was trying to build a rational or empirical system of ethics independent of metaphysics or religion, but without denying the latter. No one has ever been competent to achieve this feat, and Pope was far from competent.

The poem is a crucial instance of the problematical relation of reason and prose to poetry. In his preface on "The Design" Pope recognizes this aesthetic and intellectual problem, and shows that he realized somewhat the deficiencies of his work. Certain matters, he said, needed more detail; but detail would be tedious: other parts should have been more "poetical," but that could not be gained "without sacrificing perspicuity to ornament." In other words, Pope believed in the poetry of statement; and it is obvious that in such poems as Tennyson's *In Memoriam* or in T. S. Eliot's intellectual poems, meaning is poetical but is sacrificed for sense images, which, if not ornament, surely bear some occasional relationship to ornament or to periphrasis. It was inevitable and just that the mutual incoherence of Pope's various paragraphs should be exposed; it is also just to recognize that many paragraphs taken as such are crisp and brilliant meditations on ideas that writers of many ages have treated—whether in prose or verse—somewhat fumblingly. If one believes in the possibility of intellectual poetry, the *Essay on Man* is a masterpiece—not as the "system" Pope thought it, but rather as a cluster of sparkling passages that make an obviously incoherent whole. If one holds the strange doctrine of Matthew Arnold that Pope was essentially a prose writer, one is still bound to reckon with tangible and brilliant merits in expression. And as far back as Aristotle it was thought doubtfully wise to try to trace precisely the boundaries that separate poetry from prose.

The Aesthetic Problem of Reasoning in Poetry

As early as 1729 Pope told Fenton "that for the future he intended to write nothing but epistles in Horace's manner." Such he considered the epistles that form the "Moral Essays" and the *Essay on Man*. The modern reader is likely to apply the remark rather to Pope's "imitations" (translation plus modernization) of Horace. Of these in the thirties he did almost a dozen, and with them may be associated two adaptations from the satires of John Donne and the two other poems that became the "Prologue" and the "Epilogue" to these satires. His satires are basically directed against the follies of polite society, against corruption in politics, and against false values in art, particularly the art of poetry. All three of these join at times, as in his *Epistle to Augustus* (Horace, Epistle II, i). His political position was complex. One of his closest friends was Bolingbroke, and yet while close to this leader of the Opposition, Pope was on dining terms with Sir Robert

His Imitations of Horace

Walpole. It is corruption rather than corrupt leaders that he attacks,[30] and in the *Epilogue to the Satires* (originally called *One Thousand Seven Hundred and Thirty-eight*), where he excoriates the follies of the year, he depicts (lines 141-170) eloquently the "triumph" of corruption.

His Defense of Satire

In more than one poem, evidently aware of the increasing aversion of sentimentalism to satire, Pope defends his cruel art. This is done in his "Prologue," in the "Epilogue," and in the *Imitation of the First Satire of the Second Book of Horace* (1733), which he addresses to his eminent friend in the law, William Fortescue. His best defense is his *Epistle to Dr. Arbuthnot,* ultimately called by Warburton the "Prologue" to the Satires. The poet here vividly pictures himself as pestered by applications from Grub-street authors, and justifies his defensive aggressive treatment of them by a rose-colored summary of his early career of forbearance. Here he introduces the justly famous character of Atticus (Addison), the jealous genius who, having arrived, complacently encouraged critics to keep others from like success. Presently Pope passes to a harshly caustic portrait of "Sporus," a name here applied to John, Lord Hervey, towards whom Pope felt an intense hostility of unknown cause. In 1733 and possibly earlier Hervey and Lady Mary Wortley Montagu had attacked Pope viciously: here the poet retorts, though Lady Mary gets off, as usual, with brief but scathing scorn. All that friendship was now over. Pope ends the poem with an account of his parents, since his "obscure birth" had been sneered at in Hervey's attack, and the account is composed of sincerity and pose mixed. All Pope's critics admit he was a good son, but regret, some of them, that he was aware of the fact. The poem is among Pope's most spirited and finished works, one in which much of the time mere pique transforms itself into valid universal meanings.

Publication of His Letters

These poems of self-defense, which strive to place the poet in a good light as a moral crusader, agree in aim with Pope's publication of his private correspondence, publication which went on over a period of years (1735-42). It was not "correct" to publish one's private letters, and for this reason, at least in part, Pope resorted to chicanery to make it appear that the publications were unauthorized and piratical. He at times falsified the texts of letters, but the falsification is one of general pose usually rather than of specific fact. His great rival for epistolary fame in his half-century is Lady Mary Wortley Montagu (1689-1762), whose letters published after her death [31] deal with her travels and life as ambassador's wife in Turkey, her insatiable appetite for gossip about the irregularities of polite society in Eng-

Lady Mary Wortley Montagu's Letters

[30] Lady Mary Wortley Montagu in her little known periodical, *The Nonsense of Common Sense* (eight numbers, 1737-8), written in answer to the *Common Sense* of Chesterfield, Lyttelton, *et al.,* ardently supports Walpole and at the same time attacks corruption as nobly as did the Opposition.

[31] These letters, published under strange circumstances, in four volumes, 1763-7, are to be found in Lady Mary's *Works,* ed. James Dallaway (5v, 1803); Lord Wharncliffe (3v, 1837; 2v, 1861). — Charles W. Dilke, *Papers of a Critic,* I (1875). 343-359; "George Paston" [Miss E. M. Symonds], *Lady Mary Wortley Montagu and her Times* (1907); Lewis Melville, *Life and Letters* [1925]; Helen S. Hughes. "A Letter from Lady Mary to Mr. Wortley Montagu," *RES,* IV (1928). 327-330.

land, and her residence after 1739 on the Continent. More than Pope she shows an objective interest in the world about her; more than his letters hers are valuable as a record of the life of her time. It is to be feared, however, that she is an irresponsible if sprightly gossip: one hates to believe English society was as bad as she in her letters and Lord Hervey in his *Memoirs* paint it. Pope hardly paints society at all in his letters, which are (i.e., the ones he published) largely a personal record of mental life. In his own day Pope's letters were accepted as a sincere record; in the nineteenth century there was an excessive reaction against the supposed trickery involved in the processes of publication and "cooking" the texts. To modern readers Pope's letters are usually somewhat dull and moralistic, but for his own century his deft and elegant phrase encouraged a development of the art of letter-writing that is one of the significant aspects of the century. To Pope and to *The Spectator*, which published many personal letters, should go much of the credit for this development.

As an artist Pope is remarkable for clean-cut, incisive phrasing: his verbal *Pope's* marksmanship is unparalleled. In his early poems and in the Homer he *Methods* erred from the paths of simple plainness, but after *The Dunciad* of 1728 *as Artist* he is normally elegant and conversational in tone; a studied ease is his great achievement. In versification, if not in rime, he is one of the great masters, although he worked within self-imposed limits that would have been intolerable to another of equal ability. He learned metrics from Dryden, but he excluded Dryden's somewhat obvious devices for variety—the Alexandrine and the triplet—and depended normally on subtle variations of rhythms within the closed couplet, further hampered by a common tendency to balance and antithesis. Professor Saintsbury—and not he alone—is content to illustrate Pope's metrics from the opening lines of Canto II of *The Rape of the Lock* as showing the "rocking-horse" movement of Pope's monotonously antithetical lines. The passage (lines 1-18) is really typical only in that Pope is indulging in a *tour de force* which amounts almost to a burlesque of the antithetical half-lines that he loved with conscious excess. Even in this passage there is more variety in emphasis and in placing of the caesura than Saintsbury admits. It is true, furthermore, that the "closed" quality of Pope's couplets has been exaggerated. Couplets are curiously detachable even when lacking grammatical independence. Take the most quoted couplets:

> Slave to no sect, who takes no private road,
> But looks through Nature up to Nature's God.

Or

> Damn with faint praise, assent with civil leer,
> And without sneering, teach the rest to sneer.

Grammatically these couplets must be joined to context: they are not completely self-contained in spite of end-pauses. The second couplet, it may be noted, is part of a perfect periodic sentence which includes the whole Atticus portrait and runs on for practically twenty-two lines. The *Essay on Man* is full of couplets that are linked in groups of two or three with varying pauses at the ends of lines, or in the middle. For example,

> Of Systems possible, if 'tis confest
> That Wisdom infinite must form the best,
> Where all must full or not coherent be,
> And all that rises, rise in due degree;
> Then, in the Scale of reas'ning life, 'tis plain,
> There must be, somewhere, such a rank as Man:
> And all the question (wrangle e'er so long)
> Is only this, if God has placed him wrong?

Such a passage is far more characteristic of Pope's graceful rhythms than the opening lines of Canto II of *The Rape*. Pope's manner fascinated his inferiors for almost fifty years. As Cowper put it in 1782 in *Table Talk*:

> Then Pope, as harmony itself exact,
> In verse well disciplin'd, complete, compact,
> Gave virtue and morality a grace,
> That, quite eclipsing pleasure's painted face,
> Levied a tax of wonder and applause,
> Ev'n on the fools that trampled on their laws.
> But he (his musical finesse was such,
> So nice his ear, so delicate his touch)
> Made poetry a mere mechanic art;
> And ev'ry warbler has his tune by heart.

The mechanics of Pope's art were so subtle that mere "warblers" missed them: even Cowper, delightful as he is, lacks Pope's sparkle and dignity. There was more to the art than mere mechanics, but the mechanics were so exacting and constricting that one wonders how William Walsh could ever have advised them. Those who fail, however, to hear the delicately varied rhythms in Pope are akin to music "critics" who hear nothing but mechanic skill in Mozart. In the larger traditionalism of Pope's generic patterns as well as in the preoccupation with public emotion eloquently expressed Pope is the acme of "correct" neo-classical excellence. He is, perhaps permanently, our great example in English of "the poet of reason," of intellectuality in the poetic art. It is, of course, clear, as Joseph Warton pointed out in 1756, that Pope practised only the lesser genres of poetry, but it is perhaps also clear (as Warton says) that "in that species of Poetry wherein Pope excelled, he is superior to all mankind"—in other words, the greatest of didactic and satirical poets.

IX

New Voices in Poetry

In his *Theory of Moral Sentiments* (1759) Adam Smith, not yet a famous economist, expressed the following opinions as to the state of English poetry:

In our own language, Mr. Pope and Dr. Swift have each of them introduced a manner different from what was practised before, into all works that are written in Rhyme, the one in long verses, the other in short. The quaintness of Butler has given place to the plainness of Swift. The rambling freedom of Dryden and the correct but often tedious and prosaic languor of Addison are no longer the objects of imitation, but all long verses are now written after the manner of the nervous precision of Mr. Pope.

There is much truth in these statements, but they are not, as this chapter *Were Swift* will show, altogether true. They rather express a common feeling as to the *and Pope* obsessive influence that Swift and Pope exerted. During the second quarter *Dominant?* of the century, however, at a time when Swift and Pope were in their prime, new tendencies in poetry began to appear. These tendencies were hardly rebellious against the dominance of Swift and Pope, but they do evade the influence of those poets and of their tradition as it stemmed from Dryden and others. The developments include an increasing awareness of landscape as material for poetry, coupled, curiously enough, with an increased use of philosophical reflections in poetry. More noticeable than heretofore and parallel to the Dryden-Pope school is a Miltonic tradition, manifest metrically in the use both of blank verse and of the tetrameter couplet of *L'Allegro* and *Il Penseroso*. The idiom of Milton also is increasingly cultivated.

When in 1731 Edward Cave (1691-1754) founded the most interesting magazine of the century, *The Gentleman's Magazine,* he assumed as editor the pseudonym of Sylvanus Urban.[1] The very name suggests the bifurcation in poetic subject matter that was taking place: description of woods and meadows of rural England might now be interspersed with reflections on the manners and morals of urban society. Among several assistants presently working for the *Magazine* Cave had Dr. Johnson, who regarded the full tide of human existence as flowing at Charing Cross, and among his poetical advisers he had Moses Browne (1704-1787), who in 1729 had published *Town and* vividly descriptive *Piscatory Eclogues* that featured successfully rural scenery *Country* and folk superstition. Though there are obviously the two tendencies, it is *Poets* not possible to divide poets thus easily into town and country bards; for

---

[1] Dr. Johnson wrote for *The Gentleman's Magazine* (February, 1754) a life of Cave. As revised in 1781 it appears in his *Works*, vi (Oxford, 1825). 428-435.

some descriptive poets lived in town, and some moral-reflective poets inhabited the country. Nor is it possible to regard descriptive poets as *ipso facto* "romantic." [2] A favorite model, loosely followed, is Virgil, both in his *Eclogues* and in his *Georgics*. The latter type divides into poems that describe objective processes—Dyer's *Fleece* is an example—and poems that are speculative, in the manner of the dozens of imitations of the *Essay on Man*. Descriptive poetry is habitually blended with moralizing, and accounts of descriptive poetry, such as the *Critical Essays on Some of the Poems of Several English Poets* (1785) by John Scott of Amwell, included Denham and Pope as well as Thomson, Dyer, and others. One must not lightly call blank verse a sign of romanticism: the escape from Gothic rime had a classical as well as a libertarian bias. The entire lack of cleavage involved between "neo-classical" and "new" tendencies at this time can be seen in the explanatory note printed in 1737 at the end of a blank-verse poem (anonymous) called *Albania: a Poem Address'd to the Genius of Scotland:*

The above Poem (*Albania*) was wrote by a Scots Clergyman some Years ago, who is since dead. The fine Spirit of Poetry which it breathes, its Classic Air, but above all the noble Enthusiasm he discovers for his Country, cannot fail to make it agreeable to such as have a Taste for that Simplicity of Nature, and that beautiful Diversification of Epithets, which constitute the principal *Excellencies of Antiquity*.

Among the more urban poets of the time we may here mention such minor writers as James Ralph [3] (1705?-1762), better known for his prose and for having been a friend of Benjamin Franklin and of Henry Fielding, than for his blank-verse descriptive poems, *The Tempest* (1727), *Night* (1728), and *Zeuma, or the Love of Liberty* (1729)—this last an American poem—or his unhappy attack on Pope, *Sawney, an Heroic Poem occasioned by the Dunciad* (1728), which won for Ralph a dubious immortality among the dunces. More friendly to Pope among poets of the urban type were Richard Savage, David Mallet, and George, Lord Lyttelton.[4] Lyttelton's second poem was *An Epistle to Mr. Pope* (1730), and one of his four eclogues on *The Progress of Love* (1732) was dedicated to Pope. His most discussed poem, the *Monody* (1747), on his wife's death, was in somewhat monotonous Pindaric form. Lyttelton, again, is better known for his prose and for his political influence with Frederick, Prince of Wales (whose secretary he was). Isaac Hawkins Browne (1706-1760) produced early poems of interest and a *magnum opus* in Latin hexameters *De Animi Immortalitate* (1754). In 1736, after preliminary circulation and piratical publication, he brought out his *Pipe of Tobacco*,[5] a masterly set of imitations of contempo-

[2] A. O. Lovejoy, "On the Discrimination of Romanticisms," *PMLA*, xxxix (1924). 229-253; Raymond D. Havens, "Romantic Aspects of the Age of Pope," *PMLA*, xxvii (1912). 297-324.

[3] On Ralph see *CBEL*, ii. 443. Also Helen S. Hughes, "Fielding's Indebtedness to James Ralph," *MP*, xx (1922). 19-34.

[4] On Lyttelton see Part iii, ch. iv, n. 2.

[5] Browne's *Pipe of Tobacco* is edited by H. F. B. Brett-Smith (Oxford, 1923).

rary poets and a masterpiece of light verse at the same time. It continues the tradition of elegant informality, of which Prior is the best exemplar.

These urban poets are surpassed in interest by the "sylvan" poets, at least by the ones devoted to description. These men, though some of them passed their "career" years in or near London, were animated by a real love of "external nature" and by memories at least of a pleasant past amid rural surroundings.[6] The most important of them, James Thomson, came from Scotland; John Dyer came from Wales, and a group of west-country poets including Lyttelton, Shenstone, Somerville, and Jago, also made their reputations during this period, though their careers lasted on to a point where they properly become "mid-century" poets. Memories and pleasures of rural life were supported in many cases by literary or artistic precedent: Dyer, being a painter as well as a poet, was influenced by the landscapes painted by Poussin, Salvator Rosa, and Claude Lorrain.[7] The literary influences came largely from the pastoral tradition, from the *Georgics,* from the topographical school of Denham involving descriptions of prospects or estates, or from the modest and ingratiating pattern of *L'Allegro* and *Il Penseroso.*

James Thomson [8] (1700-1748) was much influenced by these literary tradi- *Thomson's* tions, which reinforced a true love of natural scenery, acquired from the *Career* Scottish lowlands where he was born and from which he was sent to Edinburgh for university training—supposedly for the ministry. Hesitant for some reason to continue his theological studies, he traveled to London by boat in 1725, where, still undecided as to a future career, he became tutor to the small son of a Scottish family. He had in David Mallet and others good friends who encouraged his bent to poetry, which he had manifested as early as 1720 by then publishing three poems in the *Edinburgh Miscellany.* One of these, *Of a Country Life* (in couplets), was prophetic of *The Seasons.* Mallet and Thomson exchanged manuscripts and criticized each other's verses during these years when Thomson was writing *The Seasons* and Mallet his *Excursion* (1728). They remained lifelong friends. *The Seasons* (1726-30) established Thomson's fame, and secured for him a place as traveling tutor to young Charles Talbot, son of the future Lord Chancellor. After their return from the Continental tour Thomson was made Secretary

---

[6] On "the return to nature" see Myra Reynolds, *The Treatment of Nature in English Poetry between Pope and Wordsworth* (2d ed., Chicago, 1909); Cecil A. Moore, "The Return to Nature in English Poetry of the Eighteenth Century," *SP,* xiv (1917). 243-291; Christopher Hussey, *The Picturesque* (1927); C. E. de Haas, *Nature and the Country in English Poetry of the First Half of the Eighteenth Century* (Amsterdam, 1928); G. G. Williams, "The Beginnings of Nature Poetry in the Eighteenth Century," *SP,* xxvii (1930). 583-608; Cecil V. Deane, *Aspects of Eighteenth Century Nature Poetry* (Oxford, 1935).

[7] Elizabeth W. Manwaring, *Italian Landscape in Eighteenth Century England* (1925), esp. pp. 98-102.

[8] Thomson's *Works,* ed. George, Baron Lyttelton (4v, 1750 ff.); Sir Harris Nicholas (2v, 1830); Peter Cunningham (2v, 1860 ff.); Duncan C. Tovey (2v, 1897); *Poetical Works,* ed. Charles Cowden Clarke (Edinburgh, 1868); J. Logie Robertson (Oxford, 1908); *The Seasons* (1730, 1738, 1744, 1746); critical ed. by Otto Zippel (Berlin, 1908); John Beresford (1927). — Léon Morel, *James Thomson, sa vie et ses œuvres* (Paris, 1895); George C. Macaulay, *James Thomson* (1907); Alan D. McKillop, *The Background of Thomson's Seasons* (Minneapolis, 1942).

of Briefs in the Court of Chancery (1733-7) with a stipend of £300 a year. When the Lord Chancellor died, Thomson, who by now had become allied with the opposition poets, lost his place; but his good friend Lyttelton persuaded the Prince of Wales to give the poet a pension of £100. On this and the income from his poems and plays he lived quietly in Kew Lane, Richmond, after 1736. Here was his "Castle of Indolence," where in good-natured and almost phlegmatic mood he passed a life very different from that of such contemporaries as his neighbor (and friend) Pope at Twicken-ham or the even busier Fielding in London.

The
Seasons

The Seasons is both descriptive and philosophical in nature. Moral reflec-tion was indispensable, but description was what gave novelty and charm. Even landscape painters of the time always placed somewhere in their canvases human figures: Aristotle had announced that men in action were the proper subjects of poetry. Mere description, with no attention to manners, was juvenile. In 1756, writing about Pope, Joseph Warton remarked "that description of the external beauties of nature, is usually the first effort of a young genius, before he hath studied manners and passions." Warton may here be laboring under the prejudice of Pope's opinion that youth was the time

When pure description held the place of sense;

but the opinion lasts on, and Gibbon, for example, in his *Essai sur l'Étude de la Littérature* (1761) thought "the external beauties of nature" were not advantageous if used as substance rather than ornament.

By enlarging *The Seasons* in successive revisions Thomson made them increasingly episodic.[9] *Winter* first appeared, in 1726, as a poem of 405 lines; it went through several editions with augmentation: in the first collected edition of *The Seasons* (1730) it included 787 lines and in its final revised edition (1746) had 1069 lines. Similarly *Summer,* which in the first edition had 1146 lines, grew to 1805; *Spring* (1728) and *Autumn,* which, with the important *Hymn to the Seasons,* appeared first in the collected edition of 1730, each added about 100 lines. The evolution of the final text is com-plicated, but the essential structure, of which Thomson was perhaps more careful than most authors of his day who produced works of similar length, remained fairly fixed. *Autumn* and *Winter* are organized on a loose narra-tive pattern, following the progress of the season in time. *Summer* presents a typical day, with passages devoted to dawn, forenoon, noon, and so on through sunset to contemplation of the nightly stars and Serene Philosophy. *Spring,* finally, presents the effects of the season on the rising scale of being: "on inanimate matter, on vegetables, on brute animals, and last on Man; concluding with a dissuasive from the wild and irregular passion of Love, opposed to that of a pure and happy kind." There is, obviously, in all four poems an expository as well as a descriptive purpose, and these devices of organization are hardly more than strings upon which to hang episodes or

---

[9] Otto Zippel, *Entstehungs- und Entwicklungsgeschichte von Thomsons "Winter"* (Berlin, 1907), and Thomson's *Poetical Works,* ed. J. Logie Robertson (Oxford, 1908), pp. iii-viii.

individual landscapes. Even the episodes may be organized for expository purposes: in *Winter* the reflections on poverty (lines 322-388), appended to the brief death of the husbandman frozen in the snow, arouse sentiments of sympathy just as in the same poem the famous passage on the robin (lines 245-256) dramatizes the sympathy that should exist between man and the lower animate creation.

Thomson has doubtless favorite ideas that he wishes to express; but in his choice of materials for description it is hard to find favorite scenes. Forest, river, sky, sea, plains, mountains, meadows, valleys, flowers, and animals, are all presented with an equal eye in varying aspects: the mass of detail is most inclusive. It has been urged that his repeated use of the epithet "horrid" for mountains expresses a conventional dislike rather than a romantic love of the rougher aspects of landscape.[10] But the truth seems to be that he felt sympathy for titanic as well as for intimate details. He ranges from "the repercussive roar" of thunder to a thoroughly sentimental treatment of the domestic animals:[11] "rapturous terror" and "generous purpose" are both characteristic of his moods. Familiarity was no pedantic requisite: he gives us the wolves of the Alps and Apennines and the sand storms of the desert along with the British countryside. In general his descriptive passages are marked by motion and change and are not composed pictures of landscapes. There is a keen love of varying light and shade, of changing mood and shifting color. His colors are treated definitely in a kaleidoscopic fashion, as one sees in his apostrophe to the sun in *Summer:*

Descriptive Details

> At thee the ruby lights its deepening glow,
> And with a waving radiance inward flames.
> From thee the sapphire, solid ether, takes
> Its hue cerulean; and, of evening tinct,
> The purple-streaming amethyst is thine.
> With thy own smile the yellow topaz burns;
> Nor deeper verdure dyes the robe of Spring,
> When first she gives it to the southern gale,
> Than the green emerald shows.

Such lines are typical also of the large vague effects that he loves. He is seldom minutely particular, but he is capable both of massing specific detail and of a realistic observation unusual, and practically unknown, in his time:

> not a breath
> Is heard to quiver through the closing woods,
> Or rustling turn the many-twinkling leaves
> Of aspen tall.

---

[10] P. K. Das, "James Thomson's Appreciation of Mountain Scenery," *ESt*, LXIV (1929). 65-70. On the general topic of attitudes towards mountain scenery see Claire-Eliane Engel, *La Littérature alpestre en France et en Angleterre au XVIIIme et au XIXme siècle* (Chambéry, 1930), and Professor R. S. Crane's comment in *PQ*, XI (1932). 175-177.

[11] Dix Harwood, *Love for Animals and How It Developed in Great Britain* (1928).

Coupled with his love of motion is an exuberance in the presentation of his details that is highly significant: in Thomson it is the plenitude rather than the order of nature that arouses enthusiasm—though both principles are felt. His picture of man in the primitive state of the Golden Age "replete with bliss" as well as the benevolent aspect of nature itself is full of this mood:

> Clear shone the skies, cooled with eternal gales,
> And balmy spirit all. The youthful sun
> Shot his best rays, and still the gracious clouds
> Dropped fatness down; as o'er the swelling mead
> The herds and flocks commixing played secure.
> This when, emergent from the gloomy wood,
> The glaring lion saw, his horrid heart
> Was meekened, and he joined his sullen joy.
> For music held the whole in perfect peace:
> Soft sighed the flute; the tender voice was heard,
> Warbling the varied heart; the woodlands round
> Applied their quire; and winds and waters flowed
> In consonance. Such were those prime of days.

Thomson and Physico-Theology

Many passages like this, better in feeling than in poetic expression, suggest reflective processes going on behind the descriptions. Thomson observes and loves details in external nature; he does not much depend on the nostalgic love of scenes once dear in childhood, such as Goldsmith later was to feel for "Sweet Auburn," and he has less of the mere sense of the picturesque in nature than had Dyer and perhaps others of his day. Fundamentally his love of nature is in a large sense philosophic. There is, to be sure, a religious aspect in it, seen in the appended *Hymn to the Seasons* and in various passages such as *Summer,* lines 185-191, in which he echoes the Psalmist's theme, "All Thy works praise Thee!" This idea, much used by deistical believers in natural religion, may perhaps be called the basic warrant for the mass of descriptive detail Thomson lovingly presents. There is, however, an added attitude, derived from the physico-theologists like John Ray and William Derham, the scientific theologians like Sir Isaac Newton, and such widely read works as Shaftesbury's *Moralists*. It is difficult to disentangle the various strands of influence here involved: [12] Shaftesbury contributes the vague enthusiasm for contemplation of nature; the more scientific writers support a rational reflection upon the divine *teachings* of nature. Nature is a book to be reverentially studied:

---

[12] On Thomson's intellectual background see chiefly McKillop, *op. cit.,* and also Cecil A. Moore, "Shaftesbury and the Ethical Poets in England, 1700-1760," *PMLA,* xxxi (1916). 264-325; Raymond D. Havens, "Primitivism and the Idea of Progress in Thomson," *SP,* xxix (1932). 41-52; and several articles on the influence of Newton on Thomson by Herbert Drennon as follows: *PMLA,* xlix (1934). 71-80; *SP,* xxxi (1934). 453-471; *PQ,* xiv (1935). 70-82; *ESt,* lxx (1936). 358-372. On the philosophic aspects of Newton's work see Hélène Metzger, *Attraction universelle et religion naturelle chez quelques commentateurs anglais de Newton* (Paris, 1938), and Marjorie H. Nicolson, *Newton Demands the Muse* (Princeton, 1946).

To me be Nature's volume broad displayed;
And to peruse its all-instructing page,
Or, haply catching inspiration thence,
Some easy passage, raptured, to translate,
My sole delight.

Thomson has the curiosity of a scientist. The passage quoted about the sun
and its gem-like diffractions is not merely a passage delighting in color: it
has behind it notions as to the origin of precious stones. Many times Thomson insists that the study of nature frees us from the credulous superstition
of the ignorant. He appended his *Hymn to the Seasons* as an important
justification and explanation of the rational purpose that he fuses with
enthusiastic delight in nature. It is this latter that now captures romantic
critics: in his own day the philosophy was probably of equal importance.

Thomson's favorite ideas occur in poems other than *The Seasons*. While   Hymn on
writing these four poems he had published some smaller pieces, two of   Solitude
which are notable. His *Hymn on Solitude*,[13] published in James Ralph's
Miscellaneous Poems by Several Hands (1729), is an evening piece contemplating nature somewhat more sedately than Theocles had done at
dawn in *The Moralists*. Thomson here uses a simpler and more pleasing
idiom than in *The Seasons*. So likewise in the other poem, *To the Memory
of Sir Isaac Newton* (1727), the elegiac tone softens the blank verse, and
enables the poet to pay dignified and worthy praise to the great scientist,
to whom his mind owed so much stimulus.

It is, however, in *Liberty*, published in five parts in 1735-6, that Thomson   *Politics and
most explicitly expresses ideas concerning society and government that had   *Industry*
been incidental in *The Seasons*. The poem to Newton had been dedicated,
apparently without due response, to Sir Robert Walpole, and though in
sympathies a Whig, Thomson passed to the group of "Patriots" who under
the guidance of Lyttelton were attacking the Walpole ministry. Thomson
was an ardent nationalist and a sentimental benevolist: his political ideas
followed somewhat the line of his Patriot group and somewhat that of his
own contradictory personality. By nature indolent, he throughout his career
praises industry perhaps more often than any poet has done. In *Autumn*
there are several passages that enunciate the principle that

All is the gift of industry—whate'er
Exalts, embellishes, and renders life
Delightful.

And in the second part of his *Castle of Indolence* the Knight of Art and
Industry is the rescuing hero. *Liberty* is in a sense a "progress piece," in
which Thomson traces the development of civil liberty from Greece and
Rome to Britain—and into the future prospects. His philosophy of history,
like that of many of his contemporaries, involved a worship of primitive

[13] Abbott C. Martin, "The Love of Solitude in Eighteenth Century Poetry," *So. Atl. Quar.*
XXIX (1930). 48-59.

times and a belief, not so contradictory as it at first sight appears, in progress. The pristine days were the best man had known, but man could not retrace his steps: his best hope, then, was to "relume the ancient light" (as Pope phrased it) in some millennial day far ahead. With a divine origin behind him man could only work towards a heavenly city of the future. So Thomson repeatedly, in the best Whig fashion, condemns luxury, praises the simple virtues and the force of the arts, and, looking before and after, at times laments the decadence of man in the Walpole era and at times is optimistic concerning men, industry, and trade. Of course victims of an undue thirst for gold are, as he had shown in *Summer,* enemies of human progress:

> Ill-fated race! the softening arts of peace,
> Whate'er the humanizing muses teach,
> The godlike wisdom of the tempered breast,
> Progressive truth, the patient force of thought,
> Investigation calm whose silent powers
> Command the world, the light that leads to Heaven,
> Kind equal rule, the government of laws,
> And all-protecting freedom which alone
> Sustains the name and dignity of man—
> These are not theirs.

Here and in many other passages speaks the spirit of Illumination. Thomson, like his patron Lord Talbot, was alive to the humanitarian movements of his day. As solicitor-general Lord Talbot had acted (1729) for the crown in the prosecution of Bambridge, the inhuman warden of Fleet prison, and thereafter Thomson more than once expressed enthusiasm for prison reform, and for the work of General Oglethorpe both in that respect and in regard to the colony of Georgia. Among other humane projects he praised, in the last, prophetic part of *Liberty,* the not yet realized project of Thomas Coram for a foundling hospital—

> The dome resounding sweet with infant joy,
> From famine saved, or cruel-handed shame.

The Castle of Indolence   After *The Seasons* Thomson wrote over a period of fifteen years five tragedies, which were staged with only moderate success. His final work of distinction was his *Castle of Indolence,* published a few weeks before his death in 1748. Somewhat deficient in action (it tells merely how the wizard Indolence enticed pilgrims into his castle, and how the Knight of Art and Industry liberated them), the poem is one of the best imitations of Spenserian melody and descriptive techniques in the language,[14] and is by all odds metrically the most harmonious of Thomson's poems. It is rich in portraiture, and has fewer passages devoted to the prosaic topics treated in *Liberty.* The description of the castle and its environs at the opening of the poem is both admirable Spenser and admirable "atmosphere":

[14] Herbert E. Cory, "Spenser, Thomson, and Romanticism," *PMLA,* xxvi (1911). 51-91.

> A pleasing land of drowsyhed it was:
> Of dreams that wave before the half-shut eye;
> And of gay castles in the clouds that pass,
> For ever flushing round a summer sky:
> There eke the soft delights, that witchingly
> Instil a wanton sweetness through the breast,
> And the calm pleasures always hovered nigh;
> But whate'er smacked of noyance, or unrest,
> Was far far off expelled from this delicious nest.

The life of the enchanted idle pilgrims is like a dream—

> As when a shepherd of the Hebrid Isles,
> Placed far amid the melancholy main,
> (Whether it be lone fancy him beguiles,
> Or that aerial beings sometimes deign
> To stand embodied to our senses plain)
> Sees on the naked hill, or valley low,
> The whilst in ocean Phoebus dips his wain,
> A vast assembly moving to and fro;
> Then all at once in air dissolves the wondrous show.

From this bit of supernaturalism the poet has some difficulty recalling himself without breaking the mood: he describes some of the rooms of the castle and with stanza lvi turns to sketching the characters of some of the idlers. These stanzas—very likely among the earliest to be written—sketch actual friends of the poet, and stanza lxviii (by a friend, except for the first line) portrays Thomson himself:

> A bard here dwelt, more fat than bard beseems. . . .

Obviously here we have left the abode of Indolence for some House of Good Fun, and the spell of "drowsyhed" is gone. Though lacking in substance, the poem is in many ways the author's most poetical effort.

The individuality and merit of Thomson's work can be easily grasped if one considers the moment at which *The Seasons* appeared. Their chief rivals in immediate vogue were the seven satires by Edward Young, called *Love of Fame,* and Pope's *Dunciad.* It was a moment when poets, animated by a desire to ennoble the poetic art, were "stooping to truth" and moralizing their songs; but while both Young and especially Pope were dealing with petty particularities, Thomson was dealing with more general and fundamentally moral subjects. If Pope was in part led to write satirical epistles because of the success of *Love of Fame,* it is conceivable that in writing his *Essay on Man,* which he began during the first vogue of *The Seasons,* he was influenced by Thomson. At least the two men are expressing very similar sets of ideas—the one in rather harsh and unmelodious "rhyme-unfetter'd verse," the other in smooth and polished couplets. But Thomson anticipated Pope in expressing the benevolism of Shaftesbury in verse, and he avoided some of Pope's difficulties by being vaguely optimistic and

The Novelty and Merit of The Seasons

forbearing to attack head-on, so to speak, the problem of evil and of man's moral responsibility. Neither in blank verse nor in the Spenserian stanza was Thomson a pioneer, but his success helped to popularize these metres and to subvert the couplet. As description his work is vastly superior to *The Excursion* of his more ambitious and sensational friend Mallet. Thomson's excellence clearly lay in his sensitiveness to sense impressions and his confident use of such impressions: his blank verse is not smoothly rhythmed, and his diction is, like that of Young, greatly inferior to Pope's. Pope could never have passed a cacophonous line like

> Who nobly durst, in rhyme-unfetter'd verse;

and he would surely have pilloried (if *Liberty* had been written in time) the bathos of such another as

> And ventilated states renew their bloom.

Other oppressive artifices are his self-conscious compound epithets, which no page is without, and his love of polysyllabic monstrosities like *irriguous, contiguous, convolutions,* etc. Not Thomson's gifts of expression but rather his natural poetic sensitiveness that emerges in spite of the heavy-going style makes him a memorable part of the movement to reform poetry as the drama and prose style were being "reformed." In his preface to the second edition of *Winter* Thomson voices this objective:

That there are frequent and notorious abuses of Poetry is as true as that the best things are most liable to that misfortune. . . . To insist no further on this head, let poetry once more be restored to her ancient truth and purity; let her be inspired from heaven, and in return her incense ascend thither; let her exchange her low, venal, trifling, subjects for such as are fair, useful and magnificent; and let her execute these so as at once to please, instruct, surprise, and astonish . . . and poets [shall] yet become the delight and wonder of mankind.

In certain aspects such ideals and Thomson's application of them to his work tend towards the romantic; they more clearly tend towards the quality that Matthew Arnold aptly called "high seriousness." [15]

John Dyer

In 1726, possibly before *Winter,* appeared the one important poem by John Dyer [16] (1699-1757), *Grongar Hill.* During the year the poem was

[15] Thomson's extensive Continental influence is with justice regarded as "romantic." See K. Gjerset, *Der Einfluss von James Thomsons Jahreszeiten auf die deutsche Literatur des achtzehnten Jahrhunderts* (Heidelberg, 1898); B. G. Halberstadt, *De Nederlandsche Vertalingen en Navolgingen van Thomson's Seasons* (Leipzig, 1923); and Margaret M. Cameron, *L'Influence des Saisons de Thomson sur la poésie descriptive en France, 1759-1810* (Paris, 1927).

[16] John Dyer was born in Wales and passed much of his life there. He attended Westminster School briefly, studied law, and (after his father's death) painting—this last with Jonathan Richardson. He tried painting and farming in Wales, and eventually became a clergyman. The circumstances of publication of *Grongar Hill* are obscure. It is conceivable that the *New Miscellany: Being . . . Pieces from Bath, Tunbridge . . . in the Year 1725 . . . Written chiefly by Persons of Quality* appeared in 1725, and so represents first publication. The miscellany of David Lewis, possibly Dyer's former master at Westminster, called *Miscellaneous Poems by Several Hands,* was published in June, 1726, and Savage's *Miscellaneous Poems and Translations* was being reviewed in September. Savage's volume contained the Pindaric form of the poem and also *The Country Walk* and other small poems by or about Dyer. Dyer's

printed in at least three different miscellanies, with differing texts. In the last of the three the poem is cast in Pindaric form; but since this version is far less attractive than the tetrameter couplets of other texts, it has been assumed to be a first form of the poem: it was not the first form printed. The immediate influence of Dyer's poem is perhaps comparable to that of *The Seasons*. In a companion piece, *The Country Walk*, Dyer was less happy; for the mood of *L'Allegro* (which it affected) had less appeal at the moment than that of *Il Penseroso*, and it is in the tradition of evening contemplation that Dyer cast *Grongar Hill*. His interest in landscape was that of both painter and poet: he gives us more of settled scene than does Thomson in *Winter*, even though his confusion of background and foreground is open to criticism. He notes picturesque detail, such as "streaks of meadow" in the distance, or ancient ruined towers, but his reactions are likely to be those of common sense: ruins at a distance are picturesque, but close by they are fearful; for "there the pois'nous adder breeds." His distant purple hills tipt with golden sunset, his wide valleys in the manner of Claude, his deep shade at the river's bank, give us the ingredients of a typical painting of his day. The mood is contemplative and even melancholy. He at times surpasses his elegiac rivals with such graceful, if chilly, comment as:

> A little rule, a little sway,
> A sun beam in a winter's day,
> Is all the proud and mighty have
> Between the cradle and the grave.

His poems are most sincere, and can be astonishingly honest. In *The Country Walk*—published when our urban poets were afraid of "low" details— Dyer uses the language of the kitchen and the stable fearlessly in his depiction of an old man at work in his small garden:

> Here he puffs upon his spade,
> And digs up cabbage in the shade;
> His tatter'd rags are sable brown,
> His beard and hair are hoary grown.

Such lines are almost prophetic of the vogue of such rural scenes as Gainsborough was to popularize later in the century. They were almost unknown in 1726. The prosaic honesty of these lines serves to indicate the difficulty Dyer had in his longer poems. *The Ruins of Rome* (1740) is both too uneven poetically (it has its moments!) and too discursive to achieve great

---

friends in London included Jonathan Richardson, Aaron Hill, Richard Savage, Martha Fowke, and Benjamin Victor—all of whom are at least mentioned in Savage's Miscellany.—Dyer's *Poems* (1761, 1765, 1770); ed. Robert A. Willmott (1855); Edward Thomas (1903); Hugh I'A. Fausset (Everyman's Library, 1930); *Grongar Hill*, ed. Richard C. Boys (Baltimore, 1941) [Introduction].—William Gilpin, *Observations on the River Wye Relative chiefly to Picturesque Beauty* (1782); John Scott of Amwell, *Critical Essays on Some of the Poems of Several English Poets* (1785); Helen S. Hughes, "John Dyer and the Countess of Hertford," *MP*, xxvii (1930). 311-320; Edward Parker, "John Dyer" [biographical data], *LTLS*, July 22, 1939, p. 437.

repute, and *The Fleece* (1757) deals somewhat too bluntly with the details of sheep-raising and of the wool trade even for devoted Virgilians. It has again some good landscapes. It is landscapes, in the first place, and then the use of picturesque ruins and other devices for gentle melancholy that characterize the "newer" elements in Dyer's work. Moral reflections are a less novel staple.

Didactic
Poems

Apart from Thomson and Dyer the poets of the second quarter of the century limited themselves closely to the moralizing tradition, which of course both these poets encouraged. There were many didactic poems, among which the concrete "process" poem, remotely or closely in the manner of the *Georgics,* aroused interest long before *The Fleece.* The best of these was *The Chace* (1735) by William Somervile [17] (1675-1742), a blank-verse poem that celebrates in honest detail the joys of the hunt, the breeding and training of hounds, and the attendant outdoor pleasures of a country squire. Earlier Somervile had published fables and verse tales of rural life, and later he published *Hobbinol, or the Rural Games* (1740) and *Field Sports* (hawking) in the year of his death; but *The Chace* alone pleased greatly. All three of his sporting poems are in blank verse of a quality undeserving Dr. Johnson's prejudiced description as "crippled prose." In *The Chace* his diction is less artificial and conventional than in the other two poems. Dr. Johnson's verdict ("he writes very well for a gentle-man") suggests the probable nature of Somervile's early vogue.

Somervile's objective didacticism is less characteristic of the period than the more philosophical efforts that appeared after the *Essay on Man.* Among these, *Universal Beauty* (1735) by Henry Brooke (1703?-1783) and *The Pleasures of Imagination* (1774) by Dr. Mark Akenside [18] (1721-1770) have especial literary interest. Brooke,[19] known for his plays and better still for his novel *The Fool of Quality* (1765-70), in *Universal Beauty* shows typical influence of Shaftesbury on aesthetic minds in his harmonizing of beauty, nature, and truth. It was the plenitude and diversity of the scale of being that aroused his devout enthusiasm and (to be frank) at times upset the clarity of his couplets. Dr. Akenside's early important poem blended the influence of Shaftesbury with that of Addison and others, and was influential in preaching the importance of imagination to both poet and reader. A youthful poem, it was revised, or rather rewritten, in maturer years, which led Akenside to retrench the lushness of his earlier style. Dr. Johnson, who respected but disliked Akenside, thought that in some respects the poet was "perhaps superior to any other writer of blank verse." Pope had encouraged Dodsley to pay well for the poem, and it is obvious that neither Pope nor the poets of this chapter shared Dr. Johnson's opinion that blank verse was "in description exuberant, in argument loquacious, and in narration tiresome."

17 On Somervile see Johnson's *Lives of the Poets* (ed. G. B. Hill), III. 1-66; also Raymond D. Havens, "William Somervile's Earliest Poem," *MLN,* XLI (1926). 80-86.
18 On Akenside see Part III, ch. IV, n. 12.
19 On Brooke see Part III, ch. V, n. 11.

Far more famous in their day, but hardly more readable now than Brooke *Young's* and Akenside, the *Night Thoughts* of Edward Young [20] (1683-1765) are Night with *The Seasons* and Cowper's *Task* the most important blank-verse poems Thoughts of the century. Young "arrived" slowly. Five years older than Pope, his fame postdated Pope's *Iliad* by a decade. His satires, *The Universal Passion* (1725-8), were his first great success, and that success determined him to take holy orders and become a royal chaplain. The *Night Thoughts* (1742-5) was his masterpiece, but his prose *Centaur not Fabulous* (1754) notably strengthened the common condemnation of the follies of high society, and his *Conjectures on Original Composition* (1759) have been thought (mistakenly) to mark a revolution in criticism. Young's achievement was in seizing his moments and thus making rather common ideas strike his readers as important novelties. In this respect *Night Thoughts* "on life, death, and immortality," among other things, won European fame for a century.

The work was essentially an exercise in Christian apologetics,[21] but its appeal lay in its concentration on death, on its macabre detail. It is a poetical *memento mori,* and an argument for the truths of Christianity as guides to paradise. Young's intellectual intent was to stress apologetics; his readers loved his thrilling mortuary images—

> The knell, the shroud, the mattock, and the grave;
> The deep damp vault, the darkness, and the worm.

Such sensationalism was ably reinforced by an autobiographical back- *The Ele-* ground, in part fictitious, that made many passages seem expressions of *ment of* poignant personal grief. Death had aimed his darts freely and successfully *Auto-* at the sixty-year-old poet's closest and dearest. He had in 1731 married the *biography* Lady Elizabeth Lee (granddaughter of Charles II), and she had died in January, 1740. Young's grief over this loss may have been poignant, but within four months he was paying his aging addresses to another lady of fifty winters and some fortune—discreetly! [22] Lady Elizabeth's daughter, called Narcissa in the poem, had died in 1736, and Narcissa's husband

[20] Young, the son of the rector of Upham near Winchester, studied at Winchester, at New College, Corpus Christi, and All Souls. He became a well-known but not intimate member of London literary circles by 1713. After 1730 he was rector of Welwyn (Herts), where he led a life of dignified retirement, interspersed with trips to Bath, Tunbridge Wells, etc.— *Complete Works,* ed. J. Doran (2v, 1854); *Poetical Works* (2v, 1741; 4v, 1757, etc.); ed. J. Mitford [Aldine ed.] (2v, 1830); *Dramatic Works* (1778); *Conjectures on Original Composition* (1759); ed. M. W. Steinke (Philadelphia, 1917); Edith J. Morley (Manchester, 1918); "One Hundred and Fifty Original Letters between Dr. Edward Young and Mr. Samuel Richardson," *Monthly Magazine,* Dec. 1813-Aug. 1818. — George Eliot, "Worldliness and Other-worldliness: The Poet Young," reprinted from *Westminster Review* for January, 1857, in *Essays and Leaves from a Notebook* (1884); W. Thomas, *Le Poète Edward Young* (Paris, 1901); Henry C. Shelley, *The Life and Letters of Edward Young* (1914); Alan D. McKillop, "Richardson, Young, and the *Conjectures,*" *MP,* XXII (1925). 391-404. H. H. Clark, "The Romanticism of Edward Young," *Trans. Wisconsin Acad.,* XXIV (1929). 1-45.

[21] See the excellent article of Isabel St. J. Bliss, "Young's Night Thoughts in Relation to Contemporary Christian Apologetics," *PMLA,* XLIX (1934). 37-70.

[22] H. T. Swedenberg, Jr., "Letters of Edward Young to Mrs. Judith Reynolds," *HLQ,* II (1938). 89-100. (The death of Lady Elizabeth Young is announced in *The Daily Post,* January 30, 1740, as having taken place "yesterday.")

(Philander in the poem) had died in August, 1740. There had been other losses, but of these three Young, with a certain amount of poetic license, made his "Complaint" to Death in the first of his *Night Thoughts:*

> Insatiate Archer! could not one suffice?
> Thy shaft flew *thrice,* and *thrice* my peace was slain;
> And thrice, ere thrice yon moon had fill'd her horn.

Romantic subjectivity does not require factual accuracy, and these three, as one can see upon careful reading, turn out to be chiefly "cases" that evoke specialized reflections on death: Narcissa died young and beautiful and in her "bridal hour"; Philander, the good man, died suddenly; of Lady Elizabeth the poet tells us she

> Not early, like Narcissa, left the scene,
> Nor sudden, like Philander. What avail?

Of Narcissa's furtive midnight burial in France, where Protestants were not normally buried in consecrated ground (though in England Catholics were buried even in Anglican churches), the poet (III. 150-88) gave so lurid an account as to provoke shedding of ink in international literary recrimination. (In England, it may be noted, throughout Young's lifetime burials were customarily at night.)

Their
Moral Aim   It is this element of personal narrative with its great wealth of somewhat melodramatic woe that gave these poems vogue. The moral reflections on the duty of Being Prepared were all aimed at a possibly fictitious "silken son of pleasure" called Lorenzo—one whose "fond heart dances while the siren sings." To the reflections on sudden death, on the triumphant death of the virtuous, the pitiful deaths of the young and beautiful, the case of the ill-living Lorenzo adds an ominous note about the death of the infidel. And thus after many winged reflections through three "Nights," we have in the fourth "The Christian Triumph." These four poems, almost Christian *Georgics,* were then "collected" (1743), and ran through six editions in six months. In December, 1743, the poet resumed his profitable task with a fifth "Night," "The Relapse," and the series ran to nine "Nights" by January, 1746. The later group confined itself more closely to theological argument, and hardly achieved the popularity of the earlier parts.

Intellectually Young is conventional. His neo-puritan antipathy for the silks and sirens of wealthy sinners and for what he calls "art, brainless art," has led to a hasty association of him with evangelical or even Wesleyan tendencies. He holds, rather, a normal latitudinarian position. He touches but lightly on the doctrine of the entire corruption of man, and rather stresses the seeds of natural virtue or even the nobility of man. He emphasizes neither the doctrine of grace nor the importance of a conscious act of conversion. He does stress the necessity of strong faith built upon a foundation of sound reason. Night IV comes nearest to evangelicalism, but even it accords with latitudinarian ideas. Young's eloquence in all these argumentative parts of the *Night Thoughts* was doubtless impressive; for a century after his poems appeared virtuous young Christians were instructed to "think much on death," and the *Night Thoughts* were a useful stimulant in that good work.

It is, then, the pious gloom and the seemingly personal feeling of these *Graveyard* poems that gave them their European vogue. The melancholy tradition *Poetry* in England was of long standing.[23] In *Tatler* No. 89 Steele had remarked that "That calm and elegant satisfaction which the vulgar call Melancholy, is the true and proper Delight of Men of Knowledge and Virtue." Many poets from the time of *Il Penseroso* had agreed, and the wealth of funeral elegies in the eighteenth century forms an impressive background for *Night Thoughts*.[24] Young's own early poem, *The Last Day* (1713), and Parnell's *Night Piece on Death* (1722) anticipate *Night Thoughts;* and *The Grave* by Robert Blair (1699-1746) [25] achieved fame in 1743 along with Young's masterpiece. It is also notable that Thomas Gray began work on his *Elegy Written in a Country Churchyard* during the time when *Night Thoughts* was being completed. In prose the tradition of pious melancholy is interminable: in the eighteenth century two very popular works of the sort were Mrs. Elizabeth Rowe's *Friendship in Death* (1728) and James Hervey's *Meditations and Contemplations* (1746), the first part of which was called "Meditations among the Tombs."

Young's poetic art is most uneven. His diction and his rhythms can be flatly prosaic. Witness his enumeration of themes that puzzle him:

> The importance of contemplating the tomb;
> Why men decline it; suicide's foul birth;
> The various kinds of grief; the faults of age;
> And Death's dread character. (v, 295-298)

He, like Thomson, is victimized by heavy phrases such as the "feculence *Young's* of falsehood," and he is also unfortunate in his metaphors: *Diction and Eloquence*

> Lean not on earth; 'twill pierce thee to the heart.

Or

> Fired is the Muse? and let the Muse be fired.

He warns that the delights of the flesh pall; that the roué gets no pleasure even from memory:

[23] On this tradition see Raymond D. Havens, "Literature of Melancholy," *MLN*, xxiv (1909). 226-227; Harry H. Clark, "A Study of Melancholy in Edward Young," *MLN* xxxix (1924). 129-136, 193-202; Amy L. Reed, *The Background of Gray's Elegy: a Study in the Taste for Melancholy Poetry, 1700-1751* (1924); P. Van Tieghem, "La Poésie de la nuit et des tombeaux," *Le Préromantisme*, série 2 (Paris, 1930); also Oswald Doughty, "The English Malady of the Eighteenth Century," *RES*, ii (1926). 257-269.
[24] John W. Draper, *The Funeral Elegy and the Rise of English Romanticism* (1929).
[25] Robert Blair was born in Edinburgh and was educated there and in Holland. Having prepared for the ministry he in 1731 received the living of Athelstaneford, East Lothian, and there spent the remainder of his life, as minister and student of poetry and botany.—*Poetical Works of Beattie, Blair, and Falconer*, ed. G. Gilfillan (Edinburgh, 1854).—W. A. Drake, "A Note on Robert Blair." *Freeman*, viii (1924). 516-518.

> On cold-served repetitions he subsists,
> And in the tasteless present chews the past;
> Disgusted chews, and scarce can swallow down.

And again he warns Lorenzo:

> A languid, leaden iteration reigns,
> And ever must, o'er those whose joys are joys
> Of sight, smell, taste.

He has the gift of his century for sententiousness, and many a "familiar quotation" comes from his pen:

> Procrastination is the thief of time.

> Who does the best his circumstance allows,
> Does well, acts nobly; angels could no more.

> How blessings brighten as they take their flight.

> Death loves a shining mark, a signal blow.

In sustained passages Young is best when indulging a clerical bent for stately, if emotional, eloquence. A good example is the prayer (lines 36-54) with which *Night Thoughts* begins. His style lacks all the unassuming tenderness that Dyer had: it is formal and somewhat overbearing. To explain the European vogue of *Night Thoughts* one must recall the thirst for melancholy as well as the growing love of personal emotion.[26] The poems blended "what oft was thought" with what the circumstances of the moment led the poet personally to feel. Then too, Young had a real gift in sensationalism: he was frequently absurd here, but he evidently captured the taste of the time perfectly. His artifices, after all, were no more obvious and self-conscious than those of Macpherson's Ossian, which also pleased all Europe.

New Tones and Tendencies   International reputations in poetry are perhaps unaccountable, but one of the important aspects of the history of European civilization is the fact that during the eighteenth century southern Europe awoke to the artistic existence of the northern countries. At the beginning of the century almost all of the Elizabethans were unknown in the Latin countries. Boileau pretended to a total ignorance of English poetry and even of the name of his contemporary, John Dryden. During the first half of the century this ignorance of English poetry ceased. Milton and Pope led the way, and Thomson and Young were not far behind in vogue. Romanticism, and more than romanticism, came out of England to change the course of European poetry. Roman eloquence, notable in all four of these poets, was soon to lose its prestige in favor of a more personal expression of subjective emotion; the tradition of ancient models for poetry—desiccated through petty rules— gave way to new tones and modified patterns in writing. The transformation did not take place rapidly; it came about rather slowly and unob-

---

[26] J. L. Kind, *Edward Young in Germany* (1906); Fernand Baldensperger, "Young et ses *Nuits* en France," *Études d'histoire littéraire* (Paris, 1907), pp. 55-109.

trusively. Without the noble Roman tone and the use of generic classical patterns familiar throughout Europe English poets would not have had a Continental hearing. But the patterns and the tones were being modified. The models, for example, first substituted for the Virgilian pastoral tradition, as we have seen in this chapter, were in no way hostile to Virgilian ideals: all they did was gently to push the *Eclogues* and the *Georgics* more to the background as models, and to attempt, at times awkwardly and unskilfully, to forsake the pattern of the ancient poems while still preserving their spirit of true poetry. By the middle of the century these new tendencies were no more than tendencies, tentatives reaching out without conscious program—other than the desire to make poetry more noble by making it more philosophical—and without conscious rebellion against the tyranny of tradition that had operated so long.

X

The Mid-Century Novel

Three
Masters
of the
Novel

By the middle of the century (1740-54) three great novelists had permanently modified the art of English fiction:[1] of these Richardson dilated
the short story or "novel," as it was called before his day, by means of
psychological or sentimental detail; Fielding added structure, style, and a
realistic attitude towards life; and Smollett excelled in the invention and
crisp presentation of unforgettably vivid burlesque episode. Through these
men fiction acquired a sense of pattern or structure, richness of varied
detail, and gravity as well as comedy. All three were critics of manners.
Fielding was both an artist and a critic of his art, which he analyzed in
brilliant essays or prefaces and which he dignified by associating it with
the noblest of narrative forms, the epic. As psychologists the three vary
considerably, but each has his excellences. Their purposes were avowedly
moral; they taught men to know themselves and their proper "spheres"
and appropriate manners.

Lesser
Writers of
Narrative

This last aspect of their work differs somewhat from that of their immediate predecessors. Defoe, to be sure, made great pretensions to moral
instruction; but his real interest, like that of any inspired story-teller, was
in the ingenious thrills of his rogues. Life stimulated the telling of such
adventure stories, and Defoe's tales were hardly more "strange and surprising" than the adventures of Count Grammont in high society,[2] of
James Annesley,[3] heir perhaps to an Irish earldom but "trepanned" into
America by a wicked uncle, or of Elizabeth Canning,[4] servant girl in the
city of London. Life—or appetite for "innocent" libel—also stimulated

---

[1] For bibliographies of the prose fiction of this period see *CBEL*, II. 488-553. The fullest
history is that of Ernest A. Baker, *The History of the English Novel*, Vols. III and IV (1930).
Good short histories are Sir Walter Raleigh, *The English Novel* (1894); Wilbur L. Cross, *The
Development of the English Novel* (1899); George Saintsbury, *The English Novel* (1913);
Robert M. Lovett and Helen S. Hughes, *The History of the Novel in England* (Boston, 1932);
and Edward Wagenknecht, *Cavalcade of the English Novel* (1943).

[2] Anthony Hamilton, *Memoirs of the Life of Count de Grammont* (in French, 1713; trans.
by Abel Boyer, 1714); ed. Sir Walter Scott, Bohn Library (1846); ed. Gordon Goodwin
(1908); ed. Peter Quennell (1931). See also Ruth Clark, *Anthony Hamilton* (1921).

[3] *The Case of James Annesley* (1743); Andrew Lang, *The Annesley Case* (1912). The
story is used by Sir Walter Scott in *Guy Mannering* (1815), by Charles Reade in *The Wandering Heir* (1872), and by Robert Louis Stevenson in *Kidnapped* (1886). Annesley was made
hero of an anonymous contemporary novel, featuring sentimental distress, called *Memoirs of
an Unfortunate Nobleman Return'd from a Thirteen Years Slavery in America* (2v, 1743).

[4] Of the scores of pamphlets concerning the disappearance of Elizabeth Canning in 1753 one
may cite Henry Fielding's *Clear State of the Case of Elizabeth Canning* (1753) in his *Works*,
ed. Wm. E. Henley, XIII (1903). 221-255. For modern accounts see Arthur Machen, *The
Canning Wonder* (1926); Barrett R. Wellington, *The Mystery of Elizabeth Canning* (1940),
and Lillian de la Torre Bueno, *"Elizabeth is Missing"* (1945).

the production of gossip tales called "scandal chronicles." Mrs. Mary Dela-riviere Manley (1663-1724) was the early leader in this genre. Her master-piece, *Secret Memoirs and Manners of Several Persons of Quality ... from the New Atalantis* (1709-10), was a daring satire on great personages of her day—the names concealed transparently under pseudonyms, which are sometimes explained at the end in a "key." [5] Mrs. Eliza Haywood (1693?-1756), who had begun her long career as a playwright and novelist (i.e., short-story writer), inherited Mrs. Manley's love of scandal in her *Memoirs of Utopia* (2 volumes, 1725), in which she indulged in slurs on Lord Boling-broke, Mrs. Howard (the royal mistress), and Martha Blount, a procedure which, since these were all friends of Pope, won Mrs. Haywood a mean rôle in *The Dunciad.* [6] She later learned much from her betters, and such novels as her *Fortunate Foundlings* (1744), which was based remotely on scandals in the family of the Duke of Rutland but was also a good historical novel in Defoe's manner with sentiment added, *Life's Progress through the Passions* (1748), and especially her *Betsy Thoughtless* (1751) and her *Jemmy and Jenny Jessamy* (1753), are interesting pieces of work, verging towards excessive pathos and melodrama. She had a long and voluminous career.

What Defoe and the writers of short "novels" lacked was emotional appeal. This element was perhaps acquired from France. Both Mrs. Manley and Mrs. Haywood used French sources at times, and the tradition of *grands sentiments,* which Ménage found in the romances of his friend Mlle Scudéry, was in French fiction well established. [7] During the decade after Defoe's death the best fictional reading the English had came from France and from the pens of the comic writer Marivaux and the senti-mental Prévost. The first part of Marivaux's *Vie de Marianne,* which was in English by 1736, is thought by some to have influenced Richardson's *Pamela,* [8] and there is no doubt that Fielding knew Marivaux's *Paysan Parvenu,* translated in part in 1735. Prévost's masterpiece, *Manon Lescaut,* had little vogue in eighteenth-century England; but it as well as his other two important novels—*Cleveland, the Natural Son of Cromwell* and *The Dean of Coleraine*—was translated into English before 1743. Prévost's periodical *Pour et Contre* (1733-40) was an important vehicle in conveying a knowledge of current English literature to France. His novels must have stimulated the sentimental love of pathos already known in the drama, and he in turn was to be the translator of Richardson into French.

Emotional Appeal of French Fiction

[5] Paul B. Anderson, "Delarivière Manley's Prose Fiction," *PQ*, XIII (1934). 168-188.

[6] George F. Whicher, *The Life and Romances of Mrs. Eliza Haywood* (1915).

[7] Edith Birkhead, "Sentiment and Sensibility in the Eighteenth-Century Novel," *E&S,* XI (1925). 92-116; Paul Van Tieghem, "Le Roman sentimental en Europe de Richardson à Rousseau," *RLC,* XX (1940). 129-151.

[8] See Helen S. Hughes, "Translations of the *Vie de Marianne* and their Relation to Con-temporary English Fiction," *MP,* XV (1917). 491-512; Ronald S. Crane, "Richardson, War-burton, and French Fiction," *MLR,* XVII (1922). 17-23; George R. Havens, *L'Abbé Prévost and English Literature* (Princeton, 1921); J. R. Foster, "The Abbé Prévost and the English Novel," *PMLA,* XLII (1927). 443-464. Prévost's first novel, *Memoires et aventures d'un homme de qualité qui s'est retiré du monde* (7v, 1728-31), contains episodes that take place in England. These have been translated and published with an interesting introduction by Mysie E. I. Robertson, *The Adventures of a Man of Quality* (1930).

Richardson and the Distresses of Love

French fiction at any rate makes a plausible bridge to carry one from the relatively unemotional, ingenious adventures of Defoe's characters to the intense distress to which the central persons in Samuel Richardson's novels are subjected. If Richardson [9] (1689-1761) were a lone phenomenon, one might credit the access of emotion to his own personal bent, which obviously accounts for much. He had been an industrious apprentice and had risen to be one of the most reputable and prosperous printers in London. Long before that, however, as a boy in Derbyshire, he had been the confidential adviser for damsels despondently in love. He had written their love letters for them, had in the process acquired a curiosity about the feminine emotional life, and had developed an imagination that delighted in projecting in extreme detail fantasies concerned with the distresses of love. One suspects that he must have read stories of the sort; for his own love life seems to have been steady and (with all respect to his prudently chosen and dutiful wives, each of whom bore him six children) unimaginative. His loving care in building up fantasies with complex emotional situations is his chief asset as a novelist. He had also defects: "Surely, Sir, Richardson is very tedious," protested a friend to Dr. Johnson, and the Doctor in his famous reply conceded, "Why, Sir, if you were to read Richardson for the story, your impatience would be so much fretted that you would hang yourself. But you must read him for the sentiment." Besides tediousness (which implies a deficiency in sense of style), Richardson also suffered from a total lack of humor, a naïve and snobbish veneration of rank and respectability, and an undue devotion to the principle of poetic justice. These are almost insuperable limitations, but his minute imaginative construction of his central situations was so careful and so detailed that if read in small portions any one of his novels in his own day was bound to be impressive. The general love of elegance in literature as well as his own neo-puritanism kept him from handling his sex situations with blunt realism or crudity; but his prolix fondling of episodes was even more indecent than vulgarity would have been.

He specialized in the portrayal of divided minds, and the materials got him always into a dilemma from which he was not clever enough to escape

---

9 Richardson's *Works* have been edited by Edward Mangin (19v, 1811); by Sir Leslie Stephen (12v, 1883-4); his *Novels* are found edited by Austin Dobson and Wm. L. Phelps (18v, 1901-3), by Ethel M. M. McKenna (20v, 1902); Blackwell ed. (19v, Oxford, 1930). — *Letters Written to and for Particular Friends, Directing the Requisite Style and Forms...in Writing Familiar Letters* (1741); ed. Brian W. Downs (1928), as *Familiar Letters ...* [this is Richardson's manual of letter-writing]. *The Paths of Virtue Delineated* (1756), a condensation in 250 pages of Richardson's three novels, "adapted to the capacities of youth," who thus early found the originals far too long. *The Correspondence of Samuel Richardson*, ed. Anna L. Barbauld (6v, 1804); *The Letters of Dr. George Cheyne to Samuel Richardson* (Columbia, Mo., 1943). A highly useful volume is Wm. M. Sale, *Samuel Richardson: A Bibliographical Record* (New Haven, 1936). Also Clara L. Thomson, *Samuel Richardson* (1900); Aleyn L. Reade, "Samuel Richardson and his Family Circle," *N&Q*, Sept. 2, 1022 to June 30, 1923; Brian W. Downs, *Richardson* (1928); Paul Dottin, *Samuel Richardson, imprimeur de Londres* (Paris, 1931); Alan D. McKillop, *Samuel Richardson, Printer and Novelist* (Chapel Hill, 1936); and the same author's "Samuel Richardson's Advice to an Apprentice," *JEGP*, XLII (1943). 40-54.

without fundamental imaginative self-contradiction. He saw the central *His Por-*
problem of each story very simply—perhaps too simply. In 1739 while *trayal of*
working on a manual of letter-writing that two booksellers had asked him *Indecisive*
to do, Richardson took time off to write his first novel, *Pamela, or Virtue* *Minds*
Rewarded. The problem posed in a series of letters was one of decorum:
how was the fifteen-year-old servant girl Pamela to resist the improper
advances of her mistress' son now that her mistress was dead, and what
would be the reward of decorous resistance? The novel, published in two
volumes in 1740, was an enormous success; a continuation came out a year
later, and here the problem in simplest terms was, how would Pamela, now
virtuously wedded to her young master, succeed socially in "high life"?
Presently (1744-8) Richardson was at work on a second novel, *Clarissa*
(1747-8), and again the central problem was clearly conceived: can Clarissa,
a paragon of virtue and decorum, violated by an earl's nephew (Lovelace)
who believes no woman truly chaste, be rewarded for her virtue on earth
or must she look to a better world for justice? Any indecision here exists
not in Clarissa's mind but in that of Lovelace—and of the reader! In his
third and last novel, *Sir Charles Grandison* (1753-4), Richardson's hero,
the fine gentleman, must decide which of two young ladies would make
the appropriate wife. In all three cases there is a problem of indecision, a
divided mind: should Pamela quit her master's house or stay to complete
embroidering his waistcoat and to finish other assigned tasks? Is Lovelace
merely a brutal investigator of chastity or does he truly love Clarissa? Can
she marry Lovelace and thus become an "honest woman" or should she
droop and die like a broken flower? Which of two ladies did Sir Charles
prefer with all his heart and with all his mind, the Lady Clementina della
Porretta (an Italian Catholic) or Harriet Byron, a nice English girl?

The central problems may be simple in all senses of that word, but the *Problems*
difficulties arise in the process of vivid and realistic dilation. We suspect *of Detail*
the disinterestedness of Pamela's virtue when we see her disinclination to
leave Squire B——'s house after her complete awareness of extremities
to be expected if she remains. She is to be sure very young; but she is
also very clear-eyed, is said to be intelligent and capable. Her attempts
to escape from the Lincolnshire estate are inept. Unsympathetic readers
(Fielding, for example) regarded Pamela as a shrewd schemer, determined
all along to marry her master. The possibility of such calculation is suggested by Richardson himself in various remarks. Early in the continuation
it occurs to Pamela (now a lady), and to Richardson, that her letters to
her parents narrating vividly the various attempts on her honor are being
shown to all the neighboring gentlemen, who may form strange ideas from
her love of explicit detail. Lady Davers reassures her by saying that

except one had known these things, one could not have judged of the merit of
your resistance, and how shocking those attempts were to your virtue, for that
life itself was endangered by them: nor, let me tell you, could I, in particular,
have so well justified him for marrying you (I mean with respect to his own

proud and haughty temper of mind), if there had been room to think he could have had you upon easier terms.

There is inevitably a danger of compromise between sentimental ideals and selfish "terms" in all Richardson's fully expanded plots.

This is least true, of course, of his masterpiece, *Clarissa*. Here we have more direction in narrative movement, less wavering. The story is easily likened to a five-act tragedy with a rising and falling action, a crisis in the rape of Clarissa, and a dual tragic catastrophe. There is a considerable use of dramatic mannerism in writing. Sentences take the form of stage directions such as "(Enter Dorcas in a hurry)"; parenthetical adverbs often indicate the precise tone of a speaker's voice, and at times epistolary form is so far forgotten that the author gives us dialogue presented as in a play. More important, however, is the fact that in *Clarissa* Richardson's imagination functions substantially without self-contradiction: the details here "click," and if the novel is read slowly and reflectively, as it must be if read at all, its effect is even today overwhelming. Few novels in any language have the wealth of organic detail, the focus on a rather simple train of events, and the emotional power of *Clarissa*.

His Heroines   The dilemmas of Richardson's novels are usually psychological, and the modern reader must consider the vastly changed status of women and maintain a historical attitude in part. But even to Fielding Pamela and possibly also Clarissa (though *Clarissa* he praised highly in print) seemed as heroines too passive and helpless. Sophia Western is in almost as great distress as Clarissa; but one has perfect confidence in Sophia's abilities to evade danger. Clarissa is so perfect a creature that in spite of Richardson's exceedingly deft exposition of the situation in the Harlowe family at the start of the novel, one is a little surprised to find her writing to Miss Howe most caustic criticisms of her brother and sister. One is not surprised, of course, at her refusal to compromise her ideals with the "respectable" mores of high society in the falling action; but one is here, more than elsewhere, bored by the prolongation of distress. With Lovelace the dilemma was reversed: Richardson's respect for rank and his ready belief in the combinations of vice and merit that were to be expected in the heirs to earldoms, led him to make Lovelace too charming for the good of his lady readers, and he had to blacken the portrait.[10] Lovelace must attract Clarissa, but she must recognize and shun (shall we say?) his cloven hoof. Unlike Clarissa, Lovelace does not suffer from the need of self-exposition imposed on epistolary heroines. Pamela, Clarissa, and Harriet Byron all have to make clear their more than modest merit, and they record in some detail at times their triumphs and the various pretty compliments paid them. This dilemma, heightened by the need of frank criticism of her family by Clarissa and the need of something very like moral blind-

---

[10] H. G. Ward in his "Richardson's Character of Lovelace," *MLR*, VII (1912). 494-498, suggests that Lovelace is drawn after the "gay Lothario" of Nicholas Rowe's *Fair Penitent*. Miss Matthews in Fielding's *Amelia* more than once associates herself with Lothario's Calista.

ness on the part of Pamela, is perhaps inevitable in the epistolary method of story-telling.

Through focus on a single situation such as might heretofore have been treated in a short novel, Richardson created the "dilated novel," and his *His In-* performance was revolutionary so far as material and structure went. His *fluence* success led to a great vogue of epistolary novels, though he himself used the letter form loosely.[11] The early letters of *Pamela* are reasonably brief; letters XVII-XXXI become longer, and are followed by an interruption not in epistolary form. Thereafter, in Lincolnshire, Pamela's "letters" become a very detailed journal. Even in *Clarissa* and *Grandison* the letters frequently turn into journal form, and at no time in his novels did Richardson imagine that he was writing model letters. That function was performed in his manual of *Familiar Letters* (1741). For the rest Richardson's great influence was due to his focus on sensational love problems, his use of the highest and purest ideals in morals, his adoption of the moral clichés popularized by benevolists and sentimental dramatists, and his unquestioning faith that

> What nothing earthly gives, or can destroy,
> The soul's calm sunshine, and the heart-felt joy,
> Is virtue's prize.

It very likely did not occur to him, as it did to his Yankee contemporary, Benjamin Franklin, that "to be proud of one's virtue is like poisoning one's self with the antidote."

Franklin's view did appeal to Henry Fielding [12] (1707-1754), whose social outlook might well have been complementary to Richardson's, but seems in many respects antithetical. Great-grandson of an earl, son of a general, *Fielding's* educated at Eton and (briefly) at the University of Leyden, Henry Fielding *Moral and* was a gentleman more experienced both in society and in books than was *Social Bias*

[11] Helen S. Hughes, "English Epistolary Fiction before *Pamela*," *Manly Anniversary Studies* (Chicago, 1923), pp. 156-169; Godfrey F. Singer, *The Epistolary Novel* (Philadelphia, 1933); F. G. Black, "The Technique of Letter Fiction from 1740 to 1800," *Harvard Studies and Notes*, xv (1933). 291-312; Paul Dottin, "Samuel Richardson et le roman épistolaire," *Revue Anglo-américaine*, XIII (1936). 481-499; Katherine Hornbeak, "Richardson's *Familiar Letters* and the Domestic Conduct Books," *Smith College Stud. in Mod. Lang.*, XIX, ii (1938). 1-50; and see also Miss Hornbeak's "Complete Letter-Writer in English, 1568-1800," *ibid.*, xv (1934). 1-150; Frank G. Black, *The Epistolary Novel in the Late Eighteenth Century* (Eugene, Oregon, 1940).

[12] On Fielding's career as dramatist see Part II, ch. VI. Fielding's *Works* are edited as follows: by Arthur Murphy (4v, 1762, etc.); Sir Leslie Stephen (10v, 1882); George Saintsbury (12v, omitting much, 1893); Sir Edmund Gosse (12v, novels only, 1898-9); Wm. E. Henley, *et al.* (16v, 1903); Basil Blackwell ed. of novels (10v, Oxford, 1926). The novels have been often reprinted separately; *Joseph Andrews* is notably edited by J. Paul de Castro (1929). Parts of *The Covent-Garden Journal* are edited by Gerard E. Jensen (2v, New Haven, 1915). — G. M. Godden, *Henry Fielding* (1910); Wilbur L. Cross, *The History of Henry Fielding* [with a bibliography] (3v, New Haven, 1918); Aurélien Digeon, *Les Romans de Fielding* (Paris, 1923; in English, 1925); Hiran K. Banerji, *Henry Fielding* (Oxford, 1929); Ethel M. Thornbury, *Henry Fielding's Theory of the Comic Prose Epic* [reprints the sale catalogue of Fielding's library] (Madison, Wis., 1931); Maria Joesten, *Die Philosophie Fieldings* (Leipzig, 1932); Benjamin M. Jones, *Henry Fielding: Novelist and Magistrate* (1933); Annelise Studt, "Fieldings Charakterromane," *Britannica*, XIII (1936). 101-118; Richard Haage, "Charakterzeichnung und Komposition in Fieldings *Tom Jones* in ihrer Beziehung zum Drama," *Britannica*, XIII (1936). 119-170; Howard P. Vincent, "The Childhood of Henry Fielding," *RES*, XVI (1940). 438-444.

Richardson. Yet Fielding was definitely *déclassé*. He was poor, and he had a rugged contempt for the social and political corruption of his day. To Richardson high society was either "calm sunshine" or titillating vice: Fielding's comment in *Tom Jones,* xiv, i, was that "the highest life is much the dullest, and affords very little humor or entertainment." Nor would Fielding think of virtue as merely a state of being. He regards virtue (*Tom Jones,* xv, i) as "a certain relative quality, which is always busying itself without-doors, and seems as much interested in pursuing the good of others as its own." Poverty and contempt are as likely to be the reward of virtue as is felicity; and if he agrees with Mrs. Heartfree, whose burlesque adventures in *Jonathan Wild* end with her surest conviction "that Providence will sooner or later procure the felicity of the virtuous and innocent," he agrees with the reservation that one may not surely expect just rewards in this life.

Shamela and Joseph Andrews

Richardson's extravagant pride in Pamela's virtue as well as his critics' extravagant praise of the morality of the novel evidently annoyed Henry Fielding, and made him in his first burlesque of the novel, *Shamela* (1741), take the attitude that this type of virtue was a sham. The highly indecent boisterousness seen in this burlesque became more refined and truly comic in a second attempt, *The History of the Adventures of Joseph Andrews, and of His Friend Mr. Abram Adams Written in Imitation of the Manner of Cervantes* (1742). Here Pamela's newly invented brother Joseph refuses the overtures of Squire Booby's sister-in-law, and, promptly dismissed from her service, takes the road to Somersetshire where lives the damsel of his heart, Fanny. On the way he meets the parish parson, the quixotic Adams, and their adventures occupy the middle half of the novel. In Book iv they reach Lady Booby's country house, where in a burst of delicious snobbery Pamela arrives to plead with Joseph to marry Lady Booby and thus elevate the station of the Andrews family additionally. This last book shows a doubtless excessive influence of stagecraft on Fielding's art. The farcical revolutions and discoveries come thick and fast. The real art, however, lies not in the puppet-like manipulation of the persons but in their psychology. Parson Adams is the first of Fielding's portraits of "the good man," and easily the best. Heartfree in *Jonathan Wild* lacks Adams's brains, as indeed does Tom Jones's foster father Allworthy. Dr. Harrison in *Amelia* has learning but he has no witty fecundity of argument or happiness in self-contradiction such as Adams shows. Parson Adams is guileless as an apostle; his naïve virtue busies itself without-doors as well as within; it seeks the good of others always—and occasionally the means of defraying his own expenses of travel. The element of paradoxical discussion that he introduces into the novel gives the book its true character, and we forget the Boobys gladly. The novel is full of high spirits, rough horse-play, and a healthy sense of the comedy of life.

The burlesque *Life of Mr. Jonathan Wild the Great,* published in Fielding's *Miscellanies* (1743), continues, in reverse, the intellectual attitudes of

Parson Adams.[13] The central formula here is the ironical contrast between **Jonathan** "goodness" and "greatness."[14] Wild the criminal, hanged in 1725, had **Wild** become the symbol of political knavery, and Fielding capitalizes on the tradition. In *Joseph Andrews* he had followed (except for the burlesque of Richardson) the quixotic pattern of master and man meeting adventure on the road. In *Jonathan Wild* the pattern is that of biography with a feminine burlesque of voyage adventures added for Mrs. Heartfree. The intention is chiefly moral. The good man, Heartfree, virtuously free from suspicion of others, is easily victimized. The "great man," whether conqueror or prime minister, or thief, is thoroughly selfish—"a bold heart, a thundering voice, and a steady countenance" make up his transcendent nature. "Mankind," Fielding tells us prophetically, "are first properly to be considered under two grand divisions, those that use their own hands, and those who employ the hands of others" (i, xiv). The great thief, like a prime minister, works through a cabinet or gang. In spite of much evidence to the contrary Fielding avows that he is not here attacking a particular prime minister (Walpole was just out of office). "Roguery, not a rogue," is his game. Rich in irony, this book is primarily a moral apologue with wounding cuts at political and economic abuses. The persons tend, under these aims, to become mere intellectual formulae.

For both *Joseph Andrews* and *Jonathan Wild* Fielding had written very **Tom Jones** important prefatory statements about his artistic and moral intentions.[15] He was first to make his ideas effective in his masterpiece, *The History of Tom Jones, a Foundling* (1749). In his preface to *Joseph Andrews* Fielding had talked both of structure and of characterization, and had used the notable phrase "the comic epic poem in prose." The epic was the only narrative form to have been much the object of critical formulation: it had a central plot idea; it moved steadily towards a desired terminal objective; it used episodes, but the episode contributed to the general narrative pattern. In *Tom Jones* application of these doctrines produced one of the best-plotted novels in English. Obviously Fielding had learned much from the drama as well as from the epic tradition, and he had learned much also from life. Foundlings in the decade after the Hospital in Bloomsbury was opened were a popular social problem, and Tom as a foundling had to discover his birth—which must be such as to make him worthy of his lovely Sophia Western. The pattern followed is biography, with unusual stress placed upon the boyhood of Tom. The word *history,* found in the title, suggests an avoidance of the lofty, the marvelous, and the fantastic, and the adherence to "the plain and simple workings of honest nature" as seen in real life. The focus of incident resembles somewhat that of *Joseph Andrews*. The first third takes place at the house of Squire Allworthy in Somersetshire; the middle section deals with adventures on the

13 William R. Irwin, *The Making of "Jonathan Wild"* (1941).
14 F. McD. C. Turner, *The Element of Irony in English Literature* (Cambridge, 1926).
15 Richmond C. Beatty, "Criticism in Fielding's Narratives and his Estimate of Critics," *PMLA* XLIX (1934). 1087-1100.

roads to London; and the last third takes place in that city. At the exact middle of the narrative in Books IX and X we reach a comic (if not farcical) plateau of dramatic episode in the inn at Upton-on-Severn. But the high jinks of these books are all neatly woven into the organic structure of the whole in a fashion not attempted in the complications of the farcical elements in the last book of *Joseph Andrews*.

Inter-weaving Detail and Episode

It is the skilful interweaving of small detail or episode that best characterizes the economy of Fielding's art in this story. Every appearance of Attorney Dowling, for example, signals information to the reader clearly but not too obviously. The bank note appropriated by Black George becomes gradually a significant device in complicating and unraveling the plot. And most of the episodes illustrate some favorite idea of the author's. Human characters are mixed, good and bad, he thinks, and the world is most obtuse in perceiving true merit. Thus at first Blifil is preferred to Tom. Though a member of a military family, Henry Fielding did not like soldiers as a class; though a resident of London, he had little respect for the high society of that city. Consequently Ensign Northerton and Lady Bellaston will be unsavory types. Tom must, so his foster father Allworthy tells him, acquire prudence and religion, and when Tom leaves what has been home he matures rapidly: he lectures the hard-hearted Quaker at Hambrook, and the Man of the Hill near Upton, and young Nightingale in London. He becomes a sound Christian apologist on the subject of misanthropy. In or near London he meets, among others, an honest highwayman, Mrs. Miller, and Mr. Fitzpatrick, who in his hour of deepest disfavor become indispensable witnesses to the real goodness of his nature. A wealth of highly diversified episode is fitted together by the hand of a master craftsman into a perfectly organized whole. Practically everything except the introductory essays to the eighteen books is organic; and since these essays are as brilliantly written as any essays in this essay-writing century, only harassed undergraduates wish them away.

Human Nature and Psychological . Clichés

Here as in all his novels Fielding devises his persons from observation or from psychological clichés. Virtue is easily deceived, he thinks; and thus Squire Allworthy (whom he designs, so he says, in compliment to his patrons Ralph Allen and George, Lord Lyttelton as prototypes) becomes a mere formula, not a live person. Allworthy's opposite, Squire Western, is the classic Tory country squire of the century, so truly and roughly is he drawn. Lady Bellaston is the hardened female commonly seen on the Drury Lane stage; her opposite, Molly Seagrim, smells of Somerset loam. The balance between characters taken from life and those taken from Fielding's intellectual preconceptions dips probably in favor of the latter source. In the principal pair of opposites, Tom and Blifil, Fielding seems to be playing with the problem of fate or predestination, which fascinated him. These two lads have the same mother, similar fathers (though Tom's is superior), the same environment and education. Yet one is fated to be a sneak and a villain and the other, though young, rash, full of impulse, is full also of benevolence and what Fielding calls "good nature." In the prologue to Part v of *The Cry* his sister Sarah well expresses a common view of psychological determinism:

Altho' it might be absurd to assert that any man is entirely bad, or completely good; yet there is surely no absurdity in declaring, that every individual possessed of rationality is absolutely in the path to goodness, or in the road to corruption. . . . There appears to be but two grand master passions or movers in the human mind, namely, LOVE and PRIDE. . . . Thus a man may be more or less proud; but if PRIDE be his characteristic, he cannot be a good man. So a man may be more or less attracted by love, and rouzed to benevolent actions; but whilst he preserves LOVE as the characteristic of his mind, he cannot be a bad man.

According to some such theory of master passions, Tom and Blifil move apart. Another contrasting pair are Thwackum and Square, the former a typical polemical divine stressing total depravity and redeeming grace, whereas the latter, a Stoic deist, cants of "the natural beauty of virtue," "the unalterable rule of right, and the eternal fitness of things"—and both have long since discarded benevolence and "all natural goodness of heart." Fielding prefers Square over Thwackum, but Square's final on-stage appearance in Molly Seagrim's attic chamber is a quaint comment on the "eternal fitness of things." The intellectual by-play in *Tom Jones* is far more a matter of careful intention than the casual reader imagines.

Certainly in Fielding's last novel intellectual and social intentions are obvious. *Tom Jones* and *Joseph Andrews* had appealed because written generally in high spirits and with nimble wit. But when Fielding wrote of London life, as in his comedies of manners and in the last part of *Tom Jones,* his picture was grim and his tone lacking in spirit and comedy. And so *Amelia* (1751), awaited with great expectation, was a disappointment. In some ways it is Fielding's most pretentious and yet his least finished work.[16] He had been appointed justice of the peace for Middlesex in 1749 and his daily duties in court thereafter left him little time for careful writing. He defended the novel warmly in his *Covent-Garden Journal,* remarking in No. 8 (January 28, 1752): *The Epic Quality of Amelia*

I go farther, and avow, that of all my Offspring she [*Amelia*] is my favourite Child. I can truly say that I bestowed a more than ordinary Pains in her Education; in which I will venture to affirm, I followed the Rules of all those who are acknowledged to have writ best on the Subject; and if her Conduct be fairly examined, she will be found to deviate very little from the strictest Observation of all those Rules; neither Homer nor Virgil pursued them with greater Care than myself, and the candid and learned Reader will see that the latter was the noble model, which I made use of on this Occasion.

Thus designedly the epic action of *Amelia* really begins *in medias res* with the modern Dido (Miss Matthews) listening to Captain Booth's military adventures and seducing him in the "cave" of Newgate prison. It is an

---

16 George Sherburn, "Fielding's *Amelia:* an Interpretation," *ELH,* III (1936). 1-14.

unheroic beginning, but this is an epic *in prose,* with the "proposition" articulated in the first sentence: "The various accidents which befel a very worthy couple after their uniting in the state of matrimony will be the subject of the following history." This prosaic announcement is a product of Fielding's theory of realism. In his autobiographical *Voyage to Lisbon* (1754) he says:

I must confess I should have honoured and loved Homer more had he written a true history of his own times in humble prose, than those noble poems that have so justly collected the praise of all ages; for though I read these with more admiration and astonishment, I still read Herodotus, Thucydides and Xenophon, with more amusement and more satisfaction.

Its Social and Moral Themes

The events of this prose epic, "accidents" that befell a very worthy couple, are shaped largely from two sources of motivation. As in an epic, there is a national theme: the hardness of a social system that keeps Booth from getting back his commission. There is also a personal theme; and for the wrath of Achilles and the piety of Æneas we have Booth's lack of courage to battle against the social system and make a living for his family and for his courageous wife, Amelia. After Parson Adams, Booth is easily Fielding's best educated protagonist; he has an excellent army record, and his chief faults before the story begins are his desire to appear as a gentleman rather than a mere farmer and his lack of courage for the struggle of life: he is a fatalist of sorts—as Fielding makes evident in a crucial passage from Claudian which he did not translate for his readers. At the end of the story Amelia unexpectedly inherits a fortune, Booth suddenly "gets religion," and a happy ending is enforced. Between the events in Newgate and his final happiness the episodes are largely such as should have pleased Richardson's admirers—a series of attempts to seduce Amelia, who, however, is a courageous mother and a faithful wife. Yet the scenes of extreme poverty, the lack of luck that attends all Booth's actions, and other things such as his somewhat American willingness to do a part of the housework make the story unattractive, and certainly the general hardness of life for the underprivileged offers no catharsis. Booth's personal failing is remedied at the end by a reading of Dr. Barrow's sermons and a sort of conversion; but the public problem of the story—the lack of patronage for merit—is, naturally, unsolved. Noble lords will get commissions for their footmen pimps, but for a demobilized officer of distinguished record in the service they will do nothing. The reader must exclaim with Amelia:

"Good Heavens! ... what are our great men made of? are they in reality a distinct species from the rest of mankind? are they born without hearts?"

"One would, indeed, sometimes," cries Booth, "be inclined to think so. In truth, they have no perfect idea of those common distresses of mankind which are far removed from their own sphere. Compassion, if thoroughly examined, will, I believe, appear to be the fellow-feeling only of men of the same rank and degree of life for one another, on account of the evils to which they themselves are liable. Our sensations are, I am afraid, very cold towards those who are at a great distance from us, and whose calamities can consequently never reach us. ... Where ambition, avarice, pride, or any other passion [than benevolence], governs the man and keeps his benevolence down, the miseries of all other men affect him no more than they would a stock or a stone. And thus the man and his statue have often the same degree of feeling or compassion." (x, ix)

Here Fielding touches one of the social sores in a period that was by turns vaguely benevolist and brutally hard. Similar comments can be found in other novels—notably Smollett's—as well as in Johnson's *Life of Richard Savage* and his celebrated letter to the Earl of Chesterfield. Fielding does not organize *Amelia* either for mere entertainment or for any revolutionary action: he simply presents grim truths in uncolored prose.

Fielding and Richardson gave form and pattern to the novel. Fielding added dignity to the art of fiction by imitating the epic and by cultivating serious criticism of manners. Tobias Smollett (1721-1771) was to excel in vivid human detail rather than by structure.[17] Like Richardson and Fielding he was a critic of manners; but being a "lousy Scot" and a surgeon to boot he lacked entrée to high society and wrote always as an external observer and critic. A born storyteller, he paid little attention to premeditated effects; his narrative and descriptive gifts were sufficient to keep readers keenly interested and amused. He expressed his conception of what a novel should be in his preface to *Ferdinand Count Fathom*:

Smollett's Achievement

A novel is a large diffused picture, comprehending the characters of life, disposed in different groups, and exhibited in various attitudes, for the purposes of an uniform plan, and general occurrence, to which every individual figure is subservient. But this plan cannot be executed with propriety, probability, or success, without a principal personage to attract the attention, unite the incidents, unwind the clue of the labyrinth, and at last close the scene, by virtue of his own importance.

[17] Smollett's *Miscellaneous Works* (6v, Edinburgh, 1790, 1796; 12v, 1824); ed. Thomas Roscoe (1841, etc.); *Works*, ed. John Moore (8v, 1797; 1870, etc.); ed. Wm. E. Henley and T. Seccombe (12v, 1899-1901); ed. George Saintsbury (12v, 1895, etc.); ed. Gustavus H. Maynadier (12v, 1902). *Novels* (11v, Oxford, 1925-6). *Letters*, ed. Edward S. Noyes (Cambridge, Mass., 1926). Apart from fiction Smollett's most popular work was *The Complete History of England* (4v, 1757-8; 11v, 1758-60). *Continuation of the History of England* (5v, 1760-5). Among Smollett's translations were *Gil Blas* (4v, 1749), *Don Quixote* (2v, 1755), *The Works of M. de Voltaire* (Smollett and others: 36v, 1761-9), *Adventures of Telemachus* (2v, 1776). He edited *The Critical Review* in its early years, 1756-63, and *The British Magazine*, 1760-67, *The Briton*, 1762-3, and contributed to other periodicals. The luckless tragedy that he brought up to London in 1739 was called *The Regicide* (1749). On it see *Roderick Random*, chs. 61-63.— Scholarly treatment of Smollett is moderately recent: Howard S. Buck, *A Study in Smollett, Chiefly "Peregrine Pickle"* (New Haven, 1925); H. S. Buck, *Smollett as Poet* (New Haven, 1927); Lewis M. Knapp, "Smollett's Early Years in London," *JEGP*, xxxi (1932). 220-227; George M. Kahrl, "The Influence of Shakespeare on Smollett," *Essays in Dramatic Literature: the Parrott Presentation Volume* (Princeton, 1935); Eugène Joliat, *Smollett et la France* (Paris, 1935); Lewis M. Knapp, "The Publication of Smollett's 'Complete History' and 'Continuation,'" *Library*, xvi (1935). 295-308; L. F. Powell, "William Huggins and Tobias Smollett" [Letters, 1756-61], *MP*, xxxiv (1936). 179-192; James R. Foster, "Smollett's Pamphleteering Foe Shebbeare," *PMLA*, lvii (1942). 1053-1100; Claude E. Jones, *Smollett Studies* (Berkeley and Los Angeles, 1942); Louis L. Martz, *The Later Career of Tobias Smollett* (New Haven, 1942); Henry W. Meikle, "New Smollett Letters," *LTLS*, July 24 and 31, 1943, pp. 360, 372; George M. Kahrl, *Tobias Smollett, Traveler-Novelist* (Chicago, 1945).

Practically all of his stories thus fall into the picaresque tradition of rambling episode, though he sometimes neglects the picaresque function of exposing the vices and follies of various social classes or professions. Sometimes for the social class he substitutes racial distinctions such as the Welsh or Irish or Scotch. This trick of racial characterization was very popular by the end of the century. For inventiveness and diversity of episode, vivid particularity of detail to the point of caricature, and energy of style Smollett is hardly excelled. He is to the eighteenth-century novel what Hogarth is to painting—a savage realist with an eye for eccentric character, which he discovers in all classes.

Roderick Random

His first novel, *Roderick Random* (1748), antedated *Tom Jones* by about a year and was, so Smollett wrongly thought, a source from which Fielding plagiarized. The novel was in part autobiographical. Like Smollett, Roderick after some training in surgery came from Scotland to London, where, after suffering from poverty, he, like Smollett, secured a place as surgeon's mate on a man-of-war and sailed away to the West Indies to take part in the unfortunate expedition against Carthagena (1740-1). Roderick's journey up to London in company with the ineffable Strap and the ghastly pictures of life aboard the *Thunder* and the *Lizard* in the West Indies are outstanding episodes, the life aboard a man-of-war being a complete novelty in English fiction.[18] He returned from these naval exploits; and after a brief episode in Sussex where he fell in love with Narcissa, military adventures on the Continent, including the battle of Dettingen, enabled Smollett to express caustic opinions of French fighters. Supported by Strap's money "Rory" next went on a hunt for a rich wife at Bath (scene of a failure on Smollett's part as surgeon). In London's Marshalsea prison Roderick listened to Melopoyn's (Smollett's) account of a luckless tragedy. Here Smollett anticipated the attack on patrons that Fielding and Dr. Johnson were soon to make. Finally—and how fortunately!—Rory discovered a long lost, wealthy father, married Narcissa, repurchased the family estate in Scotland, and showed his scorn for those relatives who had at the beginning of the story scorned him. The exile had returned triumphant.

Clearly such a tale must depend upon vividness for its appeal. In his preface Smollett tells us that he "attempted to represent modest merit struggling with every difficulty to which a friendless orphan is exposed"; but Roderick finds friends at need, and he evokes no more sympathy than does a Defoe protagonist. He, like Smollett, is fighting for a place in the sun, and he is ingenious and not too scrupulous in battling for the rights of "modest merit." Thinking Roderick's chief misfortune was his being a Scot, Smollett created for his second novel, *Peregrine Pickle* (1751), an English hero, who might well have been Roderick's twin. The supporting cast, however, is much improved. Commodore Hawser Trunnion, whose country

Peregrine Pickle

[18] Charles N. Robinson and John Leyland, *The British Tar in Fact and Fiction* (1909); Lewis M. Knapp, "The Naval Scenes in *Roderick Random*," *PMLA*, XLIX (1934). 593-598; Louis L. Martz, "Smollett and the Expedition to Carthagena," *PMLA*, LVI (1941). 428-446.

house observes the routine of a battleship, is Smollett's most sympathetic creation, but as an eccentric he is almost equaled by the man-hunting spinster Grizzle Pickle and by the misanthropic Cadwallader Crabtree. The art of caricature is here seen at its best, and burlesque episodes abound, such as, for example, the famous dinner in the manner of the ancients (chapter 44). The novel was made less readable by the insertion, doubtless at the financial instance of Lady Vane, the author, of the long interrupting section (chapter 81) called "Memoirs of a Lady of Quality." This chapter—of one hundred and fifty pages—has no connection with the rest of the story, and lacks the spice that one expects from the apologies for their lives not infrequently written about this time by ladies charged with frailty.

In his later novels Smollett was inclined to experiment. *The Adventures of Ferdinand Count Fathom* (1753) recounted the heinous deeds of a Continental villain and through appeal to the "impulses of fear" professed to hope to terrify into virtue those hesitating "on the brink of iniquity." Much of this book is mere melodrama; at times it anticipates the so-called "novel of terror." In 1760-1 he brought out *The Adventures of Sir Launcelot Greaves,* a curious attempt to adapt *Don Quixote* to the eighteenth century by creating a benevolist reformer so disinterested as to seem (and be) a madman. The *Adventures of an Atom* (1769), which pretended to be about Japan, is a coarse and virulent satire on important political issues and persons in the troubled early years of George III. In method it owed something to Charles Johnstone's *Chrysal, or the Adventures of a Guinea* (1760-5). Count Fathom

Smollett's best experiment was his last novel—and his masterpiece—*The Expedition of Humphry Clinker,* which appeared in 1771 shortly before Smollett's death. Stimulated by his prejudice against Bath and all watering places and by the poetical epistles of the witty and popular *New Bath Guide* (1766) by Christopher Anstey, Smollett designed this expedition, which started from Brambleton Hall (Wales) and journeyed through Gloucester, Bath, London, Harrowgate, Scarborough, Berwick, Edinburgh, Cameron (the Smollett "seat"), Glasgow, Carlisle, Manchester, and again home. The novelist's virtuosity in devising variety of happenings ranges from practical jokes of a dubious sort to attendance at a Methodist meeting where our footman hero is the preacher. In this book Smollett discards the method of travel narrative used in his early novels and suddenly shows himself a great master of the epistolary method. Each correspondent has a highly individual style and characterizes (or caricatures) himself with facility. Matthew Bramble is the *pater familias,* and externally, as his name indicates, he is what the world thought Tobias Smollett—thoroughly irascible; but his true self is what Smollett thought his to be—easily moved to benevolent action. Squire Bramble is making this journey in part to distract the mind of his young niece, Lydia Melford, who has fallen in love supposedly with a strolling player. Tabitha Bramble, Matt's sister, is an Humphry Clinker aging spinster in violent search for a husband, whom she finds in the priceless veteran of Indian warfare, Lismahago.[19] At Marlborough Downs, needing a new postilion, they add Humphry Clinker to the party—and Humphry turns out to be the natural son of Matt, and the devoted admirer of Winifred Jenkins, Tabitha's maid, supreme among illiterate servants. With at least three major plots to unravel and several minor episodic suspenses the book is easily Smollett's richest picture of English and Scottish life, and his most entertaining narrative. He always had viewed life as a traveler, and here his critical and descriptive powers find natural scope and blend with a somewhat less tough-minded attitude towards mankind than his earlier work had shown.

Smollett's Place in Fiction   Like Fielding Smollett wrote a great deal apart from his prose fiction. He turned out political pamphlets and periodical essays; he edited two magazines,[20] and was a voluminous translator. Almost to the twentieth century he was regarded as a rather "low" author, and no one of his novels is without vulgarity. He was from the start, however, a novelist's novelist, and many writers of prose fiction are obviously in his debt. Sterne's Uncle Toby derives in part from Hawser Trunnion, and his *Sentimental Journey* is in part a counterblast to Smollett's *Travels through France and Italy* (1766). Fanny Burney will be presently his disciple in the method of caricature, and Walter Scott, Dickens, and many another have since lifted good devices from his pages. His contribution to fiction is a fusion of ingenuity with humorous and highly particularized caricature, just as Fielding and Richardson contributed dignity, structure, and emotional psychology. *Clarissa, Tom Jones,* and *Humphry Clinker* remain among the greatest masterpieces of English fiction. In the eighteenth century only Sterne's work is comparable to these three novels. The work of Richardson and Fielding was complete by 1754, when Fielding died. Smollett had by that year established his fame, but his career was longer and outlasted that of Sterne who began significant publication in 1759.

[19] Smollett probably discovered a prototype for Lismahago in Captain Robert Stobo; see George M. Kahrl's article in the *Virginia Mag. of Hist. and Biog.,* XLIX (1941). 141-151, 254-268.
[20] See, for Smollett's work on periodicals, Part III, ch. VII.

BOOK III

The Restoration and Eighteenth Century (1660-1789)

 ⌒⌒

PART III

The Disintegration of Classicism

Guide to reference marks

Throughout the text of this book, a point • set beside a page number indicates that references to new critical material will be found under an identical paragraph/page number (set in **boldface**) in the BIBLIOGRAPHICAL SUPPLEMENT.

In the Index, a number preceded by an **S** indicates a paragraph/page number in the BIBLIOGRAPHICAL SUPPLEMENT.

I

Accentuated Tendencies

To define precisely the change that came over the second half of the *The Vogue*
eighteenth century is difficult.[1] It is not quite enough to say that the Age *of Senti-*
of Reason gave way to an Age of Sentiment. Undoubtedly there was an *ment*
access of sentimentality after the vogues of Richardson and Rousseau were
established; but sentiment had existed before their day, and the phrase
"Age of Reason" was used by Tom Paine to describe the period of the
French Revolution. Nevertheless, one chief mark of the change was not
merely an increase in sentimentality but also a modification of attitude
towards sentiment. While Richard Steele in his *Christian Hero*—and other
authors of his day as well—had perceived rather the utility of sentiment,
authors later in the century indulged in the delicate enjoyment of their
own emotional thrills. Where Addison and others had praised the rationality
of simplicity, Burns will display the picturesqueness of the quality. The
ablest men of the second half of the century still were proponents of

[1] Most of the many references given in Part II, ch. I are useful also for the latter half of
the century. Certain additions, however, may be made: Thomas Seccombe, *The Age of John-
son* (1899); William L. Phelps, *The Beginnings of the English Romantic Movement* (1893);
Henry A. Beers, *A History of Romanticism in the Eighteenth Century* (1899); John H. Millar,
The Mid-Eighteenth Century (1902); John Bailey, *Dr. Johnson and his Circle* (1913); Arthur
S. Collins, *Authorship in the Days of Johnson, Being a Study of the Relationship between
Author, Patron, Publisher, and Public, 1726-1780* (1927); David Nichol Smith, *Shakespeare
in the Eighteenth Century* (Oxford, 1928); Robert W. Babcock, *The Genesis of Shakespeare
Idolatry, 1766-1799* (Chapel Hill, 1931); Francis Gallaway, *Reason, Rule, and Revolt in English
Classicism* (1940); Walter J. Bate, *From Classic to Romantic: Premises of Taste in Eight-
eenth-Century England* (1946). — For the political history add William Hunt, *The Politi-
cal History of England*, Vol. x: *From the Accession of George III to the Close of Pitt's
First Administration* (1905); Basil Williams, *William Pitt, Earl of Chatham* (2v, 1913); Lewis
B. Namier, *The Structure of Politics at the Accession of George III* (2v, 1929); L. B. Namier,
England in the Age of the American Revolution (1930); Philip W. Wilson, *William Pitt the
Younger* (1933); R. B. Mowat, *The Age of Reason—the Continent of Europe in the Eighteenth
Century* (1934); Sir Charles Petrie, *The Four Georges* (1935); L. B. Namier, *In the Margin
of History* [collected essays] (1939).—For the intellectual and social background add Trueman
Wood, *Industrial England in the Eighteenth Century* (1911); Louis W. Moffit, *England on
the Eve of the Industrial Revolution* (1925); Ephraim Lipson, *Economic History of England*
(1931), Vols. II and III; *Johnson's England*, ed. A. S. Turberville (2v, 1933); J. H. Whiteley,
Wesley's England: A Study of . . . Social and Cultural Conditions (1938); H. N. Fieldhouse,
"Bolingbroke and the Idea of Non-Party Government," *History*, XXIII (1938). 41-56; Charles
Reith, *The Police Idea: Its History and Evolution* (Oxford, 1938); Wilmarth S. Lewis, *Three
Tours through London in the Years 1748, 1776, 1797* (Colver Lectures at Brown University:
New Haven, 1941); Maurice J. Quinlan, *Victorian Prelude: a History of English Manners,
1700-1830* (1941).—On the household arts see A. T. Bolton, *The Architecture of Robert
and James Adam* (1922); Oliver Brackett, *Thomas Chippendale: A Study of his Life, Work,
and Influence* (1924); Percy Macquoid and R. Edwards, *The Dictionary of English Furniture*
(3v, 1924-7); Sir Kenneth Clark, *The Gothic Revival* (1928); Sacheverell Sitwell, *Narrative
Pictures* (1937); G. C. Williamson, *English Conversation Pictures* (1931); Chauncey B.
Tinker, *Painter and Poet* (Cambridge, Mass., 1938).

reason and common sense; but they were also (Dr. Johnson or Burke, for example) likely to be men of strong emotional natures. It is significant that Hume's philosophical writing was practically done by 1750; thereafter he was to be the historian and essayist. Hume's highly logical thinking, one may say, served but to subvert the classical integrity of man's reason, and throughout the century there had been a strong anti-rational prejudice against "mere" logic. The change is at once felt if we place the leading poets of the Queen Anne group—Pope and Swift—in comparison with *fin de siècle* poets such as Cowper and Burns. It is a change obviously that does not imply an access of intellectual power but does imply increased delight in subjective emotional states. The later century tends to glorify the individual's sensations whether merely thrilling or (as they seemed at times) revelatory of new, vague truths.

The Able Conservatives

Lovers of romanticism have liked to picture this last half-century as a slow awakening to a better artistic life, an awakening from constrictive tradition. There is truth in the picture, but not the whole truth. The ablest writers and thinkers of the period were still traditionalists—Johnson, Reynolds, Gibbon, and Burke. The awakening was not altogether an advance except in the field of graphic art. In the field of music, the most purely emotional of the arts, there was something like an eclipse in the second half of the century as compared with the periods of Purcell and Handel. Waging war was almost an inveterate pursuit of the whole century, but the second half of the century produced no general comparable to Marlborough and no prime minister equal to Walpole (though the younger William Pitt was more picturesque). If the latter half-century produced no poet comparable to Pope, it did perhaps produce a larger number of writers of high importance, and it did move forward to the period of the highest regard for the dignity and transcendent nobility of the individual soul and its potentialities. Even Dr. Johnson believed in progress, and his contemporaries in general glorified the idea.

Religion and Politics

There were obvious repercussions in religion and politics. In the second third of the century the evangelical movement of Methodism became notable; by the end of the century it had softened and civilized the spirit of the lower classes, and was rapidly elevating many to a rank in the middle class that was to be so commended during the nineteenth century. This development, with its emphasis on emotional "conversion" to a Christian faith and its reassertion of the importance of the individual soul, was moving in the main channel of tendencies of the time. Such tendencies in politics were not to be viewed with equanimity by conservatives. The law of subordination, Dr. Johnson feared, was being relaxed—dangerously. While enterprising Englishmen were building a British empire across various seas, the politicians in Parliament (now regarded as "the finest club of gentlemen in Europe") were wittily or eloquently confusing themselves and the electorate over the rights of electors (notably the electors of Middlesex) and the rights of the crown as opposed to the rights of Parliament.

It was a period of argumentative vituperation and chicanery among partisans, and a field-day for not too scrupulous trouble-makers like John Wilkes
and "Junius." In such a period Edmund Burke seems to resemble a colossus
of integrity. The loss of thirteen American colonies was an episode in this
period of confused and selfish politics.

The humanitarianism of the time led to increased feeling of social re- *Humani-*
sponsibility for the underprivileged. Such feeling had stimulated the work *tarianism*
of Henry Fielding as justice of the peace for Middlesex and as author of
the *Enquiry into the Late Increase of Robbers* (1751). Henry's work was
continued with distinction by his blind brother, Sir John, and later by
John Howard (1726?-1790), whose *State of the Prisons* (1777 ff.) is a
landmark in the literature of reform, and by William Wilberforce (1759-
1833), who added to an interest in prison reform a great zeal in the cause
of anti-slavery. The career of Jonas Hanway (1712-1786) also is a typical
record of labors for the Foundling Hospital, the Magdalen House, the
Marine Society, and other similar institutions. *Humanitarian* was not a
word to be found in Johnson's *Dictionary,* but the trait was coming more
and more into existence.[2] That it was coupled with the sentimental ideas
of "universal benevolence" can be seen by the international nature of
John Howard's work, and, concretely, by the epitaph placed on his remote
Russian grave:

WHOEVER THOU ART, THOU STANDEST AT

THE TOMB OF THY FRIEND.

Prosperity as well as a strongly utilitarian bias led to the development
of such arts as made for dignified and beautiful living conditions. Architecture throve under the guidance of Sir William Chambers (1726-1796) and,
among others, James (d. 1794) and Robert Adam (1728-1792). In London
Sir William's final achievement was Somerset House—which since his *The Useful*
day has been much enlarged. Along the Thames also the Adam brothers *and*
similarly showed their finest work in the pretentious façade of their Adelphi *Fine Arts*
buildings (1768-71). These were classical buildings—Sir William being
more correctly traditionalist than the brothers, who displeased Horace Walpole by their "warehouses laced down the front." They had a touch of
rococo, but not much of it. Walpole, of course, at Strawberry Hill, was
promoting the vogue of Gothic, and between 1757 and 1762 Sir William
Chambers was adorning Kew Gardens for the dowager Princess of Wales
with the *chinoiseries* that, with Gothic, became the fantastic but modishly
popular extremes of taste. Possibly when all is said, the great architectural
achievement of the half-century is to be seen at Bath, where a most brilliant
experiment in community architecture took place in the rebuilding of

---

[2] Wilmarth S. Lewis and R. M. Williams, *Private Charity in England, 1747-1757* (New
Haven, 1938); Frank J. Klingberg, "The Evolution of the Humanitarian Spirit in Eighteenth-
Century England," *Pennsylvania Magazine of Hist. and Biog.,* LXVI (1942). 260-278; Frank
J. Klingberg, *The Anti-Slavery Movement in England* (New Haven, 1926); Wylie Sypher,
Guinea's Captive Kings: British Anti-Slavery Literature of the XVIIIth Century (Chapel Hill,
1942); John H. Hutchins, *Jonas Hanway, 1712-1786* (1940).

the city, chiefly on designs by John Wood (1705?-1754) and his son of the same name. Through their efforts Bath became the most stately city in England and an admirable example of the classical tradition. At a slightly later date the Adam brothers were designing beautifully and building solidly new streets, squares, public buildings, and palatial residences for the Scottish capital, Edinburgh.

Interiors of buildings were fully as lovely as exteriors. Excessive rococo ornamentation was less common in England than on the Continent, and the less ornate English interiors of the time had a cheerful repose and a spacious dignity hardly excelled. The walls of these houses were hung with the work of the greatest painters England has yet produced. In 1768 Benjamin West, a native of Pennsylvania and an historical painter who enjoyed the patronage of George III, founded, with the aid of the King and of three fellow artists, the Royal Academy of Arts, of which Sir Joshua Reynolds became the first president. These were the great days of Reynolds (1723-1792) and Gainsborough (1727-1788), who surpassed such earlier masters as Joseph Highmore, Richard Wilson, Allan Ramsay the younger, Paul Sandby, and the Cozenses, and were ably supported in a glorious second rank by such men as Romney, Beechey, Zoffany, Raeburn, Hoppner, Opie, Morland, and others. Painting was perhaps the most highly developed of the fine arts in this period, but love of beautiful interiors also stimulated the production of finely designed furniture, and an English school of cabinet-makers throve, equal almost to the painters as artists. The relative heaviness of the designs of William Kent now gave way to the lightness that the greatest of these designers, Thomas Chippendale (1718-1779), was enabled to give to mahogany—which now displaced walnut as a favorite wood. Chippendale's styles included much from earlier English traditions, much from contemporary French, and much from Chinese and even Gothic patterns. His rococo tendency was corrected in favor of a less fanciful type of classicism in the elegant designs of Robert Adam, George Hepplewhite, and Thomas Sheraton. The essential quality that marked the work of all these men and the interiors that they adorned was elegance.

In literature there was perhaps no truly comparable achievement; but literature, being more important than household arts and being more accessible for general study, has naturally been basic in all descriptions of the period. If one focuses attention merely on literature, one has to conclude that the second half of the century is still the victim of the first. Authors may now more readily disparage the rules, may seek to strike out new paths for the imagination; but they are still inhibited by excessive attention to decorum, by a fear of not being correct, of being the object of satire because of a lack of common sense. One feared to have too much epic quality in one's elegy: Gray's use of the pentameter in his *Churchyard* was suspected of this fault. One had to watch one's manners: Evelina is merely a projection of music-master Burney's daughter, who through decorum rose to be a friend and critic even of royalty. One wished to be thought exquisitely normal in action, to avoid above all being fantastic. One took refuge in *domestica facta,* in realistic matters of daily life, and rested there with little overt rebellion against the classical tradition. One simply thought about other things and gently disregarded the classical pastoral, the Punic War, classical mythology, and much else that seemed merely the stale clap-trap of schoolmasters and schoolboys.[3]

So-called classical tendencies varied in value and in the amount of approbation they received throughout the century. *Sub specie aeternitatis* their theory might be excellent; in the closets where poets wrote they received a decreasing amount of attention. Subversive and disintegrating tendencies were seldom openly or clearly opposed to classicism, but at bottom they were hostile. Three of these tendencies may be briefly described.[4] First, there was the much-vaunted English love of liberty. The French might accept Boileau in right of Horace as an absolute literary monarch: the English still kept "unconquered and uncivilised." For ancient authority the English had largely substituted the more abstract sanction of truth, reason, or nature; the ancients were now simply the best guides. As the Enlightenment advanced, there was a marked tendency to insist on the impossibility of absolute standards, to believe in progress, change, novelty—in a word, in relative if not subjective standards of excellence.

Classicism Subverted:

1. By English Love of Liberty

Secondly, doubts arose as to whether truth—poetic truth at least—*was* "one clear, unchanged, and universal light," and the belief in uniformity and universality gave way to a love of diversity that led to revolutions. Truth was less often conceived as quite external to the poet; it was seen filtered through the varying lights and shades of the poet's mood. Before the Restoration a poet's personality had had relatively little to do with understanding his art. The ancients normally had glorified art rather than artists. But Milton, Dryden, and Pope were all men of commanding personalities apart

2. By Subjective Attitudes towards Truth; by Moods

---

[3] Dr. Johnson, of course, was hardly gentle in his disregard of these matters. See Joseph E. Brown, *The Critical Opinions of Samuel Johnson* (Princeton, 1926), pp. 154-160. On the frigidity of the use of mythology by the poets of the time see Douglas Bush, *Mythology and the Romantic Tradition in English Poetry* (Cambridge, Mass., 1937).

[4] The paragraphs immediately following describe tendencies that without much meaning might be called "the beginnings of romanticism." Some years back the academic discussion of eighteenth-century literature eddied about the "romanticism" of the second half of the century. To the present writer it seems that such discussion has tended to describe the eighteenth century as seen distorted through the spectacles of the nineteenth. Furthermore, the term *romantic,* as Professor Lovejoy has clearly shown ("On the Discrimination of Romanticisms," *PMLA,* xxxix [1924]. 229-253), has been used in divergent and even self-contradictory senses. In so far as the term is a comprehensive label covering the general quality of the literature of the early nineteenth century, it has a limited but not very descriptive usefulness for that century. When it is used so loosely as to be a synonym of "imaginative" or to be merely a blanket term of approbation, it ceases to be historically or critically illuminating. Hence the term is here used infrequently and, it is hoped, cautiously. Other writers on the subject may be consulted as follows: J. G. Robertson, *Studies in the Genesis of Romantic Theory in the Eighteenth Century* (Cambridge, 1923); Harko G. de Maar, *A History of Modern English Romanticism,* Vol. i: *Elizabethan and Modern Romanticism in the Eighteenth Century* (1924); Paul Van Tieghem, *Le Préromantisme* (2v, Paris, 1924, 1930); Paul Kaufman, "Defining Romanticism: A Survey and a Program," *MLN,* xl (1925). 1-12; Fernand Baldensperger, " 'Romantique,' ses analogues et ses équivalents: tableau synoptique de 1650 à 1810," *Harvard Studies and Notes in Philology and Literature,* xix (1937). 13-105; Arthur O. Lovejoy, "The Meaning of Romanticism for the Historian of Ideas," *JHI,* ii (1941). 257-278.

from their gifts as writers; and it was natural that in a journalistic period when literature and politics were so near allied, personalities should come increasingly to influence reputation. Speedily writers developed the self-conscious sensitive mind: the cult of genius accentuated the tendency. The sensitive mind is likely to be a restless mind, and that mood characterizes authors of this period. Even Dr. Johnson's mind must be classified as restless. Serenity, however desirable, was at best a dream, at worst a delusion.

The moods of these sentimental self-tormentors most commonly operative can be roughly classified. There was the benevolist filter. This had been used even in the late seventeenth century as producing serenity: clearly it might do that. It might also be the mood of an eager and generous soul wishing to pour itself out for the improvement of the human lot, or even for the sole pleasure of outpouring. Benevolism had made for stable equilibrium; it will now begin to work for instability. One of Pope's phrases most often quoted in the fifty years after his death and quoted significantly as applying to the whole consciousness of the sensitive man is "tremblingly alive all o'er." Another mood is that of melancholy. This was not new, but it was greatly (even tediously) accentuated in the later century. To Continental observers hypochondria was notoriously *The English Malady* before 1733 when Dr. George Cheyne published his book of that title. Night, death, and the graveyard became favorite topics in poetry; and the English acquired an international reputation for suicide. ("These are the dark November days," said Voltaire, "when the English hang themselves!") A third mood much affected was that of sublimity. Founded fully as much on the rhetorical precepts of Longinus (whose thesis was that sublimity could, if one followed his precepts, be attained by conscious effort) as on the superlative achievement of John Milton,[5] the cult of the sublime subverts common-sense rationalism, and hence points in part away from so-called classical tendencies. In so far as it opened new channels for noble Roman rhetoric it is hardly so "romantic" as many have thought. Thomas Gray did some lofty and thrilling things in this mood, but more truly serviceable were those who by applying some of the enthusiasm of this mood to subjects less titanic and noisy than *The Descent of Odin* or *The Progress of Poesy* became poets of humble life, and with their mildly warming glow of imagination anticipated Wordsworth himself. The cult of Longinus stimulated perhaps this quiet antithesis to itself that is more truly characteristic of a period devoted to simplicity[6] than was the somewhat rococo sublime. Collins and Cowper illustrate this quiet and at times pedestrian mood. Increasingly poets are creatures of mood rather than the eloquent announcers of general truths.

Thirdly, we may note the tendency away from Horatian or French classicism in the less frequent and inexact attention on the part of the abler

---

[5] Arthur Barker, " '. . . And on his Crest Sat Horror': Eighteenth-Century Interpretations of Milton's Sublimity and his Satan," *Univ. of Toronto Quar.,* XI (1942). 421-436. For a more extensive treatment see Samuel H. Monk, *The Sublime: A Study of Critical Theories in XVIII-Century England* (1935).

[6] Chauncey B. Tinker, *Nature's Simple Plan* (Princeton, 1922).

poets to the imitation of established generic models. A poet like Goldsmith, conservative in many of his sympathies, could sit down to write poems like *The Traveller* and *The Deserted Village* without asking himself whether he was writing a Georgic, an elegy, or a pastoral. Such emancipation is quiet but fundamental. More learned poets, still dependent upon patterns to follow, passed from the Roman genres to other models. There was a revival of interest in Greek, which in the mid-century encouraged William Mason to attempt two plays, or, as he called them, dramatic poems "Written on the Model of the Ancient Greek Tragedy." Adaptations of both his *Elfrida* and his *Caractacus* were performed at Covent Garden long years after those poems had been printed; but both were monuments of piety to a Greek form rather than attempts at a popular success in the theatre. More than one poet of the mid-century wrote monostrophic odes of the type used in Greek tragedy.[7] Still others, like Gray in *The Descent of Odin* and in *The Fatal Sisters,* attempted to recapture the tone of primitive lyricism; Macpherson is obviously in this tradition. There was also a naturally increasing tendency to use English models, which nationalist critics approved. It is not easy to see why Spenser and particularly Milton should be thought more "romantic" than Ovid, for example; but the imitation of English models, if still imitation and still not too clearly romantic, at least broadened the field of poetic method and subject matter. Milton, known as a political revolutionary, was frequently called by critics "the assertor of English liberty" in that he freed poetry from "the bondage of rime." Of course Milton himself adopted blank verse as approximating classical metrical forms; but again, reasons apart, the cultivation of nondramatic blank verse in the early eighteenth century had certainly increased the number of standard metrical forms from which a poet *de longue halcine* might choose.

3. By Neglect of Horace and the Genres

In all these additions to poetic matter or manner was apparent an increasing love of novelty. The conservative opinion about this was stated by Henry Felton in his *Dissertation on Reading the Classics* (1713): " 'Tis easier to strike out a new Course of Thought, than to equal old Originals, and therefore it is more Honour to surpass, than to invent anew." This was, however, distinctly a minority view. A mere newspaper critic in *The Daily Gazetteer* (September 25, 1741) states the opposite position: "I would be content to inculcate a Desire of Excelling, rather by striking out new Paths, than by treading very circumspectly in the old ones. I have shewn, that it is natural for our Contemporaries to be pleased with anything that is tolerable if it be new, rather than a better Thing if it be evidently an Imitation."

Love of Novelty

That new paths were being more and more frequently trod is seen if we look at some specimens of new subject matter. It may be noted that here Horace himself seems to countenance undermining classical imitation. On one page he could advocate using known fables (*ex noto fictum carmen sequar*) and on another could urge forsaking Greek paths (*vestigia Græca*)

English vs. Classical Story

---

[7] Bernard H. Stern, *The Rise of Romantic Hellenism in English Literature, 1732-1786* (Menasha, Wis., 1940).

and using native material (*domestica facta*). This patronage of English or everyday materials was in a way forced on writers. Classical story might be excellent; but after a dozen costive poets have moaned over Hero and Leander, other writers, if wise, are likely to choose another fable for their poem. Take Orpheus, or whatever classical story you will, and the condition will be similar: the tragedies of Thomson and dozens of forgotten narrative poems all attest the fact that classical story was an exhausted vein for the moment at least. It is an attractive hypothesis that a story tradition appeals when first well known, as the classics did in the Renaissance, or when again sporadically recovered, as in the nineteenth century. In any case, by 1756, Joseph Warton was simply expressing a general desire when he said: "It is to be wished, that our writers would more frequently search for subjects, in the annals of England, which afford many striking and pathetic events, proper for the stage. We have been too long attached to Grecian and Roman stories. In truth, the DOMESTICA FACTA, are more interesting, as well as more useful...." Dr. Johnson, though the author of the pseudo-oriental *Rasselas,* expressed the same idea earlier than Warton, and more frequently. Nicholas Rowe, Aaron Hill, and John Home illustrate the tendency to use the "annals of England" popularly in ₚtragedy. Thomas Leland's *Longsword* (1762) marks the same purpose in fiction. George Lillo and his friend Henry Fielding are among the numerous authors who use "daily life" in the drama, the novel, the essay-story, or in poetry.

Medieval-ism   If a genuine thirst for novelty cannot be quenched by classical story, it is not likely to be satisfied for long by stories of one's own day. There was a turning from the "annals of England" as well as from Greece and Rome, a turning that took two lines of escape, one temporal, the other geographic. The first was a return to the Middle Ages. This sort of "revival" is always going on. Milton meditated the Arthurian legend as a subject; Dryden retold several medieval tales; Blackmore wrote Arthurian epics, and Pope added greatly to the fame of one medieval love story by his poem *Eloisa to Abelard*. He might have done more had he written his projected epic about Brutus, the founder of the British nation. This interest in medieval story was intensified by the middle of the century. Frequently it extended, as in the case of Richard Hurd, to hardly more than the chivalry of Spenser's *Faerie Queene;* at times, as in the case of Gray, it included Scandinavian lore.[8] There was also an increased interest in Welsh and Irish stories,[9] and Macpherson achieved an extravagant success in his Ossian. At times, of course, medievalism became mere clap-trap, as in Walpole's influential *Castle of Otranto.*

Oriental Exoticism   The other escapist path led to remote lands. Under the stimulus of *The Arabian Nights,* first translated into occidental languages in the first two decades of the century, and of Jesuit "relations" as well as of the literature

[8] Frank E. Farley, *Scandinavian Influences in the English Romantic Movement* (Boston, 1903).
[9] Edward D. Snyder, *The Celtic Revival in English Literature, 1760-1800* (Cambridge, Mass., 1923); Russell K. Alspach, *Irish Poetry from the English Invasion to 1798* (1943).

of travel and trade, there were definite idealizations of Chinese, Persian, Arabian, and other Oriental peoples. These again were not new, nor were they ever vividly realistic. "Local color" and particularity were not yet. In the Oriental tale we get usually a medium for philosophizing. This is most marked in *Rasselas*. The love of oriental luxury and magnificence is seldom so stressed as in Beckford's *Vathek* (1786).

Another sort of incidental material that came much into use was outdoor scenery.[10] After the example of James Thomson writers used landscape increasingly because of a deistical preoccupation with the design of the universe or of a more orthodox belief in the benevolence of the Deity as seen in His works. The use of landscape backgrounds in novels was encouraged by Rousseau's *Julie* (1761). Landscapes turn up somewhat unexpectedly in such novels as Thomas Amory's *John Buncle* (1756-66) and Richard Graves's satirical story *The Spiritual Quixote* (1773). By the time of Ann Radcliffe the use of landscape illustrates what Ruskin was to stigmatize as "the pathetic fallacy." Cowper and possibly some others felt at least a medicinal, if not a spiritual, influence from nature; but Wordsworth had yet to formulate and vivify such concepts in poetry.

Description of Landscape

Preoccupation with landscape, like other novelties in subject matter here mentioned, was induced from books as well as from life. It was an easily acquired focus of attention. The unstable equipoise of the sensitive mind—Cowper's, for example—sought tranquillity outside itself in nature, and it had not far to seek, for in the eighteenth century one could walk from central London into the country, and apart from London there were few large towns.[11] To the end of the century England was still a nation of villagers and husbandmen. Even the woolen industry was for the most part rural rather than urban: the factory system was largely the invention of the early nineteenth century, though the increase in coal mining and the mechanical inventions of Arkwright and Watt had fully prepared the way during the last third of the century for the institution of large factories. At the moment, however, industrial matters had little place in literature. In spite of Blake's prompt perception (1804) of the evil of "dark Satanic mills," even he recognized that largely England was still a "green and pleasant land." For the most part poets were to be and to remain preoccupied with greenness and pleasantness.

Approaching Economic Changes

The subject matter of literature in the later eighteenth century thus added new and varied materials, and at the same time writers became in manner

10 Alfred Biese, *The Development of the Feeling for Nature in the Middle Ages and Modern Times* (1905).

11 According to the census of 1801 London was a city of about 900,000 inhabitants. The changes in size of certain English cities were due to their positions as ports: Bristol had a population of 64,000; Liverpool had displaced Chester as a northwest port, and had grown rapidly to 78,000; Plymouth had 43,000. Of the mushroom manufacturing towns Manchester-Salford had 84,000, Birmingham 74,000, and Leeds 53,000. Of the older towns of importance Norwich, possibly in 1660 the second city of England, was now eighth with 37,000 inhabitants. Other towns that had populations of between thirty and forty thousand were Bath, Portsmouth-Portsea, Sheffield, and Hull. Twenty-five towns had populations of between ten and twenty-five thousand.

and form less dependent on classical genres. Above all, the tone became more elegant and soft. One has only to contrast Swift and Burke (both of whom knew how to inflame) or Pope and Cowper or Addison's *Cato* and Home's *Douglas* to see the effects of increasing sentiment or fervor. There is no great increase in intellectual power; there is perhaps (Blake apart) none in imaginative power; but there is an increased effort for emotional appeal. This is objectively visible if we compare the method of Hogarth with that of the popular illustrator of books Thomas Stothard (1755-1834). Stothard embodies the spirit of his time in that his every line is graceful and elegant. He lacks the harsh robustness of Hogarth—is, in fact, somewhat anemic if placed beside that great graphic satirist; but his appeal is more facile and more agreeable. So perhaps is the appeal of the latter half of the eighteenth century as compared with the earlier half.

II
Opinions of Critics

As the eighteenth century moved on, there were changes of emphasis and *Confusions* tone with regard to many critical positions. There was no small amount of *of Doctrine* confused statement, in large part due to failure of the critic to make clear whether he was talking about (*a*) the nature of literature itself, (*b*) the psychological experience of enjoying literature, (*c*) the processes involved in the creation of literature, or (*d*) the intellectual process of evaluating literary achievement. The conscious changes in doctrine were less trenchant than they seem at first sight. *Rules* and *imitation* continued a tendency to become "indecent" words; but the art of literature remained representational (mimetic) in the minds of practically all writers except Blake, and the battle between controlled and spontaneous art continued—with much of the shouting done by the believers in spontaneity.

In the case of imitation there were changes in doctrine which are not *Imitation:* easily analyzed without false simplification or systematization. Pope in the *Pope's* preface to his *Works* (1717) had modestly justified his youthful efforts by *Views* the statement, "All that is left us is to recommend our productions by the imitation of the Ancients." This statement should be compared with the more intelligent remarks on imitation in the first Observation [1] affixed to Book 1 of his translation of the *Iliad*—and with other such passages. Failing such comparisons, critics have placed Pope too easily among the supporters of servile rather than emulous imitation. That he was so placed was in part due to his official editor, pugnacious William Warburton, who expounded Pope *ex cathedra,* and was by accident or through controversies hostile to views expressed by others, such as Akenside, Spence, and Joseph Warton.

To an edition of Horace's *Epistle to Augustus* Warburton's friend Richard *Hurd on* Hurd in 1751 added a *Dissertation on Poetical Imitation,* which attempted *Imitation* to defend something more or less like Pope's true position. "Every wondrous *original,* which ages have gazed at, as the offspring of creative fancy" is, so Hurd asserts, the result of "mimetic arts"—"is itself but a *copy,* a transcript from some brighter page of this vast volume of the universe." Whatever originality we can achieve must lie in our *manner* of imitation or representation. Homer in "rosy-fingered" conveys the "precise idea," and

---

[1] "Observations," p. 5 (of the first edition): "Imitation does not hinder Invention: We may observe the Rules of Nature, and write in the Spirit of those who have best hit upon them, without taking the same Track, beginning in the same Manner, and following the Main of their Story almost step by step; as most of the modern Writers of Epic Poetry have done."

so shows original genius. "General appearances," or the "objects of imita-tion," are a common stock; it is the effect of the poet's mind operating on these objects that will show his originality. There are obviously servile imitators, whom Hurd is ready to "resign to the shame and censure which have so justly followed them in all ages." "Successful imitation" is another matter. The two types of imitators suggest the journalistic formula of lofty "Parnassians" and vile "Grubeans" so much used in the pages of the *Grub-street Journal* twenty years before Hurd wrote.

Hurd's friends at Cambridge—including Thomas Gray and William Mason—were evidently interested, and at Mason's request Hurd wrote another dissertation, *On the Marks of Imitation* (1757). This is somewhat less theoretical, but in it from various favorite passages by many poets Hurd defends parallel expressions of ideas or sentiments.

Hurd's views were by no means accepted by all his contemporaries, though clearly they were not unusual. Dr. Johnson, at about the same time, in *Rambler* No. 143, condemned plagiarism but allowed imitative echoing of the "successful" sort. The blunt dictum of *Rasselas*, chapter x, that "no man was ever great by imitation," represents another aspect of the case, which the Doctor possibly would not always support. Boswell much later speaks of Hurd's commentaries as of the "Warburtonian School," and that label would not indicate popularity. To Joseph Warton the notes of Pope's first editor are not always pleasing, but he speaks pleasantly of "the ingenious Mr. Hurd," and in his oftenest quoted piece of criticism, his *Essay on Pope* (1756), he seldom, if ever, disparages any but ineffective imitation. In the *Adventurer* No. 63 (June 12, 1753) he commended several passages in which Pope had improved hints from others, and in this paper Warton speaks of poetry as "an art whose essence is imitation." [2] In the same passage he praises originality as a superlative and inevitably rare achievement. Edward Gibbon in his *Journal* for 1762 rigorously interprets Hurd's argument as an attempt to make anything but imitation impossible. Hurd, he says, "endeavours to prove, by a very elaborate deduction, that both the ideas, and the methods, employed by the ancients, were not only *natural ones,* but the *sole natural ones;* so that if succeeding poets, endued with judgment, looked abroad into nature, they not only *might,* but *must* meet with them; while men of irregular fancies could avoid *them only* by avoiding truth and probability." Hurd's position Gibbon regards as extreme.

Young's Conjectures It was, so Warton said, Pope's remark in his preface of 1717 that led Dr. Young, author of *Night Thoughts,* to write in his old age a pamphlet called *Conjectures on Original Composition in a Letter to the Author of "Sir Charles Grandison"* (1759). Boswell records that Johnson, to whom the *Conjectures* were read before publication, "was surprised to find Young receive as

---

[2] His brother Thomas, in the preface to his *Five Pastoral Eclogues* (1745), says, "The learned reader will observe, that the author has endeavour'd to imitate the simplicity of the ancients in these pieces, as thinking it not only more particularly adapted to pastoral, but the true ornament of all kinds of poetry in general." Ancient simplicity and "romantic" simplicity are frequently indistinguishable.

novelties, what he thought very common maxims"; but in spite of this expert opinion, historians in general have regarded Young as here advanced in his views. In many respects he agrees perfectly with Warton. While "imitation must be the lot (and often an honourable lot it is) of most writers," it is one's first duty and highest possible achievement to be "original." If all the literati could have read Young's *Conjectures,* perhaps he might have achieved the banishment, not of the representational concept of literature but of the notion of imitation as copying other masterpieces. In the *Conjectures* originality is not, as sometimes elsewhere, confused with novelty. Originality to Young consists in going back to the originals of things, in not going to "copies" made by others. Unlike Pope's Maro, he finds that Homer and Nature are *not* the same, though both must be very highly regarded; and the discovery, if not precisely new, is one that in his day had to be made again and again. His other significant doctrine is his insistence on the importance of the mind of the writer. *Know thyself; reverence thyself:* these are his two remedial principles. Genius comes before learning; "the divinely-inspired enthusiast" before "the well-accomplished scholar." In spite of his high metaphorical style, Young's effectiveness lay in his enthusiastic tone rather than in much of his content. The Warburtonians did not like the pamphlet, which seems to have aroused little immediate interest in England. Its influence in Germany, where it had some vogue, has been variously estimated. Young's essential position on imitation had been more quietly stated by Burke two years earlier when he remarked that poets had been "confined in so narrow a circle" because "they have been rather imitators of one another than of nature."

The best example of the continuance of conservative ideas on imitation *Reynolds'* may be seen in the fifteen *Discourses* of Sir Joshua Reynolds, delivered *Discourses* before the Royal Academy during the years 1769 to 1790. These lectures, in spite of William Blake's contempt for them, are a distinguished statement of the case for traditionalism and mimesis in the art of painting. They apply equally well to literature. Reynolds does not too much stress rules, but thinks some attention to them is essential. "The rules by which men of extraordinary parts . . . work, are either such as they discover by their own peculiar observations, or of such a nice texture as not easily to admit being expressed in words"; but, even unexpressed, "they are still seen and felt in the mind of the artist." Artists must begin by imitating other artists, but their goal is the representation of ideal beauty in the "great style." Again and again he insists, "This idea of the perfect state of nature, which the artist calls the ideal beauty, is the great leading principle by which works of genius are conducted." What Dr. Johnson says bluntly ("Nothing can please many, and please long, but just representations of general nature") Reynolds says with elegant dignity and with noble and subtle reasoning that makes him the most impressive defender of mimesis and of tradition in his century.

Thus the question of imitation was kept alive; though Sir Joshua's reiteration of his views may indicate that he felt restatement necessary because of

Poetry and Painting

apparent lack of receptiveness on the part of the young artists of his day. The prestige of imitation had of course been undermined by more than one writer on the graphic arts, in which the inferiority of merely representing or "copying" nature was peculiarly apparent. In 1719 the Abbé Du Bos had brought out a work ultimately translated by Thomas Nugent as *Critical Reflections on Poetry, Painting, and Music* (3 volumes, 1748). Even before the translation appeared similar discourses on the allied arts were fashionable. After 1750 they were numerous. Among the most influential early works doubtless Joseph Spence's *Polymetis* (1747) should stand first. These genteel dialogues developing a parallel between Roman poetry and ancient sculpture were ushered into the world after long preparation with a list of subscribers worthy of Pope himself. In some sense this work supplanted Andrew Tooke's *Pantheon* (1698), which Swift had forced upon Lady Acheson in an endeavor to improve her taste. *Polymetis* doubtless was of aid in the Greek revival of the later century and prepared a public for the beautiful sculptures of John Flaxman. To some extent these parallels between the arts undermined false notions of mimesis and encouraged sound redefinitions of aesthetic principles in the belles lettres.

As the century progressed, talk about imitation decreased. It was agreed that imitations of masterpieces were generally inferior to direct imitations of nature, called "originals."

Talk about "genius" and "imagination" certainly increased: these were the good words. *Genius* had by the mid-century supplanted *wit* as the creative force in an author's mind. Following a remark from *Spectator* No. 253, the Abbé Yart in his critical sketch of Pope's career observes, in fashion typical of the time, that "wit consists in adorning well-known thoughts, but genius is creative." [3] More commonly genius is associated with *original* (almost a synonym of *creative*),[4] and this fact indicates a tendency to abandon the well-worn stories of Greece and Rome. Dr. Johnson himself was an ardent proponent of *domestica facta,* and disparaged the use of classical stories and even of classical allusions. The Trojans, he asserted apropos of Pope's projected *Brutus,* "were a race upon whom imagination has been exhausted and attention wearied." One remembers also his lack of interest in Catiline and the Punic Wars. This appetite for new material hardly agrees with Hurd's idea that originality can consist only in manner, and it indicates Johnson's sympathy with the popular search for new materials. Joseph Warton was on record to the same effect. The desire of novelty drove authors to escape from classical material by turning to realism or by going to exotic subject matter—Peruvian, American, Indian, Scandinavian, Mohammedan, or Chinese. Bishop Lowth's Latin lectures *De Sacra Poesi Hebraeorum* (1753), which went through several editions and were finally (1793) translated into English, certainly stimulated the already keen taste for the so-called *style oriental*. In the work of a writer lacking genius these exotic

Originality and Genius

[3] *Idée de la poësie angloise,* III (1753). 18n.
[4] Paul Kaufman, "Heralds of Original Genius," in *Essays in Memory of Barrett Wendell* (Cambridge, Mass., 1926), pp. 191-222.

materials would be classed as somewhat grotesque novelties; the "original genius" alone can effectively "explore unbeaten tracks...invent new designs, and perfect the productions of Art."

Such at least was the opinion of one of the clearest and most methodical of the many writers about genius, William Duff (1732-1815). When this pious Scot published his *Essay on Original Genius* (1767), so much had been written on the subject that he made no pretense of novelty in many of his views and hence may serve as a convenient summarizer. The most important ingredient of genius was generally thought to be imagination; but Duff, with apology, adds other elements that temper and exalt each other. The effect, Duff tells us, of "a plastic and comprehensive imagination, an acute intellect, and an exquisite sensibility and refinement of taste" in union, "will be very extraordinary." He always glorified imagination, but still judgment is once or twice mentioned as a sensible guide to the glowing and impulsive faculty. Wit and Humor are "nearly allied to true Genius," but are the offspring of "a rambling and sportive Fancy," while Genius "proceeds from the copious effusions of a plastic Imagination." Swift was a wit rather than a genius of any "exalted kind"; Ossian was obviously no wit. This dichotomy of interest, especially since Duff, suggests that "men of genius, conscious of possessing superior talents, are not very ambitious of acquiring the reputation which arises from Wit." Such ideas become the highway from the *riant* art of the classical age to the mansions of high seriousness. But Duff can still see that "Genius derives vivacity from Wit, and Wit derives justness and extent of comprehension from Genius." In view of attempts at philosophical poetry in his day it is interesting to find him asserting that while "Original Philosophic Genius is that which is distinguished by regularity, clearness, and accuracy,...Original Genius in poetry is that whose essential properties are a noble irregularity, vehemence, and enthusiasm." We later learn that to Duff the normal manifestation of irregularity is "a mixture of great beauties and blemishes," and that Shakespeare illustrates the quality. The path of Genius, "as the course of a comet, is blazing, though irregular; and its errors and excellencies are equally inimitable." The cult of correctness is losing its charm.

Duff on Genius

So also is the Renaissance idea that a poetic genius should be learned. One may depend on the force of nature as sufficient aid, and may believe in geniuses quite untaught. Joseph Spence and some Wiltshire friends had stimulated these ideas when in 1730 they sent up to court "the thresher poet," Stephen Duck. Spence's account of Magliabecchi and even his insistence on Alexander Pope's rôle as automath also indicate his obsession with the force of nature as effective inspirer. Young enthusiastically proclaims: "Many a Genius, probably, there has been, which could neither write, nor read." This would have appalled Rymer or even the dunce who asserted bluntly that Pope had not that sufficient learning necessary to make a true poet. Shakespeare again was the chief exhibit among unlearned geniuses;

Genius and Learning

but after Stephen Duck had achieved royal patronage the number of them became legion.

Imagination   The force of nature manifested itself in geniuses through imagination. This commonplace of the seventeenth century was enthusiastically reiterated by critics throughout the Augustan period. The poets of the eighteenth century seem particularly fond of stressing the creative in this connection.[5] Joseph Warton, who as a critic affected the word, used it most notably in his dedication to his *Essay on Pope* when he announced that "it is a creative and glowing IMAGINATION, *acer spiritus ac vis,* and that alone" that can entitle a writer to the name of poet.[6] There is no serious objection on the part of his contemporaries to this view, nor is there any serious analysis of the creative imagination as seen in operation. The tone and frequency of such remarks is more novel and significant than is their content. We still find in Duff's *Essay* and elsewhere insistence on the old alliance of imagination and judgment. In one passage Duff makes imagination subordinate to judgment. Unregulated imagination, he thinks, may "throw glaring colours on objects that possess no intrinsic excellence," and thus "mislead the mind." More than once this element of *glare* is mentioned by critics with disfavor.

Sympathetic   Duff's generation made perhaps its chief contribution to an understand-
Imagination ing of the imagination by adapting principles concerning the association of ideas and by a notion of intuitive, sentimental, or "sympathetic" imagination.[7] From 1749, when David Hartley's *Observations on Man* appeared, down to Archibald Alison's *Essays on Taste* (1790) and of course even to Coleridge's day, critics made increasing use of association of ideas in explaining imaginative appeal. Duff specifies also a duality of function in the imagination that harks back perhaps to the days of Hobbes: the faculty had both powers of association and powers of creation. Wit and humor are, as in the days of Hobbes, associational; but poetic genius now is creative. These views are interesting further because Duff tends, in anticipation of Wordsworth and Coleridge, to name the associative power, *fancy.*[8]

Taste and   From early in the century views of the imagination were tied up with
Judgment another favorite topic: *taste.* Addison and others had stressed the power of imagination to refine taste, to make one in some sort the *honnête homme;* and the later century, equally devoted to refined elegance, wrote interminably on the subject. It was largely accident if concepts of taste undermined neo-classical uniformity. That was not the intention. The situation was that, having like sensible men first abandoned the authority of Aristotle and the ancients for the authority of those indefinable absolutes, Truth (*Rien n'est*

---

[5] Logan Pearsall Smith, "Four Words: Romantic, Originality, Creative, Genius," *S.P.E. Tract* No. XVII (1924), pp. 21-22.

[6] See Hoyt Trowbridge, "Joseph Warton on the Imagination," *MP,* XXXV (1937). 73-87 (esp. pp. 82-84).

[7] Walter J. Bate, "The Sympathetic Imagination in Eighteenth-Century English Criticism," *ELH,* XII (1945). 144-164.

[8] John Bullitt and Walter J. Bate, "The Distinctions between Fancy and Imagination in Eighteenth-Century English Criticism," *MLN,* LX (1945). 8-15.

beau que le vrai), Nature (the source, end, and test of art), and Reason (which "wants not Horace to support it"), they were next compelled, as good empiricists, to limit their regard to the authority of experience, which was "taste." Nature methodized gave rules; experience methodized gave taste. In the realm of judicial criticism the one was to replace the other: taste was to be a faculty of judgment.

More readily, however, from the Addisonian point of approach, taste *Taste and* became a faculty of enjoyment. Taste may be innate in part, but training is *Enjoyment* likely to be stressed as an aid. Through refinement of imagination, one associates the "right" ideas—not the vulgar. Dr. John Armstrong in his poem *Taste* [9] (1753) is still echoing Pope's outcry against the crude false taste of the *nouveaux riches*. Enjoyment of the best depends on delicate sensibility. It is not, except for critical judgments, necessary to transmute sensibility into a standard. In his important essay *Of the Standard of Taste* (1757) Hume in stating a point of view different from his own makes a distinction between *Hume on* sentiment and judgment that really is not alien to his own way of thinking: *Taste*

All sentiment is right; because sentiment has a reference to nothing beyond itself, and is always real, wherever a man is conscious of it. But all determinations of the understanding are not right; because they have a reference to something beyond themselves, to wit, real matter of fact; and are not always conformable to that standard. Among a thousand different opinions . . . there is one, and but one, that is just and true; and the only difficulty is to fix and ascertain it.

Taste as a faculty of enjoyment, then, is quite subjective and unpredictable so far as particular enjoyments go. In another essay, *Of the Delicacy of Taste and Passion,* Hume praises this sensibility as desirably refined and as tempering our interest in the cruder passions of real life. He gives us the cool, well-bred point of view of the eighteenth-century Francophile.

But even if the *enjoyment* of literature can be left, within genteel limits, to individualism, taste as a faculty of *judgment* is in theory quite another thing. Hume summarizes an opinion somewhat divergent from his own as saying that "Beauty is no quality in things themselves: It exists merely in the mind which contemplates them; and each mind perceives a different beauty." For enjoyment this may do, but for the further purpose of evaluation we must search for what Hume calls "a *Standard of Taste;* a rule, by which the various sentiments of men may be reconciled; at least, a decision, afforded, confirming one sentiment and condemning another." Hume himself asserts: "Though it be certain, that beauty and deformity . . . are not qualities in objects, but belong entirely to the sentiment; . . . it must be allowed, that there are certain qualities in objects, which are fitted by nature to produce those particular feelings." It is on this correspondence between cause in the object and effect in the sentiment that Hume bases his belief

[9] *Taste* is probably the most readable of this medicinal poet's writings. For an account of his amazingly varied friendships with many literary folk see the excellent article by Lewis M. Knapp, "Dr. John Armstrong, Littérateur . . . ," *PMLA*, LIX (1944). 1019-1058.

in a standard of taste. In similar fashion Alexander Gerard in his more extensive *Essay on Taste* (1759) by implication differentiates the tasteful reader from the critic: [10] "A critic must not only *feel,* but possess that accuracy of discernment, which enables a person to *reflect* upon his feelings with distinctness, and to explain them to others." In 1759 Burke prefixed to his *Sublime and Beautiful* an introduction in which he also insists that the recording faculty is essential as an ingredient in taste. In general, so far as "taste" critics focused attention on nameless graces, on the *je ne sais quoi,* they headed towards a subjective anarchy in criticism; but with regard to other "graces" their normal aim was to replace outworn sanctions by a criterion empirically established. In his important dissertation *Of the Standard of Taste,* Hume, as a conservative disciple of French taste, was impelled towards the belief that a uniform standard of excellence exists; but, as a skeptic, he could not feel that such a standard could easily be determined. "Every voice," he says, "is united in applauding elegance, propriety, simplicity, spirit in writing; and in blaming fustian, affectation, coldness, and a false brilliancy: But when critics come to particulars, this seeming unanimity vanishes; and it is found, that they had affixed a very different meaning to their expressions." The quotation perhaps exaggerates the skeptical nature of Hume's conclusion. He goes on to show how the standard of taste is to be determined, and is able to conclude thus: "But in reality the difficulty of finding, even in particulars, the standard of taste, is not so great as it is represented. Though in speculation, we may readily avow a certain criterion in science and deny it in sentiment, the matter is found in practice to be much more hard to ascertain in the former case than in the latter." He holds that even "amidst all the variety and caprices of taste, there are certain general principles of approbation or blame," but the difficulty is that "though the principles of taste be universal, and, nearly, if not entirely the same in all men; yet few are qualified to give judgment on any work of art, or establish their own sentiment as the standard of beauty." The critic, he sees, may lack delicacy, or such sureness as comes from practice, or the skill that compares works justly, or the necessary freedom from bias. The fundamental difficulty lies in "the different humours of particular men" or in "the particular manners and opinions of our age and country."

The Galli-cism of Hume's Taste

Of this last limitation, it may be remarked parenthetically, Hume himself is a sweet example. His Francophile manners, for instance, amusingly lead him to adopt the current reservations as to Homer's heroes: "The sage Ulysses in the Greek poet seems to delight in lies and fictions.... But his more scrupulous son, in the French epic writer,[11] exposes himself to the most imminent perils, rather than depart from the most exact line of truth and veracity." Of the death of old Memnon in Rowe's *Ambitious Stepmother* it is easy for him to say, "The English theatre abounds too much with such shocking images." His encouragement of his friend and cousin,

[10] The Select Society of Edinburgh had awarded Gerard's *Essay* a prize. Hume had been one of the judges, and he helped see the *Essay* through the press.
[11] The reference is to Fénelon's *Avantures de Télémaque fils d'Ulysse* (1699).

John Home, the author of *Douglas,* is sufficient evidence of his loyalty to old Scotia's grandeur. Significantly in a letter he urged Home: "For God's sake, read Shakespeare, but get Racine and Sophocles by heart. It is reserved for you, and you alone, to redeem our stage from the reproach of barbarism." Such an adviser could readily see the French objections to Shakespeare.

This elegant, clear-eyed critic was not the man to break a butterfly on the *Analysis of* wheel; but more than one of his contemporaries was. In analyzing taste they *Beauty* could not be content with Hume's admired universals—"elegance, propriety, simplicity, spirit"—as telling adequately what qualities please the imagination. In largest terms these qualities were to them the beautiful, the sublime, and, sometimes, the picturesque.[12] The first two of these were incessantly subjected to analysis in this period. The greatest English painter of the mid-century, William Hogarth (1697-1764), gave an influential and typical account of the first in his *Analysis of Beauty* (1753), where appeal is said to arise from the following: fitness of the parts in a design, variety, uniformity, regularity or symmetry (but these can only subserve fitness or design), simplicity, intricacy, and magnitude (the cause of admiration and awe). Burke in his *Sublime and Beautiful* did not admit fitness, proportion, or perfection as sources of beauty, but named different elements in his more psychological analysis into such component parts as smallness, smoothness, variation from straight lines, delicacy, and color. Alexander Gerard, making beauty one of several principles of taste (which are, according to him, novelty, grandeur, beauty, imitation, harmony, ridicule, and virtue), analyzes it into figure (uniformity, variety, proportion), utility (fitness to design), and color.

And so, with variations, these qualities were again and again regurgitated. In 1761 Dodsley reprinted Spence's *Crito* (1752), in which beauty falls under the four heads of color, form, expression, and grace. Spence regarded virtue as the chief beauty, and it may be said in passing that most of these men, however much they expatiate on the beautiful, were at heart moralists. Lord Kames in his *Elements of Criticism* (1762) based beauty and ugliness on the emotions of pleasure and pain, after the fashion of Hume and many others; and Kames reverted to earlier theorists for the idea that beauty belongs to objects of sight and is either intrinsic or relative to other objects. The constituent parts of intrinsic beauty he found to be utility, color, figure (which depends on regularity, uniformity, proportion, order, simplicity), motion, and simplicity. He stressed most, perhaps, figure and simplicity.

---

[12] Since the "picturesque," the seeing of landscape itself or the use of it in terms of the graphic arts, is not early formalized in theory, it is not further treated here. While picturesqueness dominated the literary use of landscape for two-thirds of a century, it was theorized late chiefly by William Gilpin and Sir Uvedale Price. Its early manifestations grew out of schools of landscape painting or gardening or out of accidental personal interests uniting the graphic arts and literature in such individuals, for example, as John Dyer, Jonathan Richardson, William Mason, William Shenstone, Philip de Loutherbourg, etc. The idea of picturesqueness influenced profoundly the description of landscape, but it did not receive the repeated analysis bestowed on the beautiful and the sublime. See Elizabeth W. Manwaring, *Italian Landscape in Eighteenth Century England* (1925), Christopher Hussey, *The Picturesque* (1927), Chauncey B. Tinker, *Painter and Poet* (Cambridge, Mass., 1938).

In 1790 Archibald Alison in his *Essays on the Nature and Principles of Taste* adopted a newer method of approach, the association of ideas, upon which rather than perception he based aesthetic pleasure.

Analysis of the Sublime: Burke   Contemplation of the *disiecta membra* of beauty was not enough: the sublime must also be anatomized. Before the mid-century there were glimmerings of this attempt, and possibly the two most significant relationships stressed are the relation of the sublime to novelty or astonishment, which harks back to a baroque theory of art, and its relation to the pathetic. Writers such as John Baillie [13] (for whom chiefly vastness but also novelty and uniformity stimulate the sublime mood) and Bishop Lowth [14] (who commends agitation, amplification, and passion, as sublime) groped towards analysis; but Edmund Burke first arrived at detailed and avowed sources of the mood. In his early work, *A Philosophical Enquiry into the Origin of Our Ideas of the Sublime and Beautiful* (1757), he based the sublime emotions on terror, and on the astonishment and amazement that accompany terror. These subsidiary states of mind recall not merely Longinus but the appeal that even the early seventeenth century found in baroque art. The qualities stimulating these sublime emotions are listed as obscurity ("It is one thing to make an idea clear, and another to make it affecting to the imagination"), power, privation (i.e., vacuity, darkness, solitude, and silence), vastness, infinity (including succession, uniformity, and magnitude), difficulty (i.e., objects or effects that are the result of "immense force"), magnificence (profusion plus, sometimes, a desirable disorder), light, color, loud sounds, as well as other sensory and emotional affects. This is clearly a confusingly inclusive list, which provoked both hostility and discipleship. Burke used physiological as well as psychological data, and found the theory of the association of ideas somewhat useful. In his opinion that the strongest sublime emotion is one of distress, he came dangerously near to wedding sublimity and sentimentalism. Unsatisfactory as Burke's thought may appear, his point of view is purely scientific and disinterested. He was simply describing mental reactions to certain types of stimulation; he had no purpose either to heighten enjoyment or to guide judgment. Yet in his purely descriptive function he had no idea that he was at work on a subjective chaos. In the introduction "On Taste" he said: "If taste has no fixed principles, if the imagination is not affected according to some invariable and certain laws, our labour is likely to be employed to very little purpose; as it must be judged an useless, if not an absurd undertaking, to lay down rules for caprice and to set up for a legislator of whims and fancies." Principles, standards, even rules, are not yet intentionally replaced by "individualism," but the appeal of subject matter is rapidly being redefined in very new terms.

Burke was followed by dozens of writers and analysts. Gerard in his *Essay on Taste* relates the sublime to quantity or amplitude, to simplicity,

---

[13] *An Essay on the Sublime* (1747).
[14] Robert Lowth (1710-1787), *De Sacra Poesi Hebraeorum Praelectiones* (1753).

to vastness, etc., but not to terror. Lord Kames in his *Elements of Criticism*
devoted a conventional chapter to "Grandeur and Sublimity." Priestley's
ideas combined views of Gerard and Hartley. Blair objected, in lectures
delivered in 1759 and later, to founding the sublime solely on terror or on
vastness; he preferred "mighty force or power." It is unnecessary to list
further suggestions. The critics here mentioned show that by no psychological technique available could satisfactory principles or rules for a faculty of
judgment be deduced. Unintentionally what these analysts had accomplished
was a shift from the relatively unified sanctions of Reason, Truth, and
Nature to dozens of new and diverse qualities that appealed to imagination.
While hunting through experience for a uniform standard, they introduced
the Trojan horse, diversity.

They hardly accomplished more in the direction of a standard than to
stress such criteria as permanence and universality of appeal, but these had
already been derived at least in part from the anti-rationalist concept of
common sense (*consensus gentium*). The criterion of permanence of appeal
had an interesting development in the historical criticism which was prac-
ticed much in the later century. It centers, perhaps accidentally, on the study
of such authors as Homer, Shakespeare, and Spenser. There was in editing
masterpieces a strong scholarly tradition, paralleled by a more genteel
amateurish tradition. From Richard Bentley and Tom Hearne to Richard
Porson and Edmond Malone there were fine scholars who were good editors.
Though this sound scholarship aided the editors of Shakespeare, most of
them from Rowe to Blair were ready, as Bishop Percy was with his ballads,
to falsify without warning as well as to modernize the original texts with
which they dealt. But after the work of Pope and Theobald it was obviously
necessary to study an author's vocabulary in the light of his own generation.
Elizabethan puns and humor were explained as the result of the dramatist's
necessary appeal to the groundlings. Similarly, as we have seen in Hume's
remark on Odysseus's disregard of honesty, there were things to be explained
about Homer's heroes. These, among other matters, were discussed in such
works as Thomas Blackwell's *Enquiry into the Life and Writings of Homer*
(1735) and Robert Wood's *Essay on the Original Genius and Writings of
Homer* (1769). One remark by Wood explains his point of view: "I must
confess I am a little surprized ... that those who have affected to discover
so perfect a system of morals and politics in Homer, should have bestowed
so little consideration upon the character of the times for which this instruction was calculated." And Wood suggests that the age of Homer differed
from that of Madam Dacier "as we do ... from our Gothic ancestors in the
days of Chivalry and Romance." Relative conditions as formative of genius
were becoming important for the critic's thorough understanding of a masterpiece, not merely of its morals but of its entire nature as well. This type
of study is best illustrated by Thomas Warton's *Observations on the Faerie
Queene* (1754, 1762). To aid the critic of Spenser, Warton says, "I have
considered the customs and genius of his age; I have searched his con-

temporary writers, and examined the books on which the peculiarities of his style, taste and composition, are confessedly founded." Beside this passage may be placed his repeated belief that in criticizing our "elder poets ... not only a competent knowledge of all antient classical learning is requisite, but also an acquaintance with those books, which, though now forgotten and lost, were yet in repute about the time in which each author respectively wrote, and which it is most likely he had read." In such remarks we see the scholarly critical conscience growing; the first law of sound criticism is to be complete understanding. Thomas Warton was not a systematic historian, but his pioneer *History of English Poetry* (3 volumes, 1774-81) is full of a rich store of learning and of admiration for the Middle Ages.[15] His enthusiasm was shared by Richard Hurd, who, in glorifying "Gothic Chivalry," found, as did others of his day, its best embodiment in *The Faerie Queene.* Hurd's *Letters on Chivalry and Romance* (1762) show the same revulsion from the pedestrian life of his own day that Horace Walpole was expressing in his *Castle of Otranto.* Hurd sees that common-sense *vraisemblance* has "perfectly dissolved ... the magic of the old Romances," and he concludes with his well-known lament for the loss of "fine fabling."

The Drift of Opinion   This "romantic" observation comes from a critic who, it must be remembered, was an ardent defender of imitation. Such apparent confusion must be expected in most so-called "liberal" critics of the time. It is customary to read Joseph Warton's dedication to his *Essay on Pope* and having read no further pronounce him a revolutionary. But Warton always regarded Pope as among the half-dozen first poets of England: his dedication simply calls attention to the fact that Pope, while the greatest of poets in the genres he attempted, did not attempt the highest genres. It should be remembered also that Warton appended to the first volume of Virgil's *Works in Latin and English* (1753) "Reflections on Didactic Poetry," which, even if colored by the idea that "Men love to be moved, much better than to be instructed," is lacking neither in sympathy for this type of poetry nor in the magisterial tone sometimes associated with rules of criticism. It is, then, possible to exaggerate the conscious "romanticism" of such men as Young, Hurd, and the Wartons. It is wise to remember that the best brains of the mid-century— Hume, Gibbon, Reynolds, and Dr. Johnson—were in many respects the most fervent "classicists" of the whole century. The drift was away from authority, tradition, and formalism, to diversity, to originality, and to admiration of a "creative and glowing IMAGINATION, *acer spiritus ac vis.*" This drift, fortunately or unfortunately, was not entirely conscious: it was inconsistently maintained, and the opposition to parts of the tendency were stated with shrewdness and above all with magisterial emphasis.

15 René Wellek, *The Rise of English Literary History* (Chapel Hill, 1941), gives a comprehensive view of the beginnings of historical criticism and of Warton's place in the development. On Hurd one may compare the divergent emphasis of two articles: Audley L. Smith, "Richard Hurd's *Letters on Chivalry and Romance,*" *ELH,* VI (1939). 58-81; and Hoyt Trowbridge, "Bishop Hurd: a Reinterpretation," *PMLA,* LVIII (1943). 450-465. On another aspect of historical criticism see Donald Foerster, "Mid-Eighteenth Century Scotch Criticism of Homer," *SP,* XL (1943). 425-446.

III

Dr. Johnson

Samuel Johnson (1709-1784), who at the age of fifty-five became Doctor *Samuel*
of Laws, and was thereafter known as "Doctor," was doubtless the most *Johnson*
magisterial among the conservatives of the later eighteenth century.[1] His
very great achievement was two-fold: that of writer and that of conversationalist. One might add a third function: being the subject of the greatest
biography ever written, that by James Boswell. Largely through Boswell's
picturesque efforts Johnson still lives, and through his own gifts in conversation as well as through Boswell's gifts in retailing small anecdotes, he lives
chiefly as a psychological eccentric—which he certainly was. In thinking of
him, however, as representative of his period and in some sense of his race,
we must not forget to conceive of him as a man of typical *mind*.

A native of Lichfield, son of a provincial bookseller, he contracted

[1] *The Works of Samuel Johnson*, ed. Sir John Hawkins and others (15v, 1787-9); Arthur
Murphy (12v, 1792); Oxford English Classics (11v, 1825).—*Poems*, ed. David Nichol Smith
and Edward L. McAdam (Oxford, 1941); *The Rambler*, ed. Alex. Chalmers, *British Essayists*,
Vols. xix-xxii (1802); *Rasselas*, ed. Oliver F. Emerson (1895); Robert W. Chapman (1927);
The Idler, ed. Alex. Chalmers, *British Essayists*, Vols. xxxiii, xxxiv (1802); *A Journey to
the Western Islands of Scotland*, ed., with Boswell's *Tour*, Robert W. Chapman (1924); *The
Lives of the Poets*, ed. Mrs. Alexander Napier and John W. Hales (3v, 1890); Arthur Waugh
(6v, 1896); George Birkbeck Hill (3v, Oxford, 1905); *Johnsonian Miscellanies* (includes
Prayers and Meditations), ed. George Birkbeck Hill (2v, Oxford, 1897); *Prefaces & Dedications*,
ed. Allen T. Hazen (New Haven, 1937); *Letters*, ed. Hester Lynch [Thrale] Piozzi (2v, 1788);
George Birkbeck Hill (2v, Oxford, 1892, 1897); *The Queeney Letters* [from Johnson and Mrs.
Thrale to Hester Maria Thrale], ed. the Marquis of Lansdowne (1934). Dr. R. W. Chapman
is preparing a new edition of all Johnson's letters. The best bibliography of Johnson is that
by William P. Courtney and David Nichol Smith (1925). "A Supplement to Courtney" by
R. W. Chapman and A. T. Hazen appeared in *Proc.... Oxford Bibl. Soc.*, v (1938). 117-166
— James Boswell, *Life of Samuel Johnson* (2v, 1791); ed. Edmond Malone (4v, 1799, 1804, etc);
John W. Croker (5v, 1831); George Birkbeck Hill (6v, 1887, rev. by L. F. Powell, 6v, 1934 —
in progress), and many other eds. Other biographical works about Johnson include those by
Hester Lynch Piozzi (*Anecdotes*, 1786; in Hill's *Johnsonian Miscellanies*, 1897; ed. S. C.
Roberts, Cambridge, 1925), Sir John Hawkins (1787), Arthur Murphy (1792), John W.
Croker (*Johnsoniana*, 1836), Alexander M. Broadley (*Dr. Johnson and Mrs. Thrale*, 1910),
Aleyn L. Reade (*Johnsonian Gleanings*, 10 Parts, 1909-46), Mildred C. Struble (*A Johnson
Handbook*, 1933), Sydney C. Roberts (*Dr. Johnson*, 1935), James L. Clifford (*Hester Lynch
Piozzi*, Oxford, 1941); Joseph W. Krutch (*Samuel Johnson*, 1944). — Of general interpretative
value are the following: Thomas B. (Lord) Macaulay, "Samuel Johnson" (*Edinburgh Review*,
Sept., 1831; ed. David Nichol Smith, Edinburgh, 1900; Chester N. Greenough, 1912); Thomas
Carlyle, "Samuel Johnson" (*Fraser's Magazine*, May, 1832; reprinted separately, 1853); Sir
Walter Raleigh, *Six Essays on Johnson* (1910); Chauncey B. Tinker, *Dr. Johnson and Fanny
Burney, Being the Johnsonian Passages from the Works of Mme d'Arblay* (1912); Percy H.
Houston, *Dr. Johnson: A Study in Eighteenth-Century Humanism* (Cambridge, Mass., 1923);
Joseph Epes Brown, *The Critical Opinions of Samuel Johnson* (Princeton, 1926); David Nichol
Smith, Robert W. Chapman, and L. F. Powell, *Johnson and Boswell Revised by Themselves
and Others* (three essays, Oxford, 1928); Hugh Kingsmill (ed.), *Johnson without Boswell:
A Contemporary Portrait* (1940); Bertrand H. Bronson, *Johnson and Boswell* (Berkeley, Calif.,
1944); Sydney C. Roberts, *Samuel Johnson* (British Academy Lecture, 1944).

His Educa-
tion

scrofula in infancy from his nurse, and thereby his eyesight was impaired. Nevertheless he grew up a lad of unusual physical strength and robustness as well as an omnivorous reader. In spite of poverty he was sent briefly, it seems (1728-9), to Pembroke College, Oxford, in which "nest of singing birds" he distinguished himself for his pride as well as for his learning. Of these poverty-stricken days, when tutors and students both loved him and thought him "a gay and frolicksome fellow," he said: "Sir, I was mad and violent. It was bitterness which they mistook for frolick. I was miserably poor, and thought to fight my way by my literature and my wit; so I disregarded all authority." Poverty drove him back to Lichfield without a degree, and for six years he was a schoolmaster or bookseller and, as always, a rapid and desultory reader. In 1731 he first became a published author when his Oxford friends printed without his consent his Latin version of Pope's *Messiah,* and in 1735 a friendly bookseller employed him to translate a book on Abyssinia. In this same year he married a widow twice his age, to whom beyond her death (1752) he remained touchingly devoted. By 1737 he had written a tragedy, *Irene,* and he thereupon hopefully abandoned schoolteaching and trudged up to London with one of his pupils named David Garrick. Thereafter Johnson was to be a Londoner.

Early Years
in London

In the metropolis he made curious, amusing, and useful friends. Richard Savage, whose *Life* Johnson wrote in 1744, initiated him into the seamy life of the hack writer, and Edward Cave, proprietor of *The Gentleman's Magazine,* gave him employment of various sorts, notably (1738-43) in helping prepare the semi-allegorical and almost illegal accounts of the "Senate of Lilliput," which gave the public some notion of the speeches made in the Houses of Parliament. For another bookseller, Thomas Osborne, he used his erudition in preparing a catalogue of the famous Harleian Library (5 volumes, 1743-5), and wrote proposals and a Preface for *The Harleian Miscellany* (1744). He was making himself useful and respected both for his learning and for his poetry.

His Poetry

It was, after all, poetry that had brought Johnson to London. *Irene* was not acted until 1749 when Garrick, then famous and in power at Drury Lane, produced it.[2] In it Johnson had transformed a savage story into a fable carrying fine moral implications expressed in formal but noble eloquence that aroused respect but evoked no tears. He long believed in the play, and it is pathetic to find him years later leaving a room where it was being read aloud to friends. When asked why he left, he replied, "Sir, I thought it had been better." Johnson's reputation as a poet had been made on other pieces.[3] *London,* an imitation of Juvenal's third satire, was published in 1738 on the same day as Pope's *Epilogue* to his satires. Though the work of a new poet it was thought to compare favorably with Pope's mature eloquence. Both Pope and Johnson attacked the corruption of the times in typical fashion.

---

[2] David Nichol Smith, *Samuel Johnson's "Irene"* (Oxford, 1929); reprinted in part from *E&S,* xiv (1928). 35-53.

[3] T. S. Eliot, Introduction to *London and The Vanity of Human Wishes* (1930); R. W. Chapman, "Dr. Johnson and Poetry," *Sat. Rev. of Lit.* (Aug. 17, 1929), pp. 49-51.

Johnson's picture of the town in this poem is, however, not comparable to that given in his *Life of Savage,* which is the best account of Grub-street existence that we have. In 1747, at Garrick's request, he wrote a prologue for the opening of the season at Drury Lane, which was remarkable for its pungent and imaginative statements by way of dramatic criticism. In sixty-two lines he sketched incisively the development of English drama with particularly neat lines devoted to neo-classical tragedy. In 1749 another important poem, *The Vanity of Human Wishes,* appeared. Pessimism such as it expresses permeates Johnson's whole life. The vanity of literary or scholarly fame is colored by personal feeling in the couplet:

> There mark what ills the scholar's life assail,
> Toil, envy, want, the patron, and the jail.

Five years earlier Savage had died in a debtor's jail, and Johnson's collaborator on *The Harleian Miscellany,* William Oldys, was from 1751 to 1753 in Fleet prison for debt. The word *patron* was substituted for *attic* after Johnson's failure to get patronage from Lord Chesterfield. The magnificent and marmoreal gloom of the couplets about Charles XII remind one of later conquerors:

> He left the name, at which the world grew pale,
> To point a moral, or adorn a tale.

He could command this stately eloquence, but tenderness of strong personal emotion left him inarticulate. Even his quiet lines *On the Death of Dr. Robert Levet,* who had for many years been a member of Johnson's household, lack intimacy.

He was essentially a prose man, as he himself realized, and he won high reputation as a scholar and a prose moralist. As a scholar he had shown *His Work* *as a Scholar* ability first in his work on the Harleian Library. His major reputation in his own time was perhaps gained from his *Dictionary of the English Language* (1755), for which in 1747 he had addressed a *Plan* to the third Earl of Chesterfield. Failing to get response in the way of patronage until the work was completed, Johnson wrote in 1755 the famous (and impertinent) letter to Chesterfield denouncing patrons in general. The *Dictionary* had been composed with the aid of a half-dozen amanuenses (chiefly Scottish), employed to transcribe the illustrative quotations that were a feature.[4] Johnson had a naturally defining mind, and his definitions of words were usually excellent—though now chiefly remembered are the jocose or erratic examples cited by Boswell and others. These were at times merely playful,

---

[4] Sir James A. H. Murray, *The Evolution of English Lexicography* (Romanes Lecture, 1900); Percy W. Long, "English Dictionaries before Webster," *Bibl. Soc. of America, Papers,* IV (1910). 25-43; Stanley Rypins, "Johnson's Dictionary Reviewed by his Contemporaries," *PQ,* IV (1925). 281-286; Allen W. Read, "The Contemporary Quotations in Johnson's Dictionary," *ELH,* II (1935). 246-251; Philip B. Gove, "Notes on Serialization and Competitive Publishing: Johnson's and Bailey's Dictionaries, 1755," *Oxford Bibl. Soc.,* V (1940). 305-322; De Witt T. Starnes and Gertrude E. Noyes, *The English Dictionary from Cawdrey to Johnson, 1604-1755* (Chapel Hill, 1946).

and at times they aired Johnson's cherished prejudices. A *lexicographer* was "a harmless drudge, that busies himself in tracing the original, and detailing the signification of words." *Network* was "anything reticulated or decussated, at equal distances, with interstices between the intersections." He kept up the feud with the Scots in defining *oats*—"A grain, which in England is generally given to horses, but in Scotland supports the people." *Whig,* tersely, is "the name of a faction." And after 1762, when through his Scottish prime minister, Lord Bute, King George III bestowed a pension on Johnson, the joke was on the Doctor because of his definition of *pension*—"An allowance made to any one without an equivalent. In England it is generally understood to mean pay given to a state hireling for treason to his country." In revising the work later Dr. Johnson did not meddle with these *jeux d'esprit.* The preface to the *Dictionary,* while not the best of his notable series of prefaces, is rich in sound sense, in general observation, and in the stylistic mannerisms already demonstrated in *The Rambler* and elsewhere. His plea for mercy from critics is memorable for all such works:

> In this work, when it shall be found that much is omitted, let it not be forgotten that much likewise is performed; and though no book was ever spared out of tenderness to the author, and the world is little solicitous to know whence proceeded the faults of that which it condemns; yet it may gratify curiosity to inform it, that the *English Dictionary* was written with little assistance of the learned, and without any patronage of the great; not in the soft obscurities of retirement, or under the shelter of academick bowers, but amidst inconvenience and distraction, in sickness and sorrow; and it may repress the triumph of malignant criticism to observe, that if our language is not here fully displayed, I have only failed in an attempt which no human powers have hitherto completed.

The work, naturally, was faulty: the derivations, for example, because of the backwardness of studies in English etymology were not too creditable; but the undertaking as a whole was both highly useful and nobly monumental in scope and effect. As Carlyle remarked in his *Heroes, Hero-Worship,* etc., "Had Johnson left nothing but his *Dictionary,* one might have traced there a great intellect, a genuine man."

Shake-speare's Plays

Even before he published his *Plan* for the *Dictionary* Johnson had formed a hope of editing Shakespeare's plays. In 1745 he had shown critical insight appropriate to such a task in his *Miscellaneous Observations on the Tragedy of Macbeth;* and, again, after the *Dictionary* was off his hands, he published *Proposals* (1756) for an edition of Shakespeare.[5] Subscriptions were received, but Johnson was scandalously dilatory in performing the task. Friends tried to urge industry, and foes, like Charles Churchill in his *Ghost* (1762), added perhaps more effective jeers:

[5] Sir Walter Raleigh, *Johnson on Shakespeare* (selections edited with a preface, 1908); David Nichol Smith, *Eighteenth Century Essays on Shakespeare* (Glasgow, 1903) and *Shakespeare in the Eighteenth Century* (1928); Karl Young, "Samuel Johnson on Shakespeare: One Aspect" [i.e., source study], *Univ. of Wisconsin Studies,* XVIII (1923). 147-227; Robert W. Babcock, *The Genesis of Shakespeare Idolatry, 1766-1799* (Chapel Hill, 1931).

He for *Subscribers* baits his hook,
And takes their cash—but where's the Book?

In 1765 the volumes finally appeared, and, while attacked in part as coming from a pensioner, they were well received and greatly stimulated scholarship concerning Shakespeare. Johnson's contribution was less textual than it was interpretative and historical. He, first, pointed out many sources for the plays, and his notes on individual passages were usually sound and illuminating, and frequently provocative of comment by others. The preface was one of the best pieces of prose Johnson ever wrote—manly, incisive, and sensitively phrased.

Its doctrine was sensible rather than new. Neither Johnson nor Garrick *The Preface* nor their half-century "discovered" Shakespeare or made his reputation. *to Shake-* That was long since assured. Nor was Johnson's defense of Shakespeare's *speare* failure to follow the "rules" wholly revolutionary: Addison and Pope (with all Pope's respect for both Rymer and for rules) and many others had already indicated similar positions. But Johnson's statements concerning the nature of Shakespeare's genius and work are more complete and more explicit than those of his predecessors, and they are in general admirable. Three points may be noted: (1) Johnson appeals to the imaginative basis of literature in attacking the unities: "The objection arising from the impossibility of passing the first hour at Alexandria, and the next at Rome, supposes, that when the play opens, the spectator really imagines himself at Alexandria, and believes that his walk to the theatre has been a voyage to Egypt, and that he lives in the days of Anthony and Cleopatra. Surely he that imagines this may imagine more." And the Doctor goes on to give an exposition of imaginative truth that should cause critics that talk of the "distrust of the imagination" to read him again. (2) His conception of "general" nature is here well expressed. Johnson may be deficient in a liking for the fantastic or the particular. Shakespeare he likes because "Shakespeare always makes nature predominate over accident." To Johnson nature is essential humanity, not accidental or minute detail. On the other hand extreme attention to decorum of character leads to trivialities that are "the petty cavils of petty minds." "Just representations of general nature" require the elimination of irrelevant detail. The poet does not, as he remarks in the famous passage in *Rasselas* (chapter x), present *all* details or even irrelevant details such as the "streaks of the tulip," but rather "such prominent and striking features, as recall the original to every mind." The chosen detail must induce imaginative recall, but the detail may be small since "There is nothing, Sir, too little for so little a creature as man." The sort of imaginative recall demanded by art (in Johnson's opinion) is that which serves to lead one to general truth.[6] (3) Dr. Johnson is in regard to Shakespeare, as with regard to all literature, moralistic in his approach. Shakespeare is, he believes, a great moral teacher; but only by accident, not by effort. In general it may be confessed Johnson had an extensive conception of Shakespeare's defects--he is always a judicial

[6] Arthur Friedman and W. K. Wimsatt, Jr., in *PQ,* xxi (1942). 211-213; xxii (1943). 71-76.

critic, and must find fault—but he had a noble and manly sense of the excellences as well.

Johnson as Essayist

Apart from these works of scholarship Johnson had made a great reputation as a moral essayist before either the *Dictionary* or the edition of Shakespeare appeared.[7] "He who thinks reasonably must think morally," was with him a fundamental principle, and with him all art as well as philosophy was a guide to life. In 1748 he contributed to Dodsley's *Preceptor* an allegory called *The Vision of Theodore, the Hermit of Teneriffe*, which Johnson once said was "the best thing he ever wrote." It couples allegory with moral precept, and has interest as an early expression of Johnson's fear of habit as deadening the sincerity of religious devotion. It was inevitable that presently Johnson should try his hand at a periodical essay; and his *Rambler* (208 numbers, 1750-52) is, after *The Tatler* and *The Spectator*, the most respected effort in this form, and it did much to make his early reputation.[8] In the years 1758-60 he contributed to a newspaper, *The Universal Chronicle*, a series of nearly a hundred essays called *The Idler*, which were fully as amusing as but less meaningful than *The Rambler* had been. He contributed also essays in *The Adventurer* (1753-4), and wrote book-reviews and articles for various magazines at this period.

As a Moralist: Rasselas

The best piece of moral writing by Johnson is found in his *History of Rasselas, Prince of Abissinia*. This was an Oriental apologue related to the sort of thing he had occasionally done in *The Rambler* but nearer to his heart and more significant. It was rapidly written in January, 1759, and hastily published in April to defray the funeral expenses of his mother. It is his most appealing presentation of his ideas on the vanity of human wishes, on the impossibility of complete happiness in the imperfect human lot. Animals can eat, sleep, and be content; man who is both animal and immortal is torn by desires that this world cannot satisfy; for him a "stagnant mind" is brutal, a restless mind inevitable—and unhappy. It is interesting to see Johnson, who hated deism, here writing a book that is almost as despondent as the freethinker Voltaire's *Candide*, which was published probably in February, 1759, but did not reach England until after *Rasselas* appeared. Voltaire is content to scoff at the optimism of Leibniz and Pope, which (he mistakenly believes) denies the existence of evil. Johnson is not so much concerned in *Rasselas* with "the system of things," or with universal harmony, as he is with the imperfect ability of man to adjust himself to practical life. The two works are only superficially parallel. As a devout, though despondent, Christian Johnson might have saved the case for cheerfulness by introducing the popular orthodox idea of rewards and punishments in a future state; but this he refrains from doing. The "fable" is highly episodic; but the episodes are admirably pointed and are used to expose the vanity of many ideas current in his day apart from rationalistic optimism: he pays his respects to pastoral life, to the hermit's solitary flight from

[7] O. F. Christie, *Johnson the Essayist* (1924).
[8] On *The Rambler* see below, ch. VII.

temptation, to monastic life, to Stoic pride, to the life according to nature, and to many another recipe for happiness. His "Orientalism" like that of most Oriental tales is purely a device for effacing any bias of locality and reducing life to a sort of biblical universality.[9] The action is seldom vivid, though there are many moments that might have been dramatic. The escape from the Happy Valley is unexciting, and the ultimate return from the region of Cairo to Abyssinia—where, as Imlac had foretold, they would find themselves unknown and unregarded—is left equivocal as between the futility of their search for happiness and the aimlessness of a nondescript wandering existence. The author's reflections whether implicit or explicit are the important matter. He is sincerely and profoundly realistic about happiness, and here more than in his other prose he suffuses his reflections with emotional power.

After getting his pension in 1762 Johnson tended to write less than before. Two major works, however, appeared after that date. His *Journey to the Western Islands* (1775) is an account of a long-projected tour with Boswell, finally made in 1773 when Johnson was sixty-four years old. The journey was not merely primitive; it was at times positively dangerous. In a letter to Mrs. Thrale Johnson wrote:

Journey to the Western Islands

> You remember the Doge of Genoa, who being asked what struck him most at the French court, answered, 'Myself.' I cannot think many things here more likely to affect the fancy than to see Johnson ending his sixty-fourth year in the wilderness of the Hebrides.

His book is shaded by Boswell's *Tour of the Hebrides* (1785), which excels precisely because Boswell can feature the picturesqueness of Johnson as well as of the Hebrides. He can show us Johnson sleeping in barns with no bed except hay or Johnson dragging his feet all day astride an undersized pony guided only by a halter—and longing "to be back in a land of saddles and bridles." Johnson, however, shows an interesting eye for detail and, as one would expect, rises to nobility in his moral reflections. His historical reverence for Iona leads him to express the moral stimulus of all history:

> Whatever withdraws us from the power of our senses; whatever makes the past, the distant, or the future predominate over the present, advances us in the dignity of thinking beings. Far from me and from my friends, be such frigid philosophy as may conduct us indifferent and unmoved over any ground which has been dignified by wisdom, bravery, or virtue. That man is little to be envied, whose patriotism would not gain force upon the plain of *Marathon,* or whose piety would not grow warmer among the ruins of *Iona!*

The net result of the journey was to confirm Johnson in his opinion that Macpherson's Ossian was a fraud and that primitive life and institutions were loathsome. He had experienced "simplicity" and found it "a native of the rocks." He made some attempt to control his anti-Scottish prejudices,

[9] Geoffrey Tillotson, "*Rasselas* and the *Persian Tales*," *Essays in Criticism and Research* (1942), pp. 111-116.

Lives of the English Poets

but witticism would break through, and his caustic passages probably helped the sale of the book and temporarily increased its vogue.

His last work, the series of prefatory *Lives of the English Poets* (1779-81), has survived as easily his best. Begun in his sixty-eighth year and completed in his seventy-second, these fifty-two lives in their vigor and keenness would have been a major achievement for any author, young or old. The booksellers who employed Johnson decided that the series should begin with Cowley; Johnson suggested a few modifications of their list of authors, but in general followed their choice. Many of the briefer lives are obviously perfunctory, but Johnson was devoted to both poetry and "the biographical part of literature"—which, as he told Boswell, "is what I love most"; and his *Lives* are in general written *con amore*.[10] He had had earlier experience in writing lives for *The Gentleman's Magazine*, and his *Life of Savage* was a small masterpiece. In literature Johnson valued "what comes near to ourselves, what we can turn to use," and he found that in biography. He had a sense of both the uniformity and the diversity of mankind, and advocated the presentation of minute biographical facts. The enforced brevity of his own *Lives*, however, precluded the use of much minute detail. The *Lives* excel not so much for their intimacy as for their solid judgment and their terse, finished phrasing. They abound also in authoritative enunciations of general wisdom, such as (concerning education), "We are perpetually moralists, but we are geometricians only by chance."

Johnson regarded as most important the authors of the Restoration and the Queen Anne periods—Dryden, Pope, Swift, and Addison. These men gave scope to his moralistic approach to literature, and their works were based on the principles of "general nature" that he valued. He is illuminating in his understanding both of these men as men and of their works—though by no means blind to some of their limitations. But to many poets he was less sympathetic.[11] To Cowley and especially to Milton among his earlier poets, he was unfair, though he himself preferred his *Life of Cowley* to all the rest "on account of the dissertation it contains on the Metaphysical Poets." This dissertation is indeed a brilliant and justly famous passage, still the classic verdict on the metaphysicals. Among the later poets he was not altogether kind in his estimates of certain contemporaries, notably Gray, Lyttelton, Shenstone, and even Collins, though for Collins he had a strong personal affection. His worst case of critical blindness is Milton, for whom he had a dislike grounded on religious and political issues which carried over to the poet's language and versification. Yet it must be remembered that the *Life of Milton* is full of mixed praise and blame, and that the compliments are so noble that Milton might well have retorted, as a man of less merit did, to Johnson's two-edged praise and blame, "Nay, Sir, Alexander the Great, marching in triumph into Babylon, could not have desired to have had more said to him." It would be difficult to determine

[10] Bergen Evans, "Dr. Johnson's Theory of Biography," *RES*, x (1934). 301-310.
[11] Meyer H. Abrams, "Unconscious Expectations in the Reading of Poetry," *ELH*, ix (1942). 235-245.

whether the greatest excellence of these *Lives* lies in Johnson's fine understanding of human nature manifested as poetical genius or in his vigorous
and sensible criticism of individual poems. His comprehension of the mixed
characters of men like Savage, Swift, Pope, and Addison shows masterful
insight, kindliness, and tolerance; his views of the poetry surveyed are
normally judicious and beautifully articulated. The romantics found easy
grounds for discounting Johnson's taste, but at this distance it seems inevitable that any man's taste may be invigorated by spending his days and nights
on *The Lives of the English Poets.*

Even before he secured leisure through his pension, Johnson was well *The Club*
advanced in reputation from his other career, that of conversationalist. He
met Boswell in 1763, and thereafter we naturally have more records of his
talk. In 1764 the Club was founded, and Johnson there had the best conversation in the kingdom. Sir Joshua Reynolds first proposed the Club, and
the original members included Reynolds, Johnson, Burke, Goldsmith, and
lesser friends in their circle. "They met," Boswell tells us, "at the Turk's
Head in Gerrard-street, Soho, one evening in every week at seven, and
generally continued their conversation till a pretty late hour." Other than
charter members, in Johnson's day, were Bishop Percy, Garrick, Joseph and
Thomas Warton, Fox, Gibbon, and Adam Smith. In 1773 Boswell himself
was elected. One sees at a glance that Johnson enjoyed the company of the
most interesting men of his time. He was in a sense driven to club life and
eating abroad because of conditions at home. His wife had died in 1752, and
he gradually surrounded himself with a strange assortment of dependents
whom he received in charity but who behaved at times without that quality.
Apparently at home he could be sure of neither good-natured conversation
nor well-prepared food: hence in the years before the wealthy Thrales
rescued him (1765), club life was important.

Conversation was Johnson's greatest pleasure, and it was also a necessary *Conversa-*
anodyne. All his adult life he suffered from melancholia, at times to the *tion and its*
very point of insanity. Increasingly he hated to be alone; talk was medicinal *Functions*
to his mind. It was also a positive delight and an art conscientiously and
joyously cultivated. With his temperament conversation was bound to be
mercurial. Like the sluggish bear, whose external traits he seemed to have,
he required prodding into activity; and the resulting talk might at times be
"mad and violent" and at times hilarious and triumphant. "Well," he said
to Boswell on one classic occasion, "we had good talk." "Yes, Sir," came the
reply, "you tossed and gored several persons." Such was often the drama of
his talk, but what he said made sense, and it was said with deliberate impressiveness, with wit, and with definitive finality. The idiom of his phrasing
was picturesque and perfectly individual. According to Malone, he was "as
correct and elegant in his common conversation as in his writings." He
complimented his hearers by talking above them, and they only listened the
more attentively. In general, he "laid it down as a fixed rule to do his best

on every occasion and in every company; to impart whatever he knew in the most forcible language he could put it in." There was little doubt of his force: as Goldsmith complained, "When his pistol misses fire, he knocks you down with the butt end of it." He was essentially kind but not sensitively polite. In view of the Boswellian record it is surprising that Malone could say, "I have been often in his company, and never *once* heard him say a severe thing to anyone; and many others can attest the same." One must assume that these friends meant that he never used undeserved severity.

Boswell concludes his *Life of Johnson* with the opinion that in conversation Johnson was essentially a virtuoso, who in a group delighted in showing his dexterity even to the extent of making sophistry acceptable. But talking more privately, or on topics concerning which he had settled convictions, he was genuinely and constantly sincere. He admitted that he often "talked for victory," and Boswell's recordings of Johnson's voice are so perfect that readers of Boswell are easily led to regard Johnson's conversation as a "performance" and to forget that the talk had a mind behind it. To do this is to be unfair to the intellectual quality of the Doctor, though it is true that he talked and at times wrote rashly and that his mental processes were not always logically consistent. Boswell expresses this mental self-contradiction admirably:

His mind resembled the vast amphitheatre, the Colisæum at Rome. In the centre stood his judgement, which, like a mighty gladiator, combated those apprehensions that, like the wild beasts of the *Arena,* were all around in cells, ready to be let out upon him. After a conflict, he drove them back into their dens; but not killing them, they were still assailing him. To my question, whether we might not fortify our minds for the approach of death, he answered, in a passion, 'No, Sir, let it alone. It matters not how a man dies, but how he lives. The act of dying is not of importance, it lasts so short a time.' He added, (with an earnest look,) 'A man knows it must be so, and submits. It will do him no good to whine.'

This is a picture of a mind with judgment and emotions perpetually in unstable equilibrium, a mind capable of gladiatorial combat or of furious refusal to fight.

Johnson on Religion   Johnson's best topics—whether in conversation or in print—were religion, politics, and literature. In matters of religion his mind worked with intense feeling.[12] "Religion appears, in every state of life," he thinks, "to be the basis of happiness, and the operating power which makes every good institution valid and efficacious." In his *Vision of Theodore* and in *Idler* No. 41 he insists again that religion is the only source of whatever happiness we have. Yet his written *Prayers* and Boswell's record indicate that his own religion lacked joyfulness. He approved Hugh Blair's sermon on Devotion, but objected to Blair's "rash" assertion that "he who does not feel joy in religion is far from the kingdom of heaven." Johnson's fear of the Deity

[12] William H. Hutton, "The Religion of Dr. Johnson," *Burford Papers* (1905), pp. 277-281; Stuart G. Brown, "Dr. Johnson and the Religious Problem," *English Studies,* xx (1938). 1-17, 67; W. T. Cairns, *The Religion of Dr. Johnson and Other Studies* (1946).

outweighed his love. Much of his religious longing was "the pursuit of perfect peace," which seemed to him "the great, the necessary, the inevitable, business of human life." This passion for a divine equilibrium is frustrated by the necessity of hope, which destroys poise. "Where there is no hope, there can be no endeavour"; and endeavor is the essence of moral and religious life. Johnson believed in the necessity of regularity in both public and private devotions, and suffered greatly over his negligences or even his tardinesses in worship.

The second half of the eighteenth century was a period wearied by the theological acrimony of the preceding century and deficient in creative theology of its own. Johnson recognized and condemned its "prevailing spirit" as one of "skepticism and captiousness, of suspicion and distrust, a contempt of all authority, and a presumptuous confidence in private judgment; a dislike of all established forms, merely because they are established, and of old paths, because they are old." He himself held that "the Bible tells us in plain and authoritative terms, that there is a way to life and a way to death." Essentials were clear and not to be questioned; he had no tolerance for "private judgment" in essentials. In theory he had little tolerance for any heterodoxy. His primitive conclusion was, "Every man has a right to utter what he thinks truth, and every other man has a right to knock him down for it. Martyrdom is the test." But in practice he could be more civilized, and could, in trying days, speak with moderation of either Catholics or Methodists. He much enjoyed the conversation of his overbusy friend and fellow high-churchman, John Wesley. The two had in common a spiritual intensity that showed itself most diversely. Johnson was possibly too conscious that his own sin was idleness. Perhaps (in view of his chronic fear of death) the most touching of his prayers is the "Ejaculation Imploring Diligence": "O God, make me to remember that *the night cometh when no man can work.*"

Religion, to repeat, is "the operating power which makes every good institution valid and efficacious." Johnson has no use for primitive society, Stoic poise, or (above all) for a cloistered retreat from temptation. Man's place is in society, and in a society based on Christian submission to the fundamental principle of subordination. "Order," he held, "cannot be had but by subordination." He also scorned equality as a political principle. "There may be community," he remarks through Imlac, "of material possessions, but there can never be community of love or of esteem. It must happen that one will please more than another." Unscrupulous demagogues talked of "natural equality, the absurdity of 'many made for one,' the original compact, the foundation of authority, and the majesty of the people," and Johnson regretted their ascendency. He felt that the chain of subordination was being relaxed, but solaced himself with the notion as to the English lower classes "that their insolence in peace is bravery in war." Of the cant of his day about liberty he was contemptuous. "All boys," he said, "love liberty, till experience convinces them they are not so fit to govern themselves as they

Johnson on Subordination

imagined. We are all agreed as to our own liberty; we would have as much of it as we can get; but we are not agreed as to the liberty of others." Similar opinions are found throughout Johnson's writings.

In practical politics he was again conservative. He was reared as a Tory and a Jacobite; but by the time of George III he had concluded that long establishment of the Hanoverian family justified their claim to the throne. In his early London years he had written mildly against Walpole in his

*His
Toryism*

Marmor Norfolciense (1739), for example; but his chief political attitudes developed later, and concerned colonial possessions and the constitutional crisis in Parliament. Johnson was a violent anti-imperialist. In his *Observations of the State of Affairs in 1756* he condemns war with the French over boundaries in America on the ground that neither the French nor the English have any just title since both were robbers of the Indians. This basic injustice to the aborigines will, he thinks, make America "a perpetual ground of contest." In his *Political State of Great Britain* he disparages the motives of colonists, men either disaffected or bankrupt, who, loving adventure and enterprise, settled in "Canada, a cold, uncomfortable, uninviting region, from which nothing but furs and fish were to be had, and where the new inhabitants could only pass a laborious and necessitous life, in perpetual regret of the deliciousness and plenty of their native country." In his later outbursts about colonies he showed a prudential legalistic attitude rather than any economic awareness of the advantage of imperial outposts. He castigated the "howling violence of patriotick rage" over the Falkland Islands, which had "exasperated to such madness, that, for a barren rock under a stormy sky, we might have now been fighting and dying, had not our competitors been wiser than ourselves." For the most part he was sure the Islands would be but "a station for contraband traders, a nursery of fraud, and a receptacle of theft." In view of such opinions it is not surprising that when thirteen American colonies proved "disloyal" he poured forth scorn on the passion of the hypocritical "slave-drivers" for liberty. He had some awareness of the constitutional inconsistencies of the colonists but little comprehension of their economic grievances. He did not "take to" his fellow club-member, Adam Smith, and like Burke might on occasion couple economists with "sophisters."

At home he attacked vehemently rabble-rousers like John Wilkes. His *False Alarm* (1770) defended Parliament for refusing to seat Wilkes on the ground that a man convicted of "sedition and impiety" should not serve as "one of the guardians and counsellors of the church and state." In *The Patriot* (1774), written to aid his friend Thrale get elected to Parliament, he delivers his best blows at "false" patriotism and defends admirably the toleration of Catholicism in Quebec—six years before the Gordon Riots. In his earlier pamphlet on Falkland's Islands (1771) he had paid his respects to the ablest of the rabble-rousers, the mysterious Junius. It is perhaps Junius's "blaze of impudence" that appealed to Johnson, who condemned his morals but not his faculties:

It is not by his liveliness of imagery, his pungency of periods, or his fertility of allusion, that he detains the cits of London, and the boors of Middlesex. Of style and sentiment they take no cognizance. They admire him, for virtues like their own, for contempt of order, and violence of outrage; for rage of defamation, and audacity of falsehood. The supporters of the bill of rights feel no niceties of composition, nor dexterities of sophistry; their faculties are better proportioned to the bawl of Bellas, or barbarity of Beckford; but they are told, that Junius is on their side, and they are, therefore, sure that Junius is infallible. Those who know not whither he would lead them, resolve to follow him; and those who cannot find his meaning, hope he means rebellion.

There is more than alliterative pomposity in this passage. Johnson could not stem the rising tide of democracy, and that he wished to do so was doubtless due to his keen perception of the imperfections of democratic procedure as of 1771. He turned shuddering from such corruptions to fly, like Goldsmith, from lesser tyrants to the impartial protective authority of the throne. He was blindly conservative, and in politics he had an unfortunate knack of starting from sound principles and ending in conclusions quite mistaken.

Johnson as a Literary Critic This knack betrayed him in the field where he was most at home—literary criticism. His blindness and prejudice in respect to Milton, his neglect of the Elizabethans [13] (except Shakespeare), and his dislike of contemporaries have cost him reputation as a critic. He is often outrageously wrong but seldom corruptingly wrong: his errors are gross, open, and palpable. His strength lies in his directness and clarity of insight, in his defined and articulate thinking, in his typically eighteenth-century insistence that life is the best commentary on art. "Books," he quotes Bacon as saying, "can never teach the use of books." And he adds: "The student must learn to reduce his speculations to practice, and accommodate his knowledge to the purposes of life." The function of criticism was "to form a just estimate" of a work. The critic-judge must understand the case before him and the principles, rules, or laws applicable to it. Principles or rules are essential but relative: they are "the instruments of mental vision, which may indeed assist our faculties when properly used, but produce confusion and obscurity by unskilful application." Principles were an aid to perception, but no substitute for it. More than once he speaks of "the cant of those who judge by principles rather than perception." The real enemies of just criticism, however, were in his opinion not the rules so much as "the anarchy of ignorance, the caprices of fancy, and the tyranny of prescription." One can recognize in these enumerated faults the errors of Johnson himself as well as of all critics.

His Conception of Poetry His conception of the nature and function of poetry is of his age. Its end is "to instruct by pleasing." It is the work of genius, and genius is "that power which constitutes a poet; that quality without which judgment is cold and knowledge is inert; that energy which collects, combines, amplifies, and animates." Genius includes invention, imagination, and judgment, and Johnson while affirming that "no man ever yet became great by imitation"

[13] Dr. Johnson read them at least! See Walter B. C. Watkins, *Johnson and English Poetry before 1660* (Princeton, 1936).

of his predecessors merely, believes that genius must be trained by study. In *Adventurer* No. 85 he eloquently denounces a recent statement of an author who had "been able to learn nothing from the writings of his predecessors." "The highest praise of genius is original invention," he says elsewhere; but he makes imagination merely a recombining, not a creative, faculty. It is not reasonable, however, to cite such *loci* as chapter XLIII of *Rasselas* on "The Dangerous Prevalence of Imagination" (frequently only this title is cited) as showing that Johnson distrusted poetical imagination. In practical or philosophical matters it is to be distrusted when it prevails over reason and becomes insanity or practical delusion—as in the chapter cited.[14] To Johnson imagination in poetry is a vivifying and delightful faculty: it objectifies truth, recombines experience, "and produces novelty only by varied combinations." Finally, we should recall the noble passage in *Rasselas,* chapter x, where it is said that the poet "must write as the interpreter of nature, and the legislator of mankind, and consider himself as presiding over the thoughts and manners of future generations; as a being superiour to time and place." Johnson has no truck with such notions as the unhappy bit of insincerity expressed by the youthful Alexander Pope in his first preface about "poetry and criticism being by no means the universal concern of the world, but only the affair of idle men who write in their closets, and of idle men who read there." After religion and morality poetry was to Johnson the most important thing in the world. It was, in fact, the attendant and indispensable servant of both religion and morality. It is consequently not strange that he should show prejudice towards the writing of the anti-episcopal republican, John Milton, or against the metaphysicals whose calculated playfulness of wit failed, in his opinion, to achieve either the pathetic or the sublime. His prejudices were strong; but his values—sense, morality, power, novelty, and durability—are manly, sound, and usually judiciously applied.

On Poetic Diction   Johnson is especially competent and interesting as a critic of diction. He is a purist, and that fact makes him condemn the artificial re-creation of Latinate idiom that Milton used in *Paradise Lost*. Dryden forced language to the very "brink of meaning" and loved to "hover over the abyss of unideal vacancy." In diction Pope is preferred to Dryden. With regard to Gray's diction probably prejudice again operated, though one may well recall that Wordsworth as well as Johnson objected to Gray's artificiality or inexactness. Johnson had a real if clouded interest in poetic diction, and might have made history if he could have paused in his preoccupation with morality long enough to have thought through his theories as to the language proper for poetry.

[14] Irving Babbitt's "Dr. Johnson and Imagination," *Southwest Rev.*, XIII (1927). 25-35, should be read only as preliminary to F. B. Kaye's trenchant comment on it in *PQ*, VII (1928). 178; Raymond D. Havens, "Johnson's Distrust of the Imagination," *ELH*, x (1943). 243-255; Stuart G. Brown, "Dr. Johnson, Poetry, and Imagination," *Neophilologus*, XXIII (1938). 203-207; W. B. C. Watkins, "Dangerous Prevalence of the Imagination," *Perilous Balance* (Princeton, 1939), pp. 71-98.

His own prose style is perhaps the greatest of his achievements.[15] It con- *His Prose*
stantly and aptly expresses the essential directness of his mind. A typical bit *Style*
of his idiom is his characterization of Otway's bottle companions: "Their
fondness was without benevolence, and their familiarity without friendship."
This has significant balance, conscious structure and rhythm; it has pithiness
(the phrasal components of his sentences are normally brief); and it has
exquisite precision in its choice of abstract nouns. It also has an illusion of
Latinity. By habit he writes in abstract terms, and such terms tend to seem
Latin even when they are not. His fondness for polysyllables produced the
heaviness of style that has unjustly been called Johnsonese. The same tendency is visible in Congreve's plays, in Thomson's blank verse, and in Walter
Scott's novels, in all of which it is less appropriate than in Johnson's more
abstract disquisitions. His choice of words is at least correct, and both his
example and his *Dictionary* begot correctness in others. Arrangement of
clauses consciously in parallel or balanced patterns is also typical of his prose.
He almost never uses parenthetical clauses, but builds short members into
complex but easily grasped sentences. An unusual proportion of his sentences
are periodic in structure: he forms subjects from infinitives or "that" clauses,
which are then elaborated and finally concluded by a brief, forceful predicate.
Objective "that" clauses are piled up. His lives of Roscommon and Pitt each
have a sentence ending with a series of five such clauses, and the concluding
sentence of the life of Cowley has six. A more famous example of balanced
elaboration comes in the well-known letter to Chesterfield:

> The notice which you have been pleased to take of my labors
>   had it been early,   had been kind;
> but it has been delayed
>   till I am indifferent,   and cannot enjoy it;
>   till I am solitary,   and cannot impart it;
>   till I am known,   and do not want it.

Johnson's position in the history of eighteenth-century prose is individual
and influential. Among the stylists of his day Hume, Gibbon, Burke, and
Johnson himself are eminent for care, vigor, and elegance of expression. All
four are notable practitioners of the grand or formal style. They mark a
general revulsion against the easy, fluent, unobtrusive style which Addison
had made perfect, and which his followers had made commonplace. To that
style Johnson pays high tribute in his *Life of Addison,* and of William
Whitehead's opposite style he expresses the immortal opinion that "grand
nonsense is insupportable." Yet his own manner is definitely of the formal
or noble sort. It varies with the subject, but it is always dignified and never,
for long at least, colloquial. He was doubtless consciously avoiding the errors

---

15 W. V. Reynolds, "Johnson's Opinions on Prose Style," *RES,* ix (1933). 433-446, and
"The Reception of Johnson's Prose Style," *RES,* xi (1935). 145-162; William K. Wimsatt,
Jr., *The Prose Style of Samuel Johnson* (New Haven, 1941); Morley J. Mays, "Johnson and
Blair on Addison's Prose Style," *SP,* xxxix (1942). 638-649.

of his predecessors; his clauses are of Attic brevity; his arrangement of clauses might be Ciceronian, but he economizes on connective words—omitting conjunctions with increasing frequency as he grows older—and he substitutes for the Ciceronian suavity a vigorous directness. His sentences have a more apparent structural unity than those of his seventeenth-century masters. In severity of design they are true Palladian; they lack any Corinthian or baroque ornateness. With the other great stylists of his day Johnson signalizes a moment of architectural formality and correctness that had been preceded by the easy journalistic prose of the early periodical essayists or by the rather facile Ciceronianism of Shaftesbury or Bolingbroke. It was followed in the early nineteenth century by the intimate and charming but highly careless prose of the romantic essayists. No writer in the eighteenth century achieved a style at once so nobly dignified and so individual as Samuel Johnson.

IV

Mid-Century Poets

Dodsley's Collection

The taste of readers of poetry in the mid-century is revealed by Dodsley's *Collection of Poems, by Several Hands,* which first appeared in three duodecimo volumes in 1748. Robert Dodsley,[1] the footman poet, who by the middle of the century had become a fashionable bookseller and the leading publisher of English poetry, was so successful with this *Collection* that by 1758 it had grown to six volumes, and between 1748 and 1782 it was reprinted eleven times. It was in these volumes largely that people of the day read their "contemporary" poetry. The authors included Dodsley's friends, especially those for whom he was publisher, and other poets who were pleased to be included. One or two, like Robert Nugent (1702-88) and George, Lord Lyttelton, were there perhaps less as poets than as men of fashion and of influence in the world of letters.[2] Shenstone and Akenside got generous recognition because they were Dodsley authors; Collins, Gray, and others were doubtless there because they were eminent in public esteem. Poets such as Beattie or Chatterton, considered in this chapter along with these Dodsley protégés, emerged just too late to be included in the *Collection.*[3]

[1] Robert Dodsley (1703-1764), though more important as an editor and publisher than as a writer, began his career as a footman who turned poet just as Stephen Duck, the thresher poet, was acquiring fame. Of Dodsley's early poems *The Muse in Livery* (1732) and *An Epistle to Mr. Pope* (1734) won favorable attention. In the years 1735-58 he wrote a half-dozen theatrical pieces, of which *The Toy-Shop* (1735) and *The King and the Miller of Mansfield* (1737) were the most esteemed. In 1735 Pope set him up as a bookseller and publisher, and he published for Pope, Young, Laurence Sterne, and many others. In addition to his *Collection of Poems* he published *A Select Collection of Old Plays* (12v, 1744), perhaps his greatest service to literature, since the *Collection* served to keep in mind the lesser Elizabethans. With the aid of Edmund Burke he began to publish in 1759 his *Annual Register.* Some of his pieces were collected as *Trifles* (1745; 2v, 1777). See also Alex. Chalmers, *British Poets* (1810), Vol. xv.—Ralph Straus, *Robert Dodsley* (1910); William P. Courtney, *Dodsley's Collection of Poetry, Its Contents and Contributors* (1910), is superseded by R. W. Chapman, "Dodsley's *Collection of Poems,*" *Oxford Bibl. Soc.,* iii, iii (1933). 269-316.

[2] George Lyttelton (1709-1773), however, was fully represented in the *Collection* by no less than thirty-three poems—all of his significant verse. His early epistles and songs seem now perfectly conventional. His *Monody* (1747) written in memory of his first wife was one of the most discussed irregular odes of the mid-century. Lyttelton, for a time secretary to the Prince of Wales, was an essayist as well as a poet. He turns up in literary circles as the friend of Pope, Thomson, and Fielding, the object of attack by Smollett, and in other connections. He is, as Gray called him in a letter to Horace Walpole reviewing Dodsley's *Collection,* "a gentle elegiac person"—as were too many writers of verse in his day. See Sydney C. Roberts, *An Eighteenth-Century Gentleman* (Cambridge, 1930); Ananda V. Rao, *A Minor Augustan* (Calcutta, 1934); and Rose M. Davis, *The Good Lord Lyttelton* (Bethlehem, Pa., 1939).

[3] For further accounts of the poetry here treated see William Minto, *The Literature of the Georgian Era* (1895), ch. VII; John H. Millar, *The Mid-Eighteenth Century* (1902), ch. v; William J. Courthope, *A History of English Poetry,* Vol. v (1905), esp. ch. XII; *CHEL,* Vol. x, ch. VI, VII, and x; Thomas Seccombe, *The Age of Johnson* (1899), ch. x; Oliver Elton, *A Survey of English Literature, 1730-1780* (2v, 1928), ch. XIII, XIV, XV. Inferior texts of these poets can

More illuminating historically if one is not obsessed with the idea that poetry was steadily tending towards romanticism, the *Collection* reveals no marked sense of cleavage with the past. After all, Dodsley owed his start in life both as poet and as publisher to Pope's kindness, and he was hence likely to admire Pope's work. He was not permitted to include much of it in his *Collection,* but the influence of Pope is pervasive. There are Mason's *Musaeus* and a half-dozen other poems chiefly concerned with Pope, and still others mention him with high respect. From the early century are reprinted poems by William King (1663-1712), Abel Evans, Dr. Arbuthnot, Lord Bolingbroke, William Harrison, and Thomas Tickell. With these appear the leading poets of the mid-century: Akenside, Collins, William Whitehead (the laureate), the Wartons, Shenstone, Mason, and Gray. There is nothing from Edward Young. Thomson is represented by three short poems, among which is his admirable *Hymn on Solitude.* The Thomson influence, however, is apparent neither in extended description of landscape nor in the use of his type of blank verse.

Its Typical Subject Matter

The tone and subject matter are seldom novel: there is much moralizing, if not so much satire; there are epistles, though these tend to be less formal than those of Horace and Pope; there are sedate elegies, but not much compelling grief; there is little landscape, but much "rural elegance"; there are poems of humble life, which tend to be realistic and jocose rather than idyllic. The many songs are likely to be neatly turned and witty—almost as witty as the numerous epigrams. Most of the poems could in 1750 easily be classed according to one or another tradition then well recognized. Possibly Roman-French devices decline in favor of native English or classic Greek forms. There is much prettiness, sweetness, and softness; there is relatively little robustness save in the attempts after sublimity and in the moralizing couplet poems (Dr. Johnson's three most important poems are here) and in the poems of rural life that remotely resemble the fabliau. Still we find chiefly "poems on occasions," and the occasions are public and the poetic manner is usually rhetorically effective rather than intimate or private.

Its Metrical Habits

In general the metres used are what we should expect. Of the poems that run to over twenty pages in length, eleven are in the heroic couplet; four in the Spenserian stanza, and two in blank verse, at least in part. Most of the blank-verse poems are short and tend to a simpler, less sublime idiom than that of *The Seasons* or *Paradise Lost.* The rimed poems, especially those in tetrameter couplets, abound in phrasal echoes of Milton's shorter poems. There are dozens of odes, which range from the Horatian to the Cowleyan, to the "true" Pindaric, and to poems in non-classical stanza forms. The Cowleyan odes here are likely to be called "irregular." The other most popular metres are the tetrameter couplet (used for fables and for light as well as pensive effects), the various standard quatrains, and six-line stanzas of varying structure.

---

be found in *The Works of the British Poets,* ed. Robert Anderson (13v, 1792-5) and in *The Works of the English Poets from Chaucer to Cowper,* ed. Alexander Chalmers (21v, 1810). These collections in other notes for this chapter will be cited as Anderson or Chalmers.

By the middle of the century, then, if one may judge from Dodsley's *Collection,* the divergence from traditional metres and materials is not marked. What is notable is that one or two real geniuses appear in Dodsley, who have either new subjects to treat or new voices with which to speak. High among these would surely be William Collins (1721-1759) and *William* Thomas Gray. Collins,[4] naturally, does not occupy many pages, for his total *Collins* poetic output was a scant score of poems; but he is represented here by five poems somewhat strangely chosen. His *Epistle Addresst to Sir Thomas Hanmer* is his longest poem included, and it, in spite of its common neglect by romantic critics, is a striking poem to come from a university undergraduate. It is not typical Collins, however. His other poems used by Dodsley are the elegiac *Ode to a Lady on the Death of Colonel Ross,* the small but perfect *Ode Written in the Beginning of the Year 1746,* the *Ode to Evening,* and the early *Song from Shakespeare's Cymbeline.* Probably all of Collins's poems were available to Dodsley, and it is perhaps significant that he neglected to use the more complex odes. The two longer poems used had an obvious topical appeal through their connections with Hanmer and Colonel Ross. The three shorter poems are certainly among Collins's best so far as delicacy of feeling, clarity, and structure are concerned. The first of these qualities Collins evinces in all his poems; the other two he less often achieves.

His first published poem appeared in 1739 when he was still a boy in *The Brevity* Winchester College, and his last written ode, *On the Popular Superstitions* *of His* *of the Highlands of Scotland,* was at least sketched in 1749. A career of a *Career* decade, terminating before Collins was thirty years old, and productive of only about a score of poems, cannot be expected to show much development, or great range and diversity. We can now see more easily than could Dodsley or Dr. Johnson the quality of Collins's art, because his methods embody a type of romanticism with which poetry since 1800 has been more or less familiar. Although it is untrue that Collins was in his own century neglected, it is probable that he was not completely and sympathetically understood.

Among his immediately popular poems were his youthful *Persian* *His Man-* *Eclogues,* which had, as he himself saw, a merely conventional prettiness *nerisms* and grace under the thinnest of "Persian" veneers. His later poems frequently offer what seems like a quite new poetic idiom. The aphoristic didacticism, the chiseled phrases of Dryden and Pope are absent—though more than once his phrases are based on those of Dryden or Pope. His style

---

[4] Collins's *Poems* are found in Anderson, Vol. IX and in Chalmers, Vol. XIII. The best modern eds. are those by Walter C. Bronson (Boston, 1898), Christopher Stone (1907, rev. 1917, rev. 1937), and Edmund Blunden (1929). Bibliographies are available in Bronson's edition and in Iolo A. Williams's *Seven XVIIIth Century Bibliographies* (1924). See Samuel Johnson, *Lives of the English Poets* (1781); ed. George Birkbeck Hill (Oxford, 1905), III. 334-342; John W. Mackail, "Collins and the English Lyric," *Trans. Royal Soc. of Lit.* (1921), reprinted in *Studies of English Poets* (1926), pp. 135-156; John Middleton Murry, "William Collins," *Countries of the Mind* (1922), pp. 81-99; H. O. White, "The Letters of William Collins," *RES,* III (1927). 12-21; Alan D. McKillop, "The Romanticism of William Collins," *SP,* XX (1923). 1-16; Heathcote W. Garrod, *Collins* (1928); Edward G. Ainsworth, *Poor Collins* (Ithaca, N. Y., 1937); Arthur S. P. Woodhouse, "Collins and the Creative Imagination: A Study in the Critical Background of his Odes," *Studies in English by Members of University College, Toronto* (Toronto, 1931), pp. 59-130.

is exclamatory rather than reflective; it is full of emotional apostrophe: "Oh thou" or its equivalent can be found in almost every poem, and more than once. Next, one notes that, in his longer odes, freed from couplet-control, his sentences drift on until they become so involved or so lost among parentheses that doubtless even the poet himself could hardly untangle them. Smaller mannerisms are his love of personifications (which, were they not so frequently statuesque evocations in highly particular poses, would be strictly neo-classical) and his perpetuation of the seventeenth-century habit of suffixing the letter *y* to adjectives ("the folding-star's *paly* circlet," for example). More important and equally clear is it that Collins had the true poetic gift of myth-making, of bodying forth his impressions in phrases fused with delicate and individual imagination. This is done in fragmentary flashes, possibly because he lacked the gift of sustained imaginative constructions and possibly because he chose to work with sudden strokes. To line 82 of his *Ode to Liberty* he appends a footnote recounting a traditional mermaid story about the Isle of Man. Many a poet of his inclinations would have made a whole poem out of this story: Collins makes one line—and a line quite unintelligible without the footnote. It is this condensed, at times incoherent, imaginative fusion that sets Collins apart from the placid poets of his day.

The Poetical Character

Poetry to him—as he tells us in his *Ode on the Poetical Character*—is essentially imaginative; it is divine in origin, wild and impassioned in method and insight; and its approved exemplars are Shakespeare, Spenser, and, most of all, Milton. He disparages gently "Waller's myrtle shades," and obviously he is not of the Dryden-Pope tradition. The form affected in most of his poems is the ode, both in simple Horatian stanza and in the strict Pindaric or the monostrophic form. In spite of superficial appearances of irregularity Collins's odes are metrically well controlled except in *The Passions* and in the irregular (and unfinished) *Ode on the Popular Superstitions of the Highlands*.[5] In a sense he belongs to the line of ode-writers who, after Congreve, reacted against the irregularities popularized by Cowley. His unrimed *Ode to Evening* is not free verse but is a skilful classical imitation in metres used by Horace and Milton. All told, his appeal is to our love of dim, dreamlike effects; and if he does not warm us with poignant humanity, he delights by his ornate and curious fantasy.

Christopher Smart

The poetic idiom of Collins is fantastic but not really mad. That of Christopher Smart[6] (1722-1771), does at best actually approach the insane. Domi-

---

[5] Arthur S. P. Woodhouse, "Collins and Martin Martin," *LTLS*, Dec. 20, 1928 (concerns the sources of this Ode).

[6] *Poems* (omitting much, 2v, Reading, 1791); also in Anderson, Vol. xi and Chalmers, Vol. xvi. *A Song to David* (1763) has been edited by John R. Tutin (1898), Richard A. Streatfield (1901), Edmund Blunden (1924); Oxford facsimile reprint (1926); *Rejoice in the Lamb*, ed. William Force Stead (1939).—George J. Gray, *A Bibliography of the Writings of Smart*, in *Trans. Bibl. Soc.*, vi (1903); reprinted separately (1903).—Sir Edmund Gosse, "Smart's Poems," *Gossip in a Library* (1891), pp. 183-199; K. A. McKenzie, *Christopher Smart, sa vie et ses œuvres* (Paris, 1925); C. D. Abbott, "Christopher Smart's Madness," *PMLA*, xlv (1930). 1014-1022; F. T. Wood, "Christopher Smart," *ESt*, lxxi (1936). 191-213; Edward G. Ainsworth and Charles E. Noyes, *Christopher Smart, A Biographical and Critical Study* (Columbia, Mo., 1943).

ciled as student and fellow in Pembroke Hall, Cambridge, in the years 1740-49 (before Thomas Gray moved across from Peterhouse), this wildly convivial genius, who was about the most delightful alehouse companion in Cambridge, seemed to Gray in 1747 to be headed for a debtor's prison or for Bedlam. In the fashion of needy authors, he migrated to London; and although his early fame rested upon his pious blank-verse Seatonian Prize poems, his meager income in London was that of a periodical essayist, pamphleteer, wit, and satirist.

After years of avoiding the debtor's jail and after having been privately confined for a year as mentally unbalanced, Smart achieved the madhouse in 1757. His mania was largely religious: he was obsessed by the command to "pray without ceasing," and upon impulse would kneel in the traffic of busy streets. Probably he was liberated a few weeks before the publication in 1763 of his masterpiece, *A Song to David*. Although without contemporary favor, the poem has enjoyed belated repute since Browning's *Parleyings with Certain People* (1887) appeared. More than some admirers admit, the poem relates to eighteenth-century traditionalism, with obvious debts to *Paradise Lost, The Seasons,* the *Essay on Man,* the Boyle lectures, and Smart's own earlier blank-verse poems. Regard for the vast scale of being directs David's choice of themes and man's adoration. Despite its rambling structure, small groups of stanzas within it are beautifully and deftly interrelated. Verbal play—the shifting position, for example, of the repeated phrase *for adoration*—is quite in keeping with the eighteenth-century love of ingenious effects. But in sustained lyric intensity, in bold transitions from the homely to the sublime, in exotic imagery, and in its piercing, mystical piety, it is unique in the century. Although Smart's madness may not have been such as to prevent his writing the *Song* while confined, there is no evidence that it was written during his confinement for madness. But his *Rejoice in the Lamb, a Song from Bedlam* (Smart's own title was *Jubilate Agno*) was so composed. It lacks the form of the *Song to David,* but it is a rich document in imaginative madness, and may even be regarded as in some sense prophetic of Blake. The tradition of literary madness from the *Hurlothrumbo* (1729) of Samuel Johnson of Cheshire through Collins, Smart, and Cowper, to William Blake, is both amazing and alluring. In this tradition and in any tradition of religious lyricism, *A Song to David* is a glowing achievement. It appeared too late for use by Dodsley.

More typical of the normal lyric mood of the mid-century was the work *The Wartons* of Collins's friend Joseph Warton. Collins and Warton had talked of publishing their odes in a joint volume, but eventually (December, 1746) they published separately, and two years later some of their poems were found together in Dodsley's *Collection*. The Wartons, three of them, have been given perhaps an exaggerated rôle in the development of a romantic tradition. Thomas the father (*c.* 1688-1745), who was Professor of Poetry at Oxford in the years 1718-28, showed at least a slight primitivistic tendency in choosing to write *An American* [Indian] *Love-Ode* and *A Runic Ode*.

These, with other poems,[7] were edited by his elder son, Joseph, in 1748. In general the volume is Horatian and biblical in tone, with phrasal echoes also from the greater English poets; on the whole, it is a typical and not a very distinguished collection of early eighteenth-century verses. Warton's sons, Joseph and Thomas, are somewhat more clearly romantic at times, but they are far from being complete romanticists.

Joseph Warton   Joseph Warton (1722-1800) is a sort of focus of transitional tendencies.[8] We have already seen certain ambivalences in his criticism, and it may be again recalled that his reputed hostility to Pope was a source of grief to him. He always admired Pope, and in his old age edited Pope's *Works* (1797). In his own poems, however, Warton avoided didactic materials, and cultivated idyllic moods. Both he and his brother Thomas preferred rural to urban subjects. The preface to Thomas's *Five Pastoral Eclogues* (1745) shows this preference diffidently, and it is stressed in Joseph's *Enthusiast* (1744). In this last poem, however, the most primitivistic passages (lines 79 ff., 87 ff., 104 ff., and 119 ff.)[9] are quite in the Roman tradition, being based, as the first edition points out in footnotes not commonly reprinted, on Lucretius, Tibullus, and Horace. *The Enthusiast* combines other "romantic" traits with its borrowed primitivism,[10] such as the praise of idyllic simplicity, the preference of nature to art, the delight in objective natural beauty, the innocence of America, aesthetic irregularity, and sentimental melancholy in the vein of *Il Penseroso*. Its blank verse is quieter than that of Thomson and the followers of *Paradise Lost*. Quietness, placidity, are qualities that mark pleasingly most of Joseph's poems. His *Ode to Evening* as compared with that of Collins is relaxed, and is without imaginative perplexity.

Thomas Warton the Younger   The younger Thomas Warton (1728-1790), similarly, cultivates the relaxed mood of *Il Penseroso* in his *Pleasures of Melancholy* (1747).[11] But in more than one poem he preserves the neo-classical love of gayer, lighter verse; for example, in his *Panegyric on Oxford Ale,* which Dodsley placed in his *Collection*. In their odes as well as in their other poems the Wartons seek new materials, but they lack high imaginative gifts and intellectual strength; for the most part they fail to rise above the timid but graceful conventions

---

[7] *Poems on Several Occasions* (1748; reprinted by Facsimile Text Society, 1930).—D. H. Bishop, "The Father of the Wartons," *So. Atl. Quar.*, XVI (1917). 357-368; E. E. Willoughby, "The Chronology of the Poems of Thomas Warton, the Elder," *JEGP*, xxx (1931). 87-89; Leo Kirchbaum, "The Imitations of Thomas Warton the Elder," *PQ*, XXII (1943). 119-124; XXIV (1945), 89-90.

[8] In Chalmers, Vol. XVIII; for selections see also *The Three Wartons: a Choice of their Verse*, ed. Eric Partridge (1927).—John Wooll, *Biographical Memoirs* (1806); Hoyt Trowbridge, "Joseph Warton on the Imagination," *MP*, xxxv (1937). 73-87.

[9] In most later texts the passages in question begin with lines 87, 97, 115, 135.

[10] A. O. Lovejoy, in *PMLA*, xxxix (1924). 237-245, discusses incidentally the "romanticism" of *The Enthusiast*. See also Audley L. Smith, "The Primitivism of Joseph Warton," *MLN*, XLII (1927). 501-504.

[11] In Chalmers, Vol. XVIII. See also Eric Partridge, *The Three Wartons* (1927).—Clarissa Rinaker, *Thomas Warton, a Biographical and Critical Study* (Urbana, 1916); Raymond D. Havens, "Thomas Warton and the Eighteenth-Century Dilemma," *SP*, xxv (1928). 36-50; René Wellek, *The Rise of English Literary History* (Chapel Hill, 1941), esp. ch. VI, "Thomas Warton."

of their day. Thomas, to be sure, was one of the few writers of sonnets in his century, and he is to be remembered as a medievalist notable in his day and as the first historian of English poetry.

The last two volumes (1758) of Dodsley's *Collection* begin with fifty or   *Akenside* more pages of poems by William Shenstone and Dr. Mark Akenside,[12] respectively. Both had been Dodsley authors for years. Akenside (1721-1770) is represented in the *Collection* by typically dignified odes and "Inscriptions," full of naiads, dryads, nymphs, classical allusions, and frequent exhibitions of what Dr. Johnson termed "an unnecessary and outrageous zeal for what he called and thought liberty." These poems now have lost most of their charm. Some of the mythology is used gracefully:

> Tonight retired the queen of Heaven
> With young Endymion stays;

but most of it is perfunctory. Years before, Dodsley had printed Akenside's *Pleasures of Imagination* (1744), and for Dodsley during 1746-7 Akenside had supervised, and written for, a not uninteresting periodical called *The Museum.*

William Shenstone (1714-1763), represented in Dodsley's *Collection* by   *Shenstone* no less than forty-seven poems,[13] is chiefly known for his Spenserian imitation, *The Schoolmistress,* for his *Pastoral Ballad,* and for the concluding quatrain of his lines *Written at an Inn at Henley:*

> Whoe'er has travell'd life's dull round
> Where'er his stages may have been,
> May sigh to think he still has found
> The warmest welcome at an inn.

His prose essays contain interesting observations on literature, and his sprightly letters, addressed to a wide circle of literary friends, are still entertaining. His *ferme ornée,* Leasowes, was a miniature show place competing for attention with its magnificent neighbor, Hagley Park, residence of Lord Lyttelton, and, in spite of its somewhat cluttered prettiness, deserving a place alongside of Gothic Strawberry Hill in the newer modes of gardening already in vogue. Dr. Johnson's unkind remark that "the pleasure of Shen-

---

[12] *Poetical Works* in Anderson, Vol. ix; in Chalmers, Vol. xiv; also ed. Alexander Dyce, Aldine ed. (1835, 1894); R. A. Willmott (1855).—Johnson's *Lives* (ed. George Birkbeck Hill, Oxford, 1905), iii. 411-420; Iolo A. Williams, *Seven . . . Bibliographies* (1924), pp. 75-97; George R. Potter, "Mark Akenside, Prophet of Evolution," *MP,* xxiv (1926). 55-64; Howard S. Buck, "Smollett and Dr. Akenside," *JEGP,* xxxi (1932). 10-26; Alfred O. Aldridge, "The Eclecticism of Mark Akenside's "The Pleasures of Imagination'," *JHI,* v (1944). 292-314; Charles T. Houpt, *Mark Akenside: A Biographical and Critical Study* (Philadelphia, 1944).

[13] *Works* (2v, 1764; 3v, 1769); ed. George Gilfillan (Edinburgh, 1854); in Anderson, Vol. ix, and Chalmers, Vol. xiii; *Letters,* ed. Marjorie Williams (Oxford, 1939); and by Duncan Mallam (Minneapolis, 1939).—Iolo A. Williams, *Seven . . . Bibliographies* (1924), pp. 41-71.— Richard Graves, *Recollections of . . . the late William Shenstone, Esq.* (1788) and *Columella* (1779), a novel about Shenstone's life; Samuel Johnson, *Lives* (ed. George Birkbeck Hill), iii. 348-359; Marjorie Williams, *William Shenstone, a Chapter in Eighteenth-Century Taste* (Birmingham, 1935); Helen S. Hughes, "Shenstone and the Countess of Hertford," *PMLA,* xlvi (1931). 1113-1127; A. R. Humphreys, *William Shenstone* (Cambridge, 1937).

stone was all in his eye" implies a more serious deficiency of mind behind the eye. Shenstone's poems, like those of other minor bards of his day, are "rather the sport than the business" of a mind, and serve to prophesy that romantic poetry is to be sensuous rather than intellectual. An admirer and acquaintance of James Thomson, Shenstone continued the tradition of descriptive poetry, loving above all, as he said, "odd picturesque description." He was averse to Thomson's Miltonic grandeur, to the "present pomp and haughtiness of style instead of sentiment"; and he consciously cultivated an artificially simple and pretty style. Like many a sentimentalist he was emotionally timid, and excused his *Schoolmistress* to the critical by means of its jocose and burlesque details. He felt a need repeatedly to "spruce up" the "trivial" poem, and so he recast it more than once. Similarly he defended the genuineness of feeling in his *Elegies* by insisting that they were about his own farm and his own sheep! He belonged to the conscious admirers (so numerous in his day) of simplicity, rural elegance, picturesqueness, informality, melancholy, and ornate prettiness. His liking for ballads led him not merely to compose poems in that form (the best of which is doubtless *Jemmy Dawson*) but also to aid his friend Thomas Percy in the preparation of the *Reliques of Ancient English Poetry* (1765). He used a diversity of metres pleasingly; his early success, *The Judgment of Hercules* (1741), was in the heroic couplet, but that was a metre which in general he avoided. The pentameter quatrains of his too numerous elegies reflect the popularity of James Hammond's *Love Elegies* (1743) and perhaps also of Gray's *Churchyard*.[14] For the grand style, the lofty, conscious art, Shenstone had little affection. "The public," so he writes to a friend, "has seen all that art can do, and they want the more striking effects of wild, original, enthusiastic genius."

Thomas Gray

With the last part of this opinion Shenstone's greatest mid-century contemporary, Thomas Gray, would have agreed; but Gray was also and above all a poet of art.[15] Among the most learned of English poets, he was widely

[14] J. Fisher, "James Hammond and the Quatrain of Gray's *Elegy*," *MP*, xxxii (1935). 301-310, and "Shenstone, Gray, and the 'Moral Elegy'," *MP*, xxxiv (1937). 273-294.

[15] Thomas Gray (1716-71), son of a London exchange broker, entered Eton in 1725, where he formed a friendly "quadrumvirate" with Horace Walpole, Richard West, and Thomas Ashton. In 1734 he went on to Peterhouse, Cambridge, but left in 1738 without a degree. In 1739 he accompanied Horace Walpole on a tour of France and Italy, and as a result of a quarrel returned to England alone in 1741. The next year he was back at Cambridge studying law; and most of the rest of his career is associated with that place. In 1745 his friendship with Walpole was renewed, and Walpole ultimately printed some of Gray's pieces on his Strawberry Hill press. As a result of a practical joke by undergraduates Gray left Peterhouse (1756) and moved to Pembroke College. During the years 1759-61 he settled in London in order to read in the newly opened British Museum. In 1768 he was appointed Professor of Modern History at Cambridge. He visited the Scottish Highlands in 1765, and in 1769 made a tour of the English lakes, which he described in his journal kept for Dr. Wharton. In 1771 he was contemplating a journey to Switzerland to visit his young friend Charles Victor de Bonstetten, but death prevented the journey.—Clark S. Northup, *A Bibliography of Thomas Gray* (New Haven, 1917).—Gray's *Poems* have been edited by William Mason (York, 1775, etc.); Gilbert Wakefield (1786); John Mitford (1814). His *Works* have been edited by John Mitford (2v, 1816; 4v, 1835-7); Sir Edmund Gosse (4v, 1884); William Lyon Phelps (Selections, Boston, 1894); Duncan C. Tovey (Cambridge, 1898); A. L. Poole and Leonard Whibley (Oxford, 1937). His *Correspondence* has been rather badly edited, but the best edition is easily that of Paget Toynbee and Leonard Whibley (3v, Oxford, 1935).—Samuel Johnson, *Lives* (ed.

and intelligently read in the Romans, in the Greek lyrists and tragedians, in his great English predecessors, and, significantly, in such versions of Old Norse and Welsh poems as were available in his day. He typifies the transitional poet who loved tradition yet courted novelty. He excelled his contemporaries in meticulous workmanship and in ability to use new materials—medieval Welsh or Scandinavian—with dramatic imaginative power. He sought sublime moods, *sensations fortes,* and elevated even primitive materials to noble Roman or heroic levels.

Various explanations have been offered of the quantitative limitation of Gray's output. Perhaps he felt that devotion of all of his leisure to mere versifying would annul his position of genteel amateur. Gray, furthermore, could savor his refined sensations without the urge to share them with strangers. His delight in Alpine scenery led to no Coleridgean *Hymn before Sunrise;* and his pleasure in the English Lake region would not have made him a Wordsworth, had he lived longer. He did not "pour himself out": he was perceptive and receptive rather than publicly articulate. Although his letters to his intimates are easy and informal, his public appearances in print are dignified, stately, "official." He was certainly learned; that he was intellectually very creative is doubtful in view of his small prose output and of his appetite for "eternal new romances of Marivaux and Crebillon." Whether at Cambridge, Stoke Poges, or the newly opened (1759) British Museum reading-room, he was absorbed and stimulated by books. Unlike Walpole or Fielding, and unlike any typical poet of his day, he was shy. While hardly more melancholy than other lovers of *Il Penseroso,* he was a true hypochondriac, and both his character and his poetry were affected somberly by sorrows—such as, for example, the death of his closest friend, Richard West. Lastly, he was a fastidious exquisite. He perceived and delighted in beauty; over the exacting expression of beauty in poetry he labored as few English poets have done. His *Churchyard*—not really a long or complex poem—occupied his creative hours during perhaps six years. Of his projected but unwritten history of English poetry Walpole wrote, "If he rides Pegasus at his usual foot-pace, [he] will finish the first page two years hence." *Gray's Limitation*

Slow, stately, and impersonal as Gray's genius was, some of his earlier poems are nevertheless derived chiefly from his personal experience of life; they are, like those of so many "bards" of his day, actually "poems on several occasions." A distant prospect of Eton College, where ten years before he *His "Occasional" Poetry*

George Birkbeck Hill, Oxford, 1905), III. 421-442; Charles V. de Bonstetten, *Souvenirs* (Paris, 1832); Matthew Arnold, "Thomas Gray," *Essays in Criticism* (Second Series, 1888); Duncan C. Tovey, *Gray and His Friends* (Cambridge, 1890); Charles Eliot Norton, *Gray as a Naturalist* (Boston, 1903); Amy L. Reed, *The Background of Gray's Elegy* (1924); Roger Martin, *Essai sur Thomas Gray* (Paris, 1934); Robert W. Ketton-Cremer, *Thomas Gray* (1935); La Rue Van Hook, "New Light on the Classical Scholarship of Thomas Gray," *AJP*, LVII (1936). 1-9; William Powell Jones, *Thomas Gray, Scholar* (Cambridge, Mass., 1937); Herbert W. Starr, *Gray as a Literary Critic* (Philadelphia, 1941); M. H. Griffin, "Thomas Gray, Classical Augustan," *Classical Jour.*, XXXVI (1941). 473-482; Geoffrey Tillotson, "Gray the Scholar-Poet," *Essays in Criticism and Research* (Cambridge, 1942), pp. 124-126.

had been a schoolboy, led in 1742 to the composition of an ode on the subject that involved obviously heartfelt reflections on the hidden future sorrows awaiting the happy youngsters seen at play. Here, as in his *Ode on the Spring,* the diction is ornately Augustan, as indeed Wordsworth found it also in the *Sonnet on the Death of Richard West.* The *Ode on the Death of a Favourite Cat* (belonging to Horace Walpole) is a neat and laughing *jeu d'esprit* that Gray could approve. Another such, *The Long Story* (1753), was less pointed and finished; and it Gray excluded from the 1768 edition of his poems. Cowper knew this tune better; there was little of the *riant* in the genius of Gray.

*His
Elegy*

The greatest of Gray's poems—possibly the greatest of his century—is his *Elegy Written in a Country Churchyard.* Though perhaps motivated in part by sorrow over the death of West, the poem is not "particular": it is an Elegy for Man, or at least for all "average" and obscure men. Both in its attempt to work thus in universal terms and in its unrivaled purity, propriety, and harmony of diction the poem is a great realization of the ideals of its day: in its placid melancholy and its rustic setting it is perhaps slightly romantic. In its treatment of the common man it is heroic and even majestic; it has not the tone of Wordsworth. The poem is compact of what Tennyson called "divine truisms," and these are universally, if decorously, affecting. Among poems embodying the noble ideal of

What oft was thought but ne'er so well expressed,

this *Elegy* must always rank high. Persons with an aversion to reflective commonplaces in poetry may, as T. S. Eliot has done, question the subtlety of the *Churchyard;* but critics who admit *both* clarity and subtlety as merits will be content with the noble and finished transparency of this poem. Its achievement is, of its very nature, the opposite of facile: *"divine* truisms" are not so easily come by!

*Inspiration
from Books*

After 1751 Gray derived poetic stimulus from his reading of books rather than from life itself. After the *Elegy* came his two regular Pindaric odes, *The Bard* and *The Progress of Poesy.* Although his contemporaries appreciated the clarity and reflective moralizing of the *Elegy,* they found the energetic and rhapsodical quality of these odes difficult. The imagery of *The Progress of Poesy* dazzled more readers than Dr. Johnson; [16] the frequent classical allusions in Milton's vein recalled to them the schoolroom rather than the glory and grandeur of Greece or Rome; and the management of persons in *The Bard* required a sort of study familiar to Browning's readers but unfamiliar in 1757. Yet neither ode is so obscure as it at first seemed; both have unusual energy and imaginative shimmer. The medieval fable in *The Bard* has dramatic power hardly equaled between Milton and Byron. These odes approach the sublime as do few others in this age that adored Milton and Longinus. Though their rhythms at first sound dithyrambic, they are rigidly correct within the true Pindaric form. Gray published in his

16 W. P. Jones, "The Contemporary Reception of Gray's *Odes,*" MP, XXVIII (1930). 61-82.

lifetime no poems in the heroic couplet, though he had used it in a few brief translations and had begun in it his didactic *Education and Government*. Yet his achievement in other metres and his critical interest in them give him high importance in the history of English metrics. His range from the somewhat cold pomp of the heroic quatrains in his *Elegy* to the energetic outburst of his Pindarics and his later primitive chants is unparalleled in his century.

As historian and antiquary, Gray had long been interested in early verse forms and medieval poetic materials. Paul Henri Mallet's *Introduction à l'Histoire de Dannemarc* (1755) drew him to Norse antiquities and poetry; Bartholin's *De Causis Contemptae ... Mortis* (Copenhagen, 1689) offered two Norse poems which Gray translated as *The Fatal Sisters* and *The Descent of Odin;* and Evans's *Some Specimens of the Poetry of the Ancient Welsh Bards* (1764), viewed in manuscript by Gray in 1760, furnished materials for *The Triumphs of Owen* and *The Death of Hoel*. Gray and others significantly turned, as Gibbon did not, from the Graeco-Roman tradition to Northern antiquities, from classically correct elegies and Pindarics to the primitive minstrelsy of the North.[17] In 1768, when Gray for the last time carefully edited his poems, he also became Professor of Modern History at Cambridge; and it is remarkable that learning and poetry marry so perfectly in the wild "runic" chants of these last products of his muse.

His Scandinavian and Celtic Poems

Gray, however, was not the first to exploit heroic Celtic story.[18] He was a distinguished, if independent, admirer of Macpherson's Ossian, and Ossian importantly reinforced Sir William Temple's view that all nations, not merely Greece and Rome, had their artistic distinction. "Imagination," as Gray wrote after reading Ossian, "dwelt many hundred years agoe in all her pomp on the cold and barren mountains of Scotland. ... she reigns in all nascent societies of Men, where the necessities of life force every one to think & act for himself." The cult of imagination, the belief in cycles of culture outside the Graeco-Roman tradition, the belief in primitive nature (seen in "nascent societies of Men") as more potent than formalized art—all these influences and more had been long preparing the way for James Macpherson (1736-1796) and his supposed versions of Ossianic poems.[19] The aesthetic rightness of the moment is seen if we remember how unpopular

Macpherson's Ossian

17 George L. Kittredge, "Gray's Knowledge of Old Norse," *Selections from Gray,* ed. William L. Phelps (Boston, 1894), pp. xli-l.
18 Edward D. Snyder, "Thomas Gray's Interest in Celtic," *MP,* xi (1914). 559-579.
19 *The Works of Ossian,* ed. William Sharp (Edinburgh, 1896); *Ossian. Faksimile-Neudruck der Erstausgabe von 1762/63 mit Begleitband: die Varianten,* ed. Otto L. Jiriczek (3v, Heidelberg, 1940); *Fragments of Ancient Poetry* (1760); ed. Otto L. Jiriczek (Heidelberg, 1915); *Fingal. An Ancient Epic Poem* (1762); *Temora. An Ancient Epic Poem* (1763).—G. F. Black, "Macpherson's Ossian and the Ossianic Controversy: A Contribution towards a Bibliography," *Bull. New York Public Library,* xxx (1926). 424-439; 508-524.—Hugh Blair, *A Critical Dissertation on the Poems of Ossian* (1763); Thomas B. Saunders, *The Life and Letters of James Macpherson* (1894); John S. Smart, *James Macpherson* (1905); Paul Van Tieghem, *Ossian et l'Ossianisme dans la littérature européenne au XVIIIᵉ siècle* (Groningen, 1920) and "Ossian et l'Ossianisme au XVIIIᵉ siècle," *Le Préromantisme* (Paris, 1924), II. 197-284; Edward D. Snyder, *The Celtic Revival in English Literature* (Cambridge, Mass., 1923), ch. IV.

Scots were in London in the days of Lord Bute, John Wilkes, Charles Churchill, and the arch-enemy, Dr. Johnson, and if we remember how Scottish poets had recently failed to "take" in London. For unpretentious homely geniuses such as Allan Ramsay (1686-1758) and Robert Fergusson (1750-1774) one need not expect a fashionable vogue; but John Home, author of *Douglas,* had not overwhelmed London, as he had Edinburgh, in his rôle of "the Scottish Shakespeare," and William Wilkie (1721-1772), author of *The Epigoniad* (1757), had been even less welcomed as a "Scottish Homer." But Macpherson fared better—fared beyond all expectation, so that his success became even embarrassing.

As early as 1749, when John Home, not yet a Shakespeare, was returning to Scotland, Collins in his unpublished *Ode on the Popular Superstitions of the Highlands* had urged him to sustain the "rural faith," "the themes of simple, sure effect," and to collect legendary materials in the Highlands both from the "well-taught hind" and from the more credulous shepherd.

> Old Runic bards shall seem to rise around,
> With uncouth lyres, in many-colour'd vest,
> Their matted hair with boughs fantastic crown'd. . . .

Ten years later Home met James Macpherson and found in him the man who should answer the wishes not merely of Collins but of all well-disposed antiquaries, nationalists, and primitivists. Under encouragement of Home, Hugh Blair, and other patriotic Scots, Macpherson in 1760 published in Edinburgh a small volume of *Fragments of Ancient Poetry Collected in the Highlands of Scotland*. An instant success, it lighted a poetic fire that for a half-century was to rage throughout all Europe. The widespread appetite for primitive poetry found its fullest gratification in Ossian.

Insistent Scottish supporters forced Macpherson to collect and "translate" other Gaelic poems. Ignorant of Gaelic and perhaps confused as to the relation of his fragments to each other and to their romantic cycles, Macpherson was reluctant; but, fired with the enthusiasm of his backers, he continued his work. Challenged by Dr. Johnson and others to authenticate the antiquity of his fragments, he could produce no ancient manuscripts, and lacked, in the discussion of oral transmission, any scholarly understanding which might have aided him. The controversy over the genuineness of his poems became bitter, but it did not, at least for some years, greatly affect their popular vogue.

The Melancholy of Ossian   The materials which he had gathered from the mouths of not too well-taught hinds bore, in general, relationships to the Fenian cycle of Celtic romance. Macpherson adapted or even invented his episodes, as any eighteenth-century "translator" might have done. The Ossianic poems were in one respect peculiarly fitted to his needs. They were retrospective in method. Macpherson found in the dark backward and abysm of time, Ossian: Ossian, in turn, sang mournfully of glories that had vanished before his day. The effect of remoteness was doubled, and the tender melancholy implicit in all reminiscence added a touch of sentiment, without which in 1760 there was little chance of success. The method and style of this poetic prose may be called Macpherson's own in spite of the fact that it is largely biblical in coloring and owes much to Homer, Milton, Pope's *Iliad,* and even to bits of more recent authors. A happy invention, it answered to the full the eighteenth-century concept of primitive objectivity, naturalness, and sublimity. Designed to show that, ages long ago, Ossian on the cold and barren mountains of Scotland had equaled, if not surpassed, Homer on Scamanderside, it actually achieved almost the full synthesis of romantic primitivism.

Thomas Percy (1729-1811) was more of an antiquarian than was Macpherson, and certainly more of a scholar; but he also was hardly more than an amateur in the work of "old runic bards," and his chief success was to be less their editor than their popularizer.[20] Aware of the public's avidity for the exotic, he sponsored the translation of a Chinese novel, *Hau Kiou Choaan,* and wrote two other volumes concerning China; stimulated by Macpherson's success, he brought out *Five Pieces of Runic Poetry* (1763) from the Icelandic and *Northern Antiquities* from the French of Mallet. As late as 1775 he was preparing a volume of *Ancient Songs ... Translated from the Spanish.*[21] His greatest work, the enhancing of popular regard for early English ballads, began about 1758, when he had secured from his friend Humphrey Pitt of Shifnal a folio manuscript volume of old ballads. With the encouragement of Shenstone, Thomas Warton, and others, Percy assembled enough ballads to make three volumes called *Reliques of Ancient English Poetry* (1765). As an editor of ballads Percy had had more than one predecessor in the earlier eighteenth century; but since the sixties had witnessed an increase in the appetite for "ancient poetry," he had more success and influence than his predecessors. The volumes stimulated an extensive rehabilitation of the repute of English balladry. Percy does not belong to the tradition of good editing in his century—that of Tom Hearne and Edmond Malone—but to that of the popularizers and improvers of texts, the tradition of Pope among others. He selected his materials capriciously, frankly mixing old ballads, such as *Chevy Chase, Edom o' Gordon,* and *Sir Patrick Spens* with political songs of the seventeenth century, and

Thomas Percy

[20] There is no collected edition of Percy's writings; his *Reliques* is edited by Henry B. Wheatley (3v, 1886) and by M. M. Arnold Schröer [a critical edition] (2v, Berlin, 1889-93). For a bibliography see L. F. Powell, "Percy's *Reliques,*" *Library,* IX (1928). 113-137.—Alice C. C. Gaussen, *Percy, Prelate and Poet* (1908); Hans Hecht, "Kleine Studien zu Graves, Shenstone und Percy," *Anglia,* LVIII (1934). 103-112, 131-154; Clarissa Rinaker, "Percy as a Sonneteer," *MLN,* XXXV (1920). 56-58; Leah Dennis, "The Text of the Percy-Warton Letters," *PMLA,* XLVI (1931). 1166-1201 and "Percy's Essay 'On the Ancient Metrical Romances'," *PMLA,* XLIX (1934). 81-97; Vincent H. Ogburn, "Thomas Percy's Unfinished Collection, *Ancient English and Scottish Poems,*" *ELH,* III (1936). 183-189; "Further Notes on Thomas Percy" [biographical], *PMLA,* LI (1936). 449-458; and "A Forgotten Chapter in the Life of Bishop Thomas Percy," *RES,* XII (1936). 202-208; Irving L. Churchill, "William Shenstone's Share in the Preparation of Percy's *Reliques,*" *PMLA,* LI (1936). 960-974; Walter J. Bate, "Percy's Use of his Folio Manuscript," *JEGP,* XLIII (1944). 337-348; *The Percy Letters,* general editors, David Nichol Smith and Cleanth Brooks: *Correspondence of Percy & Edmond Malone,* ed. Arthur Tillotson (Louisiana State Univ., 1944); *Correspondence of Percy & Richard Farmer* (Louisiana State Univ., 1946). Other vols. will follow.

[21] First published with a preface by David Nichol Smith (Oxford, 1932).

with ballads by his contemporaries, and by himself. He used certain interesting devices of "salesmanship," such as the transference of *Chevy Chase* at the very last moment from Volume III to the beginning of the first volume, where this song about a Percy followed a dedication to the Countess of Northumberland, "in her own right Baroness Percy," etc. Thus the son of the Bridgnorth grocer capitalized on the accident of his own name, and began his rise to the spiritual lordship of Dromore.[22]

Beattie's Minstrel

To his *Reliques* he added essays historical and critical on various aspects of English verse, essays which interested and encouraged Thomas Warton in his *History of English Poetry* and one of which, on ancient minstrels, stimulated James Beattie [23] (1735-1803) to one of the longest and certainly one of the best poems of the century in the Spenserian stanza, *The Minstrel* (1771-4). Here we find a sketch of the training of Edwin (Beattie himself), a modern "minstrel." In the first Book the simplicities of rural life ánd the beauties of landscape seem educational:

> Lo! where the stripling, wrapt in wonder, roves
> Beneath the precipice o'erhung with pine;
> And sees, on high, amidst th' encircling groves,
> From cliff to cliff the foaming torrents shine:
> While waters, woods, and winds, in concert join,
> And Echo swells the chorus to the skies.

The "mighty masters of the lay" also instruct the youth, and in Book II philosophy and history aid in the task apparently still essential of curbing "Imagination's lawless rage." The poem in some passages seems a graceful but not compelling predecessor of Wordsworth's *Prelude.* Beattie's *Essays* are of more interest than his poems apart from *The Minstrel;* for the latter tend to be conventional odes, elegies, and translations.

Thomas Chatterton

The cults of genius and of medieval minstrelsy, so enthusiastically fostered by these poets in the sixties, meet in the tragic career of Thomas Chatterton (1752-1770), "the marvellous boy" who began publishing poems before he was twelve, and ended with suicide before he was eighteen.[24] To the succeeding great romantics Chatterton became the myth or symbol of "heaven-born

22 Leah Dennis, "Thomas Percy: Antiquarian vs. Man of Taste," *PMLA,* LVII (1942). 140-154.
23 Beattie's poems are found in Chalmers, Vol. XVIII, and in the Aldine edition, ed. A. Dyce (1831, etc.).—Sir William Forbes, *An Account of the Life and Writings of James Beattie, Including Many of his Original Letters* (2v, Edinburgh, 1806); Margaret Forbes, *Beattie and his Friends* (1904); E. A. Aldrich, "James Beattie's *Minstrel:* Its Sources and Influence," *Harvard Summaries of Theses* (Cambridge, Mass., 1931), pp. 117-119.
24 *Works,* ed. Thomas Tyrwhitt [*The Rowley Poems*] (1777); Robert Southey and J. Cottle (3v, 1803); Walter W. Skeat (2v, 1871); Henry D. Roberts (2v, 1906); Maurice E. Hare, *The Rowley Poems* (Oxford, 1911).—Francis A. Hyett and W. Bazeley, *Chattertoniana* [bibliography] (Gloucester, 1914).—Helene Richter, *Thomas Chatterton* (Vienna and Leipzig, 1900); Eduard H. W. Meyerstein, *A Life of Thomas Chatterton* (1930); Esther P. Ellinger, *Thomas Chatterton, the Marvellous Boy* (Philadelphia, 1930); L. F. Powell, "Thomas Tyrwhitt and the Rowley Poems," *RES,* VII (1931). 314-326; A. Watkin-Jones, "Bishop Percy, Thomas Warton and Chatterton's Rowley Poems (1773-1790)," *PMLA,* L (1935). 769-784; Eduard H. W. Meyerstein, "Chatterton: his Significance To-day," *Essays by Divers Hands (Transactions of the Royal Society of Literature),* XVI (1937). 61-91; Wylie Sypher, "Chatterton's *African Eclogues* and the Deluge," *PMLA,* LIV (1939), 246-260.

Genius" suffering from "want and the bleak freezings of neglect." Dull as Bristol schoolboy and attorney's apprentice, he brightened in his favorite haunt, the church of St. Mary Redcliffe. Among the muniments of this church, of which his family were almost hereditary sextons, he learned according to myth to read black letter before he knew Roman type, and to adore illuminated parchments. His "medievalism," since it began before he was twelve, may well have been spontaneous rather than owing to the *ersatz* of Ossian or *The Castle of Otranto;* but it flowed in somewhat similar channels. Endowed with a gift for lyric, satire, and literary mimicry, Chatterton composed work supposedly by poets of Chaucer's day and later, chief among them a feigned Bristol monk, Thomas Rowley. Chatterton's counterfeiting of spelling and diction has been disparaged; yet the style was archaic enough to delight many contemporary readers, though Gray, Mason, Walpole, and others—made wary by Macpherson's work—remained unconvinced and unsympathetic. Such counterfeiting wore out its success easily, and Chatterton, denied both bread and fame, in bitter pride and despondency drank arsenic and died.

The real quality of Chatterton's gifts is difficult to dissociate from his tragic career. Actually his stimulus was Elizabethan and Spenserian rather than Chaucerian or fifteenth-century. This is especially true of his best poem, *An Excelente Balade of Charitie.* Here we have colorful Renaissance imagery and the stateliness of rime royal modified by a Spenserian Alexandrine. Always Chatterton showed a pretty gift in his figurative and decorative language and in the warm tunefulness of his lines. More than Macpherson, Percy, or Gray, he could emancipate himself from the mannerisms of his own century, and escape to the imaginary world of fifteenth-century Bristol, his own created city of refuge. It is, after all, this frustrated escape rather than the achievement of poems actually written that became important to his romantic idolaters. They praised his gifts rather than his poems; he was regarded by them as first among "the inheritors of unfulfilled renown." The transition from Chatterton to Coleridge, Shelley, or Keats is in many ways a short step.

Another able poet, whose career like Chatterton's postdated Dodsley's *Collection,* was Charles Churchill (1731-1764), a dissipated clergyman, who during the last four years of his life acquired notoriety and fame as a satirist.[25] His first important poem, *The Rosciad* (1761), attacked theatrical personalities with a verve that made the poem, in the opinions of some later critics, the outstanding success in personal satire between Pope's *Dunciad* and Byron's *English Bards and Scotch Reviewers.* It was soon supported by an attack on Smollett in Churchill's *Apology to the Critical Reviewers*

Charles Churchill

---

[25] Churchill's *Poems* were collected in 1763 and thereafter; they are found in Anderson, Vol. x, and Chalmers, Vol. xiv, and are edited by James Laver (2v, 1933). For biographies (there is no first-rate life of Churchill) and special articles on Churchill see *CBEL*, II. 340-342, especially the biographical articles there listed as by Joseph M. Beatty. See also George Nobbe, *The North Briton, a Study in Political Propaganda* (1939), and Wallace C. Brown, "Charles Churchill: A Revaluation," *SP*, XL (1943). 405-424.

(1761) in the form of an epistle to his close friend Robert Lloyd [26] (1733-1764). This attack in turn led to an alliance with the author of *The North-Briton*, John Wilkes, that shaped much of Churchill's later poetry. *The Prophecy of Famine* (1763) continued Wilkes's outcry against the Scotch; the *Epistle to Hogarth* (1763) was a bitter revenge on the aging artist for his caricature of Wilkes drawn in the courtroom; *The Duellist* (1764) was a defense of Wilkes's rôle in his duel with Samuel Martin; and *The Candidate* (1764) renewed onslaughts on Wilkes's hypocritical enemy, the fourth Earl of Sandwich. *The Times* (1764) was an unsavory depiction of the vices of the day with emphasis at times on vices to which Churchill himself was perhaps not a stranger. Less satirical was his rambling *Gotham* (1764), which expounded ideas of political and social freedom and gave way to humanitarian reflections that pleased his former schoolmate, William Cowper. That Churchill had a remarkable gift for satirical portraiture is attested by his laughter at Dr. Johnson (Pomposo) in *The Ghost* (1762-3) and his more virulent satire on Wilkes's enemies, Warburton and Lord Sandwich, in *The Duellist*. As favorite metres he used both the four- and the five-stressed couplets, and was happier in his use of the latter. For some reason—possibly because he hated Pope's editor, Warburton—he disliked Pope, and cultivated the vigorous flow of Dryden, which more suited his genius. In *Gotham* he remarks

> Nothing of Books, and little known of men,
> When the mad fit comes on, I seize the pen,
> Rough as they run, the rapid thoughts set down,
> Rough as they run, discharge them on the Town.
> Hence rude, unfinish'd brats, before their time,
> Are born into this idle world of rime....

In substance and manner the passage is typical, though the poet's gross energy and power are better seen in his acrid and mordant personalities. But satire's preoccupation with the "Sons of Sin" (Churchill's phrase), when stressed by such a sinner, was naturally suspect. That vein had been worked out; [27] and Churchill remains a journalist, a savage and incisive editorial commentator or propagandist who happened to write best—and it was very well—in eloquent couplets. His art looks backward to a rhetorical school, whereas Chatterton and others, looking farther back, were renewing aged and unfamiliar poetic strains.

---

[26] On Robert Lloyd see *CBEL*, II. 370, and Austin Dobson's essay on Lloyd in *At Prior Park and Other Papers* (1912); also I. R. Halsband, "The Poet of *The North Briton*," *PQ*, XVII (1938). 389-395.

[27] Worked out, but not abandoned! Witness the frequently lively and witty attacks on Pitt and his partisans by members of the Esto Perpetua Club in their burlesque epic, *The Rolliad*, with also the *Criticisms on The Rolliad* that furthered the burlesque in 1784 and for a decade thereafter. The multitudinous lampoons that, during the last quarter of the century, poured from the pen of John Wolcot (1738-1819), or "Peter Pindar," as he called himself, show also that energy still endured in satire though deftness and elegance had ceased to be notable traits

V

The Novel After 1760

Excessive articulation of the rules of poetry, constricting one to the traditions of Homer, Aristotle, and Horace, might stimulate subversion of such rules, but since tradition in the English novel was brief and relatively unformulated, no similar revolution in taste is here to be expected. The very popularity of a new form, of course, tended to withdraw attention from the classical traditions. In the novel, changes in form or emphasis will relate to changes in attitude towards the phenomenon *man* and his daily life and not to remote literary precedent.[1]

The function of the novel remained the study of man and his manners *Manners,* and morals. The most notable developments are those due to emphasis on *Morals, and* the emotions or sentiments of men—and of women!—rather than on their *Sentiments* rational endowments. But just as the light of reason was regarded as uniform in all right-minded men, so were the sentiments of the heart. Rousseau's Julie reproaches her lover for his preoccupation with "those peculiarities of manners and decorum, which ten years hence will no longer exist" and for his neglect of "the unalterable springs of the human heart, the constant and secret workings of the passions." It is these last which, under the influence of Richardson and Rousseau, engrossed novelists increasingly, though study of manners was by no means excluded. Manners were found interesting among humble folk as well as among aristocrats, in *domestica facta* as well as in foreign society.[2] The problem of how far the particular (the *trivial,* novelists and critics termed it frequently) might augment or diminish universality was seldom faced by writers. They seem, however, conscious that changeable manners and values that were only relative possessed the appeal of novelty and diversity. Strange Rousseauistic moral ideas crept into novels. Julie avowed, "My virtue is unblemished, and my love has left behind no remorse. I glory in my past life." But such a view was foreign to English sense of decorum; no English heroine of comparable behavior thus regarded her eccentricities. If highly particular psychological reactions were to be depicted, they must normally be kept in some way "universal." So Sterne managed

[1] For additional details on the novel of this period consult Ernest A. Baker, *The History of the English Novel,* Vols. IV (1930) and V (1934); J. M. S. Tompkins, *The Popular Novel in England, 1770-1800* (1932); Charlotte E. Morgan, *The Rise of the Novel of Manners* (1911); Robert M. Lovett and Helen S. Hughes, *The History of the Novel in England* (Boston, 1932). For further bibliography see *CBEL,* II. 488-490, 521-553.

[2] See Houghton W. Taylor, *The Idea of Locality in English Criticism of Fiction, 1750-1830* (Chicago, 1936), and his "Modern Fiction and the Doctrine of Uniformity," *PQ,* XIX (1940). 225-236; and again by the same author, " 'Particular Character': An Early Phase of a Literary Evolution," *PMLA,* LX (1945). 161-174.

his Shandean sentiments; so Fanny Burney shaped her notorious and specialized "character-mongering."

Virtuosity in Structure

In practice there were also other modifications. The neat, suspensive structure formulated by Fielding and Richardson, through its very excellence perhaps, led virtuosos like Sterne and his imitator Mackenzie (in *The Man of Feeling*) to play tricks with structure. Normally, of course, matrimony remained the terminal point in plots, but frequently writers discard plot and affect the loose patterns in vogue in Defoe's time. Setting became definitely more important: medieval or Oriental or other remote backgrounds indicated a superficial interest in the exotic and, more significantly, a disgust with trivial daily life as matter for fiction. The introduction of landscape backgrounds that were peacefully idyllic or wildly sublime or mysterious was a development important for the future though at first used—by Ann Radcliffe, for example—somewhat artificially. This "poetic" tendency illustrates a natural desire on the part of the undervalued art of storytelling to elevate its status, a desire seen also in the habit of inserting poems in the text to give a "literary" tone or in the use of a style at times excessively dignified or polysyllabic. These last habits, for better or worse, carried over into the next century, and are all to be seen in the work of Sir Walter Scott among others.

Feminine Influences

The incurably sentimental tone of most novels of this period is in part due to feminine influence. Women were the novel-reading public, and there were a surprising number of women novelists.[3] Among these were Mrs. Charlotte Lennox (1720-1804), the American, whose work was approved by Dr. Johnson; Mrs. Sarah Scott (1723-1795), author of one very successful book, *Millenium Hall* (1762); Mrs. Frances Sheridan (1724-1766), the dramatist's mother, whose *Miss Sidney Bidulph* (1761-7) and *History of Nourjahad* (1767) went through several editions; Mrs. Frances Brooke (1724-1789), author of *Lady Julia Mandeville* (1763), and a further train of other ladies somewhat too seriously sentimental for long popularity. These would include Mrs. Elizabeth Griffith, Clara Reeve, Charlotte Smith, and the romantic Mrs. Elizabeth Inchbald. So many women tried their hands at elegant tales of feminine distress that in Smollett's *Humphry Clinker* (1771) Tim Cropdale's failure is excused because novel-writing "is now engrossed by female authors, who publish merely for the propagation of virtue, with so much ease, and spirit, and delicacy, and knowledge of the human heart, and all in the serene tranquillity of high life, that the reader is not only enchanted by their genius, but reformed by their morality." Tobias Smollett, horse of another color, thus paid his ironic respects to the gray mare of the moment.

Sterne's Sense of Comedy

The basic attitude of the most eminent novelist of the period, Laurence Sterne,[4] was by nature not very different from Smollett's with regard to this

[3] R. B. Johnson, *The Women Novelists* (1918); also Miriam R. Small, *Charlotte Ramsay Lennox* (New Haven, 1935); Walter M. Crittenden, *The Life and Writings of Mrs. Sarah Scott* (Philadelphia, 1932); William McKee, *Elizabeth Inchbald, Novelist* (Washington, D. C., 1935); Florence M. A. Hilbish, *Charlotte Smith, Poet and Novelist* (Philadelphia, 1941).
[4] Laurence Sterne (1713-1768) was born in Ireland, son of an English army officer and

facile ease, spirit, and "knowledge of the heart," affected by his contemporaries. At the beginning of his brief literary career, at least, he saw all these matters as materials for comedy, if not for grotesque farce. In his first, unsuccessful attempt (May, 1759) to sell Volume I of *Tristram Shandy* to Dodsley, he described the work as "taking in, not only, the Weak part of the Sciences, in which the true point of Ridicule lies—but every Thing else, which I find Laugh-at-able in my way." He thought, so he wrote Garrick, that a "Cervantic comedy" might be drawn from Volumes III and IV. The first volumes were certified by Cambridge friends as the "best & truest & most genuine original & new Humour, ridicule, satire, good sense, good nonsense ever put forth." But even before sending the manuscript to Dodsley, Sterne had learned by reading parts of the story to his convivial and tolerant friends at Stillington Hall [5] that much of it was too gross. Even after revision the work, when published, was widely condemned as too indelicate for a clerical pen. In later volumes he in part curbed his salacious bent, and wrote, with or without his tongue in his cheek, something more apparently sentimental. But the "serene tranquillity of high life" at Shandy Hall has little in common with that of Rousseau's Eloisa at Clarens—or with the scenes depicted by Sterne's female contemporaries: the Shandy brothers led a life that was essentially tranquil—and essentially comical.

Sterne's significant output was limited to two pieces of fiction, seven small volumes of *Sermons* (1760-69), and his correspondence, which includes the *Letters from Yorick to Eliza* (1773). To modern readers he is the author of *The Life and Opinions of Tristram Shandy* (1759-67) and its by-product

Tristram Shandy

---

an Irish mother. His early years were spent moving about with the regiment; during the years 1723 to about 1731 he was in school in Yorkshire. Receiving the B.A. in Jesus College, Cambridge, in 1737, he took orders the same year, and in 1738 obtained the vicarage of Sutton-in-the-Forest, near York. He later received other livings, and resided chiefly in or near York itself. His great-grandfather had been Archbishop of York, and an uncle was archdeacon in the diocese during Sterne's career. A chapter quarrel indirectly led to Sterne's first imaginative writing, *A Political Romance* (1759), later called *The History of a Good Warm Watch Coat*. In 1760, upon the publication of the first of *Tristram Shandy*, he was lionized by London society. Ill health—he had long been consumptive—made advisable a visit to France in 1762; but here despite his health he plunged into fashionable society. Again in 1765 London fêted him, and again recuperation required a seven-months' tour of France and Italy. While in London in 1768 to superintend publication of the *Sentimental Journey*, he died. He had married Eliza Lumley in 1741; but the match was completely incompatible. During his last hectic winter in London Sterne indulged in a passionate but Platonic intrigue with Mrs. Eliza Draper, the young wife of a Bombay official in the East India Company. Sterne's letters to this Eliza, written after she sailed for Bombay, became his *Journal to Eliza*.—Of his works the edition by Wilbur L. Cross (12v, 1904) and that from the Shakespeare Head Press (7v, Oxford, 1926-7) are standard. His *Letters* (3v, 1775) are best edited by Lewis P. Curtis (Oxford, 1935). The standard life is by Wilbur L. Cross (2v, 1925); other lives by Percy Fitzgerald (2v, 1864) and H. D. Traill (1882) are of some value. For Sterne's Continental vogue see Harvey W. Hewett-Thayer, *Sterne in Germany* (1905); Francis B. Barton, *L'Influence de Sterne en France* (Paris, 1911); Gertrude Hallamore, *Das Bild Laurence Sternes in Deutschland von der Aufklärung bis zur Romantik* (Berlin, 1936); and F. Louise W. M. Buisman-de Savornin Lohman, *Laurence Sterne en de Nederlandse schrijvers van c. 1780-c. 1840* (Wageningen, 1939). See also Lewis P. Curtis, *The Politicks of Laurence Sterne* (Oxford, 1929).

[5] This was the seat of John Hall-Stevenson, the original of Eugenius in *Tristram Shandy*, and author, among other things, of *Crazy Tales* (1762).

A Sentimental Journey through France and Italy (1768), and these works are a most highly individual achievement. It was Sterne's intention to bring out *Tristram Shandy* in annual installments during the rest of his life.[6] This his health did not permit; but the method of the story is in part dictated by the plan for interminable serial publication. As in comic-strip drawings in present-day newspapers, it was essential here to husband one's material, to work with minutiae—in short, to get nowhere. The structural results are apparent. Sterne used small scenes—snapshots one might call them—and cultivated variety and surprise to the utter neglect of continuity or progress. The art of digression was never so continually or successfully cultivated.

> Digressions [Sterne tells us], incontestably, are the sunshine;—they are the life, the soul of reading;—take them out of this book for instance,—you might as well take the book along with them;—one cold eternal winter would reign in every page of it; restore them to the writer;—he steps forth like a bridegroom,— bids All hail; brings in variety, and forbids the appetite to fail.

After the close organization of *Tom Jones* and the tragic rise and fall of complication in *Clarissa,* such apparent chaos would be intolerable except in the hands of a great genius.

Its Time Scheme

The chaos is more apparent than actual. There was both a method and a (concealed) plan. On the original title-page Sterne announced in a Greek tag from Epictetus that not deeds but the teachings of deeds are what concern men. So his pages are devoted to adumbrations of trivial occurrences, and his overtones are both rich and amusing, if not logically arranged. Furthermore, although he conceals the fact, he does have a complete chronological conception of the events he is presenting, and he does live up to his title, *The Life and Opinions of Tristram Shandy,* more fully than a casual reader realizes. Since the nine published volumes are only a beginning, Tristram's elders naturally occupy the center stage, but in the sequel Tristram would have come to that position himself. As matters stand, we know the dates of Uncle Toby's and Trim's active military careers and the years of the campaigns on the bowling-green at Shandy Hall. We know that the maneuvers relating to the Widow Wadman fall chiefly in the years 1713-14; that Tristram was born on November 5, 1718; that after attending Jesus College, Cambridge, he made the grand tour—and that, like a good comic-strip artist, Sterne planned to send with him most of the male dramatis personae of the book: how many volumes that might have made! We know that in 1741 Tristram attended Mr. Noddy's son as governor in Denmark; that in 1748 Parson Yorick died; and that Tristram supposedly began his latest volume on or about August 12, 1766.[7]

But chronology or "plot" was not the principle on which *Tristram Shandy* was built. Not deeds but the implications of deeds engrossed Sterne: it is

---

[6] The facts concerning the composition and history of the novel are admirably summarized in the edition prepared for the Odyssey Press (1940) by James A. Work.

[7] Theodore Baird, "The Time-Scheme of *Tristram Shandy* and a Source," *PMLA,* LI (1936), 803-820.

the emotional aura of these things and especially their comic aspects that he was dramatizing. He was much influenced by John Locke's theory as to the irrational nature of the association of ideas; Tristram calls Locke's *Essay* "a history-book ... of what passes in a man's own mind"; and since association is thought an accidental or whimsical process, it easily lends itself to a comedy of intellectual incoherence. Hence the casual, digressive motion of the work; hence the tragicomic interruption in the first chapter and other *non-sequiturs* in many other chapters. When Dr. Slop avers, "It would astonish you to know what improvements we have made of late years in all branches of obstetrical knowledge," Uncle Toby wistfully replies, "I wish you had seen what prodigious armies we had in Flanders." At Lyons when the commissary of the post politely asks, "And who are you?" Tristram *en philosophe* replies, "Don't puzzle me!" When at the visitation dinner the learned Kysarcius—his very name a monument to Locke's theory—triumphantly summarizes the weighty proofs that led all ecclesiastical authorities to agree that the Duchess of Suffolk was not of kin to her own child, Uncle Toby, with human eagerness, cries out, "And what said the Duchess of Suffolk to it?" This interplay of pedantry and natural humanity is one of Sterne's favorite sports: it has both comic and sentimental aspects.

Comedy from the Association of Ideas

Comedy also arises from fundamental idiosyncrasy of character. Corporal Trim learned his catechism in a military fashion, so to speak; and so he must deliver it. Uncle Toby, who devoted his waking hours to war games, was nevertheless the most pacific of mortals with "scarce a heart to retaliate upon a fly." At the start of the painful story of LeFevre, he sighed, "I wish, Trim, I was asleep." With preparations befitting a foreign embassy he waited upon the Widow Wadman to tell her he was in love; but at that moment taking up the Bible and happening upon the siege of Jericho, he forgot completely the rest of his intended discourse. Uncle Toby's "hobby-horse" (war) furnished Sterne with the best possible burlesque of the popular eighteenth-century doctrine of the "ruling passion."

Comedy from the Ruling Passion

Sterne's forte is in the sensitive perception of the comedy that goes on in our minds; there are less attractive aspects of his fooling. One tolerates his use of blank pages, black pages, and marbled pages, his placing his preface in the middle of the book, his dots, dashes, and index hands, and other tricks that Joseph Addison would have classed as "false wit." It is less easy to tolerate his recurrent grossness. Quite possibly the comedy of the human mind depends much upon the grotesquely indecent associations found even in the purest minds. In general, however, Sterne's grossness is not subtly psychological; it derives from the sort of stimulus that moves the urchin to scrawl with chalk upon a sidewalk—the desire to be bold and shocking, to evoke a snigger. His prurience is, however, by intention and in effect comic rather than corrupting.

Sterne's Indecency

Adverse criticism resulted, and there was less indecency later. If one compares Volume vii of *Tristram* (1765), the record of Tristram's tour of

France, with Yorick's travels as recounted in *A Sentimental Journey through France and Italy* (1768) one appreciates readily this increasing refinement. The grotesque tricks of *Tristram*—its first illustrator was appropriately William Hogarth himself [8]—are replaced by something approaching elegance; the comedy of mental processes becomes more sweetly tender. The use of *sentimental* in the title puzzled English as well as Continental readers. Sterne himself perhaps conveyed its meanings when he wrote to a friend: "I told you my design in it was to teach us to love the world and our fellow creatures better than we do—so it runs most upon those gentler passions and affections." Similarly in the work itself he says, " 'Tis a quiet journey of the heart in pursuit of NATURE, and those affections which arise out of her." Yorick was not the philosophical traveler like Goldsmith, nor the "proud traveler" like Dr. Samuel Sharp, whose *Letters from Italy* (1766) won him Sterne's notice as "Mundungus," nor yet the jaundiced traveler such as Smollett ("Smelfungus"), whose *Travels through France and Italy* were anathema to Sterne. Yorick savored the situation of the moment—usually as trivial as fiction could produce—with sweet emotion, the result in part of Sterne's consumptive hyperesthesia. Long a very sick man, he was throughout the composition of his last work face to face with death.

Of Sterne's *Sermons* it may be said that their publication brought him money; of his letters that they show him carrying on his inveterate clowning, delicate or indelicate by turns, off stage as well as on. Those addressed to Mrs. Eliza Draper and published as his *Journal to Eliza* in a synthetic text enjoyed much popularity in an age that overvalued emotional facility. His epistolary style has charm of the same sort as that seen in his public works, but not of the same degree; for before publishing his stories Sterne revised, recast, and filed his phrases in order to perfect the apparently spontaneous effervescence that is his glory. He writes the language of conversation with a finished and economic sureness and an attention to overtones that are with him unique.

As he had no important and close predecessors—though there is the intriguing *Life and Memoirs of Mr. Ephraim Tristram Bates, Commonly Called Corporal Bates* [9] (1756)—he had likewise no worthy followers. Most novelists of his time, to be sure, featured emotions of obvious stimulus, ranging from domestic tenderness and the sorrows of abandoned beauty, such as those of Sterne's Maria of Moulines, to more self-conscious public emotions, such as love of liberty, symbolized by Sterne's caged starling. But other sentimentalists had neither his ingenious facility nor his light sureness of touch. Sentimental clichés are of course found everywhere in the novels and plays of the time. Goldsmith's *Vicar,* commonly regarded as a sentimental achievement, contains no comedy worthy of Sterne, and seems more or less earnest in dramatizing a virtuous fortitude in the face of distress

---

[8] Thomas Cary Duncan Eaves, *Graphic Illustration of the Principal English Novels of the Eighteenth Century* (unpub. Harvard diss., 1944), pp. 211-261.

[9] Helen S. Hughes, "A Precursor of *Tristram Shandy*," *JEGP*, XVII (1918). 227-251.

rather than any abandonment to mere tenderness. Closest to Sterne, perhaps, but far behind him, is "the Northern Addison," Henry Mackenzie,[10] whose *Man of Feeling* (1771) imitates *Tristram* in a pretended structural incompleteness, a reminiscent pathos, and a certain quality of dreamlike fantasy. Mackenzie's hero, Harley, faced with the hard facts of existence, exhibits a sentimental incompetence, which, though common in literature at this time, is not characteristic of the Shandys nor altogether of Goldsmith's Vicar—though Dr. Primrose can be inept on occasion. Harley seems rather akin to Rousseau's St. Preux and Goethe's Werther (1774). In general *The Man of Feeling* is crammed with sentimental motifs, such as the loneliness of the delicate soul (not the delicate female soul!), unhappy love, the hardness of life for a private soldier and for the victims of the enclosure movement or of business trickery; it is also filled with the customary glorification of benevolence.

Henry Mackenzie

Mackenzie's companion-piece to his first novel is the more luridly melodramatic *Man of the World* (1773). The villainous protagonist is significantly named Sindall, and he is a cruder descendant of Richardson's villains; the heroine, naturally of mysterious birth, is the perfection of innocence in extremes of distress; and the hero, true to type, is a "friend of humanity." Both *The Man of Feeling* and *The Man of the World* are set down in an extremely stilted and inflexible style. The love scenes are as formal in diction as they are in human conduct.

More effectively theatrical is Mackenzie's third novel, *Julia de Roubigné* (1777), obviously a Puritan's reworking of the basic story of Rousseau's *Julie*. Mlle de Roubigné is preserved chaste, is separated from her true love, Savillon, is married through family pressure to the Count de Montaubon, who upon Savillon's return from Martinique imitates not Wolmar but Othello and in groundless jealousy brings tragedy upon Julia and himself. Little is new or subtle in this, but the motives are well sustained, and the story—granted its author and tradition—is not too baldly narrated. Sir Walter Scott reports that in this novel Mackenzie tried to avoid using the devices of melodramatic villainy. In his substitution of complications resulting from misunderstanding or bad timing of actions he is in accord with the better practice of his day, as Fanny Burney was shortly to show. He gives us bits of romantic scenery as background—following Rousseau here— and motivates the whole upon the principle that "memoirs of sentiment and suffering, may be found in every condition," not merely among the great.

One of the richest fictional storehouses of sentimental clichés is by another contemporary of Sterne's, the Irishman Henry Brooke.[11] His *Fool of Quality*

---

[10] Henry Mackenzie (1745-1831) was born, was educated, and lived most of his life in Edinburgh, where he was from the time of David Hume to that of Sir Walter Scott a notable leader in the political, legal, literary, and social activities of the northern capital. He produced three novels and four plays—the four are of no great distinction—and won reputation by his essays contributed to *The Mirror* (1779-80) and to *The Lounger* (1785-87). His life has been written by Harold W. Thompson in *A Scottish Man of Feeling* (Oxford, 1931).

[11] Henry Brooke (*c.* 1703-1783), was the son of an Irish Protestant clergyman. After studying in Trinity College, Dublin, he went to London to study law in 1724, but turned rather

as a narrative is complex and confused; it includes in a seventeenth-century manner transverse episodes and biographies, and it pauses for set discussions of economic, political, religious, and educational problems. Except possibly for Sarah Fielding's *Governess* (1749) it is the first important English educational novel, and it follows the English sentimental tradition as well as that of Rousseau in his *Émile* (1762) and other works. It presents, as Charles Kingsley remarked, "the education of an ideal nobleman by an ideal merchant prince"; and it teaches that "all virtues, even justice itself, are merely different forms of benevolence." From this book nonconformists as well as churchmen learned (in Kingsley's ardent phrase) "more which is pure, sacred, and eternal, than from any which has been published since Spenser's *Faerie Queene*." In so extreme a benevolist there is bound to be not a little naïveté. His hero, young Harry Moreland, destined to become Earl of Moreland and to marry a Princess of Morocco, from childhood showers guineas—seldom less—on all the needy, so thoroughly is he imbued with "generosity." Cosmopolitanism readily extends to marriage with a blond African princess who has a twin brother "of sable hue." The power of sympathy agitates the merchant-prince when seated in a side-box at the Paris opera next to "one of the loveliest young fellows I ever beheld"—who turns out to be a future brother-in-law. "The truth is," our author remarks, "that people live incomparably more by impulse and inclination than by reason and precept." "Even the wild Indians" feel "the sweet compunctions and emotions of the human heart." It is such opinions that make the *Fool of Quality* an interesting "document," and not its superfluity of episode, of thrilling heroism, of astonishing coincidence, or revolutions, discoveries, and deferred, heart-melting reunions. Its teachings commended the work even to so austere a mind as that of John Wesley, who in 1781 issued a condensed edition of it.

The strong set of the time was doubtless towards all these "sweet compunctions" and benevolences; but there were many readers and some writers who protested that while nature might be nature "wherever placed," it was
more effective in drama and novel if highly placed, if aristocratic. Horace Walpole [12] was one. It is easy to isolate excessively so-called "Gothic" or "terror" fiction from the sentimental tendencies of the time. Walpole in his second preface to his *Castle of Otranto* (1765) states that his story was "an attempt to blend the two kinds of romance, the ancient and the modern."

---

to letters, became acquainted with Pope, Lyttelton, and others, and in opposition to George II became a zealous adherent of Frederick, Prince of Wales. His tragedy *Gustavus Vasa* was forbidden to be acted because of political bias. In 1740 he returned to Ireland, where he lived the life of a country gentleman noted for his benevolence and generosity.—His works have been collected as *A Collection of Plays and Poems* (4v, 1778) and as *Poetical Works* (4v, Dublin, 1792). These include, in part, *Universal Beauty, A Poem* (1735); *Gustavus Vasa* (1739); *The Farmer's Six Letters to the Protestants of Ireland* (Dublin, 1745); *The Secret History and Memoirs of the Barracks of Ireland* (1745); *The Case of the Roman Catholics of Ireland* (Dublin, 1760); *The Fool of Quality; or the History of Henry Earl of Moreland* (5v, 1764-70; 2v [condensed by John Wesley], 1781); ed. Charles Kingsley (2v, 1859); ed. Ernest A. Baker (1906); *Juliet Grenville; or, The History of the Human Heart* (3v, 1774).
[12] For Walpole's career and his other writings see below, ch. VIII, n. 23.

By this he seems to mean an attempt to revive in briefer compass the marvelous or supernatural elements of seventeenth-century French romance, on which he had been reared, and to avoid any too "strict adherence to common life." Of Richardson and Fielding he had no great opinion. He stopped at the fourth volume of *Sir Charles Grandison:* "I was so tired of sets of people getting together, and saying, 'Pray, Miss, with whom are you in love?'" His own work would be more brief, more exotic, less bourgeois.

But his persons in *Otranto* are still the children of his own day rather than of the Middle Ages. Manfred, the blood-stained usurper, is Sindall in a costume rôle; Hippolita is a tearful, subservient wife of 1765; Conrad, the sickly heir, might be Harry Moreland's elder brother; Mathilda is the idyllic heroine hopelessly in love; Isabella is persecuted eighteenth-century innocence; and Theodore, the mysterious heir—"a lovely young prince, with large black eyes, a smooth white forehead, and manly curling locks like jet." This exquisite personage must, like Tom Jones, establish his birth and thus win estate and love. The ground bass of this performance, then, is familiar; it is the descant that is fantastically "Gothic," supernatural, and full (so the author hoped) of terror. With the supernatural causes of terror, however— his giant swords and helmets, his bleeding statues and walking portraits— Walpole was not too effective; with natural causes he was happier. His use of gloomy cloisters, strange sounds, and breathless flights—with the fragile Isabella panting out in the very nick, "Oh transport! here is the trap-door"— these were new and alluring; these chiefly his followers imitated. A less effective but much copied device is the attempt to get comic relief through excessive and ill-timed loquacity of servants, who here and in later tales are drawn after Dogberry, Verges, and Juliet's Nurse, but so feebly that they fail almost totally in comic power.

Otranto a "Costume" Piece

His significant Gothicism derives from medieval architecture, the theatrical gloom and mystery of which had been more slightly exploited in a scene in Congreve's *Mourning Bride* and in Pope's *Eloisa.* By rebuilding his house, Strawberry Hill, in Gothic style Walpole stimulated others to regard that style more favorably, but in literature his uses of Gothic background are less new or picturesque than sensational.[13] He knew something about medieval life, doubtless, but he embodied little knowledge in his story. A Gothic castle with subterranean passages, gloomy stairways, long corridors, and remotely slamming heavy doors—plus supernatural happenings—rescued one from "common life" and furnished thrills. Walpole's chief contribution to fiction is his reliance on exotic stage-sets; his primary aim was to avoid vulgar triviality. For novel-writers this medieval escape was never antiquarian, seriously historical, or learned; it simply provided a no-man's-land where startling, thrilling, sensational happenings might be frequent. In this vein Walpole was imitated by Clara Reeve, Ann Radcliffe, and many others.

Its Medievalism

13 Wilmarth S. Lewis, *The Genesis of Strawberry Hill* (Metropolitan Museum Studies, v [1934]) and W. H. Smith, *Architecture in English Fiction* (New Haven, 1934). The best life of Walpole is that by Robert W. Ketton-Cremer (1940).

His *Castle of Otranto* was crammed with absurdities not manipulated with any real finesse; but the story was highly regarded, and its influence was enormous.[14]

Oriental Tales

Another similar escape was to the Oriental.[15] Early in the century translations and pseudo-translations of Arabic, Persian, Turkish, and Chinese tales flooded England, and thereafter the Oriental story or the essay with Oriental background had great vogue. Usually these Oriental stories are short and imbued with a moral-philosophical aim or with criticism of manners. At times they are fantastic and horrible and relate thus to the novel of terror; at times again they are merely sentimental with an exotic background used to make displays of emotion plausible. Of such attempts in this vein as those of John Hawkesworth (*Almoran and Hamet*, 1761), Mrs. Sheridan (*Nourjahad*, 1767) Charles Johnstone (*Arsaces*, 1774), and Robert Bage (*The Fair Syrian*, 1787) little need be said; the tradition produced in this period only two indubitable and yet very different masterpieces—Johnson's *Rasselas*, which excels, as we have seen, not in its veneer of orientalism, but in its dignity and wisdom of life, and William Beckford's *Vathek*, which excels in its varied, theatrical fantasy.

Beckford's Vathek

Beckford,[16] born to great wealth, social eminence, and idle amateurism, expressed himself exotically. The enormous structure of his rebuilt palace, Fonthill Abbey, represented an extreme of Gothicism, and the gloom of its great hall has been said to have inspired his dreams of the Hall of Eblis in *Vathek*. His later architectural creation, Lansdown Tower, near Bath, was exotic if not Gothic. In literature his one notable achievement is *Vathek, an Arabian Tale* (1786). This was written first in French, of which Beckford had a fairly competent command, and was translated into English for him by the Reverend Samuel Henley, who, contrary to Beckford's injunctions, published his English version before the French had appeared. Beckford, long afterwards, told his first biographer:

I wrote Vathek when I was twenty-two years old. I wrote it at one sitting, and in French. It cost me three days and two nights of hard labour. I never took my clothes off the whole time. This severe application made me very ill.

---

14 This influence is studied in *Le Roman terrifiant* (Paris, 1920, 1923) by Alice M. Killen.
15 Martha P. Conant, *The Oriental Tale in England in the Eighteenth Century* (1908).
16 William Beckford (1760-1844), son of a Lord Mayor of London and heir to great wealth, was born at Fonthill-Gifford, Wiltshire, was privately educated, traveled extensively, and after 1784, despite frequent trips to the Continent, was, except for the years 1795-1805, a Member of Parliament until 1820. Before that date he had long secluded himself at Fonthill. He twice rebuilt the house on an increasingly grand scale, and added a tower 300 feet high, which, when it soon fell, he replaced with another. Extravagance and neglect of business matters forced him in 1822 to sell Fonthill, and he retired to Bath, where he died.—Guy Chapman and John Hodgkin, *A Bibliography of William Beckford* (1930).—*Vathek* (translated into English by Samuel Henley as *An Arabian Tale*, 1786; in French, Lausanne, 1787; Paris, 1787; ed. [English text] Richard Garnett, 1893, 1900; ed. [French text] Guy Chapman, 2v, 1929); *Modern Novel Writing* (2v, 1796); *Italy, with Sketches of Spain and Portugal* (2v, 1834); *The Episodes of Vathek* (translated into English by Sir F. T. Marzials, ed. "Lewis Melville" [L. S. Benjamin], 1912; the French text is in Chapman's *Vathek*, 2v, 1929); *The Travel-Diaries*, ed. Guy Chapman (2v, 1928); *The Vision, Liber Veritatis*, ed. Guy Chapman (1930).—Cyrus Redding, *Memoirs* (1859); "Lewis Melville," *Life and Letters of Beckford* (1910); John W. Oliver, *Life of Beckford* (1932); Guy Chapman, *Beckford* (1937).

Conceivably but not too probably this is true concerning a first draught of
the story: Beckford's letters show him at work on the tale for a period of
several weeks early in 1782, and it undoubtedly received from him all the
care of which he was capable. On the three *Episodes* (first in English in
1912) designed for ultimate insertion towards the end of *Vathek* he worked
intermittently over a longer period. They are far less inspired than *Vathek*
itself. The story of how that sensual and sadistic young caliph sold his
soul to the devil is a somewhat cynical, witty contribution to the literary
satanism of a generation that also produced Goethe's *Faust* and the adoles-
cent horrors of Lewis's *Monk*. Its prose has a brittle brilliance and is slyly
ironical; in the final scene where the hearts of the newly damned are suddenly set aflame with infernal fire it achieves a superb theatrical quality that
has been more than once mistaken for a sudden moral qualm on the part of
the author. Beckford's Orientalism derived largely from the *Arabian Nights*
and its train of imitations; he antedates the scholarly interest in the Orient
fostered notably by Sir William Jones (1746-94), but by some happy accident
of natural sympathy for his material his *Vathek* is the most successfully
imaginative piece of exotic fiction in his century.

All these Gothic and Oriental tales form a small current in the stream of
English fiction. Preoccupation with "common life" and with manners, in *Contempo-*
spite of Walpole, dominated novel-writing, and a fairly large number of the *rary Man-*
novels of manners escaped the drug of sentimentalism, and preserved, if not *ners Still*
a high sense of human comedy, at least a satiric attitude. Both Mrs. Haywood *Preferred*
in her *Betsy Thoughtless* (1751) and Sarah Fielding in her *Countess of
Dellwyn* (1759) maintain a generally critical attitude towards female difficulties and dangers. True comedy is found at its best in this field in the
work of Fanny Burney; but social satire abounds elsewhere. The curious
thing about many of these satirical novels is their lack of technical progress.
They hark back to the picaresque pattern—particularly to that of *The Golden
Ass* of Apuleius, encouraged perhaps by Le Sage, by *The Sopha* (1742) of
Crébillon *fils,* and by much of Smollett. Instead of a human adventurer
they, like Apuleius, frequently substitute some unhuman piece of "currency";
Smollett used an atom; Francis Coventry in *Pompey the Little* (1751) used
a lap-dog; an anonymous author (1760) produced *The Life and Adventures
of a Cat;* and in *Chrysal* (1760-65) Charles Johnstone used a guinea. All
these devices enabled authors to pass in satiric review various classes and
professions in corrupt society. A persisting theme was the insensibility of the
patron to humble merit, but in these tales the hard-hearted man of wealth
is not treated with true sentimental horror. *Chrysal* was perhaps the most
notable, or even notorious, of this type, with its glimpses of corruption in
high places, its scandals about the Medmenham "monks," and its relations
to the career of John Wilkes.

Other rambling satirical novels persisted in attempts at the pattern of *Don Novels of*
Quixote.* Among these were Smollett's *Sir Launcelot Greaves* (1760-61), *Episodic*
Mrs. Lennox's *Female Quixote* (1752), in satire of the novel-reading girl, *Pattern*

and, more interesting, Richard Graves's *Spiritual Quixote* (1773), in which Whitefield and Methodist preachers are satirized in the adventures of Sir Geoffrey Wildgoose. This novel is also notable for its charming and frequent uses of English landscape backgrounds. Graves has a pretty gift of ridicule; he is neither too savage nor too absurd. There were also numberless novels of the loose biographical pattern, such as Thomas Amory's *John Buncle* (1756-66) or the fictional lives turned out by Edward Kimber.[17]

Fanny Burney

Fanny Burney [18] in her social attitude belongs to the courtesy-book tradition. She was no careless workman, and, aware of the traditions of her great predecessors, fashioned her neat plots with matrimony as a terminus, and formed her perfect characters on Richardsonian ideals, her eccentrics in the mode of Smollett. Perhaps instinctive and extreme decorum was naturally strong in her; in any case circumstances developed such instincts. Her father was a music master—a distinguished one, to be sure, and famous in his own right as author of a notable *History of Music* (1776-89)—but still a music master, and hence on the very edge of polite society. Socially the Burneys watched their steps and particularly Miss Fanny, who, like her heroines conscious of an insecure position, sought something more assured. She was a sensible, sensitive, decorous maiden with a very just feeling for social values—and a resulting tincture of snobbishness. Her sense of the socially ridiculous was acute and comprehensive. After all, her contemporaries were trying to live up to their setting—to their grand houses and magnificent gardens, to their furniture by Chippendale, Heppelwhite, Sheraton, or Adam, to their portraits by Reynolds, Gainsborough, or Romney, to their ruffles and laces, which required delicate gestures. No English generation before her day had been called upon to grace an environment so exquisite. Miss Burney saw, valued, and shared the attempt—and laughed at its incongruities.

Evelina

Evelina (1778), her first and most regarded novel, appeared at an auspicious moment when little or no coolly decorous and elegant fiction—in contrast to sentimental ardors—was being produced. It appeared anonymously, most of her family pretending at least ignorance of her authorship.

[17] F. G. Black, "Edward Kimber: Anonymous Novelist," *Harvard Studies & Notes in Phil. & Lit.*, XVII (1935). 27-42.

[18] Miss Burney (1752-1840) was the daughter of Dr. Charles Burney (1726-1814), organist and historian of music. Among Dr. Burney's early friends of influence was Fulke Greville (proud but second son of the fifth Lord Brooke), whose wife, Walpole's "pretty Fanny Macartney," was Fanny Burney's godmother. Another friend of Dr. Burney's, Samuel Crisp, became the "adopted father" (called "Daddy Crisp") of the Burney girls. He was Fanny's closest confidant and doubtless a prototype of Evelina's Mr. Villars. With the success of *Evelina* Miss Burney, aged 26, became the admired friend of Dr. Johnson and all his circle, particularly of Mrs. Thrale, who introduced her widely in society. (See James L. Clifford's *Hester Lynch Piozzi*, 1940). During the years 1786-91 Fanny was second keeper of the robes to Queen Charlotte. In 1793 she married a refugee from France, General d'Arblay, and during the decade 1802-1812 they lived in France. After their return to England, and especially after his death in 1818, Mme d'Arblay lived out her long old age in quiet retirement.— Apart from her novels she wrote *Memoirs of Dr. Burney* (3v, 1832), *The Diary and Letters of Madame d'Arblay* (7v, 1842-46), and *The Early Diary of Frances Burney* (2v, 1889). Biographical studies have been written by Austin Dobson (1903), by Constance Hill (*Juniper Hall*, 1904; *The House in St. Martin's Street*, 1907; *Fanny Burney at the Court of Queen Charlotte*, 1912), by R. B. Johnson (1926), and by Christopher Lloyd (1936).

It was an instant and enormous success among the best people. All the world from Dr. Johnson, Sir Joshua Reynolds, and Edmund Burke to Mrs. Delany and the Duchess of Portland were most complimentary—as one can see from Miss Burney's *Diary* where their favorable comments are carefully recorded. In *Evelina* as elsewhere Miss Burney wisely limited herself to a field that she understood, and she published only after a long apprenticeship. The story is in most senses an antithesis to *Tom Jones*. Evelina, with a stigma on her birth, must be owned by her father and show herself socially worthy of her paragon of masculine decorum, Lord Orville. The plot device most commonly used is summed up in the French term *contretemps*: unseasonable coincidence complicates many a simple circumstance. A vulgar grandmother intrudes most unhappily; people hear and misinterpret half-heard remarks or catch glimpses of seemingly equivocal but actually innocent situations. The inexperience of Evelina constantly gets her into small difficulties from more than one of which the impeccable Orville somewhat frigidly rescues her. The reader is ultimately almost as much surprised as Evelina herself to find that his lordship is in love with her.

Among her vulgar characters Miss Burney is happiest. Mr. Smith, the "gentleman *manqué*," was a great favorite, and the Branghtons, Evelina's crude kinfolk, were a great cause of mirth. Here the author's sense of ridicule and insight into degrees and kinds of "low" behavior serve her well. She is unhappy in her practical-joking sea-captain, Mirvan, and is not altogether sure in her handling of the "French" grandmother, Mme Duval, but for the rest her gallery of eccentrics is full, varied, and convincing. As her *Diary*—perhaps her greatest work after all—shows, she almost transcribes more than one eccentric from real life. Certainly she forgets "universality" in the face of an original character.

Evelina is effectively cast in epistolary form; only *Humphry Clinker* uses letters to better effect. But in her second novel, *Cecilia* (1782), which deals   Cecilia with similar material, she discarded letters, and wrote in ten "books" subdivided into chapters of greatly varying lengths. The reason very possibly is that after *Evelina* she was urged to write a comedy. Significantly, she shrank from the stage as unsuitable for a lady; but in her second novel she wished perhaps to show that she could build up highly dramatic scenes of some length, and this could not be done well in letters. Even in *Evelina* she is as much interested in dramatic situation as she is in the sort of emotional analysis that made the letter a good form for Richardson and others.

Cecilia Beverley's difficulty is that her fortune has been left her on condition that she marry a man who will take her name. By *contretemps* she falls in love with young Delvile, who ardently returns her affection; but his family is proud of its antiquity, and he alone can perpetuate its name; hence their love is frustrated through four volumes and unspeakable agonies. Then a secret marriage takes place, but again misunderstandings, baseless jealousies, separate them until Cecilia runs mad at night in the streets of London and is only recovered by Delvile through a shopkeeper's notice inserted in

an early "agony column" of *The Daily Advertiser*. *Cecilia* has less of grotesquely comic vulgarity than *Evelina,* but the heroine has a galaxy of three
guardians each in his way unbelievable, and there is a mad moralist, Albany,
who appears at the oddest moments to utter diatribes against the follies of
fashionable life. The story is more melodramatic than *Evelina,* more sentimental, less comic, but equally thrilling.

*Miss
Burney's
Later
Novels*

With *Cecilia* Miss Burney's career as novelist really stopped. *Camilla*
(1796) and *The Wanderer, or Female Difficulties* (1814) were tediously
lacking in narrative interest, and were in fact courtesy books rather than
stories. Her years at court in the service of the Queen had increased her
regard for formality; and the horrors of the French Revolution doubtless
heightened her belief in the best people. She was proud of having made the
novel a valued and respectable vehicle for social instruction, and this pride
with an increasing sense of the dignity of her function expressed itself in a
cumbrous style that has been blamed on her personal admiration for Dr.
Johnson. If a similar style were not to be found in other novelists who strove
to be literary, the explanation might be satisfactory. But as the letter to her
father prefixed to *The Wanderer* shows, she had come to regard the novel
as by no means trivial in nature though of "frivolous exterior." Her late
attempt to dignify this exterior was unfortunate; her early success in writing
letters in a natural style and in portraying social correctness and social eccentricities, in creating a type of novel that, through manipulation of accidental
misunderstanding or unseasonable coincidence, delineated "female difficulties" thrillingly, is undoubted. This fictional genre she passed on to her great
superior, Jane Austen; and it is notable that a moral passage in the last
chapter of *Cecilia* gave not merely the theme but even the title to *Pride and
Prejudice*.

VI

The Drama, 1740-1785

The year 1740 saw the publication of Colley Cibber's *Apology*, which included an account of the drama from 1660 to the time in the thirties when the old Drury Lane company of actors finally disappeared.[1] In 1741 emerged the greatest theatrical genius of the century, David Garrick whose success in *Richard III* at the unlicensed theatre in Goodman's Fields made him instantly the idol of theatre-goers. With him emerged a more natural method of acting; but increased dependence on histrionic skill did not tend to promote literary quality in the drama. With such performers as Macklin, Quin, Barry, J. P. Kemble, Kitty Clive, Peg Woffington, and, lastly, the tragedy queen, Sarah Siddons, who after 1782 dominated performances at Drury Lane, it was not necessary to have great playwrights, and almost none appeared. Three or four theatres at most easily accommodated patrons. Drury Lane, under the distinguished management of Garrick[2] (till 1776), of Sheridan (till 1788), and thereafter of J. P. Kemble, Mrs. Siddons' brother, was the "first" theatre normally. Covent Garden was in general less distinguished, but George Colman the Elder while in charge there (1767-77)

Personalities of the Theatre

---

[1] For the drama of this period histories with varying amounts of detail are as follows: David E. Baker, Isaac Reed, and Stephen Jones, *Biographia Dramatica* (3v, 1812); John Genest, *Some Account of the English Stage* (10v, Bath, 1832); Percy H. Fitzgerald, *A New History of the English Stage* (2v, 1882); George H. Nettleton, *English Drama of the Restoration and Eighteenth Century (1642-1780)* (1914); Ernest Bernbaum, *The Drama of Sensibility* (Boston, 1915); Alwin Thaler, *Shakspere to Sheridan* (Cambridge, Mass., 1922); Allardyce Nicoll, *A History of Late Eighteenth Century Drama, 1750-1800* (Cambridge, 1927). For two volumes of invaluable theatrical records of this period see Dougald MacMillan, *Drury Lane Calendar, 1747-1776* (Oxford, 1938) and, by the same scholar, *Catalogue of the Larpent Plays in the Huntington Library* (San Marino, Calif., 1939).

[2] David Garrick (1717-1779) was born at Hereford and educated in Lichfield and in Samuel Johnson's "academy" at Edial. In March, 1737, he came up to London with Johnson. Presently he and his brother started a wine business, but this proving unsuccessful David, already interested in dramatic writing, tried acting. His speedy success enabled him in 1747 to purchase a part of the patent for Drury Lane, and his career as manager began. He did much to revive the popularity of Shakespeare, and he wrote himself numerous pieces—many of them afterpieces or farces and others light comedies that furnished good rôles for himself and his company. Their literary merit was, on the whole, inconsiderable. After 1766 he ceased to act much, but continued as manager. In 1769 he organized the Shakespeare Jubilee at Stratford, and in 1773 he was elected to Johnson's Club. In 1776 he took leave of the stage by playing once again a complete round of his favorite characters.—*Dramatic Works* (3v, 1798); *Poetical Works* (2v, 1785); *Private Correspondence*, ed. James Boaden (2v, 1831-2); *Some Unpublished Correspondence*, ed. George P. Baker (Boston, 1907); *Pineapples of Finest Flavor* [letters], ed. David M. Little (Cambridge, Mass., 1930).—Thomas Davies, *Memoirs of Garrick* (2v, 1780; rev. S. Jones, 2v, 1808); Arthur Murphy, *Life of Garrick* (2v, 1801); Sir Joshua Reynolds, *Johnson and Garrick* (1816); ed. R. B. Johnson (1927); Percy H. Fitzgerald, *Life of Garrick* (2v, 1868; rev., 1899); Florence Parsons, *Garrick and his Circle* (1906); Dougald MacMillan, "David Garrick as Critic," *SP*, xxxi (1934). 69-83; Elizabeth P. Stein, *David Garrick, Dramatist* (1938).

staged both of Goldsmith's comedies, which had been refused by Garrick, and thus gave the house distinction. In the sixties, the supreme mimic of the period, Samuel Foote, got control of the Little Theatre in the Haymarket, famous earlier for Fielding's robust farces, and there in midday performances indulged his gifts for impersonations, farces, musical shows, and other entertainments. Whereas Drury Lane and, to a less degree, Covent Garden, stuck to the stereotyped sort of comedy and tragedy, the Little Theatre in the Haymarket was "experimental" (if one wishes to be polite)— or scurrilous. Foote's impersonations made him many enemies. Dr. Johnson, when asked how he escaped exhibition, replied of Foote: "Sir, fear restrained him; he knew I would have broken his bones." But Foote in spite of the libelous quality of his satire preserved a vital if unorthodox theatrical tradition.

Stagecraft

Except with new or very popular plays theatres normally offered as an evening's entertainment a major piece, either tragedy or comedy, and an afterpiece [3] of contrasting character. Between the acts frequently appeared singers, dancers, acrobats, or strong men—to keep the audience quiet. Afterpieces and even the major piece might frequently be musical comedies, such as Bickerstaffe's *Love in a Village* (1762) or Sheridan's *Duenna* (1775). In stagecraft the period shows some advance in lighting methods, and, after the coming of the Alsatian De Loutherbourg to Drury Lane in 1771, a considerable advance in the realism of scene painting.[4] The costumes usually made little pretense to historicity. Any lesser lady of the stage was proud to act "in a *cast* gown of some person of quality." Fashion rather than history was attended to. In 1764 *Richard III* was performed "in the Habits of the Times," and in 1773 *Macbeth* was staged in Scottish costumes: "modern dress," however, was the normal thing. Exotic performances or spectacles got special treatment. In 1785 John O'Keeffe and De Loutherbourg staged at Covent Garden a pantomime called *Omai, or a Trip round the World,* a landmark in the stagecraft of local color.[5] Omai, a noble savage from the South Seas, had visited England (1774-6) as a result of Captain Cook's second voyage to the South Seas, and had been a notable social success. With him had been brought back drawings of local costumes, weapons, and utensils, all of which were later used to give this pantomime a great pretense of local authenticity. It was at once a symbol of the cult of the noble savage, of British empire-building, and of the apparent intellectual bankruptcy of the London theatre. Outward realism already was a frequent substitute for sound psychology and good plotting in these days of pantomimes.

The more legitimate plays of the period were less novel than *Omai*. They were usually of obvious derivation and story. During the period of Garrick's

[3] C. R. Baskervill, "Play-lists and Afterpieces of the Mid-Eighteenth Century," *MP*, XXIII (1926). 445-464.
[4] W. J. Lawrence, "The Pioneers of Modern English Stage Mounting: De Loutherbourg," *The Magazine of Art* (March, 1895). Also Russell Thomas, "Contemporary Taste in the Stage Decorations of London Theaters, 1770-1800," *MP*, XLII (1944). 65-78.
[5] William Huse, "A Noble Savage on the Stage," *MP*, XXXIII (1936). 303-316; Thomas B. Clark, *Omai* (San Francisco, 1940).

dominance the tragedies and romantic comedies of Shakespeare [6] and other *Dramatic* Elizabethans were frequently revived or, even more frequently, reworked. *Fare of the* Restoration comedies had to be made moral: Garrick himself made Wycher- *Time* ley's country wife a decent woman in his own *Country Girl* (1766), and there were numerous similar moral improvements. Translations of French plays—those of Destouches, Voltaire, Diderot, and many others—were a chief source throughout the period, and after 1786 German plays were adapted with success, with the work of Kotzebue having enormous vogue in the last decade of the century. The narrow vein of stereotyped comedy of manners was nearing exhaustion, and neo-classical tragedy practically had reached that point. The result was that not merely sentimental comedy but also pantomimes, musical comedies, and burlettas, throve—and these last are almost never drama in any literary sense.

The tragedies of this period lacked both novelty and freshness. As in the *Tragedies* first fifty years of the century, there were attempts to use native historical stories for tragic plots, but this was usually done without great success. To be sure, Henry Brooke's use of the worn story of *The Earl of Essex* (1750) had still some individuality. Hall Hartson's *Countess of Salisbury* (1767) was a sentimental yet successful adaptation of the novel *Longsword* (1762) written by Hartson's tutor, Dr. Thomas Leland; Thomas Francklin reworked a play by J.-F. de la Harpe called *The Earl of Warwick* (1766); William Woodfall, the journalist and actor, reworked Richard Savage's *Sir Thomas Overbury* with success in 1777, and Hannah More's pseudo-historical *Percy* was well received at the end of the same year. Some of Shakespeare's historical plays were very popular, but no new tragedies on English stories held the boards really well.

More successful were a few plays based upon a more modern interpretation of *domestica facta* that encouraged the writing of "domestic" or bourgeois tragedy. Edward Moore's prose *Gamester* [7] (1753) was a proper successor to *George Barnwell*. The hero, Beverley, confirmed in the vice of gaming, loses his whole fortune through the machinations of a melodramatic villain-friend (who remotely recalls Iago and Jonathan Wild), is accused of murder, and poisons himself just before learning that he has succeeded to the wealth of his uncle. The tears of the virtuous Mrs. Beverley doubtless seemed both affecting and "natural." Similarly in the very successful *Douglas* (1756), the masterpiece of "the Scottish Shakespeare," John Home [8] (1722-1808), Lady Randolph's ever fresh grief for an infant son lost twenty years ago, and now recovered only for a tragic fate, marks the play as devoted to "simple nature." Its emotional power kept it on the stage for a century or more in spite of obvious defects. Richard Cumberland's prose tragedy, *The Mysterious Husband* (1783), with a plot based on secret marriages, was somewhat less lurid than Walpole's unacted *Mysterious Mother*

[6] On the adaptations of Shakespeare see George C. D. Odell, *Shakespeare from Betterton to Irving* (2v, 1920), and Hazelton Spencer, *Shakespeare Improved* (Cambridge, Mass., 1927).
[7] John H. Caskey, *The Life and Works of Edward Moore* (New Haven, 1927).
[8] Alice E. Gipson, *John Home* (Caldwell, Idaho, 1917).

(1768), but not powerful enough to strengthen the domestic tradition in tragedy, which was doing better in France and Germany than in its native England. Remotely lofty plots were still in demand; and if stories from English history were used with increasing frequency, Orientals, Peruvians, royal slaves, and noble Romans still made highly acceptable tragic heroes. The continued influence of Voltaire, from whom, for example, Arthur Murphy's *Orphan of China* (1759) derived, may account in part for the Oriental vogue. Pretentious poets, like William Whitehead, might still use classical stories, but the swing was away from that cult. William Mason, to be sure, used Greek tragedy as a model for his British stories of *Elfrida* and *Caractacus,* thus combining two traditions. But tragedy lacked the freshness necessary to hold its own against the increasing popularity of sentimental comedy.

Not that all comedy was sentimental. Comedy of manners was frequently attempted with success, and the loosely wrought comedy (or farce) that was topical and personal in its satire continued to find a home in the theatre where Henry Fielding had domesticated it, the Little Haymarket. The *Samuel* libelous work of Samuel Foote [9] (1720-1777) in the third quarter of the *Foote* century illustrates this at its most sensational limit. His plays are frequently devised to give the author-actor opportunity to show his gifts of impersonation, not merely in his noonday skits *The Diversions of the Morning* (1747), *An Auction of Pictures* (1748), and *Taste* (1752)—which are all practically identical except for their titles—but in his "scandal-chronicle" comedies as well. In *The Minor* (1760) he indulges in the popular sport of satirizing George Whitefield the Methodist; in *The Patron* (1764) he depicts Bubb Dodington (1691-1762), and in *The Maid of Bath* (1771) he derides the pre-Sheridan suitors of Miss Elizabeth Linley, the beautiful singer soon to be Mrs. Sheridan. These are but specimens. All of Foote's pieces are loosely constructed and, through their personalities, cheaply effective—grand vehicles for his talents in mimicry. The vitality of his performances can be judged in part by the influence they had on Garrick and even on Sheridan's play, *The Critic.*

It is usual to classify the comedies of this period, on the one hand, as old-fashioned witty plays that aimed to provoke laughter and amusement, *Laughing* and, on the other hand, as sentimental plays that avowed morality as their *and* object and at least secured tears as a response. Actually all comedies of the *Weeping* time have rid themselves of Restoration looseness of morals: the real diver-*Comedies* gence is between laughter and sentiment. Managers—Garrick and Colman, for example—were officially in favor of mirth; but their commercial instincts

[9] Foote spent three years (1737-40) in Worcester College, Oxford, and thereafter had a career in London as young man about town. Having dissipated his fortune, he became an actor and was a great success because of his astonishing gifts of mimicry. In 1766 he obtained from the Duke of York the patent for a theatre in Westminster as compensation for a practical joke that had cost him his leg. He built the new Haymarket Theatre the following year, and continued to hold it until 1777, when he sold it to Colman.—*Works* (4v, 1786); ed. John Badcock (3v, 1830).—Percy H. Fitzgerald, *Samuel Foote: A Biography* (1910); Mary M. Belden, *The Dramatic Work of Samuel Foote* (New Haven, 1929).

made them very tolerant of "the luxury of tears." Playwrights found it somewhat easier to produce sentimental plays, which depended more on mystery and plot, than to turn out plays rich in sparkling wit, incisive and novel perception of faulty manners, and pointed situations. Even the best Restoration comedies lacked story and neat plot construction: in days of less witty genius when taste was returning to the story-drama of Shakespeare's age, a sentimental plot was both a refuge and an asset.

There were, however, many plays that relied on *vis comica*. Among these *Arthur* may be ranged those of Arthur Murphy [10] (1727-1805), who between 1756 *Murphy* and 1777 produced over a dozen farces or comedies. Tired of life as a bank clerk Murphy set up as journalist-essayist in 1752, and two years later began appearances as an actor. His brief career as such contributed something to his first play, a farce called *The Apprentice* (1756). His best afterpiece, *The Citizen* (1761), and a rewritten farce, *Three Weeks after Marriage* (1776), bring to the old sport of baiting citizens a new edge due to Murphy's own brief sojourn in a banking house. Drugget, in *Three Weeks,* one of Murphy's best characters, is the parvenu citizen of taste, a belated expert in topiary work, who wishes to cut two fine yews to represent Gog and Magog, because, as he says, "I won't have anything in my garden that looks like what it is." His best five-act comedies are *The Way to Keep Him* (1760) and *Know Your Own Mind* (1777). In this last-named play Murphy presents three well-contrasted ladies—Miss Neville, who arouses our pity for poor relations of charm; Lady Jane and Lady Bell, the shy and witty pair of sisters. Lady Bell speaks out to her shy sister: "You may let 'concealment feed on your damask cheek.' My damask cheek, I hope, was made for other purposes." Even these best of Murphy's comedies owe much to French sources; they are true comedies of manners, but are somewhat deficient in lightness, ease, and elegance of dialogue. Though at his real best in comedy, Murphy produced a half-dozen successful tragedies. The earliest was his *Orphan of China* (1759), adapted from Voltaire, and his best were *The Grecian Daughter* (1772) and *Alzuma* (1773), which blends classical and Peruvian elements. Habitually in most of his plays Murphy took his inspiration from books, but he usually adapted his borrowings effectively to the taste of the moment.

In native ability George Colman the Elder [11] (1732-1794) surpassed

[10] Murphy was born in Ireland and educated at the English College in St. Omer (France). He returned to England and Ireland for commercial employment, became interested in both the theatre and the law, entered Lincoln's Inn (1757), and although devoting most of his time to dramatic writing, continued to practise law until his retirement from the bar in 1788. He was Commissioner of Bankrupts, and at the end of his life had an annual pension of £200.—*Works* (7v, 1786). His periodical essays include *The Gray's Inn Journal* (52 nos., 1753-4; reprinted 2v [104 nos.], 1756); *The Test* (with Henry Fox and others, 35 nos., 1756-7); *The Auditor* (43 nos., 1762-3).—Jesse Foot, *Life of Arthur Murphy* (1811); John Homer Caskey, "Arthur Murphy and the War on Sentimental Comedy," *JEGP*, xxx (1931). 563-577; Howard H. Dunbar, *The Dramatic Career of Arthur Murphy* (1946; *MLA Revolving Fund Ser.,* xiv); John P. Emery, *Arthur Murphy, an Eminent English Dramatist of the Eighteenth Century* (Philadelphia, 1946).

[11] Colman the Elder was born in Florence, where his father was British envoy. He was educated at Westminster, Christ Church, Oxford, and in Lincoln's Inn. During the middle fifties, with other friends of Westminster days—notably Bonnell Thornton, Robert Lloyd, and William Cowper—he formed a "Nonsense Club." He became intimate with Garrick (1758),

Murphy, but the early promise of Colman's career was not fulfilled. After a half-dozen years (1760-66) of producing comedies and farces of vivid reality and vigor, managerial duties, or some other cause, brought about a decline in the quality of his plays. Although he wrote a variety of pieces during the years 1760 to 1786, many of these are so obviously derivative that he hardly deserves the credit for them. One of his most significant adaptations was Beaumont and Fletcher's *Philaster* (1763), which remained popular for years. In 1777 his *Spanish Barber* was based on *Le Barbier de Séville*, the famous new comedy by Beaumarchais; and his last play, *Tit for Tat* (1786), was based on a recent Dublin success, which in turn derived from Marivaux. Colman's first work, *Polly Honeycombe* (1760), was a gay afterpiece satirizing the novel-reading girl and warning that soon, if not already, it would be more reprehensible to read novels than plays. Polly, like her descendant, Lydia Languish (and also, vaguely, Lydia Melford in *Humphry Clinker*), frequents the circulating library—"that evergreen tree of diabolical knowledge." [12] In 1761 in *The Jealous Wife* Colman contrived a somewhat novel plot in the distresses of Harriot Russet, whose initial situation reminds one of Sophia Western in London: Harriot escapes from the advances of Lord Trinket in her aunt's house, and finds shelter with the Oaklys; Mrs. Oakly is the jealous wife, but all turns out happily when her husband reduces her jealousy to ridicule, and then Harriot and young Charles Oakly, true lovers, are made happy. *The Jealous Wife* was one of the most popular and most truly comic plays of the century. Its equal in character interest and skilful construction was the play in which Colman had the considerable aid of David Garrick, *The Clandestine Marriage* (1766). Here Lord Ogleby has brought his nephew, Sir John Melvil, to arrange a marriage with the elder daughter of the newly rich Sterlings. Both nephew and uncle, however, successively are smitten with the younger daughter, Fanny, who is already secretly married to her father's clerk, Lovewell. Much of the comedy depends on the matriarchal Mrs. Heidelberg, on the superannuated foppishness of Lord Ogleby, and on satire of the *nouveau riche* taste in gardening and other foibles of the day. The serious complications come to a thrilling climax, and when the clerk Lovewell announces that he is "the happiest of men," the faithful maid Betty sobs, "I could cry my eyes out to hear his magnimity." It has been suspected that the audience shared in this benevolent sobbing. The seriousness of the suspense in the Fanny-Lovewell action brings to the play the mixture of comic and sentimental elements that is the normal characteristic of the drama at this time.

devoted himself increasingly to dramatic writing, and upon the death of his uncle, William Pulteney, Earl of Bath (1764), he abandoned the law. For the years 1767-77 he was manager of the Covent Garden theatre and during 1777-89 of the Haymarket theatre. He became insane shortly before his death.—*Dramatic Works* (4v, 1777).—George Colman the Younger, *Random Records of my Life* (2v, 1830); Richard B. Peake, *Memoirs of the Colman Family* (2v, 1841); Joseph M. Beatty, "Garrick, Colman and *The Clandestine Marriage*," *MLN*, xxxvi (1921). 129-141; Eugene R. Page, *George Colman the Elder* (1935); Howard P. Vincent, "Christopher George Colman, 'Lunatick'," *RES*, xviii (1942). 38-48.

[12] Austin Dobson, " 'Polly Honeycombe'," in *Eighteenth Century Vignettes, Third Series* (1896), pp. 83-103.

Chief among the sentimental playwrights were Hugh Kelly (1739-1777) *Hugh*
and Richard Cumberland (1732-1811). Kelly's career was brief and very *Kelly*
successful.[13] A needy Irishman, for the first years of his residence in London,
1760-67, he relied on contributions to periodicals and work on newspapers
for a living. Garrick took him into protection, and he won fame by his first
comedy, *False Delicacy* (1768), which was staged in successful rivalry with
Goldsmith's first play, *The Good Natur'd Man. False Delicacy* was acted
over twenty times the first season, and within the year ten thousand printed
copies of it were sold. The plot employs a triple intrigue, giving rise to
much complexity of situation. Lady Betty, a young widow, too delicate for
the impropriety of a second marriage, will not have Lord Winworth, whom
secretly she loves. He consequently turns to her protégée, Miss Marchmont—
who, though in love with Sidney, is under obligations to Lady Betty, who
seems to wish Miss Marchmont to make Lord Winworth happy. Meanwhile
Miss Rivers, in love with Sir Harry, must have the delicacy to obey her
father and marry Sidney. The false delicacy of these three ladies is cured
by the two anti-sentimental characters, Mrs. Harley and Cecil, who furnish
the comedy in the play. As a result of his new fame it was alleged that Kelly
received a pension from the unpopular minister Lord North, and when his
second comedy, *A Word to the Wise* (1770), was brought on, it was at once
damned by political cabal. After a negligible tragedy, *Clementina* (1771),
The School for Wives (1773), the least sentimental of Kelly's plays, was
successfully produced. It, like *False Delicacy,* ends in three weddings after
misunderstood situations. In 1774 Kelly produced his last play, was called to
the bar, and gave up literature—both the theatre and newspaper work. The
play, *The Romance of an Hour,* is a two-act afterpiece, in which Zelida, a
petite Hindoue, "a character of perfect simplicity," finally marries the man
she loves rather than the Colonel to whom her father had bequeathed her.
The comedy comes largely from a near-admiral whose manners and language, as his wife judiciously remarks, are those of the forecastle. In concern
over the distress of Zelida this would-be wit hopes that the arrival of the
Colonel "will prevent the worms of her sorrow from eating into the planks
of her constitution."

Richard Cumberland[14] had a longer, more distinguished, and more

---

[13] *The Works of Hugh Kelly, to which is Prefixed his Life* (1778).—Mark Schorer, "Hugh
Kelly: His Place in the Sentimental School," *PQ,* XII (1933). 389-401.

[14] Richard Cumberland, son of the Master of Trinity College, Cambridge, and- grandson
of a more famous Master of the College (Richard Bentley), was born in the Master's Lodge,
February 19, 1732. He was educated in Bury St. Edmunds, Westminster, and Trinity College,
Cambridge. His brilliant record as a student helped him to both academic and civic employments. His work was concerned with the Board of Trade and with various American colonies.
He was briefly (1780-1) Ambassador to Spain, from which mission he returned distressed in
health and in finances. His last years were spent in Tunbridge Wells, where he devoted most
of his time to varied literary work. He died in 1811, the acquaintance of Byron, Tom Moore,
and Scott.—Five from his forty plays (never collected in one edition) are found in Vol.
XVIII of Mrs. Inchbald's *British Theatre* (1808). He also published translations, poetry, religious
tracts, essays, conducted *The London Review* (2v, 1809), wrote two novels, *Henry* (1795)
and *John de Lancaster* (3v, 1809), and published his own *Memoirs* (2v, 1806-7). Stanley T.
Williams has written the standard biography, *Richard Cumberland* (New Haven, 1917), and
has published additional articles in *MLN* during 1920 and 1921.

Richard Cumberland

quarrelsome career than did Kelly. His eye for good materials was both covetous and furtive, and although he borrowed plots or situations freely, he was from the beginning of his career sensitive to accusations of such thefts. Thus he was easily identified as the original of Sir Fretful Plagiary in Sheridan's *Critic*. He first achieved success in his comedy *The Brothers* (1769), and while he produced a half-dozen tragedies and a few musical comedies, his real success lay in sentiment. *The Brothers* is typical of its day in its complicated plot, its deep-dyed villain contrasting with a completely virtuous younger brother, its use of a secret marriage, of a quarrelsome married couple, and its enveloping gloom of distress. His best comedy, *The West Indian* (1771), introduces an element notable in several of his plays, the defense of character types formerly treated as ridiculous. In his *Memoirs* he explains his object: "I introduced the characters of persons who had been usually exhibited on the stage as the butts for ridicule and abuse, and endeavoured to present them in such lights as might tend to reconcile the world to them, and them to the world." In *The West Indian* these puffed characters are the Irishman O'Flaherty, who is made genteelly winsome, and Belcour, the West Indian, a child of nature in Rousseau's pattern. Belcour is certainly one of the most attractive heroes of sentimentality. The same method of characterization is used in other plays: in *The Fashionable Lover* (1772) he combats the prejudice against Scots by creating the virtuous steward, Colin Macleod; and in *The Jew* (1794) he created Sheva to combat anti-Semitism. Allied with this element of purpose Cumberland had an obvious tendency to melodrama. *The Wheel of Fortune* (1795), his most appealing play of this sort, was long enormously successful. Its central character, Penruddock, is an interesting summation of much in the whole period. He is the Man of the Hill in *Tom Jones* and a dozen other places: the unsocial hermit, here devoted to the thought of revenge for long past wrongs, but (since this is a moment for facile moral reform) here to be converted to ultimate benevolence. The character of mixed good and evil, with good bound to win through ultimately, made Penruddock one of the best emotional rôles of the day. The moving performance of J. P. Kemble, who created the rôle, doubtless gave the play much of its power. Cumberland's last comedy, *The Widow's Only Son,* was staged in 1810. His death in the following year and burial in the Poet's Corner in the Abbey ended one of the longest careers known for an English dramatist.

Opposition to Sentimental Comedy

Throughout his fifty years as playwright there had been notable objection to the sort of play called comedy by Cumberland and his admirers. Garrick himself passed jokes about the advisability of putting a steeple on the playhouse now that it was a temple of virtue, and sneered gently at "these our moral and religious days." Avowedly it was a warfare between two schools, one stressing the desire to promote morality and the other a desire to promote mirth and entertainment. But the contrast thus stated is surely too strong. If Hugh Kelly and Cumberland made obvious concessions to mirth, so Goldsmith and Sheridan, the two great writers supposed hostile to "weeping .

comedies," made concessions to morality. All plays, one may rashly say, were now moral; but some preached more explicitly than others. In general, also, the morality of the sentimentalists was excessively facile: from Cibber's *Love's Last Shift* (1696) to Cumberland's *First Love* (1795) the erring are shamed into virtue with surprising—and unconvincing—ease. The situation, suggesting at times a not too sincere didacticism, is simply explained by the fact that audiences were readier to pay for tears than for laughter.

The subservience of the managers to their own commercial interests was what first moved Goldsmith to animosity,[15] and his attack on the managers in the chapter "Of the Stage" in his *Enquiry into the Present State of Polite Learning in Europe* (1759) was not forgiven by Garrick. He declined both *Goldsmith's* Goldsmith's plays for Drury Lane, and in 1768 injured the success of *The* *Views* *Good Natur'd Man* by producing in competition with it Hugh Kelly's new comedy, *False Delicacy*. Shortly before submitting *She Stoops to Conquer* to public censure, Goldsmith published in *The Westminster Magazine*[16] his essay *A Comparison between Laughing and Sentimental Comedy*. He bluntly queries "whether the exhibition of human distress is likely to afford the mind more entertainment than that of human absurdity?" He asserts that "the distresses of the mean by no means affect us so strongly as the calamities of the great." "While we melt for Belisarius, we scarcely give halfpence to the beggar." Goldsmith thinks that the success of so-called sentimental comedies, "in which the virtues of private life are exhibited, rather than the vices exposed, and the distresses rather than the faults of mankind make our interest in the piece," may be due to novelty or to "their flattering every man in his favorite foible." But he thinks such plays deficient in *vis comica,* and thinks audiences likely by being "too fastidious" to banish humor from the stage.

In his *Good Natur'd Man* Goldsmith had not been too fastidious; he had *Goldsmith's* instead offensively put fine sentiments about generosity into the mouth of a *Plays* low bailiff—and of that scene the exquisite auditors forced the excision. But as a partial concession to such possible critics he had combined in his hero, Young Honeywood (as he had in Beau Tibbs and the Man in Black in his essays), both sentiment and criticism of sentiment. Young Honeywood, to his uncle's disgust, "loves all the world"; and such "love" is undiscriminating. "His good-nature arises rather from his fears of offending the importunate, than his desire of making the deserving happy." Thus Goldsmith preaches, here as elsewhere, a *prudent* benevolism. Honeywood, like Fielding's good men, is unsuspicious and easily deceived: the play is the history of his education, and in the process Miss Richland aids more actively than most eighteenth-century heroines could have done. The subplot resembles that of Bevil Junior and Indiana in *The Conscious Lovers*: it is, if anything, less carefully constructed than Steele's story. Croaker—an obviously "humorous" character of the late Elizabethan type—is used to subvert sentimentality:

[15] For treatment of Goldsmith's nondramatic works see below, ch. VII.
[16] For January, 1773; also in his *Works* (ed. J. W. M. Gibbs), I. 398-402.

"Ah! my dear friend," he croaks, "it is a perfect satisfaction to be miserable with you." The play got little recognition from its early audiences, since in spite of its easy dialogue the whole lacks focus and structure, and even the comic effect its author sought.

She Stoops to Conquer (1773), on the other hand, was an immediate success, and has always remained one of the half-dozen most popular comedies in English. From the start it was recognized as almost farce; but even in days when it was ill-bred to laugh loudly, this play made Horace Walpole and the other exquisites "laugh very much." All English audiences since 1773 have joined in the laughter, and in spite of defects in structure, plausibility, and characterization, its appeal has hardly waned. Enjoyment here is not much heightened by analysis. One sees the improbability of the continued misapprehension that the Hardcastle mansion is a country inn; one can accept the comic bashfulness of Young Marlow, but not his inability to distinguish a barmaid from a young lady; one is pleased with Tony Lumpkin's ability to display his Latinity in his song on The Three Pigeons in Act I, but surprised to find him practically illiterate in Act IV (he is of course stupid or shrewd as the individual situation demands); and one finds Mrs. Hardcastle's kneeling to her own husband in her own garden and fancying herself forty miles away on Crackskull Common face to face with a highwayman—one finds this a strain on the bedazzled imagination. These defects would kill any other comedy, and yet they count as nothing in this jolliest of all plays. Whatever its absurdities, the action seems to move naturally and among natural homely people—not the artificially sensitive persons found in sentimental comedy nor the hard, brittle wits of high comedy. The characters are all easily individualized—drawn again in the "humorous" Jonsonian fashion—and they are all individuals new to the drama of their day. The historic excellence of the work lies not in the fact that it is apparently anti-sentimental or that it is obviously attempting a revival of the comedy of manners. It is *sui generis,* not sentimental and not overtly anti-sentimental. It has been likened to the work of Farquhar, but it is better written and is morally innocent. Like much of Goldsmith's work, it is casually rather than carefully organized; and it is not too surely prophetic of more dramatic masterpieces from Goldsmith. He died a twelvemonth after its success. The play has succeeded perfectly in being what its author hoped it would be—one of the most entertaining plays in English.

Sheridan   Richard Brinsley Sheridan,[17] ordinarily regarded as Goldsmith's aid and

[17] Sheridan (1751-1816) was the grandson of Swift's friend, Dr. Thomas Sheridan. His father was an actor, who, when Richard was not yet twenty, left London for Bath, where he taught elocution. Richard's mother, Frances Sheridan (1724-66), was the author of two novels and of three plays. Some translations, popular verses, and an unacceptable farce were the products of her son's early years. In 1772 the beautiful singer, Elizabeth Linley, persecuted by undesired suitors, persuaded young Richard to escort her to a refuge in a religious house in France. In France they allegedly married, the ceremony being repeated in England a year later. Meanwhile Sheridan fought two duels with a less fortunate suitor, and was "rusticated" at Waltham Abbey by his father. In the late summer of 1774 he wrote *The Rivals,* and for the next five years his chief activities were theatrical. In 1776 he became part owner and manager of the Drury Lane theatre, and in 1777 he was elected a member of

successor in the attempt to restore comedy to its own province of mirth, had almost as brief a career as Goldsmith. In the years 1775-79 he produced five plays and two afterpieces. One of these was a very successful comic opera, *The Duenna* (1775), which beat all records for full-length plays with seventy-five performances in its first season. Its long popularity was due to ingenious plotting and to its music rather than to any notable brilliance or wit in the lines. Another play, *A Trip to Scarborough* (1777), is a competent sterilized version of Vanbrugh's *Relapse*. The sex of the bawd Coupler is changed; Loveless and Berinthia overstep the bounds of decorum but not of morality, and the ingenious double plot is preserved effectively. Sheridan's last play, *Pizarro* (1799), adapted from the popular Kotzebue, adds nothing to his fame.

There remain, then, three original comedies, and since the last of these, *The Critic* (1779), is least important, it may be first disposed of. In method it is a "rehearsal" in the tradition instituted by the Duke of Buckingham in 1671, brought to its cleverest development by Fielding's *Tom Thumb* (1730), and used by various playwrights, among them Garrick in his *Peep behind the Curtain* (1767). It is highly significant, as Mr. Rhodes has shown, that the methods of Sheridan involve caricature rather than parody, of which last there is little in *The Critic*. The verbal dexterity of Buckingham and Fielding is discarded for impersonation and mimicry: the result is perhaps more theatrical but less literary. By the same token it tends to be more perishable because of its topical nature. Sir Fretful Plagiary is Richard Cumberland, but since here the burlesque is good satire, it transcends the personality of one man, and becomes a lasting symbol of the vanity and irritability of bards born without thick skins; and yet it remains Cumberland. Lesser burlesques are traceable, but less tangibly. The play is also a "war" play: Spain had declared war on England three or four months before *The Critic* with its rehearsal of a new tragedy called "The Spanish Armada" was presented. Thus the immediate success of the piece was topical in part; the ultimate value lies in the theatrical wisdom shown in the implicit and explicit observations made on the nature of tragedy and in the element of robust good fun that dominates every scene. Sheridan was already looking forward in 1779 to a political career, and this farcical treatment of tragedy and of public affairs came as an appropriate transition.

Sheridan's great service to English drama lies in his two high comedies.

The Critic

---

the Club on motion of Dr. Johnson himself. He was in Parliament from 1780 to 1812, and politics withdrew his attention from the theatre. His gifts as orator equaled those as playwright. With Burke he was very active in the impeachment of Warren Hastings, and his speeches were as much enjoyed as Burke's were admired. He was long the confidential adviser of the Prince Regent, who remained his generous friend to the time of Sheridan's death. Personally Sheridan was a brilliant wit of charm and fascination. Although his later years were financially perplexed, he lived gaily, drank to excess, and was an artful and scheming gallant "among fine ladies." Wit and charm made these faults venial in the Regency period. —Much myth has arisen among the facts of Sheridan's life. The best biography perhaps is *Harlequin Sheridan* by R. Crompton Rhodes (1933). Other lives, among many, are those by Walter Sichel (2v, 1909) and W. A. Darlington (1933). For the standard text see *The Plays and Poems of Sheridan*, ed. R. C. Rhodes (3v, Oxford, 1928).

The Rivals   *The Rivals* [18] and *The School for Scandal* are amazing for their period and excellent for any period. They represent a return to the ideals of witty, elegant comedy, purged of its Restoration impurities, but a return that preserves an amusing consciousness of contemporary sentimental absurdities. *The Rivals* was soundly damned at its first performance on January 17, 1775. While in rehearsal the play had been puffed as "the *ne plus ultra* of comedy," and this boast for a new playwright not yet twenty-four years old may have antagonized other literati. The title, with the knowledge that the scene was Bath, may have suggested that the squabbles over the fair Elizabeth Linley, "The Maid of Bath," were to be served up again, and that idea might stimulate to opposition Sheridan's rivals in love. But the performance was inadequate, and the play faulty. Shuter as Sir Anthony Absolute made little pretense of having learned his lines, and Lee as Sir Lucius O'Trigger was ineptly cast. The rôle of Sir Lucius, furthermore, was regarded as insulting to the Irish gentry. Coming after Cumberland's gracious O'Flaherty in *The West Indian* the rôle of Sir Lucius, as first written, naturally grated on Irish sensibilities. All told, the performance had too much buffoonery and it lasted an hour longer than usual. The only parts generally liked were the sentimental scenes between Julia and Faulkland. And so the play was withdrawn that its faults might be corrected. The rôle of Sir Lucius was largely rewritten, and the dialogue much improved. Clinch replaced Lee as actor of the rôle; Shuter learned his lines; the whole was shortened, and Sheridan's personal enemies remained quiet: the net result was that the second performance (eleven days after the first) was greeted with agreeable convulsions of laughter, and the play was repeated twelve times or more that season. It became from that moment a permanent part of English dramatic repertoire.

The intrigue of *The Rivals* is not too original, but it is skilfully conducted, and the humors of Mrs. Malaprop, Sir Anthony, Bob Acres, and indeed the whole cast are triumphs of theatrical genius. Even borrowed bits—the novel-reading girl, the coward forced into a duel, the rebellious son bent on marrying to please himself and not his father and yet making love unwittingly to the very girl his father wants him to wed—all such bits, though not new, are treated so vividly that Sheridan makes them easily his own. Even more surely did he appropriate to himself the device now called "malapropism," which had been popular since the days of Mistress Quickly, and had renewed its popularity many times in the eighteenth century. Every admirer has his favorites among Mrs. Malaprop's "nice derangement of epitaphs," but her projected schooling for girls may serve as an example:

I would send her, at nine years old, to a boarding-school, in order to learn a little ingenuity and artifice.—Then, Sir, she should have a supercilious knowledge in accounts;—and as she grew up, I would have her instructed in geometry, that she might know something of the contagious countries;—but above all, Sir Anthony, she should be mistress of orthodoxy, that she might not mis-spell, and mis-pro-

18 *The Rivals* has been admirably edited by Richard L. Purdy (Oxford, 1935).

nounce words so shamefully as girls usually do; and likewise that she might reprehend the true meaning of what she is saying.—This, Sir Anthony, is what I would have a woman know;—and I don't think there is a superstitious article in it.

Auditors in the theatre catch but fragments of this word-play, but from its profusion enough is grasped to make its uproarious effect unfailing. In lightness, crispness, and elegance of point the dialogue of the play is unsurpassed, unless by Congreve, who in wit is Sheridan's only real competitor.

Two years later (1777) the only rival to the fame of *The Rivals* was staged: *The School for Scandal*. This was carefully prepared; Sheridan was now the author-manager, and could cast his own players. In the opinion of Horace Walpole, "there were more parts performed admirably ... than I almost ever saw in any play." The dialogue this time was set down with such exquisite Congreve-like precision that it enforced excellence of delivery. James Boaden thought the comedy "better *spoken,* in all its parts, than any play that I have witnessed upon the stage." Unlike *The Rivals,* then, it sailed to success with poise, dignity—and with a dazzling glitter of wit. It has indeed been urged that even the stupid characters are here made witty, that there is a surfeit of wit. The assumption seems to be that characters—particularly servants—ought to use "the language of real life," which is a strange idea if applied to eighteenth-century servants at least. Audiences seldom balk at too much wit; only critics do that.

Much in the play is partly familiar; but here it strikes us always with the pleasure of novelty: the quarrelsome couple, here the old husband and the young wife from the country; the two brothers, one impulsive and feckless like Tom Jones, the other mouthing fine sentiments like Blifil, and plotting mischief; the "scandal-club" of Lady Sneerwell—and more besides are all familiar; yet here are felt to be endowed with new life. Apart from the dialogue, the pride of the play is doubtless the perfect manipulation of the intrigue leading inevitably to the thrilling resolution in the famous screen scene. More than marital worries are here resolved: at this crucial moment Sheridan pays his cutting respects to the sentimentalists. In this play he makes no concessions to Julias and Faulklands. He presents Charles Surface, the true man of feeling who gaily eschews fine sentiments, and Joseph, the hypocritical man of feeling, who conceals malice under falsely moral or noble sentiments. Thus, early in the screen scene, Joseph has reproached Charles for having given Sir Peter cause to suspect Lady Teazle: "I'm sorry to find, Charles, you have lately given that worthy man grounds for great uneasiness"; and before the screen goes down Sir Peter has urged Charles to be like Joseph: "He is a man of sentiment.—Well, there is nothing in the world so noble as a man of sentiment!" After the screen is down, Charles makes (for Sheridan) his retort about sentiments:

Egad, you seem all to have been diverting yourselves here at hide and seek, and I don't see who is out of the secret.—Shall I beg your ladyship to inform me? Not a word!—Brother, will you be pleased to explain this matter? What! is

The School for Scandal

Morality dumb too?—Sir Peter, though I found you in the dark, perhaps you are not so now! All mute!...so I'll leave you to yourselves—[*Going*] Brother, I'm sorry to find you have given that worthy man grounds for so much uneasiness.—Sir Peter! there's nothing in the world so noble as a man of sentiment!

If Sheridan's object was to discredit sentimentalism, this retort should have accomplished it; but sentimentalism is only an ingredient in the rich sauce of his satire. He gives us the quintessence of a scandal-loving society, its brilliantly lacquered veneer, its less lovely basic substance. He can be serious, but is not too serious; he keeps to the comic aspects of the foibles of the day, and enlivens the whole with incessant sparkling wit.

Later Sentimental Plays   It is very wrong to assume that Goldsmith and Sheridan gave notable pause to sentimentalism. It went marching on, specializing at the end of the century in either melodrama as in the early plays of George Colman the Younger [19] (1762-1836) or in the drama of humanitarian purpose as in the plays of such revolutionists as Thomas Holcroft [20] (1745-1809) and Mrs. Elizabeth Inchbald [21] (1753-1821) or of Thomas Morton (1764?-1838), author of *Speed the Plough* (1800) and *The Slave* (1816). In *Such Things Are* (1787) Mrs. Inchbald portrayed the great prison-reformer, John Howard, under the name of Haswell, who in a Sumatra prison converses with a noble savage, Zedan. The Indian has stolen Haswell's pocketbook, hoping to buy his freedom. As Haswell repasses with the Keeper, there ensues the following conversation—sufficiently indicative of the persistence of sentiment:

Keeper. [*To* Zedan.] What makes you here?—still moping by yourself, and lamenting for your family? [*To* Haswell.] That man, the most ferocious I ever met with, laments, sometimes even with tears, the separation from his wife and children.

Hasw. [*Going to him.*] I am sorry for you, friend: [Zedan *looks sullen and morose.*] I pity you....Poor man! bear your sorrows nobly.—And, as we are alone, no miserable eye to grudge the favour—[*Looking round.*] take this trifle —[*Gives Money.*] it will, at least, make your meals better for a few short weeks, till Heaven may please to favour you with a less sharp remembrance of the happiness you have lost.—Farewell.

[Zedan *catches hold of him, and taking the Pocket-book from his Belt, puts it into* Haswell's *Hand.*]

Hasw. What's this?

Zedan. I meant it should gain me my liberty—but I will not vex you.

Hasw. How came you by it?

Zedan. Stole it—and wou'd have stabb'd you, had you been alone—but I am glad I did not—Oh, I am glad I did not!

Hasw. You like me then?

Zedan. [*Shakes his Head, and holds his Heart.*] 'Tis something that I never

19 Colman the Younger's *Dramatic Works* were edited, with a Life, by J. W. Lake (4v, Paris, 1827). Colman wrote an autobiography covering his life to about 1790, which he published (2v) in 1830 as *Random Records*. See also Richard B. Peake, *Memoirs of the Colman Family* (2v, 1841).

20 On Thomas Holcroft see Elbridge Colby, "A Bibliography of Thomas Holcroft," *Bull. New York Public Library* (1922), and articles by Mr. Colby as listed in *CBEL*, II. 470.

21 James Boaden, *Memoirs of Mrs. Inchbald* (2v, 1833).

felt before—it makes me like not only you, but all the world besides.—The love of my family was confined to them alone—but this sensation makes me love even my enemies.

Hasw. O, nature! grateful! mild! gentle! and forgiving!—worst of tyrants they, who, by hard usage, drive you from men's breasts.

It may gratify the reader to know that at the end of the play Zedan is given his freedom.

VII

The Periodicals and Oliver Goldsmith

In the thirties when Johnson and Smollett came up to London armed with their tragedies, the most likely openings for needy authors were in the fields of periodical literature. The same situation held in the late fifties when Goldsmith reached London. Literature, in fact, was increasingly "periodical." The lowest and most completely anonymous employments of this sort were offered by newspapers, which sooner or later got involved dangerously in politics. The most ambitious efforts in the field were put forth in following the path marked out by the *Tatler* and *Spectator,* in the periodical essay.[1] The golden mean of effort between these two extremes was solicited by the newly developing magazines and reviews. It may help if we survey developments in these fields as a background for the career of the most attractive essayist of the time, Oliver Goldsmith.

The history of the periodical essay in the later part of the century is one of decline and of absorption into newspapers as a "feature." Such an opinion is unfair to the serial which more than any one other work made the reputa-

The
Rambler

tion of Dr. Johnson—*The Rambler* (1750-52), a periodical doubtless second only to *The Spectator* and possibly to *The Tatler*. But *The Rambler* ran only for 208 numbers as compared with *The Spectator's* 555, and it appeared only twice a week instead of six times. After two years of "the anxious employment of a periodical writer," Johnson was delighted to quit. It is true that his essays were considerably longer than those of Addison and Steele, and that fact augmented their difficulty by making it more necessary to have significant content. The earlier essayists wrote playfully, like statesmen out of office, on a vacation: Johnson and many of the later essayists were more serious.[2] Bluntly, the contrast is between entertaining journalism and the ingenious display of mind. Such a contest is likely to be weighted in favor of entertainment as opposed to intellect.

Johnson displayed high intellectual quality, but he and his generation lacked lightness and informality. The "principal design" of *The Rambler* was "to inculcate wisdom or piety." Possibly, as Johnson said in his conclud-

---

[1] Information concerning the development of the essay must largely be sought in the biographies of the various essayists. In addition to the more general works cited on the periodical essay in Part II, ch. v, the following are useful for the period after 1750: Arthur S. Collins, *Authorship in the Days of Johnson* (1927); David Nichol Smith, "The Newspaper," *Johnson's England,* ed. Arthur S. Turberville (2v, Oxford, 1933), II. 331-367; Benj. C. Nangle, *The Monthly Review (1749-89): Indexes of Contributors and Articles* (Oxford, 1934); Laurence Hanson, *Government and the Press, 1695-1763* (Oxford, 1936); George Nobbe, *The North Briton: A Study in Political Propaganda* (1939).

[2] O. F. Christie, *Johnson the Essayist* (1924).

ing paper, he produced some essays "of which the highest excellence is harmless merriment," but gaiety of tone is not here really obtrusive. He had little assistance, and that little came also from persons of sobriety: Elizabeth Carter, Catherine Talbot, Hester Mulso (later Mrs. Chapone), each wrote one or two, and Samuel Richardson, the novelist, wrote No. 97, which is said to have outsold all other numbers. Significantly, Richardson suggests that more attention be paid in *The Rambler* to ridicule of "fashionable follies" in the manner of *The Spectator*. Johnson recognized this lack of lightness and variety, and at the end feared that "the severity of dictatorial instruction has been too seldom relieved, and that he [the reader] is driven by the sternness of The Rambler's philosophy to more cheerful and airy companions"; but if the author "can be numbered among the writers who have given ardor to virtue and confidence to truth," he will rest content. He has some amusing papers: No. 16, about the woes of eminence in authorship, is facetious in tone, and so is the project analogous to Fielding's "univorsal register" in No. 105. He gives us also allegories, Oriental tales, and sketches—not too vivid—of London life. It is the critical essays that have most permanent interest: No. 4 on modern romance, No. 60 on biography, No. 93 on prejudice in criticism; No. 125 on tragedy and comedy, No. 152 on letter-writing, and Nos. 156 and 158, in which he attacks the rules—all these and others demonstrate Johnson's ability. These, standing out above the Johnsonian average, are among the best brief critical essays of the century; they are models of thoughtfulness. Later Johnson wrote at least twenty-five essays [3] for *The Adventurer* (1752-54) of his friend John Hawkesworth (1715?-1773), Swift's editor and a notable figure in the periodical literature of the day.

Other writers of periodical essays that appeared independent of news or other condiments fared less well in general than Johnson. *The World* (209 nos., 1753-56), conducted by Edward Moore, the dramatist, would seem to have been the most popular series, and if we can believe its claims its circulation at times reached 2500. *The Rambler,* which averaged less than 500, was, however, far more highly regarded in reprinted editions. *The World* probably at first had a considerable snob appeal as well as undoubted merit; for its contributors included Lord Chesterfield, Horace Walpole, Richard Owen Cambridge, Soame Jenyns, and others of note. [4] If Johnson could find

Other Periodical Essays

---

[3] L. F. Powell, "Johnson's Part in *The Adventurer*," RES, III (1927). 420-429.

[4] The blue-stocking ladies called the last three of these gentlemen "the old wits"; and the group represents a stately tradition soon to be discarded for something less formal. Cambridge (1717-1802) led an amiable, pious, and complacent life, passed chiefly at Twickenham Meadows on the banks of the Thames. He was an amateur poet and essayist, but achieved distinction chiefly through elegant and kindly hospitality. His *Works* were collected into a quarto volume with a life by his son George in 1803, and his career has recently been well depicted by Richard D. Altick in *Richard Owen Cambridge: Belated Augustan* (Philadelphia, 1941).—Soame Jenyns (1704-1787) did not, like Cambridge, shun public employment, and he made more pretense to intellectuality than most of his group. He was not, however, capable of profound reasoning, and his *Free Enquiry into the Nature and Origin of Evil* (1757) was the object of a famous review by Dr. Johnson that is somewhat surprising for its extremely caustic tone. Jenyns's *View of the Internal Evidence of the Christian Religion* (1776) was much read and was at the time overvalued by the orthodox.

a Hawkesworth and these aristocratic personages find a Moore who would shoulder responsibility for a periodical, the tradition was still possible; but such editors were rare. Lesser successes were achieved by Fielding in his various essay newspapers and by Arthur Murphy in his *Gray's-Inn Journal* (1753-4) where one may find some excellent criticism, especially on the drama. The Nonsense Club (Bonnell Thornton, George Colman, Robert Lloyd, William Cowper, *et al.*) in their *Connoisseur* (1754-6) met with less success than one would have expected. In Edinburgh, where many of the most distinguished thinkers and writers lived, the novelist Henry Mackenzie won distinction as chief author of *The Mirror* (1779-80) and *The Lounger* (1785-87).

Newspapers   The truth is that long before the time of *The Grub-street Journal* (1730-37) and *The Universal Spectator* (1728-46) newspapers had begun to absorb essay writers and use them as authors of leading articles, frequently of a literary character. Such "leaders" need not have merit sufficient to stand alone, and need not always appear regularly. The drudgery was therefore less than in "the anxious employment" of the independent essayist, who constantly faced a deadline. After 1750 many essay series, literary in character, appeared in newspapers. Sir John Hill's *Inspector* (1751-3) was printed in *The Daily Advertiser;* the *Idler* essays, to the number of 104, all but twelve of which were by Johnson, graced the front page of John Payne's *Universal Chronicle* for two years (1758-60); and Goldsmith's "Chinese Letters" were read first in *The Public Ledger.* Hardly any newspaper of considerable duration failed to have an essayist among its contributors some of the time, and though such writers naturally tended to be topical or political or religious, they were often literary.

It may perhaps here be remarked that while in the second half of the century newspapers continued to be usually very short-lived, stability was definitely emerging. No newspaper, except the official *Gazette,* had weathered the whole period 1700-50; but at least two tri-weekly evening papers founded before 1750 continued beyond the end of the century. These were *The London Evening Post* (1727-1806) and *The General Evening Post* (1733-1813). *The Daily Advertiser* (1730-98) had the longest life of any daily. Of the papers founded in the second half of the century *The London Chronicle* (1757-1823), for which Dr. Johnson wrote the first leader, had notable literary interests. "It was," so Boswell tells us, "constantly read by Johnson himself; and it is but just to observe, that it has all along been distinguished for good sense, accuracy, moderation, and delicacy." John Newbery's new daily, *The Public Ledger* (1760-) during its first twenty months of existence, featured Goldsmith's "Chinese Letters," as indicated above, and *The Chronicle* at much the same time (1760-62) carried a series called "The Schemer." At almost the same moment (1761) Bonnell Thornton and George Colman started *The St. James's Chronicle,* in which Colman published essays called "The Genius." Of greater commercial and political weight in the nineteenth century were *The Morning Chronicle* (1769-1862),

The Morning Post (1772-1937), and finally *The Times* (1788), which survives to the present day. The battle for "freedom of the press" was largely won in the eighteenth century, but in times of stress the journalist was still precariously placed. It will be recalled that in 1719 John Matthews was hanged, drawn, and quartered, for a technically treasonable piece of journalism; John Wilkes's troubles over his *North Briton* No. 45 (1763) were notorious,[5] and in the last decade of the century James Perry was repeatedly prosecuted for sarcasms in his *Morning Chronicle*. But Perry in general defended himself with ease and success. There had been great progress in this important matter.

If the newspapers continually featured poems, stories, and essays, that was in part due to competition arising from the development of magazines and reviews in the period. In the history of magazines the landmark doubtless was the founding in 1731 of *The Gentleman's Magazine* [6] by Edward Cave (1691-1754), its publisher. This magazine appeared monthly until 1907, and was at its inception a pioneer influence. Its contents were most miscellaneous, including a section devoted to poetry, another to news summaries for the month—births, deaths, marriages, preferments, lists of books published during the month—and a third section, the magazine's real specialty, abridgments or quotation of interesting essays printed in the newspapers. In the introduction to the first volume Cave announced his aim as "to give Monthly a View of all the Pieces of Wit, Humour, or Intelligence, daily offer'd to the Publick in the News-Papers, (which of late are so multiply'd, as to render it impossible, unless a Man makes it a Business, to consult them all)." Naturally he was accused of plagiarism, but the "plagiarism" proving profitable was speedily and often imitated by rivals. Of these *The London Magazine* (1732-85) was a powerful and closely imitative competitor. In it Boswell published his "Hypochondriack" essays (1777-83). *The Scots Magazine* (1739-1817), which carried the "digest" idea to Edinburgh, had a long run; as did also *The Universal Magazine* (1747-1814). By the middle of the century two obvious developments took place. *The Magazine of Magazines* (1750-51) instituted the further plagiaristic synthesis of all monthly periodicals; and, secondly, by this time original material formed a notable part of the matter of each number of the well-established magazines. Original poetry from the start was included by Cave, and by 1735 letters from readers were frequently printed. Johnson was an early contributor of verse in the *Gentleman's*, and early was concerned in writing up the debates in Parliament for Cave. He also contributed ten biographies of distinguished persons, most of them recently deceased. Other prominent contributors were (Sir) John Hill, Christopher Smart, John Hawkesworth, Sir John Hawkins, and John

The Gentleman's Magazine (side note)

---

[5] See George Nobbe's book on *The North Briton* (1939).

[6] John Nichols, "An Account of the Rise and Progress of *The Gentleman's Magazine*," in *A General Index to The Gentleman's Magazine* [*from 1731 to 1818*] (4v, 1789-1821), Vol. III (1821). Also Carl Lennart Carlson, *The First Magazine: A History of The Gentleman's Magazine, with an Account of Dr. Johnson's Editorial Activity and of the Notice Given America in the Magazine* (Providence, R. I., 1938; *Brown University Studies*, Vol. IV). Review article by Donald F. Bond, *MP*, xxxviii (1940). 85-100.

Duncombe. After Cave's death successive editors included David Henry (Cave's brother-in-law), Francis Newbery, and the eminent antiquarian, John Nichols (1745-1826). The magazine eventually depended less and less on abridgments from the newspapers, and came to be a miscellany with considerable emphasis on science, religion, and politics as well as on literature.

Specialized Magazines

Along with the imitations came specialization. Perhaps to relieve pressure for the publication of religious material, the resourceful John Newbery founded in 1760 *The Christian's Magazine,* apparently the first to be devoted to popular religious topics. *The Arminian Magazine* (1778-97) was the organ of the Wesleyan Methodists. Various short-lived periodicals were devoted to theatrical matters. *The Town and Country Magazine* (1769-96) specialized in literary and aristocratic entertainment. In literature its most famous contributor was the boy Thomas Chatterton. Since the days of Richard Steele the fair sex had been reading periodicals, and now there were magazines for ladies. It is amusing that no less a person than Goldsmith himself, under the pen-name of the "Honourable Mrs. Caroline Stanhope," [7] edited for a while *The Lady's Magazine; Or, Polite Companion for the Fair Sex* (1759-63), and there were several other magazines for this clientele. So also lawyers, builders, farmers, musicians, and other particular groups all had their own magazines.

The Annual Register

Hardly a magazine in the usual sense but still an important example of a specialized periodical is *The Annual Register,* founded in 1758 with Dodsley as publisher and the youthful Edmund Burke as first author. The annual volume thus published contained a retrospective account of the year, even including reviews of a few chosen books. Somewhat imitative in concept of earlier registers, such as John Meres's *Historical Register* for the years 1714-1738, it transcended its predecessors by being more inclusive and more literary. Burke was "during the space of one-and-thirty years, the principal conductor" of this undertaking, of which he made an enormous success.[8]

Soon after the eager market for magazines was evident, reviews also entered the popular field. Throughout the first half of the century there had been reviews devoted to learned publications, especially in the field of theology and of classical literature. For contemporary belles-lettres reviewing had been casual and rare. Compliments to fellow authors appear not infrequently in *The Spectator* and in other periodical essays; but usually reviewing in the early period would be found in unfriendly pamphlets. A

The Monthly Review

periodical devoted to reviewing relatively untechnical books was instituted by Ralph Griffiths in his *Monthly Review* (1749-1845). At first, under the influence perhaps of the magazine plan of abridgments, the accounts of books tended to be summaries, with a minimum of critical comment. This is not the worst possible fault since reviewers can hardly summarize without reading. In fact, one of the merits of Griffiths' review articles is that

---

[7] Ronald S. Crane, *New Essays by Oliver Goldsmith* (Chicago, 1927), pp. xxxii, n. 2 and 89, n. 1.

[8] An admirable account of Burke and the *Register* may be found in Thomas W. Copeland's "Burke and Dodsley's *Annual Register*," *PMLA*, LIV (1939). 223-245.

they focus attention on the nature of the work rather than on the nature of the anonymous critic's response. That emphasis would come in the reviews later in the century and in the early nineteenth century. Griffiths' bias was that of a nonconformist, and several of his assistants were dissenting clergymen. It was this anti-ecclesiastical tendency that made Johnson give so unfavorable an account of the undertaking to the King. Griffiths, in spite of Goldsmith's opinion, apparently paid well, was the sole responsible chief, and secured, when possible, genuine experts to write for him.[9] These he protected normally by a complete anonymity. His classical reviewers, as we know, were Porson, Parr, and Fanny Burney's brother Charles—three of the best classical scholars of the day. For drama he had Arthur Murphy [10] and George Colman the elder; for belles-lettres, Goldsmith (very briefly!), John Langhorne, John Hawkesworth, John Wolcot ("Peter Pindar"), and others. Science, theology, Oriental studies, and other fields were similarly well covered. In the spring of 1757 Goldsmith was resident in Griffiths' house as an important and adequately paid assistant on the *Monthly*. The arrangement proved unsatisfactory at the end of six months, though Goldsmith contributed four reviews to the *Monthly* for December 1758 before quarreling with Griffiths the following month. When Goldsmith's *Enquiry* (1759) appeared, it was reviewed by a new writer for the *Monthly*, William Kenrick (1725?-1779), a man whose libelous asperities foreshadowed—and surpassed—the savagery of early nineteenth-century reviewers. Griffiths' chief assistant at the start was the cultivated dissenter William Rose; at the very end of the century the revolutionary William Taylor of Norwich was beginning in the *Monthly* a career as critic with an enthusiasm for things Continental, especially German. According to the exaggerated compliments of the day Taylor stimulated Walter Scott to be a poet and Hazlitt to be a critic.

The cultural superiority of the *Monthly* did not escape challenge. Dr. *Other* Johnson edited and wrote much of *The Literary Magazine: or Universal* *Reviews* *Review* (1756-8); his contributions constitute some of his best writing, especially on political subjects. Church and Tory interests joined in support of the real rival of the subversive *Monthly*, which was *The Critical Review* (1756-1817). This was edited at first by Tobias Smollett with the aid of three or four others of doubtful identity. There was no admitted chief as in the case of Griffiths. Joseph Robertson (1726-1802) informs us that he contributed to *The Critical Review* more than 2600 articles between the years 1764 and 1785. William Guthrie (1708-1770) and Percival Stockdale (1736-1811) were successively important staff members in the years after Smollett left the *Critical*. Less able than the *Monthly*, the *Critical* had nevertheless notable

---

[9] Aubrey Hawkins, "Some Writers on *The Monthly Review*," RES, VII (1931). 168-181; also Benj. C. Nangle, *The Monthly Review (1749-89): Indexes of Contributors and Articles* (Oxford, 1934).

[10] In 1757-8 Murphy may have been contributing to a section in *The London Chronicle* called "The Theatre." See J. P. Emery, "Murphy's Criticisms in *The London Chronicle*," PMLA, LIV (1939). 1099-1104.

contributors. Johnson wrote at least three good articles, and Goldsmith in 1759 and 1760 wrote over fifteen reviews. Presently the rows between the rival reviews were aired in the satirical *Battle of the Reviews* (1760); and Charles Churchill (1731-1764), in his *Apology Addressed to the Critical Reviewers* (1761) and in others of his satires, ridiculed Smollett and his collaborators. Smollett's health forced him to withdraw from the *Critical* in 1763, and Kenrick at the end of 1765 left writing for the *Monthly*. In 1775 in his own periodical, *The London Review of English and Foreign Literature,* Kenrick continued decrying and even libeling Johnson, Goldsmith, and most of the geniuses of the age. Among other notable reviews of the period were Gilbert Stuart's *English Review* (1783-95), published by John Murray, and Thomas Christie's *Analytical Review* (1788-99), which attracted the revolutionary literati. Other leading conservative reviews included *The British Critic* (1793-1826), edited by William Beloe and Robert Nares, and *The Anti-Jacobin Review and Magazine* (1798-1821), edited by "John Gifford" (i.e., James R. Green) and Robert Bisset. Among all such periodicals Griffiths' *Monthly* continued the leader until in 1802 *The Edinburgh Review* was founded.

Goldsmith as "An Author to be Let"

Periodicals such as these here presented formed the background for the career of the foremost of hackwriters, Oliver Goldsmith.[11] Bibliographies of his work indicate that in the years 1757 to 1762 Goldsmith contributed to at least ten periodicals of differing kinds. The serial miscellany that he himself wrote, *The Bee* (1759), ran to only eight weekly numbers, but these early years of magazine writing in general served him well. He made many friends, and in 1764, when his first signed work, *The Traveller,* was published, he was already one of the original members of Dr. Johnson's Club. The magazines and reviews, however, were not sufficiently lucrative, and

[11] Oliver Goldsmith (1730?-1774) was born in Ireland, where he received most of his education. From Trinity College, Dublin, he received the degree of B.A. in 1749. He studied medicine in Edinburgh, 1752-3, but took no degree there. He continued his medical studies at the University of Leyden, and traveled on the Continent through France, Switzerland, and Italy. After his return to London in 1756 he attempted for two strenuous years to establish himself as a physician in Southwark and to augment his meager earnings by writing reviews for the magazines. In 1759 he published his first book, *An Enquiry into the Present State of Polite Learning in Europe,* and by this time was launched on a busy career as writer. By steady use of his facile pen he eventually made a good income, but he was apparently improvident, and died leaving debts amounting to about £2000. On these debts Dr. Johnson made the proud comment: "Was ever poet so trusted before?"—Goldsmith's *Works* (4v, 1801); ed. Sir James Prior (4v, 1837); J. W. M. Gibbs (5v, 1884-6); *Plays,* ed. Austin Dobson (1893, 1901); *Complete Poetical Works,* ed. Austin Dobson (1906); *New Essays by Oliver Goldsmith,* ed. Ronald S. Crane (Chicago, 1927); *The Collected Letters of Oliver Goldsmith,* ed. Katharine C. Balderston (Cambridge, 1928).—Iolo A. Williams, "Oliver Goldsmith," *Seven XVIIIth Century Bibliographies* (1924), pp. 117-177; Temple Scott, *Oliver Goldsmith Bibliographically and Biographically Considered* (1928); R. S. Crane, "Oliver Goldsmith," in *CBEL,* II. 636-650 (the most complete list of writings by and about Goldsmith).—Thomas Percy, "The Life of Dr. Oliver Goldsmith," in *The Miscellaneous Works of Oliver Goldsmith,* Vol. I (1801); see Katharine C. Balderston, *The History and Sources of Percy's Memoir of Goldsmith* (Cambridge, 1926); Sir James Prior, *The Life of Oliver Goldsmith* (2v, 1837; still the most authoritative life); John Forster, *The Life and Adventures of Oliver Goldsmith* (1848), with notes as *The Life and Times of Oliver Goldsmith* (2v, 1854); Austin Dobson, *Life of Oliver Goldsmith* (1888); Arthur L. Sells, *Les Sources françaises de Goldsmith* (Paris, 1924). For many special studies of the canon and sources of Goldsmith see *CBEL.*

once his reputation was established Goldsmith took to translation and compilation as a means of further income. Among the many works in which he
was concerned at least as reviser may be listed an abridgment of Plutarch's
Lives in five volumes (1762), a *History of England* (1764) in two volumes,
another in four volumes (1771), *The Roman History* in two volumes (1769),
The Beauties of English Poesy in two volumes (1767), *The Grecian History*
in two volumes (1774) and, most extensive and perhaps most interesting of
all his compilations, *An History of the Earth and Animated Nature* (1774)
in eight volumes.[12] During the fifteen years that elapsed between his first
original book, his *Enquiry into the Present State of Polite Learning in
Europe* (1759), and his death, Goldsmith must have either written, revised,
translated, compiled, or supervised over two score volumes. No one will
accept Horace Walpole's verdict that "Goldsmith was an idiot, with once
or twice a fit of parts"; but it is evident that he was a professional maker of
books, who affords high delight from a relative few of his writings.

As an essayist he achieved his earliest and perhaps his greatest success.[13] *Goldsmith*
In his own days his essays could be read in the original periodicals or in *as an*
three collections, to the sum of which later additions have been made. These *Essayist*
collections were *The Bee* (not a reprint), *The Citizen of the World* (1762),
collected from *The Public Ledger,* in which they had appeared serially as
"Letters" (1760-61); and the *Essays by Mr. Goldsmith,* assembled from the
magazines and newspapers into a volume in 1765.

Before these volumes appeared Goldsmith's *Enquiry* had helped readers *The*
to understand certain typical positions of its author. The book, to be sure, *Enquiry*
lacks the charm of the essays partly because, as Davies said, "the Doctor
loved to dwell upon grievances." It is one of the long series of complaints
made by writers that their art is both unappreciated and unrewarded. The
mid-eighteenth century was vocal in its complaints of this sort. From another
point of view the volume might seem to be a prose "progress of poesy"; for
"polite learning" is here belles-lettres. Goldsmith's survey of the cultural
state of the countries of Europe anticipated his *Traveller,* and is typically
facile and moralistic. Everywhere he finds decay of the arts, and, since he
thus seems an "ancient" rather than a "modern," one might think him a
pessimist negating the popular belief in progress. Actually he believes in a
theory of cyclic change with new achievement compensating for the obvious
decay of parts. Almost a *philosophe* in his devotion to finite causes of the
human state, he blames the decline of the arts on faulty education (he is
typically for the elegant, the humane, and opposes the technical and pedan-

---

12 James H. Pitman, *Goldsmith's Animated Nature* (New Haven, 1924); Winifred Lynskey,
"The Scientific Sources of Goldsmith's *Animated Nature,*" *SP,* XL (1943). 33-57.
13 The publication of Professor Ronald S. Crane's *New Essays by Goldsmith* (Chicago, 1927)
has greatly stimulated a mass of research concerning the sources and the canon of Goldsmith's
essays. This work has been done by A. J. Barnouw, H. J. Smith, A. L. Sells (pioneers in the field),
and by R. W. Seitz, J. H. Warner, and Arthur Friedman. The extensive record of these
researches may be found in the excellent bibliography of Goldsmith in *CBEL,* II. 636-650. The
results of the work make it apparent that Goldsmith was capable of frequent, interesting
plagiarisms. Professors Crane and Friedman are preparing an edition of Goldsmith's works.

tic), on lack of patronage by the aristocrats, and, perhaps most surprisingly, on the literary critics, who discourage genius and malign all innovation. These positions, like many of Goldsmith's, are easily taken and not thoroughly considered. The author himself was making an income as a critic; and such remarks as "The author who draws his quill merely to take a purse, no more deserves success than he who presents a pistol," somewhat naturally provoked sneers from his former employers on *The Monthly Review*.

His Methods as Essayist

His essays were less querulous and more varied in tone. *The Bee,* a periodical miscellany in octavo format, which appeared on eight Saturdays in October and November, 1759, contains some of his best small poems as well as an amusing diversity of prose—dramatic criticisms, moral tales, serious or fanciful discourses. Among the last perhaps the most famous is the *Resverie* ("The Fame Machine"), in which he compliments *The Rambler* highly. Goldsmith excels in human details. In *The Bee* and in his other groups of essays we find interesting ideas expressed and we meet such amusing personages as the Strolling Player, who reminds us of Goldsmith himself as well as of George Primrose in the later *Vicar;* the Private Sentinel, that colossal monument to human distress and fortitude; and, above all, the immortal Beau Tibbs, surely one of the most delightful brief characterizations of the century. The Strolling Player and the Private Sentinel remind one at least vaguely of Addison's Political Upholsterer in *Tatler* Nos. 155, 160, and 178. The methods of Addison and Goldsmith can be studied illuminatingly in these essays. The earlier writer is more definitely pointed and more brilliant in his satirical concept; the Upholsterer was a clearer comment on an age recently exposed to newspapers and their wild daily rumors. Goldsmith, on the other hand, is contentedly preoccupied with vivid and rich human detail; he creates his persons not merely as mouthpieces or as gorgeous eccentrics: strange as they are, he really likes them as people.

He does, of course, at times use persons as topics or as mouthpieces. Mistress Quickly in the *Reverie at the Boar's Head Tavern,* certainly one of Goldsmith's happiest efforts, is vivaciously human, but she is obviously borrowed from Shakespeare for the purpose of avowing that it is futile to mourn over the degeneracy of the age, since "every age is the same." There is neither progress nor regress: there is compensated change always. Similarly, the figure of *Asem the Man Hater* merely is a personal center for a fantasy of various favorite ideas. Asem is taught the necessity of having the life of pure reason stimulated by emotion. He is taught the complementary lesson of the necessity of controlling one's rash benevolence by prudence. He illustrates the theory of cyclic change embodied in an individual life. Almost alone among the eighteenth-century descendants of Timon, Asem is cured of his misanthropy—by means of regenerated social emotions. At the end of the tale he is starting on a new cycle dominated again by benevolence; but the new round is to be an improvement; for his benevolence now is to be not rash, like Timon's, but prudent.

The Citizen of the World [14] is perhaps Goldsmith's best sustained work. It is certainly the best example in English of the essay device so popular at the time in France, which made the essayist a foreign traveler (preferably Oriental; for philosophy came from the East) who wrote letters to his home country describing and criticizing the strange customs of the lands through which he passed. The device, initiated in the late seventeenth century by G. P. Marana's *L'Espion Turc* and perfected in Montesquieu's *Lettres Persanes* (1721), throve in France where the critics of established institutions sheltered themselves behind the pretense of being foreigners. From Montesquieu's imitator, the Marquis d'Argens, author of a series of *Lettres Chinoises* (1739), Goldsmith drew much inspiration and even many small plagiarized passages.[15] Long before D'Argens such writers as Le Comte and Du Halde had started a Chinese tradition that was invaluable to both D'Argens and Goldsmith. As this tradition developed, the Chinese were made into a race of philosophers, embodiments of simple reason and common sense; people who lived in a patriarchal society or under an absolute but perfectly benevolent emperor. They honored men of letters above conquerors and military heroes, and were in religion rationally devout, tolerant—and altogether void of bigotry and "superstition." In a word, the Chinese traveler embodied the pure light of reason, and his mind played effectively over the customs of England and of Christendom in an impartial and at times devastating fashion. To him nothing established had an absolute validity: in the Orient, as these essayists all loved to remark, polygamy was perfectly respectable; in Christendom the marriage customs were frequently shocking. All things were relative. The *philosophe* had quite emancipated himself from the ecclesiastical interpretation of the universe. The excellence of all customs was to be estimated according to human and common-sense standards. If Goldsmith's "Chinese Letters" are less brilliantly trenchant than the best of his French models, it is in part due to the fact that England was, by definition almost, the land of liberty, and the English, unlike the French, did not have "God and the king to pull down"—to borrow Walpole's phrase. Goldsmith is more playful, more relaxed, more superficial, more of the literary man, less of the revolutionary.

Thus these Chinese letters are most useful in giving a picture of Goldsmith's mind and the temper of his time. From the very beginning of his career he had loved to set the qualities of one country over against the quali-

The Citizen of the World

---

14 *The Citizen of the World*, ed. Austin Dobson (1891); Hamilton J. Smith, *Oliver Goldsmith's "The Citizen of the World"* (New Haven, 1926); also Martha P. Conant, *The Oriental Tale in England in the Eighteenth Century* (1908).

15 Ronald S. Crane and Hamilton J. Smith, "A French Influence on Goldsmith's *Citizen of the World*," *MP*, XIX (1921). 83-92. A noteworthy English link between Montesquieu and Goldsmith was the *Letters from a Persian in England* published in 1735 by George (later Baron) Lyttelton. This youthful and undistinguished piece of writing Lyttelton revised for a fifth edition (1744). It contains interesting political and social criticisms, and had obvious but not very important influence on Goldsmith. Lyttelton tried his hand at another popular type of essay in 1760 when he brought out his *Dialogues of the Dead*. Mrs. Elizabeth Montagu of Blue-Stocking fame contributed three dialogues to this volume. On Lyttelton's *Letters from a Persian* see Samuel C. Chew, "An English Precursor of Rousseau," *MLN*, XXXII (1917). 321-337.

ties of another. He is a patriot, but a patriot who is sure each nation has its individual and superlative merit—as well as a contrasting defect. Upon this concept his poem *The Traveller* is based. The philosophic mind, he thinks, will attempt to absorb the diverse goods of all nations. It was, then, appropriate to call the "Chinese Letters," when they were reprinted, by a title that haunted Goldsmith, *The Citizen of the World*. This phrase, picturesque and cogent from the ancient moment when Dionysius put it into the mouth of Plato, had a particular appeal to the illuminati, who abhorred the parochial. Goldsmith had used the phrase in his essay on *National Prejudices* (1760), in his *Memoirs of M. de Voltaire* (1761), and in the twentieth and the twenty-third of his series of Chinese letters. The title is philosophical rather than political in implication; for Goldsmith, like many another proponent of cosmopolitanism in his day, believed that one should be aware and tolerant of the curious opinions and customs of strange nations, but he did not deny the duty of a local allegiance; he rather insisted that local allegiance be subordinated to allegiance to the Whole.

In these "Chinese Letters" as well as elsewhere Goldsmith is also typical of his day in his praise of simplicity. Here Nature's "simple plan" (Letter III) is the catchword. To be sure, he is at times equivocal. Where wealth accumulates, men decay; but where there is no wealth, there are no arts, no graces of civilization; and these last are what the century really valued. Plain living and rigid intellectualism might easily become to Goldsmith a meager, bleak existence. He certainly tends to idealize something like an opulent patriarchal society, but even in his picture of "Sweet Auburn" or of the Vicar's family of Wakefield, he forgets his dictum that "every age is the same," and shares the predilection of his time for the simple, though not for the truly primitive.

Goldsmith excelled in other types of writing as well as in the essay, and the mental processes seen in these essays carry over into his plays,[16] his one novel, and even into his poems. He illustrates the economic methods of the less shrewd authors of his day in his magazine work, and he also illustrates

The Vicar — the curious equivocal emancipation of mind typical of many men in his day. His attitude towards sentimentalism and towards "trade" are cases in point, and can be studied in *The Vicar of Wakefield*.[17] The plot of the *Vicar* is not complex: clouds gather more and more blackly over the poor Primroses; finally when their complete misery seems assured, the sun shines out, all woes vanish, and we leave the family living happily ever afterwards. Goldsmith loved to portray simplicity, but his love of idyllic simplicity was curiously modified by economic considerations. After the South Sea Bubble a conservative reaction towards a trust in the land as the source of wealth and well-being prepared the way for the idealized farmer-philosopher. Consequently, when *The Vicar of Wakefield* finally appeared in 1766 (it was at

---

16 On Goldsmith's plays see Part III, ch. VI, n. 15.

17 Among the very many editions of the *Vicar* may be mentioned for their introductions and notes those by Austin Dobson (1883) and by Oswald Doughty (1928).

least partly written four years earlier), its public was prepared for a "hero" who united in himself "the three greatest characters upon earth:...a priest, an husbandman, and the father of a family." There is, obviously, a connection here with sentimentalism, but the sentimental bearings of the *Vicar* are difficult to grasp justly.[18] Here as elsewhere—especially in the "Distresses of a Private Sentinel" (*Citizen of the World,* cxix)—Goldsmith lavishly uses "distress" as material; but his attitude towards distress demands acute attention. The distresses of the Sentinel are so gross as to be absurd: they are far from moving tears, and at the end of the essay one can see the logical conclusion: "Thus saying, he limped off, leaving my friend and me *in admiration of his intrepidity and content;* nor could we avoid acknowledging that an habitual acquaintance with misery is the truest school of fortitude and philosophy." We are not invited to weep; we are asked to admire intrepidity. Similarly we are told in the *Vicar* that "after a certain degree of pain, every new breach that death opens in the constitution, nature kindly covers with insensibility." Submission, intrepidity, fortitude, these are the lessons Goldsmith wishes us to learn from the distresses of the virtuous. The tone of the novel is emotional and benevolist, but it must be noted that the good vicar himself is habitually caustic as to the absurdities of his socially ambitious females. The popularity of the book was and is doubtless due not to its overt moral purpose but to the author's attitude towards his material. Like his vicar, he seems "by nature an admirer of happy human faces"— preferably faces distinctly self-conscious in their happiness. One thinks of Greuze and the *Accordée de Village.* Both author and painter are self-conscious; their sentimentalism is intended to serve a moral or even divine purpose—not, however, quite too deep for tears.

Dr. Johnson's opinion of the *Vicar* was expressed to Fanny Burney: "It is very faulty; there is nothing of real life in it, and very little of nature. It is a mere fanciful performance." This verdict is surprisingly severe, but not altogether unjust. The faults of the *Vicar,* like those of *She Stoops to Conquer,* are palpable, and yet for most people these works make still very pleasant reading. The charm is in part due to the imaginative glow that Goldsmith so effortlessly casts over the action of the *Vicar* (after all *Daphnis and Chloe* has its absurd side!), and to his flexible and easy style.

Much praise has been given to his style, which is indeed attractive. It *Goldsmith's* lacks the coldness of the aristocratic manner, and it escapes the tendency of *Prose* his generation to follow Johnson into excessive heaviness of diction and *Style* balanced formality of sentence structure. The unfriendly review [19] of his *Enquiry* in *The Monthly Review* shows that Goldsmith's former colleagues were aware of his criteria of style—his avoidance of "the quaintness of antithesis, the prettiness of points, and the rotundity of studied periods"; and yet they professed to feel a "remarkable faultiness" in expression. Probably even for them Goldsmith was hardly bookish enough to be a "fine writer."

18 W. F. Gallaway, "The Sentimentalism of Goldsmith," *PMLA,* xlviii (1933). 1167-1181.
19 *Monthly Review,* xxi (1759). 381-389. The reviewer was William Kenrick.

It is precisely for this lack of formality and for his graceful and sensitive ease, fluency, and vividness that we value his style.

His Poems   At his death Goldsmith was commended usually for his poems; obituaries mentioned *The Traveller* and *The Deserted Village* rather more frequently than any of his prose works. Apart from these two masterpieces, and perhaps *Retaliation,* which is remembered for biographical rather than aesthetic reasons, his verse is interesting but unimportant. In these two poems he succeeds signally in the couplet tradition, in which most of his contemporaries were commonplace. *The Traveller* contains glowing statements of his cosmopolitanism, of his patriotic Toryism, and of his favorite notion of compensation; *The Deserted Village* presents the economic difficulties of rural life, the dangers of luxury and "trade's unfeeling train." [20] These two are eighteenth-century masterpieces of the poetry of statement: in them current ideas and attitudes are caught and are suffused sufficiently with genuine feeling to make them stir our imaginations to this day. They are the work of a gifted author, happy in not too much education but richly endowed with human insight. Aesthetically he was a traditionalist; mentally he was of the Enlightenment; he was too hard-headed to be a thorough sentimentalist, and too sympathetic to be an outright satirist. In spite of the pot-boiling nature of most of his books, his complex personal endowments with his especial gifts of flexible expression enabled him in several of his works to achieve fame as one of the most readable writers of his century.

[20] On the general background of *The Deserted Village* see Julia Patton, *The English Village: A Literary Study, 1750-1850* (1919). For a literary antecedent by Goldsmith in prose see Ronald S. Crane, *New Essays by Oliver Goldsmith* (Chicago, 1927), pp. 116-124 and the introduction. See also Howard J. Bell, Jr., "*The Deserted Village* and Goldsmith's Social Doctrines," *PMLA,* LIX (1944). 747-772.

VIII
Biography and Letter-Writing

To a century devoted to the proper study of mankind biography was a natural medium.[1] To a century devoted to communication in the coffee-house and by means of rambles through the countryside to gracious Georgian country seats, letter-writing was a natural means of conversing with absent friends. In many periods biographies and letters are merely invaluable sources for historical study, but in the eighteenth century they frequently serve for a delight as well. The didacticism of the age led to an insistence on the significant, the morally useful; a sense of realism, furthermore, encouraged scrupulous attachment to truth and to a love of picturesque detail; and an insatiable human curiosity encouraged a love of trivial anecdotes, which added an element of drama to the universality and uniformity that characterized most views of human nature at the time. Thus grew up a belief that the lives even of "average" men might furnish materials for virile, witty, and perhaps even noble personal writing.

In biography the century had a long way to go before it reached Johnson and Boswell, the greatest practitioners of the art. It developed away from the distant formality advised by Addison in *Freeholder* No. 35 and towards the judicious realism advised by Johnson. Addison had correctly condemned the Grub-street authors who added a new terror to death by rushing to "Curll's chaste press" with garbled and jumbled "lives." Although these works are now usually negligible, often valuable are such brief lives as are found in the biographical dictionaries of the time. A thirst for information about celebrities is marked in the *Life of Francis Bacon* (1740) by David Mallet, the "beggarly Scotchman" who later published Bolingbroke's *Works* (1754), and in such pedestrian compilations as John Jortin's *Erasmus* (2v, 1758-60) and Ferdinando Warner's *Sir Thomas More* (1758). New techniques gradually mingled with established methods. The noble Roman style of Conyers Middleton's *Life of Cicero* (1741), at which Fielding sneered but which Fanny Burney and others thought "manly and elegant," was less significant than Middleton's effective use of Cicero's letters as jewels set in

The Development of Biography

[1] The following general sources on biography may well be consulted: Anna R. Burr, *The Autobiography* (1909); Waldo H. Dunn, *English Biography* (1916); Mark Longaker, *English Biography in the Eighteenth Century* (Philadelphia, 1931); John C. Major, *The Role of Personal Memoirs in English Biography and Novel* (Philadelphia, 1935); Donald A. Stauffer, *The Art of Biography in Eighteenth Century England* (2v, Princeton, 1941). Stauffer's second volume contains an "Alphabetical Index of English Biographies and Autobiographies, 1700-1800."

the biographical narrative. This method was developed by William Mason [2] (1724-1797) in the "Memoirs" he prefixed to his edition of his friend Thomas Gray's *Poems* (1775). Mason used many letters and thus stimulated the tradition of combining "life and letters" which was later common, and was followed by Boswell. Unfortunately for Mason's ultimate reputation he garbled inexcusably the texts of the letters used.

Spence's Anecdotes   Joseph Spence (1699-1768) in some respects anticipated the techniques of Boswell. His type of favorite subject differed from Boswell's in that he had a predilection for natural, self-taught geniuses such as Stephen Duck, "the thresher poet," and Thomas Blacklock, a blind Scottish poet: of both these men he wrote lives. More popular was his account of the Italian Magliabecchi in his *Parallel in the Manner of Plutarch* (1758). As a definitely limited predecessor of Boswell in method, Spence attached himself after 1726 to Alexander Pope and collected supposedly verbatim records of Pope's conversation and that of other eminent persons as well. Unlike Boswell, Spence was himself too timid to make any real use of these collected materials, but Pope's editor, Warburton, and Dr. Johnson were allowed to use some of them. They were published as *Anecdotes* (1820) long after Spence's death at a time when the influence of Boswell had increased the value of such intimate matter.

Boswell's Career   James Boswell [3] (1740-1795), when first he met Dr. Johnson in 1763, was known in his native Edinburgh as a convivial and witty member of Scottish literary circles, as the friend of Lord Elibank, Lord Kames, of Robertson, Hume, and Blair among others. He was the author of certain anonymous poems and pamphlets, and was eager for literary fame. His correspondence with the Hon. Andrew Erskine, upon publication in 1763, was hailed as a

---

[2] John W. Draper, *William Mason* (1924); on Mason's handling of Gray's letters see *Correspondence of Thomas Gray*, ed. Paget Toynbee and Leonard Whibley (3v, Oxford, 1935), I, pp. xiii-xvi.

[3] James Boswell was the eldest son of Alexander Boswell, who on being raised to the bench took the title of Lord Auchinleck (pronounced *Affléck*) from the family estate in Ayrshire. Boswell studied law in Edinburgh and Glasgow, with little enthusiasm, and on a visit to London in 1763 met Johnson. After a Continental tour (December 1763-February 1766), he lived chiefly in Scotland, marrying his cousin there in 1769. Usually he visited London in the spring of the year, and saw much of Johnson at such times. After the death of his father in 1782, Boswell, having succeeded to the family estate, became politically ambitious, with no great success. At the end of 1788 he removed to London and devoted himself to seeing his *Life of Johnson* through the press. His remaining years were marked by a continual decline in health and spirits. — Apart from his *Life of Johnson* (for which see Part III, ch. III), his principal works are *Dorando, A Spanish Tale* (1767); *The Essence of the Douglas Cause* (1767); *An Account of Corsica* (1768); ed. Sydney C. Roberts (Cambridge, 1923); *The Journal of a Tour to the Hebrides* (1785), ed. George Birkbeck Hill (1887), Robert W. Chapman (1924), and from the original MS by Frederick A. Pottle and Charles H. Bennett (1936); *Letters*, ed. Chauncey B. Tinker (2v, 1924); *The Hypochondriack* (70 nos., 1777-83, reprinted from *The London Magazine*), ed. Margery Bailey (2v, Stanford University, 1928); *Private Papers of James Boswell from Malahide Castle*, ed. Geoffrey Scott and Frederick A. Pottle (18v, 1928-34, privately printed). — Frederick A. Pottle, *The Literary Career of James Boswell, Esq., being the Bibliographical Materials for a Life of Boswell* (Oxford, 1929); F. A. Pottle, *The Private Papers of James Boswell from Malahide Castle: A Catalogue* (1931); Claude C. Abbott, *A Catalogue of Papers Relating to Boswell ... found at Fettercairn House* (Oxford, 1936). — Charles Rogers, "Memoir" prefixed to *Boswelliana* (1874); Percy H. Fitzgerald, *Life of Boswell* (2v, 1891); Chauncey B. Tinker, *Young Boswell* (Boston, 1922); John L. Smith-Dampier, *Who's Who in Boswell* (1935); L. F. Powell, "Boswell's Original Journal of his Tour to the Hebrides and the Printed Version," *E&S*, XXIII (1938). 58-69.

work of "true genius"; his pamphlets about the Douglas Cause, including the allegorical *Dorando* (1767), attracted attention on the Continent as well as in England; and his writings in favor of the brave Corsicans—the result of a visit to the "enslaved" island in 1765—gave him European fame. His *Account of Corsica* (1768) is still a most readable book. Besides General Paoli, the Corsican patriot and apostle of freedom, Boswell had met in his travels Voltaire, Rousseau, and other celebrities. He returned to England in 1766 escorting thither the mistress of Rousseau, who at that time was making his unfortunate sojourn in England. By this time Boswell had probably decided to write a "great" life of his friend Johnson; but his duties as a Scottish advocate and his interest in politics make it wrong to suppose Johnson the sole center of Boswell's existence. Apart from his *Life of Johnson* Boswell had a very considerable career as writer, and as a writer of travels he was far more interesting than was Johnson. As an essayist he was inferior, but his *Hypochondriack* indicated some ability in a form of writing to which he made contributions at times jocose and at times sedate or even melancholy.

But if not the center of Boswell's existence, Johnson was certainly Boswell's best subject. Boswell excelled in insight into human nature and in ability to dramatize a situation. For such purposes Johnson was God's plenty, and when relatively rare occasions offered through the years, Boswell watched and listened and collected materials for the great work. His methods in collecting have been differently described. Rarely he perhaps made notes on the spot as conversation ran its fascinating course. Usually he recorded the day's gleanings in his journal from memory, and in the process he sometimes fell into arrears of over a fortnight.[4] He questioned Johnson himself; he pestered Johnson's friends; he visited Lichfield; and, after the Doctor's death, was indefatigable in collecting letters and anecdotes, and in verifying details not earlier settled. His memory was prodigious and accurate. He would not have thought of himself as a trained scholar, but actually his devotion to truth of detail and his ideals of thoroughness would do credit to many such. These qualities evidently, and fortunately, won the respect and aid of the ablest research scholar of the day, Edmond Malone—a man whose illuminating work on such figures as Dryden and Shakespeare still demands veneration. Boswell knew material; Malone knew a competent workman, and so gave up any desire he had to write Johnson's life and by his discreet and judicious aid helped to settle Boswell's final draught of the greatest of biographies.

Boswell was not merely a conscientious preserver of detail; he was also an inspired shaping artist. He knew, and transmits, the sound of his subject's voice to a degree unparalleled in other biographers. From the Malahide Papers we now learn that frequently Johnson's talk is more characteristically

Boswell's Method with Johnson

---

[4] Geoffrey Scott, *The Making of the Life of Johnson*, Vol. VI of *The Private Papers of James Boswell from Malahide Castle* (1929). See also Frederick A. Pottle and Charles H. Bennett, "Boswell and Mrs. Piozzi," *MP*, XXXIX (1942). 421-430.

Johnsonian in the final form Boswell gave it than it was in the first form—that in which very likely it fell from Johnson's lips. Not merely remarks but scenes doubtless undergo this artistic reshaping to give them character. At least many scenes, such as the first meeting of Boswell with Johnson and the famous dinner with Wilkes in 1776, come to mind as masterpieces of theatrical manipulation, in which every detail has been given priceless organic value. It is only to a casual reader that Boswell at first sight seems a biographical annalist swamped with magnificent detail.

His Ideal of Complete Portrayal

Completeness of portrayal was certainly Boswell's aim—and his accomplishment. For this he labored, prodding the sluggish mind of Johnson that appeared to him like a great mill needing grist; and prodding also at times the sluggish body. In his sixty-fourth year the Doctor was persuaded to visit Scotland and its Western Islands. It would have been a difficult journey for a younger man, but from all points of view the adventure was a great success. Both men wrote accounts of the journey, and, some richly Johnsonian passages apart, Boswell's *Tour,* published ten years after Johnson's *Journey* and a year after Johnson's death, is easily superior. Here his narrative flows more smoothly and is perhaps more steadily entertaining even than in the *Life of Johnson.* The work was less weighty, less rich: completeness did not oppress here as a duty—after all, the journey was a holiday.

Problems of Particularity

By his contemporaries Boswell was castigated for his fondness for petty personal detail, for exhibiting flaws and foibles as well as virtues. It was in this actually that he excelled his master, Johnson, who understood through his intellect while Boswell used also his senses and intuitions. Not that Johnson was averse to particularity. When Boswell sought his counsel, the Doctor remarked, "There is nothing, Sir, too little for so little a creature as man." Johnson excelled in a sense of human values; Boswell triumphs by means of his sense of vital particular detail that gives significant lifelike quality. Truth and particularity for him went hand in hand "in the Flemish picture which I give of my friend." "By how small a speck," he exclaims, "does the *Painter* give life to an Eye!" His friend Sir Joshua Reynolds was not so tolerant of these Flemish methods in painting, but Boswell was on the side of the future, and the remark of Hazlitt—"I did not then, nor do I now believe, with Sir Joshua, that the perfection of art consists in giving general appearances without individual details, but in giving general appearances with individual details"—was a remark that Johnson and Boswell would have endorsed for biography. It was a crucial part of Boswell's magic to give significance and vitality to the apparently trivial; it is this trait, together with his notable accuracy and unparalleled completeness of portraiture, that made him, in one of the few Macaulay phrases still quotable about Boswell, "the Shakespeare of biographers."

Autobiographies

In theory at least autobiography was preferable to biography. "Those relations are therefore commonly of most value," announced Johnson in *Idler* No. 84, "in which the writer tells his own story"; and both Johnson and John Wesley continually urged their friends to keep journals. The diversity of the autobiographies of the time is astonishing. Cibber's *Apology* (1740) stimulated others to autobiographical self-defense. A revision of the alleged autobiography of Bampfylde-Moore Carew became *An Apology for the Life of Bampfylde-Moore Carew ... commonly known throughout the West of England by the Title of King of the Beggars* (1749); but this is perhaps rogue fiction rather than autobiography.[5] Cibber's youngest daughter brought out *A Narrative of the Life of Mrs. Charlotte Charke* (1755), which in robust and varied episode surpasses fiction, and gives, incidentally, one of the most authentic accounts of strolling players of the time. The theatre stimulated more egoists than Cibber to paint themselves as well as their trade: Benjamin Victor's *History of the Theatres of London and Dublin* (1761-71) and Tate Wilkinson's *Memoirs of His Own Life* (1790) are important in their material but not in their literary quality. This lack of art is also notable in the stories written by more or less lovely ladies who, having been indiscreet, desired to publish and justify their indiscretions. Among these Letitia Pilkington's *Memoirs* (1748) with its sidelights on Dean Swift, Con. Phillips's *Apology* (1748-9), and above all, Lady Vane's memoirs, inserted in *Peregrine Pickle* (1751), are significant of the marital infelicities of the day.

More significant and varied are the numberless specialized autobiographies that give accounts of voyages—round the world as in the cases of Anson and Cook—or simply to the Continent as in the work of Henry Fielding, Tobias Smollett, James Boswell, Dr. Charles Burney, William Beckford, and Arthur Young.[6] Throughout the century voyage narratives had formed an important part of the popular reading matter and had had an enormous influence on literature—witness *Robinson Crusoe* as well as *Roderick Random*. Large "Collections" of voyages had been frequently reprinted, and the enterprising publisher John Newbery (1713-1767) brought out in the second half of the century one of the largest in *The World Displayed; or, a Curious Collection of Voyages and Travels.*[7] Voyages had influence at various levels: we have seen how they affected such authors as Smollett and Sterne; it is also clear that such books as Arthur Young's *Travels in France* (1792) had notable implications for the political economy of his revolutionary times. Still another sort of possible influence is seen in such a work as the *Authentick Narrative* (1764) by Cowper's evangelical friend, the Rev. John Newton, who had pictured himself vividly as a brand plucked from the burning, and as a sailor sinful and repentant he foreshadowed a type transcendently treated by Coleridge in *The Ancient Mariner*.

Of the less adventurous autobiographies written in this half century the

Narratives of Voyages

---

[5] The *Apology* is edited by C. H. Wilkinson (Oxford, 1931) under the more usual title, *The King of the Beggars*.

[6] It is doubtless invidious to mention these few and omit many others. For extensive classified lists of voyages one should consult the admirable bibliography prepared by R. W. Frantz for *CBEL*, II. 739-757.

[7] 20v, 1759-61; 1774-8; 1790.

Edward Gibbon

subtlest and smoothest was that of the historian Edward Gibbon,[8] who was so fascinated by the problem of self-portrayal that he left six draughts of his own life, which his friend Lord Sheffield blended for publication in Gibbon's *Miscellaneous Works* (1796). The reserved honesty of the portrayal and the crystal hardness and clarity of the style make this work a masterpiece. Unlike most autobiographers Gibbon is no obvious eccentric. "My name may hereafter be placed among the thousand articles of a Biographia Britannica," he writes; "and I must be conscious that no one is so well qualified as myself to describe the series of my thoughts and actions." Of his native endowments he says bluntly, "Wit I have none"; but his gift of phrasing and of incisive arrangement of details furnishes a very fair imitation. Unforgettable is his comment on his second tutor at Oxford, who "well remembered that he had a salary to receive, and only forgot that he had a duty to perform." The termination of his romance—by parental edict—with the lady who later was to be the mother of Mme de Staël is equally characteristic: "I sighed as a lover, I obeyed as a son." Elegant and cool irony is surely an acceptable ingredient of wit. A more obvious limitation is confessed when he says, "My temper is not very susceptible of enthusiasm"; and yet no one has conveyed more justly the genuine thrill a true neo-classicist felt upon first visiting the *fons et origo,* the eternal city of Rome. Nor have historians ever recorded with truer emotion the moments of conception or termination of an enormous piece of work. "It was at Rome, on the 15th of October 1764, as I sat musing amidst the ruins of the Capitol, while the barefooted fryars were singing vespers [what sacrilege!] in the Temple of Jupiter, that the idea of writing the decline and fall of the city first started to my mind." The emotions of deliverance from the task, twenty-three years later, on the night of June 27, 1787, are equally fine. Certainly the dramatic impact of Rome on Gibbon represents one of the supreme moments in neo-classicism. But the autobiography of Gibbon is a part of an essentially rhetorical tradition: it is done in the forum rather than in the closet; it is personal without being extremely intimate; it has all the reserve and composure of a public performance.

Less designed for the public were the diaries and private letters of the time: these were the raw materials for biography, and according to traditions well established were not to be published until revised and purged of intimate details in which only gossips might have a natural interest. Probably none of these diaries or correspondences was first published without excision or adaptation. It is natural that the *Memoirs of the Reign of George the Second,* actually an autobiography of John, Lord Hervey (1696-1743) for the years 1727-37, should have been kept from publication for a century, since his frankness and brilliant wit, which at times is almost brutal in its hardness, especially in his reflections on his good friends of the royal family, would have been offensive at an earlier period. Of other journals the very

Lord Hervey's Memoirs

---

[8] For bibliographical references for Gibbon see below, ch. IX, n. 6. All six versions of the autobiography are printed in *The Autobiographies of Edward Gibbon,* ed. John Murray (1896).

bulk as well as their uneven interest has hindered complete publication. No one in the age is a Samuel Pepys.

For about fifty-five years John Wesley (1703-1791), the founder of Method- *John* ism, kept a journal which, while its entries are fragmentary and brief for *Wesley* the general reader, has for historians enormous social and religious impor- tance.[9] In 1729, while a fellow of Lincoln College, Oxford, Wesley joined with his brother Charles and a group of like-minded young men in system- atic ("methodic") devotions and undertook preaching to prisoners and doing religious work among undergraduates. In spite of opposition the work of the group prospered. Wesley's *Journal* begins in 1735 with his embarkation for Georgia on an unsuccessful two-year mission. After his return in 1738 he began his lifelong, stupendous activity in preaching and organizing religious societies. For fifty years or more he traveled on an average of 4500 miles a year, preaching almost every day three times (the first at five A.M.), writing letters about his work, and doing a mammoth job of organization. He throve on persecution, and met riots and mobs with indomitable com- posure. Gradually he won his way. Soldiers, respecting his courage, came to listen and, if need be, defend. Colliers venerated him, and the upper classes were in the end usually respectful. He was miraculously active to the age of eighty-five, and continued preaching, on occasion held up in the pulpit by assistants, almost up to his death at the age of eighty-seven.

He represents a curious combination of emotional, intellectual, and prac- tical tendencies. He regarded fervent spirituality as of more importance than theological dogma, which he neglected. While remaining to the end a loyal high-churchman, he stressed a belief in the necessity of conversion, in par- ticular Providence, and in good works. He was a scholarly gentleman, an astonishing reader of ancient and modern literature, and in his travels keenly observant of architecture, parks, gardens, and works of art. Oxford was always his norm of beauty. Returning there at the age of eighty-two he notes: "I once more surveyed many of the gardens and delightful walks. What is wanting but the love of God to make this place an earthly para- dise?" But from this paradise he was self-exiled to a life arduous beyond belief, devoted to illiterate and brutalized colliers, felons, tradesmen, and, when they would listen, "the better sort of people." Whether one believes in modern wise that Wesley "set back the clock" of progress by preventing a proletarian revolution in England comparable to that in France,[10] or whether one regards him as a man who labored, not entirely in vain, to realize the Kingdom of Heaven on this earth and among humble folk, one

[9] Wesley's *Works* (32v, Bristol, 1771-4; 11th ed., 15v, 1856-62); *Journal* (4v, 1827); ed. Nehemiah Curnock (8v, 1909-16); *Letters,* ed. John Telford (8v, 1931). — Richard Green, *Bibliography of the Works of John and Charles Wesley* (1896). — Biographies are numerous: John Whitehead (2v, 1791-93), Robert Southey (2v, 1820), Luke Tyerman (3v, 1870-71), John H. Overton (1891), Caleb T. Winchester (1906), William H. Hutton (1927). Brief dis- cussions of the *Journal*, with extracts and with other examples of this type of writing, may be found in the volumes by Arthur, Baron Ponsonby, *English Diaries* (1923), *More English Diaries* (1927), and *Scottish and Irish Diaries* (1927).

[10] Wellman J. Warner, *The Wesleyan Movement in the Industrial Revolution* (1930).

Thraliana

must recognize and admire the magnificent personal achievement recorded in his *Journals*.

Less important but more amusing than Wesley's writing are the diaries of two ladies, who are in part coadjutors of Boswell in preserving Dr. Johnson's life and the manners of his day. These are the *Thraliana* of Mrs. Hester Lynch Thrale, later Mrs. Piozzi, and the diaries of Fanny Burney, later Mme d'Arblay. Only recently has *Thraliana* been published in its entirety, so that its total effect has been until now unappreciated. It is more than a source for anecdotes about Johnson; it is a partly unconscious piece of realistic self-portraiture of high value. Mrs. Thrale [11] kept other journals and wrote hundreds of letters, not for the most part published. *Thraliana* begins in 1776, and its last entry dates 1809. It is not a mere diary; it is a "repository" of anecdotes, jests, poems by herself or others, as well as a record of her life and emotions. "Strange Farrago as it is," she writes, "of Sense, Nonsense, publick, private Follies—but chiefly my own— & *I* the little Hero &c. Well! but who should be the Hero of an *Ana?*" So she rambles on, fluttering from records that concern all members of the Johnson circle to inferior verses of her own composing and to jests that savor at times almost of the bawdy house. She sets down voluminously and interestingly, perhaps not too scrupulously, the "small talk" of a gossiping age. Her taste is as far from being impeccable as her conduct was from being stately: she gives an unvarnished portrait of herself and astonishing glimpses into the society of her day. The total effect is one of liveliness and surprising charm: we see her defects, but see also the gaiety and unstable warmth that led Johnson in his more generous moments to call her "the first of women."

Fanny Burney's Diaries

Mrs. Thrale's protégée and friend, Fanny Burney, [12] is of course practically always impeccable. Her diaries, covering most of her long life after she was sixteen, show a discretion in her recordings that Mrs. Thrale never

[11] Mrs. Thrale (1741-1821) was born Hester Lynch Salusbury, in a distinguished but impoverished Welsh family. She was educated at home by her mother and by Dr. Arthur Collier (1707-77), who also taught Sarah Fielding, Henry's learned sister. In the fifties Miss Salusbury began to keep diaries, of which some thirty odd, covering much of her later life, have been at least in part preserved. In 1763 she was married to the wealthy brewer, Henry Thrale, and thereafter lived for many years either in Southwark or in Streatham. She became the mother of many children, only four of whom (daughters) survived to maturity. In 1765 Johnson was first entertained by the Thrales, who thereafter for about fifteen years afforded him a sort of second home. After Mr. Thrale's death (1781) Johnson and Mrs. Thrale saw less of each other, and when the wealthy widow married Gabriel Piozzi (1784), she was temporarily estranged from Johnson, her family, and from many friends. After 1795 she lived chiefly in Wales or at Bath. — With more facility than distinction she wrote several books for publication. Her *Anecdotes of the Late Samuel Johnson* (1786), ed. in *Johnsonian Miscellanies* by G. B. Hill (Oxford, 1897) and separately by Sydney C. Roberts, (Cambridge, 1925), is her most valued book. She also edited (badly) Johnson's *Letters* (2v, 1788). Apart from *Thraliana*, ed. Katharine C. Balderston (2v, Oxford, 1942), other diaries or journals have been published: *Observations and Reflections Made in the Course of a Journey through France, Italy, and Germany* (2v, 1789); her Welsh journal of 1774 in *Dr. Johnson and Mrs. Thrale* by A. M. Broadley (1910); her *French Journals*, ed. Moses Tyson and Henry Guppy (Manchester, 1932); her *Autobiography, Letters, and Literary Remains*, ed. Abraham Hayward (2v, 1861), and Percival Merritt, *Piozzi Marginalia* (Cambridge, Mass., 1925). The standard biography is that by James L. Clifford, *Hester Lynch Piozzi* (Oxford, 1941).

[12] For bibliographical references regarding Miss Burney see Part III, ch. v, n. 18.

coveted. To be sure, Mme d'Arblay in her old age erased and expunged, and left us texts both improved and imperfect; but doubtless even the indiscretions excised would not if extant undermine the natural dignity and poise of "little Burney." She is far less occupied with herself than with the pageant of life about her, and since her part of the pageant included the most important figures of a long and thrilling period, her record is priceless. Her attitude towards others was reserved, sophisticated, even critical. Possibly a sense of social limitation—after all her father, known through Europe later as a musicologist, started life as a mere music master—led her to be amusedly critical of the manners and minds of others. She was herself a "junior" blue-stocking, but she could see the comedy of their self-important prosy remarks. A gem from the lips of Mrs. Vesey is perfect Burney:

"Did you know Mr. Wallace, Mr. Cambridge?" [Mrs. Vesey asks.]
"No, ma'am."
"It's a very disagreeable thing, I think," said she, "when one has just made acquaintance with anybody, and likes them, to have them die."

This speech set me grinning so irresistibly, that I was forced to begin filliping off the crumbs of the macaroon cake from my muff, for an excuse for looking down.

She records long conversations naturally; her characterizations are incisive and revealing. Obviously more prudish than Mrs. Thrale, her prudery is never annoying; she perceives that she herself also has comical aspects. If she records all the compliments that she ever heard of as paid to her *Evelina,* she must be pardoned as being in general the most self-effacing of diarists. She is by habit the demure but shrewd spectator, whether reporting by letter to her sisters or to Daddy Crisp or recording the opinions of the literati gathered by the Thrales at Streatham or the horrors of the ogress Mrs. Schwellenberg, her *bête noire* at Court during the period when she served as second Mistress of the Robes to Queen Charlotte, or later the troubles of the French *émigrés,* one of whom, General d'Arblay, she married when she was forty-one. Her *Early Diaries* (1768-77) are the more easy and sprightly, more full of "worldly dross"; as she grew older, her natural sedateness developed at times into something remotely resembling a heavy self-consciousness; but her materials are everywhere interesting and her methods pleasantly dramatic.

Letter-writing was more commonly approved than the writing of diaries *Blue-* or journals, which at least one early adviser of Miss Burney regarded as *stocking* "the most dangerous employment young persons can have." One was taught *Letters* to write letters; and, in fact, many pages of Miss Burney's diaries were really transcripts of her long journal-like letters. She, her sisters, and all the sobering company of her intellectual friends were notable correspondents. The "Blue-stocking Club," an unorganized circle of ladies who loved literary or intellectual conversation ("Babels" these gatherings seemed to Horace Walpole), was at its prime in the early sixties.[13] Some of these ladies

13 Chauncey B. Tinker, *The Salon and English Letters* (1915).

published essays, frequently in epistolary form, or poems; Hannah More even wrote plays. Mrs. Elizabeth Montagu, "Queen of the Blues," achieved her loudest fame as writer by her exasperating defense of Shakespeare against Voltaire in her *Essay on the Writings and Genius of Shakespeare* (1769). But it is by recording vivid impressions of men, manners, and books in private letters that these ladies and their friends, Mrs. Mary Delany (1700-1788), Mrs. Elizabeth Vesey, called "The Sylph" (1715?-1791), Elizabeth Carter (1717-1806), and Hester Mulso Chapone (1727-1801), have achieved their permanent modicum of repute.[14]

The Queen of the Blues   Mrs. Montagu [15] (1720-1800), though she wrote letters by the thousand, probably will always be best remembered as a charming hostess. In her luxurious houses in Hill Street and in Portman Square, she gathered London literary society about her and acquired fame as a patroness of the arts, without perhaps too much strain on her purse-strings, considering the fact that she was about the wealthiest woman in England. She was allowed to add three dialogues to the *Dialogues of the Dead* (1760) by Lord Lyttelton, always a close friend, who was defended by her and her feminine myrmidons when Johnson's *Lives of the Poets* seemed not sufficiently aware of his lordship's merits. In this case as well as in that of her patronage of James Beattie, she exaggerated her own literary influence: doubtless she had influence, but her real place is rather in social than in literary history.

Chesterfield's Letters   Among the more specialized letter-writers of the period must be placed one of the leading statesmen of the reigns of the first two Georges, the fourth Earl of Chesterfield (1694-1773). The general correspondence of this noble lord,[16] so famous for being, and for not being, a patron of letters, must

---

14 *Autobiography and Correspondence of Mary Granville, Mrs. Delany*, ed. Lady Llanover (6v, 1861-62); *A Series of Letters between Mrs. Elizabeth Carter and Miss Catherine Talbot . . . To which are added Letters from Mrs. Carter to Mrs. Vesey*, ed. Montagu Pennington (4v, 1809); *Letters from Mrs. Elizabeth Carter to Mrs. Montagu*, ed. Montagu Pennington (3v, 1817); Hester Chapone, *Letters on the Improvement of the Mind, Addressed to a Young Lady* (2v, 1773); *The Works of Mrs. Chapone* (2v, Dublin, 1786; 4v, 1807); *Posthumous Works of Mrs. Chapone* (2v, 1807); *Letters of Elizabeth Montagu*, ed. Matthew Montagu (4v, 1809-13); other volumes are edited by John Doran (1873), Emily J. Climenson (2v, 1906), R. Blunt (2v, 1923), and Maud Wyndham (2v, 1924).

15 René Huchon, *Mrs. Montagu* (1907).

16 Philip Dormer Stanhope, fourth Earl of Chesterfield, may be said to have inherited his interest in courtliness, since his mother was the Lady Elizabeth Savile for whom the Marquis of Halifax had written his *Advice to a Daughter* (1688). Largely privately educated, the future fourth Earl at twenty traveled on the Continent, and speedily was embarked on one of the more distinguished diplomatic and administrative careers of the century. After serving as Ambassador to the Hague (1728-32) he returned to England, accompanied by his mistress; their son, Philip, on whose education the Earl was to spend unusual effort, was born two months later (May, 1732). His lordship was long in public employment, but becoming deaf and ill he continued an interest in politics only for the sake of his son, who died in 1768. Thereafter his lordship concentrated on the education of his godson and presumptive heir to his title, who also was named Philip. The arts of life, particularly literature, had always interested the fourth Earl. In youth a friend of Pope, Arbuthnot, Gay, and others, he later cultivated Voltaire, Rousseau, and Montesquieu. His interest in writers was normally so generous that his neglect of Samuel Johnson was probably not intentional and certainly was not characteristic. — His *Letters to his Son* were published (1774) immediately after his death by his son's widow, and they have often been republished. *Miscellaneous Works*, ed. Dr. Matthew Maty and John O. Justamond (2v, 1777; 4v, 1779); *Letters* (2v, 1774); ed. Lord Mahon (5v, 1845-53); John Bradshaw (3v, 1892); Bonamy Dobrée (6v, 1932). The *Letters to his Godson* were first edited by the Earl of Carnarvon (1890). — Sidney L. Gulick, *A*

have been dominantly political; but his fame will probably always rest on the series of courtesy-book letters addressed to his illegitimate son, Philip. A similar series, addressed to his godson (1761-73) and first published in 1890, serves to reinforce the doctrines of the earlier series. Chesterfield in many ways was a belated Ciceronian in life as in epistolary style. His counsels to his son are based on the noblest "Roman" principles; but the object is policy. According to his contemporary, the Philadelphia printer, Dr. Franklin, honesty was the best policy; according to Chesterfield, manners were the best policy. To his bookish, shy, and awkward son, he preaches in his letters the art of pleasing—always for a purpose: he wished his son to have a distinguished political or diplomatic career. Young Philip had excellent training for this end, but he lacked grace, social charm, and even the inclination to win by diplomacy. His father has been castigated as worldly and insincere; he seems merely to be at times cynical about public intelligence. At least he realized that a compromise between ideals and conduct is inevitable in public life. That he was himself an honest and amiable diplomat and an affectionate parent is indubitable. His knowledge of men was wide and shrewd: "Whatever poets may write, or fools believe, of rural innocence and truth, and of the perfidy of Courts, this is most un-doubtedly true—that shepherds and ministers are both men; their nature and passions the same, the modes of them only different." Such worldly wisdom is deftly stated; but the primitivists and sentimentalists of 1774 regarded such opinions as insensitive and artificial, and probably even fellow peers felt that Chesterfield worked too hard at being noble. He certainly lacked warmth of style but not sound perception of social values. His Augustan spirit is seen when he applies Horace's precepts for the poet to a wider field: "To avoid extremes, to observe propriety, to consult one's own strength, and to be consistent from beginning to end, are precepts as useful for the man as for the poet." The ideal of noble diplomacy has hardly found a sounder proponent in English.

In violent contrast to the special province of Chesterfield is that of Gilbert White [17] (1720-1793), who in his thirties retired from a useful career as an Oxford don to his native and ancestral Hampshire village, Selborne, there to pursue his real career as natural historian. His letters (1767-87) to his fellow observers of nature, Thomas Pennant and Daines Barrington, which were first published in 1789 under the title *The Natural History of Selborne*,

Gilbert White

Chesterfield Bibliography to 1800 (Chicago, 1935; *Papers of the Bibl. Soc. of America*, Vol. XXIX). — Samuel Shellabarger, *Lord Chesterfield* (1935); Sidney L. Gulick, "The Publication of Chesterfield's Letters to his Son," *PMLA*, LI (1936). 165-177; Willard Connely, *The True Chesterfield* (1939); Virgil B. Heltzel, "Chesterfield and the Anti-Laughter Tradition," *MP*, XXVI (1928). 73-90.

[17] Gilbert White's *Writings* (incomplete), ed. H. J. Massingham (2v, 1938); *The Natural History and Antiquities of Selborne* (1789; 2v, 1802, with "A Naturalist's Calendar"), ed. Edward T. Bennett, *et al.* (1837); Sir Wm. Jardine (Edinburgh, 1829); Frank Buckland (2v, 1876); John Burroughs (2v, 1895); Grant Allen (1900); L. C. Miall and W. Warde Fowler (1901); World's Classics (Oxford, 1902); B. C. A. Windle (Everyman's Library, 1906). — *Life and Letters of Gilbert White*, ed. Rashleigh Holt-White (2v, 1901); *Journals*, ed. Walter Johnson (1931). — Edward A. Martin, *A Bibliography of Gilbert White* (1934); Walter Johnson, *Gilbert White: Pioneer, Poet, and Stylist* (1928).

embody a world of curious fact about the weather, the soil, the animals, and the birds of the secluded and beautiful region in which he lived. At first sight the letters take us quite out of the world of men; nature is their subject, and while the villagers appear briefly, White never deviates into "world topics" of the day. A young neighbor, "a young gentleman in the service of the East-India Company," is mentioned, not as an empire-builder, but as one who "has brought home a dog and a bitch of the Chinese breed." White's observations, especially of birds, are said to have notable value to science. His literary charm depends largely on his obvious but unconscious and restrained affection for what he sees, and on his interest in the instincts and almost human behavior of birds and animals. On the instinctive anger of fangless, unborn vipers torn from the belly of their dam, just dead, he comments: "To a thinking mind nothing is more wonderful than that early instinct which impresses young animals with the notion of the situation of their natural weapons, and of using them properly in their own defense, even before those weapons subsist or are formed." Of unwieldy, disproportioned, newly hatched swifts he says: "We could not but wonder when we reflected that these shiftless beings in a little more than a fortnight would be able to dash through the air almost with the inconceivable swiftness of a meteor; and perhaps, in their emigration must traverse vast continents and oceans as distant as the equator. So soon does nature advance small birds to their ἡλικία, or state of perfection; while the progressive growth of men and large quadrupeds is slow and tedious!" Accurate and diverse curiosity and an unceasing wonder at the mysteries of creation, together with a "thinking mind," have in these letters created that rarity, a scientific literary masterpiece.

But most letter-writers are not so specialized as Lord Chesterfield or Gilbert White. Most of them are content, without plan, to make their letters merely friendly communications. This is especially true of literati, among whom for the moment we may place the great actor and less great playwright, David Garrick (1717-1779). Although preoccupied in his letters with the details of his career as actor and manager, Garrick writes from the time he is sixteen amiable, natural, sprightly letters that at times rise to wit and brilliance.[18] He approaches the task of letter-writing normally with a special point of view, if not a new histrionic individuality, for each important effort. He is sincere, but shows the emotional flexibility of a great actor, even though, as he says, he writes "upon the gallop." His letters gain interest in part from the fact that his correspondents included not only theatrical celebrities and members of the Johnson circle (Burke is his closest friend here), but also other leaders of the social and political life of the day. His chief interest, however, in spite of his wide acquaintance is to students of theatrical history.

Among the poets more than one is distinguished for epistolary charm: perhaps the three most commonly praised are William Shenstone, Thomas

---

[18] On Garrick see Part III, ch. VI, n. 2.

Gray, and William Cowper. Of these Shenstone [19] is in all respects the least, *Poets as* but he is by no means contemptible. From the ornamented rusticity of *Letter-* Leasowes he wrote interestingly on literary topics to the publisher Robert *Writers:* Dodsley, to Bishop Percy, to Richard Graves, author of *The Spiritual* *Shenstone* *Quixote,* to the Edge Hill poet Richard Jago, and to William Somervile, author of *The Chace.* To his neighbor fifteen miles away, Lady Luxborough (half-sister of Lord Bolingbroke), he confided his emotional state and his gardening projects. Apart from gardening, his "rural allusions" in his letters, as in his poems, suffer from self-consciousness. His epistolary style is easily overpraised: his sentences straggle and sprawl—inelegantly at times but almost always interestingly and naturally.

Thomas Gray is in all respects a greater epistolary artist.[20] Gray, in fact, *Thomas* seems more natural and easy in his letter-writing than elsewhere. Here the *Gray* true warmth and fineness of his personality are evident. Frequently erudite, a trait unavoidable in "the most learned man in Europe," he was even more frequently colloquial, witty, and genuinely affectionate. There is none of the stiffness that his normal reserve in company would lead one to expect. The mere fact that he called his friend the Rev. William Mason "Scroddles" alone speaks volumes of his gift for affectionate informalities. Mason, Nicholls, and the young Swiss Bonstetten all won Gray's affections as young men. Such major correspondents as Horace Walpole and Richard West had been boyhood friends at Eton. At Cambridge Dr. Thomas Wharton, Fellow of Pembroke College from 1739 to 1747, became Gray's closest friend, and to him in 1769 Gray sent as an account of his tour of the Lake Region a series of letters that of itself would establish the poet's epistolary fame.[21]

Apart from the unconscious revelation of himself, Gray's letters have at least three notable topics: antiquities, literature, and the beauties of land- scape. The letters are a chief clue to his great learning, and they also con- stitute him, in well-chosen excerpts, a notable critic of poetry and prose fiction. Most interesting, because unusual, is his ability to convey his delight in the wilder aspects of nature. It is absurd to imagine that Gray was the first Englishman really to feel the titanic beauty of the Alps or the quieter loveliness of the English lakes; but he is perhaps the first to express this beauty in words of distinction. Thomas Amory, for example, in his fantastic *John Buncle* (Volume I, 1756) had made the attempt, and he shows that Westmorland already had a reputation for wild natural beauty. He also shows that a taste for the sublime may exist without gifts of expressing the sublime. Throughout his life Gray's mind recorded delicate impressions of

[19] On Shenstone see Part III, ch. IV, n. 13.

[20] In addition to the references on Gray given in Part III, ch. IV, n. 15, see Geoffrey Tillotson, "On Gray's Letters," in *Essays in Criticism and Research* (Cambridge, 1942), pp. 117-123.

[21] Dr. Wharton had planned to accompany Gray, but asthma prevented. Consequently Gray kept for his friend a detailed journal of the tour in pocket note-books, from which letters were extracted and sent to Wharton. See Gray's *Correspondence,* ed. Paget Toynbee and Leonard Whibley (Oxford, 1935), III. 1074 ff.; esp. the footnote on pp. 1074-5. Gray's interest in nature at times approached the purely scientific. See, for example, Charles Eliot Norton's *The Poet Gray as a Naturalist* (Boston, 1903), which publishes some of his learned marginalia.

beautiful landscapes, and, unlike others, he had a special gift for conveying his impressions through words. His letters record a rich experience of books, men, and nature, and the record is warmly intimate yet restrained; informal yet, of its epoch, dignified.

William Cowper

William Cowper,[22] in spite of his intermittent periods of mental derangement, led a more serene and winsome existence than did busy intellectuals like Gray or Shenstone; and this quiet life of virtue and piety is beautifully mirrored in his letters. For over forty years he sent his friends charming accounts of his life—his country walks, his adventures with "Puss" and his other hares and pets, his religious agonies, his reading, and his own labors as a poet, together with observations on the life of the parish in which he happened to be living. As Johnson represents the literary life in town, so Cowper symbolizes the refined aspects of village life of the late century. In his letters, he writes with an ease, limpidity, naturalness, and elegance that is hardly found elsewhere in letters. It is perhaps true that one remembers Cowper for a relatively small number of superlatively excellent letters—those in which ease is spiced by his exquisite humor rather than made painful by his religious depression; but the average quality of his prose is high and the total effect of self-portrayal is most attractive. Doubtless he is the most lovable of letter-writers.

In the opinion of his editor Thomas Wright, Cowper "is universally acknowledged to be the greatest of English letter-writers." Such assertion will provoke opposition from the many admirers of Gray or, more evidently,

Horace Walpole

of Horace Walpole [23] (1717-1797), though they will probably admit that in many ways Cowper had a quiet integrity and personal charm that Walpole lacks. But Walpole has everything else: brilliance, wit, humor, knowledge of society, politics, literature, architecture, painting, and an ability always to be—at some slight cost of conscious effort—extremely entertaining. Among the thousands of his letters there are relatively few that are not enlivening. He was personally "spirits of hartshorne" to his intimates. At first sight Walpole seems merely a superficial, elegant amateur, to whom no high human experience came. From another point of view, however, all experi-

22 On Cowper see references given below, ch. x. To these may be added articles by Kenneth Povey: "The Text of Cowper's Letters," *MLR*, XXII (1927). 22-27; "Notes for a Bibliography of Cowper's Letters," *RES*, VII (1931). 182-187; VIII (1932). 316-319; X (1934). 76-78; XII (1936). 333-335.

23 *The Works of Horatio Walpole*, ed. Mary Berry *et al.* (9v, 1798-1825). Apart from his letters his major contribution to the history of his own time is made in his *Memoirs of the Last Ten Years of . . . George the Second*, ed. Lord Holland (2v, 1822) and in his *Memoirs of the Reign of George the Third*, ed. Sir D. Le Marchant (4v, 1845). His *Correspondence* has been often edited since 1820 when four volumes appeared. The best editions are by Peter Cunningham (9v, 1857), Mrs. Paget Toynbee (16v, Oxford, 1903-5; Supplements by Paget Toynbee, 3v, Oxford, 1918-25; 2v, Oxford, 1915). These, however, are to be supplanted by the magnificent Yale Edition now in progress, edited by Wilmarth S. Lewis. This began in 1937, and to date 12 volumes have appeared. The completed edition may run to over fifty volumes. — Austin Dobson, *Horace Walpole, a Memoir* (1890, 1927); Paul Yvon, *La Vie d'un dilettante: Horace Walpole* (Paris, 1924); Leonard Whibley, "The Foreign Tour of Gray and Walpole," *Blackwood's Magazine*, CCXXVII (1930). 813-827; Warren H. Smith, *Architecture in English Fiction* (New Haven, 1934); Robert W. Ketton-Cremer, *Horace Walpole, a Biography* (1940); Isabel W. U. Chase, *Horace Walpole, Gardenist* (1943).

ence came his way, and found in him an attentive and amused observer and recorder. His most famous remark was, "The world is a comedy to those who think, a tragedy to those who feel." He chose to be a comic artist.

Born the youngest son of the great prime minister, Horace was in his ninth year sent to Eton, where he formed ardent boyish friendships with Thomas Ashton and two other boys—Richard West (1716-1742) and Thomas Gray. This "Quadruple Alliance" lasted for some years. Another Eton group was called "The Triumvirate": it included George Montagu, *His Early* later Walpole's correspondent to whom social gossip was confided, and *Years* Charles Lyttelton, brother of the "good" Lord Lyttelton and later Bishop of Carlisle. The years (1727-34) at Eton meant much to Walpole—far more than the succeeding years at Cambridge (1735-9), though there he continued his friendship with Ashton and Gray. Both Gray and Walpole were intended for the law, but neither fancied that fate, and both welcomed the opportunity of making the grand tour together. Before they got to Calais differences in temperament between the volatile and theatrical Walpole and the shy, proud Gray manifested themselves; but together they delighted in Paris, the Alps, Florence, and Rome, and perhaps had no more psychological rubs than befall the average fellow travelers. At Florence they met and enjoyed the hospitality of Horace Mann, destined, in spite of the fact that Walpole never saw him after this tour, to receive the most voluminous and valued of Walpole's correspondences. In the spring of 1741 the two travelers parted company for some unknown and probably unimportant reason: the coolness was not removed until late in 1745. This tour through France and Italy was most influential in the development of Walpole's social and artistic tastes.

During the period 1741-68 Walpole was a member of Parliament, and though he seldom spoke in the House, he was active and even influential in discreet and respectable wire-pulling. The most trying moment in his career came at its beginning when his father in 1742 was forced to resign by means so treacherous, Horace felt, as to be eternally unforgivable. Other tense moments came at crises in the career of his cousin, the Hon. Henry Seymour Conway, who as member of Parliament and even as Secretary of State deferred—but not always—to Walpole's advice. In 1747 Walpole acquired in Twickenham a small house, presently rechristened Strawberry Hill, and set about a career first as gardener and by 1750 as architect.

To the surprise of some of his friends he decided to do the house in *Strawberry* Gothic style. There was nothing really revolutionary in the decision. Gothic *Hill* was never totally "out"; antiquarians had almost consistently praised it, and clergymen and others sporadically throughout the first half of the century had been pointing the windows of their cottages and at the same time adding "Chinese" porches to their doorways. For music and dining *al fresco* one of the most fashionable places of resort after 1732 was Vauxhall Gardens, and here Gothic design had been freely used. The distaste for this style came normally from those who loved simplicity and plainness. The chapel of

Henry VII in the Abbey had seemed to John Evelyn "lace . . . cut-work, and crinkle crankle." The ingenuity of baroque ornamentation and the artifice of decorative Gothic were regarded, however, as akin rather than as hostile. In 1717 that true Palladian architect, Colin Campbell, had charged that post-Palladian "Italians can now no more relish the antique simplicity, but are entirely employed in capricious ornaments, which must at last end in the Gothick." The vexed problem of ornamentation in art rather than any love or even understanding of pure Gothic forms is at the bottom of most eighteenth-century controversy over architectural styles. Since practically all architectural revivals are easily dated fifty years after the fact, it need surprise no one that Walpole's somewhat rococo Gothic was, to say the least, impure. He had no intention of making his house a perfect period piece devoid of modern convenience: being naturally an exotic, somewhat disillusioned with the life of his own day, he sought a remote style that would gratify his antiquarian tastes and also give play to the multiplicity of decorative effects that were his delight. By 1753 the first stage of his gothicizing was accomplished, but at intervals for twenty years he greatly enlarged the house, adding a cloister, towers, and several spacious rooms and other architectural features. If he did not originate the Gothic revival either in architecture or in literature, he certainly gave aristocratic sanction and popular vogue to both. Curious visitors became so frequent that tickets were issued and rules of visit established. Walpole's house aroused more interest in his own day than did any of his other activities.

The Straw-
berry Hill
Press

Near his house Walpole's experimental nature led him to set up a private printing press, and the press stimulated him to authorship. Here he published his friend Gray's two great odes (the first productions of the press; brought out in 1757), as well as other works not by himself.[24] Of his own writings he did not publish all at Strawberry Hill. Naturally the anonymously produced *Castle of Otranto* (1765) did not come from his own press, but his *Fugitive Pieces in Verse and Prose* (1758) and his tragedy, *The Mysterious Mother* (1768), did. Although this last work, dealing with a morbid story of incest, was unfitted for stage production, it is his most powerfully written imaginative work.

Even in his original writing Walpole was the amateur medievalist, and the most regarded works of the Strawberry Hill press that came from his pen were genteelly historical. His *Catalogue of the Royal and Noble Authors of England* (2 volumes, 1758) was an amusing compilation of literary and antiquarian gossip, and his *Historic Doubts on Richard III* (1768), which was not printed at Strawberry Hill, was an interesting if unsoundly argued attempt to clear Richard from his alleged murders and other misdeeds. It was in part, as Mr. Ketton-Cremer says aptly, a work of "disdainful amateurishness." Of far different merit and far more typical of Walpole's

---

[24] Allen T. Hazen and J. P. Kirby, *A Bibliography of the Strawberry Hill Press, with a Record of the Prices at which Copies have been Sold* (New Haven, 1942). This excellent work supersedes all other secondary sources of information about Walpole's press.

natural interests was his production, on the Strawberry Hill press, of his *Anecdotes of Painting in England* (4 volumes, 1762-71). This work, based on the valuable note-books of the famous engraver George Vertue (1684-1756), which Walpole had purchased from Vertue's widow, made Walpole a pioneer in the history of English painting; and when in the twentieth century a society was founded for the promotion of the historical study of English art, it was appropriately named the Walpole Society.

As the son of a notable prime minister Walpole had naturally an interest in the political history of his own day. Before he bought Strawberry Hill he had begun to envisage himself as a historian of his own time; and in this difficult rôle he produced his *Memoirs,* covering much of the latter half of his century. These show his limitations (a capricious hatred of his father's enemies being one), and yet show also his keen observation and wide knowledge of the political alignments of his day, a knowledge invaluable for its frequent illumination of the tortuous political quarrels and friendships so perplexing to later historians. *Walpole's Memoirs*

Possibly, as has been suggested, Walpole came to regard his voluminous correspondences not merely as the raw materials for memoirs but as themselves the best memoirs he could bequeath to posterity. If so, he thought wisely. He was an artist in miniature work; for the large canvas of formal history he lacked the indispensable quality of settled industry and the ability to make coherent and large interpretations. In letters he becomes legitimately the vivid and intelligent reporter of the specific scene. At present scholars believe that Walpole selected his correspondents as worthy recipients of specialized materials: to Horace Mann in distant Florence was consigned the matter of politics; to George Montagu went society gossip, and to William Cole talk of antiquities. One can perhaps exaggerate this conscious and somewhat pedantic specialization in correspondences, but clearly to some degree it existed. It enabled Walpole to leave a diversified record of the life of his time, and his concentration on the specialized aspect of the moment helped to make each letter an individual and artistic achievement. *His Letters as Memoirs*

Historically the letters have the value of a thousand examples of that modern work the "documentary film"; artistically the letters are superior to any graphic portrayal of their time. He gives us "shots" of everyone—the beautiful Countess of Coventry, the chivalrous highwayman, M'Lean, the notorious Fanny Murray, clapping the despised gift of a twenty-pound note between two pieces of bread and eating it!—they are all there. We have pictures of the trials and executions of the Jacobite lords, of the funeral of George II, of a score of other historic—and possibly grotesque—moments. He recaptures for nostalgic minds a whole social era in a sentence: "Old Cibber plays tonight, and all the world will be there." His art, formed on the model of Madame de Sévigné's, is at its best in focused episode or anecdote. At times he certainly has the modern journalistic defect of overconfidence in the authenticity of his information; yet he was not intentionally the irresponsible gossip, and he doubtless was the best informed gossip of

his century. His deftness and lightness—tinged at times with cynicism—
together with a keen sense of humor make him supreme among the wits of
a decreasingly witty period. His personality, his artifice, have been decried;
but from one point of view his personality is negligible: it is the wealth of
his material that counts. From another point of view, however, the catholic-
ity of his perceptions *is* his personality. Life for him was a "dome of many-
colored glass" and from it he caught a myriad of brilliant diffractions. Of
the serious religious or intellectual life of his time he is, like a good popular
journalist, almost totally unaware: in *comédie humaine* he would rank near
the top in any period. He is the most voluminous and, by all odds, the most
entertaining practitioner of the art of letter-writing in the period that is
clearly the golden age of that art.

IX

Intellectual Prose

In David Hume, Edward Gibbon, and Edmund Burke are seen tendencies that indicate significant, if diversely individual, developments in style and in modes of thinking. Their very diversity suggests intellectual disintegration in the period, but all three seem alike in that they mark a transition from the mechanistic a priori thinking of many early Augustans towards a new organic concept of man and of human institutions. The first two of our trio were skeptics; Burke was a man of faith, but he too tended to rely on a psychological pragmatism or opportunism rather than on abstract theory— a position that subverted trust in reason. "Reason," as a matter of fact, was claimed as on the side of the French Revolution: Burke was not. We must ask, then, how do these three men illuminate the movements of their day?

Hume's [1] preëminence is supremely that of a philosopher; but he was also an historian and an essayist of worth. His philosophy was embodied in early works that won recognition too slowly to suit their ambitious author.

[1] David Hume (1711-1776) was born in Edinburgh, and was educated there in the University. He spent the years 1734-7 in France, where he wrote his first *Treatise*. After publishing it in London, he returned to Scotland, but failing to secure a professorial appointment, he became (1745-6) a nobleman's tutor, and presently he was with General Sinclair at Lorient and later in Vienna and Turin. In 1749 he returned to Scotland, where he wrote (1751) his *Dialogues concerning Natural Religion* (1779). Because of clerical opposition he failed (1752) of appointment as successor to Adam Smith in the chair of logic at Glasgow. From 1752 to 1757 he was Keeper of the Advocates' Library, and became a leader in the distinguished intellectual society of Edinburgh. After serving (1763-66) as secretary of the British Embassy in Paris, where he was a great social success, he returned to England, escorting the philosopher Rousseau to an English refuge. A famous quarrel between the two resulted. In 1767 Hume was Conway's under-secretary of state; but most of the rest of his life was spent among his Scottish friends, who included Hugh Blair, John Home, Adam Ferguson, Lord Kames, William Robertson, and Adam Smith. In his autobiography, dated April 18, 1776, he expects "a speedy dissolution." The calm cheerfulness of his demise four months later greatly annoyed the orthodox. His character was both upright and amiable; his life attempted a demonstration of a proposition very dear to the free-thinkers of his century: that virtue could exist independent of religion. — Rudolf Metz, "Bibliographie der Hume-Literatur," in *Literarische Berichte aus dem Gebiete der Philosophie*, xv-xvi (1928). 39-50; Thomas E. Jessop, *A Bibliography of David Hume*, etc. (1938). — Hume's writings have been collected as *Essays and Treatises* (4v, 1753-6; 1758, 1760, etc.); as *Philosophical Works* (4v, 1826, etc.); as *A Treatise of Human Nature*, ed. Thomas H. Green and T. H. Grose (2v, 1874) and *Essays Moral, Political, and Literary*, ed. Thomas H. Green and T. H. Grose (2v, 1875). His histories have been published as follows: *History of Great Britain*, Vol. 1 [Reigns of James I and Charles I] (Edinburgh, 1754); Vol. 11 [The Commonwealth, Charles II, and James II] (1757); *History of England under the House of Tudor* (2v, 1759); *History of England from the Invasion of Julius Caesar to the Revolution of 1688* (8v, 1763; and many eds. thereafter; after 1793 with continuations by Smollett to 1760 and by others later for later periods). — *The Life of David Hume, Esq., written by Himself* (1777; and in most eds. of the *Essays* thereafter); *The Letters of David Hume*, ed. John Y. T. Greig (2v, Oxford, 1932). The standard biography is that of John H. Burton, *Life and Correspondence of David Hume* (2v, 1846); Ernest C. Mossner gives an illuminating account of Hume's personal relations with contemporaries in *The For-*

The core of his thinking was precociously formed, and was expressed in a *Treatise of Human Nature,* completed when he was twenty-five and published anonymously in 1739. "It fell *dead-born from the press"* was the author's pained comment. In his final edition of his *Essays* (1777) he included an Advertisement requesting that only pieces published later than the *Treatise,* a "juvenile work," be "regarded as containing his philosophical sentiments and principles." His later work in philosophy, however, is by and large a restatement and development, in more polished and strategic form, of positions taken in the *Treatise.* The most inclusive single reworking was his *Enquiry concerning Human Understanding* (1748), the second edition of which was the first volume to bear the author's name. In his *Four Dissertations* (1757) that on the passions frankly uses material drawn verbatim from the *Treatise,* and these ideas had already been fundamental to the work that was his favorite, his *Enquiry concerning the Principles of Morals* (1751). It was chiefly in posthumous works, particularly the smoothly written *Dialogues concerning Natural Religion* (1779), that Hume trenchantly extended his skepticism (always outspoken in other directions) to the field of religion.

Hume's Skepticism   Beyond doubt Hume was the most thoroughgoing and strategically logical skeptic to come out of Great Britain. Carrying the empiricism of Locke and Berkeley to its extreme conclusion, Hume held that nothing can be known by the mind but its own "impressions" (sensations) and "ideas" (faint copies of impressions). He is opposed to all a priori thinking and to most metaphysical concepts. He builds inductively from psychological data; but his service is less the erection of a new system than it is the destruction of doctrines to him either irrelevant or baseless. He combats such arguments from "design" as the physico-theologists had indulged in; and in his *Dialogues concerning Natural Religion* he ridicules current speculation about the divine attributes. His logical legerdemain is everywhere dazzling, and perhaps nowhere more so than in the sections of his *Human Understanding* which analyze the concept of Causation. Naturally he will have no traffic with supernaturalism in religion; and if he does admit—somewhat strangely—an idea of "necessary connection" or even at rare moments "an eternal inherent principle of order" that ranges and rules our "impressions," he rigorously opposes any analogy between this principle and intelligence whether human or divine. He clears the way, in metaphysics, for the positivism of the nineteenth century. In ethics he as clearly prepares for utilitarianism. He proves to his own satisfaction that while the passions cause actions, reason is neither a guide nor a controlling force in the face of passion. Ethical choice he bases altogether on utility, on a *sentiment* that declares a preference of pleasure to pain. Reason and the earlier concepts of

gotten *Hume* (1943). On the trouble with Rousseau see Albert Schinz, *État présent des travaux sur J.-J. Rousseau* (New York, 1941) and H. Roddier in *RLC,* XVIII (1938). 452-477. — Charles W. Hendel, *Studies in the Philosophy of David Hume* (Princeton, 1925); André Leroy, *La critique et la religion chez David Hume* (Paris, 1930); John Laird, *Hume's Philosophy of Human Nature* (1932); Norman K. Smith, *The Philosophy of David Hume* (1941).

conscience are modified in nature and in power. Belief itself in Hume's eyes is a *sentiment,* "which depends not on will, nor can be commanded at pleasure." If there ever was an age of reason in Matthew Arnold's sense of the phrase, surely Hume with skilful logic was its treacherous, subversive high priest. In his thinking "eternal verities" disappear, and his probable answer to the question as to what kept his world from being merely a chaos of sensation would be "the principles of the association of ideas." "Common sense" was the answer later urged by some of his Scottish compatriots and critics.

Hume's early works, as we have said, were less cordially received than his thirst for fame desired. This was due less to an immediate realization that, if he was right, all the theologians and a priori rationalists were hopelessly wrong, than it was to the fact that he wrote in a cool, quiet fashion when the reasoners of the moment (like William Warburton and his school) were excitingly abusive or paradoxically or ironically entertaining. Hume's *Philosophical Essays concerning Human Understanding* was, he said, eclipsed by Conyers Middleton's *Free Enquiry into the Miraculous Powers,* an unintentionally subversive work of the same year. Possibly the excitement over Bolingbroke's posthumous *Works* (1754) held back readers from Hume; but he was gradually coming into his own, and presently was to be spoken of as "the fashionable Hume." Eventually he acquired a comfortable income through the very large sale of his books.

Vogue of the "fashionable" sort he doubtless sought, but he wisely sought *Hume's* it through literary efforts in the form of essays. In 1741-2 Hume brought out *Essays* two volumes of essays, which he had accumulated with the unrealized intention of using them in a weekly periodical; some were social and moral—remotely patterned after *The Spectator;* others were political, somewhat in the manner of *The Craftsman.* One of these latter was an uncomplimentary "Character of Sir Robert Walpole"—discreetly published just after the great statesman's fall. Of the two types the political essays, especially those on economic subjects,[2] have been at times highly regarded, though their cool moderation would hardly have fired readers used to *The Craftsman* or *The Daily Gazetteer.* Hume was practising to gain an elegant style fit for *salons;* but he lacked the lightness, the playfulness, and the wit, as well as the feeling for details of human interest that are required of the journalist-essayist. Almost ten years before *The Rambler* he was demonstrating the unfitness of the clear, abstract thinker for the task so well performed by Steele and Addison. The net result of the experience gained through these twenty-seven essays was that Hume effectively cast his *Human Understanding* in brief essay-like sections. The most readable of his *Essays* are those on literary topics or his sketches ("characters") of the Epicurean, the Stoic, the Platonist, and the Skeptic. The style usually is unadorned, but where it departs from the simplicity and refinement that he normally sought and achieved, it departs

---

[2] Hume's influence on Adam Smith is perhaps exaggerated by James Bonar, *Philosophy and Political Economy* (1893), pp. 105-129.

in the tradition of classical oratory or history. His most finished writing is found in the *Dialogues concerning Natural Religion*, which was suppressed until after his death.

Strangely enough this gifted thinker was to achieve his greatest popular success in the field of history, where his endowments were less remarkable than in philosophy. An appointment (1752) as Keeper of the Advocates' Library (now the National Library of Scotland) put at his disposal what *His* History seemed large resources for writing in the neglected field of history, and thus encouraged him to realize long-cherished ambitions to shine as an historian of Great Britain. His first volume, dealing with the early seventeenth century, which was to him "the most curious, interesting, and instructive part of our history," was not well received. Hume as a Scot was naturally pro-Stuart;[3] but he had thought himself open-minded and impartial. Reactions to his work were disappointing. "I was assailed," he writes, "by one cry of reproach, disapprobation, and even detestation; English, Scotch, and Irish, Whig and Tory, churchman and sectary, free-thinker and religionist, patriot and courtier, united in their rage against the man, who had presumed to shed a generous tear for the fate of Charles I and the Earl of Strafford." This extreme picture is hardly congruent with his further complaint that only forty-five copies of the work were sold during a year. The second volume, with Charles I out of the way and the glorious Revolution of 1688 as terminal point, was less offensive, and "helped buoy up its unfortunate brother" (Volume 1). The next installment, on "The House of Tudor," was criticized; but when the whole was completed in 1762, and became in the following year the *History of England from the Invasion of Julius Caesar to the Revolution of 1688* in eight volumes, Hume had achieved the first satisfactory history of England to be written. Its defects are now obvious: it is not very soundly based in careful study or research; the Middle Ages are ignorantly defamed and in later fields there is bias. The organizing purpose—Hume's desire to illustrate the dangers of violent faction to a state—had more appeal in his time than in later days. But the work supplied a great lack, and it was readable. Its fame outlived that of Hume's contemporary rivals, Robertson[4] and Smollett, and was for over a century the most read history of England. In 1828 Macaulay[5] admitted that Hume was "the ablest and most popular" of English historians, and a more recent historian, the

[3] E. C. Mossner defends Hume's position in "Was Hume a Tory Historian?" *JHI*, II (1941). 225-236, and in "An Apology for David Hume, Historian," *PMLA*, LVI (1941). 657-690, gives a more general account of Hume as historian, and gives a good bibliography of other accounts of Hume's work as historian. These papers are shrewdly reviewed by William Davidson, *PQ*, XXI (1942). 206-209.

[4] William Robertson (1721-1793), a Scottish Presbyterian minister, was a charter member (1754) of the "Select Society," a club of fifteen eminent Scots, including David Hume, Adam Ferguson, Monboddo, Kames, and Adam Smith. His fame was established by his *History of Scotland during the Reigns of Queen Mary and of King James VI* (2v, 1759), and was sustained by his *Charles V* (3v, 1769), and his *History of America* (2v, 1777). Both in style and in scholarship his work is comparable with Hume's, but his subjects were less popular in appeal. For Smollett see above, Part II, ch. x, n. 17.

[5] In a review article on Neele's *Romance of History* in the *Edinburgh Rev.*, XLVII (1828). 331-367.

Right Honorable Winston Churchill, has called the work his "boyhood's manual."

In 1752 Viscount Bolingbroke brought out his much read *Letters on the Study of History*. These in England and—much more significantly—the work of Montesquieu and Voltaire in France and Vico in Italy were modifying the concept of history. Hume would have agreed with the fundamental precept of Bolingbroke, borrowed from the ancients, that "history is philosophy teaching by examples." For although he did not write history like a philosopher, Hume's purpose was fundamentally didactic. Unlike the French illuminati, who stressed the criminal wrongs of the past, Hume was a pioneer giving an account of a great nation that had recently emerged as a power and a cultural force in Europe.

Curiously enough the historian Gibbon [6] is somewhat more philosophical than the historian Hume, and even more typical of the aristocrats of his age. *Gibbon's* Like Hume and Voltaire, Gibbon was anticlerical; his mind had "emerged *Decline* from superstition to skepticism." Like Voltaire he inclined to the tragedy *and Fall* rather than the comedy of man's past. He was less keen than Voltaire on finding ideas behind actions, but was far more interested in causal sequences than was Hume. Above all, he was in coolness of temperament and in his veneration for the civilization of ancient Rome the perfect neo-classicist. The fascination that the pageantry of imperial Rome had for Gibbon stimulated him to spend more than twenty years of his life in the research for and composition of his great masterpiece, *The Decline and Fall of the Roman Empire*. In his *Autobiography* he remarked:

My temper is not very susceptible of enthusiasm, and the enthusiasm which I do not feel I have ever scorned to affect. But, at the distance of twenty-five years, I can neither forget nor express the strong emotions which agitated my mind as I first approached and entered the *eternal city*. After a sleepless night, I trod, with a lofty step, the ruins of the Forum; each memorable spot where Romulus *stood*, or Tully spoke, or Caesar fell, was at once present to my eye; and several days of intoxication were lost or enjoyed before I could descend to a cool and minute investigation.

[6] Edward Gibbon (1737-1794) was born in Putney, near London, of a well-to-do family. His youth was sickly, and his early education irregular. After fourteen months at Magdalen College, Oxford (1752-53), he became a convert to Catholicism and was dismissed. His father thereupon placed him under the care of a Calvinist minister in Lausanne, and Gibbon soon abandoned the Roman faith—and all faith. Lausanne became a second home to him, and French a second language. In 1757 he returned to England, where he served two years as captain in the Hampshire Militia (1760-62), and then devoted himself to historical studies and writing. In 1764 he visited Rome, and there conceived the project of writing the history of the decline and fall of the city. In 1774 he was admitted to Dr. Johnson's "Club," and became a Member of Parliament. He served on the Board of Trade and Plantations 1779-82, but retired from politics when the coalition government of 1783 was formed. Thereafter he lived at Lausanne; but in 1793 he paid a visit to his friend Lord Sheffield in England, became ill, and died there. — Jane E. Norton, *A Bibliography of the Works of Edward Gibbon* (Oxford, 1940). — *Miscellaneous Works*, ed. the first Earl of Sheffield (5v, 1814). — J. B. Black, *The Art of History* (1926); Vernon P. Helming, "Edward Gibbon and Georges Deyverdun," *PMLA*, XLVII (1932). 1028-1049; Shelby T. McCloy, *Gibbon's Antagonism to Christianity* (1933); Edmund Blunden, *Edward Gibbon and his Age* (1935); Robert B. Mowat, *Gibbon* (1936); David M. Low, *Edward Gibbon* (1937); I. W. J. Machin, "Gibbon's Debt to Contemporary Scholarship," *RES*, xv (1939). 84-88.

Years of this cool and minute research followed; for Gibbon far surpassed the historians of his time in devotion to careful study: Rome merited such consecration of effort. If he found history brick and left it nobly marble, the change doubtless was due to inspiration from that ancient civilization the decay of which was his tragic theme. He was among the last and among the best of the true Augustans.

Its Scope   Through the years of his labor the scope of Gibbon's project steadily enlarged itself. His first idea was to write "the decline and fall of the city" of Rome. He early expanded this to include the fall of the Western Empire, a field covered in the first three volumes of the published work (1776-81). Then after a year of hesitation and of political confusion (1783), he began work looking towards a history of the fall of the Eastern Empire, which he completed at Lausanne, June 27, 1787. After all those years the great work was done, and a "sober melancholy," as if at losing "an old and agreeable companion," was Gibbon's natural mood. Seldom has so extensive and prolonged a piece of study been so thoroughly a labor of love.

The effect on his readers is that of dignified and magnificent pageantry. The narrative unfolds in smooth, living details—not details that are full of vague overtones: they are sharply defined and register in the mind without much imaginative repercussion. Imaginative impressiveness comes less from individual pictorial passages than from the tremendous and complete marshaling of great masses of material. Gibbon's aim is to *portray* fully and accurately; he makes the somewhat austere remark that "Diligence and accuracy are the only merits which an historical writer may ascribe to himself." To a surprising extent even after 150 years the accuracy of much of his wealth of fact is not impugned. Nowadays a scholarly historian might evaluate sources more carefully, and nowadays more sources are available; but if one recognizes on Gibbon's part a failure to understand Byzantine civilization or the play of economic forces, if one sees and regrets a too frequent bias through anticlericalism or other limitations of Gibbon's mind and day, one still finds an amazing amount of sound fact and shrewd interpretation.

History and   Authenticity and the ability to unfold a stupendous panorama clearly and
Causation   smoothly have been granted Gibbon, but there have been regrets that he lacked "philosophy." This is in part a Victorian indictment of all eighteenth-century skeptics; and it must be admitted that they lack metaphysics. But Gibbon is precisely the first great English historian to stress causation as a philosophic basis for the writing of history. He does not use the causes of decline and fall as devices for organization, but he does pause at times in his narrative for formal discussions of this or that cause. At other times a cause is briefly, almost slyly, adverted to in the course of narrative or description. Only in his last chapter does he summarize methodically.

After a diligent inquiry, I can discern four principal causes of the ruin of Rome, which continued to operate in a period of more than a thousand years. I. The injuries of time and nature. II. The hostile attacks of the barbarians and Christians. III. The use and abuse of the materials. And, IV. The domestic quarrels of the Romans.

These causes of the ruin of the city of Rome suggest the causes of imperial ruin—which obviously would be more complex. It is notable that while all these causes are informally and briefly introduced into Montesquieu's work translated in 1734 as *Reflections on the Causes of the Grandeur and Declension of the Romans,* the extensive development and application of them is Gibbon's own. One of his editors (J. B. Bury) has stressed Gibbon's remark about cause III: "In the preceding volumes of this History, I have described the triumph of barbarism and religion." To isolate this remark as indicating total cause is debatable justice. In his summary Gibbon carefully subordinates the subversive rôle of Christianity; but his anti-Christian remarks occur *Gibbon and* slyly, frequently, and pervasively; and they constitute evidence that prej- *Christianity* udices the rôle of religion as villainous. Byron expressed a widespread awareness that Gibbon was

> Sapping a solemn creed with solemn sneer.

To evaluate the relative importance in Gibbon's mind of the manifold causes of decline would be difficult, because this summary for the city of Rome is the nearest to a complete summary that we get. Causes normally are expressed recurringly, like *leitmotivs* or themes in a symphony. Such a method in historical discourse is obviously diplomatic if one is subverting religion; and while the method in the hands of a journeyman might be dangerous to logic and clarity, in the hands of a masterworkman it is adroit. He has made "diligent inquiry," and a diligent reader will find plenty of causes emerging effectively. To present a unique cause would falsify.

The art of Gibbon is nowhere more noticeable than in his manner of expression. This is marked by a clear flow of narrative expressed in diction of unvarying nobility. Like a true neo-classicist he shuns "low" everyday words: a physically small man himself, he compensates with a pompous *Gibbon's* style of rhythmic sonority, definitely "noble Roman." It is obvious that he *Art* frequently writes as he does merely for the sake of the sound. Conscious effort here succeeds: the sound is always musical, and the pomp has true majesty. His phrasing is not especially decorative. One has to forgive excessive melodramatic heightening such as the murder of Probus (chapter XII) or the theatrical apparition of the King of the Goths:

A victorious leader, who united the daring spirit of a Barbarian with the art and discipline of a Roman general, was at the head of an hundred thousand fighting men; and Italy pronounced, with terror and respect, the formidable name of Alaric.

In general the style, vivid in description and fluid in narration, enlarges and elevates the mind of the reader in spite of a chill formality. Its idiosyncrasy is doubtless irony—seen at its most devastating in the offensive chapters (xv and xvi) that terminated his first volume and with covert sacrilege pictured the rise of Christianity. Of the early saints he could write, four years before the Gordon riots:

It is a very ancient reproach, suggested by the ignorance or the malice of infidelity, that the Christians allured into their party the most atrocious criminals, who, as soon as they were touched by a sense of remorse, were easily persuaded to wash away, in the water of baptism, the guilt of their past conduct, for which the temples of the gods refused to grant them any expiation.... The friends of Christianity may acknowledge without a blush that many of the most eminent saints had been before their baptism the most abandoned sinners. Those persons who in the world had followed, though in an imperfect manner, the dictates of benevolence and propriety, derived such a calm satisfaction from the opinion of their own rectitude, as rendered them much less susceptible of the sudden emotions of shame, of grief, and of terror, which have given birth to so many wonderful conversions.

It is this suave, almost unctuous, irony that gives the Gibbon tone quality. His external mannerisms are typical of the day: there is much antithesis, though it is more sinuous and varied than Dr. Johnson's type, much aphorism, and much beautiful design in his finely chiseled sentences. A common mannerism here is the "Attic"[7] tendency to economize on subordinate clauses, to omit connectives, and to make logical relations implicit yet plain simply by arrangement of detail. Of Bernard of Clairvaux he remarks:

A philosophic age has abolished, with too liberal and indiscriminate disdain, the honours of these spiritual heroes. The meanest amongst them are distinguished by some energies of the mind; they were at least superior to their votaries and disciples; and in the race of superstition they attained the prize for which such numbers contended.

Clearly, in artistic conscience, as well as in lucid order and conscious elevation, Gibbon is among the foremost neo-classic stylists. He owed much to Livy and Tacitus; he owed more to his own personality and to the age in which he lived, to the elegant, cool and spacious drawing-room environment, in which he existed. With successful artifice he fused congruous elements into a manner that was highly individual. The small details of the work are as clearly executed as the design of the whole is architecturally unified. Gibbon gave distinction to historical writing by his style just as he gave meaning to historical thinking through his focus on the organizing idea of "decline and fall." Rome was the world's greatest art object in institutional civilization; Gibbon believed in progress, and the lesson of Rome was that man's progress

has been irregular and various, infinitely slow in the beginning, and increasing by degrees with redoubled velocity; ages of laborious ascent have been followed by a moment of rapid downfall.... The splendid days of Augustus and Trajan were eclipsed by a cloud of ignorance; and the Barbarians subverted the laws and palaces of Rome.

[7] See M. W. Croll, " 'Attic Prose' in the Seventeenth Century," *SP*, xviii (1921). 79-128.

In passing from Gibbon to Burke,[8] we pass from history to actuality. In *Edmund* the Restoration period it was possible to believe that even at that moment *Burke* England was renewing the splendid days of Augustus. By Burke's day—and before—the consciousness was growing that what had happened to Roman liberty could also happen to the English. To Gibbon, obviously, Rome was remote, and was an awful warning. Burke was not especially interested in history;[9] he was devoted to the processes of administering government rather than to tracing its origins. He was both a political philosopher and a practical politician; and as such he fell upon relatively evil days—days of constitutional crisis, of selfish intrigue, of covertly shifting personal allegiances, and even of corruption. His mind was too good for its tasks: he was set to "cut blocks with a razor." The blocks were too hard for him, but although he was normally in the minority in the House of Commons, he exercised through his intellectual quality, his evident integrity, and his fervid logic, a far-reaching influence.

The method of his thinking combined practical empiricism with a neo-*A Practical* classical veneration for established precedent and for Law that was com-*Statesman* patible with a faith in metaphysical absolutes. As an empiricist he appealed to "the wisdom of our ancestors" as if to established authority. He abhorred

---

[8] Edmund Burke (1729-1797) was the son of an Irish Protestant attorney. He was educated in Trinity College, Dublin, and in 1750 entered the Middle Temple. He now, with introductions by William Burke (always his closest friend), became a typical literary Templar, frequenting coffee-houses and the society of writers. His marriage in 1757 made publication a financial necessity, and his important connection with the *Annual Register* resulted. He was in 1763 an original member of the Club, and in 1765 he became secretary to the prime minister, the Marquis of Rockingham, and entered Parliament. He was a leader among the Rockingham Whigs, and when in 1782 the coalition ministry fell and Rockingham became again, briefly, prime minister, Burke was Paymaster of the Forces—his highest office. After 1783 he was in the opposition, and in 1794 he retired from Parliament. — *Works*, ed. F. Laurence and W. King (8v [quarto], 1792-1827; 16v [octavo], 1803-27; 12v, Boston, 1897; 8v, 1901-6). The best editing of Burke is that of Edward J. Payne, *Select Works* (3v, Oxford, 1874-8). The six volumes in the World's Classics (1906-7) are useful and moderately priced. — *A Vindication of Natural Society* (1756); *A Philosophical Enquiry into the Origin of our Ideas of the Sublime and Beautiful* (1757 and [with the *Discourse on Taste* added] 1759); *An Account of the European Settlements in America* (with William Burke, 2v, 1757); *Thoughts on the Cause of the Present Discontents* (1770); *Speech on American Taxation* (1774); *Speech on Conciliation with the Colonies* (1775); *A Letter to the Sheriffs of Bristol* (1777); *Two Letters on Ireland* (1778); *Speech on Oeconomical Reformation* (1780); *Speeches at the Bristol Election* (1780); *Speech on Mr. Fox's East India Bill* (1784); *Speech on the Nabob of Arcot's Debts* (1785); *Articles against Warren Hastings* (1786); *Reflections on the Revolution in France* (1790); ed. Edward J. Payne (1875); ed. Walter A. Phillips (1875); *A Letter to a Member of the National Assembly* (1791); *An Appeal from the New to the Old Whigs* (1791); *A Letter to Sir Hercules Langrishe on the Subject of the Roman Catholics of Ireland* (1792); *A Letter to a Noble Lord* (1796); *Two Letters on the Proposals for Peace with the Regicide Directory of France* (1796; Third Letter, 1797; Fourth Letter, 1812); *Correspondence*, ed. Earl Fitzwilliam and Sir R. Bourke (4v, 1844); *Correspondence with William Windham*, ed. J. P. Gilson (Roxburghe Club, 1910). — Robert Bisset, *The Life of Burke* (1798; 2v, 1800); Sir James Prior, *Memoir of Burke* (1824, 5th ed., 1854); Thomas Macknight, *History of the Life and Times of Burke* (3v, 1858-60); John (Viscount) Morley, *Edmund Burke* (1867, 1893); John MacCunn, *The Political Philosophy of Burke* (1913); A. P. I. Samuels, *The Early Life, Correspondence, and Writings of Burke* (1923); Dixon Wecter, "The Missing Years in Edmund Burke's Biography," *PMLA*, LIII (1938). 1102-1125; D. Wecter, "Edmund Burke and his Kinsmen," *Univ. of Colorado Studies* (Boulder, Colo., February, 1939) ["A Study of the statesman's financial integrity and private relationships"]; Thomas W. Copeland, "Burke and Dodsley's *Annual Register*," *PMLA*, LIV (1939). 223-245; Donald C. Bryant, *Edmund Burke and his Literary Friends* (St. Louis, 1939).

[9] For mention of Burke's interest in literary criticism see Part III, ch. II.

the doctrinaire notions of Rousseau and others concerning the natural rights of man: man, he thought, had only such rights as continuous precedent gave him in a civil state. The appeal to experience was attended by a reverence for continuity, for institutions developed through agelong trial; and this sense of the value of continuity became a fundamental part of Burke's method of thought. As a practical politician he was insistent on the necessity for lawmakers to understand the state of mind of the governed. In such matters he was a social psychologist, and in a sense an idealistic opportunist. "The temper of the people amongst whom he presides ought," he urged, "to be the first study of a statesman." This is the crux of the matter in his doctrine of conciliation with the American colonies. A governor must choose between practical wisdom and unsound theory. Sound theories, so Burke thinks, will fit the facts.

A strong common-sense dislike of unproved theory was on the whole convenient in the confused and tortuous years of Burke's career. But common sense was not all: study was essential, and no member of Parliament gave more time to study of the great problems of the day than did Burke. Among *His Fields* the political problems upon which he brought his powers to bear, one may *of Activity:* isolate five. First would come the constitutional crisis precipitated when *1. Domestic* King George III attempted to choose ministers responsible to himself rather *Issues* than to Parliament. This imbroglio was a part of the loose construction of constitutional rights that led the Commons to deny John Wilkes a seat in Parliament in spite of his repeated elections to that House.[10] Burke's respect for legal procedure is the high ground here on which he attacks both the King and "the King's Men" in his *Thoughts on the Present Discontents,* one of his early major efforts. His enemies retorted with the specious charge that Burke was the concealed author of the *Letters of Junius,*[11] which were *2. America* appearing in the *Public Advertiser* (1769-72). Secondly, Burke dealt with the more unified problem of the American colonies. Here his gospel is expediency. Not the natural rights but the natural grievances of the colonists were what he wished to satisfy. He had studied American conditions thoroughly, and was convinced that the practical course was conciliation. Ultimately he hoped for a system that might preserve both English superiority and colonial liberty. In favor of the cause of the Americans Burke composed two great speeches—that on *American Taxation* (1774) and that on *Conciliation with America* (1775). For his resolution in favor of conciliation his speech won only 58 votes, but it has generally been regarded as one of the great examples of classical eloquence in English. Burke continued

10 The story of Wilkes and his rôle in the fight for a free press has been interestingly told by George Nobbe, *The North Briton* (1939).

11 Junius himself chose 69 letters from the series for a collected edition in 1772. Before 1812 at least 70 reprintings of this collection had been issued. The identity of Junius has never been determined. Over 40 people have been accused of writing the letters. The most generally favored "victim" is Sir Philip Francis. Junius evidently had access to highly confidential official information, which he used against the ministers who alone should have had the information. The unsolved authorship is one of the most fascinating mysteries of the century. See *CBEL,* II. 630-632.

his support of the colonies even after they took up arms, in his *Speech on the Address to the King* (1777) and his *Letter to the Sheriffs of Bristol* (1777), as well as in the House of Commons. Thirdly, Burke faced crises in matters of trade. The unjust restrictions upon Irish trade concerned him *3. Irish* in 1779 and later, and naturally the problems of his native country were *Trade* always close to his heart. In 1780 he presented an elaborate bill for Economic Reform, and on February 11 made one of his most brilliant speeches on the subject. His proposals at that time were rejected. Presently he was advocating, without immediate success, humane regulation of the Negro slave trade, and was supporting justice for Roman Catholics in the face of the rabid intolerance that led in June 1780 to the anti-Catholic Gordon riots. In the autumn these various activities cost him the support of his Bristol constituency, which he quitted with triumphant dignity: "The charges against me are ... that I have pushed the principles of general justice and benevolence too far." Bristol trade would not be augmented by these activities as it would have been by prevention of war with the colonies! Burke was of course promptly chosen by another borough.

The fourth great field that exercised Burke's genius was India. Of this *4. India* domain like that of America Burke was a profound student, and from 1783 through much of the rest of his career in Parliament it engrossed his attention. At the end of 1783 he eloquently supported Fox's bill to reform Indian administration, a bill that so annoyed the King that he dismissed his ministers who had supported the rejected bill, and chose William Pitt the younger, aged twenty-four, to be his prime minister. Early in 1785 Burke countered a royal desire to keep Indian issues quiescent by one of his most eloquent speeches, that on the Nabob of Arcot's debts (February 28, 1785). To the present day this speech is still full of dynamite for statesmen concerned with the exploitation of "backward" peoples. Burke had long been critical of the administration of the Governor-General of India, Warren Hastings, and in January 1786 he with others began to draw up charges. Fox and R. B. Sheridan (the dramatist) were Burke's coadjutors, and the trial was a series of field-days for orators. Sheridan's most glowing attack was his speech on the Begum charge (February 7, 1787). For four days, February 15-19, 1788, Burke spoke on an average of three hours daily, and in 1794 (for the trial was interminable—with evidence far off in Asia) he spoke in summing up for nine days in succession. On April 23, 1795, the lords voted a verdict of acquittal. The scenes in Westminster Hall had been theatrical beyond belief. Seats were in great demand—£50 being "cheerfully" given for one; beautiful ladies fainted; and the histrionic Sheridan himself at the end of one speech collapsed into the arms of Burke with the words, "My Lords, I have done!" Burke's motives were certainly those of integrity: he wished justice and sound administrative procedure. He had here a relatively popular cause at first, but favor veered to Hastings, and Burke lost the verdict—as so often happened in his career.

Before the Hastings trial was over, Burke had become involved in his fifth and last great public effort, opposition to the French Revolution. No one in England was more astounded and horrified than Burke by the Fall of the Bastille and the subsequent irregular proceedings. He had a high admiration for the brilliant and intellectual aristocrats whom he had met in Paris, and he was totally ignorant of the grievances of France as a whole. Sound administration and dutiful obedience to such administration were the highest public duties, and he had no doubts as to the abilities of French rulers. Furthermore, *continuity* in institutional life was in his eyes the great test of merit: it was to him almost a religion. He loved civil liberty, and the revolution seemed to him to have substituted the capricious tyranny of a riotous mob for the settled government, which, to his way of thinking, should have been amended, not destroyed. During and after the summer of 1789 Burke privately in conversation and in his letters expressed hostility to the Revolution. Early in 1790 he broke off his friendship with Sheridan, who in Parliament endorsed the new freedom and found Burke's animosity to it inconsistent with his earlier American sympathies. Later Burke renounced friendship with Fox also on the same disagreement in views. The behavior of the revolutionaries became an obsession, and in November 1790 he published a formal and eloquent explanation of his attitude, *Reflections on the Revolution in France*.

Cast in the form of a letter (volume-long!) to a French gentleman who sought his views, it took occasion for offense from the fact that the well-known dissenter, Dr. Richard Price [12] (1723-1791), had just preached a sermon before the Revolution Society (founded to commemorate the English Revolution of 1688) in which he felicitated the French on their achieving liberty. Burke was enraged that the glorious and orderly change of 1688 should be connected with the mob riots of the French. "I flatter myself," he writes, "that I love a manly, moral, regulated liberty as well as any gentleman of that society." But before he congratulates a mob on its "liberty," he feels one must ask, What are you going to do with your liberty? That question he felt sure the followers of doctrinaires like Voltaire and Rousseau, believers in natural rights, could not answer wisely. Among the most picturesque and emotional passages in the book are those that narrate the violation of Versailles on October 6, 1789, or describe the young Queen, Marie Antoinette, as he had seen her long ago "glittering like the morning star." His sincere grief is summed up in the sentences: "But the age of chivalry is gone. That of sophisters, economists, and calculators has succeeded; and the glory of Europe is extinguished forever." Burke's *Reflections* in its magnificence of rhetoric surpassed all other attacks on the Revolution; and in argumentative force also, in spite of his obvious ignorance of conditions in France and in spite of its emotional bias in favor of the grace and elegance of the *ancien régime*, the work compares favorably with other attacks. The chief reply was

---

12 This "apostle of liberty" was invited in 1778 by the American Congress "to consider him as a Citizen of the United States," and if possible to remove to America, where his services as a financial expert were badly needed. He of course did not accept the invitation. See Roland Thomas, *Richard Price* (Oxford, 1924).

Tom Paine's *Rights of Man,*[13] which defended the bases of the Revolution, asserted that every civil right is derived from a natural right, and reproached Burke's love of monarchical pageantry: "He pities the plumage and forgets the dying bird." Possibly the most cogent answer was Arthur Young's *Travels in France* (1792), in which is revealed the actual condition of France, which was unknown to Burke. Among all the thinkers and writers of Europe Burke was immediately preëminent as champion of the old order. He continued his attacks, notably in his *Letter to a Member of the National Assembly* (1791), in his *Appeal from the New to the Old Whigs* (1791), and in his *Letters on a Regicide Peace* (1796). Of this last prophetic vision of woes to come he remarked, "It may have the weakness, but it has the sincerity of a dying declaration." He died a year later (July 9, 1797).

Burke's fame is that of a thinker and of a superb rhetorician. As a thinker his doctrines were practical but idealistic common sense. Bolingbroke's friend Pope had achieved a popular witticism in his *pensée*: "Party is the madness of Many for the gain of a Few." Party was faction. This favorite idea of *The Craftsman,* embodied in Bolingbroke's *Dissertation upon Parties* (1735), angered Burke. One of his functions was to popularize somewhat a better concept: *Burke as a Thinker*

Party is a body of men united for promoting by their joint endeavours the national interest upon some particular principle in which they are all agreed.

He was firmly insistent that a party in power must govern with an unselfish regard for the welfare of the nation. In a period of confused personal alliances in politics and of loose concepts as to the constitutionality of measures, Burke's influence here was most salutary. Again it may be repeated that he was a practical psychologist. As applied to America this method is exhibited in his remark, "The question with me is, not whether you have a right to render your people miserable; but whether it is not your interest to make them happy." The value that he set upon continuity as a test of efficiency need not be further stressed. Mr. Brailsford has given a brief summary of the doctrines of William Godwin which were in a sense the intellectual background of the English romantics in their revolutionary mood. The summary may well serve to indicate most of the things at the turn of the century that Burke abhorred:

perfectibility, non-resistance, anarchism, communism, the power of reason and the superiority of persuasion over force, universal benevolence, and the ascription of moral evil to the desolating influence of "positive institution."[14]

Two or three of these, with different connotations, Burke might favor, but the attitudes of the two men towards institutions and government were antithetical. All Burke's doctrines were recognized as those of a man highly respected for his integrity. This respect came from his disinterested, modest

[13] Hastily but vigorously written and published (1791-2) in two parts within four months after Burke's *Reflections* appeared.
[14] H. N. Brailsford, *Shelley, Godwin, and their Circle* [1913], p. 219.

Burke as a Rhetorician

action and also from the lofty plane upon which his mind and his rhetoric habitually moved.

During a career of over forty years as writer Burke's command of all the arts of persuasion steadily increased. In 1794, disheartened and despondent, embittered against his former satellites, Sheridan and Fox, for their sympathy with revolution, Burke withdrew from Parliament after nearly thirty years of distinguished services. A year later these were recognized by royal grants of pensions, and the reward caused repercussions even in the House of Lords, where the radical Duke of Bedford, whose enormous family fortunes were due to royal favor dating from the sixteenth century, attacked the grants—and Burke. Burke replied in what is perhaps the masterpiece of decorative classical rhetoric in English—his *Letter to a Noble Lord* (1796). Reply to his grace was easy, almost superfluous; and Burke indulges in arguments of the moment and for the man. The wealthiest of dukes was an improper person to object to royal rewards; an improper person to object to Burke's attacks on levellers and revolutionaries. The rhetoric used is typical. In one of the finest passages Burke weaves together the ideas that the British Constitution is both a citadel and a temple, the symbol of Law, Order, and Security for wealthy dukes and all British subjects. *As long as* it endures, the "dykes of the low, fat Bedford level will have nothing to fear from all the pickaxes of all the levellers of France." Like a symphonic composer Burke allows his central theme on this subject—*continuity*—to announce itself repeatedly in parallel clauses beginning *as long as;* and he concludes in a burst of extra-rational rhetoric:

as long as these endure, so long the Duke of Bedford is safe: and we are all safe together—the high from the blights of envy and the spoliations of rapacity; the low from the iron hand of oppression and the insolent spurn of contempt. Amen! and so be it: and so it will be,

> Dum domus Aeneae Capitoli immobile saxum
> Accolet; imperiumque pater Romanus habebit.

It is typical of Burke's mind that, sure of itself, its point well made, it should, so to speak, overflow in a purely emotional climax. He borrows the majestic lines from the ninth *Aeneid,* where Virgil prophesies that the fame of two young heroes, Nisus and Euryalus, shall endure

> Long as th' imperial capitol shall stand,
> Or Rome's majestic lord the conquer'd world command!

and transfers the permanence of heroic fame to the duration of British rights of property. As pure poetry the borrowing is effective; but it is a beautiful dilation of mood rather than a triumph of logic. The echo from Virgil may serve to remind us that Burke's art came from the ancients, and that with the figured and fervent mood of his last works eighteenth-century prose goes out in a blaze of noble artifice. One may say justly of Edmund Burke's mind that it too was both a citadel and a temple.

X

Cowper and Burns

By 1780 the mid-century poets were mostly gone, and a new generation was arising. In it among the most distinguished were William Cowper, Robert Burns, William Blake, George Crabbe, and Samuel Rogers.[1] Cowper and Burns alike mark a tendency to use subjective, autobiographical material and to write of rural domesticity: they were among the latest flowerings in the eighteenth century of the cult of simplicity. Since it chances that Cowper's dates (1731-1800) are exactly a century later than John Dryden's, it is interesting to compare these last voices in the neo-classic choir (if indeed they belong there) with the tones of Dryden and Pope, the partial founders of the tradition. Obviously the century elapsed has grown tender; Burns and Cowper both write satires, but these are relatively good-humored— perhaps too good-humored. Cowper's satire in particular lacks hardness, flash, and cutting edge. Burns, like Dryden and Pope, has sympathetic, generalized observations to make about man, but like Blake and Cowper he is most aroused concerning underprivileged men. Burns and Blake have faith in progress and in the ability of man to achieve his own destiny. Cowper, like Dryden and Pope, has a sense of man's limitations; but Cowper would have man rely on God's help, on a divine plan, whereas Pope had fitted man into a philosophic chain of being, in which duty urges him to be a competent link or a submerged atom. There is, however, little in the observations of these later poets about man that would revolt Dryden or Pope, and both Cowper and Burns echo the *Essay on Man* with some sympathy—though Cowper could tolerate no attempt (such as Pope's fundamentally seemed) to build up a moral philosophy independent of religion. The earlier poets had featured impersonal material, "what oft was thought"; Cowper and Burns stress what *they* have thought and felt, though they value impersonal aphoristic wisdom. The later poets tend to talk to themselves or to a small audience; they lack—Cowper always and Burns usually— the loud, noble eloquence of the earlier poets. The tendency is increasingly subjective and lyrical; it expresses not so eagerly an acquired wisdom of life as it does a personal experience of life. The later poets are less intellectual than Dryden and Pope, more intimately emotional. Cowper and Burns are transitional poets.

The important part of Cowper's [2] career as poet was relatively brief. His

---

[1] Blake, Crabbe, and Rogers are here regarded as members of a later generation of poets.
[2] William Cowper (1731-1800) came of distinguished ancestors. Since his mother, a descendant of the Elizabethan John Donne, died before Cowper was six, he was then sent to

first extant poem, *On the Heel of a Shoe,* was written in 1748, and in the years following he addressed poems to his cousin Theodora, and wrote essays and witticisms in the period (1754) of the Nonsense Club. But poetry as a professional recreation—its major function to Cowper—began to occupy him after he had lived in rural Olney for some years. His first independent volume was his *Poems* (1782), which included various lyrics but chiefly his eight moral essays—discursive, reflective poems in the heroic couplet. These rapidly written, carefully revised essays in verse reflect the activities of Cowper's mind. Quite suddenly in the winter of 1780-81 he had begun to amuse himself by putting on paper *The Progress of Error* and *Truth* (together over 1200 lines, composed in December and January), and speedily thereafter *Table Talk* and *Expostulation* were completed. *Hope, Charity, Conversation,* and *Retirement* were products of the summer of 1781, the period of the poet's first friendship with Lady Austen. These poems are all reflective rather than descriptive. *Table Talk* has interesting comments on the poetry of the century; *Conversation, Retirement,* and *The Progress of Error* attack the follies of high life; *Expostulation* condemns anti-Semite prejudice; and the others represent the religious thinking of the poet. They are all medleys of reflective passages, with very serious and very obvious moral purpose. The volume, unpretentious and pious, met in general with a favorable reception.

Under the stimulus of success and of new-found encouragement from Lady Austen, Cowper continued to write. In 1782 he composed his noble patriotic lyric *On the Loss of the Royal George* as well his humorous master-

---

a boarding school, where he was persecuted by one of the older boys. Later (*c.* 1741-48) he was happier at Westminster School, where his friends included Robert Lloyd, Charles Churchill, George Colman the Elder, Bonnell Thornton, and Warren Hastings. His favorite master here, Vincent Bourne, was perhaps the best Latin poet of the century in England. Later, in the Middle Temple, Cowper studied law, and was called to the bar in 1754. He had fallen in love with his cousin Theodora ("Delia" in his poems), whom, in 1756, presumably because already he had suffered one lapse from sanity, he was forbidden to marry or to see. In 1763, overwhelmed by an approaching examination for a clerkship in the House of Lords, he went mad a second time, and attempted suicide. After a long convalescence, he settled for two years at Huntingdon as a lodger in the house of the Rev. Morley Unwin. Upon Mr. Unwin's death (1767) Mrs. Unwin ("My Mary"), her daughter, and Cowper moved to Olney, where they lived for almost twenty years, then removing to Weston Lodge, a mile outside the town. At Olney the vicar was, until 1780, the Rev. John Newton (1725-1807), who became one of Cowper's closest friends and upon removal to London a frequent correspondent. In 1773 another period of madness resulted from a terrible dream, "before recollection of which all consolation vanishes," and thereafter he suffered intermittently from melancholia, most seriously in 1787 and 1794. At East Dereham, Norfolk, where they spent their last years, Mrs. Unwin died in 1796, and Cowper less than four years later. — *Works,* ed. John Newton (10v, 1817); ed. with a "Life" by Robert Southey (15v, 1835-7; 8v, Bohn Library, 1853-5); ed. Thomas S. Grimshawe (8v, 1835, 1836), with the Life and Letters by William Hayley and an Essay on Cowper by John W. Cunningham; *Poems* (2v, 1782-5; 3v, 1815); ed. John Bruce (Aldine ed., 3v, 1865); ed. Sir Humphrey S. Milford (1905 ff.); ed. Hugh L'A. Fausset (Everyman's Library, 1931); *Letters,* with a Life by William Hayley (4v, Chichester, 1809); ed. Thomas Wright (4v, 1904); *Unpublished and Uncollected Letters,* ed. Thomas Wright (1925). — There are biographies by William Hayley (3v, Chichester, 1803-4); Goldwin Smith (1880); Thomas Wright (1892; rev. 1921); Hugh I'A. Fausset, *William Cowper* (1928); Lord David Cecil, *The Stricken Deer; or, The Life of William Cowper* (1929); Gilbert Thomas, *William Cowper and the Eighteenth Century* (1935). See also Robert E. Spiller, "William Cowper: A New Biographical Source: Rev. J. Johnson's Holograph Memorandum Book, 1795-1800," *PMLA,* XLII (1927). 946-962; cf. Hoxie N. Fairchild, *PMLA,* XLIII (1928). 571-572.

piece, *John Gilpin's Ride.* The first of these, strangely enough, was published only after Cowper's death; but *John Gilpin,* sent to a newspaper in November 1782, was instantly a popular success. Humor was becoming rare and precious in poetry. In July, 1783, Lady Austen urged Cowper to attempt blank verse, and upon his protest that he had no subject, she replied, "Oh, you can never be in want of a subject; you can write upon any—write upon that sofa!" Accepting the assignment, Cowper was able somewhat over a year later to send the result, called *The Task,* to the printer. It was over 5000 lines in length. In composing this poem Cowper strengthened his animus against the couplet and Pope, and thus was persuaded to set about (1784-91) rescuing Homer from the clutches of rime and artificial elevation. Homer, he thought, was more remarkable than any book except the Bible "for that species of the sublime that owes its very existence to simplicity." If his translation fails in competition with Pope, the failure is not due to lack of simplicity but rather to inability to capture the vigor of the ancient epics.

For thirty-five years William Cowper lived as retired a village life as one could imagine, but he took an intelligent, if mild, interest meanwhile in the outside world, and the issues of the day form a noticeable part of the more impersonal subject matter of his verses. A typical passage is the opening of Book IV ("The Winter Evening") of *The Task.* The post rides into the village bringing news of all the world—received with tolerant interest:

Cowper's Interest in Public Affairs

> have our troops awak'd?
> Or do they still, as if with opium drugg'd,
> Snore to the murmurs of th' Atlantic wave?
> Is India free? and does she wear her plum'd
> And jewell'd turban with a smile of peace,
> Or do we grind her still? The grand debate,
> The popular harangue, the tart reply,
> The logic, and the wisdom, and the wit,
> And the loud laugh—I long to know them all;
> I burn to set th' imprison'd wranglers free,
> And give them voice and utt'rance once again.
>   Now stir the fire, and close the shutters fast,
> Let fall the curtains, wheel the sofa round,
> And, while the bubbling and loud-hissing urn
> Throws up a steamy column, and the cups,
> That cheer but not inebriate, wait on each,
> So let us welcome peaceful ev'ning in.   (ll. 25-41)

Here is quiet and gentle curiosity—no burst of eloquence. Such is Cowper's usual reaction to outside stimuli, whether the subject is India, America, prison reform, slavery, or the French Revolution. On many of these topics he is very intelligent; but unlike Dryden, Swift, or Pope, he is rarely an eager crusader for a cause. He does appear such in his lines *On the Loss of the Royal George;* in his castigation of war as the sport of kings in Book V of *The Task;* and in such passages as his defense (*Hope,* ll. 554-593) of the eminent Methodist, George Whitefield (1714-1770), who had in his lifetime been grossly slandered.

His Religion

Cowper's ardent, evangelical Calvinism led to expressions of despair, of hope, and of firm doctrinal assertion typical of his day. Biographers have found in religion the key and cause of Cowper's melancholia. The most terrifying moment of his life came on January 24, 1773, when in a "fatal dream" a word, apparently of divine condemnation, seemed to enjoin eternal and complete despair. "Nature," he wrote to Newton years later, "revives again, but a soul once slain lives no more." At other times, however, there were glimpses "of heavenly light by the way" or whispers saying "Still there is Mercy." Critics ought to remember constantly that if religion was an undoubted cause of despair to Cowper, it was also a great source of comfort. Doctrinally he was true to type. Much of his didactic verse about religion is anti-deistic and anti-philosophical. In *Charity* come the lines—

> That man, in nature's richest mantle clad,
> And grac'd with all philosophy can add,
> Though fair without, and luminous within,
> Is still the progeny and heir of sin.
> Thus taught, down falls the plumage of his pride;
> He feels his need of an unerring guide....

Pride is, as he shows in *Truth,* the most insidious foe of the Gospel. Being no deist, he substitutes for man's philosophizings

> Heav'n's easy, artless, unincumber'd, plan!

and his Calvinism rejects as "outrageous wrong" the idea of

> Ten thousand sages lost in endless woe,
> For ignorance of what they could not know.

In many passages he stresses the sole efficacy of grace, and doctrinal points turn up at times even in his hymns.

His Hymns

It is one of the contradictions of history that the eighteenth century, known as an age of doubt and skepticism, is also the great age of English hymnody, and Cowper is notable as a writer of great hymns.[3] Earlier in the century hymns such as those by Isaac Watts tended to be "congregational" in point of view, but the best known hymns of Charles Wesley and of his brother John are more personal, intimate, and evangelical. Cowper's "Oh! for a closer walk with God" is comparable, and superior, to Wesley's

---

[3] Cowper contributed 67 hymns to John Newton's *Olney Hymns* (1779). Newton included 281 of his own, among the most popular of which is "Glorious things of thee are spoken." Charles Wesley was doubtless the greatest of the hymn-writers of the time, and the Wesleyan love of music did much to promote congregational singing. Among Charles Wesley's famous hymns are the well-known "O for a thousand tongues to sing," "Hark! the herald angels sing," "Arise, my soul, arise," "Love divine, all loves excelling," and "Jesus, Lover of my soul." John Wesley's notable contributions are translations of German hymns. Among other well-known hymns of this period may be mentioned Augustus Toplady's "Rock of Ages," and Edward Perronet's "All hail the power of Jesus' name." See John Julian, *A Dictionary of Hymnology* (1892; rev. ed., 1921).

popular "Jesus, Lover of my soul"; and the tone of "Sometimes a light surprises" reminds one—as some other of his hymns do not—that

> True piety is cheerful as the day.

The frequent fault of hymn-writers is their incongruous mixture of secular metaphor with biblical symbolism. Cowper is not an outrageous offender here except in "There is a fountain filled with blood." Cheerful or not, his religious poems, while doctrinally sound, are sufficiently emotional to avoid the heaviness of theological argument. The language is always that of un-affected and sincere devotion.

Religion and current public issues as treated in Cowper's verse have less *Nature as* appeal than do his descriptions of nature. Unlike his predecessors Cowper *an Escape* describes and reflects about landscape details, but rather seldom philosophizes about the abstraction "Nature." In a few such passages as *The Task,* Book VI, lines 198-261, to be sure, he urges that there can be no Law of Nature apart from God's law:

> The Lord of all, himself through all diffus'd,
> Sustains, and is the life of all that lives.
> Nature is but a name for an effect,
> Whose cause is God.

But it is not the theological aspect of the creation that preoccupies and con-soles Cowper: it is rather the extra-theological innocence of Nature; for Na-ture is free from the primal curse, depravity; and a consciousness of this happy fact encourages Cowper in his escape from the moral to the natural world. From another point of view Cowper's love of rural life resembles the common-sense attitude of the Sabine farmer, Horace, or of people who, like Henry Fielding, did not love "the town." In any case, the gambols of Cowper's hares or the antics of his many other pets as well as the spring zephyr or the slow-winding Ouse were innocence itself. The inanimate world was to Cowper a plaything, a "bauble," as he loved to call it, to dis-tract his mind from manic gloom. The moral world was full of terrors; the amoral, full of innocent delights that

> Exhilarate the spirit, and restore
> The tone of languid Nature.

And so, in his most famous aphorism, he could say,

> God made the country, and man made the town.

The "Not-me" is then a broad and tranquilizing stream that flows peace-fully through his consciousness. It is panorama, motion, normally—not the static picturesque. Nature dreads

> An instant's pause, and lives but while she moves....

> Oceans, rivers, lakes, and streams,
> All feel the fresh'ning impulse, and are cleans'd
> By restless undulation: ev'n the oak
> Thrives by the rude concussion of the storm.

His Taste in Land-scape

Being thoroughly individual, Cowper avoids the common predispositions of his day. He recognizes that the creation is "an effect whose cause is God," but he does not play with the rationalist tradition that places "the Book of Nature" beside the Bible. Nor does he affect the dramatic or thrilling arrangement of detail that constituted the Italian picturesque. Even less does he, loving tranquillity, gratify any romantic appetite for the "delightful horrors" of the artificial sublime promoted by Burke and others. He loves tame nature and everyday phenomena—*domestica facta.* After his visit in 1792 to Hayley at Eartham, he wrote to Newton:

> The cultivated appearance of Weston suits my frame of mind far better than wild hills that aspire to be mountains, covered with vast unfrequented woods, and here and there affording a peep between their summits at the distant ocean. Within doors all was hospitality and kindness, but the scenery *would* have its effect; and though delightful in the extreme to those who had spirits to bear it, was too gloomy for me.

Cowper's evocation of the sights and sounds of the "tame" Olney region was delicate, precise, and full of placid glamour. Neither he nor his neo-classic predecessors normally cultivated *sensations fortes,* and in romantic days to come this fact was held a limitation by lovers of intense effects. Certainly a violent and "outrageous thirst for stimulation" was no source of Cowper's art. The homely household occupations, images such as the dancing light on his shaded pathway, sounds such as that of small streams

> chiming as they fall
> Upon loose pebbles—

these were the simple natural facts of experience that moved him delicately. There is no great admixture of strangeness in his beauty and no intense neurotic passion for nature: simply a genuine, normal, and constant attachment. If there had never been a Wordsworth, Cowper would be more highly and justly regarded.

The Task

In its day *The Task* seemed a masterpiece: it satisfied the taste (soon to vanish) for long poems. It preserved the discursive rambling structure that the eighteenth century liked in such poems, but it added to reflection what Cowper's "moral essays" lacked—description of nature. The poet in Book I soon left the assigned topic ("The Sofa"), and started describing a morning walk to Weston. Delightful bits of typical English landscape are simply and naturally presented:

> hedge-row beauties numberless, square tow'r,
> Tall spire, from which the sound of cheerful bells
> Just undulates upon the list'ning ear,
> Groves, heaths, and smoking villages, remote. . . .

In Book II he relapses into moral reflection—on Sicilian earthquakes, on "our own late miscarriages" ("England, with all thy faults, I love thee still"), on the necessity of discipline in education, and on various other topics. In Book III comes the famous passage

> I was a stricken deer, that left the herd
> Long since; with many an arrow deep infixt
> My panting side was charg'd . . .

and here he celebrates "domestic happiness" and gardening as giving "blest seclusion from a jarring world." The last three books, written in winter, describe the tranquillity of home in "The Winter Evening" (IV), and walks at morning (V) and at noon (VI). In these books again description is pleasingly blended with reflection.

The art of the poem seems transparent. Cowper in general avoids the "poetic diction" long stereotyped for objective detail. Usually simple and precisely plain, he employs a characteristic idiom, which at best prophesies Wordsworth and at second best tries to recapture the tones of Thomson. But unlike Thomson and Young, Cowper has a nice word sense, and the polysyllables which he evidently loves could not be better chosen had Johnson himself culled them. One suspects that at times Cowper fell into polysyllables out of slight poetic embarrassment; for example, in his dutiful account of the gardener's dunghill in *The Task* (III, 463-475). *Yardley Oak* illustrates his most effective use of such diction.

In the blank verse of *The Task* and of *Yardley Oak* Cowper achieves *His Blank* more individuality than in the couplet. He may have believed that he as *Verse* well as "every warbler" had Pope's tune by heart, but actually his couplets, as compared with those of Dryden and Pope, are languid and lack both edge and, above all, vigorous variety. In blank verse he is a pioneer in the humble vein in which Wordsworth (perhaps alone) achieves distinction. Cowper's lines are relaxed and are rhythmically much less constricted in blank verse than in the couplet. He had not learned Pope's art of building two or three couplets, each technically closed, into a unified easy period; but in blank verse, though too many lines are still end-stopped, he works with more ease and grace.

From the brevity of Cowper's creative period in the early eighties one *His Merits* must not expect much in the way of artistic development. Furthermore, *and Defects* another cause impeding development was the poet's essential amateurishness. His reflections may rise out of deep conviction, but his poems as such are casual. He can "write upon the sofa" or on any topic assigned. He is in love with "baubles"; and apart from religion most topics are to him equally significant. He keys his flights so low that he frequently achieves mere prose.

> Who loves a garden loves a green-house too,

he chants; and he seems frequently thus in love with platitude or bathos. His very gift of raising, not always but usually, obvious everyday life into the realm of the poetic is the quality that makes him in many ways the most typical poet of his century. Fidelity to truth is a fundamental neo-classic ideal seen in Cowper as admirably as anywhere except perhaps in Gray's *Churchyard*. He achieves the Horatian *simplex munditiis,* but lacks the Horatian finish, felicity, and pleasing acidity. At times he is delicately and placidly lyrical. His painter's eye is excellent, and his ear is one of the nicest.

> The poplars are fell'd, farewell to the shade
> And the whispering sound of the cool colonnade

is an excellent beginning. It is, however, with the vice of moralizing, immediately watered down to insipidity. Most pathetically personal is the tragic final lyric, *The Castaway*. Although one of Cowper's less typical pieces, this poem through autobiographical intensity has to this day an appeal that his more placid verses lack. He is, like his favorite beverage, at best cheering, never inebriating. After the French Revolution there was a demand rather for poetical *aqua vitae*.

Robert Burns: A Natural Genius

Robert Burns,[4] like Cowper, is largely a poet of domestic emotion; but whereas Cowper loved environment for its own sake, Burns loved it for the human relationships implied in it. *The Cotter's Saturday Night* is an obvious illustration. Burns also found his local background a grim stimulus towards an escape to a larger life, a life which he rebelliously believed the just destiny of all men in a state of freedom. A great difference between the two poets lies in the fact that while Cowper came of a distinguished family of notable ability and of rich cultural opportunity, Burns was a "sport" in a family of humble uprightness and poverty-stricken integrity, but without a spark of genius except in Robert. Burns was an untaught genius, or, to use his epithet applied to Fergusson, "Heaven-taught." As such he was the realiza-

---

[4] Robert Burns (1759-1796) was born at Alloway in Ayrshire, a county in which most of his life was passed. His father William Burnes (as he spelled it) was a tenant farmer in a region where rentals were so high as to make certain the poverty of the tenant. At Mount Oliphant (1765-77), Lochlie (1777-84), and at Mossgiel, it was the same story of heart-eating labor, and poverty its reward. In 1781 Burns spent some months in Irvine learning to dress flax, but that work proving unattractive, he returned to the farm. Upon the death of his father (1784), Robert and his younger brothers moved the family to Mossgiel in Mauchline parish. Before this time Robert had commenced writing verses and making love. His sexual activities were promiscuous as well as fruitful. Jean Armour of Mauchline, whom he married in 1788, if not earlier, bore him twins in 1786 and again in 1788. Mary Campbell ("Highland Mary") apparently died in childbirth in 1786. There were several others also. In 1786 appeared his first book, *Poems, Chiefly in the Scottish Dialect*, printed at neighboring Kilmarnock. This brought local fame, and during the following winter Burns was in Edinburgh, where he conducted himself with dignity even though in more intellectual or aristocratic society than he had hitherto seen. Two reprintings of his poems, with some additions, were made in Edinburgh in 1787, and a second winter there was devoted in part to adjusting financial returns, which were considerable. The volume was also brought out in London, and within two years piracies appeared in Dublin, Belfast, Philadelphia, and New York. Burns now decided, after brief vacation tours in the summer of 1787, to return to the farm, and presently to marry Jean Armour. They settled at Ellisland, near Dumfries, and after a last unsatisfactory attempt to make a rented farm pay, removed in 1791 to Dumfries itself, where Burns got a place as an officer in the excise. In spite of gossip to the contrary, and in spite of ill health, it is certain that the last five years of Burns's life were those of a valued and respected citizen, of a well-known poet, who up to the last was busy in his attempt to aid George Thomson in his projected *Select Scottish Airs*, designed to glorify Scots song-writing. — The most scholarly *Life of Robert Burns* is that by Franklyn B. Snyder (1932); those by Hans Hecht (trans. by Jane Lymburn, 1936) and by John De Lancey Ferguson (*Pride and Passion*, 1939)

tion of an eighteenth-century dream that went back even further than *Spectator* No. 160. At the beginning of Alexander Pope's career a hostile critic could assure him: "You have not that sufficient learning necessary to make a poet." The idea of learning as essential to a poet perished in the eighteenth century. Stephen Duck, the thresher poet, Ann Yearsley, the milkmaid, and Thomas Chatterton all aspired to the rôle of natural genius— and to the grief of possible sponsors seemed deficient in quality. Robert Burns consciously attempted the part, and succeeded beyond all rivals. His outcry against such college wits as "think to climb Parnassus / By dint o' Greek" would have annoyed Pope's critic:

> Gie me ae spark o' Nature's fire,
> That's a' the learning I desire;
> Then, tho' I drudge thro' dub an' mire
>   At pleugh or cart,
> My Muse, tho' hamely in attire,
>   May touch the heart.

Burns was by no means so untaught as this would seem to say, but the stanza constitutes at least a declaration of poetical independence of learning. It is, on the other hand, implicitly a reaffirmation of the favorite dogma of the century, "Nature is nature wherever placed." The ability of "the force of Nature" to arrive at heights, if unimpeded, or even to arrive in spite of impediment, had been a cherished notion throughout the period of Illumination, and Burns was a complete demonstration of the idea. Later, it may be noted, natural genius will be regarded as "spontaneous" rather than untaught; but Burns was proud of his careful revision of his poems: they came from the heart rather than the head, but they are no "profuse strains of unpremeditated art." His career, however, as well as the idea of spontaneity, encouraged the romantic heresy that a true genius could bloom into a finished poet overnight.

An untaught genius naturally had to be proletarian—a thresher, a milkmaid, a farmer. Burns's pride in his humble origin is no self-conscious literary pose, as we shall see, but fitted into a tradition glorifying the farmer that went back to the days (1728) when Lord Bolingbroke had rakes, hoes, and other farm implements painted on the walls of the entrance hall of his house, named, in mock modesty, Dawley Farm. Bolingbroke, of course, had his eye on the rôle of Cincinnatus. The tradition was promoted by the later physiocrats, and echoed, for example, in the "Advertisement" in Goldsmith's *Vicar,* where Dr. Primrose is said to unite in himself "the three greatest characters upon earth"—the priest, the farmer, and the father of a family.

---

are also excellent. Most lives are quite unreliable. The most authentic text of the poems is found in *Robert Burns, The Poems,* ed. Charles S. Dougall (1927). The one-volume Cambridge Edition (Boston, 1897), a condensation of the four-volume edition by William E. Henley and T. F. Henderson (1896-7), is useful except for the untrustworthy introduction. Professor Ferguson has well edited *Selected Poems of Robert Burns* (1926) and has published the only reliable edition of the *Letters* (2v, Oxford, 1931).

The world was ready for a genius like Burns, who should be a farmer, a family man, and a great poet.

Hard Labor and Books
The farming was inevitable; his father and grandfather before him had struggled to wrest a livelihood from the farms of Ayrshire, and the poet followed the family tradition. It was a hard life, and was—both for the boy at Mount Oliphant, overworking and thus undermining his health, and later for the married man with children—a losing fight. Almost from the start there were three worlds closing and opening on the poet bewilderingly. The first was the back-breaking world of hard work. Farm life to Burns was never sincerely idyllic. The second was the world of books; for his father and many another Ayrshire man were "reading people," and the poet early and always loved books. He cherished a schoolbook, Arthur Masson's *Collection of Prose and Verse,* which gave him his first knowledge of bits of Shakespeare, Dryden, Addison, and others. Later he knew well the work of Milton, Pope, Thomson, Gray, Shenstone, Beattie, and Goldsmith; and his bias to sentiment is seen in his love for Sterne's and Mackenzie's novels. Even more important was his affection for his Scottish predecessors, Allan Ramsay and Robert Fergusson, and his long passion for Scots songbooks encouraged his great lyric gift. In various other unrelated fields he read widely—in theology, philosophy, and even in agriculture. From this reading in prose as well as from the controversies between the "Auld Lichts" and the "New Lichts" current throughout Scottish life in his day and violent in the more rustic parishes, Burns very likely acquired his anti-Calvinistic belief in the natural goodness of man—a belief that did much to develop a sense of the injustice of the poor farmer's lot and to make him what he speedily became—a social rebel.

Love vs. Law
This attitude was stimulated not merely by philosophy and by exhaustion from "the thresher's weary flingin-tree," but also through influence of the third world that opened so maddeningly upon the high-strung youth, when, as his Muse in *The Vision* says—

> youthful Love, warm-blushing, strong,
> Keen-shivering, shot thy nerves along.
>
> .   .   .   .
>
> I saw thy pulse's maddening play,
> Wild-send thee Pleasure's devious way,
> Misled by Fancy's meteor-ray,
>   By passion driven;
> But yet the light that led astray
>   Was light from Heaven.

The young poet, rebelliously guilty, disclaims moral responsibility in these last lines; but his whole psychology belies such fatalism: his loves were consciously sinful, and he rationalizes excuses by blaming Heaven or by such brilliant satire on the faults of others as is found in *The Holy Fair*—to which Fair he represented himself as going accompanied by the "hizzie" Fun, to keep an eye on Superstition and Hypocrisy. He concludes:

> There's some are fou o' love divine;
>   There's some are fou o' brandy;
>   An' monie jobs that day begin
>   May end in houghmagandie
>   Some ither day.

The poet eagerly makes us feel the comedy of the sinful hypocrites; open sin seems thus the less reprehensible. His amours have obvious if inadequate excuse in the drabness of the life to which he seemed unjustly condemned.

> There's nought but care on ev'ry han',
>   In every hour that passes, O:
>   What signifies the life o' man,
>   An' 'twere nae for the lasses, O.

Burns thus begins his career with an apologetic and allegedly heaven-authorized defiance of convention, due in part to the rigorous morality his father had attempted to instill, in part to his conscious rationalizing of his own errors, in part to his growing class-consciousness; and ultimately to his political heterodoxy. This last was somewhat notorious after 1788 when he became an exciseman in the employ of His Majesty the King. By this time class-consciousness was reinforced by a rational love of freedom, a sympathy first with the American colonies and later with the French revolutionaries— and, natural to a Scot, a not too serious notion that Charles III or his daughter "the bonie lass of Albanie" would fill the throne of England with more grace than a mad Hanoverian. His Jacobitism is negligible, but his anger at political or social injustice is true, eloquent, and pervasive. It may be seen in *The Twa Dogs, A Dream, Is there for Honest Poverty,* and in the romantic anarchy of the last chorus of *The Jolly Beggars.* *Burns's Politics*

From the worlds of work, love, and books, there was, then, this other opening that he had found: the world of poetry. Probably in 1781 occurred the episode recorded in his letter to his friend Richard Brown, December 30, 1787:

Do you recollect a Sunday we spent in Eglinton Woods? you told me, on my repeating some verses to you, that you wondered I could resist the temptation of sending verses of such merit to a magazine: 'twas actually this that gave me an idea of my own pieces which encouraged me to endeavour at the character of a Poet.

His first volume assured his fame and indicated fully the nature of that fame. He, like Cowper, was to be a poet of rural, daily life. He aimed humbly "at the character of a Poet," and his notion of that character was thoroughly that of his time: *A Poet of Rural Life*

> . . . manners-painting strains,
>   The loves, the ways of simple swains—

these were to be his subjects, and one might add to them the portrayal of the hypocrisies of the townsfolk of Ayrshire and, occasionally, the injustices of the larger world of statecraft. But chiefly he focused on men and their interrelations—their loves, their revels, their labors, and their sorrows. Landscape is incidental. As in *The Holy Fair,* he frequently commences with a bit of description; he uses imagery with brief poignant effect, but almost unawares—

> The wan moon sets behind the white wave,
> And Time is setting with me, O.

If he writes of animals or flowers, they are companions—the farmer's mare Maggie, the child's pet sheep Mailie, or the Mouse, or the Mountain Daisy—to all of whom (*which* would be improper!) he ascribes human traits, a human lot.[5] The focus is on Man still, and from many of his poems—the less glowing ones perhaps—one could deduce parts which, if grouped, would show that Burns, still of his century, conceived his work, his "manners-painting strains," as an essay on man. The final injunction in *The Vision* is,

> Preserve the dignity of Man
> With soul erect;
> And trust the Universal Plan
> Will all protect.

His subject matter, then, is what we might expect: love songs, drinking songs, humorous satires on the religious hypocrites of the Mauchline region, glowing eloquence on the theme of the rights of man, and the pervading incidental use of bits of rural life that becomes only slightly artificial even when self-consciously idyllic as in *The Cotter's Saturday Night.* He is never far from the soil, and never fails in a human sympathy for whatever subject he treats.

His Use of Folk Superstitions   Even when he makes use of the folk superstitions of the Ayr region he shows these same qualities of homeliness and humanity. For sophisticates like Matthew G. Lewis or (at a proper interval) Wolfgang von Goethe, Satanism was a taste largely acquired from books. But Burns, or rather his neighbors, believed firmly that a personal devil, who lived "in yon lowin heugh," might be met casually and frightfully in many "lanely glens"; and it was well established, they were certain, that he and his witches haunted the ruined Alloway Kirk, less than a mile away from the house where the poet was born. Burns himself evidently took his devils with several grains of humor, as one can see in his Halloween poems or in his account of the peripatetic mores of "Auld Hornie" in the *Address to the Deil:*

> Whyles, ranging like a roarin lion,
> For prey, a' holes an' corners tryin;
> Whyles, on the strong-wing'd tempest flyin,
> Tirlin the kirks;
> Whyles, in the human bosom pryin,
> Unseen thou lurks.

[5] On the treatment of animals in literature see the interesting book by Dix Howard, *Love for Animals and How it Developed in Great Britain* (1928).

Auld Hornie himself seems to share the poet's high spirits, and possibly in the prank of "tirlin the kirks" his sense of humor also. Any poet deserves acclaim whose imagination can evoke witches in the road that runs past his own house, and that is substantially what Burns did in his narrative masterpiece of *Tam o' Shanter,* a triumph of creative imagination through its vividness, its vigor, and its combination of local color with the supernatural. He makes us hear Nannie and her infernal crew come galloping from the kirk to the river in full cry after poor Tam. The reader is left wide-eyed and breathless—and at the same time, highly amused. It is one of the best fusions of diverse grotesque elements to be found in the century.

In his handling of all his created persons, from "the deil" to Tam Glen, *His Adap-* Burns's method is flexible, rich, and supremely sure. One is always confident *tation of* that Burns will not fumble, no matter in what varied genre he chooses to *Genres* write. In view of his exquisite humor his frequent use of the elegy is surprising. His admiration for Shenstone was doubtless excessive, and this, with his own tendency to melancholy, led him to write such pieces as *Man was Made to Mourn, To a Mouse,* and other despondent pieces. He is, however, especially delightful in mock-elegies such as those for Poor Mailie and Tam Samson. His satire also is cut by humor, though *Holy Willie's Prayer* (which was published posthumously) is savagely caustic. *The Holy Fair* is perhaps his most typical assault in satire on the hypocrisy that so offended him. His epistles are notably independent in form and conversational in tone: he knew Pope's work in this sort, but his own is perfectly independent of the Horatian tradition, though his *Epistle to J. Lapraik* is in some sense an *ars poetica.* The eighteenth century had been fond of humorous verse—"the Muse in a good humor"—but Burns stood on the threshold of the era of high seriousness, and while he may not have been the last British humorous poet, no poet since his day has surpassed him in rich and varied gaiety.

His lyrics are also diverse in mood and method. His songs of wooing *His Songs* range from the tender in *Mary Morison* to archness in *Tam Glen,* to a jocose treatment of bashfulness in *Duncan Gray,* and to uproarious delight in the story of *Last May a Braw Wooer.* There are happy songs of married life, such as *Contented wi' Little* and the salvaged treasure of *John Anderson my Jo,* among others. Absence, though not his common theme, is sweetly treated in *Of a' the Airts,* and the elegiac tone of *Banks o' Doon* and *Highland Mary* expresses beautifully the tragedy of lost love. *Tam o' Shanter* alone would prove that Burns had superlative gifts in poetic narrative, but in his songs he seldom relies on story for substance. In *Auld Rob Morris, Open the Door,* and *Tam Glen,* however, story is exquisitely implied. The lover at parting perhaps protests too much in *Ae Fond Kiss,* but in the fervidly hyperbolic *Red, Red Rose* we surely have authentic passion if ever words conveyed it. His more "public" songs, such as the reworked *Auld Lang Syne, Is there for Honest Poverty,* and above all the battle song of *Scots Wha Hae* are in their respective modes supremely eloquent.

It was a principal function of Burns to add dignity and life to the folk-song of his people. He was almost a learned expert as well as a poetic genius in this field, and to such collections as James Johnson's *Musical Museum* (1787-1803) and George Thomson's *Select Scottish Airs* (1793-1841) he gave much of the labors of his last years. Unfortunately the settings of *Select Scottish Airs* by Haydn and Beethoven, among others, transformed the folk-song into the art-song; and the nineteenth-century poets, lacking Burns's sure sense of recurring rhythms, turned from the song to the "art lyric" that was quite independent of song. After Burns, Tom Moore and Mrs. Hemans represent the tradition of song: Shelley, Keats, and Tennyson the art lyric.

Universality and Ayrshire Life   Burns's high and individual achievement depended largely on his intense and tender insight into social relations. In these his scope was wide: they might be as private as love or as public as monarchy; but at his best Burns drew from the social problems keenly felt in the laborious farm life that was his lot. His literary ambitions were two-fold: he hoped to be a poet like Thomson, Gray, or Shenstone (*The Vision*), but he distrusted his abilities; he hoped more confidently to be a local poet following a Scottish muse and singing the scenes from which "old Scotia's grandeur springs." The two ambitions get mixed. To be a universal poet, he thought, required the ability to strike out aphoristic reflections; but this art had perished, and in such lines as

Anticipation forward points the view,

Burns showed that he could not recapture it. No more could Byron, of whom Goethe remarked, "The minute he reflects, he is childish." It is not that Burns could not write well in English; his letters would do credit to any writer of English, and show conclusively that it was as natural for him to write English as it was to speak Scots. But to Burns poetry was rhythm and sound as well as meaning; and the sound of his native Scots gave him courage, and gave his writing life, vigor, and savor. He got his more un-usual stanza forms from Ramsay's *Ever Green* (1724) or from songbooks; his superbly firm and fine sense of musical rhythm was presumably native with him. He was always excessively modest, and after a pleasant winter in Edinburgh society, including duchesses, he was content to retire to the misty moors of Ayrshire and do his duty by Jean Armour. His "ain countree" gave him courage to be himself and integrity to win, in spite of his moral flaws, the respect of the best people with whom he came in contact. His personality was vibrant and glowing, and it had life-giving power to bestow on the essentially and frankly autobiographical and local material that con-stitutes his best poetry. On a more serene level Cowper's achievement was similar. The stage was well set for the autobiographical Wordsworth.

BOOK III. THE RESTORATION AND EIGHTEENTH CENTURY (1660-1789)

The following abbreviations are used for various *Festschriften:*

Carré Festschrift. Connaissance de l'Étranger: Mélanges offerts à la mémoire de Jean-Marie Carré (Paris, 1964).

Jones Festschrift. The Seventeenth Century: Studies in the History of English Thought and Literature from Bacon to Pope, by Richard Foster Jones and Others writing in his Honour (Stanford, Calif., 1951).

McKillop Festschrift. Restoration and Eighteenth-Century Literature: Essays in Honor of Alan Dugald McKillop. Ed. Carroll Camden (Chicago, 1963).

Nicolson Festschrift. Reason and the Imagination: Studies in the History of Ideas, 1600-1800. Ed. J. A. Mazzeo (1962).

Pottle Festschrift. From Sensibility to Romanticism: Essays presented to Frederick A. Pottle. Ed. Frederick W. Hilles and Harold Bloom (1965).

Powell Festschrift. Johnson, Boswell and their Circle: Essays presented to Lawrence Fitzroy Powell in Honour of his Eighty-fourth Birthday (Oxford, 1965).

Sherburn Festschrift. Pope and His Contemporaries: Essays presented to George Sherburn. Ed. James L. Clifford and Louis A. Landa (Oxford, 1949).

Tinker Festschrift. The Age of Johnson: Essays presented to Chauncey Brewster Tinker (New Haven, 1949).

Willey Festschrift. The English Mind: Studies in the English Moralists presented to Basil Willey. Ed. Hugh Sykes Davies and George Watson (Cambridge, 1964).

Woodhouse Festschrift. Essays in English Literature from the Renaissance to the Victorian Age presented to A. S. P. Woodhouse, 1964. Ed. Millar MacLure and F. W. Watt (Toronto, 1964).

Part I: The Rise of Classicism

I. The Spirit of the Restoration

699 Additional general studies: Alan D. McKillop, *English Literature from Dryden to Burns* (1948); Louis I. Bredvold, "The Literature of the Restoration and Eighteenth Century," in *A History of English Literature,* ed. Hardin Craig (1950), pp. 343-459; Stanley J. Kunitz and Howard Haycraft, *British Authors before 1800: a Biographical Dictionary* (1952). Gilbert Highet's *The Classical Tradition: Greek and Roman Influence on Western Literature* (1949) has special relevance for this period, both as a survey and a bibliography. An important side of Restoration publishing is treated by Roy M. Wiles, *Serial Publication in England before 1750* (Cambridge, 1957). In addition to the MHRA *Annual Bibliography, The Year's Work in English Studies* (1921—) contains chapters surveying the scholarship of the Restoration and eighteenth century, and the *Annual Bibliography* in the Spring issue of *PMLA* provides (from 1956) a comprehensive coverage of scholarship. A supplementary Vol. v of *CBEL*, ed. by George Watson, was published in 1957 (for errors see the review by Gwin J. Kolb in *MP*, LVI (1959). 197-203). Of major importance for the Restoration period is Donald Wing's *Short-Title Catalogue, 1641-1700* (for supplements and additions see Donald F. Bond, *A Reference Guide to English Studies* (Chicago, 1962), pp. 82-83). Annual surveys of scholarship in this period also appear in *SEL*: the first, by Donald J. Greene, "Recent Studies in the Restoration and Eighteenth Century," *SEL*, I (1961). 115-41 (continued by other scholars). Beljame's classic work appeared in English translation by E. O. Lorimer in 1948 (New York, 1953), with introduction and notes by Bonamy Dobrée. For the influence of the King see James Sutherland, "The Impact of Charles II on Restoration Literature," *McKillop Festschrift* (Chicago, 1963), pp. 251-63.

700 G. N. Clark (Sir George Clark), *The Later Stuarts, 1660-1714*, has appeared in a revised ed. (Oxford, 1955).

For the influence of science see also Francis Christensen, "John Wilkins and the Royal Society's Reform of Prose Style," *MLQ*, VII (1946). 179-187, 279-290; Marie Boas, *Robert Boyle and Seventeenth-Century Chemistry* (Cambridge, 1958); R. F. Jones, "The Rhetoric of Science in England of the Mid-Seventeenth Century," *McKillop Festschrift* (Chicago, 1963), pp. 5-24.

Sprat's *History of the Royal Society* has been edited by Jackson I. Cope and Harold W. Jones (St. Louis, 1958); see the important review of this by R. S. Crane in *PQ*, XXXIX (1960). 357-359. Newton's *Correspondence* is being edited by H. W. Turnbull (Cambridge, 1959—), of which three volumes (to 1694) have appeared. Andrew Motte's (1729) translation of Newton's *Mathematical Principles of Natural Philosophy and his "System of the World,"* rev. and ed. by Florian Cajori (2v, Berkeley, 1962). For early expositors of Newton see E. W. Strong, "Newtonian Explications of Natural Philosophy," *JHI*, XVIII (1957). 49-83. A useful survey is provided by I. Bernard Cohen, "Newton in the Light of Recent Scholarship," *Isis*, LI (1960). 489-514.

R. F. Jones's *Ancients and Moderns*, (rev. ed., St. Louis, 1961).

701 Ernest L. Tuveson, *Millenium and Utopia: A Study in the Background of the Idea of Progress* (Berkeley, 1949).

702 George Williamson, *The Senecan Amble: A Study in Prose Form from Bacon to Collier* (1951).

703 G. R. Cragg, *From Puritanism to the Age of Reason: A Study of Changes in Religious Thought within the Church of England, 1660-1700* (Cambridge, 1950). On the Quakers: Catherine Owen Pearce, *William Penn: A Biography* (Philadelphia, 1957); *The Journal of George Fox*, rev. ed. by John L. Nickalls (Cambridge, 1952); Jackson I. Cope, "Seventeenth-Century Quaker Style," *PMLA*, LXII (1956). 725-754.

The importance of John Tillotson (1630-1694), Archbishop of Canterbury 1691-1694,—both in the religious thought of the time and in his influence upon prose style—has been underlined in a number of recent studies: Louis G. Locke, *Tillotson: A Study in Seventeenth-Century Literature* (Copenhagen, 1954); Norman Sykes, "The Sermons of Archbishop Tillotson," *Theology*, LVIII (1955). 297-302; David D. Brown, "The Text of John Tillotson's Sermons," *Library*, XIII (1958). 18-36, and "John Tillotson's Revisions and Dryden's 'Talent for English Prose,' " *RES*, n.s. XII (1961). 24-39; Irène Simon, "Tillotson's Barrow," *ES*, XLV (1964). 194-211, 273-288.

704 D. G. James, *The Life of Reason: Hobbes, Locke, Bolingbroke* (1949). Alfred O. Aldridge, "Polygamy and Deism," *JEGP*, XLVIII (1949). 343-360.

705 Filmer's *Patriarcha and Other Political Works*, ed. Peter Laslett (Oxford, 1949).

706 *Locke's Travels in France, 1675-79, as related in his Journals, Correspondence and Other Papers*, ed. John Lough (Cambridge, 1953); *Essays on the Law of Nature*, ed. W. von Leyden (Oxford, 1954); *A Letter concerning Toleration: Latin and English Texts* rev. and ed. by Mario Montuouri (The Hague, 1963). On Locke see also Gabriel Bonno, *Les Relations intellectuelles de Locke avec la France* (Berkeley, 1955); John Hampton, "Les Traductions françaises de Locke au XVIIIᵉ siècle," *RLC*, XXIX (1955). 240-251; Maurice Cranston, *John Locke: A Biography* (1957); Theodore Redpath, "John Locke and the Rhetoric of the Second Treatise," *Willey Festschrift* (Cambridge, 1964), pp. 55-78.

708 David Green, *Grinling Gibbons: His Work as Carver and Statuary, 1648-1721* (1964).

II. Literary Criticism of the Restoration

710 R. S. Crane's "Neo-Classical Criticism" is reprinted ("English Neo-classical Criticism: An Outline Sketch") in *Critics and Criticism* (Chicago, 1952), pp. 372-388. Cf. also his article, "On Writing the History of English Criticism, 1650-1800," *UTQ*, XXII (1953). 376-391, apropos of the book by J. W. H. Atkins, *English Literary Criticism: 17th and 18th Centuries* (1951). Other books dealing with particular aspects: Marjorie H. Nicolson, *The Breaking of the Circle: Studies in the Effect of the "New Science" upon Seventeenth Century Poetry* (Evanston, 1950; rev. ed., New York, 1960), and Alexander W. Allison, *Toward an Augustan Poetic: Edmund Waller's "Reform" of English Poetry* (Lexington, Ky., 1962). The most comprehensive work on the subject is Alexandre Maurocordato, *La Critique classique en Angleterre de la Restauration à la mort de Joseph Addison: Essai de définition* (Paris, 1964). Some of the French critical essays are collected in *The Continental Model: Selected French Critical Essays of the Seventeenth Century, in English Translation*, ed. Scott Elledge and Donald Schier (Minneapolis, 1960). Other important items: Harold F. Brooks, "The 'Imitation' in English Poetry, especially in Formal Satire, before the Age of Pope," *RES*, XXV (1949). 124-140; H. V. S. Ogden, "The Principles of Variety and Contrast in Seventeenth Century Aesthetics, and Milton's Poetry," *JHI*, X (1949). 159-182; Louis I. Bredvold, "The Rise of English Classicism: Study in Methodology,"

CL, II (1950). 253-268; George Williamson, *The Proper Wit of Poetry* (1961); K. G. Hamilton, *The Two Harmonies: Poetry and Prose in the Seventeenth Century* (1963).

714 Hugh Macdonald and Mary Hargreaves, *Thomas Hobbes: A Bibliography* (1952). George Watson, "Hobbes and the Metaphysical Conceit," *JHI*, XVI (1955). 558-562 (comment by T. M. Gang, *Ibid.*, XVII (1956), 418-421); Samuel I. Mintz, *The Hunting of Leviathan: Seventeenth-Century Reactions to the Materialism and Moral Philosophy of Thomas Hobbes* (Cambridge, 1962); J. W. N. Watkins, *Hobbes's System of Ideas* (1965).

716 Dryden's critical essays have been edited by George Watson (*Of Dramatic Poesy and Other Critical Essays*) in Everyman's Library (2v, 1962) with excellent notes. On this early masterpiece see Frank L. Huntley, *On Dryden's "Essay of Dramatic Poesy"* (Ann Arbor, 1951) and Dean T. Mace, "Dryden's Dialogue on Drama," *Jour. Warburg and Courtauld Inst.*, XXV (1962). 87-112; and for Dryden's revisions in this essay Irène Simon in *RES*, n.s. XIV (1963). 132-141, and Janet M. Bately, *Ibid.*, XV (1964). 268-282. Also on Dryden's criticism: Max Nänny, *John Drydens rhetorische Poetik* (Bern, 1959); Barbara M. H. Strang, "Dryden's Innovations in Critical Vocabulary," *Durham Univ. Jour.*, LI (1959). 114-123; John M. Aden, *The Critical Opinions of John Dryden, A Dictionary* (Nashville, 1963); Niall Rudd, "Dryden on Horace and Juvenal," *UTQ*, XXXII (1963). 155-169. For the "Heads of an Answer to Rymer" see George Watson, "Dryden's First Answer to Rymer," *RES*, n.s. XIV (1963). 17-23.

719 *The Critical Works of Thomas Rymer*, ed. Curt A. Zimansky (New Haven, 1956).

721 Wesley's *Epistle to a Friend concerning Poetry*, with an Introduction by Edward N. Hooker (1947; *ARS*, No. 5).

III. The Poetry of Dryden

723 Dryden's *Poetical Works*, ed. Noyes (rev. and enlarged ed., Boston, 1950); *Dryden: Poetry, Prose and Plays*, ed. Douglas Grant (1952). The first volume of the new California edition of Dryden, ed. E. N. Hooker, H. T. Swedenberg, and others, is devoted to *Poems, 1649-1680* (1956). *The Poems of John Dryden*, ed. James Kinsley (4v, Oxford, 1958). *The Prologues and Epilogues of John Dryden: A Critical Edition*, ed. William B. Gardner (1951).

For bibliography: Samuel H. Monk, *John Dryden: A List of Critical Studies published from 1895 to 1950* (Minneapolis, 1950); cf. review by W. R. Keast in *MP*, XLVIII (1951). 205-210. Single volume studies include: David Nichol Smith, *John Dryden* (Clark Lectures, 1948/9) (Cambridge, 1950); Kenneth Young, *John Dryden: A Critical Biography* (1954); Charles E. Ward, *The Life of John Dryden* (Chapel Hill, 1961); and George R. Wasserman, *John Dryden* (1965). Cf. Pierre Legouis, "Ouvrages récents sur Dryden," *Études anglaises*, XVII (1964). 148-158. On the poetry: Guy Montgomery, *Concordance to the Poetical Works of John Dryden* (Berkeley, 1957); Arthur W. Hoffman, *John Dryden's Imagery* (Gainesville, Fla., 1962); Earl Miner, "Some Characteristics of Dryden's Use of Metaphor," *SEL*, II (1962). 309-320; Reuben A. Brower, "Dryden and the 'Invention' of Pope," *McKillop Festschrift* (Chicago, 1963), pp. 211-233; Alan Roper, *Dryden's Poetic Kingdoms* (1965).

724 Bruce A. Rosenberg, "*Annus mirabilis* Distilled," *PMLA*, LXXIX (1964). 254-258.

725 John Harrington Smith, "Some Sources of Dryden's Toryism, 1682-84," *HLQ*, XX (1957). 233-243; Bernard N. Schilling, *Dryden and the Conservative Myth: A Reading of "Absalom and Achitophel"* (New Haven, 1961) (rev. by Samuel H. Monk in *MP*, LXI (1964). 246-252).

727 On *Mac Flecknoe:* G. Blakemore Evans, "The Text of Dryden's *Mac Flecknoe*," *Harvard Library Bull.*, VII (1953). 32-54; Vinton A. Dearing, "Dryden's *Mac Flecknoe:* The Case for Authorial Revision," *Stud. in Bibliography*, VII (1955). 85-102; George McFadden, "Elkanah Settle and the Genesis of *Mac Flecknoe*," *PQ*, XLIII (1964). 55-72.

On *Religio Laici:* Edward N. Hooker, "Dryden and the Atoms of Epicurus," *ELH*, XXIV (1957). 177-190; David R. Brown, "Dryden's 'Religio Laici' and the 'Judicious and Learned Friend' [Tillotson]," *MLR*, LVI (1961). 66-69; Elias J. Chiasson, "Dryden's Apparent Scepticism in *Religio Laici*," *Harvard Theological Rev.*, LIV (1961). 207-221; Thomas H. Fujimura, "Dryden's *Religio Laici:* An Anglican Poem," *PMLA*, LXXVI (1961). 205-217; Victor M. Hamm, "Dryden's *Religio Laici* and Roman Catholic Apologetics," *PMLA*, LXXX (1965). 190-198.

728 Clarence H. Miller, "The Styles of *The Hind and the Panther*," *JEGP*, LXI (1962). 511-527; Earl Miner, "The Wolf's Progress in *The Hind and the Panther*," *Bull. N.Y. Public Library*, LXVII (1963). 512-516; Donald R. Benson, "Theology and Politics in Dryden's Conversion," *SEL*, IV (1964). 393-412.

730 A. D. Hope, "Anne Killigrew or the Art of Modulating," *Southern Rev.* [Adelaide], I (1963), 4-14; Mother Mary Eleanor, S. H. C. J. "*Anne Killigrew* and *Mac Flecknoe*," *PQ*, XLIII (1964). 47-54; David M. Vieth, "Irony in Dryden's Ode to Anne Killigrew," *SP*, LXII (1965). 91-100.—Jay Arnold Levine, "Dryden's *Song for St. Cecilia's Day, 1687*," *PQ*, XLIV (1965). 38-50.

731 William Frost, *Dryden and the Art of Translation* (New Haven, 1955); L. Proudfoot, *Dryden's "Aeneid" and its Seventeenth-Century Predecessors* (Manchester, 1960); Wolfgang B. Fleischmann, *Lucretius and English Literature (1680-1740)* (Paris, 1964); Mary Gallagher, "Dryden's Translations of Lucretius," *HLQ*, XXVIII (1964), 19-29.

IV. Minor Poets of the Restoration

734 Josephine Bauer, "Some Verse Fragments and Prose *Characters* by Samuel Butler not included in the *Complete Works*," *MP*, XLV (1948). 160-168; Norma Bentley, "Another Butler Manuscript," *MP*, XLVI (1948). 132-135; Ricardo Quintana, "Samuel Butler: A Restoration Figure in a Modern Light," *ELH*, XVII (1951). 7-13; Ward S. Miller, "The Allegory in Part I of *Hudibras*," *HLQ*, XXI (1958). 323-343.

739 Cooper R. Mackin, "The Satiric Technique of John Oldham's *Satyrs upon the Jesuits*," *SP*, LXII (1965). 78-90.

740 On the Court Poets: John Harold Wilson, *The Court Wits of the Restoration: An Introduction* (Princeton, 1948).—V. de Sola Pinto's *Rochester* appeared in a revised edition (1962) as *Enthusiast in Wit: A Portrait of John Wilmot, Earl of Rochester, 1647-1680. Rochester's Poems on Several Occasions* (a facsimile of the Huntington Library copy), ed. James Thorpe (Princeton, 1950); *Poems by John Wilmot, Earl of Rochester,* ed. Vivian de Sola Pinto (1953; 2 ed, 1964; *Muses' Library*); *The Famous Pathologist, or, The Noble Mountebank* [by Rochester and Thomas Alcock], ed. Vivian de Sola Pinto (Nottingham, 1961). On Rochester: Lucyle Hook, "The Publication Date of Rochester's *Valentinian,*" *HLQ*, xix (1956). 401-407; Thomas H. Fujimura, "Rochester's 'Satyr against Mankind': An Analysis," *SP*, lv (1958). 576-590; Jean Auffret, "Rochester's *Farewell,*" *Études anglaises*, xii (1959). 142-150; David M. Vieth, *Attribution in Restoration Poetry: A Study of Rochester's "Poems" of 1680* (New Haven, 1963; rev. by V. de S. Pinto in *PQ*, xliii (1964). 381-384, and in *MLR*, lx (1965). 253-256); Ronald Berman, "Rochester and the Defeat of the Senses," *Kenyon Rev.,* xxvi (1964). 354-368.

743 Margaret P. Boddy, "The 1692 *Fourth Book of Virgil,*" *RES*, n.s. xv (1964). 364-380 (evidence for Sedley's authorship).

745 *Poems of Charles Cotton,* ed. John Buxton (1958, Muses' Library).

746 *Poems on Affairs of State: Augustan Satirical Verse, 1660-1714* (New Haven, 1963—). Vol. i, *1660-1678,* ed. George de F. Lord (1963); Vol. ii, *1678-1681,* ed. Elias F. Mengel, Jr. (1965). See Ruth Nevo, *The Dial of Virtue: A Study of Poems on Affairs of State in the Seventeenth Century* (Princeton, 1963).

747 Additional minor Restoration poets: Richard Leigh: *Poems, 1675.* Repr. with Introduction by Hugh Macdonald (Oxford, 1947). George Stepney: *George Stepney's Translation of the Eighth Satire of Juvenal,* ed. Thomas and Elizabeth Swedenberg (Berkeley, 1948). See also H. T. Swedenberg, Jr., "George Stepney, my Lord Dorset's Boy," *HLQ*, x (1946). 1-33.

V. Restoration Drama: I. Heroic Plays and Tragedies

748 The most valuable addition to our knowledge of Restoration and eighteenth-century drama is *The London Stage, 1660-1800: A Calendar of Plays, Entertainments & Afterpieces, together with Casts, Box-Receipts and Contemporary Comment, compiled from the Playbills, Newspapers and Theatrical Diaries of the Period,* ed. William Van Lennep, Emmett L. Avery, Arthur H. Scouten, George Winchester Stone, Jr., and Charles Beecher Hogan (Carbondale, Ill., 1960—). Vol. i (1965) ed. by William Van Lennep covers the period of the Restoration. Harbage's *Annals of English Drama, 975-1700* has appeared in a revised edition by S. Schoenbaum (1964). The histories by Allardyce Nicoll have been reissued in revised form as *A History of English Drama 1660-1900* (6v, Cambridge, 1952-1959); Vol. vi: *A Short-title Alphabetical Catalogue of Plays produced or printed in England from 1660-1900* (1959). Also useful is *A Check List of English Plays, 1641-1700* by Gertrude L. Woodward and James G. McManaway (Chicago, 1945); *Supplement* by Fredson Bowers (Charlottesville, Va., 1949). See also William S. Clark, *The Early Irish Stage: The Beginnings to*

1720 (Oxford, 1955). A much-needed *Biographical Dictionary of Actors and Actresses* is in preparation by the editors of *The London Stage*. A good account of the actresses of the Restoration is to be found in John Harold Wilson's *All the King's Ladies* (Chicago, 1958). On the general aims of the drama of the period see Sarup Singh, *The Theory of Drama in the Restoration Period* (Calcutta, 1963).

752 Kathleen Lynch, *Roger Boyle, First Earl of Orrery* (Knoxville, 1965).— Vol. VIII of the California edition of Dryden includes *The Wild Gallant, The Rival Ladies, The Indian Queen*, ed. John Harrington Smith and Dougald Mac-Millan (1962); cf. review by V. de Sola Pinto in *PQ*, XLII (1963). 342-344. On Dryden's heroic plays and early tragedies: Dougald MacMillan, "The Sources of Dryden's *The Indian Emperour*," *HLQ*, XIII (1950). 355-370; Scott C. Osborn, "Heroical Love in Dryden's Heroic Drama," *PMLA*, LXXIII (1958). 480-490; John A. Winterbottom, "The Place of Hobbesian Ideas in Dryden's Tragedies," *JEGP*, LVII (1958). 665-683; Thomas H. Fujimura, "The Appeal of Dryden's Heroic Plays," *PMLA*, LXXV (1960). 37-45; Michael W. Alssid, "The Perfect Conquest: A Study of Theme, Structure and Characters in Dryden's *The Indian Emperor*," *SP*, LIX (1962). 539-559; Jean Gagen, "Love and Honor in Dryden's Heroic Plays," *PMLA*, LXXVII (1962). 208-220; Bruce King, "Heroic and Mock-Heroic Plays," *Sewanee Rev.*, LXX (1962). 514-517; Arthur C. Kirsch, "Dryden, Corneille, and the Heroic Play," *MP*, LIX (1962). 248-264; Eugene M. Waith, *The Herculean Hero in Marlowe, Shakespeare and Dryden* (1962); John A. Winterbottom, "Stoicism in Dryden's Tragedies," *JEGP*, LXI (1962). 868-883; Arthur C. Kirsch, *Dryden's Heroic Drama* (Princeton, 1965); Bruce King, "Dryden, Tillotson, and *Tyrannic Love*," *RES*, n.s. XVI (1965). 364-377; Selma Zebouni, *Dryden: A Study in Heroic Characterization* (Baton Rouge, 1965).

755 On Buckingham and *The Rehearsal*: Hester W. Chapman, *Great Villiers: A Study of George Villiers, Second Duke of Buckingham, 1628-1687* (1949); V. C. Clinton-Baddeley, *The Burlesque Tradition in the English Theatre after 1660* (1952); John Harold Wilson, *A Rake and his Times: George Villiers, 2nd Duke of Buckingham* (1954). On *Aureng-Zebe*: Arthur C. Kirsch, "The Significance of Dryden's *Aureng-Zebe*," *ELH*, XXIX (1962). 160-174; Michael W. Alssid, "The Design of Dryden's *Aureng-Zebe*," *JEGP*, LXIV (1965). 452-469.

756 On Dryden's later plays: John Robert Moore, "Political Allusions in Dryden's Later Plays," *PMLA*, LXXIII (1958). 36-42; Otto Reinert, "Passion and Pity in *All for Love*: A Reconsideration," in *The Hidden Sense and Other Essays*, by Maren-Sofie Røstvig and others (Oslo, 1963), pp. 159-195; L. P. Goggin, "This Bow of Ulysses," *Essays and Stud. in Lang. and Lit.* (Pittsburgh, 1964; *Duquesne Stud., Philol. Ser.*, 5), p. 49-86; Bruce King, "The Significance of Dryden's *State of Innocence*," *SEL*, IV (1964). 371-391; D. T. Starnes, "Imitation of Shakespeare in Dryden's *All for Love*," *Texas Stud. in Lit. and Lang.*, VI (1964). 39-46.

757 On John Banks see the monograph by Hans Hochuli (Bern, 1952). *The Works of Nathaniel Lee* have been edited by Thomas B. Stroup and Arthur L. Cooke (2v, New Brunswick, N.J., 1954-55). On this edition see the review by Fredson Bowers in *PQ*, XXXV (1956). 310-314.

758 Aline M. Taylor, *Next to Shakespeare: Otway's Venice Preserved and*

The Orphan and their History on the London Stage (Durham, N.C., 1950);
David R. Hauser, "Otway Preserved: Theme and Form in *Venice Preserv'd*,"
SP, LV (1958). 481-493; William H. McBurney, "Otway's Tragic Muse De-
bauched: Sensuality in *Venice Preserv'd*," *JEGP*, LVIII (1959). 380-399; André
Lefèvre, "Racine en Angleterre au XVIIᵉ siècle: 'Titus and Berenice' de Thomas
Otway," *RLC*, XXXIV (1960). 251-257.

VI. Restoration Drama: II. Comedy

762 On Restoration Comedy: John Harrington Smith, *The Gay Couple in
Restoration Comedy* (Cambridge, Mass., 1948); David S. Berkeley, "The Penitent
Rake in Restoration Comedy," *MP*, XLIX (1952). 223-233; Thomas H. Fujimura,
The Restoration Comedy of Wit (Princeton, 1952); a series of articles by David
S. Berkeley: "The Art of 'Whining' Love," *SP*, LII (1955). 478-496; "Préciosité
and the Restoration Comedy of Manners," *HLQ*, XVIII (1955). 109-128; "Some
Notes on Probability in Restoration Drama," *N&Q*, CC (1955). 237-239, 342-344,
432; C. D. Cecil, "Libertine and Précieux Elements in Restoration Comedy," *EIC*,
IX (1959). 239-253; Norman H. Holland, *The First Modern Comedies: The Sig-
nificance of Etherege, Wycherley, and Congreve* (Cambridge, Mass., 1959); P. F.
Vernon, "Marriage of Convenience and the Mode of Restoration Comedy," *EIC*,
XII (1962). 370-387; Irène Simon, "Restoration Comedy and the Critics," *Revue
des langues vivantes*, XXIX (1963). 397-430; Charles O. McDonald, "Restoration
Comedy as Drama of Satire: An Investigation into Seventeenth-Century Aes-
thetics," *SP*, LXI (1964). 522-544; D. R. M. Wilkinson, *The Comedy of Habit:
An Essay on the Use of Courtesy Literature in a Study of Restoration Comic
Drama* (The Hague, 1964); R. C. Sharma, *Themes and Conventions in the
Comedy of Manners* (1965). *Restoration Theatre* (*Stratford-upon-Avon Stud.*, 6),
ed. John Russell Brown and Bernard Harris (1965) contains first-rate papers on
Etherege, Wycherley, Dryden, and Congreve, as well as studies of relevant sub-
jects including the influence of Molière. Jean E. Gagen's *The New Woman: Her
Emergence in English Drama, 1600-1730* (1954) also deals in part with Restora-
tion drama.

764 H. J. Oliver, *Sir Robert Howard (1626-1698): A Critical Biography*
(Durham, N.C., 1963).

765 Dryden: Frank Harper Moore, *The Nobler Pleasure: Dryden's Comedy
in Theory and Practice* (Chapel Hill, 1963).—Etherege: Thomas H. Fujimura,
"Etherege at Constantinople," *PMLA*, LXII (1956). 465-481; Dale Underwood,
Etherege and the Seventeenth-Century Comedy of Manners (New Haven, 1957);
The Poems of Sir George Etherege, ed. James Thorpe (Princeton, 1963).

766 Wycherley: T. W. Craik, "Some Aspects of Satire in Wycherley's Plays,"
ES, XLI (1960). 168-179; K. M. Rogers, "Fatal Inconsistency: Wycherley and *The
Plain-Dealer*," *ELH*, XXVIII (1961). 148-162; J. Auffret, "Wycherley et ses maîtres
les moralistes," *Études anglaises*, XV (1962). 375-388; Carl Wooten, "*The Country
Wife* and Contemporary Comedy: A World Apart," *Drama Survey*, II (1963).
333-343; Rose A. Zimbardo, *Wycherley's Drama: A Link in the Development of
English Satire* (New Haven, 1965).

769 Shadwell: John Harrington Smith, "Shadwell, the Ladies, and Change in Comedy," *MP*, xlvi (1948). 22-33; P. F. Vernon, "Social Satire in Shadwell's *Timon*," *Studia Neophil.*, xxxv (1963). 221-226; Gunnar Sorelius, "Shadwell Deviating into Sense: *Timon of Athens* and the Duke of Buckingham," *Ibid.*, xxxvi (1964). 232-244.

772 Congreve: *The Way of the World*, ed. Kathleen M. Lynch (Lincoln, Nebr., 1965). Emmett L. Avery, *Congreve's Plays on the Eighteenth-Century Stage* (1951); Kathleen M. Lynch, *A Congreve Gallery* (Cambridge, Mass., 1951); John C. Hodges, *The Library of William Congreve* (1955); Paul and Miriam Mueschke, *A New View of Congreve's "Way of the World"* (Ann Arbor, 1958); Robert G. Noyes, "Congreve and his Comedies in the Eighteenth-Century Novel," *PQ*, xxxix (1960). 464-480; Clifford Leech, "Congreve and the Century's End," *PQ*, xli (1962). 275-293; Paul T. Nolan, "Congreve's Lovers: Art and the Critic," *Drama Survey*, i (1962). 330-339; *William Congreve: Letters and Documents*, ed. John C. Hodges (1964); John Barnard, "Did Congreve Write *A Satyr against Love?*" *Bull. N.Y. Public Library*, lxviii (1964). 308-322 [with text of the Satyr]; Jean Gagen, "Congreve's Mirabell and the Ideal of the Gentleman," *PMLA*, lxxix (1964). 422-427; Charles R. Lyons, "Congreve's Miracle of Love," *Criticism*, vi (1964). 331-348 [on *Love for Love*].

776 Farquhar: *The Beaux' Stratagem*, ed. Vincent F. Hopper and Gerald B. Lahey (Great Neck, N.Y., 1963); Willard Connely, *Young George Farquhar: The Restoration Drama at Twilight* (1949); Kaspar Spinner, *George Farquhar als Dramatiker* (Bern, 1956); Eric Rothstein, "Farquhar's *Twin-Rivals* and the Reform of Comedy," *PMLA*, lxxix (1964). 33-41; Eugene N. James, "The Burlesque of Restoration Comedy in *Love and a Bottle*," *SEL*, v (1965). 469-490.

VII. Patterns in Historical Writing

780 Pepys: *The Letters of Samuel Pepys and his Family Circle*, ed. Helen Truesdell Heath (Oxford, 1955); John Harold Wilson, *The Private Life of Mr. Pepys* (1959); Cecil S. Emden, *Pepys Himself* (1963); Ivan E. Taylor, "Mr. Pepy's Use of Colloquial English," *Coll. Lang Assoc. Jour*, vii (1963). 22-36; Marjorie H. Nicolson, *Pepys' "Diary" and the New Science* (Charlottesville, 1965).

784 Evelyn: *The Diary of John Evelyn*, ed. E. S. de Beer (6v, Oxford, 1955; also in 1 vol. (Oxford, 1959); W. G. Hiscock, *John Evelyn and Mrs. Godolphin* (1951) and *John Evelyn and his Family Circle* (1955).

786 William Matthews, *British Diaries: An Annotated Bibliography of British Diaries written between 1442 and 1942* (Berkeley, 1950).—Clarendon: Herbert Davis, "The Augustan Conception of History," *Nicolson Festschrift* (1962), pp. 213-229 [discusses Clarendon, but is mainly on Swift and Pope].

788 Burnet: W. Rees Mogg, "Some Reflections on the Bibliography of Gilbert Burnet," *Library*, iv (1949). 100-113.

790 Autobiography: Wayne Shumaker, *English Autobiography: Its Emergence, Materials, and Form* (Berkeley, 1954); William Matthews, *British Autobiographies: An Annotated Bibliography of British Autobiographies Published or Written before 1951* (Berkeley, 1955); Margaret Bottral, *Every Man a Phoenix:*

Studies in Seventeenth-Century Autobiography (1958).—Duchess of Newcastle: Douglas Grant, *Margaret the First: A Biography of Margaret Cavendish, Duchess of Newcastle, 1623-1673* (1956); Jean Gagen, "Honor and Fame in the Works of the Duchess of Newcastle," *SP*, LVI (1959). 519-538.

791 Winstanley, *Lives of the Most Famous English Poets (1687)*: Facsimile Reproduction, with Introduction by William R. Parker (Gainesville, Fla., 1963).

792 Petty: Emil Strauss, *Sir William Petty: Portrait of a Genius* (1954).— Aubrey: *Aubrey's Brief Lives*, ed. Oliver L. Dick (1949; Ann Arbor, 1957); John Powell, *John Aubrey and his Friends* (1948).

VIII. Types of Prose Fiction

793 Charles C. Mish, *English Prose Fiction, 1600-1700: A Chronological Checklist* (Charlottesville, Va., 1952); Sidney Gecker, *English Fiction to 1820 in the University of Pennsylvania Library* (Philadelphia, 1954).

795 *The Adventures of Lindamira, A Lady of Quality*, ed. Benjamin Boyce (Minneapolis, 1949).

796 Strickland Gibson, *A Bibliography of Francis Kirkman, with his Prefaces, Dedications and Commendations (1652-80)* (Oxford, 1950).

797 Bunyan: *The Pilgrim's Progress*, ed. Wharey (rev. ed. by Roger Sharrock, Oxford, 1960); *Grace Abounding*, ed. Roger Sharrock (Oxford, 1962); Henri A. Talon, *John Bunyan, l'homme et l'oeuvre* (Paris, 1948; trans. Barbara Wall, 1951); Vera Brittain, *In the Steps of John Bunyan: An Excursion into Puritan England* (1950; U.S. title: *Valiant Pilgrim: The Story of John Bunyan and Puritan England*); Roger Sharrock, *John Bunyan* (1954); Berta Haferkamp, *Bunyan als Künstler: Stilkritische Studien zu seinem Hauptwerk "The Pilgrim's Progress"* (Tübingen, 1963).

804 Mrs. Behn: George Woodcock, *The Incomparable Aphra* (1948); Emily Hahn, *Aphra Behn* (1951); W. J. Cameron, *New Light on Aphra Behn* (Auckland, 1961); R. T. Sheffey, "Some Evidence for a New Source of Aphra Behn's *Oroonoko*," *SP*, LIX (1962). 52-63; G. M. Laborde, "Du nouveau sur Aphra Behn," *Études anglaises*, XVI (1963). 364-368 [a review of Cameron's monograph]. —Henry Neville: A. O. Aldridge, "Polygamy in Early Fiction: Henry Neville and Denis Veiras," *PMLA*, LXV (1950). 464-472.

IX. The Essay and Allied Forms

807 Cowley's Essays: Robert B. Hinman, *Abraham Cowley's World of Order* (Cambridge, Mass., 1960).

808 *Five Miscellaneous Essays by Sir William Temple*, ed. Samuel H. Monk (Ann Arbor, 1963); William Roberts, "Sir William Temple on Orinda: Neglected Publications," *Papers of the Bibl. Soc. of America*, LVII (1963). 328-336.

811 Glanvill: Richard H. Popkin, "The Development of the Philosophical Reputation of Joseph Glanvill," *JHI*, XV (1954). 305-311; Jackson I. Cope, *Joseph*

Glanvill: Anglican Apologist (St. Louis, 1956).—Burnet: H. V. S. Ogden, "Thomas Burnet's *Telluris theoria sacra* and Mountain Scenery," *ELH,* xiv (1947). 139-150; Ernest Tuveson, "The Origins of the 'Moral Sense,'" *HLQ,* xi (1948). 241-259.—Ray: Geoffrey Keynes, *John Ray: A Bibliography* (1951).

812 Halifax: Donald R. Benson, "Halifax and the Trimmers," *HLQ,* xxvii (1964). 115-134; Harold E. Pagliaro, "Paradox in the Aphorisms of La Rochefoucauld and Some Representative English Followers," *PMLA,* lxxix (1964). 42-50.

813 The Character: Benjamin Boyce, *The Theophrastan Character in England to 1642* (Cambridge, Mass., 1947) and *The Polemic Character, 1640-1661: A Chapter in English Literary History* (Lincoln, Neb., 1955). Henry Gally's "Critical Essay on Characteristic-Writings" [the introduction to his translation of Theophrastus in 1725] is No. 33 of the *ARS,* with an Introduction by Alexander H. Chorney (1952).

815 P. M. Handover, *A History of the London Gazette, 1665-1965* (1965).

816 Jean Honoré, "Charles Gildon rédacteur du *British Mercury* (1711-1712): les attaques contre Pope, Swift, et les wits," *Études anglaises,* xv (1962). 347-364. See also the same writer's "Charles Gildon et la Grammaire de Brightland," *Ibid.,* xviii (1965). 145-165.

817 *The Turkish Spy*: William H. McBurney, "The Authorship of *The Turkish Spy,*" *PMLA,* lxxii (1957). 915-935; Joseph E. Tucker, "The *Turkish Spy* and its French Background," *RLC,* xxxii (1958). 74-91, and "On the Authorship of the *Turkish Spy*: An *État Présent,*" *Papers of the Bibl. Soc. of America,* lii (1958). 34-47.

The London Spy: The London Spy, by Ned Ward, ed. Kenneth Fenwick (1955; *Folio Society*).

819 For *The Adventures of Lindamira,* see above, suppl. to p. 795.

Part II: Classicism and Journalism

I. Eighteenth-Century Quality

823 There is no Short Title Catalogue for the eighteenth century, but for the early years much bibliographical information is to be had from Vol. iii of Arber's reprint of the *Term Catalogues, 1668-1711* and from William T. and Chloe S. Morgan's *Bibliography of British History (1700-1715)* (5v, Bloomington, Ind., 1934-42). The incomplete but valuable registers of books in the *Bibliotheca Annua* (1699-1703), the *Monthly Catalogues* (1714-17, 1723-30), and the *Register of Books* (1728-32) from the *Monthly Chronicle,* have been reprinted (1964) under the editorship of David Foxon. *The Rothschild Library*—the catalogue of eighteenth-century books and manuscripts formed by Lord Rothschild—(2v, Cambridge, 1954) is also of great value. See further Stanley Pargellis and D.J. Medley, *Bibliography of British History: The Eighteenth Century, 1714-1789* (Oxford, 1951). Additional surveys of the literature: John Butt, *The Augustan Age* (1950); Roger P. McCutcheon, *Eighteenth-Century English Literature*

(1950); R. C. Churchill, *English Literature of the Eighteenth Century* (1953); A. R. Humphreys, *The Augustan World: Life and Letters in Eighteenth-Century England;* (1954; 2ed, 1964); and Vol. vii of the *Oxford History of English Literature*: Bonamy Dobrée, *English Literature in the Early Eighteenth Century, 1700-1740* (Oxford, 1959), for which see the review by Donald F. Bond in *MP*, LX (1962). 138-141. A useful survey of recent scholarship is contained in the article by James L. Clifford, "The Eighteenth Century," *MLQ* XXVI (1965). 111-134. For recent works on various aspects of the background see Leon Radzinowicz, *A History of English Criminal Law and its Administration from 1750* (Vol. I, 1948); Ernest Cassirer, *The Philosophy of the Enlightenment,* trans. F.C.A. Koelln and J. P. Pettegrove (Princeton, 1951); G.M. Trevelyan, *Illustrated English Social History* (Vol. III, 1951); Ronald N. Stromberg, *Religious Liberalism in Eighteenth-Century England* (1954); L. W. Hanson, *Contemporary Printed Sources for British and Irish Economic History, 1701-1750* (Cambridge, 1963). M. D. George's *London Life in the XVIIIth Century* reached a 3rd rev. ed. in 1951. *Aspects of the Eighteenth Century,* ed. Earl R. Wasserman (Baltimore, 1965), contains several important essays dealing with this period: George Boas, "In Search of the Age of Reason"; J. A. Passmore, "The Malleability of Man in Eighteenth-Century Thought"; René Wellek, "The Term and Concept of 'Classicism' in Literary History"; R. Wittkower, "Imitation, Electicism, and Genius"; Edward E. Lowinsky, "Taste, Style, and Ideology in Eighteenth Century Music"; Henry Guerlac, "Where the Statue Stood: Divergent Loyalties to Newton in the Eighteenth Century."

825 On Shaftesbury see the articles by A. O. Aldridge: "Shaftesbury, Christianity, and Friendship," *Anglican Theological Rev.* XXXII (1950). 121-136; "Two Versions of Shaftesbury's *Inquiry concerning Virtue,*" *HLQ,* XIII (1950). 207-214; "Shaftesbury and the Deist Manifesto," *Trans. Amer. Philos. Soc.,* XLI (1951). 297-385; and "Shaftesbury and Bolingbroke," *PQ,* XXXI (1952). 1-16; R. L. Brett, *The Third Earl of Shaftesbury: A Study in Eighteenth-Century Literary Theory* (1951); Ernest Tuveson, "The Importance of Shaftesbury," *ELH,* XX (1953). 267-299; Robert B. Voitle, "Shaftesbury's Moral Sense," *SP,* LII (1955). 17-38; Erwin Wolff, *Shaftesbury und seine Bedeutung für die englische Literatur des 18. Jahrhunderts: der Moralist und die literarische Form* (Tübingen, 1960) (cf. Irène Simon in *Revue des langues vivantes,* XXVII (1961). 200-215); Jerome Stolnitz, "On the Significance of Lord Shaftesbury in Modern Aesthetic Theory," *Philosophical Quar.* XI (1961). 97-113; J. B. Broadbent, "Shaftesbury's Horses of Religion," *Willey Festschrift* (Cambridge, 1964) pp. 79-89; Robert Marsh, *Four Dialectical Theories of Poetry* (Chicago, 1965); Ernest Tuveson, "Shaftesbury on the not so simple Plan of Human Nature," *SEL,* V (1965). 403-434. The pioneering article by Cecil A. Moore (1916) has been reprinted in Moore's *Backgrounds of English Literature, 1700-1760* (Minneapolis, 1953).

826 F. B. Kaye's edition of Mandeville (2v, Oxford, 1924) is still authoritative. The *Fable* has also been edited by Irwin Primer (1962). See further, J. C. Maxwell, "Ethics and Politics in Mandeville," *Philosophy,* XXVI (1951), 242-252; Thomas R. Edwards, Jr., "Mandeville's Moral Prose," *ELH,* XXXI (1964). 195-212.

828 Berkeley's *Works* have now been edited by A. A. Luce and T. E. Jessop

(9v, 1948-1957). Luce is also author of a biography (1949) and *The Dialectic of Immaterialism: An Account of the Making of Berkeley's "Principles"* (1963). See also Paul Kaufman, "Establishing Berkeley's Authorship of 'Guardian' Papers," *Papers of the Bibl. Soc. of America*, LIV (1960). 181-183; Donald Davie, "Berkeley and the Style of Dialogue," *Willey Festschrift* (Cambridge, 1964), pp. 90-106. There is a useful survey of scholarship by Claude Lehec, "Trente années d'études berkeleyennes," *Revue Philosophique*, CXLIII (1953). 244-265.

829 William Law: Henri Talon, *William Law: A Study in Literary Craftsmanship* (1948); P. Malekin, "Jacob Boeheme's Influence on William Law," *Studia Neophil.* XXXVI (1964). 245-260.—Byrom: *Selections from the Journals and Papers of John Byrom, Poet, Diarist, Shorthand Writer, 1691-1763*, ed. Henri Talon (1950).

831 The Arts and Gardening: Margaret Jourdain, *The Work of William Kent* (1948); Dorothy Stroud, *Capability Brown* (1950, rev. 1957); Laurence Whistler, *The Imagination of Vanbrugh and his Fellow Artists* (1954); Miles Hadfield, *Gardening in Britain* (1960); Edward Hyams, *The English Garden* (1964).—Hogarth: *The Analysis of Beauty, with the Rejected Passages from the Manuscript Drafts and Autobiographical Notes*, ed. Joseph Burke (Oxford, 1955); Robert E. Moore, *Hogarth's Literary Relationships* (Minneapolis, 1948); Peter Quennel, *Hogarth's Progress* (1955); Frederick Antal, *Hogarth and his Place in European Art* (1962).

832 E. F. Carritt, *A Calendar of British Taste from 1600-1800* (1949).

II. The Critical Temper and Doctrine, 1700-1750

833 *Eighteenth-Century Critical Essays*, ed. Scott Elledge (2v, Ithaca, N.Y., 1961); Samuel Kliger, *The Goths in England: A Study in Seventeenth and Eighteenth Century Thought* (Cambridge, Mass., 1952) (cf. review by Alan D. McKillop in *PQ*, XXXII (1953). 247-250); A. Bosker, *Literary Criticism in the Age of Johnson* (rev. ed:, Groningen, 1953); Emerson R. Marks, *Relativist and Absolutist: The Early Neoclassical Debate in England* (New Brunswick, N.J., 1955); A. M. Kinghorn, "Literary Aesthetics and the Sympathetic Emotions— A Main Trend in Eighteenth-Century Scottish Criticism," *Studies in Scottish Literature*, I (1963). 35-47; Martin Price, *To the Palace of Wisdom: Studies in Order and Energy from Dryden to Blake* (Garden City, N.Y., 1964); Paul Fussell, *The Rhetorical World of Augustan Humanism: Ethics and Imagery from Swift to Burke* (Oxford, 1965); Robert Marsh, *Four Dialectical Theories of Poetry: An Aspect of English Neoclassical Criticism* (Chicago, 1965) [Shaftesbury, Akenside, Hartley, and James Harris].

834 Hooker's edition of Dennis' *Critical Works* has been reprinted (2v, Baltimore, 1965).

837 Shaftesbury as Critic. See above, suppl. to p. 825.

839 Lee A. Elioseff, *The Cultural Milieu of Addison's Literary Criticism* (Austin, Texas, 1963).

840 On Hutcheson see Alfred Owen Aldridge, "A French Critic of Hutcheson's Aesthetics," *MP*, xlv (1948). 169-184 [Charles Louis de Villette]; William Frankena, "Hutcheson's Moral Sense Theory," *JHI*, xvi (1955). 356-375; George Dickie, "An Examination of Hutcheson's Alleged Emotivism," *Research Stud. of the State College of Washington*, xxvi (1958). 55-73.

841   Raymond D. Havens, "Simplicity, a Changing Concept," *JHI*, xiv (1953). 3-32. On ballad criticism see Albert B. Friedman, *The Ballad Revival* (Chicago, 1961), chap. iv.

842   Pope as Critic: Edward N. Hooker, "Pope on Wit: the *Essay on Criticism*," *Jones Festschrift* (Stanford, 1951), pp. 225-246; Robert M. Schmitz, *Pope's Essay on Criticism, 1709: A Study of the Bodleian Manuscript Text, with Facsimiles, Transcripts, and Variants* (St. Louis, 1962). Vol. i of the Twickenham Edition, containing the *Essay on Criticism*, appeared in 1961 (see below, suppl. to p. 921).

844   Donald M. Foerster, *Homer in English Criticism: The Historical Approach in the Eighteenth Century* (New Haven, 1947); Douglas Duncan, *Thomas Ruddiman: A Study in Scottish Scholarship of the Early Eighteenth Century* (1965).

845   Gildon and others: Corbyn Morris' *Essay towards fixing the True Standards of Wit, Humour, Raillery, Satire, and Ridicule . . .* (1744) appeared as No. 10 of the *ARS*, with an Introduction by James L. Clifford (1947); Part 1 of Bysshe's *Art of English Poetry* as No. 40, with an Introduction by A. Dwight Culler (1953); and John Oldmixon's *Essay on Criticism* (1728) as Nos. 107/8), with an Introduction by R. J. Madden, C.S.B. (1964); H. Rossiter Smith, "Matthew Green, 1696-1737," *N&Q*, cxcix (1954). 250-253, 284-287. See also Paul Fussell, Jr., *Theory of Prosody in Eighteenth-Century England* (New London, Conn., 1954); Beate Wackwitz, *Die Theorie des Prosastils im England des 18. Jahrhunderts* (Hamburg, 1962).

III. Defoe and Journalism

847   Ian Watt, "Publishers and Sinners: The Augustan View," *Stud. in Bibliography*, xii (1958). 3-20.

848   Rodney M. Baine, "The Apparition of Mrs. Veal: A Neglected Account," *PMLA*, lxix (1954). 523-541, and "Defoe and Mrs. Bargrave's Story," *PQ*, xxxiii (1954). 388-395 (both articles reviewed by Arthur W. Secord in *PQ*, xxxiv (1955). 282); Arthur H. Scouten, "An Early Printed Report on the Apparition of Mrs. Veal," *RES*, n.s. vi (1955). 259-263; Arthur W. Secord, "A September Day in Canterbury: The Veal-Bargrave Story," *JEGP*, liv (1955). 639-650; Arthur H. Scouten, "At that Moment of Time: Defoe and the Early Accounts of the Apparition of Mistress Veal," *Ball State Teachers College Forum*, ii, No. 2 (1961/2), pp. 44-51; Rodney M. Baine, "Daniel Defoe and *The History and Reality of Apparitions*," *Proc. Amer. Philos. Soc.*, cvi (1962). 335-347.

849   For surveys of Defoe scholarship see the articles by Gerhard Jacob in *Wissenschaftliche Zeitschrift der Karl-Marx-Universität Leipzig (Gesellschafts— und sprachwiss. Reihe*, Heft 5), iv (1954/55). 517-526, and *Archiv*, cxcvii (1960). 126-35. For Defoe bibliography see John Robert Moore, *A Checklist of* the Writings of Daniel Defoe (Bloomington, Ind., 1960) and reviews of this by William B. Todd in Book-Collector, x (1961). 493-494, 497-498, and by James Sutherland in Library, xvii (1963). 323-325. Meditations, ed. George H. Healey (Cummington, Mass., 1946); An Essay on the Regulation of the Press, ed. John Robert Moore (Oxford, 1948); Letters, ed. George H. Healey (Oxford, 1955) (cf. review by A. W. Secord in MP, liv (1955). 45-52). See also Bonamy Dobrée, "Some Aspects of Defoe's Prose," Sherburn Festschrift (Oxford, 1949), pp. 171-184; William Freeman, The Incredible Defoe (1950); Francis Watson, Daniel Defoe (1952); Benjamin Boyce, "The Question of Emotion in Defoe," SP, l (1953). 45-58; Brian Fitzgerald, Daniel Defoe: A Study in Conflict (1954); Spiro Peterson, "Defoe's Yorkshire Quarrel," HLQ, xix (1955). 57-79; John Robert Moore, Daniel Defoe: Citizen of the Modern World (Chicago, 1958); Arthur W. Secord, "Robert Drury's Journal" and Other Studies (Urbana, 1961); Maximillian E. Novak, Economics and the Fiction of Daniel Defoe (Berkeley, 1962) and Defoe and the Nature of Man (1963); John Robert Moore, "Daniel Defoe: Precursor of Samuel Richardson," McKillop Festschrift (Chicago, 1963), pp. 351-369; Richard Gerber, "Zur Namengebung bei Defoe," Festschrift für Walter Hübner (Berlin, 1964), pp. 227-233; Maximillian E. Novak, "Defoe's Theory of Fiction," SP, lxi (1964). 650-668; G. A. Starr, Defoe & Spiritual Autobiography (Princeton, 1965).

850 Godfrey Davies, "Daniel Defoe's A Tour thro' the Whole Island of Great Britain," MP, xlviii (1950). 21-36.

852 On The Review see the three books by William L. Payne: Mr. Review: Daniel Defoe as Author of the "Review" (1947); Index to Defoe's Review (1948); The Best of Defoe's "Review": An Anthology (1951).

853 Robinson Crusoe: Edward D. Seeber, "Oroonoko and Crusoe's Man Friday," MLQ, xii (1951). 286-291; Ian Watt, "Robinson Crusoe as a Myth," EIC, i (1951). 95-119; Dewcy Ganzel, "Chronology in Robinson Crusoe," PQ, xl (1961). 495-512; Maximillian E. Novak, "Crusoe the King and the Political Evolution of his Island," SEL, ii (1962). 337-350; J. Paul Hunter, "Friday as a Convert: Defoe and the Accounts of Indian Missionaries," RES, n.s. xiv (1963). 243-248; Maximillian E. Novak, "Robinson Crusoe and Economic Utopia," Kenyon Rev. xxv (1963). 474-490; William H. Halewood, "Religion and Invention in Robinson Crusoe," EIC, xiv (1964). 339-351.—Captain Singleton: Gary J. Scrimgeour, "The Problem of Realism in Defoe's Captain Singleton," HLQ, xxvii (1963). 21-37.—Moll Flanders:. Terence Martin, "The Unity of Moll Flanders," MLQ, xxii (1961). 115-124; Robert R. Columbus, "Conscious Artistry in Moll Flanders," SEL, iii (1963). 415-432; Denis Donoghue, "The Values of Moll Flanders," Sewanee Rev., lxxi (1963). 287-303; Howard L. Koonce, "Moll's Muddle: Defoe's Use of Irony in Moll Flanders," ELH, xxx (1963). 377-394; Arnold Kettle, "In Defence of Moll Flanders," Of Books and Humankind: Essays and Poems presented to Bonamy Dobrée (1964), pp. 55-67; Maximillian E. Novak, "Conscious Irony in Moll Flanders," College English, xxvi (1964). 198-204.—Journal of the Plague Year: Ernst Gerhard Jacob, "Die medizingeschichtliche Bedeutung des Robinsondichters," Die Medizinische Welt, i (1962). 1-20; F. Bastian, "Defoe's Journal of the Plague Year Reconsidered," RES, n.s. xvi (1965). 151-173.—Colonel Jacque: There is an ed. by Samuel H. Monk (1965);

William H. McBurney, "Colonel Jacque: Defoe's Definition of the Complete Gentleman," *SEL*, II (1962). 321-336.—*Roxana*, ed. with Introduction by Jane Jack (1964); Spiro Peterson, "The Matrimonial Theme of Defoe's *Roxana*," *PMLA*, LXX (1955). 166-191.

855 The Picaresque Tradition: Robert Alter, *Rogue's Progress: Studies in the Picaresque Novel* (Cambridge, Mass., 1964).

IV. Jonathan Swift

857 Scholarship on Swift is surveyed critically in Milton Voigt's *Swift and the Twentieth Century* (Detroit, 1964), which also contains an introductory chapter on "Nineteenth-Century Views." See also Harold Williams' essay, "Swift's Early Biographers," *Sherburn Festschrift* (Oxford, 1949), pp. 114-128. H. Teerink's *Bibliography of the Writings of Jonathan Swift* has now appeared in a second edition, revised and corrected, by Arthur H. Scouten (Philadelphia, 1963), reviewed by George P. Mayhew in *PQ*, XLIII (1964). 394-396. The Guthkelch-Nichol Smith edition of the *Tale of a Tub* has appeared in a revised edition (Oxford, 1958). Herbert Davis has edited the *Prose Works* (Oxford, 1939-1962) in 13 volumes, with an index volume to follow. A second edition of the *Poems*, ed. by Sir Harold Williams was published in 1958; in the same year the *Collected Poems*, ed. Joseph Horrell, appeared in the *Muses' Library* (2v). Other important editions: the *Journal to Stella*, ed. Harold Williams (2v, Oxford, 1948); *An Enquiry into the Behaviour of the Queen's Last Ministry*, ed. Irvin Ehrenpreis (Bloomington, Ind., 1956); *Swift's Polite Conversation*, ed. Eric Partridge (1963); and the *Correspondence*, ed. Sir Harold Williams (5v, Oxford, 1963-65).

Vol. 1 of *Swift: The Man, his Works, and the Age*, by Irvin Ehrenpreis (the standard life), was published in 1962. Among general studies may be cited: F. R. Leavis, "The Irony of Swift" in *The Common Pursuit* (1952); John M. Bullitt, *Jonathan Swift and the Anatomy of Satire* (Cambridge, Mass., 1953); Martin Price, *Swift's Rhetorical Art* (New Haven, 1953); William B. Ewald, Jr., *The Masks of Jonathan Swift* (Cambridge, Mass., 1954); Louis A. Landa, *Swift and the Church of Ireland* (Oxford, 1954); J. Middleton Murry, *Jonathan Swift* (1954); R. Quintana, *Swift: An Introduction* (1955); Irvin Ehrenpreis, *The Personality of Jonathan Swift* (1958); Kathleen Williams, *Jonathan Swift and the Age of Compromise* (Lawrence, Kans., 1958); Oliver W. Ferguson, *Jonathan Swift and Ireland* (Urbana, 1962); Edward W. Rosenheim, Jr., *Swift and the Satirist's Art* (Chicago, 1963); Herbert Davis, *Jonathan Swift: Essays on his Satire and Other Studies* [contains *Stella, The Satire of Jonathan Swift*, and shorter reprinted pieces] (1964).

859 James L. Clifford, "Swift's *Mechanical Operation of the Spirit*," *Sherburn Festschrift* (Oxford, 1949), pp. 135-146; Miriam K. Starkman, *Swift's Satire on Learning in "A Tale of a Tub"* (Princeton, 1950); Robert C. Elliott, "Swift's *Tale of a Tub*: An Essay in Problems of Structure," *PMLA*, LXVI (1951). 441-455; Harold D. Kelling, "Reason in Madness: *A Tale of a Tub*," *PMLA*, LXIX (1954). 198-222; Ronald Paulson, *Theme and Structure in Swift's "Tale of a Tub"* (New Haven, 1960); Phillip Harth, *Swift and Anglican Ra-*

tionalism: The Religious Background of "A Tale of a Tub" (Chicago, 1961); Curtis C. Smith, "Metaphor Structure in Swift's *A Tale of a Tub*," *Thoth*, v (1964). 22-41; Ricardo Quintana, "Emile Pons and the Modern Study of Swift's *Tale of a Tub*," *Études anglaises*, xviii (1965). 5-17; William J. Roscelli, "*A Tale of a Tub* and the 'Cavils of the Sour,'" *JEGP*, lxiv (1965). 41-56.

860 On the Bickerstaff pamphlets see George P. Mayhew, "The Early Life of John Partridge," *SEL*, i (1961). 31-42; Richmond P. Bond, "John Partridge and the Company of Stationers," *Stud. in Bibliography*, xvi (1963). 61-80; George P. Mayhew, "Swift's Bickerstaff Hoax as an April Fools' Joke," *MP*, lxi (1964). 270-280.

860 On Swift's pamphleteering 1708-14: J. Béranger, "Swift en 1714: position politique et sentiments personnels," *Études anglaises*, xv (1962). 233-247; and the articles by Richard I. Cook: "The 'Several Ways of Abusing One Another,'" *Speech Monographs*, xxix (1962). 260-273; "Swift as a Tory Rhetorician," *Texas Stud. in Lit. and Lang.* iv (1962). 72-86; "The Uses of *Saeva Indignatio*," *SEL*, ii (1962). 287-307; "The Audience of Swift's Tory Tracts, 1710-1714," *MLQ* xxiv (1963). 31-41; "Swift's Polemical Characters," *Discourse*, vi (1962-3). 30-38, 43-48.

861 Swift's helpers on the *Examiner*: Gwendolyn B. Needham, "Mary de la Rivière Manley: Tory Defender," *HLQ*, xii (1949). 253-288, and "Mrs. Manley: An Eighteenth-Century Wife of Bath," *HLQ*, xiv (1951). 259-284; Robert J. Allen, "William Oldisworth: 'the Author of *The Examiner*,'" *PQ*, xxvi (1947). 159-180.

862 Irvin Ehrenpreis, "Swift's 'Little Language' in the *Journal to Stella*," *SP*, xlv (1948). 80-88.

864 Among the numerous (and frequently controversial) items on *Gulliver* may be cited: Harold Williams, *The Text of "Gulliver's Travels"* (Cambridge, 1952); Paul O. Clark, "A *Gulliver* Dictionary," *SP*, l (1953). 592-624; Ellen D. Leyburn, *Satiric Allegory: Mirror of Man* (New Haven, 1956); Irvin Ehrenpreis, "The Origins of *Gulliver's Travels*," *PMLA*, lxxii (1957). 880-899; George Sherburn, "Errors concerning the Houyhnhnms," *MP*, lvi (1958). 92-97; Edward Wasiolek, "Relativity in *Gulliver's Travels*," *PQ*, xxxvii (1958). 110-116; Pierre Danchin, "The Text of *Gulliver's Travels*," *Texas Stud. in Lit. and Lang.*, ii (1960). 233-250; R. S. Crane, "The Rationale of the Fourth Voyage," in *Gulliver's Travels*, ed. Robert A. Greenberg (1961), pp. 300-307, and "The Houyhnhnms, the Yahoos, and the History of Ideas," *Nicolson Festschrift* (1962), pp. 231-253; W. B. Carnochan, "The Complexity of Swift: Gulliver's Fourth Voyage," *SP*, lx (1963). 23-44, and "*Gulliver's Travels:* An Essay on the Human Understanding?" *MLQ*, xxv (1964). 5-21; E. Pons, "Gulliver ou l'Utopie-Bouffe: les 'Voyages travestis' d'un philosophe du moi," *Carré Festschrift* (Paris, 1964), pp. 429-439.

866 On the poems: Herbert Davis, "A Modest Defence of 'The Lady's Dressing Room,'" *McKillop Festschrift* (Chicago, 1963), pp. 39-48; Barry Slepian, "The Ironic Intention of Swift's Verses on his own Death," *RES*, n.s. xiv (1963). 249-256; Marshall Waingrow, "*Verses on the Death of Dr. Swift*," *SEL*, v (1965). 513-518.

867 On Vanessa: Sybil Le Brocquy, *Cadenus: A Reassessment in the Light* *of New Evidence of the Relationships between Swift, Stella and Vanessa* (Dublin, 1963), on which see the review by E. Pons in *Études anglaises*, xvi (1963). 187-188; Peter Ohlin, " 'Cadenus and Vanessa': Reason and Passion," *SEL*, iv (1964). 485-496.

V. Addison, Steele, and the Periodical Essay

870 On the Periodical Essay see Melvin R. Watson, *Magazine Serials and the Essay Tradition, 1746-1820* (Baton Rouge, 1956), and Richmond P. Bond, Introduction to *Studies in the Early English Periodical* (Chapel Hill, 1957). The last-named contains six essays on eighteenth-century periodicals: Robert W. Achurch, "Richard Steele, Gazeteer and Bickerstaff"; William F. Belcher, "The Sale and Distribution of the *British Apollo*"; Nicholas Joost, "The Authorship of the *Free Thinker*"; W. O. S. Sutherland, Jr., "Essay Forms in the *Prompter*"; James Hodges, "The *Female Spectator*, a Courtesy Periodical"; and George P. Winship, Jr., "The Printing History of the *World.*"

871 Rae Blanchard has ably edited *The Occasional Verse of Richard Steele* (Oxford, 1952) as well as *The Englishman: A Political Journal* (Oxford, 1955) and *Richard Steele's Periodical Journalism, 1714-16: The Lover, The Reader, Town-Talk* (Oxford, 1959). *The Theatre, 1720*, has been edited by John Loftis (Oxford, 1962). For *The Spectator* see below, suppl. to p. 875. On Steele see also: John Loftis, *Steele at Drury Lane* (Berkeley, 1952); Rae Blanchard, "Richard Steele and the Secretary of the S.P.C.K.," *McKillop Festschrift* (Chicago, 1963), pp. 287-295; Calhoun Winton, *Captain Steele: The Early Career of Richard Steele* (Baltimore, 1964).

872 Robert D. Horn, "Addison's *Campaign* and Macaulay" *PMLA, LXIII* (1948). 886-902, and "The Early Editions of Addison's *Campaign*," *Stud. in Bibliography*, iii (1950/1). 256-261; Lillian D. Bloom, "Addison as Translator," *SP*, xlvi (1949). 31-53; Edward A. and Lillian D. Bloom, "Addison's 'Enquiry after Truth,' " *PMLA*, lxv (1950). 198-220; J. Lannering, *Studies in the Prose Style of Joseph Addison* (Uppsala, 1951); Peter Smithers, *The Life of Joseph Addison* (Oxford, 1954); Edward A. and Lillian D. Bloom, "Addison on 'Moral Habits of the Mind,' " *JHI*, xxi (1960), 409-427; Jean Wilkinson, "Some Aspects of Addison's Philosophy of Art," *HLQ*, xxviii (1964). 31-44; John C. Stephens, Jr., "Addison as Social Critic," *Emory Univ. Quar.* xxi (1965). 157-172.

873 William B. Todd, "Early Editions of The Tatler," *Stud. in Bibliography*, xv (1962). 121-133; Donald F. Bond, "Armand de la Chapelle and the First French Version of the *Tatler*," *McKillop Festschrift* (Chicago, 1963), pp. 161-184; Richmond P. Bond, "Isaac Bickerstaff, Esq.," *Ibid.*, pp. 103-124, and "The Pirate and the *Tatler*," *Library*, xviii (1963). 257-274. On the *Tatler* and *Spectator* Fritz Rau has two important articles: "Texte, Ausgaben und Verfasser des 'Tatler,' und 'Spectator': Forschungsbericht," *Germanisch-Romanische Monatsschrift*, viii (1958). 126-144, and "Zur Gestalt des 'Tatler' und 'Spectator': Kritischer Bericht," *Ibid.*, x (1960). 401-419.

875 *The Spectator*, ed. Donald F. Bond (5v, Oxford, 1965). See also Robert D. Chambers, "Addison at Work on the *Spectator*," *MP*, lvi (1959). 145-153.

879 On continuators and imitators of the *Tatler* see Robert C. Elliott, "Swift's 'little' Harrison, Poet and Continuator of the *Tatler*," *SP*, XLIV (1949). 544-559; John Harrington Smith, "Thomas Baker and the *Female Tatler*," *MP*, XLIX (1952). 182-188.

881 *The True Patriot* of Fielding: Facsimile Text, ed. Miriam A. Locke (University, Ala., 1964).—*The Champion*: The 13 "Job Vinegar" essays comprise No. 67 of the *ARS*, with Introduction by S. J. Sackett (1958). See also William B. Coley, "The 'Remarkable Queries' in the *Champion*," *PQ*, XLI (1962). 426-436; John B. Shipley, "A New Fielding Essay from the *Champion*," *PQ*, XLII (1963). 417-422; "Henry Fielding's 'Defense of the Stage Licensing Act," *ELN*, II (1965). 193-96.

VI. The Drama, 1700-1740

883 Parts 2 and 3 of *The London Stage* (see above, suppl. to p. 748) are of first importance here: Part 2, *1700-1729*, ed. Emmett L. Avery (2v, 1960); Part 3, *1729-1747*, ed. A. H. Scouten (2v, 1961). See further Charles B. Hogan, *Shakespeare in the Theatre, 1701-1800: A Record of Performances in London* (2v, Oxford, 1952-57); Richard Southern, *Changeable Scenery: Its Origin and Development in the British Theatre* (1952); F. S. Boas, *An Introduction to Eighteenth-Century Drama, 1700-1780* (Oxford, 1953); James J. Lynch, *Box, Pit, and Gallery: Stage and Society in Johnson's London* (Berkeley, 1953); George Speaight, *The History of the English Puppet Theatre* (1955); George C. Branam, *Eighteenth-Century Adaptations of Shakespearean Tragedy* (Berkeley, 1956); Leo Hughes, *A Century of English Farce* (Princeton, 1956); John Loftis, *Comedy and Society from Congreve to Fielding* (Stanford, 1959), and *The Politics of Drama in Augustan England* (Oxford, 1963); William S. Clark, *The Irish Stage in the County Towns, 1720-1800* (Oxford, 1965).

884 On Sentimental Comedy (and Tragedy) see Lewis M. Magill, "Poetic Justice: The Dilemma of the Early Creators of Sentimental Tragedy," *Research Stud. of the State College of Washington*, XXV (1957). 24-32; Arthur Sherbo, *English Sentimental Drama* (East Lansing, Mich., 1957); Richard H. Tyre, "Versions of Poetic Justice in the Early Eighteenth Century," *SP*, LIV (1957). 29-44; Paul E. Parnell, "The Sentimental Mask," *PMLA*, LXXVIII (1963). 529-535.

885 Paul E. Parnell, "Equivocation in Cibber's *Love's Last Shift*," *SP*, LVII (1960). 519-534; Albert E. Karlson, "The Chronicles in Cibber's *Richard III*," *SEL*, III (1963). 253-267. Leonard R. N. Ashley, *Colley Cibber* (1965).

886 Rae Blanchard, "The Songs in Steele's Plays," *Sherburn Festschrift* (Oxford, 1949), pp. 185-200.

889 Mrs. Centlivre: John W. Bowyer, *The Celebrated Mrs. Centlivre* (Durham, N.C., 1952); J. E. Norton, "Some Uncollected Authors. XIV: Susanna Centlivre," *Book-Collector*, VI (1957). 172-178, 280-285.—Fielding's Plays: L. P. Goggin, "Development of Techniques in Fielding's Comedies," *PMLA*, LXVII (1952). 769-781, and "Fielding and the *Select Comedies of Mr. de Moliere*," *PQ*, XXXI (1952). 344-350; Sheridan Baker, "Political Allusion in Fielding's *Author's Farce, Mock Doctor*, and *Tumble-Down Dick*," *PMLA*, LXXVII (1962).

221-231; Edgar V. Roberts, "Henry Fielding's Lost Play *Deborah, or A Wife for You All* (1733)," *Bull. N.Y. Public Library*, LXVI (1962). 576-588; and articles by Charles B. Woods: "The 'Miss Lucy' Plays of Fielding and Garrick," *PQ*, XLI (1962). 294-310; "Cibber in Fielding's *Author's Farce*," *PQ*, XLIV (1965). 145-151; "Theobald and Fielding's 'Don Tragedio,'" *ELN*, II (1965). 266-271.

891 Edgar V. Roberts, "Fielding's Ballad Opera *The Lottery* (1732) and the English State Lottery of 1731," *HLQ*, XXVII (1963). 39-52.

893 Alfred Schwarz, "An Example of Eighteenth-Century Pathetic Tragedy: Rowe's *Jane Shore*," *MLQ*, XXII (1961). 236-247; Lindley A. Wyman, "The Tradition of the Formal Meditation in Rowe's *The Fair Penitent*," *PQ*, XLII (1963). 412-416.

894 Paul E. Parnell, "*The Distrest Mother,* Ambrose Philips' Morality Play," *CL*, XI (1959). 111-123.

895 John Robert Moore, "Hughes's Source for *The Siege of Damascus*," *HLQ*, XXI (1958). 362-366.

896 *Le Marchand de Londres:* Edition critique, traduction, préface et notes de J. Hamard (Paris, 1962); *The London Merchant*, ed. W. H. McBurney (Lincoln, Nebr., 1965). Lawrence M. Price, "George Barnwell Abroad," *CL*, II (1950). 126-156.

VII. Traditions in Early Eighteenth-Century Poetry

898 James Sutherland, *A Preface to Eighteenth-Century Poetry* (Oxford, 1948), the best general treatment of the subject; Bonamy Dobrée, *The Theme of Patriotism in the Poetry of the Early Eighteenth Century* (1949); Donald J. Greene, "'Logical Structure' in Eighteenth-Century Poetry," *PQ*, XXXI (1952). 315-336; Norman Maclean, "From Action to Image: Theories of the Lyric in the Eighteenth Century," *Critics and Criticism* (Chicago, 1952), pp. 408-460; W. K. Wimsatt, Jr., "The Augustan Mode in English Poetry," *ELH*, XX (1953). 1-14; Geoffrey Tillotson, *Augustan Poetic Diction* (1964) (four chapters, reprinted with corrections from Tillotson's *Augustan Studies*, 1961).

899 Satire: Ian Jack, *Augustan Satire: Intention and Idiom in English Poetry, 1660-1750* (Oxford, 1952); Bertrand A. Goldgar, "Satires on Man and 'The Dignity of Human Nature,'" *PMLA*, LXXX (1965). 535-541; Alvin B. Kernan, *The Plot of Satire* (New Haven, 1965) discusses Dryden, Gay, Swift, and Pope; Howard D. Weinbrot, "The Pattern of Formal Verse Satire in the Restoration and the Eighteenth Century," *PMLA*, LXXX (1965). 394-401.—Blackmore: Richard C. Boys, *Sir Richard Blackmore and the Wits* (Ann Arbor, 1949); Albert Rosenberg, *Sir Richard Blackmore* (Lincoln, Nebr., 1953); W. J. Cameron, "The Authorship of 'Commendatory Verses,' 1700," *N&Q*, CCVIII (1963). 63-66.

900 Pastoral: Thomas Purney's *Full Enquiry into the True Nature of Pastoral* (1717), with Introduction by Earl R. Wasserman (1948; *ARS*, No. 11). See also J. E. Congleton, *Theories of Pastoral Poetry in England, 1684-1798* (Gainesville, Fla., 1952) and review of this by L. P. Goggin in *MP*, LI (1953). 137-140; Dorothy S. McCoy, *Tradition and Convention: A Study of Periphrasis in English Pastoral Poetry from 1557-1715* (The Hague, 1965).

901 Aaron Hill's Preface to *The Creation* has been reproduced by the *ARS* (No. 18), with an Introduction by Gretchen Graf Pahl (1949).

902 On Ramsay's possible share in the *Collection of Old Ballads* see Albert B. Friedman, *The Ballad Revival* (Chicago, 1961), chap. v. Ramsay's *Works* have been edited: Vols. I, II, ed. Burns Martin and John W. Oliver (Edinburgh, 1951-3); Vol. III (*Poems: Miscellaneous and Uncollected*), ed. Alexander Kinghorn and Alexander Law (Edinburgh, 1963).

904 Harry Escott, *Isaac Watts, Hymnographer: A Study of the Beginnings, Development, and Philosophy of the English Hymn* (1962); Peter B. Steese, "Dennis's Influence on Watts's Preface to *Horae Lyricae*," *PQ*, XLII (1963). 275-277.

908 W. J. Cameron, "Two New Poems by Ambrose Philips (1674-1749)," *N&Q*, CCII (1957), 469-470.—Welsted: Daniel A. Fineman, *Leonard Welsted, Gentleman Poet of the Augustan Age* (Philadelphia, 1950).—Prior: *The Literary Works of Matthew Prior*, ed. H. Bunker Wright and Monroe K. Spears (2v, Oxford, 1959); cf. review by Maynard Mack in *Sewanee Rev.*, LXVIII (1960). 165-176. See also the articles by Spears: "Matthew Prior's Attitude toward Natural Science," *PMLA*, LXIII (1948), 485-507; "Matthew Prior's Religion," *PQ*, XXVII (1948). 159-180; "Some Ethical Aspects of Matthew Prior's Poetry," *SP*, XLV (1948), 606-629.

914 Additional Poet: William Diaper. *The Complete Works of William Diaper*, ed. Dorothy Broughton (1951).

VIII. Pope and His Group

916 Phyllis Freeman, "William Walsh and Dryden: Recently Discovered Letters," *RES*, XXIV (1948). 195-202, and "Two Fragments of Walsh Manuscripts," *RES*, n.s. VIII (1957). 390-401.

917 *Memoirs of the Extraordinary Life, Works, and Discoveries of Martinus Scriblerus*, ed. Charles Kerby-Miller (New Haven, 1950); Robert A. Erickson, "Situations of Identity in the *Memoirs of Martinus Scriblerus*," *MLQ*, XXVI (1965). 388-400.

918 Gay: *The Present State of Wit* (1711) was reproduced as No. 7 of the *ARS*, with Introduction by Donald F. Bond (1947). Two editions of *Three Hours after Marriage* (by Gay, Pope, and Arbuthnot) were published in 1961, one by Richard Morton and William M. Peterson (Painesville, Ohio) and the other by John Harrington Smith (*ARS*, Nos. 91-92). Both are reviewed by Curt A. Zimansky in *PQ*, XLI (1962). 593-595. See also James Sutherland, "John Gay," *Sherburn Festschrift* (Oxford, 1949), pp. 201-214; Sven M. Armens, *John Gay, Social Critic* (1954); John M. Aden, "The 1720 Version of *Rural Sports* and the Georgic Tradition," *MLQ*, XX (1959). 228-232; William D. Ellis, Jr., "Thomas D'Urfey, the Pope-Philips Quarrel, and *The Shepherd's Week*," *PMLA*, LXXIV (1959). 203-212; John Fuller, "Cibber, *The Rehearsal at Goatham*, and the Suppression of *Polly*," *RES*, n.s. XIII (1962). 125-134; C. F. Burgess,

"The Ambivalent Point of View in John Gay's *Trivia*," *Cithara*, IV (1964). 53-65; Adina Forsgren, *John Gay, Poet "of a Lower Order": Comments on his Rural Poems and Other Early Writings* (Stockholm, 1964), and "Some Complimentary Epistles by John Gay," *Studia Neophil.* XXXVI (1964). 82-100; Bertrand H. Bronson, "The True Proportions of Gay's *Acis and Galatea*," *PMLA*, LXXX (1965). 325-331; Patricia M. Spacks, *John Gay* (1965).

921 The Twickenham edition (6v in 7, Oxford, 1939-61) is now complete, except for the translations of Homer which are to be added. Some of the volumes have appeared in revised editions, and there is a one volume edition of the Twickenham text with selected annotations ed. by John Butt (1963). Another major edition is the *Correspondence*, ed. George Sherburn (5v, Oxford, 1956): reviews by Donald F. Bond in *MP*, LVI (1958). 55-59; by John Butt in *N&Q*, CCII (1957). 463-466; by Maynard Mack in *PQ*, XXXVI (1957). 389-399; by Robert W. Rogers in *JEGP*, LVI (1957). 615-619. Additional letters, chiefly to Sir William Trumbull, were published by Sherburn in *RES*, n.s. IX (1958). 388-406. A critical edition by Edna L. Steeves of *The Art of Sinking in Poetry* appeared in 1952. For criticism see Norman Ault, *New Light on Pope* (1949), with review by George Sherburn in *RES*, n.s. II (1951). 84-86; Maynard Mack, "'Wit and Poetry and 'Pope': Some Observations on his Imagery," *Sherburn Festschrift* (Oxford, 1949), pp. 20-40; "'The Shadowy Cave': Some Speculations on a Twickenham Grotto," *McKillop Festschrift* (Chicago, 1963), pp. 69-88; "A Poet in his Landscape: Pope at Twickenham," *Pottle Festschrift* (1965). pp. 3-29; and "*Secretum Iter*: Some Uses of Retirement Literature in the Poetry of Pope," in *Aspects of the Eighteenth Century*, ed. Earl R. Wasserman (Baltimore, 1965), pp. 207-243; Agnes M. Sibley, *Alexander Pope's Prestige in America, 1725-1835* (1949); George Sherburn, "Pope and 'the Great Shew of Nature'," *Jones Festschrift* (Stanford, 1951), pp. 306-315; John Butt, "Pope's Poetical Manuscripts," *Proc. Brit. Acad.* XL (1954). 23-39; Rebecca P. Parkin, *The Poetic Workmanship of Alexander Pope* (Minneapolis, 1955); Robert W. Rogers, *The Major Satires of Alexander Pope* (Urbana, 1955); Malcolm Goldstein, *Pope and the Augustan Stage* (Stanford, 1958); Goeffrey Tillotson, *Pope and Human Nature* (Oxford, 1958); Reuben A. Brower, *Alexander Pope: The Poetry of Allusion* (Oxford, 1959); Benjamin Boyce, *The Character Sketches in Pope's Poems* (Durham, N.C., 1962) and "Mr. Pope, in Bath, Improves the Design of his Grotto," *McKillop Festschrift* (Chicago, 1963), pp. 143-153; Thomas R. Edwards, Jr., *This Dark Estate: A Reading of Pope* (Berkeley, 1963); Jacob H. Adler, *The Reach of Art: A Study in the Prosody of Pope* (Gainesville, Fla., 1964); Peter Dixon, "'Talking upon Paper': Pope and Eighteenth Century Conversation," *ES*, XLVI (1965). 36-44; Donald J. Greene, "'Dramatic Texture' in Pope," *Pottle Festschrift* (1965), pp. 31-53; W. K. Wimsatt, Jr., *The Portraits of Alexander Pope* (New Haven, 1965).

922 Robert M. Schmitz, *Pope's "Windsor Forest," 1712: A Study of the Washington University Holograph* (St. Louis, 1952); Earl R. Wasserman, *The Subtler Language* (1959), chap. IV.

923 Aubrey Williams, "The 'Fall' of China and *The Rape of the Lock*," *PQ*, XLI (1962). 412-425; L. P. Goggin, "La Caverne aux Vapeurs," *PQ*, XLII (1963). 404-411.

924 Douglas Knight, *Pope and the Heroic Tradition: A Critical Study of his "Iliad"* (New Haven, 1951); Norman Callan, "Pope's *Iliad:* A New Document," *RES,* n.s. IV (1953). 109-121 [the proof-sheets of Books I-VIII, with Pope's corrections]; R. Sühnel, *Homer und die englische Humanität* (Tübingen, 1958); R. M. Schmitz, "The 'Arsenal' Proof Sheets of Pope's Iliad: A Third Report," *MLN,* LXXIV (1959). 486-489.

925 Theobald's Preface to Shakespeare forms No. 20 of the *ARS,* with an Introduction by Hugh G. Dick (1949). See also P. Dixon, "Pope's Shakespeare," *JEGP,* LXIII (1964). 191-203.

926 Aubrey L. Williams, *Pope's "Dunciad": A Study of its Meaning* (1955); Charles D. Peavy, "The Pope-Cibber Controversy: A Bibliography," *Restoration and 18th Century Theatre Research,* III (1964). 51-55.
On the "Moral Essays" see H. C. Collins Baker and Muriel I. Baker, *The Life and Circumstances of James Brydges, First Duke of Chandos* (Oxford, 1949); Earl R. Wasserman, *Pope's "Epistle to Bathurst": A Critical Reading with an Edition of the Manuscripts* (Baltimore, 1960).

928 *An Essay on Man: Reproduction of the Manuscripts in the Pierpont Morgan Library and the Houghton Library, with the Printed Text of the Original Edition,* with Introduction by Maynard Mack (1962; *Roxburgh Club*); Robert W. Rogers, "Critiques of the 'Essay on Man' in France and Germany, 1736-1755," *ELH,* XV (1948). 176-193, and "Alexander Pope's *Universal Prayer,*" *JEGP,* LIV (1955). 612-624; Ernest Tuveson, "*An Essay on Man* and 'The Way of Ideas,'" *ELH,* XXVI (1959). 368-386; F. E. L. Priestley, "Pope and the Great Chain of Being," *Woodhouse Festschrift* (Toronto, 1964), pp. 213-228.

929 Maynard Mack, "The Muse of Satire," *Yale Rev.,* XLI (1951). 80-92 (repr. in *Studies in the Literature of the Augustan Age,* ed. R. C. Boys [1952]); Aubrey L. Williams, "Pope and Horace: The Second Epistle of the Second Book," *McKillop Festschrift* (Chicago, 1963), pp. 309-321; Thomas E. Maresca, "Pope's Defense of Satire: The First Satire of the Second Book of Horace, Imitated," *ELH,* XXXI (1964). 336-394.

930 *The Nonsense of Common-Sense, 1737-1738,* ed. Robert Halsband (Evanston, 1947). See also Robert Halsband, *The Life of Lady Mary Wortley Montagu* (Oxford, 1956) and "Lady Mary Wortley Montagu as Letter Writer," *PLMA,* LXXX (1965). 155-163. Professor Halsband is editing Lady Mary's correspondence. (Vol. I, covering the years 1708-1720, has appeared [Oxford, 1965]).

IX. New Voices in Poetry

933 John Arthos, *The Language of Natural Description in Eighteenth-Century Poetry* (Ann Arbor, 1949); Bertrand Bronson, "The Pre-Romantic or Post-Augustan Mode [in English Poetry]," *ELH,* XX (1953). 15-28; Chester F. Chapin, *Personification in Eighteenth-Century English Poetry* (1955); Marjorie H. Nicolson, *Mountain Gloom and Mountain Glory: The Development of the Aesthetics of the Infinite* (Ithaca, N.Y., 1959); Patricia M. Spacks, *The Insistence of Horror: Aspects of the Supernatural in Eighteenth-Century Poetry*

(Cambridge, Mass., 1962); Geoffrey Tillotson, "The Methods of Description in Eighteenth- and Nineteenth-Century Poetry," *McKillop Festschrift* (Chicago, 1963), pp. 235-238; Karl Heinz Göller, "Die *Poetic Diction* des 18. Jahrhunderts in England," *Deutsche Viertelpahrsschrift für Literaturwissenschaft und Geistesgeschichte*, xxxviii (1964). 24-39.

934 *The Poetical Works of Richard Savage,* ed. Clarence Tracy (Cambridge, 1962). Professor Tracy is also author of the standard life of Savage (*The Artificial Bastard*, Toronto and Cambridge, Mass., 1953) and an article on the bibliography of Savage (*Book-Collector*, xii [1963]. 340-349). *An Author to be Lett* (1729) is reprinted with Introduction by James Sutherland by the *ARS*, No. 84 (1960).

935 *James Thomson (1700-1748): Letters and Documents,* ed. Alan D. McKillop (Lawrence, Kans., 1958); see also McKillop, "Two More Thomson Letters," *MP*, lx (1962). 128-130. The best general study is Douglas Grant's *James Thomson: Poet of "The Seasons"* (1951).

936 Patricia M. Spacks, *The Varied God: A Critical Study of Thomson's "The Seasons"* (Berkeley, 1959); Ralph Cohen, "Literary Criticism and Artistic Interpretation: Eighteenth-Century English Illustrations of *The Seasons*," *Nicolson Festschrift* (1962), pp. 279-306; John Chalker, "Thomson's *Seasons* and Virgil's *Georgics*," *Studia Neophil.* xxxv (1963). 41-56; Ralph Cohen, *The Art of Discrimination: Thomson's "The Seasons" and the Language of Criticism* (Berkeley, 1964).

938 F. E. L. Priestley, "Newton and the Romantic Concept of Nature," *UTQ*, xvii (1948). 323-336; William Powell Jones, "Newton Further Demands the Muse," *SEL*, iii (1963). 287-306 [stresses the *Principia* rather than the *Opticks*].

939 Alan D. McKillop, *The Background of Thomson's "Liberty"* (Houston, 1951).

940 *The Castle of Indolence and Other Poems,* ed. Alan D. McKillop (Lawrence, Kans., 1961). See also William B. Todd, "The Text of *The Castle of Indolence*," *ES*, xxxiv (1953). 115-121.

942 Ralph M. Williams, *Poet, Painter, and Parson: The Life of John Dyer* (1956).

945 Henry Pettit, "A Check-List of Young's 'Night-Thoughts' in America," *Papers of the Bibl. Soc. of America*, xlii (1948). 150-156 (additions in xliii. 348-349, and xliv. 192-195). Professor Pettit is also author of *A Bibliography of Young's Night-Thoughts* (Boulder, Col., 1954), *The English Rejection of Young's "Night-Thoughts"* (Boulder, 1957), "Edward Young and the Case of Lee v. D'Aranda," *Proc. Amer. Philos. Soc.*, cvii (1963). 145-159, and has in preparation an edition of Young's correspondence. See further C. V. Wicker, *Edward Young and the Fear of Death: A Study in Romantic Melancholy* (Albuquerque, 1952); Catharine K. Firman, "An Unrecorded Poem by Edward Young," *N&Q*, ccviii (1963). 218-219; H. B. Forester, "The Ordination of Edward Young," *ELN*, i (1963). 24-28.

947 Allan D. McKillop, "Nature and Science in the Works of James Hervey," *Univ. of Texas Stud. in English*, xxviii (1949). 124-138.

X. The Mid-Century Novel

950 On the eighteenth-century novel two important surveys have appeared: Alan D. McKillop, *The Early Masters of English Fiction* (Lawrence, Kans., 1956) and Ian Watt, *The Rise of the Novel: Studies in Defoe, Richardson, and Fielding* (Berkeley, 1957). William H. McBurney has published *A Check List of English Prose Fiction, 1700-1739* (Cambridge, Mass., 1960) (additions and corrections by Donald F. Bond in *MP*, LIX (1962). 231-234) and (with assistance of Charlene M. Taylor) a check-list of *English Prose Fiction 1700-1800 in the University of Illinois Library* (Urbana, 1965). He has also edited *Four Before Richardson: Selected English Novels, 1720-1727* (Lincoln, Nebr., 1963), including Mrs. Haywood's *Philidore and Placentia* and Mary Davies' *Accomplished Rake*. See also Robert D. Mayo, *The English Novel in the Magazines, 1740-1815, with a Catalogue of 1375 Magazine Novels and Novelettes* (Evanston, 1962); Sheridan Baker, "The Idea of Romance in the Eighteenth-Century Novel," *Papers of the Michigan Acad.* XLIX (1964). 507-522; Robert B. Pierce, "Moral Education in the Novel of the 1750's," *PQ*, XLIV (1965). 73-87.

951 William H. McBurney, "Mrs. Penelope Aubin and the Early Eighteenth-Century English Novel," *HLQ*, XX (1957). 245-267, and "Edmund Curll, Mrs. Jane Barker, and the English Novel," *PQ*, XXXVII (1958). 385-399.

952 *Selected Letters of Samuel Richardson*, ed. John Carroll (Oxford, 1964). A complete edition of the correspondence is in preparation by T. C. D. Eaves and Ben Kimpel. On Richardson: William M. Sale, Jr., "From *Pamela* to *Clarissa*," *Tinker Festschrift* (New Haven, 1949), pp. 127-138; Frank Kermode, "Richardson and Fielding," *Cambridge Jour.*, IV (1950). 106-114; William M. Sale, Jr., *Samuel Richardson, Master Printer* (Ithaca, N.Y., 1950) (cf. review by A. D. McKillop in *PQ*, XXX (1951). 285-287); T. C. Duncan Eaves, "Graphic Illustrations of the Novels of Samuel Richardson," *HLQ*, XIV (1951). 349-383; Alan D. McKillop, "Epistolary Technique in Richardson's Novels," *Rice Institute Pamphlet*, XXXVIII (1951). 36-54; George Sherburn, "Samuel Richardson's Novels and the Theatre: A Theory Sketched," *PQ*, XLI (1962). 325-329, and "Writing to the Moment: One Aspect," *McKillop Festschrift* (Chicago, 1963), pp. 201-209; John Carroll, "Richardson on Pope and Swift," *UTQ*, XXXIII (1963). 19-29; Morris Golden, *Richardson's Characters* (Ann Arbor, 1963); Leo Hughes, "Theatrical Convention in Richardson: Some Observations on a Novelist's Technique," *McKillop Festschrift* (Chicago, 1963), pp. 239-250.

953 *Pamela:* Richardson's Introduction, omitted in most recent editions, is reproduced as No. 48 of the *ARS*, with Introduction by Sheridan W. Baker, Jr. (1954). See also Robert A. Donovan, "The Problem of Pamela, or, Virtue Unrewarded," *SEL*, III (1963). 377-395; Owen Jenkins, "Richardson's *Pamela* and Fielding's 'Vile Forgeries,'" *PQ*, XLIV (1965). 200-210 [on the second part of *Pamela* as a reply to *Shamela*].

954 *Clarissa, or the History of a Young Lady*, abridged and ed. with an Introduction by George Sherburn (Boston, 1962). Richardson's Preface, "Hints of Prefaces for Clarissa," and Postscript, comprise No. 103 of the *ARS*, with an

Introduction by R. F. Brissenden (1964). See also *Critical Remarks on Sir Charles Grandison, Clarissa and Pamela* (1754) [by Alexander Campbell?], with an Introduction by A. D. McKillop (1950; *ARS*, No. 21); Norman Rabkin, "*Clarissa*: A Study in the Nature of Convention," *ELH*, XXIII (1956). 204-217; William J. Farrell, "The Style and the Action in *Clarissa*," *SEL*, III (1963). 365-375; Christina Van Heyningen, *Clarissa: Poetry and Morals* (Pietermaritzburg, 1963; Mystic, Conn., 1965).

955   E. L. McAdam, Jr., "A New Letter from Fielding," *Yale Rev.*, XXXVIII (1948). 300-310 [to Richardson, on *Clarissa*]; James A. Work, "Henry Fielding, Christian Censor," *Tinker Festschrift* (New Haven, 1949), pp. 139-148; F. Homes Dudden, *Henry Fielding: His Life, Works, and Times* (2v, Oxford, 1952) (rev. by George Sherburn in *Sewanee Rev.*, LXI (1953). 316-321); A. B. Shepperson, "Additions and Corrections to Facts about Fielding," *MP*, LI (1954). 217-224; George Sherburn, "Fielding's Social Outlook," *PQ*, XXXV (1956). 1-23; Maurice Johnson, *Fielding's Art of Fiction* (Philadelphia, 1961); Dietrich Rolle, *Fielding und Sterne: Untersuchungen über die Funktion des Erzählers* (Münster, 1963); Sheldon Sacks, *Fiction and the Shape of Belief: A Study of Henry Fielding, with Glances at Swift, Johnson and Richardson* (Berkeley, 1964); Philip Stevick, "Fielding and the Meaning of History," *PMLA*, LXXIX (1964). 561-568; W. B. Coley, "Fielding's Two Appointments to the Magistracy," *MP*, LXIII (1965). 144-149; Andrew Wright, *Henry Fielding: Mask and Feast* (Berkeley, 1965).

956   *An Apology for the Life of Mrs. Shamela Andrews* has had two recent editions: by Sheridan W. Baker, Jr. (Berkeley, 1953) and by Ian Watt (1956; *ARS*, No. 57).

On *Joseph Andrews* see Martin C. Battestin's *The Moral Basis of Fielding's Art: A Study of "Joseph Andrews"* (Middletown, Conn., 1959) and the same author's articles: "Fielding's Changing Politics and *Joseph Andrews*," *PQ*, XXXIX (1960). 39-55; "Fielding's Revisions of *Joseph Andrews*," *Stud. in Bibliography*, XVI (1963). 81-117; "Lord Hervey's Role in *Joseph Andrews*," *PQ*, XLII (1963). 226-241. See further Homer Goldberg, "Comic Prose Epic or Comic Romance: The Argument of the Preface to *Joseph Andrews*," *PQ*, XLIII (1964). 193-215; J. T. McCullen, "Fielding's Beau Didapper," *ELN*, II (1964). 98-100; Bernard N. Schilling, *The Comic Spirit* (Detroit, 1965) contains two essays on *Joseph Andrews*.

On the *Miscellanies* and *Jonathan Wild*: Bernard Shea, "Machiavelli and Fielding's *Jonathan Wild*," *PMLA*, LXII (1957). 55-73 (cf. review by R. S. Crane in *PQ*, XXXVII (1958). 328-333); Allan Wendt, "The Moral Allegory of *Jonathan Wild*," *ELH*, XXIV (1957). 306-320; Henry Knight Miller, *Essays on Fielding's "Miscellanies": A Commentary on Volume One* (Princeton, 1961); Donald D. Eddy, "The Printing of Fielding's *Miscellanies* (1743)," *Stud. in Bibliography*, XV (1962). 247-256.

On *Tom Jones*: R. S. Crane, "The Plot of *Tom Jones*," *Jour. of General Education*, IV (1950). 112-130 (repr. as "The Concept of Plot and the Plot of *Tom Jones*" in *Critics and Criticism* (Chicago, 1952), pp. 616-647); William Empson, "*Tom Jones*," *Kenyon Rev.*, XX (1958). 217-249; Alan D. McKillop, "Some Recent Views of *Tom Jones*," *College English*, XXI (1959). 17-22; Lyall H. Powers, "*Tom Jones* and Jacob de la Vallée [Marivaux, *Le Paysan parvenu*],"

Papers of the Michigan Acad., XLVII (1962). 659-697; Michael Bliss, "Fielding's Bill of Fare in *Tom Jones,"* ELH, XXX (1963). 236-243; I. Ehrenpreis, *Fielding: "Tom Jones"* (1964); Oliver W. Ferguson, "Partridge's Vile Encomium: Fielding and Honest Billy Mills," *PQ,* XLIII (1964). 73-78; Eleanor N. Hutchens, *Irony in Tom Jones* (University, Ala., 1965).

959 A. R. Towers, *"Amelia* and the State of Matrimony," *RES,* n.s. v (1954). 144-157; John S. Coolidge, "Fielding and 'Conservation of Character,' " *MP,* LVII (1960). 245-259; Arthur Sherbo, "The Time-Scheme in *Amelia,"* *Boston Univ. Stud. in English,* IV (1960). 223-228; Allan Wendt, "The Naked Virtue of Amelia," *ELH,* XXVII (1960). 131-148; E. D. H. Johnson, *"Vanity Fair* and *Amelia,"* *MP,* LIX (1961). 100-113; Sheridan Baker, "Fielding's *Amelia* and the Materials of Romance," *PQ,* XLI (1962). 437-449; D. S. Thomas, "The Publication of Henry Fielding's *Amelia,"* *Library,* XVIII (1963). 303-307, and "Fortune and the Passions in Fielding's *Amelia,"* *MLR,* LX (1965). 176-187.

960 *The Journal of a Voyage to Lisbon,* ed. Harold E. Pagliaro (1963).

961 Fred W. Boege, *Smollett's Reputation as a Novelist* (Princeton, 1947); Lewis M. Knapp, *Tobias Smollett: Doctor of Men and Manners* (Princeton, 1949), the standard life; Carmine R. Linsalata, *Smollett's Hoax: "Don Quixote" in English* (Stanford, 1956); cf. review by Lewis M. Knapp in *JEGP,* LVII (1958). 553-555; M. A. Goldberg, *Smollett and the Scottish School* (Albuquerque, 1959); Ronald Paulson, "Satire in the Early Novels of Smollett," *JEGP,* LIX (1960). 381-402; C. Aubrun, "Smollet et Cervantès," *Études anglaises,* XV (1962). 122-129; William B. Piper, "The Large Diffused Picture of Life in Smollett's Early Novels," *SP,* LX (1963). 45-56; Donald Bruce, *Radical Doctor Smollett* (1964); Lewis M. Knapp, "Smollett's Translation of Fénelon's *Télémaque,"* *PQ,* XLIV (1965). 405-407.

962 *Peregrine Pickle,* ed. James L. Clifford (1964). See also Ronald Paulson, "Smollett and Hogarth: The Identity of Pallet," *SEL,* IV (1964). 351-359.

963 James R. Foster, "Smollett and the *Atom,"* *PMLA,* LXVIII (1953). 1032-1046; Lewis M. Knapp, "The Keys to Smollett's *Atom,"* *ELN,* II (1964). 100-102. —Sheridan Baker, *"Humphry Clinker* as Comic Romance," *Papers of the Michigan Acad.,* XLVI (1961). 645-654; Byron Gassman, "The *Briton* and *Humphry Clinker,"* *SEL,* III (1963). 397-414; Thomas R. Preston, "Smollett and the Benevolent Misanthrope Type," *PMLA,* LXXIX (1964). 51-57.

Part III: The Disintegration of Classicism

I. Accentuated Tendencies

967 E. S. de Beer, "Gothic: Origin and Diffusion of the Term; the Idea of Style in Architecture," *Jour. Warburg and Courtauld Inst.,* XI (1948). 142-162; A. O. Aldridge, "The Pleasures of Pity," *ELH,* XVI (1949). 76-87; René Wellek, "The Concept of 'Romanticism' in Literary History," *CL,* I (1949). 1-23, 147-172 [cf. review by R. S. Crane in *PQ,* XXIX (1950). 257-259]; Erik Erämetsä, *A Study of the Word 'Sentimental' and of Other Linguistic Characteristics of*

Eighteenth Century Sentimentalism in England (Helsinki, 1951); Northrop Frye, "Towards Defining an Age of Sensibility," *ELH,* XXIII (1956). 144-152; Stuart M. Tave, *The Amiable Humorist: A Study in the Comic Theory and Criticism of the Eighteenth and Early Nineteenth Centuries* (Chicago, 1960).

968 R. A. Knox, *Enthusiasm: A Chapter in the History of Religion, with Special Reference to the Seventeenth and Eighteenth Centuries* (Oxford, 1950).

969 Betsy Rodgers, *Cloak of Charity: Studies in Eighteenth-Century Philanthropy* (1949). On the Adam brothers: James Lees-Milne, *The Age of Adam* (1948).

970 *Portraits by Sir Joshua Reynolds: Character Sketches of Oliver Goldsmith, Samuel Johnson, and David Garrick, together with Other Manuscripts of Reynolds Recently Discovered among the Boswell Papers and Now First Published,* ed. Frederick W. Hilles (1952); *Sir Joshua Reynolds: Discourses on Art,* ed. Robert R. Wark (San Marino, Calif., 1959); Frederick W. Hilles, "Sir Joshua's Prose," *Tinker Festschrift* (New Haven, 1949), pp. 49-60.—Allan Ramsay the Younger: Alastair Smart, *The Life and Art of Allan Ramsay* (1952). —Gainsborough: Mary Woodall, *Thomas Gainsborough: His Life and Work* (1949).

974 Thomas Leland: *Longsword, Earl of Salisbury: An Historical Romance,* ed. John C. Stephens, Jr. (1957).—Medievalism: A. L. Owen, *The Famous Druids* (Oxford, 1962); Arthur Johnston, *Enchanted Ground: The Study of Medieval Romance in the Eighteenth Century* (1964).

II. Opinions of Critics

977 Scott Elledge, "The Background and Development in English Criticism of the Theories of Generality and Particularity," *PMLA,* LXII (1947). 147-182; Earl R. Wasserman, *Elizabethan Poetry in the Eighteenth Century* (Urbana, 1947); W. K. Wimsatt, Jr., "The Structure of the 'Concrete Universal' in Literature," *PMLA,* LXII (1947). 262-280; Gordon McKenzie, *Critical Responsiveness: A Study of the Psychological Current in Later Eighteenth-Century Criticism* (Berkeley, 1949); M. H. Abrams, *The Mirror and the Lamp: Romantic Theory and the Critical Tradition* (1953); René Wellek, *A History of Modern Criticism, 1750-1950:* Vol. I, *The Later Eighteenth Century* (New Haven, 1955); Walter J. Hipple, Jr., *The Beautiful, the Sublime, & the Picturesque in Eighteenth-Century British Aesthetic Theory* (Carbondale, Ill., 1957); Ernest L. Tuveson, *The Imagination as a Means of Grace: Locke and the Aesthetics of Romanticism* (Berkeley, 1960); Martin Price, "The Picturesque Moment," *Pottle Festschrift* (1965), pp. 259-292.

980 Jean H. Hagstrum, *The Sister Arts: The Tradition of Literary Pictorialism and English Poetry from Dryden to Gray* (Chicago, 1958).

981 *William Duff: An Essay on Original Genius:* Facsimile Reproduction, ed. with an Introduction by John L. Mahoney (Gainesville, Fla., 1964; *SF&R*).

982 Wilma L. Kennedy, *The English Heritage of Coleridge of Bristol, 1798: The Basis in Eighteenth-Century English Thought for his Distinction between*

Imagination and Fancy (New Haven, 1947); Earl R. Wasserman, "Another Eighteenth-Century Distinction between Fancy and Imagination," *MLN*, LXIV (1949). 23-25; Marjorie Nicolson, *Science and Imagination* (Ithaca, N.Y., 1956), containing her 1935 essay, "The Microscope and English Imagination."

983 Frances Reynolds [sister of Sir Joshua], *An Enquiry concerning the Principles of Taste, and of the Origin of our Ideas of Beauty* (1785), with an Introduction by James L. Clifford (1951; *ARS*, No. 27).

984 George Campbell, *The Philosophy of Rhetoric,* ed. Lloyd F. Bitzer (Carbondale, Ill., 1963).

985 Carl Paul Barbier, *William Gilpin: His Drawings, Teaching and Theory of the Picturesque* (Oxford, 1963).—Lord Kames: Leroy R. Shaw, "Henry Home of Kames: Precursor of Herder," *Germanic Rev.* XXXV (1960). 16-27; András Horn, "Kames and the Anthropological Approach to Criticism," *PQ*, XLIV (1965). 211-233.

986 John Baillie, *An Essay on the Sublime, 1747,* with an Introduction by Samuel H. Monk (1953; *ARS*, No. 43). Burke, *A Philosophical Enquiry into the Origin of our Ideas of the Sublime and Beautiful,* ed. J. T. Boulton (1958). Alexander Gerard, *An Essay on Taste (1759), together with Observations concerning the Imitative Nature of Poetry:* Facsimile Reproduction of the Third Edition (1780), with an Introduction by Walter J. Hipple, Jr. (Gainesville, Fla., 1963; *SF&R*).

987 Priestley: *A Course of Lectures on Oratory and Criticism,* ed. Vincent M. Bevilacqua and Richard Murphy (Carbondale, Ill., 1965); *Writings on Philosophy, Science, and Politics,* ed. John A. Passmore (1965). Homeric criticism: Donald M. Foerster, *Homer in English Criticism* (New Haven, 1947); Gustavo Costa, *La Critica omerica di Thomas Blackwell (1701-1757)* (Florence, 1959).

988 Richard Hurd, *Letters on Chivalry and Romance,* with an Introduction by Hoyt Trowbridge (1963; *ARS*, Nos. 101-2).

III. Dr. Johnson

989 For bibliography see R. W. Chapman, *Two Centuries of Johnsonian Scholarship* (Glasgow, 1945); James L. Clifford, *Johnsonian Studies, 1887-1950* (Minneapolis, 1951); "Johnsonian Studies, 1950-60," compiled by James L. Clifford and Donald J. Greene in *Johnsonian Studies,* ed. Magdi Wahba (Cairo, 1962), pp. 263-350.—Three volumes of the new Yale Edition of the *Works* have appeared: Vol. I: *Diaries, Prayers, and Annals,* ed. E. L. McAdam, Jr., with Donald and Mary Hyde (1958); Vol. II: *"The Idler" and "The Adventurer,"* ed. W. J. Bate, John M. Bullitt, and L. F. Powell (1963); Vol. III: *Poems,* ed. E. L. McAdam, with George Milne (1964).—*The Letters of Samuel Johnson, with Mrs. Thrale's Genuine Letters to Him,* ed. R. W. Chapman (3v, Oxford, 1952). For new letters see Mary Hyde, " 'Not in Chapman,' " *Powell Festschrift* (Oxford, 1965), pp. 286-319.—Biographies and general studies: L. F. Powell's revision of the Hill edition of Boswell has been completed with Vols. V-VI (Oxford, 1950; 2 ed., 1964). (For Boswell see also below, suppl. to p. 1066.) Part xi of Reade's *Johnsonian Gleanings (Consolidated Index of Persons to Parts I-X)* was published in 1952. An abridged edition, by Bertram H. Davis, of Sir John Hawkins' *Life* appeared in 1961. Other biographical and general studies: Katharine C. Balderston, "Johnson's Vile Melancholy," *Tinker Festschrift* (New Haven, 1949), pp. 3-14; Bertrand H. Bronson, "The Double Tradition of Dr. Johnson," *ELH*, xviii (1951). 90-106; E. L. McAdam, Jr., *Dr. Johnson and the English Law* (Syracuse, N.Y., 1951); R. W. Chapman, *Johnsonian and Other Essays and Reviews* (Oxford, 1953); Walter J. Bate, *The Achievement of Samuel Johnson* (1955); Hesketh Pearson, *Johnson and Boswell: The Story of their Lives* (1958); *New Light on Dr. Johnson: Essays on the Occasion of his 250th Birthday,* ed. Frederick W. Hilles (New Haven, 1959) [twenty papers, some of them reprinted, by specialists]; Bertram H. Davis, *Johnson before Boswell: A Study of Sir John Hawkins' "Life of Samuel Johnson"* (New Haven, 1960); Donald J. Greene, *The Politics of Samuel Johnson* (New Haven, 1960); Robert Voitle, *Samuel Johnson the Moralist* (Cambridge, Mass., 1961); M. J. C. Hodgart, *Samuel Johnson* (1962).

990 The early and middle years: Benjamin B. Hoover, *Samuel Johnson's Parliamentary Reporting* (Berkeley, 1953); James L. Clifford, *Young Sam Johnson* (1955), and "Some Problems of Johnson's Obscure Middle Years," *Powell Festschrift* (Oxford, 1965), pp. 99-110; Edward A. Bloom, *Samuel Johnson in Grub Street* (Providence, R.I., 1957); Joel L. Gold, "Johnson's Translation of Lobo," *PMLA*, lxxx (1965). 51-61. Marshall Waingrow, "The Mighty Moral of *Irene*," *Pottle Festschrift* (1965), pp. 79-92. *The Vanity of Human Wishes:* Susie I. Tucker and Henry Gifford, "Johnson's Poetic Imagination," *RES*, n.s. viii (1957). 241-248; Frederick W. Hilles, "Johnson's Poetic Fire," *Pottle Festschrift* (1965), pp. 67-77.

991 James H. Sledd and Gwin J. Kolb, *Dr. Johnson's Dictionary: Essays in the Biography of a Book* (Chicago, 1955); Katharine C. Balderston, "Dr. Johnson's Use of William Law in the *Dictionary*," *PQ*, xxxix (1960). 379-388; *Johnson's Dictionary: A Modern Selection,* ed. E. L. McAdam, Jr. and George Milne (1963).

993 *Johnson's Notes to Shakespeare* [the 1773 text], ed. with an Introduction by Arthur Sherbo (*ARS*, Nos. 59-60, 65-66, 71-73, 1956-58); W. R. Keast, "The Preface to *A Dictionary* . . . : Johnson's Revision and the Establishment of the Text," *Stud. in Bibliography*, v (1952/3), 129-146; Arthur Sherbo, *Samuel Johnson, Editor of Shakespeare, with an Essay on "The Adventurer"* (Urbana, 1956); Robert W. Scholes, "Dr. Johnson and the Bibliographical Criticism of Shakespeare," *SQ*, xi (1960). 163-171; Donald D. Eddy, "Samuel Johnson's Editions of Shakespeare (1765)," *Papers of the Bibl. Soc. of America*, lvi (1962). 428-444; D. Nichol Smith (ed.) *Eighteenth Century Essays on Shakespeare* (2 ed., Oxford, 1963).

994 Gwin J. Kolb, "The Structure of *Rasselas*," *PMLA*, lxvi (1951). 698-717, and "The 'Paradise' in Abyssinia and the 'Happy Valley' in *Rasselas*," *MP*, lvi (1958). 10-16; William Kenney, "*Rasselas* and the Theme of Diversification," *PQ*, xxxviii (1959). 84-89; George Sherburn, "Rasselas Returns—to What?" *PQ*, xxxviii (1959). 383-384; *Bicentenary Essays on Rasselas,* ed. Magdi Wahba (Cairo, 1959); Gwin J. Kolb, "*Rasselas*: Purchase Price, Proprietors, and Printings," *Stud. in Bibliography,* xv (1962). 256-259; Donald M. Lockhart, " 'The Fourth Son of the Mighty Emperor': The Ethiopian Background of Johnson's *Rasselas,*" *PMLA,* LXXVIII (1963). 516-528; Frederick W. Hilles, "*Rasselas,* an 'Uninstructive Tale,' " *Powell Festschrift* (Oxford, 1965, pp. 111-121.

995 Mary Lascelles, "Notions and Facts: Johnson and Boswell on their Travels," *Powell Festschrift* (Oxford, 1965), pp. 215-229.

996 Benjamin Boyce, "Johnson's *Life of Savage* and its Literary Background," *SP,* LIII (1956). 576-598; William R. Keast, "Johnson and 'Cibber's' *Lives of the Poets, 1753,*" *McKillop Festschrift* (Chicago, 1963), pp. 89-101; John Lawrence Abbott, "Dr. Johnson, Fontenelle, Le Clerc, and Six 'French' Lives," *MP,* LXIII (1965). 121-127.

997 Lewis P. Curtis and Herman W. Liebert, *Esto Perpetua: The Club of Dr. Johnson and his Friends, 1764-1784* (Hamden, Conn., 1963).

998 Chester F. Chapin, "Samuel Johnson's Religious Development," *SEL,* IV (1964). 457-474; Maurice J. Quinlan, *Samuel Johnson: A Layman's Religion* (Madison, 1964); Arieh Sachs, "Reason and Unreason in Johnson's Religion," *MLR,* LIX (1964). 519-526; John Hardy, "Johnson and Raphael's Counsel to Adam," *Powell Festschrift* (Oxford, 1965), pp. 122-136.

1000 E. L. McAdam, Jr., "Johnson, Walpole, and Public Order," *Powell Festschrift* (Oxford, 1965), pp. 93-98; Robert Shackleton, "Johnson and the Enlightenment," *Ibid.,* pp. 76-92.

1001 W. K. Wimsatt, Jr., *Philosophic Words: A Study of Style and Meaning in the "Rambler" and "Dictionary" of Samuel Johnson* (New Haven, 1948); Jean H. Hagstrum, *Samuel Johnson's Literary Criticism* (Minneapolis, 1952); W. R. Keast, "The Theoretical Foundations of Johnson's Criticism," *Critics and Criticism* (Chicago, 1952), pp. 389-407; Donald J. Greene, " 'Pictures to the Mind': Johnson and Imagery," *Powell Festschrift* (Oxford, 1965), pp. 137-158; Arieh Sachs, "Generality and Particularity in Johnson's Thought," *SEL,* v (1965). 491-511.

1004 Donald J. Greene, "The Development of the Johnson Canon," *McKillop Festschrift* (Chicago, 1963), pp. 407-427; Gwin J. Kolb, "Johnson's 'Little Pompadour': A Textual Crux and a Hypothesis," *Ibid.,* pp. 125-142; J. D. Fleeman, "Dr. Johnson and Henry Thrale, M. P.," *Powell Festschrift* (Oxford, 1965), pp. 170-189 [Johnson's assistance in Thrale's election addresses].

IV. Mid-Century Poets

1005 Wallace Cable Brown, *The Triumph of Form: A Study of the Later Masters of the Heroic Couplet* (Chapel Hill, 1948); Earl R. Wasserman, "The Inherent Values of Eighteenth-Century Personification," *PMLA,* LXV (1950). 435-463.

1007 *Drafts & Fragments of Verse,* ed. J. S. Cunningham (Oxford, 1956) (rev. by Alan D. McKillop in *PQ,* XXXVI (1957). 352-354); Alan D. McKillop, "Collins's *Ode to Evening*—Background and Structure," *Tennessee Stud. in Lit.* v (1960). 73-83; Merle E. Brown, "On William Collins' 'Ode to Evening,' "

EIC, xi (1961). 136-153; John R. Crider, "Structure and Effect in Collins' Progress Poems," *SP*, lx (1963). 57-72; R. Quintana, "The Scheme of Collins's *Odes on Several . . . Subjects*," *McKillop Festschrift* (Chicago, 1963), pp. 371-380; Oliver F. Sigworth, *William Collins* (1965); A. S. P. Woodhouse, "The Poetry of Collins Reconsidered," *Pottle Festschrift* (1965), pp. 93-137.

1009 Christopher Smart's *Collected Poems* have been edited by Norman Callan in 2v, 1949 (*Muses' Library*); and the *Poems* (a selection) by Robert Brittain (Princeton, 1950). Of major importance: *Jubilate Agno*, re-edited from the Original Manuscript by W. H. Bond (Cambridge, Mass., 1954). *A Song to David* is edited by J. B. Broadbent (1960). See also Cecil Price, "Six Letters by Christopher Smart," *RES*, n.s. viii (1957). 144-148; Arthur Sherbo, "Christopher Smart's Knowledge of Occult Literature," *JHI*, xviii (1957). 233-241; Charles Ryskamp, "Problems in the Text of Smart," *Library*, xiv (1959). 293-298; Karina Williamson, "Christopher Smart's *Hymns and Spiritual Songs*," *PQ*, xxxviii (1959). 413-424; Christopher Devlin, *Poor Kit Smart* (1961); Charles Parish, "Christopher Smart's Knowledge of Hebrew," *SP*, lviii (1961). 516-532; K. M. Rogers, "The Pillars of the Lord: Some Sources of 'A Song to David,'" *PQ*, xl (1961). 525-534; Albert J. Kuhn, "Christopher Smart: The Poet as Patriot of the Lord," *ELH*, xxx (1963). 121-136; Charles Parish, "Christopher Smart's 'Pillars of the Lord,'" *MLQ* xxiv (1963). 158-163.

1010 A. M. Kinghorn, "Warton's *History* and Early English Poetry," *ES*, xliv (1963). 197-204.

1011 Jeffrey Hart, "Akenside's Revision of *The Pleasures of Imagination*," *PMLA*, lxxiv (1959). 67-74; Robert Marsh, "Akenside and Addison: The Problem of Ideational Debt," *MP*, lix (1961). 36-48.—*Shenstone's Miscellany, 1759-1763*, ed. Ian A. Gordon (Oxford, 1952); Roy Lewis, "William Shenstone and Edward Knight: Some New Letters," *MLR*, xlii (1947). 422-433.

1012 Herbert W. Starr, *A Bibliography of Thomas Gray, 1917-1951, with Material supplementary to C. S. Northup's Bibliography* (Philadelphia, 1953); R. W. Ketton-Cremer, *Thomas Gray: A Biography* (Cambridge, 1955); Rintaro Fukuhara, *Essays on Thomas Gray* (Tokyo, 1960); Alastair Macdonald, "The Poet Gray in Scotland," *RES*, n.s. xiii (1962). 245-256; Morris Golden, *Thomas Gray* (1964); Patricia M. Spacks, "Statement and Artifice in Thomas Gray," *SEL*, v (1965). 519-532.

1014 Odell Shepard, "A Youth to Fortune and to Fame Unknown," *MP*, xx (1923). 347-373; Cleanth Brooks, "Gray's Storied Urn," *The Well Wrought Urn* (1947), pp. 96-113; H. W. Starr, " 'A Youth to Fortune and to Fame Unknown': A Reestimation," *JEGP*, xlviii (1949). 97-107; Frank H. Ellis, "Gray's *Elegy*: The Biographical Problem in Literary Criticism," *PMLA*, lxvi (1951). 971-1008; Morse Peckham, "Gray's 'Epitaph' Revisited," *MLN*, lxxi (1956). 409-411; John H. Sutherland, "The Stonecutter in Gray's 'Elegy,' " *MP*, lv (1957). 11-13; Mark Roberts, "A Note on Gray's Elegy," *ES*, xxxix (1958). 251-256; Francis Berry, "The Sound of Personification in Gray's Elegy," *EIC*, xii (1962). 442-445; and three essays in the *Pottle Festschrift* (1965): Frank Brady, "Structure and Meaning in Gray's *Elegy*," pp. 177-189; Bertrand H. Bronson, "On a Special Decorum in Gray's *Elegy*," pp. 171-176; Ian Jack, "Gray's *Elegy* Reconsidered," pp. 139-169.

1015 Derick S. Thomson, *The Gaelic Sources of Macpherson's "Ossian"* (Edinburgh, 1952).

1016 *The Poems of Robert Fergusson,* ed. Matthew P. McDiarmid (2v, Edinburgh, 1955-7); *The Unpublished Poems,* ed. William E. Gillis (Edinburgh, 1955); Sydney Goodsir Smith (ed.), *Robert Fergusson, 1750-1774: Essays by Various Hands to Commemorate the Bicentenary of his Birth* (1952). See further: David Daiches, *The Paradox of Scottish Culture: The Eighteenth-Century Experience* (1964); John Butt, "The Revival of Vernacular Scottish Poetry in the Eighteenth Century," *Pottle Festschrift* (1965), pp. 219-237. On Hugh Blair see the book by Robert M. Schmitz, *Hugh Blair* (1948).

1017 Four more volumes of *The Percy Letters* have been published (correspondence with Thomas Warton, Lord Hailes, Evan Evans, and George Paton). For an account of the Percy books and papers see D. Nichol Smith, "The Constance Meade Collection and the University Press Museum," *Bodleian Library Record,* VI (1958). 427-433. On the *Reliques* see Albert B. Friedman, *The Ballad Revival* (Chicago, 1961), chap. VII.

1018 Beattie's *London Diary, 1773* and the *Day-Book, 1773-1798* have both been edited by Ralph S. Walker (Aberdeen, 1946-9). See also two articles by Ernest C. Mossner: "Beattie's 'The Castle of Scepticism': An Unpublished Allegory against Hume, Voltaire, and Hobbes," *Texas Stud. in English,* XXVII (1948). 108-145, and "Beattie on Voltaire: An Unpublished Manuscript," *Romanic Rev.,* XLI (1950). 26-32.—Chatterton: Bertrand H. Bronson, "Thomas Chatterton," *Tinker Festschrift* (New Haven, 1949), pp. 239-255.

1019 *The Poetical Works of Charles Churchill,* ed. Douglas Grant (Oxford, 1956); *Correspondence of John Wilkes and Charles Churchill,* ed. Edward H. Weatherly (1954); Wallace Cable Brown, *Charles Churchill: Poet, Rake, and Rebel* (Lawrence, Kans., 1953); Irène Simon, "An Eighteenth-Century Satirist: Charles Churchill," *Revue belge de philologie et d'histoire,* XXXVII (1959). 645-682; William F. Cunningham, Jr., "Charles Churchill and the Satiric Portrait," *Essays and Stud. in Lang. and Lit.* (Pittsburgh, 1964; *Duquesne Stud., Philol. Ser.,* 5), pp. 110-132.

1020 Additional poets:

Christopher Anstey: William C. Powell, *Christopher Anstey: Bath Laureate* (Philadelphia, 1944); Martin S. Day, "Anstey and Anapestic Satire in the Late Eighteenth Century," *ELH,* XV (1948). 122-146.

William Falconer: M. K. Joseph, "William Falconer," *SP,* XLVII (1950). 72-101; Gordon W. Couchman, "Editions of Falconer's 'Shipwreck,'" *N&Q,* CXCVIII (1953). 439-440.

William Hamilton: Nelson S. Bushnell, *William Hamilton of Bangour, Poet and Jacobite* (Aberdeen, 1957).

V. The Novel after 1760

1021 B. G. MacCarthy, *The Later Women Novelists, 1744-1818* (Oxford, 1948); James R. Foster, *History of the Pre-romantic Novel in England* (1949); Henri Roddier, *J.-J. Rousseau en Angleterre au XVIIIᵉ siècle: l'oeuvre et l'homme* (Paris, 1950).

1022 Mrs. Sarah Scott: *A Description of Millenium Hall,* ed. Walter M. Crittenden (1955).—Charlotte Smith: Alan D. McKillop, "Charlotte Smith's Letters," *HLQ,* XV (1952). 237-255.

1023   Ernest N. Dilworth, *The Unsentimental Journey of Laurence Sterne* (1948); Lansing van der Heyden Hammond, *Laurence Sterne's "Sermons of Mr. Yorick"* (New Haven, 1948); Earl R. Wasserman, "Unedited Letters by Sterne, Hume, and Rousseau," *MLN*, LXVI (1951). 73-80; J. C. T. Oates, "On Collecting Sterne," *Book Collector*, I (1952). 247-258; Alan D. McKillop, "The Reinterpretation of Laurence Sterne," *Études anglaises*, VII (1954). 36-47; Alice G. Fredman, *Diderot and Sterne* (1955); Margaret R. B. Shaw, *Laurence Sterne: The Making of a Humorist, 1713-1762* (1957); Willard Connely, *Laurence Sterne as Yorick* (1958); Alan B. Howes, *Yorick and the Critics: Sterne's Reputation in England, 1760-1868* (New Haven, 1958); L. P. Curtis, "New Light on Sterne," *MLN*, LXXVI (1961). 498-501; Henri Fluchère, *Laurence Sterne, de l'homme à l'oeuvre: Biographie critique et essai d'interprétation de "Tristram Shandy"* (Paris, 1961) (trans. and abridged by Barbara Bray, 1965); A. E. Dyson, "Sterne: The Novelist as Jester," *Critical Quar.* IV (1962). 309-320; Peter Michelsen, *Laurence Sterne und der deutsche Roman des achtzehnten Jahrhunderts* (Göttingen, 1962); Christian Pons, "Laurence Sterne ou le génie de l'humour," *Cahiers du Sud*, LIII (1962). 425-446; Dietrich Rolle, *Fielding und Sterne* (Münster, 1963); William B. Piper, *Laurence Sterne* (1965); Arthur H. Cash, "Some New Sterne Letters," *LTLS*, April 8, 1965, p. 284; James M. Kuist, "New Light on Sterne: An Old Man's Recollections of the Young Vicar," *PMLA*, LXXX (1965). 549-553.

1024   John M. Yoklavich, "Notes on the Early Editions of *Tristram Shandy*," *PMLA*, LXIII (1948). 508-519; Wayne Booth, "Did Sterne Complete *Tristram Shandy?*" *MP*, XLVIII (1951). 172-183, and "The Self-Conscious Narrator in Comic Fiction before *Tristram Shandy*," *PMLA*, LXVII (1952). 163-185 [cf. also Booth's *The Rhetoric of Fiction* (Chicago, 1961), chap. VIII]; John Traugott, *Tristram Shandy's World: Sterne's Philosophical Rhetoric* (Berkeley, 1954); Arthur H. Cash, "The Lockean Psychology of *Tristram Shandy*," *ELH*, XXII (1955). 125-135; J. M. Stedmond, "Genre and *Tristram Shandy*," *PQ*, XXXVIII (1959). 37-51, "Style and *Tristram Shandy*," *MLQ*, XX (1959). 243-251, and "Satire and *Tristram Shandy*," *SEL*, I (1961). 53-63; Sigurd Burckhardt, "*Tristram Shandy*'s Law of Gravity," *ELH*, XXVIII (1961). 70-88; William B. Piper, "*Tristram Shandy*'s Digressive Artistry," *SEL*, I (1961). 65-76, and "*Tristram Shandy*'s Tragi-comical Testimony," *Criticism*, III (1961). 171-185; Ernest Tuveson, "Locke and Sterne," *Nicolson Festschrift* (1962). pp. 255-277; William J. Farrell, "Nature versus Art as a Comic Pattern in *Tristram Shandy*," *ELH*, XXX (1963). 16-36; Joan J. Hall, "The Hobbyhorsical World of *Tristram Shandy*," *MLQ*, XXIV (1963). 131-143; Louis A. Landa, "The Shandean Homunculus," *McKillop Festschrift* (Chicago, 1963), pp. 49-68; Arthur H. Cash, "The Sermon in *Tristram Shandy*," *ELH*, XXXI (1964). 395-417; Gardner D. Stout, Jr., "Sterne's Borrowings from Bishop Joseph Hall's *Quo Vadis?*" *ELN*, II (1965). 196-200.

1026   Gardner D. Stout, Jr., "Yorick's *Sentimental Journey*: A Comic 'Pilgrim's Progress' for the Man of Feeling," *ELH*, XXX (1963). 395-412.

1027   Dale Kramer, "The Structural Unity of 'The Man of Feeling,' " *Studies in Short Fiction*, I (1964). 191-199.

1028   Walpole: *The Castle of Otranto*, ed. W. S. Lewis (1964); Arthur L. Cooke, "Some Side Lights on the Theory of the Gothic Romance," *MLQ*, XII (1951). 429-436.

1030 William W. Appleton, *A Cycle of Cathay: The Chinese Vogue in England during the Seventeenth and Eighteenth Centuries* (1951).

1030 John H. Sutherland, "Robert Bage: Novelist of Ideas," *PQ*, xxxvi (1957). 211-220; K. H. Hartley, "Un Roman philosophique anglais: *Hermsprong* de Robert Bage," *RLC*, xxxviii (1964). 558-563.—*The Journal of William Beckford in Portugal and Spain, 1787-1788,* ed. Boyd Alexander (1954); *Excursion à Alcobaça et Batalha,* ed. André Parreaux (Paris & Lisbon, 1956): *Life at Fonthill, 1807-1822, with Interludes in Paris and London: From the Correspondence of William Beckford,* trans. and ed. Boyd Alexander (1957); *Vathek et les Episodes,* ed. Ernest Giddey (Lausanne, 1962); Sacheverell Sitwell, *Beckford and Beckfordism* (1930); H. A. N. Brockman, *The Caliph of Fonthill* (1956); André Parreaux, *William Beckford, auteur de "Vathek" (1760-1844): Etude de la création littéraire* (Paris, 1960); Fatma Moussa Mahmoud (ed.), *William Beckford of Fonthill, 1760-1844: Bicentenary Essays* (Cairo, 1961); Boyd Alexander, *England's Wealthiest Son: A Study of William Beckford* (1962); James Rieger, "Au Pied de la Lettre: Stylistic Uncertainty in *Vathek*," *Criticism,* iv (1962). 302-312; James K. Folsom, "Beckford's 'Vathek' and the Tradition of Oriental Satire," *Criticism,* vi (1964). 53-69; Reinhold Grimm, "*Vathek* in Deutschland," *RLC*, xxxviii (1964). 127-135.

1031 Garland H. Cannon, Jr.: *Sir William Jones, Orientalist: An Annotated Bibliography of his Works* (Honolulu, 1952), *Oriental Jones: A Biography of Sir William Jones (1746-1794)* (1964), and "Sir William Jones and Dr. Johnson's Literary Club," *MP*, lxiii (1965). 20-37.

1032 *Edwy and Elgiva,* ed. Miriam J. Benkovitz (Hamden, Conn., 1957); Joyce Hemlow, "Fanny Burney and the Courtesy Books," *PMLA*, lxv (1950). 732-761, and "Fanny Burney: Playwright," *UTQ*, xix (1950). 170-189; Emily Hahn, *A Degree of Prudery* (1951); Joyce Hemlow, *The History of Fanny Burney* (Oxford, 1958), the standard life; Miriam Benkovitz, "Dr. Burney's Memoirs," *RES*, n.s. x (1959). 257-268; Eugene White, *Fanny Burney, Novelist: A Study in Technique* (Hamden, Conn., 1960); Winifred Gérin, *The Young Fanny Burney: A Biography* (1961); S. Bugnot, "*The Wanderer,* de Fanny Burney: Essai de réhabilitation," *Études anglaises,* xv (1962). 225-232; James P. Erickson, "*Evelina* and *Betsy Thoughtless*," *Texas Stud. in Lit. and Lang.,* vi (1964). 96-103; Kemp Malone, "*Evelina* Revisited," *Papers on English Lang. and Lit.* (So. Illinois Univ.), i (1965). 3-19. On Dr. Burney see Roger Lonsdale, "Dr. Burney and the *Monthly Review*," *RES*, xiv (1963). 346-358; xv (1964). 27-37; and *Dr. Charles Burney: A Literary Biography* (Oxford, 1965).

VI. The Drama 1740-1785

1035 Part 4 of *The London Stage,* (*1747-1776,* ed. George Winchester Stone, Jr., 3v. 1962) deals with this period (see above, suppl. to p. 748). See also Bertrand Evans, *Gothic Drama from Walpole to Shelley* (Berkeley, 1947); Earl R. Wasserman, "The Pleasures of Tragedy," *ELH*, xiv (1947). 283-307, and "The Sympathetic Imagination in Eighteenth-century Theories of Acting," *JEGP*, xlvi (1947). 264-272; Harry W. Pedicord, *The Theatrical Public in the Time of Garrick* (1954); William W. Appleton, *Charles Macklin: An Actor's Life* (Cambridge, Mass., 1960).—Garrick: *The Letters of David Garrick,* ed. David M. Little and George M. Kahrl (3v, Cambridge, Mass., 1963); Margaret Barton, *Garrick* (1948); Dougald MacMillan, "David Garrick, Manager," *SP,* xlv (1948). 630-646; Mary E. Knapp, *A Checklist of Verse by David Garrick* (Charlottesville, Va., 1955); Carola Oman, *David Garrick* (1958); Kalman A. Burnim, *David Garrick, Director* (Pittsburgh, 1961). On Garrick's treatment of Shakespeare see three articles by George Winchester Stone, Jr.: *SP,* xlv (1948). 89-103; *J. Q. Adams Memorial Studies* (Washington, 1948), pp. 115-128; and *PMLA,* lxv (1950). 183-197. On the Shakespeare Jubilee of 1769 see Martha W. England, *Garrick and Stratford* (1962) and *Garrick's Jubilee* (Columbus, Ohio, 1964); Christian Deelman, *The Great Shakespeare Jubilee* (1964); Johanne M. Stochholm, *Garrick's Folly: The Shakespeare Jubilee of 1769 at Stratford and Drury Lane* (1964).

1039 *"The Way to Keep him" and Five Other Plays by Arthur Murphy,* ed. John P. Emery (1956); *New Essays by Arthur Murphy,* ed. Arthur Sherbo (East Lansing, Mich., 1963).

1043 Byron Gassman, "French Sources of Goldsmith's *The Good Natur'd Man,*" *PQ,* xxxix (1960). 56-65.

1044 Jean Dulck, *Les Comédies de R. B. Sheridan: Étude littéraire* (Paris, 1962).

1047 Andrew Schiller, "*The School for Scandal:* The Restoration Unrestored," *PMLA,* lxii (1956). 694-704; Cecil Price, "The Columbia Manuscript of *The School for Scandal,*" *Columbia Library Columns,* xi (1961). 25-29; Christian Deelman, "The Original Cast of *The School for Scandal,*" *RES,* n.s. xiii (1962). 257-266; Arthur C. Sprague, "In Defence of a Masterpiece: 'The School for Scandal' Re-examined," *English Studies Today,* 3rd ser. (Edinburgh, 1964), pp. 125-135.

1048 Jeremy F. Bagster-Collins, *George Colman the Younger, 1762-1836* (1946).

VII. The Periodicals and Oliver Goldsmith

1050 A. T. Elder, "Irony and Humour in the *Rambler,*" *UTQ,* xxx (1960). 57-71.

1051 W. Powell Jones, "The Romantic Bluestocking, Elizabeth Carter," *HLQ,* xii (1948). 85-98.

1052 Randolph Hudson, "Henry Mackenzie, James Beattie *et al.,* and the Edinburgh *Mirror,*" *ELN,* i (1963). 104-108. Dr. Horst W. Drescher has in preparation a study of Mackenzie's periodical essays.

Newspapers: Katherine K. Weed and Richmond P. Bond, *Studies of British Newspapers and Periodicals from their Beginning to 1800: A Bibliography* (Chapel Hill, 1946); Robert L. Haig, "*The Gazetteer," 1735-1797: A Study in the Eighteenth-Century English Newspaper* (Carbondale, Ill., 1960); G. A. Cranfield, *The Development of the Provincial Newspaper, 1700-1760* (Oxford, 1962); Robert R. Rea, *The English Press in Politics, 1760-1774* (Lincoln, Nebr., 1963); Lucyle Werkmeister, *The London Daily Press, 1772-1792* (Lincoln, Nebr., 1963);

Roy M. Wiles, *Freshest Advices: Early Provincial Newspapers in England* (Columbus, O., 1965).—Bonnell Thornton: Wallace C. Brown, "A Belated Augustan: Bonnell Thornton, Esq.," *PQ*, xxxiv (1955). 335-348.

1053 Albert H. Smith, "John Nichols, Printer and Publisher," *Library*, xviii (1963). 169-190; William B. Todd, "A Bibliographical Account of the *Gentleman's Magazine, 1731-1754*," *Stud. in Bibliography*, xviii (1965). 81-109.

1055 Benjamin C. Nangle, *The Monthly Review, Second Series, 1790-1815: Indexes of Contributors and Articles* (Oxford, 1955); Edward A. Bloom, "Labors of the Learned: Neoclassic Book Reviewing Aims and Techniques," *SP*, liv (1957). 537-563; Paul F. Fussell, Jr., "William Kenrick, Eighteenth-Century Scourge and Critic," *Jour. Rutgers Univ. Library*, xx (1957). 42-49.

1056 Arthur Friedman, "Goldsmith's Contributions to the *Critical Review*," *MP*, xliv (1946). 23-52; Edward L. McAdam, Jr., "Goldsmith, the Good-Natured Man," *Tinker Festschrift* (New Haven, 1949), pp. 41-47; Ralph M. Wardle, *Oliver Goldsmith* (Lawrence, Kans., 1957); Earl Miner, "The Making of *The Deserted Village*," *HLQ*, xxii (1959). 125-141; Macdonald Emslie, *Goldsmith: "The Vicar of Wakefield"* (1963); Arthur Friedman, "The Time of Composition of Goldsmith's *Edwin and Angelina*," *McKillop Festschrift* (Chicago, 1963), pp. 155-159; R. Quintana, "Oliver Goldsmith as a Critic of the Drama," *SEL*, v (1965). 435-454. Professor Friedman's edition of Goldsmith's *Works* is to appear in 1966 (5v).

1059 Alan D. McKillop, "Local Attachment and Cosmopolitanism—the Eighteenth-Century Pattern," *Pottle Festschrift* (1965), pp. 191-218.

VIII. Biography and Letter-Writing

1063 R. W. Ketton-Cremer, "Roger North," *E&S*, n.s., xii (1959). 73-86; James L. Clifford, "Roger North and the Art of Biography," *McKillop Festschrift* (Chicago, 1963), pp. 275-285.

1064 William Mason: Philip Gaskell, *The First Editions of William Mason* (Cambridge, 1951).—Austin Wright, "The Veracity of Spence's *Anecdotes*," *PMLA*, lxii (1947). 123-129, and *Joseph Spence: A Critical Biography* (Chicago, 1950); James M. Osborn, "The First History of English Poetry," *Sherburn Festschrift* (Oxford, 1949), pp. 230-250. Mr. Osborn is preparing a definitive edition of Spence's *Anecdotes*.

Several volumes of the Yale Boswell papers have been published, ed. by Frederick A. Pottle and others: the *London Journal, 1762-1763* (1950); *Boswell in Holland, 1763-1764* (1952); *Boswell on the Grand Tour: Germany and Switzerland, 1764* (1953); *Boswell on the Grand Tour: Italy, Corsica, and France, 1765-1766* (1955); *Boswell in Search of a Wife, 1766-1769* (1956); *Boswell for the Defence, 1769-1774* (1959); *Boswell: The Ominous Years, 1774-1776* (1963). *The Hypochondriack* has been reprinted (1951) under the title, *Boswell's Column*. See also the articles by Frederick A. Pottle: "James Boswell, Journalist," *Tinker Festschrift* (New Haven, 1949), pp. 15-25; "Boswell as Icarus" [Boswell and the College of Arcadia], *McKillop Festschrift* (Chicago, 1963), pp. 389-406; "Boswell Revalued," *Literary Views:*

Critical and Historical Essays, ed. Carroll Camden (Chicago, 1964), pp. 79-91; and "Boswell's University Education," *Powell Festschrift* (Oxford, 1965), pp. 230-253. Further: C. N. Fifer, "Boswell and the Decorous Bishop" [Boswell and Percy], *JEGP,* LXI (1962). 48-56; Donald J. Greene, "Reflections on a Literary Anniversary," *Queen's Quar.,* LXX (1963). 198-208; Douglas Day, "Boswell, Corsica, and Paoli," *ES,* XLV (1964). 1-20; James L. Golden, "James Boswell on Rhetoric and Belles-Lettres," *Quar. Jour. of Speech,* L (1964). 266-276; Ian Ross, "Boswell in Search of a Father? or a Subject?" *REL,* V (1964). 19-34; Mary M. Stewart, "Boswell and the Infidels," *SEL,* IV (1964). 475-483; Frank Brady, *Boswell's Political Career* (New Haven, 1965); Thomas I. Rae and William Beattie, "Boswell and the Advocates' Library," *Powell Festschrift* (Oxford, 1965), pp. 254-267. On the *Life of Johnson:* Edward Hart, "The Contributions of John Nichols to Boswell's *Life of Johnson,*" *PMLA,* LXVII (1952). 391-410; James M. Osborn, "Edmond Malone and Dr. Johnson," *Powell Festschrift* (Oxford, 1965), pp. 1-20.

1067 Bernard Martin, *John Newton* (1950); James M. Osborn, "Travel Literature and the Rise of Neo-Hellenism in England," *Bull. N.Y. Public Library,* LXVII (1963). 279-300; George B. Parks, "The Turn to the Romantic in the Travel Literature of the Eighteenth Century," *MLQ,* XXV (1964). 22-33; Franz K. Stanzel, "Das Bild der Alpen in der englischen Literatur des 17. und 18. Jahrhunderts," *Germanisch-Romanische Monatsschrift,* XIV (1964). 121-138.

1068 Gibbon: Roy Pascal, *Design and Truth in Autobiography* (1960); Georges A. Bonnard, "Gibbon at Work on his *Memoirs,*" *English Studies presented to R. W. Zandvoort* (Amsterdam, 1964), pp. 207-213.—*Lord Hervey's Memoirs,* ed. Romney Sedgwick (1952) [a selection from the 1931 edition]; *Lord Hervey and his Friends, 1726-1738: based on Letters from Holland House, Melbury, and Ickworth,* ed. Earl of Ilchester (1950).

1069 Mabel R. Brailsford, *A Tale of Two Brothers: John and Charles Wesley* (1954); James L. Golden, "John Wesley on Rhetoric and Belles Lettres," *Speech Monographs,* XXVIII (1961). 250-264; George Lawton, *John Wesley's English: A Study of his Literary Style* (1962).

1070 *Thraliana* (2 ed, 2v, Oxford, 1951).

1071 William H. Irving, *The Providence of Wit in the English Letter Writers* (Durham, N.C., 1955); Herbert Davis, "The Correspondence of the Augustans," *Woodhouse Festschrift* (Toronto, 1964), pp. 195-212.

1072 Katherine G. Hornbeak, "New Light on Mrs. Montagu," *Tinker Festschrift* (New Haven, 1949), pp. 349-361.—C. Price, "Five Unpublished Letters by Chesterfield," *Life and Letters,* LIX (1948). 3-10; Samuel Shellabarger, *Lord Chesterfield and his World* (Boston, 1951); Harold E. Pagliaro, "Paradox in the Aphorisms of La Rochefoucauld and Some Representative English Followers," *PMLA,* LXXIX (1964). 42-50.

1073 *The Antiquities of Selborne,* ed. Walter S. Scott (1950); Walter S. Scott, *White of Selborne* (1950); Ronald M. Lockley, *Gilbert White* (1954).

1075 Ilse D. Lind, *Richard Jago: A Study in Eighteenth Century Localism* (Philadelphia, 1945).

1076 The Yale edition of the Walpole *Correspondence* continues to appear.

To date 29 volumes have been published, the latest the three volumes of correspondence with the Countess of Upper Ossory, ed. W. S. Lewis and A. Dayle Wallace (1965). See further: Allen T. Hazen, *A Bibliography of Horace Walpole* (New Haven, 1948); Wilmarth S. Lewis, *Horace Walpole's Library* (Cambridge, 1958); Bonamy Dobrée, "Horace Walpole," *McKillop Festschrift* (Chicago, 1963), pp. 185-200.

IX. Intellectual Prose

1081   *New Letters of David Hume,* ed. Raymond Klibansky and Ernest C. Mossner (Oxford, 1954); *An Inquiry concerning Human Understanding,* ed. Charles W. Hendel (1955); *Writings on Economics,* ed. Eugene Rotwein (1955); *The Natural History of Religion,* ed. H. E. Root (1956); *An Inquiry concerning the Principles of Morals: With a Supplement: A Dialogue,* ed. Charles W. Hendel (1957). See also "Hume's Early Memoranda, 1729-40: The Complete Text," ed. E. C. Mossner, *JHI,* ix (1948). 492-518; E. C. Mossner, "Hume's *Four Dissertations:* An Essay in Biography and Bibliography," *MP,* xlviii (1950). 37-57; Teddy Brunius, *David Hume on Criticism* (Stockholm, 1952); André-Louis Leroy, *David Hume* (Paris, 1953); Ernest C. Mossner, *The Life of David Hume* (1954); Antony Flew, *Hume's Philosophy of Belief: A Study of his First "Inquiry"* (1961); Ralph Cohen, "The Transformation of Passion: A Study of Hume's Theories of Tragedy," *PQ,* xli (1962). 450-464; Ernest C. Mossner, "New Hume Letters to Lord Elibank, 1748-1776," *Texas Stud. in Lit. and Lang.,* iv (1962). 431-460; and "Adam Ferguson's 'Dialogue on a Highland Jaunt' with Robert Adam, William Cleghorn, David Hume, and William Wilkie," *McKillop Festschrift* (Chicago, 1963), pp. 297-308; John B. Stewart, *The Moral and Political Philosophy of David Hume* (1963); R. T. Broiles, *The Moral Philosophy of David Hume* (The Hague, 1964); Sebastian A. Matczak, "A Select and Classified Bibliography of David Hume," *Modern Schoolman,* xlii (1964). 70-81; Raymond Williams, "David Hume: Reasoning and Experience," *Willey Festschrift* (Cambridge, 1964), pp. 123-145; John V. Price, *The Ironic Hume* (Austin, Tex., 1965).

1085   Bolingbroke: Walter M. Merrill, *From Statesman to Philosopher: A Study in Bolingbroke's Deism* (1949); J. H. Burns, "Bolingbroke and the Concept of Constitutional Government," *Political Stud.,* x (1962). 263-276; George H. Nadel, "New Light on Bolingbroke's Letters on History," *JHI,* xxiii (1962). 550-557.—Gibbon: *Le Journal de Gibbon à Lausanne, 17 août 1763-19 avril 1764,* ed. Georges A. Bonnard (Lausanne, 1945); *The Letters of Edward Gibbon,* ed. J. E. Norton (3v, 1956); *Gibbon's Journey from Geneva to Rome: His Journal from 20 April to 2 October 1764,* ed. Georges A. Bonnard (1961); Herbert Weisinger, "The Middle Ages and the Late Eighteenth-Century Historians," *PQ,* xxvii (1948). 63-79; Lewis P. Curtis, "Gibbon's Paradise Lost," *Tinker Festschrift* (New Haven, 1949), pp. 73-90; Gavin R. De Beer, Georges A. Bonnard, and Louis Junod, *Miscellanea Gibboniana* (Lausanne, 1952); Per Fuglum, *Edward Gibbon: His View of Life and his Conception of History* (Oslo and Oxford, 1953); Michael Joyce, *Edward Gibbon* (1953); Giuseppe Giarrizzo, *Edward Gibbon e la cultura europea del settecento* (Bari, 1954); Harold L. Bond, *The Literary Art of Edward Gibbon* (Oxford, 1960); Nicolas Barker, "A Note on the Bibliography of Gibbon, 1776-1802," *Library,* xviii (1963). 40-50; J. J. Saunders, "The Debate on the Fall of Rome," *History,* xlviii (1963). 1-17.

1089   *A Note-Book of Edmund Burke: Poems, Characters, Essays and Other Sketches,* ed. H. V. F. Somerset (Cambridge, 1957). The *Correspondence,* ed. Thomas W. Copeland and others (Cambridge and Chicago, 1958—) has now reached its fifth volume: *July 1782-June 1789,* ed. Holden Furber, with assistance of P. J. Marshall (1965). (For Burke's essay on the sublime and beautiful see above, suppl. to p. 986.) On Burke: Thomas W. Copeland, *Our Eminent Friend Edmund Burke: Six Essays* (New Haven, 1949); Carl B. Cone, "Edmund Burke's Library," *Papers of the Bibl. Soc. of America,* xliv (1950). 153-172; Charles Parkin, *The Moral Basis of Burke's Political Thought* (Cambridge, 1956); Carl B. Cone, *Burke and the Nature of Politics* (2v, Lexington, Ky., 1957-64); Peter J. Stanlis, *Edmund Burke and the Natural Law* (Ann Arbor, 1958); Thomas H. D. Mahoney, *Edmund Burke and Ireland* (Cambridge, Mass., 1960); Donald C. Bryant, "Edmund Burke: A Generation of Scholarship and Discovery," *Jour. of British Stud.,* ii (1962). 91-114; James T. Boulton, *The Language of Politics in the Age of Wilkes and Burke* (1963); C. P. Courtney, *Montesquieu and Burke* (Oxford, 1963); Peter P. Stanlis (ed.), *The Relevance of Edmund Burke* (1964); William B. Todd, *A Bibliography of Edmund Burke* (1964); Harvey C. Mansfield, Jr., *Statesmanship and Party Government: A Study of Burke and Bolingbroke* (Chicago, 1965).

1092   Lennart Ågvist, *The Moral Philosophy of Richard Price* (Lund, 1960).

1094   Other prose writers:
Catharine Macaulay. Lucy M. Donnelly, "The Celebrated Mrs. Macaulay," *William and Mary Quar.,* vi (1949). 173-207.
Adam Smith. *Lectures on Rhetoric and Belles Lettres,* ed. John M. Lothian (1963). John Rae's *Life* (1895) has been reissued with an important Introduction by Jacob Viner (1965). See also C. R. Fay, *Adam Smith and the Scotland of his Day* (Cambridge, 1956).

X. Cowper and Burns

1096   "Memoir of William Cowper: An Autobiography," ed. Maurice J. Quinlan, *Proc. Amer. Philos. Soc.,* xcvii (1953). 359-382 (cf. review by Charles Ryskamp in *MP,* liii (1955). 67-70, and ensuing corespondence (liii [1956]. 213-216; liv [1957]. 284); *The Cast-Away: The Text of the Original Manuscript and the First Printing of Cowper's Latin Translation,* ed. Charles Ryskamp (Princeton, 1963). Professor Ryskamp is preparing an edition of the correspondence. On Cowper: Lodwick Hartley, *William Cowper: A List of Critical and Biographical Studies Published from 1895 to 1949* (Raleigh, N.C., 1950); Norman Nicholson, *William Cowper* (1951); Donald A. Davie, "The Critical Principles of William Cowper," *Cambridge Jour.,* vii (1953). 182-188; Maurice J. Quinlan, *William Cowper: A Critical Life* (Minneapolis, 1953); Charles Ryskamp, *William Cowper of the Inner Temple, Esq.: A Study of his Life and Works to the Year 1768* (Cambridge, 1959); Morris Golden, *In Search of Stability: The Poetry of William Cowper* (1960); Lodwick Hartley, *William Cowper: The Continuing Revalua-*

tion: An Essay and a Bibliography of Cowperian Studies from 1895 to 1960 (Chapel Hill, 1960); Harry P. Kroitor, "Cowper, Deism, and the Divinization of Nature," *JHI,* XXI (1960). 511-526, and "The Influence of Popular Science on William Cowper," *MP,* LXI (1964). 281-287; Norma Russell, *A Bibliography of William Cowper to 1837* (Oxford, 1963); Frederick M. Link, "Two Cowper Letters," *MP,* LXII (1964). 137-138.

1102 David Daiches, *Robert Burns* (1950); Maurice Lindsay, *Robert Burns: The Man, his Work, the Legend* (1954); Christina Keith, *The Russet Coat: A Critical Study of Burns' Poetry and of its Background* (1956); Thomas Crawford, *Burns: A Study of the Poems and Songs* (1960); Alan D. McKillop, "The Living Burns," *Rice Institute Pamphlet,* XLVII (1960). 1-16; G. Ross Roy, "French Translations of Robert Burns (to 1893)," *RLC,* XXXVII (1963). 279-297, 437-453, and "French Critics of Robert Burns to 1893," *RLC,* XXXVIII (1964). 264-285; Joel W. Egerer, *A Bibliography of Robert Burns* (Edinburgh, 1964; Carbondale, Ill., 1965); Raymond Bentman, "Robert Burns's Use of Scottish Diction," *Pottle Festschrift* (1965), pp. 239-258.

Index

[**Boldface numbers** indicate main reference in the text. Numbers preceded by an **S** in this Index refer to paragraph/page numbers set in boldface in the BIBLIOGRAPHICAL SUPPLEMENT. These paragraph **numbers** correspond to pages of the text.]

i